GUIDE TO LOW-PRICED CLASSICAL RECORDS

Herbert Russcol

Hart Publishing Co., Inc.
New York City

To Margalit

HOW TO USE THIS BOOK

1. Composers appear in the alphabetical order of their last names.

2. Compositions are listed in strict alphabetical order.

3. Notations as to what is contained on the back of a record appear thus: [   ]

4. Comments about each record appear directly below the record listing in the exact order of the record listing. Each record appraisal appears in a separate paragraph.

RATING SYMBOLS

* ACCEPTABLE.

** RECOMMENDED.

*** RANKED WITH THE BEST AT ANY PRICE.

Records which are unstarred are not recommended.

CONTENTS

The Composers

The Reprint Revolution

When the casual music lover strolls into a record store these days, he will find half the space for classical records now occupied by firms offering unfamilar labels such as *Odyssey, Seraphim, Mace, Nonesuch.* Many familiar names of glittering stars—Bruno Walter, Renata Tebaldi, David Oistrakh—grace these records now selling for $1.50 to $2.98.

Our music lover glances at the bins where reassuring labels such as *RCA Victor, Columbia,* et al, are kept. He observes that on this side of the aisle Walter, Tebaldi, and Oistraikh sell at $5 to $6. What's going on?

Delighted, our buyer now loads up on the low-priced records, and walks out with six records for the price he usually paid for two. At home, he discovers that two of his six records are absolutely wonderful, two are so-so—but alas! the other two are hopeless duds, musically and sonically.

This guide is written to steer you through the maze of the new labels—to point out what is especially good and what should be avoided. For today, you can build a really *first-class record* library for an average price of $2.00 a record.

The record industry today is in the throes of a revolution quite similar to that which struck the book business two decades ago when paperbacks first appeared. Little publicity attends the record revolution. Many dealers stock these low-priced labels grudgingly. Just as die-hard book dealers did 20 years ago, some record dealers today refuse to carry the new low-priced lines.

There is little mystery about it all. The new reprint-labels are often subsidiaries of the giant corporations such as *Columbia.* You just have to know that a low-priced *Odyssey* record derives from, and is manufactured by, *Columbia.* The reason for this is that the big record firms have huge investments in their "hard-back" repertory selling at $6; they are chary and wary of hurting their image with low-priced merchandise.

Unlike the book business where new writers appear every day, the classical record trade must sell the same product over and over again: Beethoven, Haydn, Debussy and company. Sales of classical records depend overwhelmingly on roughly some 50 pieces: 30 symphonies, 10 violin concertos, 10 piano concertos. As a result, the industry is built on constantly creating new performances of the same celebrated music.

What happens to the "old" performances, just recently hailed as the greatest ever? Answer: they wind up on a low-priced label. For example, ten years ago the recordings of Bruno Walter and Arturo Toscanini were the best sellers in orchestral music. It is generally agreed no conductor today approaches the genius of these two. Yet the record industry depends on selling glamorous *new* conductors; so you can obtain many of the Walter and Toscanini records at a $2.98 list price.

At times, a low-priced recording by a famous artist has been rated by the critics as better than the high-priced performance by the same artist. Take Renata Tebaldi, considered one of the two or three greatest operatic sopranos of our time, and the best *Madame* Butterfly we have. She first recorded *Butterfly* in 1950 at the height of her powers. Today, you can buy this three-record set on the low-priced *Richmond* label. Tebaldi recorded *Butterfly* again in 1956 with a lesser voice and a poorer cast. You can get this recording lavishly packaged on the *London* label, but it will cost you more than double the low-priced Richmond.

What happened with the famous Boston Symphony Orchestra? RCA Victor simply could not afford to keep up all the BSO recordings in their catalogue; for the shops, deluged with new releases, had space for only the best-sellers. Thus, the BSO recordings under its former conductor Koussevitsky, and the recent wonderful recordings in full stereo under Charles Munch were relegated to the low-priced *Victrola* label. Leinsdorf conducts the BSO today. For better or worse, his recordings will cost you about $6 a record. Leinsdorf has lately announced his resignation, and you can be reasonably sure that in a year or two, you will be able to pick up his records on a low-priced *Victrola* label.

But it's not only "hand-me-downs" that make up the thousands of inexpensive records available today. In 1964, a little record company called *Elektra,* which had hitherto made only folk music, became interested in the classical market. They noted that there were dozens of small European firms who were turning out excellent records of classical music with first-class artists who were hardly known to the American public. Would Americans, brought up on Rubenstein, Menuhin, et al, be willing to buy inexpensive recordings of good music by lesser known artists?

Nonesuch thought they would. This company then bought American pressing rights from the topmost European firms, and put out a beautifully merchandised stereo record for less than $3.00 list.

Nonesuch was an immediate success. A year later, ten other independent companies jumped on the band-wagon with recordings from Europe that otherwise would have had no place on the American market.

Today, there are more than 50 labels of low-priced classical records.

There is a new generation of music lovers in America today that seeks good music, beautifully played, at a budget price. This group is not indifferent to the genius of an Isaac Stern or a Glenn Gould, but it is sophisticated enough to know that the music comes first—not the star. It has learned that there are many wonderful artists extant. This group has discovered the bounty in the low-priced field.

If you are a 50 to 10,000 cycles-per-second hi-fi bug doting on the electronic splendor of records, this book is not for you. The reprints are, for the most part, three to five years old—a horrible thing for the stereo fan to contemplate. On the other hand, if you want brilliant performances of music with perfectly good sound for home listening, I can help you find them. As a matter of fact, during the last ten years the issuance by reliable companies of discs with inferior tonal characteristics has been a rarity.

Many recordings listed in this book are mono. Many firms, bowing to the demand for stereo, have rechanelled their low-priced records for stereo. The results may pain some of our purist colleagues: however, you may be well satisfied with the accoustical result. Generally, I have.

The trend, more and more, is for low-priced records to be original stereo masters. Labels such as *Nonesuch, Everyman,* and *Richmond* are offering European stereo recordings—freshly made—that rival the latest American product.

The future looks good. Some 250 classical records are released every month; many of them are list-priced at less than $2.50.

Happy listening!

HERBERT RUSSCOL

GRATEFUL ACKNOWLEDGMENT is made to the excellent music critics who are quoted in this volume. My especial appreciation to *High Fidelity, Stereo Review, The Saturday Review,* and *The New York Times.*

I have also cited, on occasion, opinions of those English stalwarts, Edward Greenfield, Ivan March, Denis Stevens, Edward Sackville-West, and Desmond Shawe-Taylor.

Certain reviewers are acknowledged as preeminent in their special fields: Harold Schonberg on Chopin, C. G. Burke on Haydn, the late Nathan Broder on Bach and Mozart, Irving Kolodin on the symphonic repertory, and Arthur Cohn on modern music. I have found the books of these writers to be a most excellent source of reference, and I commend their works to the serious reader.

HERBERT RUSSCOL

GUIDE TO LOW-PRICED CLASSICAL RECORDS

Adam, Adolphe-Charles (1803-1856)

The son of a well-know pianist and professor of music, Adolphe-Charles Adam had to face surprisingly strong parental objections to his musical career. Nevertheless, he studied composition with Boieldieu who led him to write comic operas, many of which were highly successful.

A musical entrepreneur as well, Adam tried in 1847 to found a new opera house which failed because of the revolution of 1848.

Ballet lovers today honor him for his *Giselle,* the earliest classic of the ballet repertory.

GISELLE: SUITE

This concert suite, featuring highlights from the ballet, contains pleasing tunes and orchestration.

* * MARTINON   *Paris Conservatoire Orch.*   LONDON   STS 15010

Martinon gives a warm, poetic reading. The English critic, Edward Greenfield, appraised this record as "a deeply felt and beautifully played reminder of the ballet itself." The sound, though old, is excellent; it maintains the quality that earned praise upon its release in 1960.

Albeniz, Isaac (1860-1909)

A child prodigy and a pupil of Liszt, Albeniz was a Catalan pianist who composed more than 500 works, most of them for solo piano. Much of this is pleasant, facile writing, redolent with Spanish-Moorish rhythms and sweet harmonies.

IBERIA (Excerpts)

Iberia consists of four sets, each of which contains three solo pieces for the piano. *Iberia* is Albeniz's masterpiece, written near the end of his life, after he had discovered Impressionism and Debussy. This is not great music, but it will appeal to listeners who enjoy the rhythms and idioms of Spain.

* * MUNCH	*French National Radio Orch.*	NONESUCH (S) 71189 [Debussy, Iberia]
* DORATI	*Minneapolis Symphony Orch.*	MERCURY M/S 18063 [De Falla, La Vida Breve (Interlude and Dance No. 1)]

Munch gives a luminous performance. The listener will find it intriguing to compare this piece with Debussy's *Iberia* on the other side of the record. The sound is good.

Dorati, far less sensuous, is more straight-forward. Recording quality is fair.

Albinoni, Tomaso (1671-1750)

The Venetian Albinoni, an extremely prolific composer and violinist, was one of the first to write concertos for solo violin. Passionately devoted to music, he arranged for a younger brother to take over the management of the family and the patrimony while he sought employment and experience as an orchestral player among the Duke of Mantua's musicians.

Albinoni's music is refined and sometimes striking. The listener senses the strong personality of the composer. Bach admired Albinoni's music and used his themes.

ADAGIO FOR STRINGS AND ORGAN

The hauntingly beautiful *Adagio for Strings and Organ,* often attributed to Albinoni, was probably not written by him. For years, it was the classical best seller in France. Lovers were wont to give it as a gift. The arrangement of the *Adagio* was concocted by musicologist Remo Giazotto from an Albinoni score discovered in Dresden.

* * FAERBER	*Wuerttemberg Chamber Orch.*	TURNABOUT TV 34135 [Mozart, Sonata No. 4, K. 144; Corrette, Organ Concerto, Opus 26, No. 6; Handel, Organ Concerto No. 13]
* WITOLD	*Sinfonia Instrumental Ensemble*	NONESUCH (S) H-71005 [Concerto a Cinque in C Major; Concerto a Cinque in C Major, Opus 5, No. 12; Concerto a Cinque in E Minor, Opus 5, No. 9]

The Turnabout disc is full-bodied, and first-rate. (The couplings are all worthwhile baroque organ works, and are played with proper vigor by the knowledgeable organist-conductor-scholar Helmuth Rilling). The sound is resonant.

The Witold entry is attractive because it is an all-Albinoni program, but both the conducting and the playing here are bland and unaffecting.

CONCERTI A CINQUE (Opus 9)

Here are beautifully worked themes, handled in Albinoni's clear, forceful style.

* * HAAS	*London Baroque Ensemble*	VANGUARD	(S)	192
* * BRYKS	*Italian Baroque Ensemble*	DOVER		5225

Haas and his ensemble have a formidable reputation for recreating eighteenth century music in a zestful manner. This disc is one of their best offerings. The sound is clean and room-sized, which it should be.

The Bryks entry is elegantly played. This performance was on the Vox Label some fifteen years ago. The sound is decent.

CONCERTI FOR OBOE AND ORCHESTRA (Opus 7, No. 3; Opus 7, No. 6)

When you listen to this vivid music you will understand why Tomaso Albinoni, until recently merely a dusty name in music dictionaries, has been coming into more and more popularity.

* * ROTHWELL, BARBIROLLI	*The London Pro Arte Ensemble*	VANGUARD (S) 191 [Marcello, Oboe Concerto in C Minor; Cimarosa, Oboe Concerto (Arranged by Benjamin)]

Tastefully played by oboist Evelyn Rothwell, the Albinoni and other works are all of decided interest. The sound, while not outstanding, is agreeable.

CONCERTO IN D MINOR FOR TRUMPET

This is entertaining music, originally written for oboe or for organ.

* ANDRE, ARTUR, BEAUCAMP	*Rouen Chamber Orch.*	PHILIPS WS (M/S) 9049 [Leopold Mozart, Concerto in D Major; Vivaldi Concerto in B-flat Major for Trumpet and Violin; Telemann, Concerto in D Minor]

These are skillful arrangements, played with ringing tone by Maurice Andre, one of the most accomplished trumpet virtuosos of Europe. The sound is spacious.

Anerio, Giovanni Francesco (1567-1630)

Anerio composed numerous motets, hymns, madrigals, and other works —primarily church music. His music, similar to that of his great contemporary Palestrina, is emotionally more intense.

MISSA PRO DEFUNCTIS

* MALCOLM	Choir of the Carmelite Priory	NONESUCH	2367 (S) 5790

A vivid performance saves the day. Indifferently performed, this music would be wearisome.

Arne, Thomas Augustine *(1710-1778)*

Arne was educated at Eton and intended to practice law. He broke away, though, studied music surreptitiously, and produced his first opera in his early twenties. He wrote an enormous amount of music, and is best remembered for his delightful settings of Shakespeare's songs.

THE JUDGMENT OF PARIS: OVERTURE

This piece is an attractive work in the English Baroque style. It is an overture to a masque—a light and elegant dramatic "entertainment."

* SURINACH	*Chamber Orch.*	HELIODOR HS 25022 [Byrd, Fantasie for Strings, No. 1; Purcell, Abdelazar Suite]

The playing is vigorous, but the stereo sound is murky. The explanation is to be found on the record label which reads: "Electronically enhanced for Stereo." This admission does not appear on the record jacket where it ought to be.

Attaignant, Pierre (? -c.1550)

Attaignant, one of the earliest French printers of music, was reportedly the first typographer in Paris to use movable type. He is responsible for having preserved much of the music of his period.

SUITE OF DANCES

These dances have historic interest, but musically, they are quite unexciting.

ISOIR   TURNABOUT   (S) 34126
                                             [Titelouze, Hymns]

Isoir plays competently, but with no special flair. The disc is primarily for listeners with a special interest in early organ music.

Auber, Daniel-Francois *(1782-1871)*

Auber wrote 45 operas in the *opera comique* style of his day, many of them enormously successful. Today, his *Fra Diavolo* is occasionally produced in Europe, but the rest of his operas are unplayed, except for a few of their overtures.

Auber has earned a small place in music history because his *La Muette de Portici* (1828) was the first of the French romantic "grand operas" of the 19th century. The plot of this opera concerns a revolt against tyranny; and a performance of it in Brussels, in 1830, touched off the revolution which won Belgian independence.

OVERTURES *(in Collection)*

Auber's overtures are lively with clever tunes, but come through as rather noisy. These pieces were not meant to be profound; they were curtain-raisers to put the audience in an agreeable mood.

* * PARAY	*Detroit Symphony Orch.*	MERCURY (S) 18058 (M) 14058 [Bronze Horse; Fra Diavolo; Masaniello; Offenbach, Orpheus in Hades: selections from Tales of Hoffmann]
* SCHERCHEN	*Vienna State Opera Orch.*	(3) WESTMINSTER (S) 1021 [Muette de Portici and mixed program of overtures]
* WOLFF	*Paris Conservatoire Orch.*	LONDON STS 15021 [Domino Noir and mixed program of overtures]

Paray's performance is spirited and affectionate, with good sound.

The Scherchen collection is of lesser interest.

Wolff's reading is satisfactory. The stereo here is better. This is a good assorted program of French overtures, with only one piece by Auber.

Bach, Carl Philipp Emanuel (1714-1788)

"C.P.E." was the second of Johann Sebastian's sons by his first wife. C.P.E. was harpsichordist to Frederick the Great, and later director of music of the five principal churches of Hamburg.

Carl Philipp Emanuel inherited a large share of his father's genius. During his lifetime, C.P.E. was much more highly esteemed than his father. In his obituary notice, the Hamburg morning paper mourned their loss with the words, "His compositions are masterpieces and will continue to be found excellent long after the confused mass of modern jingle-jangle *(Klingklang)* has been forgotten." His *galant* music, more suave to our ears than that of his great fathers, is also adventurous for its period, much of it strikingly original and beautiful.

(See also "Flute Duets by the Bach Family," and "Chamber Music of the Bach Sons," under entry, W. F. Bach.)

CONCERTOS: FOR CELLO AND ORCHESTRA, IN A; FOR FLUTE AND ORCHESTRA, IN D MINOR

For more than 25 years, for five evenings a week, C. P. E. Bach accompanied Frederick the Great's flute playing in private concerts. A model of German orderliness, Frederick played the same 300 concertos in rotation for more than 40 years. (This explains the unconscionable amount of flute music from C. P. E.) All this drove C. P. E. Bach to distraction. His cello concerto is charming writing, well suited for the instrument.

* * BEX, RAMPAL, DREYFUS, BOULEZ	*Chamber Orch.*		Vox	PL STPL	(M) 14170 (S) 514170

Both soloists play with immaculate taste. Of special interest is the name Boulez; besides being a shining figure as an avant-garde composer, his reputation as a conductor has grown enormously in the last few years. (See entry on Boulez under "The New Music.") His conducting here is certainly impressive, yielding, poised, knowledgeable, lively readings. *High Fidelity* commented on this release: "It is doubtful whether better versions of these late-baroque and early classic charmers will appear for a long time." The sound is first-rate.

FLUTE CONCERTO IN A MINOR; FLUTE CONCERTO IN G MAJOR

This is *Gebrauchsmusik,* written to order for that patron of the arts, the mildly talented composer and intrepid flutist, Frederick the Great. It is elegant music.

The admirable talents of M. Rampal and of the Phillips engineers have been duly noted in this book; they are pleasingly evident on this disc.

FOUR ORCHESTRAL SYMPHONIES WITH TWELVE OBLIGATO PARTS

These symphonies, published in 1780 when C. P. E. Bach was over 65, contain music of virile energy; but for me they do not have enough content to chew on. What is of prime interest here is to behold the symphonic form in its larval state, just ready to emerge.

* JONES   *The Little Orch.*   NONESUCH H (S) 71180
                      of London

The music is played with vitality. The sound is irreproachable.

PIANO WORKS

C.P.E. was a dazzling improviser at the piano; some of his fancies are suggested here.

* * BALSAM   MUSICAL HERITAGE SOCIETY
                                                 (M/S)   558
                                        [Rondos: in G; in E-Flat;
                                        Sonatas for Clavier: in A;
                                        in G; in F; Twelve Varia-
                                        tions on "Folies D'Es-
                                        pagne," in D Minor.]

This decorative, at times scintillating, music is played with finesse. The disc is sensitively recorded.

SONATAS FOR FLUTE AND HARPSICHORD

This music was written-to-order for the cultural evenings at which Frederick the Great starred as flute soloist.

* * RAMPAL,   NONESUCH H (M) 1034
    VEYRON-LACROIX   (S) 71034
                                        [No. 1 in B-Flat; No. 2 in
                                        D; No. 3 in G; No. 4 in D;
                                        No. 5, in B-Flat; No. 6 in
                                        G.]

England's *Stereo Record Guide* cogently reports: "This music has a fragile charm that is entirely delectable. It is beautifully played and recorded, and with the one proviso that the disc should not be played all at one go, it is ideal music for late evening listening." *Stereo Record Guide:* "A splendid bargain."

Bach, Johann Christian (1735-1782)

The youngest son of Johann Sebastian, Johann Christian was known as "The London Bach" because he lived in that city from 1762 until his death. He was music master to Queen Charlotte, wife of King George III. Like his forebears, J. C., was extremely prolific, and he composed in all forms. His music, to our ears conventionally baroque, was highly bold and original in the composer's day.

Johann Christian was also a successful promoter. He had befriended Mozart in 1764, when Mozart visited London as a boy of eight, and later, with K. F. Abel, was responsible for the performance of Mozart's first three symphonies. Mozart revered Johann Christian, and was much influenced by him.

J. C. Bach was the first master to play solos on the piano, then a relatively new instrument.

SINFONIA IN D (Opus 18, No. 3); SINFONIA IN E (Opus 18, No. 5); SINFONIA CONCERTANTE IN C

This is pleasant, tuneful, neatly worked music, intended for high-level entertainment.

| * GALWAY, WICKENS, ARMON, JONES | The Little Orchestra of London | NONESUCH H | (S) 71165 |

The music is cleanly and gracefully played, and the chaste sound is agreeable.

SINFONIA FOR DOUBLE ORCHESTRA IN E-FLAT (Opus 18, No. 1); CONCERTO FOR HARPSICHORD AND STRING ORCHESTRA IN E-FLAT (Opus 7, No. 5); SINFONIA IN D (Opus 18, No. 4); SINFONIA CONCERTANTE FOR VIOLIN AND CELLO IN A

"This music presents no problems," say the notes on the record jacket, and that statement is only too true. It is rather vapid, but holds occasional flashes of interest. The *Sinfonia for Double Orchestra* is strong and spirited.

The *Harpsichord Concerto* is of some historical interest, for it was first published as a "concerto for Cembalo or Pianoforte and accompanyment," and is one of the earliest works to give the soloist a choice between these instruments. A raging battle went on at this time between die-hard purists who were enraged at the popularity of the vulgar, new-fangled pianoforte, and way-out composers such as Mozart (and later Beethoven) who were entirely beguiled by the new instrument. J. C. Bach took to the pianoforte like a duck to water.

* SCHNEIDERHAN, LEONHARDT, HEUBNER, SACHER	*Vienna Symphony*	PHILLIPS WORLD SERIES PHC (S) 9009

The playing is irreproachable. The sound is roomy.

"SONS OF BACH"
JOHANN CHRISTIAN BACH: QUARTET IN F MAJOR, SYMPHONY IN G MINOR; JOHANN CHRISTOPH FRIEDRICH BACH: SEXTET IN C MAJOR; WILHELM FRIEDMANN BACH: SYMPHONY IN D MINOR

Johann Christoph Friedrich (1732-1796) was Bach's eldest surviving son by his second wife. He was a chamber musician, and Konzertmeister. His music, while hearable, is undistinguished.

* RISTENPART	*Saar Chamber Orch.*	MUSIC GUILD (S) 104

The works on this disc are agreeable, uneventful, and primarily of historical interest. The playing is proper. The sound is fair.

Bach, Johann Sebastian (1685-1750)

Johann Sebastian Bach was born into a family which for two centuries had produced well-known musicians. His first important post was that of organist in the Ducal Chapel of Weimar. It was during his nine years there, beginning in 1708, that he created most of his organ music. In 1717, he became Kapellmeister to Prince Leopold of Anhalt-Coethen. Here he wrote many of his famous instrumental pieces including the *Brandenburg Concertos.*

These pleasant years ended abruptly with the death of Bach's wife. At this time, Prince Leopold married a lady who detested music. Bach left Coethen to become cantor of the Thomasschule in Leipzig.

The year 1723 began the crowning period of Bach's career; it was then he became cantor of St. Thomas Church at Leipzig. For the church services, he wrote his soaring choral music: the *Cantatas,* the *Passions* and the *B Minor Mass.*

At Leipzig, Bach was expected to teach singing and instrumental music, Latin, and Luther's catechisms; to prepare the singers of four churches; to lead the choir at funerals and weddings; to conduct a cantata every Sunday and to compose cantats and oratorios and other types of music, as the occasion demanded.

Bach remarried in 1723. Toward the end of his life, his eyesight dimmed. He died in Leipzig after a period of blindness. He had 20 children, of whom six survived beyond childhood.

PLACE AND ACHIEVEMENT At the time of his death, Bach was known chiefly as an organ virtuoso; then both he and his music were just about forgotten. If, a half century late, anyone spoke of "the great Bach," the remark referred to Bach's son, Carl Phillip Emanuel.

As late as the middle 1820's, Johann Sebastian Bach was not considered a composer of consequence, let along greatness. Since its first performance in 1729, his *St. Matthew Passion* had made no special impression; it was not until its centenary performance, in 1829, that Europe suddenly realized Bach's true stature. That famous revival, lovingly sponsored by the young Felix Mendelssohn and supported by Robert Schumann, led directly to a revaluation of the long-forgotten master.

Today, we adore Bach. His reputation has never been higher. He is the fountainhead. Schumann declared that "music owes· as much to Bach as religion to its Founder." Bach took most forms of music then extant and brought them to a peak of perfection. He laid down guidelines that led the way for Mozart and Beethoven.

His music is of the highest intellectual caliber—more so than that of any other composer. As with Rembrandt and Shakespeare, there is no end to the study of Bach; after one has grappled with most of his masterworks, it is time to begin once again from the beginning, more stimulated and less ignorant.

THE ESSENTIAL BACH

CHORAL MUSIC: *The Passion According to St. John; The Passion According to St. Matthew; Mass in B Minor; Church Cantatas Nos. 4, 76, 80, 131, 140; Magnificat in D.*

ORCHESTRAL MUSIC: *Six Brandenburg Concertos; Four Suites; Concerto in D Minor, for Piano and Orchestra; Concertos in A Minor and E Major, for Violin and Orchestra; Concerto in D Minor, for Two Violins and Orchestra.*

CHAMBER MUSIC: *Six Suites for Unaccompanied Cello; Six Sonatas for Violin and Piano; Three Sonatas for Unaccompanied Violin.*

ORGAN MUSIC: *Passacaglia in C Minor; Toccata and Fugue in D Minor; Fantasia and Fugue in G Minor; Toccata in C Major; Chorales, Choral Preludes ("Orgelbuechlein"), etc.*

KEYBOARD MUSIC: *Six English Suites; Six Partitas; The Well-Tempered Clavier; Goldberg Variations; Chromatic Fantasy and Fugue; Italian Concerto in F.*

OTHER WORKS

CHORAL MUSIC: *Christmas Oratorio, Eastern Oratorio, Cantatas, Motets, Chorales, Magnificats.*

ORCHESTRAL MUSIC: [*Bach wrote many concertos for various instruments and orchestra.*]

ORGAN MUSIC: [*He wrote many other works for organ.*]

KEYBOARD MUSIC: *Six French Suites.* [*There are other works.*]

CHORAL WORKS   Bach's *B Minor Mass*, the *St. Matthew Passion,* and the *St. John Passion,* are the most stupendous body of choral music ever written. They can only be termed sublime.

CHRISTMAS ORATORIO (S. 248)

This oratorio is really made up of six cantatas, or "'parts," designed to be performed separately on six days around Christmas time. In consequence, the colossal, unified architectural strength of Bach's other large-scale choral works is lacking. Undoubtedly, Bach would have been astonished to hear them played in one sitting, as is the modern custom. But these works contain much somber beauty, and each contata has moving moments.

* * WERNER	*Heinrich Schuetz Choir, Heilbron, with Soloists, Pforzheim Chamber Orch.*	MUSICAL HERITAGE SOCIETY	(S) 571-73
* RATHAUSCHER, HOFSTAETTER, KREUZBERGER, BERRY, GROSSMANN	*Vienna Symphony Orch.*	2-Vox VBX	(M) 201

Fritz Werner on the MHS label turns in a reading that is entirely respectable. This is an intimate performance, with strong singers led by the indispensible Agnes Giebel, and the tasteful, light cultivated tenor of Helmut Krebs. The other soloists are good, and the choral work is responsive and clear. This set is from Erato, Paris, and as is often the case with discs of French origin, the sound is a bit dry and underamplified; but the record is still enjoyable. NOTE: MHS records are available by mail order only; see listing of record companies at front of this book.

Ferdinand Grossmann delivers a zealous, enjoyable performance on an old-time Vox relic. Fine horn and trumpet work are heard; but the soloists are of uneven quality. The old mono sound is of indifferent quality.

EASTER ORATORIO (S. 249)

This genial music, composed about 1736, is rarely performed today. Apparently, Bach first wrote this music as a secular cantata to celebrate the birthday of a German princeling. Later, the composer used the same music several times as a basis for sacred works, adapting a religious text in each instance. This music is not among the greatest of Bach's work; but as always, in the work of such a master, wonderful attractions are to be encountered.

* PROHASKA	*Akademiechor*	VANGUARD	(M) 156
* GROSSMANN	*Akademie Kamerchor, Vienna Pro Musica*	Vox	(M) 8620
* WERNER	*Pforzheim Chamber Orch. Heilbronn, Schuetz Choir*	MUSIC GUILD	(S) 144

Both the Grossmann and Prohasks recordings have been around since the early 1950's when American record companies practically supported all the musicians of Vienna and Stuttgart by churning out cheap recordings of baroque. Both conductors are well-groomed in Bach. For today's ears neither version is exceptional, although both are honest and knowledgeable. On both, the mono sound is thin, but quite hearable. The adequate Werner reading, in stereo, is indifferently recorded.

MAGNIFICAT IN D (S. 243)

This is staunch, virile, enormously satisfying music. There is no better introduction to the vocal glories of Bach than the short *Magnificat*. Bach was thirty-eight when he wrote the original version for performance in the Leipzig Thomas-Kirche at Christmas time. He revised the piece ten years later; today, the second version is generally heard.

* * * WOLF, WATTS, LEWIS, HEMSLEY	*Jones Orch. and Singers*	SERAPHIM [Purcell]	60001
* * GUNDERMANN, RUETGERS, EQUILUZ, WENK, RILLING	*Stuttgart Bach Orch.*	TURNABOUT (S) 34173 [Buxtehude, Magnificat]	
* STICH-RANDALL, CASONI, BOTTAZZO, LITTASY, RISTENPART	*Saar Chamber Orch.*	NONESUCH (S) 71011 [Cantata No. 51]	

The Geraint Jones singers deliver a stunning performance for which I have nothing but praise. Small forces are used, and the singers, led by the admirable Helen Watts and Richard Lewis, are of sterling quality. The chorus is equally inspired. In the words of Bach conductor Davis Randolph, "An air of serenity and poise persuades the music, thanks to the 'otherworldly' tone quality so special to English choruses . . . in the finest tradition of English choral singing." This is a joyous record not to be missed. The mono sound is resonant. [The Purcell backing is first-rate; the brass ensemble work on the Purcell alone is worth the price of the record.]

Just a few rungs down from this heady success, and also of admirable quality, is Rilling's vigorous and full-blooded performance. This young German conductor is one of the best Bach interpreters we have today. The sound is clean. [The Buxtehude backing is worth-whole.]

The up-and-down Nonesuch disc does not compete. The English *Stereo Record Guide* comments: "Stich-Randall is the attraction . . .. and she sings most beautifully. Her fellow soloists are not up to this standard. . . . The balance is poor." [The *Cantata 51,* on reverse, comes off far more successfully. This side contains some superb trumpet playing.]

MASS IN B MINOR (S. 232)

Here is the greatest Latin Mass ever written—and by the staunchly Protestant Bach. The *Sanctus* movement was originally written for services at Christmas, 1724; the other sections were put together later. Exactly when and why is still a matter of fierce argument. In any case, this is very great music, more formal than the intimate, poetic style of Bach's musically narrated *Passions*.

* * ALARIE, DELFOSSE, HOFFMAN, SIMONEAU, REHFUSS, GOEHR	*Amsterdam Philharmonic*	2-VANGUARD	(S) 216/7
* SAILER, BENCE, WUNDERLICH, WENK, GRISCHKAT	*Swabian Chorus*	3-VOX SVBX	57

Goehr provides a most respectable and attractive performance, even if his rendition lacks the breadth and profundity of Klemperer's on a high-priced Angel. Goehr maintains dramatic tension almost throughout. The highly-respected Nathan Broder comments: "Several of the soloists do better than average work . . . the sound is excellent, with good separation in the stereo version."

The Vox set, made at the time of the 35th German Bach Festival, sounds well rehearsed. The chorus is light-weight but accomplished, and achieves a feeling of spaciousness. Grischkat is in full command, and the male soloists, especially the late Fritz Wunderlich, are strong. The trouble is that the women soloists are *schwach*, as the Germans put it. The English *Stereo Guide* comments: "With stronger casting in the female solo parts, this version would bid fair to being one of the best available."

MASSES, "LUTHERAN" (S. 233/6)

These short *Masses* are late works by Bach; they are not on a par with the great contatas, not to speak of Bach's large choral works, but there is nevertheless much pensive beauty here. In each of these *Masses*, Bach borrows themes and harmonies from his own cantatas.

* GIEBEL, LITZ, PREY, REDEL	*Munich Pro Arte Orch.;* *Lausanne Chorus* (1, 2)	PHILLIPS WS (M/S) 9060
GRISCHKAT	*Stuttgart Tonstudio*	3-PERIOD	1073

Redel conducts firmly, with the strong sense of line needed here. The singing is attractive, although the soloists have their ups and downs.

The Grischkat set goes back more than 15 years, and is just barely adequate both in performance and in sound.

MOTETS

These are tender, heartfelt pieces, a joy to every lover of Bach. A motet was a setting of a sacred text in the current style of the period, for solo voice and/or choir, with or without instrumental accompaniment. Bach's motets are for unaccompanied double chorus, for five-part chorus, and for four-part chorus with organ continuo.

* * FORSTER	*St. Hedwigs Cathedrale, Chorus, Berlin* (Nos. 1/4, 6)	MACE	(S) 9016
* WOLTERS	*N. German Singkreis, Instr.*	NONESUCH [Motets 2, 5]	(7) 1060
GERHARD	*Stuttgart Bach Orch. and Boys' Choir*	VOX [Cantata No. 80]	(5) 14150

Karl Forster is a formidable name in Germany for performances of liturgical music, and his reputation is supported in this recording. This reading is extremely accurate and disciplined—perhaps even *too* efficient and well-drilled.

The Nonesuch entry is good; it will be preferred by those who enjoy women's voices rather than boys' voices in the treble parts. Nathan Broder comments: "Beautifully done."

The Vox disc, too, is earnest but not especially persuasive. [It is backed with the triumphant *Cantata No. 80*.]

ST. JOHN PASSION (S. 245)

We must turn to the Italian painters of the early Renaissance for art comparable in spirit to that of the *St. John Passion*. Contrasted with the celestial bliss of the *St. Matthew Passion*, this is a harsh, even savage work (especially in the crowd choruses). The *St. John Passion* also gives much sharper dramatic characterization of the principal roles. It employs starker means—only one chorus and orchestra, as compared to two of each in the *St. Matthew*. (*St. Matthew* also has an independent chorus of treble voices.)

Most musicians rate *St. John* a cut below *St. Matthew*, but there are many who would not yield a page of its terrifying music for that of the more lofty *St. Matthew*.

* * * GIEBEL, MATTHES, LEWIS, REHFUSS, VANDERNOOT	*Amsterdam Philharmonic, Chorus*	3-NONESUCH	(S) 73004
* GROSSMANN	*Vienna Symphony Orch.*	3-VOX VBX	(M) 202

The Nonesuch entry with Vandernoot is superb. The conducting is lucid and devotional. The soloists, especially Agnes Giebel and Richard Lewis, are all that one could ask. The choral work is sweeping, full-bodied, and secure, and the choral soun dis spacious—these are rare pleasures in a Bach *Passion*. *Stereo Review's* report commented: "Performance, first rate; recording, very good."

The Grossmann album is an honorable relic that some of us grew up with, when it practically stood alone as the only recorded version within our financial grasp. Grossmann is an outstanding interpreter of Bach, and his performance is at all times vivid. His soprano, Gisela Rathauscher, comes off very well indeed—better than many more famous names on other sets. I cannot hear this album without my judgment being blurred by many sentiments from the past; yet I am aware that the choral singing is rough, and that the sound is not good by today's merciless standards.

ST. MATTHEW PASSION (S. 244)

Bach is believed to have composed no less than five settings of the Passion story. The *St. Matthew Passion* is elaborate and exalted. Many listeners consider it the most deeply moving of all the music of our precious cantor of Leipzig. This work towers above the many other compositions in its genre. Albert Schweitzer once groped to describe its grandeur, and finally said that "the opening movement of the *St. Matthew Passion* is a great portal through which one enters into sublimity."

The *St. Matthew Passion* is the most widely performed of Bach's *Passions*. Its popularity can be measured by the listing in Mr. Schwann's indispensable catalogue, which indicate 11 complete recordings of *St. Matthew!*

* * * STICH-RANDALL, ROESSL-MAJDAN, KMENTT, BRAUN, BERRY, WOELDIKE		2-VANGUARD	(S) 269/72
* GROSSMANN	*Akademie Kammerchor, Vienna Chamber Orch.*	3-VOX VBX	(M) 200
FERRIER, JACQUES	*Orch. and Chorus*	3-RICHMOND	(M) 43001

The illustrious recording by Mogens Woeldike has been praised as being little short of divine revelation. When this set was on the prestigious Bach Guild label, the New York *Times'* Harold Schonberg, commented: "The most interesting and satisfactory *St. Matthew* ever brought to records." The late, and truly great Bach scholar Nathan Broder also bestowed his accolade, adding: "A feature of this recording is the magnificently clear lifelike sound." This is a subdued, undramatic reading, simple and monochromatic. Two first-line women singers are featured: Stich-Randall, who has a reserved, singular voice that takes getting used to, and the much warmer alto of Roessl-Majdan.

The mono Grossmann relic on Vox is serviceable; "but the performance seldom rises above the plane of competence."*

The Richmond set, conducted by Reginald Jacques, is mono only, sung in English, and survives on the market only because of the gravely moving voice of Kathleen Feerier. But that is hardly enough to warrant purchasing this pedestrian performance.

CANTATAS One of Bach's tasks as choirmaster was to compose a church cantata for each main Sunday service, and also for celebrations on feast days. It is believed that he actually wrote nearly 300 of these; some 200 have survived. The texts are based on the Gospel for the particular day; they are based on plain Lutheran hymn tones that Bach loved above all else. Bach also wrote a few "secular" cantatas, on such topics as the joys of coffee. These are far less important.

Virtually ignored in America before the advent of the long-playing record, many music lovers of today adore these cantatas which represent the intimate work-a-day Bach. These cantatas are short and heartfelt, and I would not part with them for any other music.

Practically speaking, the only way to hear these cantatas played well is through long-playing records; for orchestras have vanished from most church services, and public concerts rarely provide good soloists for the short solo parts.

Many great cantatas are not represented on low-priced records, or have been done so shabbily that criticism can only retreat. The following list—an arbitrary choice—includes the most rewarding of the cantatas: No. 4, 8, 51, 56, 76, 80, 82, 106, 131, 140, 170, and 198.

CANTATA NO. 4, "CHRIST LAG IN TODESBANDEN"

Many listeners consider this solemn Easter cantata to be the greatest of all Bach's cantatas. The text, by Martin Luther, is based on medieval sources.

* * FELBERMAYER, UHL, BRAUN, PROHASKA	*Bach Guild Orch. and Chorus*	VANGUARD (M) 152 [Cantata No. 140]
* GIEBEL, HOEFFGEN, ROTZSCH, ADAM, THOMAS	*Leipzig Gewandhaus Orch. and Thomanerchor*	TURNABOUT (3) 4048 [Cantata No. 111]
WEHRUNG, HAASEMANN, HOEFFLIN, POMMERIEN, EHMANN	*German Bach Soloists, Westphalian Singers*	VANGUARD (S) 225 [Cantata No. 182]

The passionate conviction of Prohaska's reading commands first place. The mono sound is clear.

Turnabout's master of *Cantata No. 4* was once on the English label, "His Master's Voice." Here is the English *Stereo Guide's* review in full: "The performances here are not very fine ones. The best of the soloists is the tenor, but the others are adequate rather than distinguished. The intonation in the ensembles, too, is rather homely. The recording is excellent."

The Ehmann performance on Vanguard was originally on the now defunct Cantate label of Germany. Vanguard took over many of the Cantate masters when that firm went out of business a few years ago. The engineering is impeccable; Cantate was manufactured by Deutsche Grammophone. The performances are accurately *Urtext,* but the singing is pitifully weak. Most of Cantate discs ought to be skipped, but I don't know just how you can do this, as Vanguard gives no indication on the record jacket of theorigin of this series.

NOTE: Easily the best of all recordings is that of the Robert Shaw Chorale on an expensive RCA Victor.

CANTATA NO. 51, "JAUCHZET GOTT IN ALLEN LANDEN"

This famous cantata for solo soprano and orchestra also features a brilliant trumpet obbligato.

| * * SCHWARZKOPF, GELLHORN | *Philharmonic Orch.* | SERAPHIM   (M) 60013 [Mozart, Exsultate Jubilate] |
| * STICH-RANDALL, RISTENPART | *Saar Chamber Orch.* | NONESUCH   (S) 71011 [Magnificat] |

The Seraphim record, featuring Elizabeth Schwarzkopf, is a beauty. It was a stunning disc when first released, and it remains so. Schwarzkopf was at the top of her form when this was made, some 16 years ago. There is some spectacular coloratura display in the opening and closing arias, and effortless musicianship as well. The mono sound is just fair. [The Mozart on the reverse is also a famous and brilliant piece for soprano and orchestra.]

Stich-Randall is acceptable on the Nonesuch disc, but without the heady exuberance this music demands. The trumpet work is really exhilarating. The sound is good.

CANTATAS NO. 76, 84, 198, 210
(Wedding Cantata)

These are superior cantatas, of the highest importance for Bach lovers.

LASZLO,	WESTMINSTER (M/S) 1019
ROESSL-MAJDAN,	
MONTEANU,	
KMENTT,	
STANDEN, POELL,	
CHORUS,	
SCHERCHEN	

This recording was famous a few years ago; it features first-rate singing and conducting. However, the recording has now been butchered by "electronical-rechanneling for exciting stereo sound." The old mono pressings are much better; they have been cut out of the catalogue and can be picked up for as low as one dollar in some big record stores.

CANTATA NO. 80, "EIN FESTE BURG
IST UNSER GOTT"

A glorious setting of the Lutheran hymn, A Mighty Fortress is Our God. Albert Schweitzer rated this cantata with No. 140 as "a dramatic art-work of the most perfect kind imaginable."

* * FAHBERG, BENCE,	Wuerttemberg Chamber	3-Vox	(5) 14150
MAJER,	Orch.	[Motets]	
SCHAIBLE,			
RILLING			
GIEBEL, MATTHES,	Amsterdam Philharmonic	VANGUARD (S) 219	
LEWIS, REHFUSS,	Society Orch., Bach	[Cantata No. 104]	
VANDERNOOT	Chorus		

The vital, broadly-conceived Rilling version on Vox is the better of the two offerings. The soloists range from good to admirable. Nathan Broder wrote: "Here is the best recording yet of the great Reformation Cantata." The sound is fair.

After his magnificent St. John Passion, Vandernoot disappoints with a hard-driving interpretation. Irving Kolodin in the Saturday Review, "Vandernoot does not strike me as an ideal Bach conductor."

CANTATA NO. 82, "ICH HABE GENUG"

This weary, death-longing cantata, *I Have Enough*, must touch the heart of any mortal with ears.

* PREY, THOMAS	*Leipzig Gewandhaus Orch. and Thomanerchor*	TURNABOUT (M) 4020 (S) 34020 [Cantata No. 56]	
RISTENPART	*Saar Chamber Orch., Chorus*	MUSIC GUILD (S) 112 [Cantata No. 159]	

Hermann Prey has a pleasing baritone voice; he is a solidly trained singer. The music is well recorded. [The coupling with the fine *Cantata No. 56* makes this the better choice.]

Jakob Staempli, the bass soloist on the Music Guild disc, has a dark, rich voice. However, the recording balance is off; the soloist seems to be way back somewhere, with the oboe covering everything.

Neither of these soloists plumbs the depths of this work as does Fischer-Dieskau on the expensive Archive label.

CANTATA NO. 106, "GOTTES ZEIT IST DIE ALLERBESTE ZEIT"

God's Time is the Best Time is one of the great ones; this music is as serene as any ever penned.

* ROESSL-MAJDAN, POELL, SCHERCHEN	*Vienna Academie Kammerchor*	WESTMINSTER (M) 18394 [Cantata No. 140]

The only available version is the exciting mono disc of Scherchen, with stirring soloists. The sound is fair. [The backing is another great cantata.]

CANTATA NO. 140, "WACHET AUF!"

This glorious, heaven-inspired work is the most popular of Bach's cantatas. In a graphic manner, the text treats the parable of the ten virgins who were unready for the arrival of the bridegroom. Albert Schweitzer comments on *Cantata No. 140:* "Not until Berlioz shall we meet with any dramatic-pictorial music comparable to this."

* * FELBERMAYER, UHL, BRAUN, PROHASKA	*Bach Guild Choir*	VANGUARD (M) 152 [Cantata No. 4]
* BUCKEL, STAMPFLI, RISTENPART	*Saar Chamber Orch.*	NONESUCH (S) 71029 [Cantata No. 57]

| * LASZLO, KMENTT,
POELL,
SCHERCHEN | *Vienna Akademie*
Kammerchor | WESTMINSTER   (M) 18934
[Cantata No. 106] |

Prohaska provides a first-rate recording, alive and forward-moving from the first bar. The soloists range from good to excellent. The mono sound is quite acceptable.

The only stereo entry is Ristenpart, and I find his reading sluggishly sung, although the sonics are good. The *Stereo Record Guide* comments: "Enjoyable, if not memorable."

Scherchen has a thrilling soloist in Magda Laszlo. The sound is only mono, but clear. (Avoid the tubby "enhanced stereo" version of this record.)

CANTATA NO. 206, "SCHLEICHT, SPIELENDE WELLEN."

This secular (not sacred) cantata was written for the birthday festivities of the Saxon Elector August III. This is not Bach at his most gripping, but it will mildly interest those who already love his cantatas.

| * KIRSCHSTEIN,
BENCE, EQUILUZ,
WENK, GALLING,
RILLING | *Chorus of the*
Gedaechtniskirche,
Bach-Collegium, Stuttgart | NONESUCH   (S) H 71187 |

Rilling is never pretentious, but always entirely authentic in Bach. The soloists and small-sized chorus are most musical. *Stereo Review:* "Performance: commendable; recording: very good."

CANTATA NO. 211, "COFFEE CANTATA"

Believe it or not, this secular cantata is all about the new craze for coffee—a lively topic in Bach's day. The humor is heavy, and the work is of little musical interest.

* SPEISER, JOCHIMS, OCKER, EWERHART	*Wuerttemberg Chamber* *Orch.*	TURNABOUT (3) 4071 [Cantata No. 203]
* WEBER, KREBS, HAUCK, KOCH	*Berlin Radio Chamber* *Ensemble*	NONESUCH (S) 71008 [Cantata No. 212]
* SAILER, FEYERABEND, MUELLER, REINHARDT	*Stuttgart Pro Musica*	VOX (M) 8980 [Cantata No. 203]

The Turnabout version is simply and pleasingly sung.

The Nonesuch disc is also appealing, with good deadpan humor by the soloists.

The old mono-only Vox version is still lively. Vocal expert Philip Miller comments: "By absolute standards, very good."

ORCHESTRAL MUSIC This is rich, varied music mostly featuring vivid writing for solo instruments.

BRANDENBURG CONCERTI (S. 1046/51)

In the spring of 1718, Prince Leopold of Anhalt-Coethen went to Carlsbad to take the medicinal baths. He traveled in princely style. Included in his retinue were five members of his household orchestra, and his staff composer and harpsichordist, one Johann Sebastian Bach. There was another aristocrat present at Carlsbad at this time—the Margrave of Brandenburg, who was impressed with Bach, and commissioned from him a set of concertos for his own orchestra. Unwittingly, the Margrave of Brandenburg also gained undying fame.

The exhilarating Brandenburg Concertos are today perhaps the most popular of all Bach's enormous output, firm favorites with both concert audiences and record collectors. There are, at this writing, 24 complete recordings of the Brandenburgs in Mr. Schwann's catalogue—an incredible number.

For the neophyte, there is no better introduction to the glories of Bach.

* * * RISTENPART	*Saar Chamber Orch.*	2-Nonesuch (S) 73006
* * * PROHASKA	*Vienna State Opera Chamber Orch.*	2-Vanguard (S) 171/2
* * REDEL	*Pro Arte Chamber Orch. of Munich*	Musical Heritage Society (M/S) MHS 529/30
* * MUNCLINGER	*Ars Rediviva Ensemble*	2-Crossroads (M) 22 26 0003 (S) 22 26 0004
* * GOBERMAN	*New ork Sinfonia*	2-Odyssey 32260014
* GOLDBERG	*Netherlands Chamber Orch.*	2-Phillips WS (M/S) 2-004
* KLEMPERER	*Pro Musica*	3-Vox (M) 6180, 6200, 6220
* KEHR	*Mainz Chamber Orch.*	3-Vox SVBX (S) 569
* FAERBER	*Wuerttemberg Chamber Orch.*	2-Turnabout (S) 4044/45

Ristenpart's is the plum of the present offerings. Here are both élan and scholarship. The scholarship results in such touches as the rough-toned valveless French horns, tootling valiantly, in scorn of modern "improvements." The formidable soloists also set this album above the other entries: fluitist Rampal, oboist Pierlot, harpsichordist Veyron-Lacroix, and others of comparable stature. The sound is dry but lively, as on most releases emanating from the Club Francais du Disque in Paris. *High Fidelity* comments: "One of the finest sets of Brandenburgs to be had at any price."

Bach is also very well served in the Prohaska performance. Prohaska sticks to the original instrumentation, utilizing the violino piccolo and viola di gamba. This is a scholarly, yet enormously stimulating, reading. The sound is clean.

Another admirable choice is the Kurt Redel performance. Redel uses a very small ensemble, thus making the complex counterpoint of this music much clearer. Modern instruments are used.

The Munclinger album is spirited and assured, and the playing is irreproachable—a highly satisfying performance. The sound is clean.

The Goberman set has verve and ebullence, top New York players, and for those who insist on getting the Tablets precisely as they were engraved on Sinai, the instrumentation is almost exactly that used by Bach. Some earlier versions that Bach tried out for *Concertos No. 1* and *5* are also included. The sound is fairly bright. *High Fidelity* comments: "In the budget category you could scarcely go wrong with this excellently played set of *Brandenburgs*."

The Dutch players under Goldberg are fine; the conducting is unobtrusive. The sound, however, is a bit thickish.

Klemperer is authoritative, but the playing is sometimes ragged, and the sonics of this venerable set seem aged. For those who seek Klemperer, his later performance on an expensive Angel is far more worthy.

Kehr's players have stylistic consistency, but I miss the joyful exuberance communicated in the top choices of this list.

Faerber is respectable, but on the dullish side—unforgivable in this vivid, sparkling music. The solo playing is good.

CONCERTO IN A MINOR FOR FLUTE, VIOLIN, HARPSICHORD (S. 1044)

This is an eloquent, poised baroque concerto, with lovely and serene writing for flute.

* * MOEHRING, LAUTENBACHER, GALLING	*Stuttgart Soloists*	TURNABOUT (S) 34219 [Orchestra Suite No. 2]

* BECKENSTEINER, FERNANDEZ, LARDE, PAILLARD	Jean-Marie Leclair Instrumental Ensemble	MUSICAL HERITAGE SOCIETY (M/S) 535 [Concerto for Harpsichord and Orchestra No. 6 in F (S. 1057)]
* CROMM, HENDEL, KIND, RISTENPART	Saar Chamber Orch.	NONESUCH (S) 71057 [Concerto for 3 Violins]

Galling delivers a glowing performance, faithful to Bach. [The coupling is excellent.]

The Paillard reading seems hurried, even brusque, and there goes the charm. The sound is only so-so.

The terse nonstop review of the *Stereo Record Guide* on the Ristenpart disc commented: "These performances are spirited in a trundling sort of way but the three violins are very wiry as recorded and in BWX 1044 the harpsichord jangles."

CONCERTO IN C MINOR FOR 2 HARPSICHORDS (BWV 1062); CONCERTO IN D MINOR FOR 3 HARPSICHORDS (BWV 1063); CONCERTO IN C FOR 3 HARPSICHORDS (BWV 1064); CONCERTO IN A MINOR FOR 4 HARPSICHORDS (BWV 1065)

Here is more highly enjoyable, linear fantasizing for the harpsichord.

* * NEUMEYER, BERGER, BURR, URBUTEIT, RISTENPART	Chamber Orch. of the Saar	NONESUCH	H-71019

All four concertos receive extremely good performances. The tempos are assured. The sound is spacious even when the works get dense or complicated. The stereo effect, however, is faint.

CONCERTO IN C MINOR FOR VIOLIN AND OBOE (S. 1060)

This lovely, poignant concerto shows Bach at his most tender.

* * FENYVES, HOLLIGER, AUBERSON	Geneva Baroque Orch.	MONITOR (S) 2088 [Marcello, Oboe Concerto in D minor; C.P.E. Bach, Oboe Concerto in E flat major; Bellini, Oboe Concerto in E flat major]

| * * LEHMAN,
JANUNET,
LARDROT,
DE STOUTZ | *Zurich Chamber Orch.* | VANGUARD   (S)   198
[Suite for Flute and Strings,
No. 2, in B minor, S. 1067;
Brandenburg Concerto No.
2, in F, S. 1047] |

Both entries are enjoyable. Some critics may quibble over the fast tempos on the Vanguard set, and with the thin tone of violinist Lorand Fenyves. But Fenyves more than makes up for it in musicianship—his playing is excellent and extremely knowledgeable. The oboist, too, is first-rate. The sound is pleasant. [Couplings may well decide the choice here. The Monitor disc is made up of excellent oboe works.]

The Vanguard disc is also attractively done; the oboist Lardrot is rated even better than the equally famous oboist on Monitor. The Vanguard sound is highly agreeable. [Vanguard's disc is entitled "The Bravura Bach," and contains a shrewdly compiled program of some of his most popular pieces which feature a solo wind instrument. The *Suite No. 2* has ingratiating writing and playing on the flute, and the *Second Brandenburg Concerto* shows off the iron lip of famous trumpeter Adolph Scherbaum.]

CONCERTO IN D FOR 2 VIOLINS (S. 1043)

The *Double Concerto* is a perennial concert favorite—one of Bach's great works. This is vivid, staunchly satisfying music.

* * DAVID AND IGOR OISTRAKH, BARSHAI	*Chamber Orch.*	MONITOR (M) 2009 [Sonata No. 6 in G Major for Violin and Piano; Sara- sate, Navarra for Two Vio- lins and Piano; Hindemith, Sonata No. 1 for Violin and Piano, Opus 11]
* * CYROULNIK, ARMAND, AURIACOMBE	*Toulouse Symphony Orch.*	COUNTERPOINT (M) 610 (S) 5610 [Violin Concertos Nos. 1 and 2]
* LAUTENBACHER, VERHOLZ, KEHR	*Mainz Chamber Orch.*	VOX 5-11540 [Violin Concerto No. 1 and 2]
* SUK, JASEK, SMETACEK	*Prague Symphony Orch.*	CROSSROADS (M) 22 16 0037 (S) 22 16 0038 [Violin Concerto]

The Oistrakhs, father and son, are a bit overly suave, but nevertheless thrilling. The mono sound is all right. [The coupling consists of unimportant small pieces.]

Counterpoint offers a full-bodied, well-executed reading, with warm sound.

The playing on the Vox disc is graceful and pleasing.
Crossroads has a hearable dic, but violinist Suk seems too light-weight for my taste.

CONCERTO NO. 1 IN D MINOR (FOR HARPSICHORD AND ORGAN) (S. 1052)

This splendid, buoyant music is the most popular of Bach's concertos for keyboard instruments. The music belongs to the harpsichord, even though it is also firmly entrenched in the piano repertory.

* * RUZICKOVA, LEHEL	*Prague Chamber Orch.*	CROSSROADS	(M) 22 16 0027 (S) 22 16 0028 [Concerto No. 2]
* * RICHTER, SANDERLING	*USSR State Orch.*	MONITOR	(M) 2050 [Schumann, Concerto]
DEMUS, REDEL	*Vienna State Opera Orch.*	WESTMINSTER	(M) 18925 (S) 14109 [Concerto No. 2]

I would take Ruzickova without hesitation; she plays with excellent élan and assertiveness. The stereo sound is good, although the balance between soloist and ensemble could have been much better. *High Fidelity* comments: "Miss Ruzickova is one of today's finest harpsichordists. Her playing has a hypnotic clarity . . ." [Her disc also contains the first-rate *Concerto No. 2.*]

The great pianist Richter is unimpeachable—his lines, a model of clarity; his rippling fingers, incredible. The sound is decent mono.

Demus' interpretation is unassuming and academic.

HARPSICHORD CONCERTOS 1-7 (BWV 1052/8); THREE DOUBLE HARPSICHORD CONCERTOS (BWV 1060/2); TWO TRIPLE HARPSICHORD CONCERTOS (BWV 1063/4); QUADRUPLE HARPSICHORD CONCERTO IN A MINOR (BWV 1065); TRIPLE CONCERTO FOR FLUTE, VIOLIN AND HARPSICHORD (BWV 1044)

This is a staggering tour de force—Bach's complete concertos for harpsichord and orchestra in one album. In today's low-priced record business it is much more profitable for a company to sell three or four records in one album than a single disc. Pressing a record does not involve much expenditure; but the cost of designing a cover, making color separations, and printing the cover is considerable.

| * GERLIN and others, DOUATTE | *Paris Collegium Musicum* | 5-NONESUCH | (S) 73001 |

With all respect for the boldness of this enterprise, the playing varies widely from concerto to concerto; on many sides, the quality dips below par. Another serious drawback is the jangly sound. When the recording stage gets crowded, the sound seems to go out of control. The *Stereo Record Guide* points out that "Only the most hardened harpsichord enthusiast will manage to sit through these ten sides with aplomb." But why play them all at one sitting *ad seriatim?*

HARPSICHORD CONCERTO NO. 4 IN A (S. 1055)

Concertos No. 3 and 4 are perhaps not quite as exhilarating as the first two, but both are worthwhile. Both have poised lyrical slow movements that only Bach could have achieved.

| * * RUZICKOVA, NEUMANN | *Prague Chamber Orch.* | CROSSROADS (S) 22 16 0180 [Concerto No. 3] |

Ruzickova is lucid, crisp, and stimulating. The sound on my copy was tubby and blurry—better hear this disc first, if possible.

MUSICAL OFFERING (S. 1079)

Bach paid a visit to Frederick the Great in 1747, and the king gave him a theme to improvise upon. After returning home, Bach used it as the basis of a dazzling series of contrapuntal studies which he dispatched to Frederick as his *Musical Offering*. The extremely beautiful climax of this music, *the Ricercare,* is often played alone.

* * * MUENCHINGER	*Stuttgart Chamber Orch.*	LONDON	STS 15063
* *	*Munich Instrument Ensemble*	VOX	(500) 490
* SCHERCHEN	*Scherchen Ensemble*	WESTMINSTER 9005 (M) 19089 (S) 17089

The superbly stylish, cool and searchingly played performance of Muenchinger and his men has been praised ecstatically by *Saturday*

Review, The New York Times, and just about everyone else. There is an uncanny sense of linear polyphonic clarity here. The 1955 early stereo era sound is chaste and realistic. If you love Bach, or want to love Bach, don't miss this one. It is one of the greatest Bach performances ever recorded.

The Munich Ensemble brings out the subtle and complex lines of this score, with musical intelligence. The sound is satisfactory.

Scherchen's impressive reading is more personalized, less linear. Regrettably, the sound is only mono, but quite hearable.

SUITES FOR ORCHESTRA (S. 1066/9)

Desmonde Shawe-Taylor has written a pungent *precis* of Bach's suites: "Bach's four orchestral suites are also known as 'overtures,' in the old-fashioned sense of that word: a long first movement, consisting of a solemn introduction and a fugal allegro, followed by a series of dance movements. Like the *Brandenburg Concertos,* the *Suites* are scored for various combinations of instruments. All are enjoyable, but *No. 2* and *3* are justly the most popular. *No. 2 in B Minor* is written for the deliciously cool combination of solo flute and strings, and concludes with the enchanting piece called *Badinerie; No. 3,* richly and impressively scored, with parts for trumpets and drums, contains the famous *Air* for strings alone, one of the most beautiful long-breathed melodies ever written. During the nineteenth century this *Air* became immoderately popular in a transcription."

* * KEHR	*Mainz Quartet*	2-Vox SVUX	(S) 52000
* SCHERCHEN	*English Baroque Orch.*	2-Westminster	(M) 18012/3
* RISTENPART	*Saar Orch.*	2-Counterpoint	(5) 603/4

The best bet is the vivid, well-paced version of Kehr. The sound is clean.

Scherchen's mono version, in its day, produced much admiration; it also provoked arguments among *echt-Bach* partisans who agonized over his lack of double-dotting, and his other unconventional pepping-up of the music. The sound, today, is thin.

The Ristenpart reading is straightforward, but on the dullish side. This set started its career on mono, and the sound is only so-so.

"THE ANNA MAGDALENA NOTEBOOK"

Anna Magdalena was Bach's second wife. The musical notebook she compiled in 1725 contains many bits and pieces of her own selection. This is something of a musical curiosity. Until lately, it was widely believed that all the music was written by Bach himself. Lately, however, eager research has unearthed the fact that Bach copied some entries into the book, and that much here was written by other composers as well. Embarrassment and amusement in musicological circles followed the revelation that beautiful arias purported to be "only possible by Bach's genius" were indeed composed by the low rated G. H. Stoelzel.

Individual selections in the book include: *Polonaise in G Minor; Marches: in E-Flat; in G; in D; Minuets: in G; in G minor; Willst Du Dein Herz Mir Schenken; Rondeau in B; Bist Du Bei Mir; Aria for Clavier; So Oft Ich Meine Tabakspfeife; Allemande in D Minor; Dir, Dir, Jehova, Will Ich Singen; Prelude in C; Musette in D; Ich Habe Genug; Schlummert Ein, Ihr Matten Augen; Chorale-Prelude: Wer Nur Den Lieben Gott Lässt Walten; and Ewigkeit Du Donnerwort.*

* AMELING, LINDE, TOELZER BOYCHOIR, LEONHARD, KOCH, MAY, EWERHART	Victrola VIC (M/S) 1317

The singing is dullish, and the music seems wearisome.

VIOLIN CONCERTO IN A; VIOLIN CONCERTO IN E (S. 1041/2)

Both of these lovely concertos are staunch pillars of the classical violin repertory. They were composed around 1720, when Bach conducted and composed music for the orchestra of Prince Leopold of Anhalt-Coethen.

* * SZERYNG, BOUILLON	*Pasdeloup Orch.*	Monitor	(S)	2087
* * CYROULDNIK, AURIACOMBE	*Toulouse Symphony Orch.*	Counterpoint	(5)	610
* TOTENBERG, WISLOCKI	*National Philharmonic*	Heliodor	(S)	25008
* SUK, SMETACEK	*Prague Symphony Orch.*	Crossroads	(M) (S)	22 16 0037 22 16 0038
* LAUTENBACHER, KEHR	*Mainz Chamber*	Vox (5)	(M)	11540

Hendryk Szeryng leads, with a vibrant, compelling performance. *High Fidelity* termed this disc "superbly probing." The "electronically enhanced" stereo is all right.

The Counterpoint entry is very good, although rather on the romantic nineteenth-century side in its interpretation. The sound is clear and recommendable.

Roman Totenberg, a solid musician, has an admirably serene and secure tone, appropriate for Bach. Totenberg plays with warmth, but he is outclassed by Szeryng.

Josef Suk, the gifted Czech violinist, has a small, ingratiating tone that is often pleasing—yet one frequently yearns for a more full-bodied, convincing interpretation. The sound is bright and lively.

Lautenbacher's interpretation is sensitive and entirely acceptable. The sound is fair.

VIOLIN CONCERTO NO. 1 IN A MINOR (S. 1041)

* * * MILSTEIN, BLECH	Festival Orch.	PICKWICK (S) 4013 [Mozart, Concerto No. 3]	

Don't miss this one—it's one of the most exquisite violin records anyone ever made! The sound is pleasant. Pickwick is often hard to find at record shops; you have a better chance of picking it up at your local Woolworth's. [The coupling is with Milstein's equally fine reading of Mozart's beguiling "Turkish" Concerto.]

CHAMBER MUSIC   This is intense, intellectual, and deeply penetrating music of the highest order.

ART OF THE FUGUE (S. 1080)

A holy of holies in the Bach iconology—and Bach's definitive statement on the art to which he had devoted a great part of his life, *The Art of the Fugue* consists of 14 fugues and four canons. It was left by Bach in open score—that is, we have no indication which instruments he intended us to use when performing it. There is even one school that believes Bach wrote *Die Kunst der Fuge* as a cerebral exercise for himself—with no thought of actual performance. The *19th Fugue* was left unfinished at the time of Bach's death. Several modern transcriptions have been made, and that of Roger Vuataz is highly regarded by musicians as closest to the spirit of Bach.

* * * WINOGRAD	Winograd String Orch.	2-HELIODOR (S) 25019-2 [Beethoven, Grosse Fugue]
* * RISTENPART	Saar Chamber Orch.	2-NONESUCH (S) 73013
* * MUNCLINGER	Ars Rediviva Ensemble	2-CROSSROADS (S) 22 26 0007 (M) 22 26 0008

**   Fine Arts Ouartet.   2 CONCERT DISC
N.Y. Woodwind Quintet   (M) 1230, 1250
    (S)   230,   250

1 prefer the unvarnished strength that comes through when the music is played by a small ensemble of strings. Such a performance is available in a trenchant, penetrating reading by the gifted conductor and cellist Arthur Winograd. However, this record omits the four canons.

Ristenpart uses Helmut Winschermann's arrangement, and gives a brisk, rather unpolished reading that is most enjoyable. The sound is good.

Munclinger, using his own transcription, has a more modern sound, and is also honorably dedicated to the spirit of Bach. This is an "intellectualized," serious reading of the highest interest.

The Fine Arts version uses an arrangement by Samuel Baron that is reverent in treatment, even though it boldly uses a clarinet and chromatic horn, instruments that were not developed until after Bach's death. The playing is expert. The sound is blameless.

Those who are fascinated by this music are also directed to the great organ reading by the blind pianist Helmut Walcha, recorded on the expensive Archive label.

LUTE MUSIC

The lute, a plucked instrument with a pear-shaped body, was one of the most popular instruments for solo playing and song accompaniment in the sixteenth and early seventeenth centuries. Bach's lute music is often played on a guitar: much of this music is familiar to us from the versions of guitar virtuosos such as Julian Bream.

* GERWIG   NONESUCH (7)
    (M/S)   1137

Here is one of the rare records which features Bach's lute music played on a lute instead of on a guitar.

Igor Kipnis in *Hi/Fi Stereo Review* comments: "If Gerwig is occasionally dull or lacking in temperament, his interpretations are still to be preferred. . . . Recording, excellent; stereo, natural." Individual works included are: *Prelude in C Minor* (BWV 999); *Fugue in G Minor* (BWV 1000); *Suite in E Major* (BWV 1006a); *Loure, Gavotte, Menuetts, and Gigue; Suite in A Major,* transcribed by Gerwig from *Solo Cello Suite* (BWV 1007); *Suite in E Minor* (BWV 996); *Allemande and Bourree.*

"MUSIC FOR GUITAR AND ORGAN"

The chief interest here is Segovia's own transcription of the stupendous *Chaconne* from the *Second Violin Partita*. (See discussion of this work under "Sonatas and Partitas for Violin Unaccompanied.") The gripping tension that characterizes the *Chaconne* when it is played on a violin becomes diffused when played on the guitar: the mood becomes more pensive and reflective.

* SEGOVIA, WEINRICH	HELIODOR	(M/S) 25010

The performances are quite pleasant; both the guitarist and organist are worthy musicians. *High Fidelity* commented on the sound: "Sonics on the guitar side are faded but acceptable." This master is from an MGM disc of about 1953. [Short transcriptions, mostly from lute pieces, fill out the rest of the guitar side.]

SEVEN SONATAS FOR FLUTE, HARPSICHORD
(S. 1030/35, 1020)

Here is cool, poised, linear fantasy. Bach clearly indicated that *No. 1-3* are "Sonatas for Clavier and Flute" and that *No. 4-6* are for "Flute and Clavier." The nice distinction means that in the first three the harpsichord is a full partner of the flute; but, that in the following three, the harpsichord has merely a lowly *continuo* or accompanying role. The *Seventh Sonata* is a "challenged" work, as the musicologists say.

* * WUMMER, VALENTI	2-WESTMINSTER [Flute Sonata]	(M) 18351/2

Wummer, a subtle, gifted musician, is a polished flutist, and Valenti, his partner, is much admired. Wummer is in top form—shows spirit, imagination, and virtuosity. The mono sound is quite all right. Harold Schonberg of the New York *Times* praised this set; so, undoubtedly, will you. [The Wummer disc also includes the *Sonata for Unaccompanied Flute in A Minor*.]

SIX SONATAS FOR VIOLIN AND
HARPSICHORD (S. 1014/9)

These sonatas are among the most engaging works Bach ever wrote. This music, not at all forbidding, provides an excellent introduction to Bach's chamber music.

| * * * SCHNEEBERGER, MUELLER | 2-NONESUCH   (S) 73017 |
| * * GRUMIAUX, SARTORI | 2-PHILLIPS PHM (M) 2-597 (S) 2-997 |

The Nonesuch set is a beauty; *High Fidelity* called violinist Schneeberger's performance "a source of endless delight." The sound is alive and warm. The élan and beautiful unanimity give the Nonesuch set (originally Baerenreiter label, Switzerland) a decided edge.

Grumiaux, a fine French violinist, is nearly as good. The *Stereo Record Guide* wrote: "He conveys a sure sense of style throughout and his tone and phrasing have moments of beauty."

SIX SUITES FOR CELLO UNACCOMPANIED (S. 1007/12)

Little else in music can approach the profound simplicity of Bach's cello suites, probably completed in 1720. For what purpose they were written remains a mystery.

No other works for solo string instrument are move revered. The suites should certainly not be listened to all at once; each suite should be played and pondered individually.

* * * GENDRON	3-PHILLIPS WS PMC 3-010
* * STARKER	2-PERIOD (M) 543, 582 [No. 1, 3, 4, 6]
* JANIGRO	3-WESTMINSTER (M) 9001/3

The French cellist Gendron is compelling. *Hi Fi Stereo Review* went all out on this set, enthusing: "The playing here is close to ideal. . . . The recorded sound is as rich and full-bodied as Gendron's tone."

Starker is on mono, but hardly less dazzling; here is great playing, as well as assertive musicianship.

Janigro, a fine cellist, is outclassed by the formidable competition.

The celestial Casals reading, on a high-priced Angel record, remains the awesome criterion.

THREE SONATAS AND THREE PARTITAS FOR VIOLIN UNACCOMPANIED (Complete) (S. 1001/6)

Bach composed six works for violin without accompaniment. *No. 1, 3,* and *5* are called sonatas; *No. 2, 4* and *6* are in the form of arrangement called "'partita." The famous *Chaconne,* the most highly regarded single piece by Bach, is one movement of the *Partita No. 2.* This music is austere, dazzling, moving, and intellectual; it stands on a par with Bach's unaccompanied cello suites.

| * * * SZERYNG | 3-ODYSSEY   (M) 32 36 0013 |
| * BRESS | 3-MACE   (S) 9056/8 |

Henryk Szeryng is superb. This is an utterly "simple" and reverent reading of difficult music; there is no showing-off, no pyrotechnics. This is all Bach and nothing else. Martin Bookspan, in *Stereo Review,* wrote of this achievement: "A flawless violin technique . . . a source of continuing wonder." This album was awarded the Grand Prix du Disque in France. The sound is excellent.

Young Hyman Bress is all right, but lacks the maturity prerequisite in playing this sublime music—for which the only substitute is the gift of God, an inexplicable special talent which alone can account for Yehudi Menuhin's performance of this music in his *wunderkind* days.

THREE SONATAS FOR VIOLA DA GAMBA AND HARPSICHORD (S. 1027/9)

This sonorous music is usually played today by a cello, rather than on the more dulcet, now antiquated viola da gamba.

* * TORTELIER, VEYRON-LACROIX	MUSICAL HERITAGE SOCIETY MHS (M/S) 586
* DOKTOR, VALENTI	WESTMINSTER (M) 9004
NAVARRA, VEYRON LACROIX	WESTMINSTER (M) 9000
KURTZ, PELLEG	MONITOR (S) 2108

The vivid French cellist Tortelier, highly admired abroad, gives an exciting reading—perhaps too exciting. The sound is clear. NOTE: The MHS disc with Tortelier is available by mail order only. (*See listing at beginning of this book.*)

The violist Doktor, with Valenti, gives a rather impersonal reading, yet this interpretation seems to be closest to Bach's intention. The mono sound is quite hearable.

Navarra does not dig into this music as well as the others.

Kurtz and Pelleg are accomplished, and they play cleanly. However, they are outclassed by the top two recordings.

ORGAN MUSIC   During his lifetime, Bach made his reputation as an organist. Today, the organ repertory is built upon Bach's music. His grand, imposing organ pieces are widely admired for their power and architectural strength. The music lover is urged to discover Bach's tender, meditative chorale preludes for the organ.

ORGELBUECHLEIN (LITTLE ORGAN BOOK), WITH CANTATA CHORALES AND OTHER CHORALE SETTINGS

The *Orgelbuechlein* was composed, in Bach's words, "for the glory of the Most High God, and for the instruction of my neighbor." The music consists of chorales or hymns, covering the chorales traditional for the services of each Sunday of the church year.

In this grouping, the *Little Organ Book* of Bach is interspersed with choral settings by Bach and by some other composers, in order to demonstrate the relation of the organ compositions to the Lutheran liturgy. The texts are by Martin Luther and other worthies.

* * * RILLING	*Choir of the Gedaechtniskirche, Stuttgart*	4-NONESUCH	HD 73015

I have nothing but praise for this album. The devoted singing and sonorous sound are both exemplary, and the total emotional effect is quite considerable. This is a truly religious performance. Bach himself intended the *Orgelbuechlein* as music for "Purification," dealing with "Christian Conduct and Experience; In The Time of Trouble; Death and the Grave; The Life Eternal." He would have been pleased with this recording. This is consummate music indeed, and the Nonesuch compilation is admirable in every respect.

ORGAN MUSIC RECITALS

* * * WALCHA	HELIODOR	(S) 25068
* * DUPRE	PHILLIPS WS	(S) 9017
* * SCHWEITZER	2-ODYSSEY	(M) 32 26 003
* * HEILLER	CARDINAL [Orgelbuechlein]	(M) 10026 (S) 10027
* * REINBERGER	CROSSROADS	(S) 22 16 0068
* ALAIN	MUSICAL HERITAGE SOCIETY	(S) 626
KRAFT	3-Vox SVBX [Vol. 1]	(S) 5441
KRAFT	3-Vox SVBX [Vol. 2]	(S) 5442
KRAFT	3-Vox SVBX [Vol. 3]	(S) 5443
KRAFT	3-Vox SVBX [Vol. 4]	(S) 5444

The blind German musician, Helmut Walcha, whose compelling, heart-felt playing on both organ and harpsichord has made him one of Europe's most treasured players, turns in a splendid recording, playing with authority. The sound is spacious.

Marcel Dupre, a world-famous interpreter of Bach, has published a complete edition of Bach's organ music. His recording, *Choral Preludes,* is meditative rather than grandiose. This disc is first-rate.

Albert Schweitzer was the doyen of Bach organists. These two discs were recorded about 1952, at a time when Dr. Schweitzer was much past his best abilities as an organist. I enjoy these records, even though there are many slips of finger and foot. Schweitzer plays without frills—the music stripped bare, so to say—and he is utterly unglamorous. Critical opinion is sharply divided about this performance. *High Fidelity* comments: "By the time Albert Schweitzer made these recordings for Columbia, his keyboard technique had deteriorated past the point of charitable endurance." England's perceptive critic, Sackville-West says: "There may be a stumble or two, but I would give all of Mlle. Desessieuz's nimble-fingered and sure-footed brilliance for one choral prelude played by Albert Schweitzer." The mono sound is not bad. NOTE: This set is not to be confused with other records by Schweitzer, made much earlier in his career.

Anton Heiller is also a Bach expert, and his discs are devoted to the *Little Organ Book*. Here is measured, authoritative Bach, with superb sound.

Jeri Reinberger, a music professor at Prague, is likewise impressive and convincing.

Marie Claire Alain is a lightweight performer of Bach, lucid rather than profound.

The awesome series of discs by Kraft are solid, unimaginative performances, but well recorded. Kraft has been organist at the Marienkirche at Luebeck, and thus the successor, across three centuries, of the great Buxtehude. Kraft plays on organs of the northern baroque style, and the resultant tones are a good approximation of the sound of the organs used by Bach. As can be seen from the above, Walter Kraft has produced no less than 12 organ records of Bach. Many of these are enjoyable, but the listener is never elevated, as when listening to Walcha. *High Fidelity* sums up the first nine records in this series by saying: "Kraft is plodding when he needs to be incisive or even brilliant."

TOCCATA AND FUGUE IN D MINOR FOR ORGAN (S. 565)

In our day, this is perhaps the most widely known of all Bach's works, thanks to the famous do-it-yourself orchestral transcription by Leopold

Stokowski. I would dare say that Stokowski's gorgeous treatment which enraged purists brought Bach to millions who would otherwise never have dreamed of going out of their way to hear his music. *The Toccata* sounds great on the organ, for which it was indeed intended, and it is a tried-and-true demonstration piece for hi/fi stereo buffs.

* * REINBERGER	PARLIAMENT	(S) 169
* KRAFT	VOX	(5) 11440
* WEINRICH	WESTMINSTER	(S) 14043

Reinberger is the best choice; the sound is imposing.
Kraft and Weinrich are both serviceable but unremarkable.

MUSIC FOR SOLO CLAVIER   Sweeping Bach, not to be missed.

CHROMATIC FANTASY AND FUGUE IN D FOR HARPSICHORD (S. 903)

This is audacious music, and the "fantasy" can be really fantastic, as it is under the hands of Wanda Landowska on her classic record on an expensive Angel.

| HEILER | MACE | (S) 9011 |
| BADURA-SKODA | 3-WESTMINSTER (S) 1005 [Harpsichord Concerto; Beethoven, Sonatas Nos. 15, 17; Brahms, Sonata] |

Slim pickings here. Heiler tinkles in a superficial way.
Badura-Skoda, on a three-record piano album, is hard-driving and energetic, rather than fanciful. The sound is bad.

GOLDBERG VARIATIONS FOR HARPSICHORD (S. 988)

This "Aria with Thirty Variations" is one of the most fascinating pieces of music ever penned. Bach had a pupil named Goldberg who served the insomniac and neuralgiac Count von Kayserling. The *Variations* were commissioned to distract the hapless count. We read that Kayserling was delighted. "Dear Goldberg, Please come and play me one of my Variations," he used to say.

In our own time, the *Variations* have become, perhaps, the most known and loved of any "intellectual" piece of music. Its popularity is due to the miracle of the long-play record and also to two supreme artists, Wanda Landowska and Glenn Gould, who have both bequeathed to us spectacular (and expensive) recordings that are marvels of subtlety and controlled passion. Both are musts for the serious Bach collector. Landowka's rendition on the harpsichord is issued by RCA; Gould's famous piano version will be found on Columbia. These two records invite endless and intriguing comparison.

| * LEONHARDT | Vanguard | (S) 175 |
| GALLING | Turnabout | (3) 4015 |

Gustave Leonhardt, to quote Harold Schoenberg of the New York *Times,* "is technically accurate but limited in emotional reseources." In short, an unremarkable performance.

Martin Galling, known for his excellent ensemble work on many recordings, will just barely do. But it is my stern duty to report on *High Fidelity's* comment: "So dull that I can't imagine myself ever wanting to hear it again." I agree.

INVENTIONS, 2 and 3 Part (S. 772/801)

These *Inventions* were written as exercises for one of Bach's sons, and pianists still struggle with them. They are rarely played at concerts.

* * * MALCOLM	Nonesuch	(7) 1144
* VEYRON-LACROIX	Westminster	9329
GALLING	Vox	(5) 12330
GALLING	Vox SVBX	(S) 5436
	[Well-Tempered Clavier]	

George Malcolm is both exciting and splendid; in such hands the *Inventions* can be heady music. *Hi/Fi Stereo Review* comments: "Performance is knowing and attractive." The sound is live and highly satisfying.

Veyron-Lacroix, on mono, is knowledgeable but much less stimulating. Galling is correct, but little more.

ITALIAN CONCERTO IN F FOR HARPSICHORD (S. 971)

This fascinating work, a "Concerto in the Italian Style," imitates the then new vogue of the Italian concerto with orchestra. The keyboard suggests the contrast between the soloist and the *tutti* (group passages).

| * * KATZ | Vanguard | (S) 253 |
| | [Harpsichord Concertos No. 1, 5] | |

* HEILER	MACE (S) 9010 [Couperin, Pieces; D. Scar- latti, Harpsichord Sonata]
GULDA	MACE (S) 9060 [Chopin, Andante; Mozart, Piano Sonata No. 15; Schu- bert, Scherzos]

Katz gives a worthy interpretation on piano, played with dash and temperament. [The couplings are excellent.]

The Concerto is played objectively and prettily by Heiler on the harpsichord; the disc is well recorded, with room-size sound.

Gulda plays with a heavily romantic style, including long ritards. The piano sound is uncomfortable to hear.

PARTITA NO. 1, IN B-FLAT; ENGLISH SUITE, NO. 2 IN A MINOR; FRENCH SUITE, NO. 5, IN G

* * RUZICKOVA	MUSICAL HERITAGE SOCIETY (M/S) 621

Crossroads has begun to release many recordings of this young Czech artist, Zuzana Ruzickova, who is already rated in Europe as one of the best harpsichordists. She provides lucid, vivacious playing. Here is a highly rewarding disc on the MHS label, for anyone who cares just to dip into Bach's various forms for solo keyboard. The sound is excellent.

SIX ENGLISH SUITES FOR HARPSICHORD (S. 806/11)

The six English Suites were composed at an unknown period in Bach's life, most likely in his earlier years. They are rewarding, but by no means top-drawer Bach.

* * WALCHA	MACE (S) 9036 [Vol. 1—No. 1/3]
* * WALCHA	MACE (S) 9033 [Vol. 2—No. 4/6]
* * VALENTI	2-WESTMINSTER 9327/8

Walcha offers earnest playing and supreme musicianship, although his reading is a bit academic. The sound on these discs is superb. This master originally came from "Electrola."

Valenti is far more vivid, with a sense of forward thrust. The sound is good.

SIX FRENCH SUITES FOR HARPSICHORD

Bach wrote the six suites called *Suites pour le Clavessin* when he was Kapellmeister to Prince Leopold of Anhalt-Coethen. The title *French Suites* was appended by later hands, because of the taut elegance and dance-like treatment of the music. This is gracious harpsichord music, but not on a par with Bach's *Partitas*.

* * VALENTI	2-WESTMINSTER (M) 9300/1 [Complete]
* WALCHA	2-MACE (S) 9072/3 [Complete]
* HEILER	MACE (S) 9011 [No. 5; Bach Program]
* GALLING	3-Vox SVBX (S) 5434 [Bach Program]

The most exciting and imaginative reading is on mono by Valenti.

Mace offers a complete version by the superb Helmut Walcha who seems rather cut-and-dried here.

On a mixed program, Ingrid Heiler plays one of the suites prettily.

Galling exhibits confident musicianship and metronomic technique; but as pointed out by the formidable Nathan Broder, "what is lacking, in short, is imagination, fantasy, which we now know, thanks to artists such as Landowska and Kirkpatrick, is just as vital in playing Bach as in any type of music."

SIX PARTITAS FOR HARPSICHORD (S. 825/30)

The *Partitas* are among the most dazzling of Bach's works for solo keyboard. Glenn Gould's stunning reading on piano, on an expensive Columbia, is the modern yardstick; since that event, few other artists have dared to record these pieces.

* GALLING	3-Vox SVBX (S) 5435 [Fantasy; Preludes; Fugue and Allegro]

Martin Galling is the only low-priced entry and plays commendably. But after hearing Gould, one has the uneasy knowledge of how much more there is behind the notes. The sound on the Galling disc is agreeable.

WELL-TEMPERED CLAVIER (S. 846/93)

According to the famous remark of conductor Hans von Buelow, these compositions are "The Old Testament of Music," the "New Testament" being Beethoven's *32 piano sonatas*. Bach composed his *48 Preludes and Fugues* (in two books of 24 each) in order to demonstrate the advantages of "equal temperament" of the tones of keyboard instruments—a hotly debated question in his day. There is little of Bach's work that reveals more brilliantly his extraordinary powers of invention.

For the last hundred years, pianists and harpsichordists have lived with this music under their pillow, so to speak. (An amusing note on custom: Bach would have been amazed at our habit of presenting a whole evening's concert devoted to his 24 preludes and fugues of the *Well Tempered Clavier*.)

Landowska on harpsichord has left us historic recordings that stand alone, and Glenn Gould has recorded *Book One* on piano in his superbly exciting manner.

* * HAMILTON	6-EVEREST	(M)	6134
		(S)	3134
* GALLING	3-Vox SVBX [Book 1]	(S)	5436
* GALLING	3-Vox SVBX [Book 2]	(S)	5437
* DEMUS	5-WESTMINSTER		9332/6

Malcolm Hamilton delivers a first-rate reading on harpsichord. He has style and scholarship, as well as a facile technique. His rather methodical approach, sans poetry, would be the only possible complaint. This is perhaps a bit unfair, but after the definitive performance of Landowska, and the excitement and authority of Glenn Gould, such invidious comparisons are unavoidable. The sound is strikingly good.

Galling has linear freedom and intelligence—and a fatal dullness. The sound is fine.

Demus is well-drilled and academic—in a piano version. The mono sound is clear.

Balakirev, Mily (1837-1910)

In the late 1800's, Balakirev was considered one of the "Mighty Five" of Russia. The other stormy members of the clique were Borodin, Rimsky-Korsakov, Mussorgsky, and Cui. Balakirev, the guiding spirit of the cadre, convinced the others that Russian music should be clearly Russian in character. His music is lush and romantic, in the spirit of Rimsky-Korsakov and the early Tchaikovsky.

Although unhesitatingly generous, Balakirev seems to have been a fussy, hypercritical chap; he did not hesitate to offer advice to his colleagues on just about every bar of music.

SYMPHONY NO. 1 IN C

Balakirev began this symphony as a young man but did not finish it until some forty years later. The music is constructed on the grand scale, with exotic overtones. Sir Thomas Beecham called it "a tremendous work." I would deem that judgment doubtful.

     * BEECHAM   *Royal Philharmonic*   SERAPHIM   (S) 60062

Beecham's performance is sparkling, filled with glowing colors and nuances. The sound is luscious and clean. Said the *London Observer:* "Beecham and the recording staff have here excelled themselves."

Barber, Samuel (1910-   )

Barber ranks with Aaron Copland at the head of the list of contemporary American composers. He was born in Pennsylvania. He won the Pulitzer Prize for music in 1935 and 1936. His music is civilized and comparatively easy to grasp. His "Adagio for Strings" has achieved wide popularity.

THREE REINCARNATIONS (Opus 16)

The piece is expertly made and is entertaining. Copland's work is a setting of the Book of Genesis, also expertly tailored. The most impressive of these three numbers is William Shumann's "Carols of Death" which a setting to a text by Whitman. It is a striking choral work.

| GREGG SMITH SINGERS | *Gregg Smith Singers* | EVEREST   (S) 3129
[Copland: In the Beginning;
Schuman: Carols of Death] |

The Gregg Smith Singers are first-rate, and so is the stereo spread. This is a good disc for anyone who wants a sampler of three accomplished American composers once considered very daring.

Bartok, Bela *(1881-1945)*

Born in Nagyszentmiklos, Hungary, Bartok began to compose at nine, and appeared in public as a pianist at ten. He studied at the Royal Hungarian Musical Academy in Budapest, where, at twenty-six, he became a teacher of the piano. Bartok became intensely interested in Hungarian folk music, and traveled throughout Hungary collecting thousands of songs. In 1917, he achieved his first success as a composer with a ballet, *The Wooden Prince*. During World War II, Bartok settled in the United States. In poor health, and ill at ease in his new country, he nevertheless continued to compose until his death in New York City in 1945.

PLACE AND ACHIEVEMENT   Bela Bartok was one of the greatest composers of the last hundred years. A more resolute and single-minded composer never lived. He headed no school; he cannot be seen as the successor and inheritor of any of those who came just before him, in the sense that Brahms is the inheritor of Beethoven, and Richard Strauss the successor of Wagner.

Bartok was a quiet loner, even in his private life. His early studies in folk music, which was a passion with him, became the dominant influence upon his style. He really belongs with those composers—Smetana in Bohemia, de Falla in Spain, Mussorgsky in Russia, Copland in America —who sought inspiration from the folklore and folk music of their native lands and who welded it into their own nationalistic art.

With Bartok, this insistence upon folk music as the basis of his art was more than mere nationalism. He well knew, as did the other greats of this century—Stravinsky, Schoenberg, and others—that the old forms and conceptions of music had become played out. In other words, after the great nineteenth-century romantic composers, there was no place to go. Music had to take a new turn, find new avenues for its mainstream.

"To understand Bartok better," wrote the brilliant musicologist Hugo Leichtentritt, "we must realize that it was his purpose to revivify the already exhausted, over-refined music of Europe with a transfusion of new blood from the peasant music of Hungary."

The music of Bartok becomes accessible, without difficulty, if the listener is willing to concentrate and *listen*. A powerful personality is at work here; a tenacious strength and an exquisite sensitivity of a great composer who is one of the true, original voices of our time. There are grave and haunting melodies in Bartok; there is the anguish and bitter tension of a world of hunger and cruelty and concentration camps. There is also another side to Bartok: at his best he conjures up a nocturnal world of strange and terrible beauty.

THE ESSENTIAL BARTOK

ORCHESTRAL MUSIC: *Concerto for Orchestra; Concerto No. 3 for Piano and Orchestra; Concerto for Violin and Orchestra (1938).*

PIANO MUSIC: *Mikrokosmos.*

CHAMBER MUSIC: *6 String Quartets; Music for Strings, Percussion, and Celesta; Contrasts for Clarinet, Violin, and Piano; Sonata for Violin Unaccompanied; Sonata for 2 Pianos and Percussion.*

OTHER WORKS

ORCHESTRAL MUSIC: *Concertos for Piano and Orchestra; Concerto No. 1 for Violin and Orchestra (Opus Posthumous); Concerto for Viola and Orchestra; 2 Rhapsodies for Violin and Orchestra; Divertimento, for Strings; Miraculous Mandarin, Suite.*

VOCAL MUSIC AND FOLKSONGS: *Hungarian Folk Songs (transcribed and arranged); Bluebeard's Castle; Cantata Profana.*

ORCHESTRAL MUSIC   The listener who seeks something more from music beyond agreeable sounds, or who wishes to become familiar with the great music of the last half century, must come to terms with the esoteric music of Bela Bartok. Those who are intimidated by his harsher, more forbidding works may approach his music most easily through his compositions for orchestra — in particular the *Concerto for Orchestra,* the *Violin Concerto No. 2,* and the *Piano Concerto No. 3.*

CONCERTO FOR ORCHESTRA

This concerto, one of Bartok's last works, was composed in 1943 for the Koussevitsky Foundation. The *Concerto for Orchestra* is by far the most popular of Bartok's compositions. A brilliant, mellow, virtuoso piece, it is designed to show off individual players as well as the brass, woodwind, string, and percussion sections.

* * * REINER	*Chicago Symphony Orch.*	VICTROLA VIC	(S)	1110
* * STOKOWSKI	*Houston Symphony Orch.*	EVEREST	(M)	6069
			(S)	3069
_* HOLLREISER	*Bamberg Symphony Orch.*	TURNABOUT [Concerto 3]		4082
	Czech Philharmonic Orch.	PARLIAMENT	(S)	602

† version is to be heard on a historic performance
'hicago Orchestra. This disc also illustrates why
ductor's conductor." The music is ruthlessly
s—not usually heard—come through with
'hatever your taste. The knowledgeable
'tion of passion, fantasy, and rhythmic

surge is altogether remarkable in this performance, and the execution by the Chicago Symphony, at the height of its resurgence under Reiner, little short of fantastic. The recorded sound was always exceptional."

Stokowski delivers a predictably exhibitionistic reading, and a romantic one. But it can certainly be recommended.

Hollreiser's version is effective. [The record has the added attraction of the striking *Third Piano Concerto*.]

The Czech reading is warm, but without the vibrancy or high voltage that Bartok's music demands.

CONCERTO NO. 1 FOR PIANO

This is taut music, with a remarkable dialogue for piano and percussion—not one of Bartok's most important works.

* SANDOR, REINHARDT	*South-West German Radio Symphony Orchestra*	TURNABOUT TV (M) 4065 (S) 34065 [Stravinsky, Concerto for Piano and Wind Orchestra]
SANDOR, REINHARDT	*South-West German Radio Symphony Orch.*	Vox (5) (S) 11350 [Rhapsody Opus 1]

Sandor is biting and tough-fibered in both performances; he seems to feel this music in his bones. *Hi/Fi Stereo Review* commented: ". . . The Bartok fascinates almost all the way, but it will do little to warm the cockles of your heart. . . . The recorded sound and stereo are both good." As to the reverse sides of these two records, the Turnabout coupling with the astringent, strange, brittle Stravinsky concerto of 1923-24 is the more worthwhile. The Vox coupling is the *Rhapsody No. 1,* a very early, romantic, Liszt-influenced piece with only fair appeal.]

CONCERTO NO. 2 FOR PIANO

This waspish concerto, dating from 1931, is percussive, dynamic music

* SANDOR, GIELEN	*Vienna Pro Musica*	TUR [2
SANDOR, GIELEN	*Vienna Pro Musica*	

Sandor, a pupil of Bartok, is passionately
the two records present the same performanc
The piano tone on the Vox disc, to duc
comment, "sounds as if it had been

CONCERTO NO. 3 FOR PIANO

This rich, symphonic composition of 1945 is Bartok's most popular piano concerto. It marks a return to the diatonic idiom (the use of traditional scales) of his earlier years. He had completed all but the last 17 bars at the time of his death; indications for these were left in shorthand notes, and they were consequently scored by Bartok's noted disciple and interpreter, Tibor Serly. Tempo and expression marks were suggested by several hands, including Eugene Ormandy. This is most approachable music.

* * SANDOR, GIELEN	*Vienna Pro Musica*	TURNABOUT (S) 4082 [Concerto for Orchestra]	
* SANDOR, GIELEN	*Vienna Pro Musica*	VOX (5) (S) 11490 [Concerto No. 2]	
* BERNATHOVA, ANCERL	*Czech Philharmonic*	ARTIA (7) (S) 199 [Viola Concerto]	

Sandor made a name for himself with this dramtic, dedicated reading. [The Turnabout coupling is preferable to the reverse side of the Vox.] Eva Bernathova is competent. The sound is fair.

CONCERTO FOR VIOLA AND ORCHESTRA

This patchwork concerto, completed by Tibor Serly from the composer's sketches, nevertheless provides a subtle, luminous score.

* KARLOVSKY, ANCERL	*Czech Philharmonic*	ARTIA (7) 199 [Piano Concerto No. 3]	

Karlovsky plays the music lyrically. As to the sound, the acerbic Mr. Frankenstein comments: "The recording makes his instrument sound like an oboe d'amore or an English horn at many points."

For the definitive reading, listen to Primrose on high-priced Bartok Records. Bartok composed the piece for him.

CONCERTO NO. 2 FOR VIOLIN AND ORCHESTRA

Many devotees consider this concerto of 1938 to be in the class of Beethoven and Brahms. This is spectacular music of lyrical intensity. Yehudi Menuhin championed this work after World War II, and played the piece around the world until it became accepted. His performance (available on the expensive Angel) still stands alone.

* * GERTLER, ANCERL	*Czech Philharmonic*	2-CROSSROADS (S) 22 26 0012 [Concerto No. 1; Violin Rhapsodies]	

OISTRAKH,   *Moscow State*   PERIOD SHO   (ST2)   338
ROZHDESTVENSKY   *Philharmonic Orch.*   [Prokofiev, Concerto No. 1]

The admirable Andre Gertler, who knew the composer well, gives a fine performance as part of a two-record set. Two records, however, may be a bit much for listeners who are not Bartok enthusiasts.

Although Oistrakh himself is dazzling, the sound on the Oistrakh reading is too hazy and undefined to claim serious attention.

CONCERTOS FOR VIOLIN AND ORCHESTRA: NO. 1 (Opus Posthumous); NO. 2 (1938); TWO RHAPSODIES FOR VIOLIN AND ORCHESTRA

The *Concerto No. 1* is a posthumous resurrection. It was written in 1907 for Stefi Geyer, with whom Bartok was in love. The manuscript appeared publicly only after her death, some 50 years later. This is very early Bartok, fervent, elegiac music with overtones of early Schoenberg and of Richard Strauss.

The *Two Rhapsodies* are colorful and attractive works—good music, but not Bartok's most inspired pages.

The great music here is the *Violin Concerto No. 2*—one of the very best of our century—an unforgettable work.

* GERTLER, ANCERL,   *Czech Philharmonic Orch.*   CROSSROADS
  FERENCZIK   *Brno State Philharmonic*   (M) 22 26 0011
                    Orch.   (S) 22 26 0012

Andre Gertler, a personal friend of Bartok, plays with penetration and sober musicianship. Ancerl and Ferenczik both handle their orchestras well. This is a two-record set, commended only for Bartok devotees. The sound is resonant. [For further discussion of the great *Violin Concerto No. 2*, see entry under that heading.]

DANCE SUITE

Hungarian, Slovak, and Rumanian native song and dance are coalesced into Bartok's musical language, in this 1923 composition. This work is a good example of Bartok's transfigurations of folk music into concert music.

FERENCSIK   *London Philharmonic*   EVEREST   (M) 6022
                                                      (S) 3022
                                          [Kodaly, Psalmus Hungaricus]

Ferencsik keeps everything moving. The sound is agreeable. [The coupling is worthy.]

DIVERTIMENTO FOR STRING ORCHESTRA

This "thesaurus of string orchestra techniques," written in 1939, has proved to be one of Bartok's most durable pieces.

* FOSS	*Zimbler Sinfonietta*	TURNABOUT TV (S) 34154 [Ives, Unanswered Question; Milhaud, String Symphony No. 4; Skalkottas, Little Suite]

Composer-conductor Lukas Foss has the equipment to wring everything possible out of this score, and the Zimbler Sinfonietta (members of the Boston Symphony) toss it off with ease. The sound is crisp. [The couplings are all vivid twentieth-century pieces.]

MIRACULOUS MANDARIN: SUITE

This suite, from a ballet of 1919, concerns an aged Chinese who has been hacked to bits by a prostitute's male accomplices, but who refuses to die until the woman grants him his desire. When she shows pity and embraces him, his desire is appeased and he dies. This is violent, spectacular music.

* REINHARDT	*South-West German Radio Symphony Orch.*	TURNABOUT (3) 4068 [Wooden Prince (Ballet)]

Reinhardt, a Bartok specialist, is effective and appropriately colorful. [*The Wooden Prince* is a weak ballet of 1915, with thin inspiration—hardly worthwhile music.]

A stunning reading of the *Mandarin,* coupled with the first-rate *Music for Strings, Percussion, and Celesta,* is to be had on an expensive London record with George Solti.

MUSIC FOR STRINGS, PERCUSSION, CELESTA

This music provides a number of intriguing experiments in contrapuntal texture and in the manipulation of bizarre sonorities. This is somber, beautiful music of the highest order.

* * WAND	*Cologne Philharmonic*	COUNTERPOINT (M) 607 (S) 5607 [Divertimento for Strings]

Wand, a profound conductor of knotty modern scores, delivers a brilliant performance. The sound is all right.

CHAMBER MUSIC Bartok's chamber music is personal, deeply-felt music, superbly written. The awesome *Six Quartets* are the very heart of Bartok's writing. In the words of the critic Desmonde Shawe-Taylor, "It is no exaggeration to say that no composer since Beethoven has done more than Bartok to enlarge the scope of the form." The *Sonata for Solo Violin*, the *Contrasts,* and the *Sonata for Two Pianos and Percussion* are all fascinating works, and seem certain to endure.

CONTRASTS FOR CLARINET, VIOLIN, PIANO (1938)

The *Contrasts* were written specifically for the combined talents of violinist Joseph Szegeti (Bartok's fellow-Hungarian, who, with Hungarian conductor Fritz Reiner, was responsible for getting Bartok out of wartime Europe), and clarinetist Benny Goodman. This is off-the-track, intriguing, modern music.

* * GOODMAN, SZIGETI, BARTOK	ODYSSEY (S) 3216 0220 [Mikrokosmos]

Here is the authoritative performance—Szigeti and Goodman themselves are playing, and Bartok himself is at the piano. The New York *Times:* "For all generations to admire." The sound is very thin, but hearable. [On the reverse of the record, Bartok himself plays excerpts from his piano music, *Mikrokosmos.*]

44 DUOS FOR TWO VIOLINS

Bartok wrote these duos for teaching purposes, and employed his usual transformations of folk music. These pieces range from the extremely simple to the bewilderingly complex. This is not great Bartok, but it will certainly be of interest to his admirers.

* GERTLER, SUK	CROSSROADS (S) 22 16 0208

Though these two utterly serious violinists apparently do whatever they are supposed to do, the whole to-do has limited appeal for me. *Saturday Review* comments: "A wealth of fine artistry from Gertler and Suk. Pedagogues of the instrument have a special interest and will find it well served."

SIX QUARTETS *(Complete)*

The six quartets of Bela Bartok provide a cross-section of his life from 1907 to 1939. They are the most-discussed and most publicized quartets of our century. Without question, their fame is due to the long-playing record; for without having been recorded, music of such a new and forbidding nature could never reach world fame in such a short time.

The *Quartets* are a tremendous achievement. This is savage, dissonant, agonized music, which, to some ears, represents the pain of our time. The perceptive Sackville-West comments: "To this very intimate form Bartok confided, as to a diary, the hopes and fears, the technical discoveries, the melodic fantasies, the furious anger and love, of his most intimate experience."

* *	**Fine Arts Quartet**	3-Concert-Disc
		(M) 1501 (1207/9)
		(S) 501 (207/9)
* *	**Ramor Quartet**	3-Vox SVBX (S) 519

The stunning performance of the Juilliard Quartet of this incredibly difficult music (on a high-priced Columbia disc) is celebrated, and must, despite its age, remain the criterion.

Quite a few rungs below this, and yet quite successful, is the severe, architectonic reading of the Fine Arts Quartet. The stereo sound is decent.

The Ramor Quartet gives a somewhat more romantic and impetuous interpretation. Albert Frankenstein comments: "Powerful . . . nicely proportioned and beautifully thought out." The sound is acceptable.

SONATA FOR TWO PIANOS AND PERCUSSION

A new world of sound, or rather of timbre, opens up here. The piano is used percussively, as part o fan array that calls for pitched and non-pitched pulsatile instruments of every description. The result is heady and exciting.

* LEJSKOVA, LEJSEK,	*Piano Chamber Ensemble*	Crossroads
KRSKA, MACAL,		(M) 22 16 0073
PALENICEK,		(S) 22 16 0074
BURGHAUSER		[Janacek, Concertino for Piano and Chamber Ensemble; Sonata for Piano]
* BARTOK, DITTA		Turnabout (M) 4159
PASZTORY BARTOK,		[For Children, Sz. 42. Ten
BAKER, RUBSAN		excerpts; Ten Easy Pieces, Sz. 39, Evening in Transylvania; Bear's Dance]

The best low-priced rendition is included in a three-record album, Vox SVBX 426. That set is listed and reviewed in this volume, under BARTOK, *"Piano Music."*

The Crossroads disc offers a vivid reading of the Bartok work, coupled with the original *Concertino* by Janacek—an extremely worthwhile combination. The sound is only so-so.

Bartok and his wife play on the Turnabout disc. The percussive playing of the Bartoks was summed up in *Stereo Review's* phrase: "The
performance here is acidic, and, at appropriate moments, a little
mean." The sound is still surprisingly bright. [The children's music on
the other side consists largely of Hungarian peasant melodies, tastefully
arranged for pedagogic purposes. It is of limited appeal for the collector.]

SONATA FOR VIOLIN UNACCOMPANIED

This profound, knotty music, dating from 1944, demands a virtuoso violinist, and has even been termed "a symphony for a single violin."

* GERTLER	ARTIA [Violin Sonata]	(S) 711

The Gertler performance does not approach the celebrated reading
by Robert Mann (on high-priced Bartok Records), but Gertler nevertheless gives a steely, incisive reading. [The coupling makes this a worthwhile disc for those who want to hear two chamber music masterpieces
of our time.]

SONATAS FOR VIOLIN AND PIANO NO. 2

Here is complex music, which almost sounds barbaric. The piano throws
off cascades of color; the violin sings with gypsy abandon. Strange music
indeed.

* * GERTLER, ANDERSON (No. 2)	ARTIA [Unaccompanied Sonata]	(S) 711
* * DRUIAN, SIMMS	2-PHILLIPS WS	(M/S) 2-002

Gertler plays with a bitter conviction that sounds right. [His version
is backed with the fascinating *Sonata for Unaccompanied Violin.*] The
sound is good.

Druian and Simms play the *Second Sonata* with strength and slashing
rhythm, in a two-record set that also offers the complete violin sonatas
of Charles Ives. The sound is resonant.

PIANO MUSIC   This is extremely difficult music for many listeners, but
these compositions were not written for the general auditor. Bartok is
often deliberately percussive. Much of this music was originally intended
as teaching material for children.

"FOR CHILDREN," VOL. 1 AND 2; FIFTEEN HUNGARIAN PEASANT SONGS; SONATA FOR PIANO; PETITE SUITE; ALLEGRO BARBARO; RUMANIAN CHRISTMAS CAROLS; THREE RONDOS ON FOLK TUNES; OUT OF DOORS; SIX RUMANIAN FOLK DANCES; SONATA FOR TWO PIANOS AND PERCUSSION

This is a collection of varied and considerable interest. To the uninitiated, the savage *Allegro Barbaro* may sound like a blindfolded composer wandering down a blind alley. However, Arthur Cohn has called it "one of the most important contributions to contemporary piano literature." Cohn comments further: "Bartok's music thunder-strikes the ear; it haunts the memory."

Out of Doors is good impressionistic writing. The *For Children* suites are of innocuous appeal; the *Rumanian Christmas Carols* and other small works are mild. The *Sonata for Two Pianos and Percussion,* however, is a masterpiece.

* * SANDOR, REINHARDT, SCHAD, SOHM	3-Vox SVBX (S) 426	

The *Sonata for Two Pianos and Percussion,* played by two dedicated Bartokians, receives its best low-priced performance. The sound is brittle —all right for this work. The playing of Sandor has been much admired; Herbert Glass calls it "one of the best piano recordings of twentieth-century music."

MIKROKOSMOS (1935)

There are six volumes, and 153 pieces, in the *Mikrokosmos.* They progress from the most elementary to the virtuoso level. These pieces were intended as teaching materials for children, but they are nevertheless "pure music." The appeal for the general listener is mild, but very great for the student or pianist.

* * SANDOR	3-Vox SVBX 5425 [Complete]
* BARTOK	ODYSSEY (S) 32 16 0220 [Excerpts; Contrasts for Clarinet, Violin and Piano]
* PASZTORY-BARTOK	MACE 9007 [Excerpts]

Sandor plays with force and directness, and he knows this music intimately.

The Odyssey disc, with the composer himself at the piano, has poor sound but historic appeal. Bartok was a fine pianist, and it is not generally remembered that he placed second to Wilhelm Backhaus in the International Rubinstein Competition for Pianists in 1905.

Bartok's second wife, Ditta Pasztory Bartok, who often played her husband's music in concert when they lived in America, has less technical strength.

Beethoven, Ludwig Van (1770-1827)

Beethoven's grandfather and father were musicians at Bonn. Beethoven studied the violin, viola, harpsichord, and organ. He was harpsichord-player in the court orchestra of the Elector of Cologne at Bonn in 1783, and second court organist in 1784.

In 1792, at the age of twenty-two, Beethoven moved to Vienna where he spent the rest of his life. There he studied with Haydn and Albrechts-berger. In 1795, he made his first public appearance in Vienna as composer and pianist.

Beethoven was barely thirty when the first symptoms of deafness appeared. Despite medical attention, his hearing became gradually worse. The despair of Beethoven is to be read in his diary and in the famous "Heiligenstadt Testament," a letter to his brothers. No more moving document exists in all the letters written by composers. His growing deafness obliged him to cease performing in public, and to devote himself entirely to composition.

From 1800 to 1815, before he became totally deaf, Beethoven finished eight of his nine symphonies, five piano concertos, the opera *Fidelio,* and other masterpieces.

In the latter part of his life, he also suffered the burdens of guardianship over his somewhat delinquent nephew Karl.

As a personality, Beethoven was excessively brusque. He never married, and his frustrated, love-starved relations with women have been a source of interest to psychologists.

He revolted against the eighteenth-century system of patronage by which a musician was linked to the service of an employer. Nevertheless, he socialized with aristocrats, and was quite ready to accept their financial support. His active sympathy with the liberal ideas of his time is shown in works like *Egmont, Fidelio,* and the *Ninth Symphony*.

In his business dealings with publishers he was usually distrustful, and more than once, unscrupulous.

At the time of his death, Beethoven was a famous man. All Vienna mourned; schools were closed; thousands watched his funeral procession.

Today, Beethoven is the most universally cherished of all musicians. Though his personal life may have been a failure, in his one overpowering ambition he succeeded supremely. He left the world a testament of beauty with a legacy for every man. He stepped outside the frame of his art to live wholly and heroically in the world. He was not content merely to write music; unrest was in his soul, and the flames of liberty, equality, and fraternity blazed within him, searing his life, rendering him unhappy, goading him to rebellion.

PLACE AND ACHIEVEMENT Beethoven has been called "The Man Who Freed Music". This "Titan wrestling with the Gods" was one of the most original composers who ever lived, and he had an overpowering influence on the course of music. In our own day, his music, by and large, remains the dominating criterion for symphonic works, for concertos, and for string quartets.

He composed with difficulty, revising his original sketches over and over again until he was satisfied. But his most significant trait—that which has made him the very symbol of freedom and liberty—was his passion, his tempestuousness. He rebelled against convention both in music and in life as no musician before him ever had. For him the French and American Revolutions were deep inspirations. He was the first musician to refuse to be treated as a servant. He insisted on eating with "the quality."

In the musical world of Haydn and Mozart, Beethoven represents a sharp break with tradition almost unique in the history of music. The composers who lived before him accepted the establishment; Beethoven envisioned himself as a hero struggling for liberty and equality. These ideas for him were paramount and this passion permeates his music.

Beethoven found in the symphonic form the medium to his monumental concepts. His symphonies are titanic, and to this day, tower above all others. Only Brahms has approached their nobility.

Beethoven's own Promethean struggle against deafness, his insistence on being regarded as a creator rather than as a lackey purveying music, the noble beauty that breathes in his art—all these place him at the very pinnacle in the pantheon of music. Some music lovers may prefer Bach or Mozart; others may prefer the nineteenth-century romantics, but few will gainsay that the colossal image of Ludwig van Beethoven overshadows them all.

THE ESSENTIAL BEETHOVEN

ORCHESTRAL MUSIC: *9 Symphonies; Leonore Overture No. 3; Overture to Egmont; Concerto for Violin and Orchestra; 5 Concertos for Piano and Orchestra.*

PIANO MUSIC: *32 Sonatas.*

CHAMBER MUSIC: *16 String Quartets; Grosse Fugue, for String Quartet; 10 Sonatas for Violin and Piano; 5 Sonatas for Cello and Piano.*

OPERA: *Fidelio.*

CHORAL MUSIC: *Missa Solemnis.*

OTHER WORKS

ORCHESTRAL MUSIC: *Coriolanus Overture; Fidelio Overture; Leonora Overtures, No. 1, 2 and 3; Romance, No. 1 and 2, for Violin and Orchestra; Concerto for Piano, Violin, Cello and Orchestra.*

CHAMBER MUSIC: *8 Trios, for Piano, Violin and Cello; String Trios; Quintet for Piano and Winds.*
PIANO MUSIC: *Variations on a Theme by Diabelli; Thirty-Two Variations.*
CHORAL MUSIC: *Mass in C.*
SONGS: *Beethoven wrote many short songs.*

ORCHESTRAL WORKS The nine symphonies of Beethoven are, in a word, the backbone of the modern orchestral repertory.

FANTASIA IN C MINOR FOR PIANO, CHORUS, ORCHESTRA (Opus 80)

This interesting work for solo piano, chorus, and orchestra, dates from 1808. The *Choral Fantasia* may be regarded as Beethoven's study for his colossal *Ninth Symphony;* the style and sentiment are highly similar, and the *Fantasia,* too, ends with a chorale.

* * RICHTER, SANDERLING	*State Radio Orchestra and Academy Chorus*	MONITOR (M) 2060 [D. Scarlatti, Piano Sonata]
* * BRENDEL, BOETTCHER	*Stuttgart Philharmonic Orchestra and Chorus*	VOX (5) (S) 14160 [Liszt, Wanderer Fantasy]

The attraction on the Monitor disc is the poetry of the great Russian pianist Richter. The mono sound is decent.

Brendel is far more reserved; he sounds like a young Rudolph Serkin. This is a worthwhile disc, if you care for the flamboyant Liszt piece on the back.

OVERTURES

Beethoven's Overtures are stirring, heroic works. In a sense, these short pieces epitomize the defiiant, turbulent Beethoven that the world so much admires. Based on noble themes, they stand by themselves as artistic accomplishments. The three *Leonore* overtures that Beethoven wrote for his sole opera, *Fidelio* (and a fourth *Fidelio* overture), *Egmont, Coriolan, Prometheus,* are firm ornaments of the concert hall.

* * * TOSCANINI	*NBC Symphony Orch.*	8-VICTROLA VIC (M) 8000 [Consecration of the House; Coriolan; Creatures of Prometheus; Egmont; Quartet 16; Septet; Symphony]
* * * MUNCH	*Boston Symphony Orch.*	2-VICTROLA VIC (S) 6003 [Coriolan; Fidelio; Leonore 3; Symphony 9]

* * KONDRASHIN	*Moscow Philharmonic Orch.*	SERAPHIM (S) 60061 [Prometheus; Symphony 4]
* * ANSERMET	*Orchestra Suisse Romande*	LONDON (S) STS-15055 [Coriolan; Symphony 4]
* * ANSERMET	*Orchestra Suisse Romande*	LONDON (S) STS-15064 [Prometheus; Symphony 6]
* * TOSCANINI	*BBC Symphony Orch.*	3-SERAPHIM 6015 [Leonore 1; Symphony 1, 4, 6; Brahms, Tragic; Mozart, Overture]
* * MONTEUX	*London Symphony Orch.*	VICTROLA VIC (S) 1170 [Fidelio; King Stephen; Symphony 2]
* DORATI	*Minneapolis Symphony Orch.*	MERCURY (S) 18016 [Coriolan; Egmont; Leonore 3; Symphony 5]
KRIPS	*London Symphony Orch.*	8-EVEREST (S) 3065 [Leonore 3; Egmont; Complete Symphonies]
KRIPS	*Vienna Festival Orch.*	VANGUARD S-214/5 [Coriolan; Egmont]

Whip-driven, spine-tingling classic performances are to be had from Toscanini-NBC in his famous 8-record album of Beethoven symphonies and overtures. The sound is decidedly thin.

Sweeping fervor marks Munch's recording of three overtures; the sound is modern.

Kondrashin delivers a solid, forceful *Prometheus* with ringing sound.

Ansermet provides a meticulous, polished *Coriolan Overture*. His *Prometheus Overture* is also satisfying.

The Toscanini BBC set is composed of transfers from short-play records, and the vivid playing is foggy.

Monteux is both trenchant and heartfelt, and the sound is good.

Dorati is exciting and well-drilled. The sound is pretty good.

In his reading of *Leonore 3* and the *Egmont* on Everest, Krips is assuring, shipshape, and without high drama. The same can be said for his *Egmont* on the Vanguard disc.

SYMPHONIES: COMPLETE RECORDINGS

There are at present three complete recordings of the glorious Nine on low-priced discs.

* * * TOSCANINI	*NBC Symphony Orch.*	8-VICTROLA VIC (M) 8000
* * WALTER	*N. Y. Philharmonic Orch.*	6-ODYSSEY (M) 3266 0001
* KRIPS	*London Symphony Orch.*	8-EVEREST (M) 6065 (S) 3065

The Toscanini legacy stands supreme, a monument to this great conductor, who more than any other man, captured the Protean quality of Beethoven. To quote *Stereo Review,* the Toscanini set rates: "Performance: historic; sound; passable." By modern standards, the sound is poor.

The Bruno Walter readings are much warmer and humanitarian, and have their many admirers. A strong plea for Walter as against Toscanini is entered by *High Fidelity's* pundit Conrad Osborne: "Indeed, after a fair number of hours of direct comparison listening, I am not so sure but what Walter emerges as the really sane, mature interpreter . . . ; Toscanini's Beethoven has excited me enormously in the past, but just now, it more or less annoys me—such a hectic pressing on the music, such a feeling of trying to get something off his chest." Walter recorded all the Beethoven symphonies in two separate cycles. The first, which we list here, was made over a period running from 1942 to 1953. In California during his retirement years, Walter recorded the nine symphonies in stereo. If you want Walter's warm, mellow, humanitarian Beethoven, my reluctant advice is to get the expensive, later, better-sounding version. The sound on the first version is poor—even more so than on the Toscanini discs.

The Joseph Krips entry is honorable if hardly monumental, with far more modern sonics. The performances are correct, sometimes gracious and sometimes dull, and always Central European conceptions.

SYMPHONY NO. 1 IN C (Opus 21)

Beethoven's *First Symphony* was introduced at the composer's first concert in Vienna in 1800. The work opens with a startling dominant seventh chord in the different, closely related key of F major; but after a few bars, we are back in the traditional vein.

For those who complain of the wearisome lengths of concerts which present Mahler and Wagner, the musical program at Beethoven's concert in 1800 is worth pondering. It began at 6:30 P.M. and was rendered under his own auspices and for his sole financial benefit. Here it is:

1) Grand symphony by the late Kapellmeister Mozart.
2) Aria from Haydn's *Creation.*
3) A grand concerto for piano, played and composed by Beethoven.
4) A septet for four strings and three wind instruments, composed by Beethoven and dedicated to Her Majesty the Empress.
5) A duet from Haydn's *Creation.*
6) Improvization by Beethoven on Haydn's *Emperor's Hymn.*
7) A new grand symphony for full orchestra by Beethoven.

* * * TOSCANINI   *NBC Symphony Orch.*   8-Victrola VIC (M) 8000
                                                       (in 8-record set)

* * ANSERMET	*Orchestra Suisse Romande*	LONDON STS [Symphony No. 8]	15032
* * TOSCANINI	*BBC Symphony Orch.*	3-SERAPHIM (M) 6015 [Symphonies No. 4, 6; Brahms, Tragic Overture]	
* BARBIROLLI	*Halle Orch.*	VANGUARD (S) 146 [Symphony No. 8]	
* PARAY	*Detroit Symphony Orch.*	MERCURY (M/S) 18062 [Symphony No. 2]	

Toscanini's NBC recording is still a paradigm of a classical reading of a classic symphony. Martin Bookspan in *Stereo Review's* 1968 "Annual Updating of the Basic Repertory" rates this the top performance regardless of price: "Toscanini's is quite simply one of his best Beethoven recordings, fresh and unhurried." The sound, however, is thin and constricted.

Ansermet is a good choice for a modern-sounding version—a clean, attractive job. [There is a very well-played *Eighth* on the reverse.]

Toscanini's BBC recording is earlier, dewier, and more poorly recorded than his NBC performance. These cherishable discs stem from the 78-rpm era.

Barbirolli offers an inviting, unruffled performance. The sound is fair.

Paray is rather impetuous, less classical than other outstanding versions listed above. But this is an entirely hearable disc with agreeable sound.

SYMPHONY NO. 2 IN D (Opus 36)

For many people this is one of the easiest Beethoven works to know. The whole symphony sparkles; there are little heroics of foreboding; and there is a lightness and singing quality that reminds one at once of Haydn or Mozart at their best. It therefore is staggering to learn that this sunny work was written during the blackest period in Beethoven's life—when he seriously contemplated suicide. It may also intrigue the listener to learn that this serene symphony was stormily opposed at its first performance, and that after it was played, Beethoven was branded as being dangerous and subversive.

* * * MONTEUX	*London Symphony Orch.*	VICTROLA VIC (S) 1170 [Overture]	
* * FERENCSIK	*Czech Philharmonic Orch.*	PARLIAMENT (S) 156 [Overture]	
* PARAY	*Detroit Symphony Orch.*	MERCURY (M/S) 18062 [Symphony No. 1]	

Monteux leads, with a sunny, buoyant reading that radiates good humor. The orchestral playing is affectionate. Bookspan said in *Stereo Review:* "In the low-priced field, the performance by Monteux is outstanding." The sound is clean.

The Czech conductor Ferencsik is bustling, and he is committed to Beethoven. In 1965, *Stereo Record Guide* commented: "Good modern stereo and first-rate performance make this a highly attractive buy."

Paray is high-spirited; very much in charge. This is a mannered reading; we are too much aware of Monsieur Paray rather than of Herr Beethoven.

SYMPHONY NO. 3 IN E-FLAT ("EROICA") (Opus 55)

The *Eroica* marks Beethoven's giant step forward; each page of the MS. is stamped with his personality and genius. This is a masterpiece that is vivid, dramatic, and almost as all-embracing as Beethoven's *Ninth*.

* * * TOSCANINI	*NBC Symphony Orch.*	8-VICTROLA VIC (in 8-record set)	(M)	8000
* * * WALTER	*New York Philharmonic*	6-ODYSSEY (in 6-record set)	(M) 3266	0001
* * * STEINBERG	*Pittsburgh Symphony Orch.*	PICKWICK	(S)	4036
* * KLEIBER	*Vienna Philharmonic Orch.*	RICHMOND	(M)	19051
* FURTWAENGLER	*Vienna Philharmonic Orch.*	3-SEPHABIM [Symphonies No. 5, 7]	(M)	6018
* DORATI	*Minneapolis Symphony Orch.*	MERCURY	(M) (S)	14047 18047
* MONTEUX	*Vienna Philharmonic Orch.*	VICTROLA VIC	(S)	1036
* VON MATACIC	*Czech Philharmonic Orch.*	PARLIAMENT	(S)	129
* BOULT	*Philharmonic Promenade Orch.*	VANGUARD	(S)	127
* BOULT	*London Philharmonic Orch.*	SOMERSET/ST. FI.	(S)	15700

Toscanini had a special attachment for the *Eroica;* he performed this symphony more often than he did any other. In this recording, Toscanini is splendid and passionate; Irving Kolodin commented: "Allowing for a lack of the best sound, Toscanini's is the inclusive *Eroica* of our time, blending vigor with control." To my ears this is *the* great recording of the *Third*—though the sound is poor, even bodiless.

Walter's noble version was famous back in the early days of LP's when we all grabbed the red album cover with the Napoleon hat. Upon rehearing it today, I find its spontaneous, heart-felt qualities still impressive, but not impressive enough to overcome the dim acoustics. If you want Walter's documentation, get it in stereo on an expensive Columbia.

Steinberg provides a solid, authoritative reading, with spirited playing and spacious modern sound.

The mono reading by Kleiber, recently discontinued and available for around a dollar, is a thrilling and authoritative disc.

Furtwaengler's *Eroica* derives from old 78's. This is a ponderous reading; structure is all, rather than tempo or drive. This historical disc is a must for the sophisticated collector who already owns three *Eroicas*. It is not a first-choice selection. The sound is poor and the treble is shrill.

Dorati offers a good performance, although the sound is a bit fuzzy.

Monteux is less remarkable than usual in this *Eroica,* a nonheroic, rather smooth version that disappoints.

Von Matacic is highly dramatic. This is a good reading, but the sound is a bit fuzzy in places.

Boult, on the Vanguard disc, is correct, little more. The Somerset disc with Boult is quite poorly recorded.

SYMPHONY NO. 4 IN B-FLAT (Opus 60)

Completed in 1806 the lyrical *Fourth* is a winning symphony, though a much more modest work than Beethoven's ground-breaking *Third*. For some reason, this gentle, reflective symphony is the least played of the nine.

* * FERENCSIK	*Czech Philharmonic Orch.*	PARLIAMENT (S) 165 [Overture]
* * MONTEUX	*London Symphony Orch.*	VICTROLA VIC (S) 1102 [Wagner, Siegfried Idyll]
* * KONDRASHIN	*Moscow Philharmonic Orch.*	MELODIYA/SERAPHIM (S) 60061
* ANSERMET	*Orchestra Suisse Normande*	LONDON (S) STS-15055 [Coriolanus Overture]
* TOSCANINI	*BBC Symphony Orch.*	3-SERAPHIM (M) 6015 [Symphonies No. 1, 6; Brahms, Tragic Overture; Mozart, Overture]

My off-beat choice for first place is Ferencsik and the Czechs on Parliament, a great performance. Before the brickbats start flying from fierce fans of Toscanini, Walter, et al, I hasten to call to aid *The Stereo Record Guide,* which states: "On the showing of this account of the *Fourth,* and of his *Second,* Ferencsik is a formidable Beethoven conductor, dramatic but not over-fierce, warm but not over-romantic, and as in the

Second, the Czech Philharmonic's playing is marvelous. . . . good modern stereo." The sound is quite acceptable.

Monteux offers a superb performance, graceful and charming, fine for this lyrical work. Bookspan in *Stereo Review's* 1968 "Annual Updating of the Basic Repertory" noted Monteux's reading the best available regardless of price. The sound is good.

The Kondrashin disc is Seraphim's first offering from the U.S.S.R. This record was recorded and mastered in Russia on the M.K. label, and is now released in the U.S. by Seraphim at $2.50. This is a good example of the bounty of first-rate musical performances now available because of the economics of the American record business. Seraphim's parent company Angel would never have been able to market this very good disc at its usual $5.00 or $6.00 price, because a Kondrashin record couldn't complete with recordings by Ormandy, Szell, or Bernstein. Also, tough competition already exists even at $2.50 in the recordings of Monteux, Toscanini, etc. Result: Kondrashin is offered to America at $2.50. The Russian disc is well-recorded, even by American standards; the playing is sonorous, and sober-minded. Judging from this disc, Moscow Philharmonic does not possess much of the grace and refinement we expect from our orchestra over here; on the other hand, a solid uniformity is evident.

Ansermet, who enjoys a well-founded reputation as a colorist and image-maker, somehow presents this Beethoven in a fussy albeit lyrical manner. The rendition lacks the rugged strength we expect. The sound is agreeable.

Bookspan in his 1968 "Updating of the Basic Repertory" in *Stereo Review* rates the early Toscanini-BBC version, available in a three-record album, "a gem of purest ray"—and better than all other versions on the market. He may be right, but I find that the tubby, dry acoustic sound from old short-play discs unenjoyable and the tape hisses will disturb all but die-hard listeners.

SYMPHONY NO. 5 IN C MINOR (Opus 67)

The *Fifth Symphony* of Beethoven is the most popular ever written. In our era, it has reached a place of pre-eminence unrivaled by any other musical work. There are symphonies more melodic and others more profound—but Beethoven's *Fifth* is easily the most beloved. Untold millions have gone to the concert hall in adolescence and have been transfixed upon first hearing those terrifying bars—the three short notes, then one long, "fate knocking at the door." If anyone shrugs at the *Fifth,* it is only because of overexposure to its greatness. However, this

82   BEETHOVEN

listener has just emerged from many hours of living with an assortment
of many recordings of the *Fifth,* and can faithfully report that he still
found this piece utterly moving and a sublime work.

There are no less than 14 renditions available in the low-priced field.

* * * TOSCANINI	*NBC Orch.*	8-Victrola VIC (M) 8000 (in 8-record set)
* * * MUNCH	*Boston Symphony Orch.*	Victrola VIC (S) 1035 [Schubert, Symphony No. 8]
* * * KLEIBER	*Concertgebouw Orch.*	Richmond (M) 19105
* * * SCHURICHT	*Paris Conservatoire Orch.*	Richmond (M) 19005
* * STEINBERG	*Pittsburgh Symphony Orch.*	Pickwick (8) 4021 [Symphony No. 8]
* * FRICSAY	*Berlin Philharmonic Orch.*	Heliodor (S) 25059
* * PROHASKA	*Vienna State Opera Orch.*	Vanguard (S) 203
* * DORATI	*Minneapolis Symphony Orch.*	Mercury (M) 14016 (S) 18016
* * ANSERMET	*Orchestra Suisse Romande*	London STS (S) 15038
* KLEMPERER	*Vienna Symphony Orch.*	Vox (M) 11870 [Mozart, Serenade K. 525]
* FURTWAENGLER	*Berlin Philharmonic Orch.*	Heliodor (M) 25078
* BOULT	*London Philharmonic Promenade Orch.*	Vanguard (S) 190 [Overture]
* ANCERL	*Czech Philharmonic Orch.*	Parliament (M) 136
STEIN	*London Philharmonic Orch.*	Somerset/St. Fi. (S) 19400

The Toscanini disc (available only in an 8-record album) remains unchallenged for its Promethean, heaven-storming quality. This is a legendary performance. However, Sackville-West in a minority report says:
"Toscanini disappoints; a hard-driven performance." The sound is dry
and boxed-in.

The Munch disc is heartfelt, even noble, and has the magnificent plus
of the Boston Symphony. If you don't want to buy the 8-record Toscanini
album, this is a superb choice. C. G. Burke in *High Fidelity* was less
impressed: "It does not give out conviction." The sound is gratifying.

Another great version is Kleiber's resounding Amsterdam Concert-
gebouw Orchestra. Bookspan in his 1968 *Stereo Review* "Annual Updating of the Basic Repertory" lists this treasurable disc as Number One
regardless of price, and hails it "unrivalled for forward thrust and cumulative energy and excitement." The mono sound is just adequate.

The Schuricht disc, now deleted from the catalogue, is a stunning, thrilling performance, with good mono sound.

Steinberg's performance is stalwart and honorable with excellent playing by the Pittsburghers. *High Fidelity* thinks less of this record than I do, and comments: "Steinberg . . . fails to deliver impact in the first movement, joining a sheaf of other respectable failures." The sound is good.

Fricsay comes up with a warm, solid reading that somehow lacks body and excitement. But this is an entirely hearable and enjoyable version.

The dependable Prohaska is full-bodied and very enjoyable. This is not a great *Fifth* but a very good one.

Dorati is crackingly good, really fine. The sound is thin, but acceptable.

Ansermet is forceful, but not unforgettable; not quite as good as the top three-star entries.

Klemperer's first version is very old. Sackville-West says of it: "Klemperer treats the work as if he had just discovered its greatness." I find the performers mediocre. The sound is boxed-in and battered. Klemperer also recorded the *Fifth* much later on a high-priced Angel.

This reading of Furtwaengler made in his later years is as slow and deliberate as Toscanini's is impatient and quick-paced. With the Berliners, Furtwaengler is stately and self-conscious, and his interpretation often becomes unbearably ponderous.

Boult is honest and unexciting and decently recorded.

The mono Ancerl disc is unremarkable.

Stein is considerably outclassed.

SYMPHONY NO. 6 IN F (Opus 68), "PASTORALE."

The *Pastorale Symphony* is Beethoven's ode to nature, and the only one of the nine which is programmatic.

This is radiant, bucolic music, and the favorite Beethoven work of many music lovers.

* * * MONTEUX	*Vienna Philharmonic Orch.*	VICTROLA VIC	(S)	1070
* * * ANSERMET	*Suisse Romande Orch.*	LONDON STS	(S)	15064
* * * STEINBERG	*Pittsburgh Symphony Orch.*	PICKWICK	(S)	4009
* * * WALTER	*New York Philharmonic*	ODYSSEY (6-record album only)		3266 0001
* * KLEIBER	*London Philharmonic Orch.*	RICHMOND	(M)	19037
* * TOSCANINI	*NBC Orchestra*	VICTROLA VIC (8-record album only)	(M)	8000

* * TOSCANINI	BBC Symphony Orch.	3-Seraphim [Overture; Symphonies No. 1, 4; Brahms, Tragic Overture]	(M)	6015
* KLEMPERER	Vienna Symphony Orch.	Vox	(5)	6960
* PARAY	Detroit Symphony Orch.	Mercury	(M) (S)	14001 18001
* BOULT	London Philharmonic Promenade Orch.	Vanguard	(S)	193
SEJNA	Czech Philharmonic Orch.	Parliament	(S)	105

There is a wealth to choose from here—four really top performances among ten commendable recordings.

The Monteux reading is serenity itself. I agree with Bookspan who comments in *Stereo Review*: "In the low-priced field, the honors go to Monteux," while in a minority report, *High Fidelity says*: "A stiff, graceless quality. . . . On the whole, something of a disappointment." The sound is agreeable.

A reading of finesse and delicacy is heard on Ansermet's most admirable disc. *High Fidelity* commented in 1960: "A classic account of the music . . . Purely from the engineering viewpoint, here is the best all-around sound of any version of this symphony you can buy today."

Steinberg's lyrical lines are outstanding along fine orchestral work. The sound is excellent.

The Bruno Walter Album of six records of Beethoven symphonies offers superbly warmhearted music-making, straight from the Wienerwald forest. However, the sound is alternately tubby and thin. Later, Walter did these symphonies again on stereo with other musicians. In this later effort on expensive Columbia discs the performance was rated Number One by *Stereo Review's* 1968 "Annual Updating of the Basic Repertory." Said Bookspan: "Bruno Walter, in a sense, 'owned' this symphony, and his recording is one of the most treasurable items in the whole catalog."

The old mono Kleiber disc, recently discontinued, is a sweet-singing reading. It is now selling for around a dollar in many record stores. The sound is clean.

Toscanini's effort for NBC is too disciplined for this gentle, bucolic work. But this reading must be admired for its imaginative quality.

Toscanini's BBC disc is far more lyrical than his later NBC version, but far more dim. The tape was taken from old 78's, and you are hereby warned.

Klemperer's record is a hoary relic of his less prestigious days, and his players are pedestrian. But here is nobility and loving care, especially in the bird song which pops in and out of the score. The sound is fair.

Paray is on the fussy and energetic side, although well recorded—in a pleasant, honest job.

Boult is gentlemanly, well-paced, and entirely hearable.

Sejna is dull and unremarkable.

SYMPHONY NO. 7 IN A (Opus 92)

When first played at the great Hall of the University of Vienna in 1813 with Beethoven conducting, the performance seems to have been disastrous, for Beethoven's advancing deafness made it impossible for him to hear any but the loudest blasts from the orchestra. One of Beethoven's most gripping and exultant works today, the *Seventh* is among his most widely played symphonies.

* * * TOSCANINI	*NBC Symphony*	VICTROLA VIC	(M) 8000
		(8-record album complete)	
* * * STEINBERG	*Pittsburgh Symphony Orch.*	PICKWICK	(S) 4022
* * * FRICSAY	*Berlin Philharmonic Orch.*	HELIODOR	(S) 25065
* * * MONTEUX	*London Symphony Orch.*	VICTROLA VIC	(S) 1061
* * FURTWAENGLER	*Vienna Philharmonic*	3-SERAPHIM	(M) 6018
		[Symphonies No. 3, 5]	
* WALTER	*N. Y. Philharmonic*	ODYSSEY	(M) 3266 0001
		(6-record album)	
* CANTELLI	*Philharmonic Orch.*	SERAPHIM	(S) 60038
* BOULT	*London Philharmonic*	VANGUARD	(S) 147
* VAN REMOORTEL	*London Symphony Orch.*	VOX	(5) 10970
		[Symphony No. 8]	

Toscanini, available only in the complete eight-record album, is superb; all steel, he drives with impetus from the first bar to the last. A little relenting tenderness would have been gratefully received, at least in the Allegretto. But you can't have everything and Toscanini came close to perfection on this reading. Irving Kolodin in the 1955 *"Guide to Orchestral Music"* wrote: "The Toscanini concept of this work survives both repetition and challenge." The 1953 sound is pretty good, rounder than in most of the Toscanini discs.

Steinberg is a hard man to beat when he is at his best, which he emphatically is here. This is a vital, high-voltage yet careful reading. I can offer no better praise than to quote Robert Marsh of *High Fidelity:* "The Steinberg performance is firmly propulsive. I approve. The lines are very open; one can hear everything. Bravo! It is eloquent but it lets the eloquence come out of the music; it is not applied like a sauce. Bravissimo!

The cumulative effect is tremendous. Right! The recording suits the performance in every way." The sound is not ample.

Ferenc Fricsay, a gifted Hungarian conductor who died in mid-career, though barely known on our shores except to discophiles, had an enormous reputation in Europe in the early 1960's. This *Seventh* is perhaps his most stirring record. This is a solid, robust, entirely convincing performance. The playing of the Berlin Philharmonic is magisterial and sonorous. The sound is good.

Pierre Monteux is at his heady best here, in a crisp, vital, often soaring reading.

The Furtwaengler disc, once regarded as little less than The Last Judgment, is still highly impressive. The tempos are deliberate and ponderous. This *Seventh* is a dubbing from short-play 78-rpm recordings, and you hear a mild but annoying grinding. Nevertheless, this disc is a historical document of the highest interest for the collector who already has two or three *Sevenths*.

Walter is surprisingly rigid, and the sound is blurry. His later stereo version, a great performance indeed on expensive Columbia, is far less metronome-bound.

Cantelli, a disciple of Toscanini's, has the Maestro's drive and clenched intensity, but I do not hear more than that.

Boult is quite enjoyable in an honest, unmannered reading.

Van Remoortel is honest, competent, but much outclassed.

SYMPHONY NO. 8 IN F (Opus 93)

Beethoven completed his *Eighth* symphony in the same year he completed the *Seventh*. This is a lighthearted work, a breather as it were before the colossal *Ninth*. Wagner described its infectious gaiety as "the games and caprices of a child." This is lovable music.

* * * ANSERMET	*Orchestra Suisse Romande*	LONDON STS [Symphony No. 1]	(S) 15032
* * TOSCANINI	*NBC Symphony*	VICTROLA VIC (8-record album)	(M) 8000
* * BARBIROLLI	*Halle Orch.*	VANGUARD [Symphony No. 1]	(S) 146
* * STEINBERG	*Pittsburgh Symphony Orch.*	PICKWICK [Symphony No. 5]	(S) 4021
* VAN REMOORTEL	*London Symphony Orch.*	VOX [Symphony No. 7]	(S) 10970

Ansermet delivers a performance which, to borrow some nouns from John Briggs' *The Collector's Beethoven*, "has the qualities of lucidity, elegance, balance, and proportion so characteristic of the playing of this fine orchestra and conductor." The stereo sound, thankfully, is excellent.

This is one of Toscanini's best. The not-to-be-denied rhythmic propulsion carries you along here whether you want to be carried or not. This sound, unfortunately, is poor.

Barbirolli is infectious; his version has an ambiance that pleases.

Steinberg's recording is beautifully tailored, and the players are first-rate. The sound is excellent.

Van Remoortel, though pleasant, is quite outclassed.

SYMPHONY NO. 9 IN D MINOR (Opus 125)
(Sung in German)

Beethoven began sketching his *Ninth Symphony* in 1815. It was completed nine years later in 1824. It appears that the idea of adding a chorus to the final movement occurred to him only in the course of the writing. He longed to set Schiller's *Hymn to Joy* to music; his *Choral Fantasie* for piano, orchestra, and chorus of 1800 actually contains the melodic idea he later used for Schiller's poem. So much has been written about the power and grandeur of the *Ninth* there is little need to add comment here. Yet Debussy's remark is worth recalling—that no other work of art except the *Mona Lisa* had inspired a greater amount of nonsensical commentary. For Western music, the *Ninth* was a summing up of all that had come before; it remains a shattering, original creation that, at times, seems almost divine.

The Beethoven *Ninth* is the great touchstone for conductors, an all-embracing work that separates the men from the boys, and the podium posturers from the musical thinkers. In sizing up a conductor musicians always ask, "His Debussy sounds okay, so does his Beethoven's *Fifth;* but how is he in the *Ninth?*" Almost always, a conductor will not presume to record this master record until he has reached the age of wisdom.

* * * TOSCANINI	*NBC Symphony*	8-Victrola VIC (M) 8000 (8-record album only)
* * * MUNCH	*Boston Symphony Orch.*	2-Victrola VIC (S) 6003
* * FRICSAY	*Berlin Philharmonic Orch.*	2-Heliodor (S) 25077
* * CLUYTENS	*Berlin Philharmonic Orch.*	Seraphim (S) 60079
* * KLEIBER	*Vienna Philharmonic Orch.*	Richmond (M) 19083
* WALTER	*New York Philharmonic*	Odyssey 3266 0001 (6-record album)

* FURTWAENGLER	*Berlin Philharmonic Orch.*	EVEREST	(S) 3241
* KRIPS	*London Symphony*	8-EVEREST	(S) 3065
* HORENSTEIN	*Vienna Pro Musica*	VOX	(5) (S) 10000
DISENHAUS	*Stuttgart Philharmonic Orch.*	PERIOD SHO	(S) 305

The Toscanini performance, offered in the complete album only, is more than a historical document. It is the Maestro at his summit, displaying a furious energy that reminds us of Beethoven himself. The astute English critic Sackville-West is worth quoting: "Nowhere, perhaps, is Toscanini's genius more apparent than in this work. At the age of 85, he had lost none of the concentration and energy which he always brought to it—the listener has the strange sensation of being at the heart of a whirlwind." The soloists are first-class and the Robert Shaw Chorale is superb. The sound is adequate.

The reading by Charles Munch is not a traditional, classical approach, but a somewhat romanticized Beethoven, warm and personal rather than heaven-shaking. You will get superb singing from a quartet led by Leontyne Price, along with the ringing bass of Giorgio Tozzi, a standout. Moreover, the sonics from Symphony Hall in Boston are entirely modern. [Three fine Beethoven overtures are also included—*Fidelio, Leonora No. 3,* and *Coriolan.*]

Below this exalted level, we have Fricsay's fine performance which in 1958 was the first *Ninth* in the American catalogue. Fricsay was in his mid-forties at the time of this recording. This is a young conductor's *Ninth,* exuberant and dynamic. Its excellent soloists are led by Fischer-Dieskau and include Irmgard Seefried, Maureen Forrester, and Ernst Haeflinger—a formidable line-up. This is not an Olympian performance, as is Toscanini's, or Klemperer's on an expensive Angel, but it is a very good one, indeed. The stereo sound is decent, except for some fuzzy choral reproductions.

The late Belgian Andre Cluytens was much esteemed in Europe for his work with the Berlin Philharmonic and other ensembles. His rather straight-forward reading is solid and does not suggest the heaven-storming passion of this colossal work. Nevertheless, a sound performance.

In the mono set by Kleiber, the soloists led by Anton Dermota are fine, and there is an authoritative ring to the singing of the Singverein der Musikfreunds, and in the work of the Vienna Philharmonic Orchestra.

The Bruno Walter version, greatly admired, holds much nobility and warmth. But the soloists are just fair, and the disc shows its age badly. If you want Walter's magisterial statement of the *Ninth,* a later, clearer version is available on a high-priced Columbia.

Furtwaengler's over-expressive, eccentric reading is not for me, although the *New York Times* found it "an extraordinary example of Furtwaengler's peculiar talent." This recording was made at a concert during World War Two, and the "simulated" stereo is just that: fake.

The concept of Krips' reading is ambitious. The total result is a well-crafted rather than inspiring recording. The sound is clear.

The Horenstein version was notable some years ago as the first successful *Ninth* to be contained on a single LP. It remains an eminent performance. But the sound is sadly dated.

The Disenhaus version is quite uneventful and badly recorded to boot.

The expensive versions most esteemed at this writing are Schmidt-serstedt on London and George Szell on Epic.

CONCERTOS   Like the symphonies of Beethoven, his concertos are among the basic works of the concert repertory. His *Violin Concerto,* and his *Piano Concerto No. 5* (*Emperor*) are more played than any other classical concertos.

Beethoven wrote seven piano concertos. An early, forgotten concerto, written at the age of 14, was not published until 1888; we have only the fragment of another early effort. The five that remain are the backbone of the classical piano repertory, as Beethoven's symphonies are the cornerstone of the orchestral repertory. In the five piano concertos we watch with fascination the evolvement of the master's musical thought.

CONCERTO IN C FOR VIOLIN, CELLO, PIANO (Opus 56)

After its premiere, this work was not played again during Beethoven's lifetime. This *Triple Concerto* is highly agreeable, but does not stand with Beethoven's other towering creations in the concerto form. The solo piano part was written to be played by Beethoven's royal pupil, the Archduke Rudolph; perhaps Beethoven did not regard the opus as a work of utmost creative seriousness. But it is melodious, by no means complex. It provides good home listening.

* GIMPEL, SCHUSTER, *Wuerttemberg Symphony*   Vox   (M) 11660
WUEHRER, DAVISON *Orch.*   [Brahms, Violin-Cello Concerto]

The Vox set is listenable; the conductor does not always hold close rein on his three high-spirited soloists. The lively, winning playing of pianist Wuehrer is a stand-out.

CONCERTO NO. 1 IN C FOR PIANO AND ORCHESTRA (Opus 15)

In 1892 a brilliant young composer and pianist from Bonn, Germany, was sent by his sponsor to study in Vienna. Soon the young man found princely patronage; he established himself in musical circles as a striking pianist, and his pupils included some of Vienna's most elegant ladies. Four years later, he went on a concert tour to Prague, where his reputation as a pianist had already spread. He composed a new concerto for that tour, which he played himself.

The composer was Ludwig van Beethoven, and the concerto is known to us as his *Piano Concerto No. 1, in C*. It was written when Beethoven was at the height of his prowess as a pianist. From contemporary sources, it would seem that he was a very impressive performer indeed. Beethoven's pupil, Czerny, declared that no player equaled his master in the rapidity of his scales, double trills, and skips.

This work was actually written in 1787, some two years after the *B-Flat Major Piano Concerto,* which we list as the second. An error in the publication of the two concertos brought about the confusion. *No. 1,* which shows the influence of Mozart and Haydn, is a delicate, joyous concerto.

* * CASADESUS, VAN BEINUM	*Concertgebouw Orch.*	ODYSSEY (M) 32 16 0055 (S) 32 16 0056 [Concerto No. 4]
* * SOLOMON, MENGES	*Philharmonia Orch.*	SERAPHIM (S) 60016 [Piano Sonata No. 26]
* GILELS, SANDERLING	*Leningrad Philharmonic Orch.*	2-PARLIAMENT (M) 138 [Concerto No. 2]

Casadesus is poised and polished; with the *Concerto No. 4* on the back, this disc is easily the best buy. *High Fidelity* comments: "An attractive and generous coupling. Casadesus's geniality is most winning in the *First Concerto,* although my own preference is for Solomon's more substanial and crisper account on Seraphim."

Solomon was Britain's greatest pianist in the 1950's. His reading is patrician, even urbane, and altogether fascinating. This is a fine record. The stereo sound is acceptable.

Gilels is exuberant and fleet-fingered. The mono sound is adequate.

I list Casadesus first because of the pleasant attraction of the *Fourth Concerto* on the other side. If you're after the *First Concerto* only, however, Solomon has the edge.

PIANO CONCERTOS NO. 1, 3, 5

BARENBOIM   *Vienna State Opera Orch.*   WESTMINSTER   (S) 1018

Really atrocious re-processed stereo sound utterly damns these gracious performances. The mono versions were far more agreeable to the ear.

PIANO CONCERTO NO. 2 IN B-FLAT (Opus 19)

Beethoven was only 25 when he wrote his *Second Piano Concerto*, yet one already hears dramatic gestures that anticipate the symphonies to come. Even the more perceptive of his contemporaries sensed that a composer of exceptional stature was emerging. One wrote, rather apprehensively, "the singular and original seems to be his chief aim in composition." Beethoven himself never cared too much for this concerto; he wrote to his publisher Hofmeister in 1801: "I value the concerto at only ten ducats, because, as I have already written, I do not give it out as one of my best." This is elegant, cheerful music; it is also one of the few major Beethoven works clearly imitative of Mozart.

* WUEHRER, DAVISSON	*Stuttgart Pro Musica Orch.*	VOX STPL [Concerto No. 3]	(S) 513060
* GILELS, SANDERLING	*Leningrad Philharmonic*	PARLIAMENT [Concerto No. 1]	(M) 138

Friedrich Wuehrer is a Viennese pianist whose mono Vox recordings in the 1950's were highly respected. He is an artist of high imagination and much brilliance in nineteenth-century music. Here he is splendid, but the orchestra is ragged and the balance of sound between pianist and orchestra is far less than ideal.

Gilels is forceful, but the sound is indeterminate.

Neither of these entries approaches Glenn Gould's dazzling record on expensive Columbia.

PIANO CONCERTO NO. 3 IN C MINOR (Opus 37)

The bold stamp of the imperious Beethoven emerges here. The composer himself gave the first performance in 1803, to an unimpressed audience. Today, the concerto is highly popular.

* * * SOLOMON, MENGES *Philharmonic Orch.*   SERAPHIM   (S) 60019

92   BEETHOVEN

* * * FISCHER, FRICSAY	*Bavarian State Orch.*	Heliodor (S) 26001 [Mozart, Concerto; Rondo K. 382]
* * BRENDEL, WALLBERG	*Vienna Pro Musica Orch.*	Vox (M) 11370 (S) 511370
* * GRAFFMAN, HENDL	*Chicago Symphony Orch.*	Victrola VIC (S) 1059
* WUEHRER, DAVISSON	*Stuttgart Pro Musica Orch.*	Von STPL-513060 [Concerto No. 2]
* FIRKUSNY, SUSSKIND	*Philharmonia Orch.*	Pickwick (S) 4019
* GILELS, KONDRASHIN	*U.S.S.R. State Orch.*	Period (M) 601 [Mozart, 2 Piano Concerto in E-Flat]

We have many plums here—an almost bewildering array of first-rate discs.

Solomon's reading is a beauty, with the pianist in excellent form. He displays, in the words of Sackville-West, that combination of virility and poetic insight which the music requires. The sound is warm.

Anne Fischer's reading is cultured and poetic. *Record Guide* comments: "Her fingerwork sparkles, the tone colour is rich and varied and there is a genuine sense of spontaneous gaiety that carries one on through phrasing and speed-changes that could with some pianists seem mannered. It is a highly attractive, if rather personal, reading. The Mozart Concert Rondo provides an extra delight."

Brendel is a lyrical pianist whom I admire; one cannot go far wrong with him, although one sometimes yearns for a more full-bodied approach. Creative musicianship is heard here, along with technical aplomb. The sound is clean, but the stereo balance is hectic.

A glittering reading is to be had from Gary Graffman, indifferently supported by Walter Hendl. The sound is fine and clear.

Wuehrer has a massive style that is almost overpowering at times; but this is a solid, virile pianist, with brains. Coupled with the *Second Concerto,* this is an attractive disc. The orchestral work, however, is indifferent. The sound is fair.

Firkusny is romantic; he has smooth rapport with the Philharmonia under Walter Susskind. The sound is good.

Gilels is sweeping, technically assured and spontaneous. The deadly drawback is the pre-Sputnik, Iron Curtain sound. *High Fidelity* comments on the sound: "This recording from Russian tape is junk."

PIANO CONCERTO NO. 4 IN G (Opus 58)

This lyrical, arresting, utterly poetic concerto was first played at a massive all-Beethoven program in 1808, with the composer as soloist. Next to the *Fifth Concerto,* this is the most popular of Beethoven's piano concertos.

* * CASADESUS, VAN BEINUM	*Concertgebouw Orch.*	ODYSSEY	(M) 32 16 0055 (S) 32 16 0056 [Concerto No. 1]
* * BACKHAUS, KRAUSS	*Vienna Philharmonic Orch.*	RICHMOND	(M) 19017
* NOVAES, SWAROWSKY	*Vienna Pro Musica*	Vox	(M) 8530 (S) 58530 [Piano Sonata No. 14]
* GILELS, SANDERLING	*Leningrad Philharmonic Orch.*	MONITOR	(M) 2032
* BRENDEL, WALLBERG	*Vienna Pro Musica Orch.*	Vox	(5) (S) 11360

Casadesus presents here an intellectualized statement of one of the most lyrical concertos in the repertory. *High Fidelity* comments: "The French pianist's immaculately played version of the *Fourth* is presently unrivaled in the budget category, and this very civilized music-making is further enhanced by Van Beinum's elegant and polished accompaniments. Sonics are sharp, bright, and clean."

William Backhaus was a giant among pianists before World War II. He also recorded extensively in the 1950's, when his powers were waning. Here he gives an extraordinary performance of a master pianist in the German classical tradition. The mono sound is clean.

Novaes has silken runs, warmth, lyricism, and high musical content. As usual, she is much less gratifying with an orchestra than she is in her solo recording. Sackville-West: "solid, substantial, and musical." [The backing is Novaes' justly famous reading of the *"Moonlight"* Sonata.] The 1952 sound is fair on the *Concerto,* better on the *"Moonlight."*

Gilels' playing is warmhearted; this is a first-rate pianist. The mono sound is only so-so.

Brendel is poetic, but the Vienna Pro Musica is hardly the Vienna Philharmonic. *High Fidelity* comments: "Technically, it exhibits such failings as high tape hiss and the thinly recorded sound of a Viennese pickup band, led without magic."

PIANO CONCERTO NO. 5 IN E-FLAT (Opus 73)

The crowning achievement of Beethoven's concertos is the transcendental *"Emperor"* Concerto. This work became the model of the ideal piano concerto, an ideal still admired by most people today. It has everything: poetry, drama, and profundity.

* * * GIESEKING, KARAJAN	*Philharmonic Orch.*	ODYSSEY	(M) 32 16 0029
* * * GIESEKING, GALLIERA	*Philharmonic Orch.*	SERAPHIM	(S) 60069
* * * BACKHAUS, KRAUSS	*Vienna Philharmonic Orch.*	RICHMOND	(M) 19072
* * * KATZ, BARBIROLLI	*Halle Orch.*	VANGUARD	(S) 138
* * BRENDEL, MEHTA	*Vienna Pro Musica Orch.*	VOX	(M) 12050 (S) 512050 [Fantasy Opus 77]
* GILELS, SANDERLING	*Leningrad Philharmonic Orch.*	MONITOR	(M) 2033
* FIRKUSNY, STEINBERG	*Pittsburgh Symphony Orch.*	PICKWICK	(S) 4006
* NOVAES, PERLEA	*Bamberg Symphony Orch.*	VOX	(M) 11930 (S) 511930
RAUCH, SEJNA	*Czech Philharmonic Orch.*	PARLIAMENT	(S) 147

The great German pianist Walter Gieseking recorded the *"Emperor"* concerto three times; the Odyssey version is the second, and, for me, the greatest. This is grand-manner, sensitive, and utterly convincing playing. Karajan's accompaniment is in his smooth, accomplished style.

The Gieseking-Galliera version was also made in 1955. There is not much difference in the playing between this and the above-mentioned disc; the orchestral work here is more assertive. The *New York Times:* "Gieseking's infinitely shaded tone and sense of pacing make the disc a model of its style."

The Backhaus record is another great performance that will be heard as long as people listen to Beethoven records. This is masculine, sweeping, authoritative playing that one must admire.

For modern-age sound, we turn to a surprisingly vibrant reading by the Roumanian pianist Mindru Katz. He is bold and assertive, with tremenduos tonal range, and Barbirolli's support with the excellent Halle Orchestra is first-rate. *High Fidelity* said of this record: "Here is an *Emperor* to share first place with the Rubinstein-Leinsdorf set on RCA Victor."

Brendel gives a strong performance, full of personality. He is firmly supported by Zubin Mehta.

Gilels is superb on a well-recorded Soviet mono disc.

Firkusny's rendition has a notable singing line; it is entirely hearable.

Novaes is beautiful, in a delicate, feminine reading. The sound is adequate.

Rauch is much outclassed.

VIOLIN CONCERTO IN D (Opus 61)

This concerto was first performed in 1806. Beethoven had long considered a work for violin and orchestra, and as early as 1788, he actually composed part of a *Konzertstueck* for violin.

The Beethoven *Violin Concerto* stands supreme in the classical literature; only the concerto of Brahms rivals its power and sweep and humanity.

* * * MILSTEIN, STEINBERG	*Pittsburgh Symphony Orch.*	PICKWICK	(S)	4037
* * * SZERYNG, THIBAUD	*Paris Conservatory Orch.*	MONITOR	(S)	2093
* OISTRAKH, GAUK	*Moscow State Symphony Orch.*	VOX	(M)	16150
* RICCI, BOULT	*London Philharmonic Orch.*	RICHMOND	(M)	1934
* LAUTENBACHER, REICHERT	*Westphalian Symphony Orch.*	VOX [Romance]	(S)	11170
* SUK, KONWITSCHNY	*Czech Philharmonic Orch.*	PARLIAMENT	(S)	169

Milstein leads with a striking reading that is near the top of everyone's list. To quote John Briggs in *The Collector's Beethoven:* "When Mr. Milstein is in the vein he is superlative, and such was the case when this recording was made." I should add that Milstein's approach to this concerto is less sweeping than that of most violinists; it is intimate, thoughtful, and quite wonderful. The orchestral backing by Steinberg is firm. The sound is clear.

The excellent Szeryng gives a highly individualized, supreme performance, in many ways equal to Milstein's. The conductor here was the famous violinist Jacques Thibaud, who was killed in an air crash in 1953. *High Fidelity* commented, in 1960: "This is one of the great recordings of the concerto. The orchestral work and sound are both outstanding.

Oistrakh, one of the great violinists of this century, is famous for his dazzling interpretation of the Beethoven concerto. Those who seek him, however, are directed to his recording on high-priced Angel, since the poor and old sound on the version here precludes serious consideration.

Ricci plays with sweetness and warmth, and immaculate technique. But the artistic penetration of Milstein and Szeryng is lacking.

Small-sized, capable readings are to be had from Lautenbacher and Suk, both fine musicians and serious players.

STRING QUARTETS   The string quartets of Beethoven are among his greatest works. They are not to be missed by anyone who loves chamber music. As with all Beethoven, they are divided into three distinct periods, invariably referred to as early, middle, and late Beethoven. The first six quartets are early Beethoven, and they are full-bodied creations, somewhat reminiscent of the style of Haydn.

The middle quartets are absorbing and refreshing; the mature, path-breaking Beethoven is boldly heard. For the listener who has gone beyond Schubert's *Trout Quartet* and some Haydn and wants to take on something more meaty, there is no better choice than Beethoven's three entirely wonderful middle-period *Razumovsky* quartets (*Quartets No. 7, 8, 9*).

The late quartets are philosophy in sound. Writers such as Thomas Mann and Aldous Huxley have groped to express in words the mystic, transcendental quality of these works. In his last years, Beethoven increasingly found the string quartet to be the vehicle best suited for his final utterances; many great composers have also done so. The string quartet does not have the sonorous sound of a symphony, nor its obvious, colorful palette. A quartet is a stark, naked, form: four players scraping on catgut. The composer has to have something to say. If he is a Beethoven, the result is a lonely profundity that stands with those other devastating works of intimate self-searching art: the self-portraits of Rembrandt.

GROSSE FUGUE IN B-FLAT (Opus 133) FOR QUARTET

Written in 1825, two years before Beethoven's death, the *Grosse Fugue* is one of the awesome, metaphysical masterpieces, ranking with Bach's *Art of the Fugue*. The *Grosse Fugue* originally was the finale of the *Quartet, Opus 130*. After Beethoven's death the *Grosse Fugue* was brought out separately, and since then musicians have regarded it with special reverence. Musicologist Tovey called it "the most gigantic fugue in existence." J.W.N. Sullivan, author of a famous book about Beethoven's spiritual development, sees it as pure philosophy: "In the *Grosse Fugue* the experiences of life are seen as the conditions of creation and are accepted. . . . To be willing to suffer in order to create is one thing; to realize that one's creation necessitates one's suffering, that suffering is one of the greatest of God's gifts, is almost to reach a mystical solution of the problem of evil." I usually am not taken with mystic and purple writing about music, but there is no other way to describe the colossus known to us as Beethoven's Grosse Fugue.

The work was written for string quartet, but is often performed by the string section of a symphony orchestra—in effect, an augmented string quartet. There is much historical precedence for this, and conductors since von Buelow and Wahler have performed in this way.

* * *	*Fine Arts Quartet*	5-CONCERT-DISC	(M)	1502
			(S)	502
		[5 "Late" Quartets]		
* * *	*Fine Arts Quartet*	CONCERT-DISC	(M)	1249
			(S)	249
		[Quartet No. 16]		
* *	*Loewenguth Quartet*	3-VOX SVBX	(S)	543
		[4 "Middle" Quartets]		
* *	*Smetana Quartet*	CROSSROADS	(M)	22 16 0055
			(S)	22 16 0056
		[Quartet No. 13]		
* *	*Hungarian Quartet*	4-SERAPHIM	(S)	6007
		[5 "Late" Quartets]		
* *	*Winograd String Orch.*	2-HELIODOR	(S)	25019
		[Bach, Art of the Fugue]		
* SCHERCHEN	*English Baroque Quartet*	WESTMINSTER	(M)	9711
		[Septet]		
* FURTWAENGLER	*Berlin Philharmonic Orch.*	HELIODOR	(M)	25078
		[Symphony No. 5]		

In the original scoring, the Fine Arts Quartet tackle this work successfully with their usual bite and clarity. Their reading is available on either a single disc or a five-record set.

The Loewenguth Quartet also approach this composition intellectually. They have a juicier tone than the Fine Arts group, and keen intensity. Their performance is admirable. The sound is well-recorded.

The Smetana Quartet approach the *Grosse Fugue* with a romantic treatment, which disturbs me. But the English *Stereo Record Guide* feels otherwise: "*The Grosse Fugue* thrives on this group's characteristic treatment, and the technical problems apparently hold no terrors for the players. The quartet's tone is specially rich and true." The sound is rather grainy.

The Hungarian Quartet play with much lush beauty, but without sufficient strength and penetration.

On the augmented versions, a vital, gutsy reading is to be had from Winograd. Coupled with Bach's *Art of the Fugue,* this set should give the intellectual listener much to think about for some time to come.

Scherchen is unconventional—and highly absorbing—on good mono.

Furtwaengler's stylized grandiose exhibition is not for me. But this is a famous, widely discussed rendition. The sound is antiquated, despite "enhancing" first aid.

QUARTETS (Complete)

* * *	Fine Arts Quartet	3-EVEREST [Early Quartets]	(S)	507
* * *	Fine Arts Quartet	3-CONCERT-DISC [Middle Quartets]	(S)	506
* * *	Fine Arts Quartet	5-CONCERT-DISC [Late Quartets]	(S)	502
* *	Hungarian Quartet	3-SERAPHIM [Early Quartets, Opus 18]	(S)	6005
* *	Hungarian Quartet	3-SERAPHIM [Middle Quartets, Opus 57, 74, 95]	(S)	6006
* *	Hungarian Quartet	4-SERAPHIM [Late Quartets, Grosse Fugue, Opus 127, 130, 131, 132, 135]	(S)	6007
* *	Loewenguth Quartet	3-Vox SVBX [Four Quartets]	(S)	544
* *	Endres Quartet	3-Vox SVBX [Early Quartets, Opus 18]	(S)	516
*	Barylli Quartet	WESTMINSTER [Early Quartets, Opus 18]	(S)	1028

Most recorded sets of the *Quartets* are available in three volumes: early, middle, and late quartets.

The Fine Arts, a group with rugged bits and vigor, suffer from hard-edged tone at times, but they have a penetrating intellectual quality that must be admired. *High Fidelity* is rather less approving: "Direct, straightforward performances, with few artful subtleties."

The Hungarian Quartet have a bland tone and are impeccably recorded. My complaint is that at times they fail to grapple with the music, but sail too smoothly across it.

The sinewy "anti-virtuistic" Loewenguth Quartet also give deeply intelligent readings. They do not look for beauty of tone, but are concerned with musical content. *High Fidelity:* "Stylistically uneven, and literal in the rather deadly sense."

Incisive playing is also heard from the Endres Quartet in the early quartets.

The Barylli are a lightweight, gracious group, highly acceptable in early Beethoven. Harold Schonberg of the New York *Times:* "Played with considerable spirit, but the leader's tone is inclined to be scratchy, and he is not at all bashful about featuring it." Despite this slap from Schonberg, this set was on *Saturday Review's* list of "Best Recordings of 1968."

On high-priced records, the vibrant readings of the Amadeus Quartet on the DGG label are most admired today.

QUARTET NO. 4 IN C MINOR (Opus 18, No. 4)

This is essentially a lyrical work, but it also contains much vibrant strength.

* MORINI, GALIMIR, TRAMPLER, VARGA	WESTMINSTER (M) 9074 [Mozart, Quartet No. 23]	

This was a notable disc in the 1950's; it is still cherishable. The mono sound is pleasant.

QUARTET NO. 5 IN A (Opus 18, No. 5)

This is a lyrical, neatly made quartet that quietly appeals.

*	*Claremont Quartet*	NONESUCH 71152 [Quartet No. 6]

The playing is orderly and uneventful.

QUARTET NO. 6 IN B-FLAT (Opus 18, No. 6)

This is the last—and perhaps the most interesting—of Beethoven's early group of six quartets. The *Scherzo* of this work contains some startling syncopation that is quite hard to play. There is also a wonderful slow introduction, and Beethoven directed that it should be played "with the greatest delicacy."

* *	*Janacek Quartet*	PARLIAMENT (S) 71152 [Quartet No. 1t]
*	*Claremont Quartet*	NONESUCH 71152 [Quartet No. 5]

Gracious, light textures are supplied by the Czech players of the Janacek Quartet.

The Claremont Quartet are rather pallid, to my ears.

QUARTET NO. 7 IN F (Opus 59, No. 1) *("RASUMOVSKY")*

This work and *Quartets No. 8 and 9* are known to all music lovers as ""The Rasumovsky Quartets," so named after their patron Count Rasumovsky, who had come to Vienna as Russian Ambassador in 1792. (He himself was a violinist, and had his own quartet.) All three quartets are marvelous music. To quote Roger Fiske in *Chamber Music:* "These Rasumovsky quarters are in some ways the most wholly successful in existence. It has been argued (not by me) that in the wonderful late quartets Beethoven overstrained the medium and attempted the impossible. But no one could deny the complete success of these three works; Beethoven found heights never before scaled by man and reached the top with triumphant ease." I can only add that all three quartets are entirely approachable, by no means forbidding, and certainly the best choice for anyone who cares to find out what all the rhapsodizing over Beethoven's quartets is all about. They provide no great strain upon the uninitiated.

* *   *Vlach Quartet*   PARLIAMENT   (S)   615

The Vlach Quartet is a first-rate ensemble from Czechoslovakia. They are expert technicians, and their attacks are dazzling. They are rather German and studious in approach, which is good for Beethoven. There is also a forward thrust and unity of thought that make this an outstanding disc.

QUARTET NO. 8 IN E MINOR (Opus 59, No. 2) *("RASUMOVSKY")*

This is the second of the three quartets commissioned by Count Rasumovsky. A superb work of romantic melancholy, it employs a Russian tune in the "trio" section. The Count had requested that Beethoven employ a Russian folk tune in each of the three quartets: Beethoven obliged in this one only.

* *   *Janacek Quartet*   PARLIAMENT   (S)   627

A fresh, alert, technically impressive reading is offered by the esteemed Janacek Quartet.

QUARTET NO. 9 IN C (Opus 59, No. 3) ("RASUMOVSKY")

The third of the *"Rasumovsky" Quartets* is filled with Beethoven's warm lyricism, and with muscular energy as well. It is immediately attractive; the *Minuet* is sheer charm and grace. In sum—enthralling music, not at all dull or uninviting.

* * *   Smetana Quartet   PARLIAMENT   (S)   634
                                            [Haydn, Quartet Opus 103]

The Smetana Quartet deliver the goods in a stunning reading that has been welcomed with open arms. *Stereo Record Guide* comments: "Even among Czechoslovakia's magnificent quartet groups the Smetana players stand out both for sensitivity and virtuosity, and here they are in scintillating form. This is one of the finest Beethoven quartet records ever issued at whatever price, and to have it at bargain price is something not to be missed." The coupling is worthwhile. The sound is ample.

QUARTET NO. 11 IN F MINOR (Opus 95)

This is the shortest of all the quartets—"not because Beethoven has less to say," as Roger Fiske puts it, "but because he says it more concisely." It is fascinating music, falling between the "middle" *Rasumovsky Quartets* and the inward-turning, late quartets. Beethoven was already quite deaf at this time. One senses here that the outside world had little of interest for him.

* *   Smetana Quartet   PARLIAMENT   (S)   614
                                          [Quartet No. 1]

Here is a strong, forceful reading, even a bit rough and unmannerly, which is perfectly appropriate and even Beethovenesque.

QUARTET NO. 12 IN E-FLAT (Opus 127)

This is the first of Beethoven's towering last quartets. It is essentially a pleasant piece without the starkness of those that follow. The slow movement can only be termed sublime.

*   Vienna Konzerthaus   WESTMINSTER   (M)   9073
                Quartet

The Vienna Konzerthaus Quartet were a famous recording group some

fifteen years ago. There is a certain stodginess to their readings, but here
they are effective, in a warmhearted manner. The sound is all right.

QUARTET NO. 13 IN B-FLAT (Opus 130)

This very great, intensely tragic quartet has six movements. The
Grosse Fugue, which today is performed separately, was originally the
finale of this work. Beethoven's publisher complained that it made an
already frighteningly long quartet even longer. With uncharacteristic
meekness, Beethoven wrote a new finale.

To try to describe the fascination of this celestial music in words is
hopeless: let me only say that when this quartet, like those that follow,
was written, Beethoven was isolated from his fellow-men by total deafness. These were the last works he wrote, and he composed no other
music at this time; his life was entirely inward. To quote Roger Fiske,
"these quartets are the expression of a man who was spiritually no longer
as other men."

* * *	*Smetana Quartet*	CROSSROADS (S) 22 16 0055
		(M) 22 16 0056
		[Grosse Fugue]

The admirable Czechs come through again with a sinewy, rich-toned
reading. *Stereo Record Guide* comments: "The vigor of the Smetana
Quartet matches the quartet's greatness much more appropriately than
any attempt at refinement." The coupling is ideal. The sound is a bit
rough-edged.

QUARTET NO. 14 IN C-SHARP MINOR (Opus 131)

This is the most original, most complex, and perhaps the most profound of all Beethoven's quartets. Little else in music reaches the sublime heights of this very great work. The timid listener is urged to put a
recording of it on his phonograph, listen casually (even while reading),
and forget all about its being "One of the Great Works of Western
Civilization." After you are familiar with the music, its greatness will
surely reveal itself.

* *	*Vlach Quartet*	PARLIAMENT	(S) 625

The Vlach Quartet are another of the remarkable chamber music ensembles with which Czechoslovakia is blessed. They have a vibrant
quality that seems to search out the music, and they are always "singing,"
with a sense of high emotion. *Stereo Record Guide* comments: "This is
a fine performance, warm and passionate." The sound is a bit thin and
gritty.

QUARTET NO. 15 IN A MINOR (Opus 132)

Here is another profound masterpiece plumbing the depths of human experience. The slow movement is titled, "Song of Thanksgiving to the Deity, on recovering from an illness."

* * *   *Yale Quartet*   Vanguard   (S) C-100005

The Yale Quartet have vigor, a dynamic approach, and a lovely burnished tone; they are beautifully recorded. *Stereo Review* comments: "A Performance of almost terrifying powe rand intensity." *American Record Guide:* "One of the finest performances ever."

QUARTET NO. 16 IN F (Opus 135)

This is a very short quartet, about half the length of the others. It seems a relaxed, almost humorous work after the dizzifying complexities of the great quartets which preceded it. Its compact unity comes almost as a relief after the drawn-out probings of the other last quartets—but it does not contain their emotional range and depths.

* *   *Janacek Quartet*   Parliament   (S)   623
                                                    [Quartet No. 6]

The Janacek Quartet play with a quiet intimacy, a reverence for the music; this is a solid reading. The sound is a bit coarse-grained.

STRING TRIOS The string trios (for violin, viola, and cello) are conservative, lightweight pieces, most of them in the tradition of Haydn and Mozart. Beethoven composed five string trios before he attempted a string quartet. After his first group of quartets, he wrote no more string trios.

COMPLETE STRING TRIOS

* * * POUGNET, RIDDLE,   Westminster WM
      PINI   (M) 1017
                                             WMS (S) 1017

This is a highly enjoyable album. The playing by three top British musicians is supple and polished. Harold Schonberg in *Guide to Records of Chamber Music* commented on the original mono version: "Stylish playing, beautifully recorded. This British Group has culture, not to mention perfect ensemble and intonation." *High Fidelity* comments:

"Westminster's budget-priced "Multiple" offers formidable competition to RCA Victor's Heifetz Primrose Piatigorsky team in this music." The rechanneled sound is acceptable, but the 1957 mono sound is far warmer and cleaner.

STRING TRIO IN D (Opus 8)

Also called *Serenade,* this gracious trio was written soon after the struggling young Beethoven arrived to conquer the big town of Vienna. It was published in 1797.

*	*Pasquier Trio*	ALLEGRO (M) 9018	
		[Trio Opus 9, No. 1]	

The Pasquier Trio play smoothly, but they are no match for the virtuoso performance by Heifetz, Primrose, and Piatigorsky on high-priced Victor. The sound here is dated and filmy.

STRING TRIOS, No. 1 and 3 (Opus 9)

These trios are clever achievements of the young Beethoven.

* KOGAN, BARSHAI, ROSTROPOVICH	ARTIA (M) 164	

The *Trios* are more than well-played by the Russians; the disc is worth having just for the exciting cellist Rostropovich. The sound is fair mono.

PIANO TRIOS   The piano trios (works for piano, violin, and cello) do not have the intellectual quality that characterizes the quartets. And the trios are uneven in quality. But the great ones are endearing pieces, middleweight Beethoven that provide excellent listening.

In Beethoven's day, these were extremely popular forms, entertainments intended for talented and aristocratic amateurs and dilettantes.

NINE PIANO TRIOS

* *	*Beaux Arts Trio*	4 PHILLIPS WS (M/S) 4-007
		[Trio Opus 11; Trio Opus 121a; Variations Opus 44]

Four records of piano trios can surfeit all but the most rapt admirer of the form. But if you collect "completes," and many people do, this is first-rate, lyrical playing with exemplary sound.

PIANO TRIO NO. 1 IN E-FLAT (Opus 1, No. 1)

This trio excited the admiration of Haydn; this is youthful, graceful Beethoven.

* * FOURNIER, JANIGRO, BADURA-SKODA		WESTMINSTER (M) 9007 [Trio No. 4]
*	Prague Trio	CROSSROADS (M) 22 16 0123 (S) 22 16 0124 [Schumann, Trio No. 2]

I still enjoy the *elan* of the durable Westminster disc. The playing is by crack musicians.

The Prague Trio are smooth here, and acceptable.

PIANO TRIO NO. 3 IN C MINOR (Opus 1, No. 3)

Beethoven's first published work was the three piano trios of Opus 1, written with an eye on the popular trio market in Vienna.

* *	Suk Trio	CROSSROADS (M) 22 16 0069 (S) 22 16 0070 [Trio No. 4]
* * FOURNIER, JANIGRO, BADURA-SKODA		WESTMINSTER (M) 9006 [Trio Opus 11]

The Suk Trio are excellent, and highly musical, as they are on the entire series of piano trios that Crossroads has given us.

The old Westminster disc is an exhilarating one, and the players are three superb musicians. The sound is still agreeable.

PIANO TRIO NO. 4 IN D (Opus 70, No. 1)

This pleasant piece was published in 1798. The solo upper voice is often played on a clarinet.

* * *	Suk Trio	CROSSROADS (M) 22 16 0069 (S) 22 16 0070 [Trio No. 3]
* * FOURNIER, JANIGRO, BADURA-SKODA		WESTMINSTER (M) 9007 [Trio No. 1]

The Suk Trio give another fine performance, with a sure sense of style. They never show off—they let Beethoven show off.

Verve, excitement, and a heady youthful quality are to be had from the three famous artists on the Westminster disc. This disc and most of the Westminster series featuring Fournier, Janigro, and Badura-Skoda were recorded when ,these artists were young and coming up fast. The 1950's sound is still very good.

PIANO TRIO NO. 6 IN B-FLAT—"ARCHDUKE" (Opus 97)

Nicknamed because of its dedication to the archduke Rudolph, this trio is one of the most glorious works in the entire chamber music literature—a broad, warmhearted, immensely satisfying work from a mature Beethoven. If you want only one Beethoven trio, it should be the "Archduke."

* * *	*Suk Trio*	CROSSROADS (M) 22 16 0021 (S) 22 16 0022
* FOURNIER, JANIGRO, BADURA-SKODA		WESTMINSTER (M) 18270
* GILELS, KOGAN, ROSTROPOVICH		MONITOR (M) 2010

The version by the Suk Trio stands with any recording ever made at any price, and there have been many great recordings. The group play simply, almost with understatement; their tempos and shadings are just right. The sound is fine.

The old Westminster recording is still eminent and fresh-sounding.

The Monitor disc is pallid and subdued, with too much spotlight on pianist Gilels. By Russian standards the sound is good.

SEPTET   This engaging music is one of Beethoven's most popular chamber music pieces.

SEPTET IN E-FLAT FOR STRINGS AND WINDS (Opus 20)

This is an extremely popular piece, and Beethoven detested its popularity. "I wish it were burned," he is reported to have said upon hearing of the *Septet's* success in England some fifteen years after its premiere. It is scored for the felicitous combination of violin, viola, cello, doublebass, clarinet, French horn, and bassoon.

* *	*Leipzig Gewandhaus Soloists*	PHILLIPS W.S. (M/S) 9013

* SIEGEL	*Fine Arts Quartet and* *New York Woodwind* *Quintet Members*	Concert-Disc (M) 1214 (S) 214
*	*Barylli String Ensemble,* *Vienna Philharmonic* *Wind Group*	Westminster (M) 9711 [Grosse Fugue]
* TOSCANINI	*NBC Symphony Orch.*	8-Victrola VIC (M) 8000 [Quartet 16; Overture]

BEETHOVEN QUARTETS (Individual Records)

Many collectors prefer to have just one or two favorite quartets. Here, individual taste must decide.

The Leipzig players give a mellow, relaxed reading. The disc is warmly recorded.
Spirited, assured playing is heard on the old mono Fine Arts disc.
The Barylli group is modestly appealing.
The Toscanini version, marshalling members of the NBC Symphony, can only be regarded as a curiosity.

SONATAS FOR CELLO AND PIANO Here is top-drawer Beethoven. The five cello sonatas are indispensable works in the cello literature, perhaps the only chamber music for that instrument that approaches Bach's unaccompanied *Cello Suites*. They were composed between 1796 and 1815.
Strangely, these sonatas are neglected by chamber music lovers — which is a pity: they are splendid pieces. One has the impression of looking over Beethoven's shoulder as he rages, exults, and explores with that burning intensity which was his alone.

SONATAS FOR CELLO AND PIANO

* * * CASALS, SERKIN	3-Odyssey (S) 3236 0016
* * SCHUSTER, WUEHRER	3-Vox SVBX (S) 58
* * STARKER, BOGIN	2-Period (M) 1002
* JANIGRO, ZECHHI	2-Westminster (M) 9010/1

We are living in an age of great cellists, and several of them are represented here.
We can start with the celestial heights of Casals and Serkin. These discs were made at the Prades Festival concerts of 1952 and 1953, and now and then you will hear the great man Casals grunt as he attacks

a phrase. Casals was 76 in 1952, and his bow arm was in less than perfect control, but this performance is classic. Sackville-West calls it "humane and wonderfully wise . . . a revelation of warm, human, profound interpretation." Harold Schonberg of the *Times* was no less rhapsodic: "Excellent both tonally and in matters of balance. Two perfectly matched musicians operate here. For every bold stroke of the Casals bow there is an equivalently authoritative gesture from Serkin." The sound today is a bit rough-edged.

Schuster offers much beauty of tone, as well as fine-grained playing, lively recording, and the highly imaginative pianism of Wuehrer.

Starker is a rich-toned cellist. His phrasing is authoritative, and one feels the stamp of an extraordinary musical intellect. This is a first-rate performance. The mono sound is dry but acceptable.

Janigro, to my ears, is less virile than his colleagues here, and overly suave.

SONATAS FOR VIOLIN AND PIANO   Most of Beethoven's ten lyrical violin sonatas are early works. Eight of them were written within a four-year period, 1798-1802. They contain little of profound utterance; these well-made, expressive pieces have been called "Beethoven's diary musings."

SONATA NO. 1 IN D FOR VIOLIN AND PIANO (Opus 12, No. 1)

This springly music was published in 1799.

* * FERRAS, BARBIZET

SERAPHIM   (S) 60048
[Brahms, Violin-Cello Concerto]

The sonata is played as freshly as though it were just written. The sensitive Christian Ferras is a fast-rising young French virtuoso.

SONATA NO. 5 IN F—"SPRING"—FOR VIOLIN AND PIANO (Opus 24)

One of the loveliest of the ten Sonatas is the serene *Spring.*

* ROSAND, FLISSLER

Vox   (5) (S) 11340
[Sonata No. 9]

The playing here is tasteful, but little else.

SONATA NO. 7 IN C FOR VIOLIN AND PIANO (Opus 30, No. 2)

This is my personal favorite of the violin sonatas; here are fire and drama.

* KOGAN, MITNIK	Monitor (M) 2011 [Mozart, Sonata, K. 376]

Kogan and Mitnik provide suave, rather small-scaled music; this is by no means the last word in interpretation of this piece.

SONATA NO. 8 IN G FOR VIOLIN AND PIANO (Opus 30, No. 3)

* * * MILSTEIN, BALSAM	Pickwick (S) 4017 [Sonata No. 9]

The brilliant singing performance by Milstein and Balsam is one of the best buys to be had in Beethoven chamber music recordings.

SONATA NO. 9 IN A—"KREUTZER"—FOR VIOLIN AND PIANO (Opus 47)

This work was dedicated to a celebrated virtuoso, one Rudolpho Kreutzer, who never played it.

* * * MILSTEIN, BALSAM	Pickwick (S) 4017 [Sonata No. 8]

Milstein delivers one of the best version extant, and there is formidable competition from high-priced discs of this popular work. Beethoven authority John Briggs rates Millstein's performance, together with Oistrakh's, as the best to be had on records at any price. This is difficult music to play, and the rapport between Milstein and Balsam is a joy. The sound is warm.

PIANO SONATAS   As with Beethoven's symphonies and his string quartets, his piano sonatas are a towering achievement. They are also a self-sufficient universe of their own, in which infinite variety is to be found. Since their earliest performances, the sonatas have intrigued listeners—not to mention pianists—because of their poetry and humanism.

Before commenting on performances, a word must be said about Arthur Schnabel. This great musical thinker and pianist (1882-1951) has had an extraordinary influence on our conception of what the Beethoven sonatas should sound like; it is his recorded performances, now on Angel, that set the standard for intellectual and lyrical musicianship. It is against this legacy of Arthur Schnabel's that all succeeding performances are measured.

PIANO SONATAS (Complete)

No complete recording of the 32 sonatas exists on low-priced records at this writing. But Alfred Brendel has recorded most of them on Vox, and he plays them, on the whole, very well. A sensitive pianist, he has a touch and grace that sometimes makes the music sound as if it was being composed under his fingers. He does not over-dramatize, as so many other pianists do. His seven 3-record albums are commendable. *High Fidelity* on the sonics: "Vox's reproduction is variable, ranging from mellifluous at best to jangly and distorted at worst."

PIANO SONATA NO. 8 IN C MINOR— "PATHETIQUE" (Opus 13)

Beethoven himself applied the subtitle here, *"Grande sonate pathetique."* This is one of the composer's more romantic sonatas.

* * RICHTER	Artia [Bagatelles]	(M)	162
* * BRENDEL	Vox [Sonatas 14, 23]	(M) (S)	4270 54270
* FIRKUSNY	Pickwick [Sonatas 14, 23]	(S)	4024
* BADURA-SKODA	Westminster [Sonatas 14, 23]	(S)	14274
* PETRI	Westminster [Sonatas 14, 23]	(M)	18255

Richter is fluent and dramatic, the man to hear. The mono sound is so-so.

Brendel is massive here, and quite impressive.

Firkusny is forceful and fervent, and is well-recorded.

Badura-Skoda's version is ruined by terrible booming sound.

Petri is studious and rather heavy-handed in what should be given a highly romantic reading.

PIANO SONATA NO. 14 IN C-SHARP MINOR— "MOONLIGHT" (Opus 27, No. 2)

The subtitle "Moonlight" was *not* supplied by the composer, but by a post-critic who said the opening movement reminded him of moonlight on Lake Lucerne. This is perhaps the most frequently played of Beethoven's piano sonatas.

* * * NOVAES	Vox	(M) 11290
	[Sonatas No. 17, 26]	
* * * NOVAES	Vox	(M) 8530
		(S) 58530
	[Piano Concerto No. 4]	
* * * BRENDEL	Vox	(M) 14270
		(S) 514270
	[Sonatas 8, 23]	
* * KLIEN	Vox	(M) 12530
		(S) 512530
	[Sonatas 8, 23]	
* * BADURA-SKODA	WESTMINSTER	(S) 14274
	[Sonatas 8, 23]	
* FIRKUSNY	PICKWICK	(S) 4024
	[Sonatas 8, 23]	

Novaes is rhapsodic and utterly fresh-sounding. In 1955 Harold Schonberg in *Guide to Chamber Music Records* rated the Novaes disc the best to be had, preferable to that of Gieseking, Horowitz, and Backhaus. The same performance is available with a choice of couplings.

The Brendel reading is lyric, more objective, and extremely enjoyable.

Klien is a fine pianist and here is firmly controlled and rather reserved. The sound is good.

Badura-Skoda is surprisingly good—poetic and gentle.

Firkusny is elegant. The sound is acceptable.

PIANO SONATA NO. 17 IN D MINOR— "TEMPEST" (Opus 31, No. 2)

Beethoven is alleged to have tacked the "Tempest" subtitle on after Schindler, his biographer, asked what the music "meant." "Read Shakespeare's play," was the growled answer.

* * HASKIL	PHILLIPS WS	(M/S) 9001
	[Sonata No. 18]	
* * NOVAES	Vox	(M) 11290
	[Sonatas 14, 26]	

Clara Haskil is subtle and firmly in control. All her ideas are deeply reasoned. *High Fidelity* comments: "Miss Haskil's perspective on this music seems to me to be just about perfect."

Novaes is also worthy, but in a fresh-sounding, improvisatory conception. Harold Schonberg: "Next to hers, the more orthodox readings of Kempff and Backhaus are prose against poetry."

PIANO SONATA NO. 21 IN G—"WALDSTEIN" (Opus 49, No. 2)

This is dedicated to the earliest of Beethoven's patrons, Count Ferdinand Gabriel von Waldstein.

* NOVAES	Vox	(M) 11990
		(S) 511990
	[Schumann, Piano Concerto]	

This is a large, athletic, exciting piece, and Novaes is not quite with it.

PIANO SONATA NO. 23 IN F MINOR— "APPASSIONATA" (Opus 57)

Beethoven's astute publisher added the sure-fire subtitle. This is a turbulent work, from Beethoven's impassioned middle years; it calls for a high-powered virtuoso.

* * BRENDEL	Vox	(M) 14270
		(S) 514270
	[Sonatas 8, 14]	
* * BADURA-SKODA	Westminster	(S) 14274
	[Sonatas 8, 14]	
* * KLIEN	Vox	(5) (3) 12530
	[Sonatas 8, 14]	
* GORODNITZSKI	Pickwick	(S) 4024
	[Sonatas 8, 14]	
* PETRI	Westminster	(M) 18255
NADAS	Period SHO	(ST-2) 328
	[Sonatas 8, 14]	
VONDROVIC	Parliament	(M) 117
	[Sonata 14]	

None of the readings here exactly bowl me over.
Brendel is vivacious, and extremely lyrical.
Badura-Skoda plays with young, dauntless sweep and assurance.
Klien has appeal and fire; he is a solid musician.

Gorodnitzski is an experienced pianist, but this is a rather too-objective reading.

Egon Petri, a pupil of Busoni, was one of the pianistic giants in the 1930's and 1940's. He plays here with much tension and drama. The sound is just barely acceptable.

Nadas and Vondrovic are quite unremarkable.

If you happen to love the *Appassionata*, get Horowitz or Rubenstein on expensive RCA Victor.

PIANO SONATA NO. 26 IN E-FLAT— "LES ADIEUX" (Opus 81a)

This is a genial, pleasant piece. The gentle subtitle applies prosaically to a departure of His Imperial Highness, Archduke Rudolph.

* * NOVAES	TURNABOUT (S) 34242 [Sonatas 14 and 21]
* * NOVAES	VANGUARD C (S) 10014 [Sonatas 14, 32]

On the Turnabout disc, Novaes is warm, tender, and lyrical.

The Vanguard is a recent recording that lacks the admirable, poetic qualities of the great lady's reading on Turnabout. The sound is resonant.

PIANO SONATA NO. 27 IN E MINOR (Opus 90)

This brief sonata is played less often than the more notable ones.

* * SOLOMON	SERAPHIM (S) 60016 [Piano Concerto No. 1]

Solomon is cooly patrician—and first-rate.

PIANO SONATA NO. 28 IN A (Opus 101)

This is a difficult, cryptic work that throws most pianists. (Even the awesome Schnabel sounds too absorbed with just hitting the right keys.)

* * BISHOP	SERAPHIM (S) 60035 [Piano Sonata No. 30]

The gifted young American pianist Stephen Bishop is vital, precise, and well-recorded.

PIANO SONATA NO. 29 IN B-FLAT—
"HAMMERKLAVIER" (Opus 106)

"Hammerklavier" simply refers to the then-new instrument whose strings were struck with hammers—what we know today as the piano. This sonata is often called the Mount Everest of the piano. It is a big, rough-hewn work.

* PETRI	WESTMINSTER	18747
BARENBOIM	WESTMINSTER	1012

Petri's lumbering, intellectualized reading comes off heroically, even though he seems to be stabbing for notes at times. This record was made around 1956, and Petri was in his seventies at the time. The sound is shabby.

The Barenboim disc, entitled "Prodigy and the Genius," includes five Beethoven sonatas. Beware of this pretentiously titled set. Barenboim was a raw youngster when it was made, and the rechanneled sound is vile.

On high-priced discs, a sweeping performance is to be had from Ashkenazi, on London records. The sonics are first-rate.

PIANO SONATA NO. 30 IN E (Opus 109)

A great, brooding, naked, all-is-dust sonata, a work possible only at the end of an incredibly anguished lifetime such as was Beethoven's.

* * BISHOP	SERAPHIM	(S)	60025
	[Piano Sonata No. 28]		
* DOHNANYI	EVEREST	(M)	6109
		(S)	3109
	[Sonata 31]		

Stephen Bishop, not yet thirty, is a Californian, and a highly lyrical, sensitive pianist. His performance here is remarkable, but he does not touch the astonishing reading by Glenn Gould on high-priced Columbia.

The ancient Dohnanyi disc is a historical document and is to be respected.

PIANO SONATA NO. 31 IN A-FLAT (Opus 110)

In the last five piano sonatas of Beethoven, especially in the last two, we are on the edge of outer space. Romance is over; metaphysics is all.

* DOHNANYI	EVEREST	(M)	6109
		(S)	3109
	[Sonata No. 30]		

Some of the heroic grandeur of this sonata is suggested on this relic.
For modern sonics, and penetrating musicianship, we turn to Glenn
Gould on expensive Victor, or Arthur Schnabel on Angel.

PIANO SONATA NO. 32 IN C (Opus 111)

The end. For this listener, this leonine work is the greatest of the
32 sonatas. The awesome strength of Michelangelo is in these noble,
defiant pages.

| * NOVAES | VANGUARD (SC) 10014 |
| | [Sonatas 14, 26] |

There is no such thing as the "best" performance of Opus 111; it is
a masterpiece to be studied, weighed, and reapproached as long as man
listens to what we call Western music. The great Novaes is poetic here,
even noble, but the massive, craggy nature of this epic is better suggested
by Schnabel and Michelangeli on expensive discs.

OTHER MUSIC FOR SOLO PIANO Beethoven wrote several works
in this category.

VARIATIONS ON A THEME BY DIABELLI
(Opus 120)

This is the last of Beethoven's piano compositions; it stands with
Bach's *Goldberg Variations* as the greatest sets of variations ever written.
In 1822, an enterprising music publisher and minor composer named
Anton Diabelli invited the leading composers of Austria to contribute
variations on a slight waltz. Among those invited were Schubert, Czerny,
Mozart's younger son, and a bright eleven-year-old lad named Franz
Liszt. Beethoven, first annoyed, then outraged, then absorbed despite
himself, flung back not a single variation but a huge volume containing
no less than thirty-three. Thus came eternal fame to the otherwise utterly
forgotten Diabelli. This is tremendous, mind-stretching music, but it is
rather cold, and does not captivate the listener as do the soaring excursions of Johann Sebastian Bach in the *Goldberg Variations*.

Ordinary pianists keep away from the formidable *Diabelli Variations*.
Besides piano virtuosity, it demands musical intellect.

* * BRENDEL	TURNABOUT (S) 34139
* * RICHTER-HAASER	SERAPHIM (S) 60027
* KATCHEN	

Brendel leads again, in a probing, deeply-thought-out reading.

Richter-Haaser, a famous German Bethoven specialist, delivers a ponderous recording that the London *Gramaphone* declared to be "The best performance in the catalog. . . . Beethoven would have played it that way himself."

Katchen is resourceful, and has plenty of power.

VOCAL MUSIC Beethoven's sole opera, *Fidelio,* is more respected than performed. His choral music contains noble pages, but it is difficult to love these works; we admire the *Missa Solemnis* respectfully, but we do not embrace it as we do Verdi's *Requiem.*

Beethoven was not an extraordinary songwriter. Much of this output in this form is unremarkable *Weltschmerz.* But he has left us a lovely song cycle, *An Die Ferne Geliebte.*

AN DIE FERNE GELIEBTE (Opus 98)

Early romantic joys and sorrows are heard in Beethoven's best songs.

* * HAEFLIGER, WERBA	HELIODOR	M/S 25048
	[Schumann, Dichterliebe]	

Haefliger is a cultured lieder singer. The English *Stereo Record Guide:* "Haefliger gives a generally imaginative performance and he is well accompanied." This record was originally on the Deutsche Gramophone label. [The coupling is excellent.] The sound is clear.

FIDELIO (Sung in German)

"I could not compose operas like *Don Giovanni* and *Figaro,*" Beethoven is reported to have remarked. "They are repugnant to me." He found a less frivolous, properly ennobling subject in *Fidelio,* his single opera. The story is an account of a woman's heroic effort to save her husband, a political prisoner. This is an uneven work, full of quirks and oddities, but in *Fidelio* Beethoven reaches pages of great heights, and'his humanity permeates the work.

* MOEDL, JURINAC, WINDGASSEN, EDELMANN, FRICK, SCHOCK, FURTWAENGLER	*Vienna Philharmonic and State Opera Chorus*	3-SERAPHIM	(M) 6022
KONETZNI, RAIF, SEEFRIED, SCHOEFFLIER, ALSEN, BOEHM	*Vienna State Opera Orch.*	3-VOX	OPBX-167

KUCHTA, PATZAK,   *North German Radio*   2-NONESUCH   (S) 73005
REHFUSS,   *Orchestra and Chorus*
BAMBERGER

The Furtwaengler set is an intense, personal reading, that becomes almost hypnotic at times. The *Fidelio* of soprano Moedl is extremely shaky, and Jurinac is splendid as Marzelline, but this is not a singer's performance; the star is Furtwaengler. Yet somehow, this is less than a satisfying set despite its drive and vitality. Perhaps the soprano here, Martha Moedl, throws me off; we could use more glorious voice, less fervent passion. This set was on *Saturday Review's* 1968 "Best Records of the Year" list. The mono sound is clear.

The old Vox set is an uneven affair. Some of the singers are better than on Furtwaengler's star-studded cast. Outstanding is "Baritone Paul Schoefflier's great characterization," to quote vocal authority Philip Miller. The trouble is with soprano Hilde Konetzni, who, says Miller, "has only too obviously seen younger days."

Nonesuch provides a fairly well-recorded, serviceable set, with little vocal or musical excitement.

MISSA SOLEMENIS IN D (Opus 123)
(Sung in Latin)

Beethoven's great solemn festival Mass was written in honor of the occasion of his friend, pupil, and patron, the Archduke Rudolph of Austria, becoming installed as Archbishop of Olmutuz in Moravia. The work is not often heard in concert; the choral parts are formidable, and acrobatic leaps are required of the soloists. But there are glorious pages here. At this writing, Toscanini's incandescent reading is not listed at all in Schwann; if it pops up on Victrola, grab it.

* * * KIRSCHSTEIN,   *Cologne Orch. and Chorus*   2-NONESUCH   ((S) 73002
      DEROUBAIX,
      SCHREIER,
      MORBACH, WAND

  * STEINGRUBER,   *Vienna Symphony Orch.*   VOX   (5) 11430
      SCHUERHOFF,
      MAJKUT, WIENER,
      KLEMPERER

  * GRAF, HOFFMAN,   *North German Symphony*   2-VANGUARD   (S) 214/5
      KRETSCHMAR,   *Orch.*
      WENK, GOEHR   *NDR Chorus*

The Nonesuch edition by Wand is most exciting. The choral work is remorselessly drilled and is first-rate. The soloists are not glamorous stars, but they are excellent. The cathedral-sized sound is resonant, even splendid.

Another good recording is Klemperer's old Vienna reading, of which Sackville-West writes, "It is seldom we hear in the concert hall a performance so clear, so fervent and so musical as that which Klemperer has obtained." The sound is boxed-in and faded. Klemperer has recorded the *Missa* again, with fine sonics, on expensive Angel records.

On a less exalted plane we have a serviceable reading from Goehr, spaciously recorded.

Bellini, Vincenz (1801-1835)

Along with Donizetti and Rossini, Bellini is one of the great names of the early 19th century Italian opera, though Bellini was not as abundantly talented as the other two masters. His music is sweet, slender, and charming, and was much admired by Chopin and Wagner.

Three of his operas have survived in the repertory: *La Sonnambula*, *Norma* and *I Puritani*. In our own time, these have been shining vehicles for Maria Callas and Joan Sutherland.

Bellini died in his early thirties, struck down just as he reached his musical maturity.

CONCERTO FOR OBOE AND ORCHESTRA

* * HOLLIGER, FENYVES, AUBERSON	*Geneva Baroque Orch.*	MONITOR (M/S) MC 2088 [A. Marcello, Concerto for Oboe and Orchestro, in D minor; Bach, Concerto for Violin, Oboe, Strings, and Continuo, in D minor; C. P. E. Bach, Concerto for Oboe and Orchestra, in E flat]

This slight, early Bellini work features pure, fluent playing by the young Swiss oboist Heinz Hollier. It is a pleasant record, with clean sound. The record also includes three much more solid oboe works. In the Bach concerto, Lorand Fenyves, formerly concertmaster with the Israel Philharmonic, proves to be a splendid violinist; he plays in the rugged scholarly style of Symon Goldberg.

LA SONNAMBULA

La Sonnambula (The Sleepwalker) was first heard in 1831; so was *Norma*. In these two operas, Bellini's lyrical gifts are fully in evidence. Here are charming, engaging, old-fashioned melodies. If you're an opera bug, you must own this piece.

* * PAGLIUGHI, TAGLIAVINI, SIEPI, CAPUANA	*Radio Italiano Opera and Chorus*	EVEREST/CETRA (S) 435/3

This set is excellent. Lina Pagliughi sings with melting charm. Ferrucio Tagliavini is silver-voiced, and in this performance, he doesn't blurt and gulp too much. Cesare Siepi is first-rate. The sound is decent. Sackville-West's comment on this set: "Beautiful."

NORMA

This opera made Bellini world famous; it is an austere, imposing work that still can engage us today. The soprano role of Norma is a juicy one; the character is one of the best of the early 19th century operatic heroines which Joan Sutherland fondly refers to as "batty dames." In 1831, when this opera was first performed, sopranos were expected to move effortlessly between "dramatic" and "coloratura" roles; there was no demarcation line between the two. In this era, perhaps only Callas and Sutherland have managed this cross-over successfully.

<table>
<tr><td>* CIGNA, STIGNANI, PASERO, GUI</td><td>*Ceiar Chorus and Orch., Rome*</td><td>EVEREST/CETRA (S) 423/3</td></tr>
</table>

Gina Cigna has the right style, but technically does not negotiate the florid passages (particularly the aria "Casta diva")in the high standard of our two glittering super-sopranos, Callas and Sutherland. However, all in all, it's a pleasant set. Stignani is in fine voice.

This relic takes us back into the record history of the 1930's, which—believe it or not—was the time that this *Norma* was first recorded.

But don't back away. As sometimes happens—although not often—in the 1950's the old shellac pressings were transferred to LP, and they took on new life and spaciousness.

The second transplant, to alleged "stereo" of the 1960's, was also somewhat successful—at least not fatal. The year 2001, the bicentenary of Bellini's birth, will probably see this indestructible recording on 8-track stereo tape.

Berg, Alban (1885-1935)

Berg was a pupil of Arnold Schoenberg whose influence on him was enormous. He abandoned a conventional career as a government employee in Vienna to become Schoenberg's disciple in the twelve-tone system of writing music. At the performance, in March, 1913, of his first orchestral work, the *Altenberg Songs,* which Schoenberg conducted, the audience so resented this new music they nearly rioted.

Berg served in the Austrian Army in World War I. Later, he completed the opera *Wozzeck* which he had been working on since 1914. *Wozzeck* made Berg famous overnight. During the last seven years of his life, Berg worked on a second opera, *Lulu,* but died before its completion. *Lulu* was later completed by scholars working from Berg's notes.

PLACE AND ACHIEVEMENT   Alban Berg is one of the most important and remarkable composers of this century. Yet, as one of the three composers who championed twelve-tone musical composition, he was derided and abused almost until his death. The other twelve-tone composers were Webern, a contemporary of Berg's, and Berg's teacher Schoenberg.

Berg's music has been played much more often than that of Schoenberg or Webern. His music conveys warm lyricism and great humanity, even within the formality of the twelve-tone system.

No other operas and few other musical compositions in any form capture the modern temper as fully as do Berg's *Wozzeck* and *Lulu.* These are works of dramatic intensity—of harsh, yet sensuous beauty—that speak of the neurotic twentieth century.

THE ESSENTIAL BERG
OPERAS: *Wozzeck; Lulu.*
ORCHESTRAL MUSIC: *Concerto for Violin and Orchestra; Lyric Suite for String Quartet; Quartet for Violin and Orchestra; Three Pieces for Orchestra.*
OTHER WORKS: *Chamber Concerto.*

CHAMBER CONCERTO FOR VIOLIN, PIANO AND 13 WINDS

The composer indulges in musical acrostics using letters in his own name— E and G—as well as letters in the names of his fellow-composers Schoenberg and Webern. These notes form the basis of the theme in the opening bars. Yet this piece is not merely cerebral; the music is warm and immediate.

The playing is shaky; frequently, apprehensive. The sound is acceptable, but much more satisfaction will be derived from Robert Craft's rendering on the expensive Columbia disc.

LYRIC SUITE FOR STRING QUARTET

The *Lyric Suite* (1926) is without question one of the great products of the twelve-tone school. I cannot quite agree with Arthur Cohn who terms it "one of the most thrilling combinations of sound to be found in any work. Its proper place is with the last great set of Quartets by Beethoven." Nevertheless, it is significant chamber music that stands impressively in the 20th century literature, combining romanticism with twelve-tone technique—no mean feat.

I concur with Arthur Cohn's judgment of this reading: "While the Ramor group has technical ability, it has far from probed the guts of this music."* The group to hear in the *Lyric Suite* is the Julliard String Quartet on an expensive Victor.

*Arthur Cohn, *20th Century Music in Western Europe*, Lippincott.

QUARTET (Opus 3)

This quartet, written in 1910, was the last work Berg composed under the supervision of Schoenberg. It is intense, emotional, and highly charged from start to finish. This is difficult music to comprehend; but with repeated playing, a listener will feel that the mist begins to rise around the jagged mountain crags.

The Kohon Quartet is far better in the *Quartet* than in the *Lyric Suite*. Terrifyingly difficult technical problems are tossed off effortlessly; the playing is luminously beautiful.

THREE PIECES FOR ORCHESTRA   (Opus 6)

This is shock music, performed by a huge orchestra, and saturated with strong chromaticism. Berg's biographer, Willi Reich, considers this one of Berg's greatest works; my own opinion is that the music is interesting, but not of permanent value.

ROSBAUD   *South West German Orch.*   WESTMINSTER   (M) 9709
[Stravinsky, Agon; Webern, 6 Pieces]

The playing of Rosbaud is intense, introverted and admirable. The sound is mono—regrettable here. Arthur Cohn evaluates the performance more favoably. His verdict: "Rosbaud's recording is nothing less then sensational."

THREE EXCERPTS FROM WOZZECK   (Opus 7)

Wozzeck is perhaps the greatest opera of the twentieth century. The phobias and diseased morality of our times are the themes. In musicologist Arthur Cohn's phrase, the music captures "ferment, decay, and death."

* * * KUHSE, KEGEL   *Leipzig Symphony Orch.*   VANGUARD   (2) (S)
C-10011/2
[Mahler, Symphony No. 5]

Berg chose these excerpts at the suggestion of conductor Hermann Scherchen. Singing and sound are all first-class. Hanne-Lore Kuhse is a sensual, haunted Marie, and makes one long to hear a complete *Wozzeck* performance with her in the role. The Berg excerpts fill only one side of this worthy two-record album.

VIOLIN CONCERTO

This concerto, a true masterpiece of the 20th century, is based on the twelve-tone system. The concerto contains warmth and compassion. The death of a young girl, the daughter of a friend, affected Berg deeply; this music delineates her life and death.

SUK, ANCERL   *Czech Philharmonic*   CROSSROADS (S) 22 16 0172
[Bach, Cantata No. 60, "O Ewigkeit du Donnerwort."]

It is a pity this disc is unacceptable. Joseph Suk, whose violin playing is much admired in chamber music, is quite at sea here. Tonal balance is unbelievably bad—a mess.

This record has received a surprising variety of reviews. *Hi-Fi Stereo*

Review: "Generally passable; recording good. The Czech musicians schmaltz it up somewhat unnecessarily, and Suk occasionally runs amok." Yet another view from *High Fidelity:* "The Suk-Ancerl reading of the *Concerto* is quite easily the best we have had on records."

My word for those who want this music now: hear Isaac Stern on the high-priced Columbia.

[The startling combination of this concerto with a Bach cantata is not as incongruous as it would appear; a Bach chorale "Es ist genug" is woven into Berg's concerto and is also employed by Bach in his cantata.]

Berlioz, Hector (1803-1869)

Berlioz was the son of a French doctor. In 1830, soon after the composition of his first major work, the *Symphonie Fantastique,* he won the Prix de Rome. In 1833, he married but the relationship proved unfortunate and resulted in virtual separation. Due to his marital problems and financial difficulties—to say nothing of fierce battles with the musical establishment of Paris—Berlioz became more and more melancholic. His last years were spent in sickness and loneliness, with the solace of drugs.

PLACE AND ACHIEVEMENT In our time, no composer's standing has shot up as rapidly as has that of Berlioz.

Gautier remarked that the romantic movement was wrapped up in a poet, a painter, and a composer — Victor Hugo, Eugene Delacroix, and Hector Berlioz. Berlioz, one of the first romantics in music, was the embodiment of the romantic image. He was a mixed-up genius, and much of his music mirrors his own ambivalence and confusion.

He was a great but very uneven composer. At its worst, his composition is as appalling as that of any romantic hack who wheeled out three choruses and a super-sized orchestra to achieve a pretentious musical effect. However, in his outstanding works—of which there are many—he was a superb orchestrator, a creator of original melodies, and an inventor of lovely harmonies.

Berlioz was a megalomaniac, and you can hear it. The Don Quixote of composers, he romantically charged ahead with a hundred brilliant ideas, not quite sure where he was going but hoping for the best. When his intuition was right, that best turned out to be very fine indeed.

THE ESSENTIAL BERLIOZ

ORCHESTRAL MUSIC: *Symphonie Fantastique; Le Carnaval Romain, Concert Overture; The Damnation of Faust, Dramatic Legend; Romeo and Juliet, Dramatic Symphony.*

CHORAL MUSIC: *Requiem; L'Enfance du Christ, Oratorio.*

SONG CYCLE: *Nuits d'Eté.*

OTHER MAJOR WORKS

ORCHESTRAL MUSIC: *Harold in Italy, Symphony; Lelia, Les Troyens, Overtures.*

OPERA: *Benvenuto Cellini.*

CHORAL MUSIC: *Te Deum.*

L'ENFANCE DU CHRIST (Opus 25)
(Sung in French)

An oratorio or "dramatic cantata," *The Childhood of Christ* contains some of the most poetic, idyllic pages Berlioz ever wrote. If you love French music, don't overlook this masterpiece.

* * KOPLEFF, VALLETTI, SOUSAY, OLIVIER, MUNCH	*Boston Symphony Orch., New England Conservatory Chorus*	2 Victrola VIC (S) 6006
* BOUVIER, NOGUERA, ROUX, MEDUS, GIRAUDEAU, CLUYTENS		2 Vox VUX (M) 2009

During the Koussevitsky-Munch era, the Boston Symphony was as close as an American orchestra may ever get to French style. Munch had an authentic feeling to the work and deep affection. The soloists are persuasive, but the New England Conservatory Chorus is hardly of the stature of the Paris Conservatoire. The sound is good. All in all, this is a worthwhile record.

The old Cluytens set is well done, but the problem here is the sound. As Philip Miller has stated in his *Guide to Vocal Records,* "Even when the Vox set was new, its shortcomings were obvious. The reproduction was noted as strangely uneven . . . ."

OVERTURES

The overtures of Berlioz are vivid, exciting, melodious, and glitteringly orchestrated. Highly popular, they are concert favorites.

* * BEECHAM	*Royal Philharmonic Orch.*	Pickwick (S) 4035 [Corsair; Mendelssohn, Overtures; Rossini, Overtures]
* * PARAY	*Detroit Symphony Orch.*	Mercury (M/S) 18071 [Corsair; Roman Carnival; Bizet, Patrie Overture; Lalo, Le Roi D'Ys Overture]
* * TOSCANINI	*NBC Symphony Orch.*	Victrola VIC (M) 1244 [Roman Carnival; Respighi, Fountains of Rome; Pines of Rome]
* * MARTINON	*Paris Conservatoire Orch.*	London STS 15031 [Beatrice & Benedict; Benvenuto Cellini; Corsair; Roman Carnival; Damnation of Faust; Hungarian March]
* FEKETE	*Prague Symphony Orch.*	Crossroads (S) 22 16 0160 [Benvenuto Cellini; Corsair; D'Indy, Istar]

* ANCERL	Czech Philharmonic Orch.	CROSSROADS (M) 22 16 0105

(S) 22 16 0106
[Roman Carnival; Liszt, Les Préludes; Rimsky-Korsakov, Capriccio Espagnol; Weber, Invitation to the Dance]

A tremendously exciting conductor and a virtuoso orchestra are both heard in the disc by the fiery Sir Thomas Beecham. Only one overture by Berlioz is included on this disc, but the other overtures are all worth-while, and done to a crisp with Sir Thomas' inimitable *brio*.

Berlioz' overtures have always been one of the *spécialités du maison Paray*. Incisiveness and dramatic impact are the virtues of this excellent-sounding disc.

Toscanini's dazzling performance of the dazzling *Roman Carnival* overture is historic. The sound, however, is thin and shallow.

Martinon gives a "good, and sometimes brilliant performance, if never quite on the highest international level," according to the *Stereo Record Guide*. I have nothing to add to this opinion, except to note that the scrappy intonation of the Paris Conservatoire Orchestra sometimes gets in the way.

Fekete is blameless, shipshape, and unexceptional.

Ancerl is also competent, and entirely hearable on an excellent program of light orchestral favorites.

SYMPHONIE FANTASTIQUE (Opus 14)

This music, by the young Berlioz, is an extraordinary outburst of genius. Many music historians see the *Fantastique* as the first significant work of 19th-century romanticism. It is a heady, exotic, full-blooded piece, brilliantly orchestrated. This is by far Berlioz' most popular work. For many years it was the only major work of his to be heard in American concert halls. Subtitled "An Episode in the Life of an Artist," it was completed in 1830 as a fervent declaration of his love for the English actress Henrietta Smithson, whom he eventually married.

* * * ARGENTA	Paris Conservatoire Orch.	LONDON	STS 15006
* * * MONTEUX	Vienna Philharmonic Orch.	VICTROLA VIC (S)	1031
* * BARBIROLLI	Halle Orch.	VANGUARD	181 (M) 181 SD
* ZECCHI	Czech Philharmonic Orch.	PARLIAMENT (S)	131
* DORATI	Minneapolis Symphony Orch.	PICKWICK (S)	4040

MITROPOULOS	*New York Philharmonic Orch.*	ODYSSEY	(S) 32 16 0204
VAN BEINUM	*Concertgebouw Orch.*	RICHMOND	(M) 19010
PERLEA	*Bamberg Symphony Orch.*	VOX	(5) 11090
DE CROSS	*Paris Promenade Orch.*	PERIOD SHO	(ST-2) 325

The Spanish conductor Ataulfo Argenta's career was cut tragically short by his sudden death in 1958. He has left us a handful of records, and this is one of his best. Fiery temperament and dramatic flair are demanded in the *Fantastique,* and Argenta had plenty of both. He also had admirable restraint, as in the *adagio* here. The sound is natural. This was a favorite demonstration disc of hi-fi buffs, about 1960. The *Stereo Record Guide* comments: "Argenta's sensitivity throughout makes for an interpretation verging on greatness."

Monteux, of course, was an old hand with Berlioz, and an exquisite interpreter of his music. Here Monteux achieves an incandescent quality, never intruding on the score—always the selfless servant of the composer. This reserved and patrician reading is very fine indeed.

Barbirolli offers a lush, extremely romantic performance that I must also commend. The *Stereo Record Guide*: "Barbirolli provides a reading which is not only exciting, but has a breadth missing in many other performances."

Zecchi is properly impetuous, highly personal, and quite effective. He just happens to be overshadowed by the exceptional discs described above.

Dorati is dependably temperamental, with little of the fine shading and sense of poetry to be heard on both the Argenta and the Monteux recordings.

Mitropoulos, who used to all but smash the podium when he played this music with the New York Philharmonic, is disappointing—the reading seems curiously leaden. The tart review of this re-issue by *High Fidelity,* those guardians of the musical public, comments: "Recirculating unsuccessful efforts by great artists does little service either to their memory or to the unsuspecting record buyer attracted by the name on the record jacket. Mitropoulos arrives in Berlioz' ballroom on two left feet, prosaically surveys the scenes in the country, plods to the gallows, and attends the Witches' Sabbath virtually *in absentia.*" The 1958 sound is also of indifferent quality.

Van Beinum's careful reading has an inexcusably sluggish first movement, but picks up brilliance as it goes along. In any case, this once-admired reading is mono only. The turbulent Hector Berlioz, who would have loved stereo, needs the finest reproduction we can give his music.

Perlea is competent. The Bambergers are efficient, as always. I have little more to add.

De Cross is much outclassed by the above competition.

For those who demand the ultimate, the stunning reading of the *Fantastique* by Colin Davis, on an expensive Phillips record, provides the work of an unsurpassed Berlioz specialist, as well as luscious sound.

TE DEUM (Opus 22)

This is a huge religious work employing, according to the composer himself, "an organ at one end of the church answering the orchestra and two choirs at the other, while a third large choir represents the mass of the people taking part, from time to time, in a vast sacred concert." The *Te Deum* was begun in 1849, when Berlioz was 46.

* YOUNG, BEECHAM	*Royal Philharmonic, London Philharmonic, and Dulwich Boys Chorus*	ODYSSEY	32 16 0206

To attempt to record the vast *Te Deum* would daunt anyone less than Sir Thomas Beecham. The result, to quote the respected English journal *The Gramaphone,* is "a splendid and glowing performance of a work that contains some of Berlioz's finest music." The re-channeled sound is just fair; the choral effects and contrasts are blurry.

Bernstein, Leonard (1918-   )

Bernstein studied at Harvard, and at the Curtis Institute in Philadelphia. He was a pupil of both Fritz Reiner and Serge Koussevitsky. He was appointed assistant conductor of the New York Philharmonic in 1943, and later became the regular conductor of this world famous orchestra.

His compositions include three symphonies, *Jeremiah*, *The Age of Anxiety*, and *Kaddish*, plus the *Chichester Psalms* for chorus and orchestra; but these efforts have not been very seriously regarded by critics. To date, Bernstein's success as a composer has been with his stunningly original popular ballets and musical comedies, such as *Fancy Free*, *On the Town*, and *West Side Story*.

TROUBLE IN TAHITI

This is small beer for Bernstein. This sophomoric operatic satire has little of the exhilaration of *Fancy Free* or *On the Town*, the latter two available only on high-priced records.

<pre>
* WOLF, ATKINSON,   HELIODOR   (M/S) 25020
   WORKMAN,
   ROGERS,
   BOLLINGER,
   WINOGRAD
</pre>

The performance is fair. *High Fidelity* magazine's comment: "The performance is adequate . . . . Effective use is made of stereo."

Bizet, Georges (1838-1875)

Bizet studied at the Paris Conservatory from 1849 to 1857, and won the Prix de Rome in 1857. His first success was with his opera *Les Pecheurs de Perles (The Pearl Fishers)*, in 1863. Other operas followed. In 1872 he wrote *Carmen*, his masterpiece. This was introduced at the Opera-Comique in Paris on March 3, 1875, and was fairly successful. Bizet died at thirty-six — too early to see *Carmen* hailed by the world.

PLACE AND ACHIEVEMENT   Bizet was the most gifted composer France had seen since Berlioz. He helped create the French lyric theatre, which before him had been given over largely to inferior melodrama and spectacle of the Meyerbeer school.

The most remarkable quality of Bizet's music, one senses, is that it can readily be *enjoyed*. There are no pretentious profundities, no showy storming of the heavens. Bizet's music is felicitous and vivacious.

THE ESSENTIAL BIZET
OPERA: *Carmen*.
ORCHESTRAL MUSIC: *L'Arlésienne Suite, Nos. 1 and 2; Symphony in C Major; Jeux d'Enfants.*

OTHER MAJOR WORKS
OPERA: *Les Pecheurs de Perles*.
ORCHESTRAL SUITE: *Jolie Fille de Perth.*

CARMEN (sung in French)

Carmen is perhaps the most popular opera on the boards today. There are opera-haters who do not go to any other work; "It's not opera, it's *Carmen*" sums up their feelings. Familiar melodic tunes tumble out one after the other; the scenes are colorful and exotic; and the story line is full of savage passions. Bizet died three months after the first performance, in 1875.

| MICHEAU, BOWSIN, JUYOL, CAUCHARD, deLUCA, GIOVANETTI, VIEUILLE, WOLFF | *Chorus and Orchestra of L'Opera-Comique (Paris)* | RICHMOND RS   (M) 63006 (3 records) |

The Richmond offering is little more than serviceable. Suzanne Juyol as Carmen is pedestrian, rough-edged, and occasionally off-pitch. The rest of the cast is just adequate, and conductor Wolff confuses frenzy with drive. Sound is agreeable. *High Fidelity* magazine is more charitable towards this album. "As a good buy for the price, *si;* as the No. 1 version, *no,*" is their comment.

Tip: Wait for the RCA Rise Stevens-Fritz Reiner album to be issued by Victoria. With the showcase Leontyne Price album on the market — also issued by RCA — the Stevens-Reiner recording is bound to be lowered in price very soon. Rise Stevens is one of the best Carmens ever to be heard on records, and Fritz Reiner's disciplined reading is a stunner.

CARMEN SUITE

The orchestral suite, compiled from the opera, leads a successful life of its own in the concert hall.

* * BEECHAM	*Columbia Symphony Orch.*	ODYSSEY (M) 32 16 0117 [mixed program]
* * TOSCANINI	*NBC Symphony Orch.*	VICTROLA VIC (M) 1263 [mixed program]
* * GIBSON	*Royal Opera House Orch.* *Convent Garden*	VICTROLA VIC (S) 1108 [Gounod, Ballet music from *"Faust"*]
* CLUYTENS	*Paris Conservatoire Orch.*	SERAPHIM (S) 60064 [L'Arlésienne Suite]
PARAY	*Detroit Symphony Orch.*	MERCURY (S) 18074 [L'Arlésienne Suite]
ROSSI	*Vienna State Opera*	VANGUARD (S) 204 [L'Arlésienne Suite]
GOLSCHMANN	*St. Louis Symphony Orch.*	PICKWICK (S) 4020 [Gounod, Ballet music from *"Faust"*]

Here is a wealth of lively performances, with Beecham and Toscanini and Gibson leading the chase.

Beecham's rendering is incredibly meticulous and thought-out for such light program music. The sound is decent, not really good.

Toscanini conducts in his usual disciplined style. The sound is atniquated.

The Gibson recording is straight-forward and provides the best sonics of the three.

The Cluytens interpretation is highly mannered, even suave and enjoyable.

Paray's recording is appropriately spirited. The sound is good.

The readings of Rossi and Golschmann sound rough to my ears.

L'ARLÉSIENNE: SUITES 1 AND 2

The *Suite No. 1,* adapted by Bizet from his incidental music to Daudet's drama, remains the composer's most successful orchestral work. This is winning music. It consists of a picturesque simulation of the folk songs and colors of the provençal city of Arles — Van Gogh's Arles.

Suite No. 2, adapted by another composer, is less successful and less frequently played.

* * PARAY	*Detroit Symphony Orch.*	MERCURY [Carmen Suite]	(S) 18074
* CLUYTENS	*Paris Conservatoire Orch.*	SERAPHIM [Carmen Suite]	(S) 60064
* MOREL	*Royal Opera House Orch.*	VICTROLA VIC [Chabrier, Espana Rhapsody]	(S) 1075
ROSSI	*Vienna State Opera Orch.* (No. 1)	VANGUARD [Carmen Suite]	(S) 204
VAN BEINUM	*London Philharmonic Orch.*	RICHMOND [Carmen Suite]	(M) 19013

The dependable Paul Paray delivers the goods here with a colorful, glowing performance.

Cluytens gives a crisp, rather dry, and less vivid interpretation.

For those who prefer a coupling with music other than the *Carmen Suite,* Morel is hearable, and the sound is spacious.

The Rossi version, though acceptable, is in no way exceptional.

The Van Beinum reading, similarly, is adequate but unspectacular.

LES PECHEURS DE PERLES

The Pearl Fishers, composed in 1863, enjoys occasional revivals. It was Bizet's best-known opera before *Carmen.*

DOBBS, SERI, BORTHAYRE, MANS, LEIBOWITHS	*Paris Philharmonic*	2 EVEREST	(S) 442/2

This is a so-so performance, not new, but notable for the singing of the American, Mattiwilda Dobbs. She is occassionally shaky; but at her best, she is lovely. Sound is fair, although the performers all sing too loud.

SYMPHONY IN C MAJOR

There is a long tale connected with this symphony, written by the 17-year-old Bizet and discovered in the Paris Conservatoire Library eighty years later. Bizet's symphony is fresh and engaging, an amazing work for a precocious 17-year-old. Also, it is startlingly similar to another recently discovered work, Gounod's *D Major Symphony* which Bizet had arranged for two pianos in 1856. If your taste is for conservative orchestral music, by all means try this.

* * BENZI	*London Symphony Orch.*	WORLD SERIES PHC (S) 9086 [Jeux d'Enfants, Opus 22, Petite Suite; La Jolie Fille de Perth, Suite]
* MUNCH	*French National Radio Orch.*	NONESUCH (S) H 71183 [Jeux d'Enfants, Opus 22, Petite Suite; Patrie Overture, Opus 19]

Benzi's performance is light and lilting, and entirely appropriate to the works recorded. Sound is acceptable.

Munch is highly mannered. The French orchestral playing sounds hurriedly rehearsed. The sound is fair, not more.

A note on the couplings: *Jeux d'Enfants* are beguiling miniatures for piano duet; Bizet transcribed five of them for orchestra. The *Patrie Overture* is banal and bombastic, and the *La Jolie* suite is an orchestral piece arranged from a tuneful opera.

Bloch, Ernest (1880-1959)

Bloch was born in Geneva, but lived many years in America. He was Director of the Cleveland Institute of Music in 1920, and of the San Francisco Conservatory from 1925 to 1930. He was the first important composer whose inspiration has been intensely Hebraic. His music is consciously Jewish in its pathos, love of color, and mysticism. As Smetana caught the Czech flavor and Mussorgsky the Russian, Bloch set out to create a Jewish musical expression.

Not long ago his music was the subject of passionate argument, with fanatical admirers and equally intense opponents. In 1937, a Bloch Society was founded in England. Today, he seems to be neglected. His chamber music is played and respected; his Hebrew Rhapsody for Cello and Orchestra, *Schelomo,* has achieved an enduring place in the literature. The *Violin Concerto,* in the hands of a Menuhin, can be a captivating experience.

CONCERTO FOR VIOLIN AND ORCHESTRA

The concerto is a lush work of 1938, suggestive of the composer's more successful *Schelomo.*

| BRESS, ROHAN | *Prague Symphony Orch.* | CROSSROADS (S) 22 16 0212 [Suite Hebraique] |

Bress' playing is rather colorless. If one has heard the searing intensity of Menuhin's recording on the high-priced Angle record, the Bress performance will not seem adequate. The sound, however, is all right. A note on the coupling: The *Suite Hebraique* is more music of Jewish influence, and of obvious lesser appeal.

ISRAEL SYMPHONY

This music, written from 1912 to 1916, attempts to depict Jewish orthodox life and religion. It contains predictable harmonies and congested scoring, and does not seem impressive today, although there are some sweeping pages.

| ABRAVANEL | *Utah Symphony Orch.* | VANGUARD (S) C 10007 |

Abravanel and his forces (five singers used with the orchestra) make it sound better than it really is.

QUARTET NO. 5

Bloch's less avowedly "Hebraic" pieces may outlast the others. The *Fifth Quartet* is a rugged, uncompromising work of 1956. This is worthwhile music, if not in a class with Bloch's *Second Quartet,* which Ernest Newman and other worthy critics were comparing a generation ago with the late Beethoven quartets. (No recording of the *Second Quartet* is available today, and it is badly needed.) The *Fifth Quartet,* however, is informed with the same looming introspection.

*	*Fine Arts Quartet*	CONCERT DISC (M) 1225
		(S) 225
		[Hindemith, Quartet No. 3]

The Fine Arts players are strong and lyrical. Sound is a bit gritty.

QUINTET FOR PIANO AND STRINGS

Here is more powerful music of Bloch, from 1923, with a somber and mysterious quality. This quintet is a good introduction to the rewarding chamber music of Bloch—if you can find a satisfactory recording.

| GLAZER | *Fine Arts Quartet* | CONCERT DISC (M) 1252 |
| | | (S)   252 |

The Fine Arts Quartet play valiantly, but fail to capture much of the brooding, powerful mystique of the work. The sound is so-so.

SCHELOMO—RHAPSODY FOR CELLO AND ORCHESTRA

Schelomo is wonderful music, composed in 1915-16; its glorious, vibrant, shrewd pages wring every quiver out of the cello. King Solomon and Ecclesiastes, "Vanity of vanities," are the themes. (The perfect jacket cover for this record would be Georges Roualt's painting *The Old King;* I'm surprised it's never been used.) Almost all cellists have taken a try at this highly emotional music.

* * NELSOVA, ABRAVANEL	*Utah Symphony Orch.*	VANGUARD (S) C 10007
		[Israel Symphony]
* JANIGRO, RODZINSKI	*London Philharmonic*	WESTMINISTER (S) 14985
		[Bruch, Kol Nidrei]

Nelsova's playing is skillfully subdued, and extremely convincing. Abravanel and his players are spirited and admirable. The sound is fine.

Janigro gives a brooding reading in mono. *Schelomo* is coupled with that other Jewish cello classic, *Kol Nidrei.*

Blow, John (1649-1708)

Blow was a composer of talent, though not of the same rank as his illustrious pupil, Henry Purcell. Blow's most appealing work is the little opera *Venus and Adonis,* probably composed around 1684. This miniature opus was performed at the court of Charles II, with one of Charles' mistresses in the part of Venus, and the woman's daughter as Cupid. These days, "Music from the Court of . . . ." is in vogue with imaginative record companies. I'm surprised they have, so far, missed *Venus and Adonis.*

ODE ON THE DEATH OF HENRY PURCELL

When Purcell died suddenly at the age of 36, London was stunned; and John Dryden, Purcell's literary collaborator, composed a heartfelt *Ode,* set to music by Blow. Two countertenors and two recorders were the doleful combination often used for lamentations, and they are effective here.

THOMAS, LE SAGE, MARK DELLER, ALFRED DELLER	*Stouer Music Festival Chamber Orch.*	VICTROLA VIC (M/S) 1276 [Bring Shepherds, Bring the Kids and Lambs ("Marriage Ode"); Chloe Found Amintas Lying; Sing, Ye Muses]

The singing is on the colorless side; even the great Alfred Deller sounds tired and dispirited. A critic at *Hi-Fi Stereo Review* evaluated the performance more favorably. His verdict: "The singing is extremely worthy . . . the recording is quite satisfactory." The sound is presentable. [The three-part songs on the reverse have some part writing that is bold for the period, but otherwise they amount to nothing much.]

Boccherini, Luigi (1743-1805)

Luigi Boccherini became famous as a boy cellist, and traveled for years throughout Europe as a virtuoso. No matter how famous a composer of the 18th century became, most of his income derived from his appearances as a soloist. Boccherini wrote two operas and 567 instrumental works, many of them admired by Haydn and Mozart. Nevertheless, when in his last years ill health forced him to give up the cello, he faced starvation.

CONCERTO IN B FLAT FOR CELLO AND ORCHESTRA

This graceful, first-rate concerto was made popular by Pablo Casals. What we really hear, in most editions, is a combination of two Boccherini concertos, put together by one Greutzmacher.

* JANIGRO, PROHASKA	*Vienna State Opera Orch.*	WESTMINSTER (M) 18406 [Haydn, Concerto in D]
* NAVARRA, PAUMGARTNER	*Salzburg Camerata*	NONESUCH (S) 71071 [Haydn, Concerto in D]
* MAINARDI	*Vienna Ensemble*	MACE (S) 9077 [Vivaldi, Concerto for Orchestra]
* CASSADO, PERLEA	*Bamberg Symphony*	VOX (S) 10790 [Haydn, Concerto in D]

Janigro, in an old record, is superb, but the sound is not; yet this disc is still listenable.

Navarra comes closest to reproducing the poised, radiant quality of this work; but after hearing Janigro—not to mention the vanished Casals recording—I find myself less satisfied with Navarra.

Cassado and Mainardi are both agreeable, but little more.

CONCERTO IN D FOR FLUTE AND ORCHESTRA
(Opus 27)

The English *Stereo Record Guide:* "This nine movement divertimento is skillfully diverse . . . and altogether makes enjoyable listening."

* COMISSIONA	*Haifa Symphony Orch.*	MACE (S) 9051 [Clementi, Symphony in D Major]

The playing is unsophisticated but live. The recording quality is fine. [The Clementi work on the reverse side is elegant, drawing-room music. Clementi (1752-1832), an Italian composer and pianist, was personally acquainted with Haydn, Mozart and Beethoven. He did more than any other composer to develop pianoforte writing, as distinguished from composition for the harpsichord.]

QUINTET IN E FOR GUITAR AND STRINGS (Opus 50, No. 3)

This is charming music.

* BOETTNER, KEHR,   Vox   (50) 1010
  KALAFUSZ, LEMMEN,   [Haydn, Guitar Quartet]
  PLAM

The English critic Edward Greenfield, writing in the *Stereo Record Guide,* said: "This skillful, professional writing is altogether suaver than the Haydn work with which it is coupled, but if the music is intrinsically rather superficial, the persuasive playing and recording offers real enjoyment."

SYMPHONY IN C; CONCERTO FOR CELLO OBLIGATO, IN D (Opus 34)

This "Symphony for Grand Orchestra" was reworked by the composer from one of his string quintets. It is a bubbly piece, with spirited solos, and it employs the guitar. The *Concerto for Cello Obligato* does not approach the famous *B Flat Concerto,* but it is nevertheless pleasant. A poignant oboe and cello duet in the slow movement is notable.

* DECROOS,   *Orchestra Accademia*   DOVER   (M) HCR 5249
  JENKINS   *dell'Orso*   [Cambini, Sinfonia Concer-
                                             tante for Oboe, Bassoon,
                                             and Orchestra, No. 1 in C]

Cellist Jean Decroos plays with much verve but not much elegance. The sound is on the thin side. [Giovanni Cambini (1746-1825) was a workmanlike Italian composer whose music Mozart considered to be "quite pretty." The Cambini piece, consisting of oboe and bassoon tootlings, is unremarkable.]

TRIOS FOR STRINGS

Boccherini wrote 12 trios for violin, cello, and viola, in addition to 48 for two violins and cello. This is agreeable chamber music.

*	*New York State Trio*	DOVER (M)	HCR 5255
		(S)	HCRST 7007

The New York Trio play with dash, and seem to enjoy themselves. The results are agreeable. The trios included on this recording are: *Opus 14, No. 4, in D; No. 5, in E-flat; Opus 38, No. 2, in D; No. 3 in F.* The stereo sound is clean.

Boito, Arrigi (1842-1918)

Boito studied in Milan, and later in France and Germany. He was an intriguing figure and the writer of brilliant librettos for Verdi — *Otello* and *Falstaff*. Boito was an intensely frustrated composer. His first opera, *Mefistofele*, was given at Milan in 1868, to an indifferent audience. He revised it, and the work became highly popular. All this happened when the composer was 26.

For the remaining half-century of his life, he slaved with misgivings on the score of *Nerone*, his only other opera. After his death, it was found to be unacceptable. In 1924, Toscanini revised it and produced it at La Scala. Despite all the excitement and fanfare that surrounded this signal event, *Nerone* soon vanished from the repertory.

MEFISTOFELE

Ernest Newman once laid out Boito's talent as "a semi-musical gift that rarely rises above the mediocre and generally dips a point or two below it." But this opera is not all that bad; it has some pleasing arias and touching duets. The role of Mefistofele was a great favorite of Chaliapin, Jounet, Plancon, and other legendary singers.

* NERI, TAGLIAVINI,   EVEREST/CETRA   (S) 409/3
POBBE, QUESTA

The bass on the Cetra set is virile, but lacks personality. Margherita is appealing, and the rest of the cast is all right. But the "enhanced" sound is poor, to put it kindly. *High Fidelity* magazine commented on the sound: "The remastering has been hopelessly bungled. . . . Quavery, distorted reproduction."

Borodin, Alexander (1833-1887)

This Russian composer was a professor of organic chemistry in St. Petersburg. He began composing as a boy, and was much inspired by meeting the composer Balakirev in 1862.

His works are not numerous: two symphonies; and a third unfinished; the highly popular *In the Steppes of Central Asia,* now generally relegated to Pops programs; two operas, *Bogatyri* and *Prince Igor;* some songs.

Borodin was a fiercely nationalistic composer drawing constantly upon Russian folk song as well as upon quasi-Oriental influences. His music, extremely melodious, is often somewhat eastern in character; his harmonies and orchestration are colorful, even picturesque. Like many other Russian composers, he was ill at ease in the discipline of instrumental formulation; and he composed operas and songs with much greater ease and consequent success. Some of his songs are accounted among the best ever written by a Russian composer.

IN THE STEPPES OF CENTRAL ASIA

Borodin's most popular piece was neatly described by Sackville-West as "a beautifully scored exercise in the sectional deployment of a single, monotonous, oriental sounding tune. It contains the essence of Borodin's talent concentrated in a brief space."

* * SANDERLING	*Saxon State Orch.*	HELIODOR (S) 25061 [Symphony No. 2; Tchaikovsky, Romeo and Juliet Overture]
* ANCERL	*Czech Philharmonic*	CROSSROADS (M) 22 16 0085 (S) 22 16 0086 [Glinka, Russlan and Ludmila; Tchaikovsky, Capriccio Italienne]
* DERVAUX	*Amsterdam Philharmonic*	AUDIO FIDELITY (S) 50025 [Glinka, Russlan and Ludmila; Tchaikowsky, Marche Slave]
* ANSERMET	*Paris Conservatoire Orch.*	RICHMOND (M) 19087

Sanderling ranks first here, with a highly romantic reading. The orchestral playing is appropriately sumptuous. [The disc also contains Borodin's popular *Symphony No. 2.*]

Ancerl is less glittering. His rendition is more straightforward.

The same comment applies to Dervaux.

Ansermet and his players offer the best performance of the four—but on mono with dimmed sound.

PRINCE IGOR

After the composer's death, this opera, sung in Russian, was completed and edited by Rimsky-Korsakov, whose fate it was to perform such tasks over and over for other composers. *Prince Igor* is a rambling, uneven work, but full of stirring, melodious music.

* MELIK-PASHAYEV, BOLSHOI THEATRE	3 Period	(M) 1023

Some of Russia's finest singers are heard here: the tenor Lemeshev, Pirogov (who can sound like Chaliapin), and the sumptuous-voiced Mark Reizen. The female voices are only fair. The sound is acceptable.

PRINCE IGOR: POLOVETSIAN DANCES

These vivid, entertaining dances from opera are a staple of innumerable Russian ballet companies, from Diaghilev until today.

* * DORATI	*London Symphony Orch.*	Mercury (M/S) 18070 [Rimsky-Korsakov, Coq d'Or]
* * GOULD	*Gould Orch.*	Victrola VIC (S) 1174 [Mixed collection]
* CHALABALA		Parliament (M) 151 [Mixed collection]
RODZINSKI	*London Philharmonic*	Westminster (M) 151 [Ippolitov-Ivanov; Caucasian Sketches; Mussorgsky, Night on Bald Mountain]
VAN BEINUM	*London Philharmonic Chorus and Orch.*	Richmond (M) 19032 [Falla, El Amor Brujo]

It's just about a toss-up between Dorati and Morton Gould; both records are colorful and sound well.

Chalabala's interpretation is on the heavy side, and the sound is just fair.

Rodzinski disappoints; his is a hurried, slap-dash reading.

Van Beinum, a conductor whose work I admire, is quite good here, but not enough to warrant buying a mono record for music that benefits so much from stereo.

QUARTET NO. 2 IN D

The Second Quartet is good music, recommended for *feinschmeckers* who turn up their noses at Borodin. Although it lacks the complexity of thought and development that most chamber music lovers expect today, the composition is melodious. Nevertheless, aside from Tchaikovsky's *D Major Quartet, Quartet No. 2 in D* is probably the most popular work in the Russian chamber music repertory.

The slow movement is the celebrated *Nocturne* which in bloated orchestral form has enjoyed great vogue in the hands of Stokowski, at the Hollywood Bowl, and in other saccharine interpretations. The melody was plagiarized to form the hit tune in *Kismet*: "This Is My Beloved."

* *	*Borodin Quartet*	LONDON STS (S) 15046 [Shostakovich, Quartet No. 8]	
*	*Endres Quartet*	VOX	10190
	Galimer Quartet	[Smetana, Quartet] PERIOD (M) 505	

The Borodin Quartet provides a glowing, affectionate reading. *Stereo Review* comments: "the performance . . . is sensitive, and the recorded sound, though of reissue vintage, holds its own very nicely." [The Shostakovich on the reverse is interesting, but hardly first-rate.]

The Endres players give with color and strength, yet are not overly soupy. The sound is acceptable.

The older Galimer version is less successful.

Boulez, Pierre (1925-   )

Boulez studied with Messiaen, and has been profoundly influenced by Schoenberg. It is also instructive to learn that he studied higher mathematics, as did several other avant-garde composers, including Xenakis. Of his first impression of the music of Schoenberg (1945) the composer has written, "I realized that here was a language of our time. It was the most radical revolution since Monteverdi."

Today, Boulez claims to have an anti-Schoenberg bias, but the super-polyorganized music of Boulez is of the highest interest to anyone analyzing avant-garde development.

Boulez is also a formidable conductor (*see entries under "Stravinsky"*). An authority on Debussy, and one of the most gifted men on the musical scene today, Boulez has had enormous influence on young composers all over the world.

LE MARTEAU SANS MAITRE

"The Hammer without a Master" is already a hallowed work in the liturgy of the New Music. Often played, the surest sign of validity, it has been called by Eric Salzman "the musical classic of the European avant-garde."

This music can be labeled neoimpressionistic serialism. It is sensual, dreamy, dark music for solo voice and six instruments. Written in 1954 and revised in 1957, the composition is more free and natural-sounding than much of the scientific-mathematical, punch-drunk work of so many of today's uninspired composers.

* * DEROUBAIX, BOULEZ	*Instrumental Ensemble*	TURNABOUT	(S) 34081
* * MACKAY, CRAFT	*Instrumental Ensemble*	ODYSSEY	(S) 3216 0154 [Stockhausen, Nr. 5 Zeitmasse for five Woodwinds]

There are two extraordinarily right-sounding performances here. The version with Boulez conducting must, of course, be given preference. The sound is crisp.

Robert Craft and alto Margery MacKay are also highly convincing. Craft is a leading exponent of contemporary music. [The coupling is a very important modern work.] The sound is good.

Boyce, William (1710-1779)

Boyce was born in 1710, about the time when Handel was establishing himself in London. He lived until 1779, long enough to see the music of Haydn and Mozart come into vogue, at least among more advanced music lovers. As a child, he suffered from deafness, the infirmity increasing as he grew older. Boyce was an organist; he was Master of the King's Music in 1755.

For two centuries Dr. Boyce has been known, chiefly to musicologists, as a very good editor of other people's church music. His own music—and there was much of it—was ignored. Only in our own time, with the tremendous new interest in seldom-heard music of the past, has Boyce come into focus. He wrote church music, cantatas, odes, and similar works, and is remembered today primarily for his eight little symphonies.

His music—light, pleasant, and quite conventional—is well worth knowing. As Dr. Burney, the indispensable music historian of this period wrote, "With all reverence for the abilities of Handel . . . , there is in Dr. Boyce an original and sterling merit."

In the 1950's, the advent of LP records catapulted Boyce unto undreamed-of popularity among the new devotees of baroque music.

EIGHT SYMPHONIES

Reminiscent of Handel's *Concerti Grossi,* these are light, delightful pieces. They are not symphonies as we understand the term, but rather *sinfonie,* or overtures or intermezzi for theatrical entertainments.

| * * FAERBER | *Wuerttemberg Chamber Orch.* | TURNABOUT | (S) (3) 4133 |
| * HAAS | *London Baroque Ensemble* | 2-WESTMINISTER | (M) 18404/5 |

The work staunchly played by Faerber with efficiency and good spirit. The sound is effective.

The Haas set, renowned in its day, is alas! sonically dim.

SYMPHONIES NO. 1, IN B FLAT; NO. 4, IN F

| * HURWITZ | *English Chamber Orch.* | LONDON (S) Sts 15013 [J. C. Bach, Symphony for Double Orchestra, Opus 18, No. 5, in E; Purcell, The Faery Queen; Chaconne; Arne, Overture No. 4, in E; Avison, Concerto No. 13, in D; Locke, Music from the Tempest] |

This album, *Music in London 1670-1770,* contains one morsel from Dr.

Boyce, the rest is a sturdy selection from the works of other London composers. This is an entertaining record for lovers of the period. The music is sensitively played, with much variety of timbre and texture. The Arne and Purcell works are both rewarding; so too, the vivacious double symphony by J. C. Bach, "The English Bach." Matthew Locke (1630-1677) was a court composer to Charles II, and later was organist to Queen Catherine. His piece, as rendered here, benefits from highly effective stereo. Charles Avison (1709-1770) was an English pupil of Geminiani, and is remembered not for his composition, but rather for his treatise *An Essay on Musical Expression.*

Brahms, Johannes (1833-1897)

The son of a double-bass player at the Hamburg Stadttheater, Brahms was a boy pianist. He earned his living by playing in sailors' cafes and brothels, and toured North Germany with the gypsy violinist, Eduard Remenyi, in 1853.

In the same year, Robert Schumann published an historic article in the *Neue Zeitschrift fuer Musik*, proclaiming Brahms a genius. A lifelong friendship developed between Brahms and the Schumanns. Brahms settled in Vienna in 1862, and remained there for the rest of his life, conducting and composing.

PLACE AND ACHIEVEMENT   A half century ago, the music of Brahms was held to be austere and forbidding. He was regarded as the apostle of classicism in music, in contrast to those lush Romantics, Liszt and Wagner. The fine English critic, Neville Cardus, tells an amusing story of his rapturous admiration of Brahms at this time, and of being reproved by his German music master: "You should *admire* Brahms, my boy, but not already is it that you can enjoy him."

Today the legend of the cold Brahms has gone, and we enjoy him almost uncritically. Ironically, we recognize him today as a great romantic, tempered and controlled by intellect and a deep respect for classicism. His special flavor of romance "looked back upon in autumn" speaks to us almost more contemporaneously than the voice of any other nineteenth-century composer. In Brahms' work, the old bottles of form and tradition were filled with the new and heady wines of ardor and philosophical reflection. He was the true heir to the Viennese tradition of Mozart and Beethoven.

THE ESSENTIAL BRAHMS

ORCHESTRAL MUSIC: *4 Symphonies; Variations on a Theme by Haydn; Academic Festival Overture; Tragic Overture; Concerto in D Major, for Violin and Orchestra; 2 Concertos for Piano and Orchestra; Concerto in A Minor, for Violin, Cello, and Orchestra.*

CHORAL MUSIC: *A German Requiem; Rhapsody, for Alto Voice, Men's Chorus, and Orchestra; Liebeslieder Waltzes, for Four Voices and Two Pianos.*

CHAMBER MUSIC: *3 Piano Quartets; Piano Quintet; Clarinet Quintet; Horn Trio; 3 String Quartets; 3 Piano Trios, 2 String Sextets; 3 Sonatas for Violin and Piano; 2 Sonatas for Cello and Piano.*

PIANO MUSIC: *Variations on a Theme by Handel; Variations on a Theme by Paganini; Ballades; Capriccios; Intermezzi; Rhapsodies; Hungarian Dances; Waltzes.*

SONGS: *Wiegenlied (Lullaby); Staendchen; Immer Leiser Wird Mein Schlummer; Die Mainacht; Vergebliches Staendchen; Der Tod, Das ist die Kuehle Nacht; Vier Ernste Gesaenge; Songs for Alto, Viola and Piano.*

OTHER WORKS

CHORAL MUSIC: *Schicksalslied (Song of Fate), for Chorus and Orchestra; Zigeunerlieder (Gypsy Songs), for Four Voices and Piano.*
CHAMBER MUSIC: *2 String Quintets; 2 Sonatas for Clarinet (or Viola) and Piano.*
PIANO MUSIC: *3 Sonatas for Piano, and other pieces.*

SYMPHONIES His four symphonies are bulwarks of the orchestra repertory. They are all great. Everyone has his own favorite — which changes as soon as he hears one of the other splendid four. The symphonies of Brahms bound in beautiful melodies. Vigorous style, a personal sense of drama, and formidable constructive power are all here; only Beethoven has surpassed this symphonic achievement.

COMPLETE RECORDINGS

* * * TOSCANINI	NBC Symphony Orch.	4-VICTROLA	VIC 6400 [Academic Festival Overture; Haydn Variations; Tragic Overture]
* * WALTER	N. Y. Philharmonic Orch.	3-ODYSSEY	(M) 3236 0007
* * KUBELIK	Vienna Philharmonic Orch.	4-LONDON	STS-15001/4
* HOLLREISER	Bamberg Symphony Orch. (No. 1);	4-EVEREST	(S) 3148
* BOULT	Philharmonic Promenade Orch. (No. 2);		(S) 3148
* SAKOWSKI	Houston Symphony Orch. (No. 3)		(S) 3148
* STEINBERG	Pittsburgh Symphony Orch. (No. 4)		(S) 3148

As the diligent reader has already grasped, the battle over Toscanini-versus-Walter readings of the classics raged during their lifetimes, and the conflict has now been transferred, *post mortem,* to the low-priced record arena. I personally much prefer Toscanini's austere, intense, classical approach here to Walter's genial, urbane, flowing *Gemuetlichkeit.* The sound is sadly faded on both sets, but it remains sharper on Victrola. The Toscanini discs were made from 1948 to 1953; the Walter readings from 1951 to 1953.

Rafael Kubelik is an imaginative Czech conductor, best known in this country for his work with the Chicago Symphony. He is a forceful personality; his interpretations are admirably controlled, and planned with boldly drawn dramatic frames for big effects. He has a firm grasp of the Germanic quality of Brahms, and yet he keeps it from becoming ponderous. The mellifluous Vienna Philharmonic is a joy to hear, and the sonics are far more modern than on the Toscanini and Walter sets. For those who insist upon clear reproduction, fairly close to today's high standards, Kubelik provides the best bet for a low-priced complete album of the Brahms symphonies.

For a serviceable stereo set, the Everest compilation will do.

SYMPHONY NO. 1 IN C MINOR (Opus 68)

Published in 1876, this symphony had taken Brahms four years to complete. This work has been praised abundantly as one of the supreme pieces in the literature. It has been called "Beethoven's Tenth Symphony," "the greatest first symphony in the history of music." With this composition, Brahms emerged as the finest symphonist since Beethoven.

* * * MUNCH	*Boston Symphony Orch.*	VICTROLA	VIC (S)	1062
* * * ANCERL	*Czech Philharmonic Orch.*	PARLIAMENT	(S)	172
* * STEINBERG	*Pittsburgh Symphony Orch.*	PICKWICK	(S)	4004
* SWAROWSKY	*Vienna State Opera*	AUDIO FIDELITY	(M) 30017 (S) 50017	
* KRIPS	*Vienna Festival Orch.*	VANGUARD	(S)	22
* HORENSTEIN	*SW German Radio Symphony Orch.*	VOX	(5)	10690
* BOULT	*London Philharmonic Orch.*	SOMERSET ST. FI.		14000

Top honors go to Munch for a firm, radiant reading. Equal praise, of course, is deserved by the rich and melodious warmth of the players of the Boston Symphony.

Ancerl and the excellent Czechs have strength and vibrancy; the music is always alive. Theirs is a first-rate disc, and has been praised by critics everywhere.

Steinberg delivers a strict, predictably traditional reading that is fine, but which, to my ears, lacks a certain sense of drama. *High Fidelity* com-

ments: "a sensitive, authoritative, and effective performance." The sound
is excellent.

Swarowsky's version is cleanly recorded, and uneventful.

Krips' Brahms is warm and ingratiating, but it lacks the core of drama
and conflict that should permeate the symphonies of this composer.

Horenstein is a first-rate conductor, and his records are always of the
highest interest, although he is barely known in this country, except to
record collectors. The less than stimulating sound here explains the low
grading.

Boult's performance is broad and lyrical, and entirely hearable. However, it is outclassed by the exceptional readings at the top of this list.

SYMPHONY NO. 2 IN D   (Opus 73)

Completed one year after the epic, stormy *First,* this is a sunny, warm-
hearted work.

* * * MONTEUX	*Vienna Philharmonic Orch.*	VICTROLA	VIC (S) 1055
* BEECHAM	*Royal Philharmonic*	SERAPHIM [Academic Overture]	(S) 60083
DORATI	*Minneapolis Symphony*	PICKWICK	(S) 4045
BOULT	*Philharmonic Promenade Orch.*	EVEREST	(M) 6149 (S) 3149

The Monteux disc has been praised abundantly by just about everyone,
for its glowing qualities. Refinement and strength are both heard in
abundance. This is a first-rate, classic interpretation. Martin Bookspan, in
his annual updating in *Hi/Fi Stereo Review* for 1968, lists this one
Number One, regardless of price: "I find the mellow lyricism of the
Monteux/Vienna Philharmonic collaboration most winning in this work."
The sound is clear, but not spectacular by today's standards.

I yield to no one in my admiration for Beecham's patrician readings of
Haydn and Mozart, but his Brahms strikes me as being overly mannered,
in a swashbuckling fashion.

Dorati injects almost too much fire and temperament. The playing is
not the most polished. The sound is acceptable.

Boult's traditional reading does not have much impact.

SYMPHONY NO. 3 IN F   (Opus 90)

The *Third* was described by the great conductor, Hans Richter, as
"Brahms' *Eroica.*" Brahms was 50 when he finished this one, in the
summer of 1883. (Renewed fame — or notoriety — came to this symphony
when it was the love-theme of the film *Aimez-cous Brahms?*) This great

symphony is less played at concerts than the other symphonies of Brahms. Reason: It ends in pianissimo, and vain conductors much prefer a slam-bang, all-out finale, that will bring the house down.

* * STOKOWSKI	*Houston Symphony Orch.*	EVEREST	(M)	6030
			(S)	3030
* LEINSDORF	*Los Angeles Philharmonic Orch.*	PICKWICK [Haydn Variations]	(S)	4007
* HORENSTEIN	*SW Germany Radio Orch.*	VOX [Haydn Variations]	(5)	10620

Despite Stokowski's occasional manhandling and coloring of the score, I hold affection for his polished, highly dramatic, and often thrilling reading. The stereo sound is excellent.

Leinsdorf is a model of propriety by comparison; he is a purist in regard to following the score scrupulously. However, his players are not up to it.

Horenstein is all impetuousness, and *Sturm und Drang*. Brahms comes out sounding like Mahler.

SYMPHONY NO. 4 IN E MINOR (Opus 98)

Always the self-critic, Brahms had grave doubts about his new *Symphony No. 4,* written in 1885. After completing the first movement, he sent the manuscript to his friend and former pupil, Elizabeth von Herzogenberg, asking for her opinion. He added a postscript, "I'm not at all eager to write a bad Number 4." He worried when she was slow to respond, and the worry was deepened by the audience's cool reaction to a performance of it in a four-hand piano arrangement made for some friends. But its reception by critics and public alike was tremendous.

* * * TOSCANINI	*NBC Symphony Orch.*	4-VICTROLA [Academic Festival Overture; Haydn Variations; Tragic Overture]	VIC 6400
* * SCHMIDT-ISSERSTEDT	*Nord-Deutscher Rundfunk Symphony Orch.*	VOX	(5) 12270
* * STEINBERG	*Pittsburgh Symphony Orch.*	EVEREST	(M) 6066 (S) 3066
* * BARBIROLLI	*Halle Symphony Orch.*	VANGUARD	(S) 183

After Toscanini's intensely surging performance, it is hard to hear much less. As Martin Bookspan said of the Maestro's *Fourth,* in *Hi/Fi Stereo Review,* "It is one of the real monuments of the recorded literature." Bookspan lists this one, in his 1968 "Annual Updating of the

Basic Repertory," as the best performance available regardless of price.

Of our entries here. Schmidt-Isserstedt well suggests the "autumnal melancholy," with both power and lyricism. The sound is good.

Steinberg's performance is beautifully controlled, warm, and dignified. A solidly paced, orthodox reading.

Barbirolli's reading is exciting and compelling, but it is marred by some very shaky brass playing in the crucial moments of the last movement.

All of the above recordings are first-rate, exceptional performances.

ORCHESTRAL MUSIC Brahms' orchestral works are shorter than his symphonies, and extremely popular.

ACADEMIC FESTIVAL OVERTURE   (Opus 80)

Mellow music of 1880, this was a grateful rejoinder to the honorary degree of Doctor of Philosophy conferred upon Brahms by the University of Breslau.

* * TOSCANINI	*NBC Symphony Orch.*	4-VICTROLA VIC 6400 [Haydn Variations; Symphonies; Tragic Overture]
* * KNAPPERTSBUSCH	*Vienna Philharmonic Orch.*	LONDON STS 15027 [Haydn Variations; Tragic Overture]
* BEECHAM	*Royal Philharmonic*	SERAPHIM (S) 60083
* VAN BEINUM	*Concertgebouw Orch.*	RICHMOND (M) 19024 [Haydn Variations; Tragic Overture]
* BOULT	*Philharmonic Promenade Orch.*	4-EVEREST (M) 6148 (S) 3148 [4 Symphonies]
* BARBIROLLI	*Halle Orch.*	VANGUARD (S) 136 [Violin Concerto]

The Toscanini reading is glorious, but the sound is thin.

Knappertsbusch provides a warm, yet vigorous interpretation on this handsomely played disc. His version is less winged than Toscanini's, but this is still a stirring reading. The stereo sound is agreeable.

Beecham is genial and idiosyncratic. The sound will not meet the standards of many hi-fi fans.

Van Beinum, an entirely convincing conductor of Brahms, gives a rugged yet glowing performance. The sound is pleasant mono of the 1950's.

Boult is honest, competent, and quite hearable.

Barbirolli offers a traditional, entirely acceptable reading, with no surprises, good or bad.

HUNGARIAN DANCES

These tremendously successful pieces were intended to be popular—they made more money for Brahms during his lifetime than did any of his symphonies or chamber music.

* * * REINER	*Vienna Philharmonic Orch.*	LONDON	STS-15009 [Dvorak, Slavonic Dances]
* * SCHMIDT-ISSERSTEDT	*Hamburg NDR Orch.*	VANGUARD	(S) 236
* * LEHEL	*Hungarian Radio Symphony Orch.* (Nos. 1/8 10)	PARLIAMENT	(S) 135
* PERLEA	*Bamberg Symphony Orch.*	VOX	(5) 11240 [Dvorak, Slavonic Dances]
HAGEN	*Austrian Symphony Orch.*	EVEREST	(M) 6102 (S) 3102

Hungarian-born, Fritz Reiner plays them like an old *Zigeuner*. This is baton magic. The sound is fine. [The Dvorak dances on the back are also warm-hearted, rhythmic pops-program music.]

Schmidt-Isserstedt is not far behind in a zestful performance, cleanly executed.

Another outstanding, supremely colorful performance is heard from Lehel and the Hungarians.

The Perlea and Hagen versions are both adequate, but they are outclassed by the unusually good performances of the first three entries on this list.

TRAGIC OVERTURE   (Opus 81)

This is a less popular piece. We don't know why it's called "Tragic."

* TOSCANINI	*NBC Symphony Orch.*	4-VICTROLA	VIC 6400 [Academic Festival Overture; Symphonies Haydn Variations]
* KNAPPERTSBUSCH	*Vienna Philharmonic Orch.*	LONDON	STS 15027 [Academic Festival Overture; Haydn Variations]

| * VAN BEINUM | Concertgebouw Orch. | RICHMOND (M) 19024 [Academic Festival Overture; Haydn Variations] |

Again, it's Toscanini for compelling reasons. The sound is not up to the standards of hi-fi fiends.

And it's Knappertsbusch for a crisp reading, and for enjoyable sound.

Van Beinum's version is glowing, but the mono sound has dimmed.

VARIATIONS ON A THEME BY HAYDN (Opus 56a)

This was written in 1873—three years before the great *First Symphony*. A version for two pianos (Opus 56b) was completed in July of that year. Brahms came across this lovely theme when the Haydn biographer C. F. Pohl showed him one of the unpublished divertimentos. Brahms was struck with the unusual scoring—for two oboes, two horns, three bassoons, and a serpent (a kind of bass horn). Brahms wrote the first version of his *Haydn Variations* for two pianos—in the nineteenth century, two-piano music was extremely salable. It is a tribute to the composer's art that the orchestral form at no place sounds like orchestrated piano music.

The idea of transforming Haydn's melody appealed to the musical intellect of Brahms. He worked very hard on the technical problems he had set for himself, and later, in his four symphonies, well applied the lessons he had taught himself in his extensive study of variation design. The *Variations* are top-drawer Brahms—immensely satisfying music. They are the first example in the literature of orchestral variations composed as an independent creation, rather than as a section of some larger work.

* * * TOSCANINI	NBC Symphony Orch.	4-VICTROLA VIC 4600 [Academic Festival Overture; Tragic Overture; 4 Symphonies]
* * * KNAPPERTSBUSCH	Vienna Philharmonic Orch.	LONDON STS 15027 [Tragic Overture; Academic Festival Overture]
* * * MONTEUX	London Symphony Orch.	VICTRO'A VIC (S) 1107 [Elgar, Enigma Variations]
* VAN BEINUM	Concertgebouw Orch.	RICHMOND (M) 19024 [Academic Festival Overture; Tragic Overture]

Toscanini's recording (in the four-record set of the symphonies) is classic, and unmatched. Sweep and grandeur are both to be heard.

Irving Kolodin: "This is a Toscanini record few would want to be without."

A solid, Brahmsian reading is to be had from Knappertsbusch, in an excellent record encompassing the three minor orchestral pieces of Brahms. The sound is clean stereo.

A rugged, lucid, measured version is heard from Monteux; the reading never becomes too personalized. The orchestral playing is highly responsive, and the sound is pleasant. This is a remarkable, most enjoyable performance.

Van Beinum gives a magisterial reading, famous in its day. The mono sound is fair.

CONCERTOS   Brahms wrote four of the finest concertos in the repertory. All are large-scale symphonic works, grand and romantic, and models of architectural splendor in sound.

CONCERTO NO. 1 IN D MINOR FOR PIANO
(Opus 15)

Brahms was soloist at the premiere of this concerto in 1859. It was apathetically received. Today it is admired for its intellectual appeal; there is little of the romance and bravura of the *Second Piano Concerto,* but this granitic, somewhat forbidding work grows upon one.

* * MALCUZYNSKI, WISLOCKI	*Warsaw National Philharmonic Orch.*	SERAPHIM	(S) 60055
* * GRAFFMAN, MUNCH	*Boston Symphony Orch.*	VICTROLA	VIC (S) 1109
* FIRKUSNY, STEINBERG	*Pittsburgh Symphony Orch.*	PICKWICK	(S) 4018

I prefer the rough-hewn, brooding playing of Malcuzynski.

Gary Graffman is serious and gifted. *High Fidelity* comments: "One hears virtually all it has to offer the first time through." His record has somewhat better sound than Malcuzynski's.

Firkusny is less trenchant, more lyrical.

CONCERTO NO. 2 IN B-FLAT FOR PIANO
(Opus 83)

This sweeping, romantic concerto, one of the very best ever penned, was first performed by Brahms himself, in Budapest, in 1881. Considering the popularity of this piece, it is surprising that there are only three low-priced entries.

* * * GILELS, REINER	*Chicago Symphony Orch.*	VICTROLA	VIC (S)	1026
* * ARRAU, GIULINI	*Philharmonic Orch.*	SERAPHIM	(S)	60052
* SANDOR, REINHARDT	*SW German Symphony Orch.*	VOX	(5)	10990

Gilels is exciting, even magnificent here, strongly backed by Fritz Reiner. The sound is excellent. This is a young man's interpretation, which is fine for this tempestuous concerto.

The Arrau reading is all restrained poetry. This admirable artist often comes off badly in the recording studio; the sensitivity that characterizes his concerts is little heard on records. But he is fine here in this introspective, quietly romantic reading. *High Fidelity* comments on this disc: "As a team, Arrau and Giulini work together magnificently. . . . Arrau is entirely convincing, with wonderfully spacious phrasing."

Sandor is fresh-sounding; he has a sure command of this music. Nevertheless, he is outclassed.

For those who wish to spend more, both Richter and Rubenstein offer superlative performances on high-priced discs from Victor.

CONCERTO IN A FOR VIOLIN AND CELLO
(Opus 102)

The Brahms "Double"—as it is known affectionately to musicians—was his last concerted work for solo instruments and orchestra. As with all his music, Brahms put in enormous study before he actually began work on the composition itself. One feels the hand of a consummate master, the vintage of years captured on paper. Today the *Double Concerto* is widely loved as music that contains the autumn poetry of the Brahms *Symphonies* themselves, but it was not always so warmly regarded. In its early days, it was considered by musicians to be "unplayable." But time and familiarity—the tools of posterity—have done their work, and now the piece is regarded as one of Brahms' strongest and most beautiful compositions.

* * * FOURNIER, JANIGRO, SCHERCHEN	*Vienna State Opera Orch.*	WESTMINSTER	(M) 9712
* * FERRAS, TORTELIER, KLETZKI	*Philharmonic Orch.*	SERAPHIM [Beethoven, Violin Sonata No. 1]	(S) 60048

* * CAMPOLI, NAVARRA, BARBIROLLI	*Halle Orch.*	VANGUARD	(S)	136
OISTRAKH, KNUSHEVITSKI, ELIASBERG	*Moscow State Symphony Orch.*	PERIOD SHO (ST-2) [Violin Concerto]		336
SUK, NAVARRA, ANCERL	*Czech Philharmonic Orch.*	PARLIAMENT	(S)	601

Fournier-Janigro-Scherchen is a combination hard to beat—an intense, gutsy reading on serviceable mono. This is a stunning performance, strongly directed. If you don't mind mono, grab this one.

Here is a glowing reading by Ferras and the marvelous French cellist Paul Tortelier, who is still remembered in Boston from his days as a member of the Boston Symphony. Ferras has a smallish tone in the concert hall but you're not aware of it on well-engineered records. Conductor Kletzki is dynamic. The sound is pleasant.

Sweeping, romantic playing is heard from Campoli and Navarra. Greenspan writes in *Hi/Fi Stereo Review:* "In the low-priced field Campoli-Navarra is especially fine." *High Fidelity:* "A very solid job."

The Russian Oistrakh disc has indifferent sound, even filmy.

Suk and Navarra are both too lightweight for this trenchant, incisive music.

CONCERTO IN D FOR VIOLIN   (Opus 77)

Brahms' only violin concerto, dating from 1876, is a supreme masterpiece, and stands together with the violin concerto of Beethoven. This is by no means a suave, virtuoso, showcase piece, it is intensely serious throughout, at times almost brusque.

* * * OISTRAKH, KONWITSCHNY	*Saxon State Orch.*	HELIODOR	(S)	25091
* * * SZERYNG, MONTEUX	*London Symphony Orch.*	VICTROLA	VIC (S)	1028
* * KOGAN, KONDRASHIN	*Philharmonic Orch.*	SERAPHIM	(S)	60059
* OISTRAKH, KONDRASHIN	*Moscow Radio Symphony Orch.*	Vox [Bach, 2 Violin Concertos]	(M)	16380
* FERRAS, SCHURICHT	*Vienna Philharmonic Orch.*	RICHMOND	(M)	19018

For violinistic fluency and personal sentiment, it's hard to beat the great Russian, David Oistrakh. This is a romantic, silky-toned perform-ance. (Those who prefer a more incisive, gutsy reading—both ways are entirely valid—will prefer the Szeryng reading.) The "enhanced" stereo on the Oistrakh disc is warm-sounding.

Another admirable choice is the handsome, intense and penetrating conception of Szeryng on Victrola. The sound is full-bodied.

The Kogan disc, with good sound, is the best if you like your violin music romantically played. As Harold Schonberg said, "This is one of the most lyric performances of this masterpiece that can be found anywhere."

Oistrakh is all warm vitality and surge. The sound on the Vox disc is only passable, but you can hear the violin.

On the mono Ferras disc, the small-bodied violin tone disturbs me, although there is first-rate musicianship.

CHAMBER MUSIC At the end of Brahms' life, when he knew that he was doomed by cancer, he locked himself up in his study and destroyed many manuscripts, making sure that they would not reach the world posthumously. Not even his biographers know how much chamber music he actually composed. He remarked once that he had torn up 20 string quartets before producing one that satisfied him. No other composer was such a ruthless critic of his own art; even as a young man, he would make annual bonfires of much of his music, and this stringent critical sense remained with him all his life. Despite this savage weeding-out, he has left us 24 pieces of chanmber music, and they are all considered to be masterpieces.

CHAMBER MUSIC FOR WINDS   (Complete)

* *	*Various artists*	3-Vox	VBX (M)	78
			SVBX (S)	578

The individual works included are: *Quintet for Clarinet and Strings, in B Minor (Opus 115); Sonatas for Clarinet and Piano (Opus 120) No. 1 in F Minor; No. 2, in E-Flat; Trio for Clarinet, Cello, and Piano in A Minor (Opus 114);* and *Trio for Horn, Violin, and Piano, in E-Flat (Opus 40).* These recordings are reviewed separately; together in this three-record package, they comprise an attractive, most reasonably priced collection of choice Brahms.

PIANO TRIO NO. 1 IN B FOR VIOLIN, CELLO AND PIANO (Opus 8)

* * FOURNIER, JANIGRO, BADURA-SKODA	WESTMINSTER (M) 9049

These are fine, spirited players in a lyric reading. The mono sound, however, is pallid.

PIANO TRIO NO. 3 IN C FOR VIOLIN, CELLO AND PIANO (Opus 101)

Opus 101 is vintage Brahms, and the last of his three piano trios. It is a spare, terse work, as bracing as a swim in a mountain lake. It was written in the summer of 1886, when Brahms was 53 and at the height of his powers. The year before, he had finished his *Fourth Symphony;* the following year he wrote his *Double Concerto for Violin, Cello, and Orchestra.* Fanny Davies, an Englishwoman, left an account of a private performance of this trio, at which she was present. "A simple room, a small upright pianino, the three giants, and Clara Schumann turning over the leaves. . . . I can see him now looking eagerly with those penetrating, clear, grey-blue eyes, at Joachim and Robert Hausmann for the start, then lifting both of his little arms high up and descending "plump" on to the first C minor chord . . . as much as to say: 'I mean that.' "

This period of his life was outwardly uneventful for Brahms; he composed, he went on concert tours, he could afford to take his holidays wherever his fancy pleased. His base was Vienna, but the first sign of spring saw him up in the mountains at one of his favorite resorts. After the summer, back to concerts, introducing his music to an ever-growing public. He had already become the familiar bearded figure seen in most of his portraits. "His hair was nearly white," a contemporary wrote, "and he had grown very stout. He wore the happy, sunshiny look of one who had realized his purpose and was content with his share in life."

* * *	*Beaux Arts Trio*	2-PHILLIPS WS-SPHC 2-013
* * *	*Suk Trio*	CROSSROADS 22 16 0178
		[Mendelssohn, Trio No. 1]

The Beaux Arts recording is available only in a two-record set. The musicians provide ravishing playing. The sound is agreeable.

Don't miss this incisive Crossroads disc, if you want only one record of Brahms piano trios.

QUARTET FOR PIANO AND STRINGS, NO. 1

This *Quartet* was the first piece in which Brahms reached mastery in chamber music.

* * SZOLCHANY	*Hungarian Quartet*	TURNABOUT	(3) 4037

The work is sweepingly played, with a pervading quality of romantic warmth. The sound is clean.

QUINTET IN B FOR CLARINET AND STRINGS
(Opus 115)

This loveliest piece of chamber music by Brahms is a work to stand with the shattering *String Quintet* of Schubert (Opus 163). It was inspired, as were his other clarinet pieces, by Brahms' admiration for Richard Muehlfeld, the clarinetist of the Meiningen orchestra.

* * * GEUSER	*Drolc Quartet*	MACE (S) 9029 [Mozart, flute quartets]
* * * RIHA	*Smetana Quartet*	CROSSROADS (M) 22 16 0079 (S) 22 16 0080 [Mozart, Duos]
* KELL	*Fine Arts Quartet*	CONCERT DISC (M) 1202 (S) 202
* MICHAELS	*Endres Quartet*	3-Vox VBX (5) (S) 78 [Clarinet Sonata; Trios Opus 40, 114]
WLACH	*Vienna Konzerthaus Quartet*	WESTMINSTER (M) 9016

Geuser's interpretation is vivid and nostalgic; the interplay between solo clarinet and string quartet is first-rate.

For a fine-sounding, passionate reading, especially in the gypsy-like slow movement, we have the ubiquitous Czechs on the Crossroads disc. As *Hi/Fi Stereo Review* put it, "One might wish for more refinement, but one could hardly ask for more vitality. . . . By any standard, this disc represents a best buy in the chamber music field."

The Kell recording on 78's, of hallowed memory, was famous; his own later version on Concert Disc disappoints. My complaint here is that we are too aware of virtuoso Reginald Kell. The sound, to boot, is gritty.

Michaels is impersonal, cool and plastic.

Wlach is accomplished, but I miss soul, and soul is a must here.

QUINTET IN F FOR PIANO AND STRINGS
(Opus 34)

"Noble" is an overworked adjective when describing the chamber music of Brahms; but that is the adjective for Opus 34.

| * * CURZON | *Budapest Quartet* | Odyssey | (M) 32 16 0173 |
| DEMUS | *Vienna Konzerthaus Quartet* | Westminster | (S) 9020 |

Clifford Curzon and the Budapest Quartet, on a notable recording, deliver "a clear performance that nobody will ever regret owning" (Harold Schonberg). If you haven't discovered the dedicated musicianship of pianist Clifford Curzon, this is a fine opportunity.

Demus and the Vienna players are correct, and phlegmatic.

SEXTET IN B FLAT FOR STRINGS (Opus 18)

The slow movement of this sextet became the hit theme-song from the French movie, *The Lovers*. It is mellow, tawny, late-romantic Brahms.

| * * * | *Berlin Philharmonic Octet Members* | Phillips WS (M/S) 9050 |
| STANGLER, WEISS | *Vienna Konzerthaus Quartet* | Westminster | (M) 9021 |

The music is splendidly played by the Berliners, and well recorded with resonant Phillips sound engineering.

The Vienna players are thickish and the sound is dry.

SEXTET IN G (Opus 36)

This work is not as alluring as the *First Sextet* (Opus 18).

| HUEBNER, WEISS | *Vienna Konzerthaus Quartet* | Westminster | (M) 9022 |

The music is ponderously played.

SONATAS FOR VIOLIN AND PIANOS NO. 2, IN A (Opus 100); NO. 3, IN D MINOR (Opus 108)

Brahms wrote three violin sonatas. The first two are gentle and lyrical; the third is more dramatic. All are satisfying.

| * * SUK, PANENKA | Crossroads (M) 22 16 0087 |
| | (S) 22 16 0088 |

Suk is anything but silken, but makes up for that in sweep and vitality. *High Fidelity* comments: "... readings that are passionate, propulsive, and charged by a continuous current of near-electric dynamism." The stereo sound is faint.

For those who care, there is a famous aristocratic version of the sonatas with Szeryng and Rubinstein on an expensive Victor disc.

SONATAS IN E FOR CELLO AND PIANO
(Opus 38 and 99)

These are two of the great works in the chamber music literature for cello. Blazing fire, even romantic abandon pereate these pages. No less than three world-famous cellists offer low-priced performances.

* * STARKER, BOGIN	PERIOD (M) 593
* NAVARRA, HOLECEK	CROSSROADS (M) 22 16 0025 (S) 22 16 0026
* JANIGRO, BADURA-SKODA	WESTMINSTER (M) 9018

I keep my battered, gritty, mono copy of Starker. Harold Schonberg, a man not exactly given to huzzahs, commented on the Starker disc: "It is hard to overpraise the playing in this release."

Navarra's reading is smooth and loving.

Janigro is fluent, and has the best pianist. In sum, you cannot go wrong with any of the three.

STRING QUARTET NO. 1 IN C   (Opus 51/1);
NO. 2 IN A   (Opus 51/2)

* *	Fine Arts Quartet	CONCERT DISC (M) 1226 (S) 226
	Amadeus Quartet (No. 1)	WESTMINSTER (M) 9019 [Schubert, Quartet No. 12]

Here is solid, serious playing from the incisive Fine Arts Quartet. The sound is decent.

The Amadeus Quartet is boomingly recorded on mono.

THREE QUARTETS FOR PIANO AND STRINGS
(Complete)   (Opus 25, 26, 60)

This is stimulating, surging music, not to be missed by lovers of chamber music.

DEMUS	Barylli Quartet	3-WESTMINSTER	9051 (1)
			9050 (2)
			9052 (3)

The works are firmly played, although Demus is not the most exciting of pianists. The old mono sound is reasonably decent.

THREE STRING QUARTETS   (Complete)

* *	Janacek Quartet	2-CROSSROADS	
			(M) 22 26 0009
			(S) 22 26 0010
*	Kohon Quartet	3 Vox	SVBX-542
		[Schumann, Quartets]	

The Janacek Quartet is both noble and passionate; it is, if anything, too spirited. The sound is intimate and warm.

Of the competent Vox entry, Edward Greenfield commented, in the English *Stereo Record Guide:* "These are accomplished performances, well recorded."

THREE TRIOS FOR PIANO, VIOLIN AND CELLO, COMPLETE

The piano trios are exhilarating; the first, the great Opus 8 is a masterpiece of the form equaled only by Beethoven's *Archduke Trio.*

| * * * | Beaux Arts Trio | 2-PHILLIPS WS-SPHC 2-013 |
| | | [Trio in A, Opus Posth.] |

The Beaux Arts Trio is first-class; all of their splendid records offer some of the best buys to be had in the chamber music field. The sound is uniformly excellent. Here in the Brahms they are warm, and vigorous, Many critics prefer their playing here to that of the more virtuistic, violin-dominated playing to be heard on the Stern-Rose-Istomin Trio recordings on expensive Columbia.

TRIO IN A FOR CLARINET, CELLO, PIANO (Opus 114)

This work was written in 1891, two months after Brahms made his will; according to some biographers, this is a death-haunted piece. Not as great as the *Clarinet Quintet* which immediately followed, but also somberly beautiful.

* * DAVID AND FRANK GLAZER, SOYER	3-Vox SVBX 587 [Clarinet Sonata]
* GEUSER, TROESTER, HANSEN	MACE (S) 9038 [Beethoven, Trio (Opus 11)]
WLACH, KWARDA, HOLETSCHEK	WESTMINSTER (M) 9017 [Horn Trio]

I like the unaffected lyrical approach of the Glazers on Vox.
Geuser is a bit too sentimental at times, but entirely hearable.
Wlach is serviceable and Teutonic.

TRIO IN E-FLAT FOR HORN, VIOLIN, PIANO (Opus 40)

One of the great ones; it is because of meditative, haunting music like
this that musicians prize Brahms' chamber music so highly.

* PENZEL, VORHOLZ, LUDWIG	3 Vox SVBX 578
KOCH, BARYLLI, HOLETSCHEK	WESTMINSTER (M) 9017 [Clarinet Trio]
SHAPIRO, KOGAN, GILELS	MONITOR (S) 2066 [Haydn, Piano Trio No. 30]

Penzel is best here, with a poignant and pensive reading. The sound
is all right.

Koch is overly solemn and academic, but the record provides a good
coupling with the equally melancholy *Clarinet Trio*.

Russian hornist Shapiro plays in a quavering, French-influenced style
that I cannot listen to. Kogan is pure silk. The sound is decent.

TWO SONATAS FOR CLARINET (OR VIOLA) AND PIANO (Opus 120)

This rather placid, monochromatic music was written in 1894. Brahms
allowed these two sonatas to be played by violists, but I prefer the
original clarinet version.

* * DAVID AND FRANK GLAZER	Vox (ST) D1-(50) 1210
* * PRIMROSE, FIRKUSNY	SERAPHIM (M) 60011
* WRIGHT, GOLDSMITH	CROSSROADS (S) 22 16 0142

* DOKTOR, REISENBERG		WESTMINSTER (M) 9053
WLACH, DEMUS		WESTMINSTER (M) 9023

Best of the clarinet field is the cultivated reading of David and Frank Glazer. Too-close clarinet sound, and rather remote piano, are drawbacks, however.

Your taste may be for viola; if so, the famous violist Primrose plays it with Firkusny as well as anyone can.

Wright and Goldsmith are intelligent musicians, but here they are too reticent for my taste.

Doktor and Reisenberg are studious, but outclassed.

Wlach and Demus give a dullish interpretation.

VOCAL MUSIC   Brahms' songs should not be missed by anyone searching for more than routinely pleasant entertainment. The *Alto Rhapsoday*, the *German Requiem*, the *Songs with Viola Obbligato*, the *Four Serious Songs* —these are all treasures—lovely, exhilarating works that appeal to the spirit as well as to the emotions. All of these are top-drawer Brahms, among his very finest works.

ALTO RHAPSODY   (Opus 53)

The *Rhapsody* for alto voice, men's chorus and orchestra is lovely music, set to a somber poem by Goethe. Brahms favored this above most of his music; he remarked that for a while he slept with the score under his pillow. Most of this music was written in 1869, when Brahms was in black despondency, possibly because of an unhappy love affair.

HOFFMAN, BAMBERGER	*Hamburg Norddeutscher* *Rundfunk Symphony* *Orch. and Men's Chorus*	2-NONESUCH (7) 3003 [Deutsche Fest; German Requiem]

Little of the beauty of this music is to be heard from Hoffman on the less than inspired Nonesuch set.

For a stunning musical experience, I suggest that you hear, now, the immortal, imperfect performance by Kathleen Ferrier on a London disc.

GERMAN REQUIEM   (Opus 45)

These very great, tender, resigned pages were finally completed in 1868, after much labor. Brahms adapted German texts from the Lutheran

Bible, instead of the customary liturgical Latin—hence "German Requiem." This is very great, very lofty music.

STICH-RANDALL, PEASE, BAMBURGER	*Hamburg North German Radio Symphony Orchestra and Chorus*	2-NONESUCH (7) 30:13 [Alto Rhapsody; Deutsche Fest]

The one set available to us is a disappointment; Stich-Randall sounds tired, or indisposed, and the choral singing is pedestrian. Either wait or get Klemperer's reading on expensive Angel.

LIEBESLIEDER WALTZES   *(Opus 52, 65)*

There are two sets of *Liebeslieder,* scored for vocal quartet and four-handed piano accompaniment. The text consists of love songs by Daumer. These are bittersweet, elegant Viennese songs, and it is difficult not to fall in love with them.

* * * MORISON, THOMAS, LEWIS, BELL, VRONSKY AND BABIN		SERAPHIM	(S) 60033
* * STEPAN, HURNIK, VENHODA	*Prague Madrigal Singers*	CROSSROADS (M) 22 16 0001	(S) 22 16 0002
WINOGRAD	*String Orch. (Opus 52)*	HELIDOR [Suk]	(S) 25026

Far and away the best performance is to be had on Seraphim, with the old-school piano team of Vronsky and Babin, and four ingratiating English singers. The sound is fine.

The Crossroads set is really good, but it uses more singers, which, for me, interferes with the intimacy of this music.

The Heliodor set is arranged for string orchestra (no singers), and also has an early *Serenade in Strings* (Opus 8) by Dvorak's son-in-law, Josef Suk. *High Fidelity* on this disc: "Winograd . . . in the long run a bit heavy-handed in the Brahms . . . stereo separation is nicely balanced. . . . [the Suk piece] is rather bland work."

SONGS   Brahms left us over 200 songs and duets, and a large number of German folk songs. (The last do not have opus numbers.) These compositions are of the highest order, and rank with the songs of Schubert, Schumann, and Hugo Wolf. The songs of Brahms are artless and melodic.

Nevertheless, Brahms' formidable craftsmanship was at work; he advised the young song writer George Henschel, "Let it rest, let it rest, and keep going back to it and working at it until it is completed as a finished work of art, until there is not a note too much or too little, not a bar you could improve on."

CHORAL SONGS

Here are nine Brahms songs—a good chance to hear nineteenth-century songs for chorus. The form was once extremely popular, but today has gone out of fashion.

* RABENSCHLAG, BLUM	*Chorus of the University of Leipzig, The Camerata Vocale*	NONESUCH	(S) H71081

This well-sung disc is a representative sampler of the impetuous, sometimes swooning style of the genre. The sound is pleasant. [Also included are choral songs by Mendelssohn, Loewe, Silcher, and Schumann.]

VIER ERNSTE GESAENGE   (Opus 121)

The *Four Serious Songs* are wonderful, moving pieces, set to biblical texts. Late, great Brahms: all is vanity, all is dust.

* * FISCHER-DIESKAU, DEMUS	HELIDOR HS (S) 25082 [Dvorak, Biblical Songs]	
* PREY	2-Vox (5) 532 [Wolf, Italienisches Liederbuch]	

The compelling voice of the greatest lieder singer of our time, Dietrich Fischer-Dieskau, is ideally suited to these somber songs. The emotional range of the man is extraordinary; and his command of mood—ranging from Biblical declamation to gentle, soft legato—is also remarkable. *High Fidelity* "I have yet to hear a better-sung version than the one contained on this disc." [The coupling is with Dvorak's seldom-heard *Biblical Songs* —(6 of the set of 10—which were composed in 1894). They are simple, almost naive pieces, with Dvorak's usual supply of fresh melody, but worlds removed from the grim grandeur of the great Brahms songs.] This disc was originally on Deutche Gramophon (1960), and the sound is quite exemplary.

The young, dark-voiced Hermann Prey gives a much less moving interpretation than does Fischer-Dieskau, but he is very good indeed, in an impetuous, poetic style. [His reading here is part of a two-record album containing a grand performance of Wolf's *Italiaenisches Liederbuch.*]

ZIGEUNERLIEDER (Opus 103); FELDEINSAMKEIT; DER KRANZ; DER SCHMIED; DER TOD, DAS IST DIE KUEHLE NACHT; THERESE; MEINE LIEBE IST GRUEN; BOTSCHAFT; DAS MAEDCHEN SPRICHT; MEIN MADEL HAT EINEN ROSENMUND

* LEHMANN,
ULANOWSKY,
BALOGH

RCA Victrola   VIC (S)
1320

Recorded over the period 1935-47, this is an up-and-down affair. The German singer Lotte Lehmann, of course, has a legendary reputation, but her exaggerated style and occasional off-pitch intonation are disturbing. (Her disc on Seraphim, selected from recordings made during her prime years, is much more rewarding.) The Victrola set has been absurdly rehabilitated for stereo, presumably not to offend the ears of any modern buyer by offering him lowly mono for a song recital. George Jellenik commented, in *Hi/Fi Stereo Review*, on the result: "The engineering of the artificial stereo disc is rather mediocre."

OTHER SONGS

The lovely *Songs for Alto, Viola, and Piano* (Opus 91) are not represented at the moment at low price; Marian Anderson and Kathleen Ferrier both have made splendid high-priced recordings of these songs.

At low-price, there is little more to be had of Brahms songs. Flagstad sings a few (Opus 91) on Seraphim 60046, but I never cared for the great Wagnerian diva's lieder singing.

Four songs well sung by the expressive Christa Ludwig may be heard on low-priced Seraphim (S) 60034.

The collector who wishes first-rate singing of Brahms songs, and is willing to pay, is referred to the many records of Fischer-Dieskau on expensive Angel and DGG.

PIANO MUSIC The piano works of Brahms are not as popular as his other compositions. The *Sonatas* and *Variations* are somewhat cold, uneven, and cerebral. The short meditative pieces of his late period, however — *Intermezzi* (Opus 117) and *Six Pieces* (Opus 118)—are great concert favorites. They are barely represented on low-priced discs at this writing·

PIANO MUSIC

* KLEIN   Vox   SVBX (S) 430/31
                                          [2 albums]

I cannot urge you to buy six records of the piano music of Brahms, but anyone who needs or likes this music, will do very well with Walter Klien. This is literate, lean, playing of the school of Schnabel and Serkin, as opposed to the romantic bravura style of Rubinstein. Both styles, of course, have their admirers. But I think for the piano music of Brahms, the intellectual approach of Austrian pianist Walter Klien is on the right track. I heard a mono edition of these albums—the sound is all right. *High Fidelity* commented on these records: "Enthusiastically recommended."

The selections included are: *4 Ballades (Opus 10); 3 Intermezzos (Opus 117); 2 Rhapsodies (Opus 79); Sonata for Piano, No. 3, in F Minor (Opus 5); 6 Stuecke (Opus 118); Variations on a Theme by Schumann (Opus 9); Variations on a Theme by Handel (Opus 24); Waltzes (Opus 39); Scherzo (Opus 4); Sonatas for Piano: No. 1, in C (Opus 1); No. 2, in F Sharp Minor (Opus 2); Phantasien (Opus 116); 8 Stuecke (Opus 76); 4 Stuecke (Opus 119); Variations on an Original Theme (Opus 21), No. 1, 2; Variations on a Theme by Paganini (Opus 35).*

"HANDEL" VARIATIONS; 2 INTERMEZZI; RHAPSODY IN G MINOR; ROMANCE IN F MAJOR; BALLADE IN G MINOR; 10 WALTZES (Opus 39)

The *Rhapsody* is a rugged, leonine piece, and so are the *Handel Variations*. The other works are romantic and poignant.

KLEIN   1-TURNABOUT   TV 34165

The music is well played. [See comments on the six-record set, immediately above.]

SONATA IN F MINOR FOR 2 PIANOS (Opus 34A)

This lovely, big-scaled two-piano writing is something of a curiosity. This music was first composed for stringed intruments, and ultimately became the distinguished *F Minor Piano Quintet*.

* BILLARD, AZAIS   PHILLIPS WS (M/S) 9067

What we hear in this version is an interim form that Brahms considered. It is played with dash, nervous excitement, and superb forward thrust by a young French team, with glittering sound. This disc was included in a "Best Records of the Year" list of *Stereo Guide*.

3 INTERMEZZOS AND RHAPSODY IN E FLAT (Opus 119); VARIATIONS ON A THEME OF SCHUMANN, IN F-SHARP (Opus 9); VARIATIONS ON AN ORIGINAL THEME (Opus 21, No. 1)

The intermezzos are lovely, short pieces, and the other selections are melodious.

* * WEBSTER   DOVER   HCRST 7005

Webster plays the works with ardor and expertise. This disc was included in the *Stereo, 1967* list of "Year's Best Recordings."

VARIATIONS ON A THEME BY HANDEL (Opus 24)

Rather cold, impersonal music, for Brahms. Whereas Handel wrote five variations on this cheerful theme, Brahms wrote 25, and Brahms furthermore topped them off with a powerful fugue.

* ANIEVAS   SERAPHIM   (S) 60049
                                                 [Paganini Variations]

Anievas plays them with finesse, verve, and thorough technical command.

VARIATIONS ON A THEME BY PAGANINI (Opus 35)

"Witch Variations," in Clara Schumann's phrase. In its day, the *Variations* were the last word in technical virtuosity for piano writing. The theme is a fascinating one, the same one that Rachmaninoff used in his *Variations on a Theme by Paganini*.

* * WILD   VANGUARD   C (S) 10006
                                                 [Liszt, Etude]

* * ANIEVAS   SERAPHIM   (S) 60049
                                                 [Variations and Fugue on
                                                 a Theme by andel (Opus
                                                 24)]

* MERZHANOV   MONITOR   2013
[Scriabin, Sonata No. 5]

Here are three amazingly good entries — this is an age of mathematically accurate pianists, all frighteningly well equipped.

I give a slight edge to the powerful playing of Earl Wild. The sound is fine. [Wild's disc also contains the *Four Ballades* (Opus 10) by Brahms; romantic, Schumannesque music. The Liszt *Study No. 2* is from *Six Grand Etudes After Paganini*. What we hear is a glittering transcription of Paganini's *17th Caprice* for violin, played in the grand style.]

The young American pianist Anievas has won almost every prize to be had, and on this record you hear why. The sound is satisfactory.

Russian Victor Merzhanov is also brilliant. The sound is good. [However, the disc contains some awful Scriabin on the reverse.]

Britten, Benjamin (1913-   )

A composer since childhood, Britten is the leading British composer of our time. At twenty-one, Britten earned his living by composing film music, documentaries, and incidental music for the theater. He spent three years (1939-1942) in the United States, composing and concertizing with Peter Pears, the noted singer. Today, Britten is active as conductor, pianist, concert organizer and extremely prolific composer.

PLACE AND ACHIEVEMENT   Britten has achieved the unlikely: he is regarded by the critics and the public alike as a monument in his own lifetime. Even people who declare themselves hostile to new music like Britten. He is rarely dull; on the contrary, he is the most *interesting* of modern composers. One senses a keen intellect at work, a mind that can range with equal assurance from the *Young People's Guide to the Orchestra* to the *War Requiem*.

Above all, the voice of Britten is a highly original voice; one never feels that his music is derivative. The voice is that of a sophisticated man of culture; his texts derive from Henry James, Herman Melville, Wilfred Owen, medieval poetry, etc. Britten's music is imaginative, melodic, and charged with taut emotion; he is probably the greatest English composer since Henry Purcell.

THE ESSENTIAL BRITTEN

OPERAS: *Turn of the Screw; Peter Grimes; Midsummer Night's Dream; Noye's Flood; The Rape of Lucretia; Albert Herring; Let's Make an Opera; Billy Budd.*

ORCHESTRAL MUSIC: *Variations on a Theme by Frank Bridge; Sinfonia da Requiem; A Young Person's Guide to the Orchestra; Serenade for Tenor, Horn, and Strings; Symphony for Cello and Orchestra.*

CHORAL MUSIC: *War Requiem; Spring Symphony.*

OTHER MAJOR WORKS

ORCHESTRAL MUSIC: *Concerto for Piano and Orchestra; Concerto for Violin and Orchestra; Les Illuminations for Solo Voice and Orchestra.*

OPERA: *Gloriana.*

CHORAL MUSIC: *A Ceremony of Carols; Hymn to St. Cecilia; Saint Nicholas, Cantata; Rejoice in the Lamb.*

CEREMONY OF CAROLS (Opus 28)

Written in 1942, this work is scored for treble voices (preferably boys) and solo harp. The music is set to old carol texts and to the work of 16th and 17th century poets. The work projects an intriguing, simulated medieval mood. This is lovable music — a statement I would make about the work of only a few 20th-century composers.

| * * KULINSKY | Prague Radio Children's Chorus | Crossroads (S) 22 16 0154 [Honegger, Chistmas Cantata] |

The singing is exuberant. The sound gets thickish in some choral passages. [The Honegger piece was finished in 1953, and makes a neat coupling. All the Honegger hallmarks are here: Contrapuntal craftsmanship, austere orchestration, and a clearly structured dramatic situation. This, too, is extremely listenable music.]

SONATA IN C FOR CELLO

This austere, impressive music was dedicated to and made famous by the great Russian cellist Rostropovich.

| APOLIN, KVAPIL | | Artia   (S)   709 [Kabalevsky, Sonata] |

This piece is sometimes referred to as "Britten's Rostropovich Sonata." While the cellist Apolin is competent, the team of Rostropovich-Britten on the expensive London record is the definitive reading. [The Kabalevsky sonata, on the flip side of the Apolin disc, is banal.]

VARIATION ON A THEME BY FRANK BRIDGE (Opus 10)

This ingenious and picturesque work of 1937 was the first music of Britten's to achieve general notice. It is scored for strings alone. Each of the variations bears a title: Viennese Waltz, Chant, etc. A poised, sophisticated exercise, the composition is highly agreeable.

| * VLACH | Czech Chamber Orch. | Crossroads (M) 22 16 0107 (S) 22 16 0108 [Stravinsky, Apollo Musagete] |

The playing on the Vlach disc is less than polished, but lively. The sound is a bit confined. [The Stravinsky work, also using string orchestra, was composed as a short ballet. This is suave, intellectualized music, and a delight. The model here is clearly Tchaikovsky, whom Stravinsky admires fervently.]

YOUNG PERSON'S GUIDE TO THE ORCHESTRA
(Opus 34)

This work became an instant classic. Composed in 1946 as an accompaniment to a film illustrating the modern symphony orchestra, this instructive music is cleverly done. The formal title of the piece is *Variations and Fugue on a Theme by Purcell.*

* VAN BEINUM	*Concertgebouw Orch.*	RICHMOND (M) 19040 [Prokofiev, Peter and the Wolf]	
* DE WILDE, SWAROWSKY	*Vienna Pro Musica Symphony*	VOX (M) 9280 [Prokofiev, Peter and the Wolf]	

The playing on both discs is nicely done, but this music is better heard on stereo rather than on the mono versions available at low prices.

Bruch, Max *(1838-1920)*

Bruch, a German of Jewish birth, who was a conductor and teacher, composed in nearly all musical forms. Although German critics believe that his finest pages lie in his many cantatas, the musical public, by and large, prefer two of his sentimental pieces: the *G Minor Violin Concerto,* and the *Kol Nidrei Variations.*

CONCERTO NO. 1 IN G FOR VIOLIN *(Opus 20)*

Although some critics turn up their noses, the public loves this emotional music. Bruch's *Concerto No. 1* appeals for the warmth of its sentiment as well as for the highly skilled writing for solo violin.

* * * MILSTEIN, STEINBERG	*Pittsburgh Symphony Orch.*	PICKWICK (S) 4023 [Mendelssohn, Concerto]	
* * LAREDO, MITCHELL	*National Symphony Orch.*	VICTROLA VIC (S) 1033 [Mendelssohn, Concerto]	
* CAMPOLI, KISCH	*New Symphony Orch.*	RICHMOND (M) 19021 [Mendelssohn, Concerto]	

Milstein offers a stunning performance, the best to be had on any record regardless of price. When reviewing this disc, Irving Kolodin said: "Menuhin and Heifetz have no lack of violinistic resource at their disposal, but Milstein had quite enough, also something more: a conviction and devotion that makes his effort much more personal." The sound is decidedly good.

Young Laredo plays with dash and sweep. His recording has the best sonics among the records listed.

Although Campoli's performance is technically admirable, the small-bore reading is on faded mono.

KOL NIDREI FOR CELLO AND ORCHESTRA *(Opus 47)*

This moving, meditative music is enormously popular with cellists.

* DOR, COMISSIONA	*Haifa Symphony Orch.*	MACE (S) 10033 [Milhaud, Candelabre a Sept Branches; Partos, Yiskor]
* JANIGRO, RODZINSKI	*London Philharmonic*	WESTMINSTER (S) 14985 [Canzone; Bloch, Schelomo]

Dor and the Israeli players create gravely moving effects. The sound is agreeable. [The Milhaud piece included on the Mace disc is fervent musical Judaica for piano, well played by Israeli Frank Pelleg. Odeon Partos, composer of the other work on the disc, is an Israeli who tries to incorporate Israeli-Jewish elements into the modern structure. His work here, for viola and orchestra, is fairly successful.]

The Janigro reading has been noteworthy since its first release years ago; he captures the profoundly serious posture of the piece even more successfully than does Dor. [On the other side of the disc you'll find Bloch's *Schelomo*, another work deeply imbued with Hebraic influence.]

SCOTTISH FANTASY FOR VIOLIN AND ORCHESTRA (Opus 40)

This violin music is lush and romantic, but decidedly second-rate.

* CAMPOLI, BOULT   *London Philharmonic*   LONDON STS   15015
[Mendelssohn, Concerto]

Campoli's technical skills rank him among the best violinists in the business. Sound is clean.

Bruckner, Anton (1824-1896)

Bruckner, an organist as well as composer, studied with Sechter in Vienna. In 1856, he became organist at Linz Cathedral. In 1863, he heard Wagner's opera *Tannhaeuser,* and from that time on the music of Wagner played a vital role in his life. He became one of the most passionate of Wagner's disciples.

After 1880, Bruckner's music, long ridiculed and abused because of its length and its naiveté, began to achieve acceptance. In 1891, he was made Honorary Doctor of the University of Vienna.

PLACE AND ACHIEVEMENT   Bruckner's work has often been linked with that of Mahler, because of their common penchant for extremely long works and for grandiose orchestral effects. Like Wagner, Bruckner made colossal attempts at grandeur—attempts that often are merely wearisome and long-winded. "Symphonic boa-constrictors" is how Johannes Brahms summed up the Bruckner symphonies.

Bruckner's claim to immortality lies in two characteristics: convincing religious harmonies, and a solid strength—traits not always apparent on first hearing. Bruckner broke no new ground. His massive music simply exists, much as do the mountains that Buckner loved so well.

THE ESSENTIAL BRUCKNER
ORCHESTRAL MUSIC: *Symphonies No. 4, 5, 7, 8, and 9.*

OTHER WORKS
ORCHESTRAL MUSIC: *Symphonies No. 1, 2, 3, and 6; Psalm 150; Three Masses; Te Deum; String Quintet.*

SYMPHONY NO. 4 IN FLAT ("Romantic")

The *Fourth Symphony* is Bruckner's most popular work, and perhaps the most easily assimilated. Bruckner himself labeled this one, "Romantic."

* KLEMPERER	*Vienna Symphony Orch.*	Vox	(M) 11200
* HOLLREISER	*Bamberg Symphony Orch.*	TURNABOUT	(M) 34107

The Klemperer performance, though very old, still creates a magical atmosphere.

Hollreiser's conception, a more recent recording, conveys the rustic beauty beloved by Bruckner.

SYMPHONY NO. 5 IN B FLAT

This vast, episodic work is often held to be a noble failure; yet there are many affecting moments, especially a most beautiful adagio introduction. The symphony is not often performed. Perhaps just as well, for this expansive music is enjoyed better in one's home than in the concert hall.

* * JOCHUM	*Concertgebouw Orch.*	2 PHILLIPS (M) PHM 2-591 (S) PHS 2-991 [Mozart, Symphony No. 36]

Jochum's interpretation is romantic and authentic. The orchestra is first-rate, especially the brass. The stereo is unusually well-balanced.

SYMPHONY NO. 6 IN A

The *Sixth* is perhaps the least familiar of Bruckner's symphonies. Compared to Bruckner's more ponderous works, the mood is light and airy.

REICHERT	*Westphalia Symphony Orch.*	TURNABOUT	34226

Reichert does his best with this sprawling work, but the whole effect is unimpressive.

SYMPHONY NO. 7 IN E

The *Seventh Symphony,* written between 1881 and 1883, is one of Bruckner's best. The adagio is designated "In Memorium" for Richard Wagner who died in February, 1883.

* * SCHURICHT	*Hague Philharmonic*	NONESUCH	71139
* HAITINK	*Concertgebouw Orch.*	2 PHILLIPS (M) PHM 2-580 (S) PHS 2-998 [Te Deum]	
ROSBAUD	*SW German Symphony Orch.*	TURNABOUT (3)	4083
ROSBAUD	*SW German Symphony Orch.*	3-Vox [Symphony No. 4]	SVBX 5117

Unlike most conductors of Bruckner, Schuricht is successfully straightforward and unpretentious. He avoids the *mysterioso* element of Bruckner, who always spoke of God in a soft and whispering tone. The sound is clean.

Haitink achieves an agreeable pastoral quality in the first and last movements; and the big climax of the second movement is wonderfully robust. [The *Te Deum* makes a congenial coupling, but the works take up two records—twice as much for you to buy.]

Rosbaud seems ill-at-ease conducting Bruckner. Commenting on his interpretation, the English *Stereo Record Guide* warns: "Bruckner veterans had better sample this 7th before purchase."

SYMPHONY NO. 8 IN C

Bruckner's *Eighth* is a wide-screen monolithic symphony of cyclopean grandeur. Some think this opus is a crashing bore; others stoutly maintain it isn't one note too long. I line up with the first opinion.

| * HORENSTEIN | *Vienna Pro Musica* | 2-Vox | VUX-2016 |

Jascha Horenstein is a specialist in making malleable the immalleable. The sound is so-so.

SYMPHONY NO. 9 IN D

The *Ninth,* begun in 1887, was never completed, although Bruckner lived nine years after he started this composition. This is one of Bruckner's more clearly organized works.

| * * SCHURICHT | *Vienna Philharmonic* | SERAPHIM | (S) 60047 |
| * JOCHUM | *Bavarian Radio Symphony Orch.* | HELIODOR | (S) 25007 |

Schuricht has bite and succinctness—no easy achievement when conducting Bruckner. Irving Kolodin comments: "The secret of Schuricht's success with Bruckner is neither mysterious nor difficult to isolate . . . for those who prefer their Bruckner with the rugged simplicity of emotion. that was inherent in the man himself, Schuricht's way will appeal." The sound is spacious.

Jochum is another old Bruckner hand; his musicians are letter-perfect and strenuously rehearsed. Yet the performance winds up as somewhat lifeless.

TE DEUM

When Bruckner realized that he might not live to finish his *Ninth Symphony,* he suggested that his *Te Deum* be used as a conclusion. The idea has been tried, and has proved unsatisfactory. Today, the *Te Deum* is played separately. For many listeners, the addition of vocal soloists makes Bruckner's music more palatable.

* AMELING,	*Concertgebouw Orch.,*	PHILIPS	(M) PHM 2-598
REYNOLDS,	*Netherlands Chorus*		(S) PHS 2-998
HOFFMANN,			
HOEKMAN, HAITINK			

The singing on this well-recorded version is dedicated, and rather chaste. [The two-record set also contatins Bruckner's *Seventh.*]

Buxtehude, Dietrich (c. 1637-1707)

Buxtehude was born in northern Germany, near what is now Denmark. His father, an organist, was probably his only teacher. Buxtehude himself became a famous organist and filled various posts as organist until his death. He wrote church cantatas, organ music, and sonatas for instrumental ensembles.

This is a composer with imagination of the highest order. For organ lovers, he is a must. And those who wish to explore the music of the period just before Bach can do no better than to become acquainted with the somber, passionate, brooding music of Buxtehude. In the year 1705, on what is perhaps the most famous walk in music history, Johann Sebastian Bach tramped from Arnstadt to Luebeck, some two hundred miles, to hear the great master Buxtehude improvise on the organ.

CHAMBER AND KEYBOARD MUSIC

Instruments used here are the violin, viola da gamba, harpsichord, and regal. A regal was a portable reed organ used in the 16th and 17th centuries. The music is light, unobtrusive, and engaging, and was probably written simply for home entertainment.

* * BRINK,   Music Guild   (S)   121
    DAVIDOFF,
    PINKHAM

Grace and authentic style mark this rendition. Here is clean stereo and intimate sound. This modest little disc has been on several "Best of the Year" lists, both in America and in England.

FIVE CANTATAS; ORGAN SUITE

Buxtehude's life-span fell between that of Schutz and Bach, and he possessed much of the seriousness and strength of both these masters — as is demonstrated in these works. This is wonderful, intimate music that I commend to you full-heartedly.

* * CUENOD,   Cambridge Festival Orch.   Westminster   (M)   114
    CONRAD,   Ensemble
    PEARSON

The singing is grave and fervent—highly recommended. Mono sound is room-size and satisfying.

MAGNIFICAT ANIMA MEA

This sturdy music suggests the austere paintings and engravings of such German artists as Holbein and Duerer.

| * KUNZ, RILLING | Instrumental Ensemble and Kantorei of The Gedaechtniskirche, Stuttgart | TURNABOUT TV [Bach, Magnificat] | 34173 |

The bass, Hanns-Friedrich Kunz, is pleasing. The mood is that of the famous *Abendmusik* — Sunday evening concerts of sacred music at Luebeck where Buxtehude worked. The sound is roomy. [On the reverse side, the Bach is also played with vigor and style.]

ORGAN MUSIC (Complete)

This is not *pomposo* organ writing. Yet the simple strength and personality of this remarkable master demand unflagging interest. Hearing this pensive, tender music, the listener will readily understand why fifty years later Bach used some of these pieces as models.

| * KRAFT | | 9-Vox (S) SVBX 527/9 |

I have no idea who buys nine records of Buxtehude organ music except perfervid organ enthusiasts — and students and teachers of organ music. The English *Stereo Record Guide* commented on a one-record excerpt from this staggering collection: "The playing is most sensitive and pleasing."

ORGAN MUSIC (Selected)

| * * * HANSEN | NONESUCH   (S) H71188 |

This Nonesuch set is a beauty. The organist Hansen, who seems to be going through the entire organ literature for the Nonesuch label, is an extraordinary organist. He is never dull; he conveys his excitement with this music; and his 1690 Copenhagen instrument is brightly baroque. The individual works included on this record are: *Toccata in F; Prelude in F Sharp Minor; Passacaglia in D Minor; Gigue Fugue in C; Canzonetta in E Minor; Magnificat Primi Toni; Chorale Preludes: Ein Feste Burg; Herr Christ der Einzig Gottes Sohn; Two Preludes on "Von Gott Will Ich Nicht Lassen."* Sound: excellent. *High Fidelity* comments: "A first rate set, further enhanced by very warm and clean recorded sound."

Byrd, William (1543-1623)

Byrd is termed the "Father of English music." The greatest English composer of his day, he was famous throughout Europe for his magnificent church music, and for his skill and innovations in counterpoint. More of his music has come down to us than that of any other Elizabethan composer. Byrd's music, which ranges through every form of composition, is ingenious, attractive, and vividly alive.

FANTASIE FOR STRINGS, NO. 1

This is a lovely example of sixteenth century polyphony.

SURINACH   *Chamber Orch.*   HELIODOR   (S) 25022
[Arne, Judgment of Paris
Overtures; Purcell, Abdela-
zer Suite]

The playing is skillful and vigorous, but the sound—"electronically enhanced for stereo"—is murky.

THE FITZWILLIAM VIRGINAL BOOK

For a good overall impression of the music of Shakespeare's day, one need only turn to the remarkable anthology of keyboard pieces known as the *Fitzwilliam Virginal Book,* which contains almost 300 compositions by some 20 of the best composers. The selections were laboriously assembled by an early 17th century scribe. The book includes music by William Byrd, Thomas Tomkins, Martin Peerson, Nicholas Strogers, Giles Fanaby, Robert Johnson, Peter Philips, John Munday, William Tisdall, and John Bull.

The virginal, a small modest member of the harpsichord family, was much favored by English writers. Dutch painters often depicted young ladies playing the instrument, while men were usually shown playing the lute.

* * WINOGRON   DOVER   (S) 7266

Blanche Winogron plays the virginal quite remarkably. She coaxes variety and color without the advantage of pedals—no small feat on this limited instrument [no pun intended]. This tinkly little disc has received inordinate praise from all quarters, especially from *Hi/Fi Stereo Review.* The sound is exemplary. [Four of the pieces included were written by Byrd. The rest of the program is largely the music of minor men whose music is quite innocuous.]

MASS IN 3 PARTS; MASS IN 4 PARTS; MASS IN 5 PARTS

These Masses were written by the devout William Byrd when the Roman Catholic Church in England was functioning almost underground. The *Mass in Three Parts* is a finely meshed, astonishing work. The other two Masses are also sonorous, and the polyphony is lucidly worked out. Those who favor this type of church music will find these Masses enormously fulfilling.

* * LITTLE   *Montreal Bach Chorus*   Vox   (S) (500)   880

The singing is worthy, with good balance between the parts. Sound is clean.

Cage, John (1912-   )

In a sense, the American John Cage is the grand old man of the New Music. His compositions are highly regarded, but not often played.

Cage uses both the "concrete" method and the "true" electronic method. He writes pieces that can be played alone or that can be played together simultaneously and listened to throught two loud speakers. In the opinion of the composer, the listener will hear viable music no matter how the music is presented, either each composition alone or each composition paired.

CONCERTO FOR PREPARED PIANO AND ORCHESTRA

This 1956 concerto of John Cage resembles, at various times, Oriental music, Schoenberg, and Webern. This is curious, reflective music of much delicacy. It is also imbued with the mystic "silences" for which Cage became famous later on. Don't expect a piano concert; Cage treats the piano rather as a gamelan.

* * FOSS   *Buffalo Philharmonic*   NONESUCH   (S) 71202
                                                    [Foss, Baroque variations.]

The playing is intense, and the orchestra seems to understand this music. [The coupling is devastating fun, with Handel and Scarlatti hurled into twentieth century idiom.]

Caldara, Antonio *(1670-1736)*

Caldara, a Venetian, served as assistant-conductor at the Imperial Court of Vienna under Charles VI; he was the really influential man to know (with J. J. Fux) at the Imperial Musical Establishment. Besides church and instrumental music, he wrote 87 operas.

CHRISTMAS CANTATA: VATICINI DI PACE

The fifty-minute Christmas cantata is an ambitious work, somewhat in Handel's Italian Style.

STOKLASSA, SABO, RUSS, JELDEN, EWERHART	*Wuerttemberg Chamber Orch.*	TURNABOUT TV	(M) 4096 (S) 34096

The Turnabout performance is fairly interesting, and everything is in good technical order. Sound is agreeable.

FOUR CANONS; IL GIUOCO DEL QUADRIGLIO; VOLA IL TEMPO; CHE DITE, O MIEL PENSIERI?

Caldara gained fame for his witty musical skits. One of his most humorous is set in a dentist's office; another represents four ladies playing cards.

LOEHRER	*Societa Cameristica di Lugano*	NONESUCH	(M) H 1103 (S) H 71103

The soloist, instrumentalists, and ensemble of the Lugano chamber society are mildly entertaining. Sound is fair.

Chabrier, Emmanuel (1841-1894)

The French composer Chabrier was largely self-taught. Chabrier is best remembered for his vivacious orchestral rhapsody, *Espana*, which is entrenched in the Pops repertory. The adventurous listener is urged to investigate Chabrier's piano music. These shrewd, light-hearted pieces have been likened in style to the insouciant sketches of Toulouse-Lautrec.

ESPANA

This is extremely brilliant musical writing, with gay melodies.

* * PARAY	*Detroit Symphony Orch.*	MERCURY (M/S) 18068	
* MOREL	*Royal Opera House Orch.*	VICTROLA VIC (S) 1057	
VAN REMOORTEL	*Vienna Symphony Orch.*	VOX (5) 18068	
ANSERMET	*Suisse Romande Orch.*	RICHMOND 19097 [Marche; Ravel, Pavane for a Dead Princess, Saint-Saens, Dance Macabre; Rouet]	

Paray is appropriately vivid. The sound is crisp. [The Paray disc also contains Chabrier's *Suite Pastorale, Fete Polonaise, Danse Slave,* and *Overture to Gwendoline* — all ebullient, high-spirited pieces.]

The Morel performance ranks next best. Morel's version has dash, but not as much as Paray's.

The Van Remoortel and Ansermet readings are so-so.

PIANO MUSIC (Complete)

Chabrier was a contemporary of the French Impressionist painters, and this music, highly coolred, gay, and tasteful, is almost impressionistic in its effects.

* KYRIAKOU, KLIEN	3-VOX VBX (M/S) 400

The pianist Rena Kyriakou is smooth and graceful, and Walter Klien, in the works for four hands, matches her verve. The only trouble is that some of Chabrier's piano music is commonplace, even banal; three records are simply too much. The piano sound is good, but my copy goes booming in places.

PIANO MUSIC: BOURREE FANTASQUE; PIECES PITTORESQUES; CIMO MORCEAUX POUR PIANO

Here is a choice selection of the best of Chabrier's piano music.

* JEAN CASADESUS   Odyssey   (M) 32 16 0071
                                               (S) 32 16 0072

The music is trenchantly and effectively played.

Charpentier, Marc-Antoine (1634-1704)

Formerly a pupil of Carissimi in Rome, Charpentier became director of music for the Jesuits of the Maison Professe in Paris. He wrote two operas, other stage pieces, several oratorios, and much church music. His work has been popular during the last fifteen years, particularly in France.

CHRISTMAS ORATORIO: PASTORALE SUR LA NAISSANCE DE NOTRE SEIGNEUR JESUS CHRIST

This grand, poignant work gives us new insights into the work of this long-neglected genius.

Roger Blanchard Vocal and   NONESUCH   H 71082
Instrumental Ensemble

The singing flows along admirably. The sound is spacious.

EPITHALAMIUM

This is a good example of 17th century ceremonial music. Music was then specially written and performed for baptisms, weddings, and other occasions. The feel of court life is well conveyed.

Roger Blanchard Vocal   NONESUCH   (S) H 71039
Ensemble; Orchestra de la   [Lalande, Concert d'Escu-
Societe des Concerts du   lape; Lully, Plaude; Laetare
Conservatoire de Paris   Gallia]

The Charpentier piece and the couplings are all graciously played, with spacious sound. [The couplings are also good examples of court ceremonial music of the time; the Lully piece was composed for the baptism of the Dauphin in 1668.

MAGNIFICAT; TENEBRAE LESSONS FOR HOLY WEDNESDAY: NO. 1, NO. 3; MOTETS: AVE REGINA COELORUM, QUAM PULCHRA ES

This is appealing music, both theatrical and meditative. All in all, it deserves to be heard.

* VESSIERES,
BLANCHARD   *Vocal & Instrumental
Ensemble*   Nonesuch   H 71040

The impeccable Roger Blanchard Ensemble and bass soloist Vessieres give a convincing performance, with good, warm sound.

MESSE POUR PLUSIEURS INSTRUMENTS AU LIEU DES ORGUES

The *Mass for Instruments in Place of Organ* is a bold, experimental work, and a good one. It has freshness and charm.

* CHAILLEY   *Ancient Instrument
Ensemble, Paris, Vocal &
Instrumental Ensemble*   Nonesuch   H 71130
[Louis XIII, Ballet de La Merlaison]

The music is well played and sung. The sound is clean stereo. [The work on the reverse of the disc is a slight, bucolic ballet, allegedly written by Louis XIII, King of France, himself.]

Cherubini, Maria (1760-1842)

Although he was born in Florence. Cherubini settled in Paris in 1788, and remained there for the rest of his life. In 1822, he became director of the Paris Conservatoire. Berlioz has written some amusing bits in his *Autobiography* about student hi-jinks and encounters with the cantankerous Cherubini at the Conservatoire.

Cherubini's dignified music was much admired by Beethoven, his contemporary, who considered the Italian to be, after Beethoven himself, the greatest composer of his day. The bulk of Cherubini's music is unplayed today, although Toscanini revived the *Symphony in D*. The *Requiem Mass* is heard from time to time.

MEDEA (sung in Italian)

Medea is the most notable of the 24 complete operas composed wholly by Cherubini himself. Written in Paris in 1797, *Medea* uses the old traditions of *opera comique*, with spoken dialogue for a tragic subject. This is dramatic writing, but it seems rather dry and formal to modern ears. One intriguing aspect of this opera: the recitatives, some twenty percent of the score, were added by the 19th-century organist, Franz Lachner.

      * CALLAS, SCOTTO,   EVEREST/CETRA (S)   437/3
        PIRAZZINI,
        GIACOMOTTI:
        SERAFIN

This recording is of interest because of the intense singing of Maria Callas. She recorded the opera again — and better — after she became famous. *Medea* has been, perhaps, her best role. Callas is regal and tigerish, and the way she weaves across Cherubini's "peculiar modulation" still dazzles the ear. The rest of the cast is of little distinction. The sound is acceptable, often very good.

Chopin, Frederic (1810-1849)

The son of a French father living in Poland and a Polish mother, Chopin was a child prodigy. He left Poland permanently in 1830, settling first in Vienna, then in Paris. In Paris, he became a darling of the salons, a successful pianist and teacher, and a friend of such musicians as Liszt, Bellini, Mayerbeer, and Berlioz. In 1837, Liszt introduced Chopin to George Sand, the famous writer. Thus began a ten-year liaison which, despite clashes of temperament, was deeply significant to both of them. He lived with her in Majorca in 1838 and 1839, and subsequently, in Paris and at Nohant from 1840 to 1846. Always frail, Chopin died of tuberculosis.

PLACE AND ACHIEVEMENT Chopin is a mysterious and fascinating composer. He never wrote an opera nor a symphony nor even a string quartet. But he was the greatest of all composers for the piano. Chopin explored his chosen ground inexhaustibly as no composer before or since has done.

He was one of the most strikingly original of composers. Upon hearing a bar or two of his music, the listener immediately senses the hand of Chopin. He was as obsessed with the search for the *mot juste* in music as Flaubert was in literature. Almost everything he turned out was painstakingly done and remarkably fine. No composer has a higher percentage of his works still alive and frequently played today. Chopin ranks as one of the very precious poets of music.

THE ESSENTIAL CHOPIN

ORCHESTRAL MUSIC: *2 Concertos for Piano and Orchestra.*
PIANO MUSIC: *Sonata No. 2, in B-Flat Minor; Sonata No. 3, in B Minor; 19 Nocturnes; 24 Etudes; 26 Preludes; 13 Waltzes; 4 Ballades; 4 Fantasias; 11 Polonaises; 54 Mazurkas; 4 Impromptus.*

OTHER WORKS

CHAMBER MUSIC: *Sonata for Cello and Piano.*
PIANO MUSIC: *Piano Trio; Scherzos; Barcarolles; Rondos; Variation; Fantasie-Impromptu for Piano.*
VOCAL MUSIC: *Songs.*

ANDANTE SPIANATO AND GRANDE POLONAISE
(Opus 22)

The *Polonaise* was written in 1830-21; the *Andante Spianato* was added in 1834. This work, originally composed for piano and orchestra, is now familiar to us in its piano form.

* * GRAFFMAN	VICTROLA VIC (S) 1077 [Ballades]
GULDA	MACE (S) 9060 [Bach, Mozart, Schubert program]

Graffman gives a tense, brilliant performance. The sound is good. Gulda's reading is studied, and not too convincing.

BALLADES 1, 2, 3, 4 (Opus 23, 38, 47, 52)

The four *Ballades,* composed between 1831 and 1842, are great music, dramatic, even tempestuous Chopin at his best.

* * * FRANKL	VOX (M) 12620 (S) 512620 [Fantasy in F]
* * GRAFFMAN	VICTROLA VIC (S) 1077 [Andante Spianato]
* KEMPFF	LONDON STS 15029 [No. 3]
* ASHKENAZY	MONITOR (M) 2048 [No. 2; Etudes, Opus 10/8, 25/6]

Peter Frankl's interpretation of the *Ballades* is justly famous. Piano authority Herbert Glass, in a survey of great piano records in *Stereo Review,* lists exactly three Chopin recordings. This is one of them.

Graffman's reserved performance is nevertheless lyrical. A formidable technician, he rarely shows off. Chopin's dynamic markings and other indications are scrupulously observed. The sound is the best for this piece on low-priced records.

Kempff gives a probing and eloquent reading but only one Ballade is included on this disc.

Ashkenazy presents a technically astonishing performance. The recording quality, though, is indifferent. The disc was made quite a few years ago, just after Ashkenazy, then all of seventeen, won a prize in the Warsaw Piano Competition. Ashkenazy recently again recorded the *Ballades*—a new, mercurial, superbly recorded reading on an expensive London.

CONCERTO NO. 1 IN E FOR PIANO (Opus 11)

Known to us as *No. 1*, this concerto was in fact the second in order of composition. It is a youthful, poetic work, one of the landmarks of the romantic movement. Few piano concertos of the nineteenth century are as satisfying as this one.

* * * LIPATTI	*Orchestra*	SERAPHIM	(M) 60007
* * * POLLINI, KLETZKI	*Philharmonic Orch.*	SERAPHIM	(S) 60066
* * NOVAES, PERLEA	*Bamberg Symphony Orch.*	VOX	(M) 10710 (S) 510710
* * GRAFFMAN, MUNCH	*Boston Symphony Orch.*	VICTROLA VIC [Mendelssohn, Capriccio]	(S) 1030
* FRANKL, WAGNER	*Innsbruck Smphony Orch.*	VOX	(M) 2640 (S) 52640
* BADURA-SKODA, RODZINSKI	*Vienna State Opera Orch.*	WESTMINSTER [Concerto No. 2]	(M) 18288
* MUSULIN, MUELLER-KRAY	*South West German Radio Symphony Orch.*	PERIOD [Concerto No. 2]	SHO-306

The place of honor goes to the historic version by the late Dinu Lipatti. Igor Kipnis *(Stereo Review)* commented on the Dinu Lipatti disc: "The natural, poetic quality of his playing can nowhere be heard to better advantage." Nearly every critic has called Lipatti's the definitive performance. The mono sound is faded but fair.

In a remarkably good field, my second choice is the young Italian-born Pollini. Martin Bookspan in *Stereo Review* raved about this record, saying: "Pollini must already be ranked as one of the outstanding Chopin players in the world." *High Fidelity* commented: "This is a happy, singing performance, certainly one of the best in the catalogue. Kletzki's lithe accompaniment is ideal, and Seraphim's top-notch sound sets it all off beautifully." The stereo sound is clean.

The superb reading by Novaes is poetry itself. The sound is just fair.

Graffman offers a first-rate interpretation with beautiful clarity of line. This is a first-class, much applauded reading. The sonics are excellent.

Frankl is poetic, and has an amazing sense of timing and phrasing. This is honest, untheatrical playing.

Badura-Skoda is technically uneven. [He offers Chopin's *Concerto No. 2* as well.]

The Musulin version is small-sized, but hearable.

CONCERTO NO. 2 IN F FOR PIANO (Opus 21)

Composed in 1829, this is on-rushing, exuberant, romantic writing, which requires a pianist of elegance and power.

* * NOVAES, KLEMPERER	*Vienna Symphony Orch.*	Vox [Schumann, Concerto]	11380
* MUSULIN, MUELLER-KRAY	*South-West German Radio Symphony Orch.*	PERIOD [Concerto No. 1]	SHO-306
* PENNARIO, GOLSCHMANN	*Concert Arts Symphony Orch.*	PICKWICK (S) [Liszt, Concerto No. 1]	4025
RAUCH, SMETACEK	*Prague Symphony Orch.*	PARLIAMENT (S) [Liszt, Concerto No. 2]	628
FRUGONI, GIELEN	*Vienna Volksoper Orch.*	Vox (M) (S) [Concerto No. 1]	11460 511460
BADURA-SKODA, RODZINSKI	*Vienna State Opera Orch.*	WESTMINSTER [Concerto No. 1]	18288

Irving Kolodin comments: "In deftness and finesse, Novaes is supreme here." (1955) Novaes comes off best. But the recording dates from 1951, and the sound is thin.

The other entries are not exciting, and certainly do not compare with the many fine performances offered in the *Concerto No. 1.* Branka Musulin is perhaps best after Novaes; The New York *Times'* Harold Schonberg said of this record in 1955: "I have heard much worse Chopin from pianists of far greater reputation."

Pennario is on the overly flashy side, but offers the best of the stereo version in our low priced range.

Ranch is quite unremarkable.

Frugoni's version is spirited, but unpoetic.

Badura-Skoda's is old disc serviceable, and squeezes in Chopin's other piano concerto, as well.

ETUDES (Opus 10 and Opus 25)

Opus 10 was written between 1829 and 1832; *Opus 25* between 1832 and 1836. The youthful, vigorous *Etudes,* though less rewarding than the *Nocturnes* or *Preludes,* are still of much interest for lovers of piano music.

* * ANIEVAS	SERAPHIM (S)	60081
* NOVAES	3-Vox SVBX-5401 [Preludes; Sonata No. 2; Waltzes]	
BADURA-SKODA	WESTMINSTER (M)	18811

The young pianist Agustin Anievas, who made a name for himself as winner in the first Mitropoulos Competition, is here revealed as a Chopin player worthy of respect. A lyrical grace, and an almost self-effacing love of Chopin, can both be sensed on this beautifully recorded disc. *Saturday Review's* Irving Kolodin comments: "Anievas is treading in the footsteps of some of the greatest Chopin performers of past decades. . . . Seraphin is doing a real service to this very considerable artist in making his fine work available at a low price." This disc appeared on *Saturday Review's* list of "Best Recordings of 1968."

Novaes disappoints. To lean on Harold Schonberg: "My guess is that she had not looked at some of the *Etudes* for many years before whipping them into shape for the recording session."

Badura-Skoda's performance is reasonable. The mono is decent.

FANTASIE IN F MINOR (Opus 49)

Here is virile, top-drawer Chopin, which is a far cry from the tuberose deathly-white image of Chopin that many people hold. This is one of Chopin's supreme works.

* * * FRANKL	Vox [Ballades]	(5) 12620
* * KEMPFF	London [Piano music]	STS-15029

The young Hungarian pianist Peter Frankl delivers a Chopin devoid of mannerisms and affectations—an almost unheard-of feat. His playing is straightforward—even restrained. In listening to this technically dazzling music, one gets above all a sense of Frankl's clarity. A remarkable disc! A rave from *High Fidelity:* "If you want to hear these noble creations played with an exemplary architectural sweep and truly Beethovenian profundity (this music is *not* typical Chopin), Frankl is our man."

Kempff gives a ruggedly authoritative performance. The 1950's stereo sound is pleasant.

The Novaes disc, a treasure, is no longer available.

FOUR IMPROMPTUS

Chopin's four inspired *Impromptus* remain among his most popular music.

* BALOGH	Lyrichord [Bolero; Berceuse]	(M) 20
* HORSZOWSKI	3 Vox [Concerto No. 1; Nocturnes]	VBX-402

Balogh gives a meticulous, careful reading.

Horszowski is also on the careful and sober side, which, for me, is frustrating.

The man to hear is Rubenstein on an expensive RCA Victor disk.

INTRODUCTION ET POLONAISE, FOR PIANO AND CELLO (Opus 3)

In a letter to a friend, Chopin shrugged off this piece of 1829 by saying: "There is nothing in it but glitter—a salon piece for ladies."

* ROSTROPOVICH	MONITOR	(S)	2119

The great Rostropovich is impressive as always. The stereo sound is agreeable.

FIFTY-ONE MAZURKAS

This is first-rate Chopin. Almost every great romantic pianist has recorded some of the tempestuous *Mazurkas* at one time or another, but almost all versions have sunk without a trace since Rubinstein, from his Olympian heights, delivered them complete for RCA Victor on stereo.

* * NOVAES	Vox [11 Mazurkas]	(5) 7920
FRUGONI	2 Vox [Complete]	SVUX-52017

The great lady, Novaes, is the best at our price. The sound is good. Frugoni is highly spirited, but quite outclassed.

NOCTURNES (20)

The *Nocturnes* are starlight music. As James Huneker wrote, "They have an agitated, remorseful countenance; others seen in profile only while many are like whisperings at dusk—Verlaine moods."

* * NOVAES	2-Vox	9632-½
* HABLER	2-Vox	SVUX 52007

After Rubinstein's supreme reading of the *Nocturnes,* it is difficult to accept any other, even that of so fine an artist as Madame Novaes. My advice is to splurge on Rubinstein's two-record set on the high-priced RCA Victor. You won't regret it.

Novaes' version, nevertheless, is quite lovely. (But Rubinstein is transcendental.)

Haebler's reading is suave, without much poetry or sensitivity.

Chopin lovers are also directed to a stunning version by the Czech pianist Moravec on a high-priced Connoisseur label.

POLONAISES

In the *Polonaises,* as with the mazurkas, the voice of the nationalist Chopin is heard. Many of the *Polonaises* are martial, patriotic pieces with the rhythms of Polish folkdances.

* * CZIFFRA   PHILLIPS WS (M/S) 9052
                                [6 Polonaises]

* * FRANKL   2-Vox   SVUX 52024
                                [Complete]

BOUKOFF   2-WESTMINSTER   18779/80
                                [Complete, No. 1-16]

Cziffra gives a splendidly bravura performance with fine sound. A noted Lisztian, he employs the same bravura approach to the *Polonaises,* and I like it.

Frankl's version is impressive, taut, analytical, and altogether absorbing. Poles apart from Cziffra's ultra-romantic version, Frankl's may be termed a cool, mod, 1960's reading.

I do not care for the hectic powerhouse playing by Boukoff.

TWENTY-FOUR PRELUDES (Opus 28)

Chopin wrote Opus 28 within the years 1836 to 1839—perhaps earlier. There are 24 preludes in Opus 28; two more preludes were discovered in 1918. The *Preludes* can be described as little poems — brief, lovely miniatures.

* * NOVAES   Vox   (M) 10948
                                              (S) 510948
                                [Sonata No. 2]

Novaes has the field to herself, as well she may. Harold Schonberg prefers her reading of the *Preludes* to that of Rubinstein, and called it (in 1955) "the best modern interpretation." The sound is agreeable.

SCHERZOS 1, 2, 3, 4 (Opus 20, 31, 39, 54)

To my mind, the *Scherzos* are less poetic and less interesting than Chopin's other excursions into solo piano forms. Most of them are turbulant, excited pieces, very popular, but not as popular as they used to be in the days when a pianist's hair swept over the keys and he turned his profile towards a gasping audience.

* NOVAES (No. 1 and 3)   Vox   (5) 15000
                                [Sonata No. 3]

Novaes again stands alone, but this is not one of her better performances. The sound is decent.

SONATA NO. 2 IN B-FLAT FOR PIANO (Opus 35)

This sonata, which contains the famous funeral march, was a puzzle to Chopin's contemporaries. Even the admiring Schumann wrote ". . . But how many beauties, too, this piece contains! The idea of calling it a sonata is a caprice, if not a jest, for he [Chopin] has simply bound together four of his wildest children, to smuggle them under this name into a place to which they could not else have penetrated."

* * GILELS	SERAPHIM	(M) 60010
	[Shostakovich, Preludes]	
* * NOVAES	VOX	(M) 10940
		(S) 510940
	[Preludes]	
* KEMPFF	LONDON	STS 15050
	[Sonata No. 3]	
BADURA-SKODA	WESTMINSTER	18854
	[Sonata No. 3]	

The Russian Emil Gilels is at his best here—lyrical and sensitive, and yet virile. This is a much-praised record.

Novaes is all temperament, in a remarkable reading in which Harold Schonberg heard "fire and color, poetry and imagination."

Wilhelm Kempff was a vastly respected German pianist a generation ago. His Beethoven renditions were admired with the awed reverence usually reserved for the Holy Grail. His Chopin, however, is of less cosmic interest. This is what can only be termed enigmatic Chopin—and unsatisfying. But Kempff is nevertheless a master pianist.

Badura-Skoda, studious rather than poetic, is outclassed.

SONATA NO. 3 IN B FOR PIANO (Opus 58)

Composed in 1844, this difficult and tempestuous writing has always attracted pianists who are proud of their octave swoops.

* * NOVAES	VOX	(M) 15000
		(S) 515000
	[Scherzos]	
* KEMPFF	LONDON	STS 15050
	[Sonata No. 2]	
REGULES	COUNTERPOINT/ESOTERIC	
		(M) 570
		(S) 5558
	[Liszt, Sonata]	

BADURA-SKODA		WESTMINSTER		18854
		[Sonata No. 2]		
SOREL	—	MONITOR	(S)	2044
		[in piano collection]		

Novaes delivers a highly personalized reading, quite impetuous and freely romantic. The sound is dated.

Kempff plays with heavy grandeur. He is a masterly technician but unconvincing in Chopin.

Regules is highly emotional—little else.

Badura-Skoda, an admirable pianist in Mozart and Bach, does not impress in Chopin.

Sorel is competent and hearable.

LES SYLPHIDES

This extremely popular ballet was built around the music of Chopin. The *Nocturne in A-Flat Major* and other favorites are effectively used here in a pleasing, highly romantic style.

| * DESORMIERE | *Paris Conservatoire Orch.* | RICHMOND | 19028 |
| | | [Ibert, Divertissement] | |

No stereo version is available at a low price at the moment. Desormiere gives a good romantic treatment, but the sound is dim.

WALTZES

Chopin wrote 15 waltzes, perhaps the most popular of all his solo piano pieces. Composed between 1829 and 1847, they were to some extent inspired by the Viennese waltzes of Johann Strauss, Senior. Strauss wrote waltzes for dancing; but Chopin, as Hunker remarked, wrote dances, "for the soul, not for the body."

* * * LIPATTI	ODYSSEY	(S) 321 600 57
* * * NOVAES	VOX	(M) 8170
		(S) 58170
* * HARASIEWICZ	PHILLIPS WS	(M/S) 9034
* HAEBLER	VOX	(M) 11970
		(S) 511970

Lipatti is supreme in a famous, classic performance. This reading has been cherished for a generation. *High Fidelity* comments: ". . . some of the most exquisite Chopin playing ever recorded. The sound on the present reissue tends to be rather tubby and claustrophobic—but with artistry such as Lipatti's, one adjusts quickly to all mechanical deficiencies." Harold

Schonberg said: "Lipatti is more direct, without the color of Novaes. His is beautifully regulated playing—and yet one wishes for just a bit more. After a while his interpretations here begin to sound metronomic and four-square." The sound is poor.

Novaes gives her usual excellent, poetic interpretation. Schonberg commented: "Novaes makes her own rules, and her ideas often take a capricious turn. No matter."

Also of much interest is the fiery, spontaneous playing of Adam Harasiewicz. This young Polish pianist is a Chopin specialist, and this is a poetic, imaginative reading with sure technical ability. His disc offers the best sound in this listing.

Haebler is better known for her Mozart, but this is nevertheless a pleasing performance.

CHOPIN PIANO RECITALS

There are no end of Chopin programs and of Chopin pieces on record collections of piano music. For some reason, these collections are not very successful.

* * KEMPFF	LONDON	STS 15029
* * NOVAES	VOX	(M) 7810
		(S) 57810
* * FOU TS' ONG	PARLIAMENT	159
* BOLET	EVEREST	6079
ALEXIS	PERIOD SHO (M) 330	
	(S) ST-2330	
SIROONI	CONCERT CLASSICS	
	(M) 4149	

The Kempff and Novaes discs can be recommended for the virtues above in my remarks about their other Chopin records.

Fou Ts'ong is highly equipped, an artist to his fingertips. These are low-keyed, cool performances.

Bolet is glittering and fiery; he will appeal to those who like their Chopin ultra-passionate rather than poetic.

Alexis is agreeable but little more.

Sirooni's version is unremarkable.

Cilea, Francesco (1866-1950)

Cilea, an Italian, taught in several conservatories in Italy. His best operatic effort, *Adriana Lecouvreur,* is still quite popular in Italy.

ANDRIANA LECOUVREUR

An accomplished work of considerable charm, this second-rate opera contains a few pleasant, melodious arias.

> * GAVAZZI,   EVEREST/CETRA   S 457/3
> PRANDELLI,
> TRUCCATO PACE,
> CLABASSI,
> SIMONETTO

The singers have light-weight voices, and Gavazzi is rather unsteady at times. But on the whole, this set is enjoyable. This recording was made some years ago, and the so-so sound varies from disc to disc.

L'ARLESIANA (The Girl from Arles)

This opera—based on an earthy, rural tale—is an attempt at realism.

> * TASSINARI,   EVEREST/CETRA   S 430/2
> TAGLIAVINI,
> GALLI, SILVERI,
> BASILE

The singing is spirited, but little more. However, Tassinari goes shrill now and then; be prepared to cut down the highs. Reprocessed sound is fairly decent.

Cimarosa, Domenico (1749-1801)

The son of an Italian bricklayer, Cimarosa was one of the foremost opera composers of his period. He worked chiefly in Rome and Naples. For a while he was in the service of Catherine II of Russia. He wrote at least 65 operas, as well as masses, oratorios, sonatas, and other works.

CONCERTO FOR OBOE AND STRINGS

Four of Cimarosa's seldom-heard harpsichord sonatas of one movement each were skillfully assembled into a tasteful oboe concerto by the Australian composer, Arthur Benjamin, in 1942. This music is astonishingly convincing, and very popular today.

> * * HOLLIGER, MAAG   *Bamberg Symphony Orch.*   VANGUARD   (S)   191
> [Bellini, Donizetti, Salieri, oboe works]

The playing is crisp and lively. The sound is good.

CONCERTO FOR 2 FLUTES IN G

The piece is entirely beguiling, in its innocuous way.

> * * NICOLET,   *Berlin Philharmonic*   HELIODOR   H 25033/
> DEMMLER,   HS 24033
> MARKEVITCH   [Corelli, Concerto Grosso in D, Opus 6, No. 1; Vivaldi, Cello Concerto in G, P. 120; Pergolesi, Concertino No. 2 in G]

Aurele Nicolet and Fritz Demmler provide graceful flute playing. Sound is acceptable. [The other works on the disc are also pleasing; the record is a good baroque sampler.]

IL MATRIMONIO SEGRETO   (The Secret Marriage)

Cimarosa's most famous comic opera is still going strong since its premiere in Vienna in 1792.

> NONI, SIMIONATO,   EVEREST/CETRA   (S) 422/3
> VALLETTI,
> BRUSCANTINI,
> WOLF-FERRARI

The singing is competent, but little more. The sound is harsh.

SONATA IN C; SONATA IN C MINOR

Here is charming, poignant music that beguiles the ear.

* * * SGRIZZI   NONESUCH   H 71117

The admirable harpsichordist, Luciano Sgrizzi, plays with taste and affection. The fine room-sized sound comes from Cycnus of Paris.

[The Sgrizzi record, actually entitled "Eighteenth-Century Harpsichord Music," includes a variety of works by long-forgotten names, some of them glittering composers in their day. Baldassare Galuppi (1806-1885), of whom Browning wrote in his famous poem *A Toccata of Galuppi,* composed no less than 112 operas. Pietro Paradies (1707-1791) taught harpsichord and singing in London. The elegant composed Giovani Rutini (1723-1797) became music teacher to the future Catherine the Great. Pietro Scarlatti (1679-1750) was the older brother of the famous Domenico. Pietro's only surviving music is a set of six keyboard toccatas, one of which is presented here. Domenico Zipoli (1688-1726) gave up composing in 1717 to become a Jesuit in Argentina. These are all worthy composers. Specific works included are: Galuppi, *Sonata No. 9 in F minor;* Paradies, *Sonata in A No. 6;* Pergolesi, *Sonata in C;* Rutini, *Sonata in F, Opus 2, No. 3;* D. Scarlatti, *3 Sonatas in F, K. 274-276 (L.297, 328, S.20);* P. Scarlatti, *Toccata in G minor;* Zipoli, *Suite in C.*]

Copland, Aaron (1900-   )

Born in Brooklyn, New York, Copland studied with Nadia Boulanger and other teachers. In 1925, he won a Guggenheim Fellowship; and in 1930, he was awarded a $5,000 RCA-Victor prize for his *Dance Symphony*.

He has been a member of the board of directors of the American League of Composers, and has played an enormous role in furthering the interests of this group. Copland has organized special concerts and festivals, and he writes and lectures extensively. He has composed music for several Hollywood films, including *Of Mice and Men* and *Our Town*.

PLACE AND ACHIEVEMENT   Copland and Samuel Barber are regarded as the two leading American composers of this generation. Copland's early works showed the influence of Stravinsky, but he found his own style when he attempted to capture the spirit and charm of American folk music. His best and most popular works, such as *Appalachian Spring* ballet and suite, are pleasantly lyrical and melodic. His more esoteric works are severe, astringent, and show the hand of a sure craftsman.

Today, in comparison to the revolutionary sounds of electronic music and "the new music," much of Copland's once-daring work sounds comfortably traditional.

THE ESSENTIAL COPLAND
ORCHESTRAL MUSIC: *Appalachian Spring; Billy the Kid; El Salón México; Symphony No. 3.*
PIANO MUSIC: *Piano Fantasy; Piano Variations.*

OTHER MAJOR WORKS
Rodeo; A Lincoln Portrait, for Narrator and Orchestra; The Second Hurricane; Danzon Cubano; Quartet for Piano and Strings; Piano Sonata; Concerto for Clarinet and Strings.

APPALACHIAN SPRING   (Suite)

This music captures the nostalgic, homespun, retrospective essence of America, the America of Carl Sandburg. One of Copeland's finest works, *Appalachian Spring* has been compared to Smetana's *Moldau,* and indeed contains some of the warm, simplistic spirit of the Bohemian piece.

Appalachian Spring was written in 1944 as a ballet for Martha Graham. From this, the composer extracted a suite of eight connected sections, the version usually played.

SUSSKIND	*London Symphony Orch.*	EVEREST (M) 6002 (S) 3002 [Gould, Spirituals]
MITCHELL	*National Symphony Orch.*	WESTMINSTER (M) 18284 [El Salón México; Billy the Kid]

Neither performance can be called exciting. The Susskind recording has better sound.

BILLY THE KID

The ballet appears to be the form most congenial to Copland. This 1938 work, another ballet extract, provides more musical Americana—even a kind of musical slang. It works.

* * JOHANOS	*Dallas Symphony Orch.*	TURNABOUT (S) 34169 [Fanfare for the Common Man; Rodeo]
* COPLAND	*London Symphony Orch.*	EVEREST (M) 6015 (S) 3015 [Statements]
MITCHELL	*National Symhony Orch.*	WESTMINSTER (M) 18284 [Appalachian Spring; El Salón México; Fanfare for the Common Man]

The Johanos disc is most satisfying. The performance is clean, and very Western in style. The sound is good. [The reverse side is also quite satisfying.]

Though conducted by Copland himself, the London musicians are too pallid for this rough-and-ready fun music.

Mitchell is less interesting.

PIANO VARIATIONS AND PIANO FANTASY

The *Piano Variation* (1930) comprise one of Copland's more technically daring works. They form a complex piece, and an important one in the development of contemporary American music. Here Copland utilizes elements of Schoenberg's revolutionary twelve-tone system while still holding on to the traditional system of keys and scale structures.

Composer-critic William Flanigan, evaluating the *Variations* in *Hi-Fi Stereo Review,* states: "No one who is familiar with the history of modern American music has to be told that Copland's *Piano Variations* is a legend in its own right and a work of prime significance in the composer's musical development. Its stature as a sort of granitic masterwork has been questioned by virtually no cultivated musician—no matter what his stylistic allegiance—since its composition."

The *Piano Fantasy,* written in 1957, is, in the composer's words, "based upon a sequence of ten different tones of the chromatic scale. . . . The *Piano Fantasy* is by no means rigorously controlled twelve-tone music, but it does make liberal use of devices associated with that technique."

* * * MASSELOS   ODYSSEY   (M/S) 32 16 0040

William Masselos has made a name for himself as an exponent of contemporary music. The playing is rugged and expert. Flanigan says: "I couldn't recommend more highly either the music itself or Masselos' performance of it at any price."

EL SALON MEXICO

This delightful, colorful souvenir of Mexico is usually relegated to Pops programs, but may yet survive the bulk of Copland's more solemn works.

* FIEDLER	*Boston Pops Orch.*	VICTROLA (LM) 1928 [Grofe, Grand Canyon Suite]
MITCHELL	*National Symphony Orch.*	WESTMINSTER (M) 18284 [Appalachian Spring; Billy the Kid]

Fiedler's version is colorful and highly spirited. [On the reverse side of the record, you'll find Grofe's light, melodious *Grand Canyon Suite,* one of the most popular orchestral pieces ever written by an American.]

The Mitchell recording offers a good program, with fair mono sound.

The most inspired performance of *El Salon Mexico* available is Bernstein on a high-priced Columbia disc.

QUIET CITY

This 1940 work, originally composed for the play of the same name by Irwin Shaw, is threnodic music for trumpet, English horn, and orchestra.

JANSSEN	*Los Angeles Symphony Orch.*	EVEREST (M) 6118 (S) 3118 [Cowell, Ancient Desert Drone; Ives, Three Places in New England]

Janssen's greatest virtue is that he evokes a nostalgic mood in this interesting program of American music; in other respects, the performance, though adequate, is not outstanding. The sound is adequate. [A note on the couplings: Henry Cowell (1897-1965), a tireless investigator, is now a patron saint of today's iconoclasts. He is best remembered for his invention of tone-clusters—successive scale-steps sounded simultaneously. He also did much to transform the piano into a percussive instrument, with plucking, pounding, etc.]

RODEO

This brilliantly orchestrated ballet suite was originally written in 1948 for Agnes de Mille.

* JOHANOS	Dallas Orch.	TURNABOUT (S) 34169
		[Billy the Kid; Fanfare for the Common Man]

Johanos does well by this spirited, rowdy music. The sound is good.

STATEMENTS FOR ORCHESTRA (1933-1935)

One of Copland's "serious" compositions, this work was originally commissioned for the now defunct League of Composers, and was performed by the Minneapolis Symphony led by Eugene Ormandy. Of only mild interest, the work is hardly heard today.

COPLAND	London Symphony Orch.	EVEREST	(M) 6015
			(S) 3015
	[Billy the Kid]		

Copland, as conductor, is just fair—but the reading, of course, is authoritative. The sound is clean.

SYMPHONY NO. 3

This tight, ambitious work of 1946 is Copland's most successful effort to escape being classified as a composer of "orchestral folklore," a role in which he proved to be successful.

* COPLAND	London Symphony Orch.	EVEREST	(M) 6018
			(S) 3018

The composer himself conducts; some collectors may choose this disc just to hear Copland. However, Dorati on an expensive Mercury provides a far more convincing performance with much better sound.

Corelli, Arcangelo (1653-1713)

Corelli had an impressive reputation both as violinist and composer. An Italian, he studied at Bologna, traveled about Germany, and returned to Rome to enjoy the patronage of Cardinal Pietro Ottoboni. Corelli is generally regarded as the creator of the concerto grosso in its final form; Bach, born 33 years later, studied Corelli as a model. Less inventive than Vivaldi, Corelli nevertheless wrote music that is vivacious, intimate, and more satisfying than most other Italian baroque. He was not very prolific, for his day; the entire list of his known works totals only 72.

CONCERTI GROSSI (Opus 6)

The twelve concerti grossi of Corelli were vastly exciting works in his day—as popular and as important as symphonies were to be in the 19th century. Corelli's *Concerti Grossi* went through innumerable editions, and were studied by all serious musicians.

* GOBERMAN	*Vienna Sinfonia*	3-ODYSSEY (M) 32 36 0001 (S) 32 36 0002
* BEAUCAMP	*Rouen Orchestra (No. 9)*	PHILLIPS WS (M/S) 9045 [W. F. Bach, Symphony; Lully, The Triumph of Love; Purcell, Married Beau]
* LEHMANN	*Bavarian State Orch. (No. 1)*	HELIODOR (S) 25033 [Cinemarosa, 2-flutes Concerto; Pergolesi, Concertinos; Vivaldi, Cello-Concerto]
WARCHAL	*Slovak Ensemble (1, 3, 6, 7)*	PARLIAMENT (S) 610

Goberman provides a spirited three-record set, which is a bit much for the casual listener. The music is certainly worth-while, however.

The Beaucamp disc has only *Concerto Grosso No. 9,* but the playing is graceful, and the rest of the program on the record is worth-while as well.

Only one Corelli piece is offered on the Lehmann disc. The playing is lilting, and the couplings include some charming small concertos.

The Warchal interpretation is too ponderous, and a disappointment.

CONCERTO GROSSO (Opus 6, No. 8)
("Christmas Concerto")

Concerto Grosso No. 8, the "Christmas Concerto," is probably the loveliest piece Corelli wrote.

* *	*Slovak Chamber Orch.*	CROSSROADS	22 16 0198
* * TATRAI	*Hungarian Chamber Orch.*	MONITOR (S) 2056 [Tartini,Cello-Concerto; Vivaldi, Symphony]	
*	*Prague Chamber Orch.*	CROSSROADS (S) 22 16 0158 [Fux, Lully, Purcell]	
AKOS	*Chicago Strings*	PIROUTTE (S) 19021 [Dvorak, Serenade in E; Mozart, Divertimentos, K. 136]	
HEILLER	*Vienna Symphony Orch.*	PERIOD SHO 301 [Mozart, Flute-harp Concerto]	

The Slovak Chamber Orchestra offers gentle, pensive Corelli, and I like it.

Tatrai and the Hungarians take a far more vigorous approach. The playing is excellent. With the Corelli "Christmas" concerto, this record is the best bet for anyone who wants a varied program.

The Prague disc is pleasant, but little more. To my ears, the other pieces are quite bland.

Akos and the Chicago Strings are undistinguished.

The playing on the Heiller record is routine, and offers nothing out of the ordinary.

SONATAS (12) Opus 1

This is striking and original music. The baroque musician in Corelli's day was expected to be a musical creator as well as performer. Improvisation was expected, especially from the keyboard player. A keyboard player was given a bare bass line and harmonic figures; he was expected to develop from these a complete harpsichord part. The soloists on the other medolic instruments also improvised to a degree—adding trills, ornaments, and other embellishments.

* * GOBERMAN, TREE, EARLE, SCHNEIDER (Opus 4)	2-ODYSSEY (M) 32 26 0005 (S) 32 26 0006

This beautifully played set offers an excellent example of baroque improvisation. The stereo sound is fair.

SONATAS FOR STRINGS, ORGAN, AND HARPSICHORD; CHURCH SONATAS (Opus 1, complete); CHAMBER SONATAS (Opus 2, complete)

This mature, elevated writing demonstrates why Corelli's music was so highly renowned throughout Europe.

Musicorum Arcadia   3-Vox DL   37

The devotee of baroque music will revel in these three records; others might find this set overmuch. The playing is elegant; the sound, pleasant.

Couperin, Francois (1668-1773)

Francois Couperin is called "Le Grand" to distinguish him from his father, uncle, and other assorted musical relatives. Born in Paris, he became organist at the church of St. Gervais. He was also organist to Louis XIV at Versailles, and he taught several children of the royal family. He wrote hundreds of much-admired small pieces for the harpsichord, as well as an excellent treatise on the art of playing the harpsichord. His church music is dignified; and at times, deeply impressive.

CONCERTS ROYAUX

Couperin's *Concerts Royaux* are simply concert music in dance form scored for an ensemble group; they are not "concerti" in the Italian sense. This is agreeable music for trios, quartets, and other ensembles. It provides good examples of French classicism.

| * RAMPAL | *Ensemble* | Music Guild | (S) | 108 |

This disc includes the *Concert Royal No. 14; Concert Royal No. 10; Sonata "L'Astree"; Sonata "L'Imperiale";* and *Concert Royal No. 6.* The playing is polished, and the sonics are acceptable.

THE FOURTH BOOK OF PIECES FOR HARPSICHORD (Excerpts)

Most of Couperin's harpsichord music is arranged in *ordres,* or suites. The pieces are nuggets of refinement, variety, and discipline; two centuries later, they cast a profound spell over Debussy and Ravel.

| * HARICH-SCHNEIDER | Mace | (S) | 9081 |

The music is imaginatively played. Sound is dry but acceptable.

HARPSICHORD WORKS

Typical of Couperin at his best, these exquisite French miniatures remind the listener of the paintings of Watteau. The fanciful titles suggest character sketches or amusing allusions from the world of the *Fete galante.*

| * * * VAN DE WIELE | Nonesuch | H 71037 |

This recording provides an excellent sampler of "Le Grand Couperin." The music is charmingly played, with spirit and sensitivity. This is a lovely, warmly recorded disc. Titles include: *L'Arlequine; L'Attendris-*

sante; Les Barricades mystèrieuses; Les Calotins et les calotines ou La Pièce à trétous; Le Carillon de Cythère; Les Fastes de la grande et ancienne Ménestrandiese; La Favorite; Les Folies française ou Les Dominos; La Garnier; Les Ombres erantes; Prelude from L'Art de toucher le clavecin; Le Rossignol en amour; Le Tic-toc-choc ou Les Maillotins.

LES GOUTS-REUNIS

This discreet chamber music is well worth hearing now and then.

* RAMPAL	MUSIC GUILD (M/S)	21

This recording presents *"Les Gouts-reunis": No. 6, in B-flat; No. 10, in A Minor; No. 14, in D Minor; Sonatas: "L'Astree"*; and *"L'Imperiale."* The ensemble provides brisk French playing, with occasional flute embellismments by M. Rampal. The recording has fine, room-sized sound.

MESSE POUR LES COUVENTS (Complete)

ROBERT	*Organ of St.-Merry, Paris*	NONESUCH H 71150 [L. Couperin, Allemande in G Minor (No. 92); Sarabande en Canon in D Minor (No. 47); Chaconne in G Minor (1658, No. 122)]

The mass is complete here, but it is better played on the Turnabout disc of excerpts, listed above. The sound is pleasant. [A note on the couplings: Louis Couperin (1626-1661), uncle to "Le Grand" Couperin, was a string player in the royal service, and an accomplished but unspectacular writer for keyboard.]

MESSE POUR LES COUVENTS (Excerpts)

Couperin's two organ masses were composed to be played in alternation with the vocal parts of the Mass. Lovers of organ music will find them of interest.

* ISOIR	*Organ of the Notre Dame de St. Etienne; Organ of the Cathedrale d'Auch*	TURNABOUT TV (S) 34074 [Lebegue, Magnificat No. 1]

Isoir shows good style and imaginative playing. The sound is fine. [A note on the couplings: Nicholas Lebegue (1630-1702), organist to Louis XIV, was an unoriginal composer; his *Magnificat No. 1* provides an adequate filler for the back of the record.]

Debussy, Claude (1862-1918)

Born in Saint-Germain-en-Laye, near Paris, Debussy became a student at the Paris Conservatory. He won the Grand Prix de Rome in 1884. He first became known for his *Quartet* composed in 1893, and then for the orchestral piece *Afternoon of a Faun*. In his life in Paris, he devoted himself to conducting, to musical criticism, and to composition. His music at first was hotly disputed, but has steadily found an ever-widening public. He died of cancer in Paris at age fifty-six.

PLACE AND ACHIEVEMENT Debussy holds in music the same esteem given to his contemporaries, the French Impressionist painters whose ideals and aims he shared. His music is refined, sensuous, subtle; it is marked by an economy of means, a search for clear and luminous orchestration, and a scorn of bathetic emotion and theatricality.

Many people today — musicians, too — are startled to hear Debussy hailed by the young men of the "New Music" of the 1960's, as a spiritual ancestor. Yet the truth is that Debussy was a great innovator. In the half-century since his death, his stature has grown remarkably.

Debussy once viewed as a lightweight water-colorist, or as a fascinatingly fastidious composer who was not quite first-rate, has now come into his own. His great qualities, very French and very subtle, derive from a firm, lucid intellect. A master of musical texture, he achieves marvelous effects of color, light and shadow, and poetic sensitivity. As Sackville-West has written, "Debussy's art belongs to the great Gallic tradition which embraces artists as various as La Fontaine and Mallarme, Claude and Seurat."

THE ESSENTIAL DEBUSSY

ORCHESTRAL MUSIC: *L'Apres-Midi d'un Faune; Nocturnes; La Mer; Iberia; Image No. 2.*

OPERA: *Pelleas et Melisande.*

PIANO MUSIC: *24 Preludes; Suite Bergamasque; Images; Children's Corner.*

CHAMBER MUSIC: *Quartet in G Minor; Sonata for Violin and Piano.*

OTHER WORKS

CANTATAS: *Le Martyre de St. Sebastian; La Demoiselle Elue.*

ORCHESTRAL MUSIC: *Gigues and Ronde des Printemps, Images Nos. 1 and 3 for Orchestra.*

CHAMBER MUSIC: *Sonata for Cello and Piano.*

PIANO MUSIC: *Pour le Piano; Masques; L'Isle Joyeuse; Estampes; 12 Etudes.*

SONGS: *Cinque Poemes de Baudelaire; Fetes Galantes; Chansons de Bilitis; Trois Ballades de Villon; Trois Ballades de Mallarme.*

IBERIA (No. 2 from IMAGES POUR ORCHESTRE)

After listening to this music, it is hard to believe that Debussy, in a lifetime, spent only three hours in San Sebastian, and never set foot in any other corner of Spain. Yet the Spanish composer Maurice de Falla remarked that this Frenchman had taught all the Spanish composers how to use the folk materials of their country. The romantic music portrays the Spain of Debussy's dreams.

De Falla described the piece by saying: "Echoes from the villages, a kind of *sevillana* — the generic theme of this work — which seems to float in a clear atmosphere of scintillating light; the intoxicating spell of Andalusian nights. . . . All this whirls in the air, approaches and recedes, and our imagination is kept awake and dazzled by the power of an intensely expressive and richly varied music."

* * REINER	*Chicago Symphony Orch.*	VICTROLA VIC (S) 1025 [Liszt, Mephisto; Tchaikovsky, Overture 1812]
* * TOSCANINI	*NBC Symphony Orch.*	VICTROLA VIC (M) 1246 [La Mer; Franck, Psyche]
* MUNCH	*French National Radio Orch.*	NONESUCH (S) 71189 [Albeniz, Iberia]
* FOURNET	*Czech Philharmonic*	CROSSROADS (S) 22 16 0188 [Rondes; Ravel, Ma Mere; Pavane for a Dead Princess]
BLOOMFIELD	*Rochester Philharmonic*	EVEREST (M) 6060 (S) 3060 [Ravel, Rapsodie; La Valse]

Reiner gives a sharply defined and colorful performance. His interpretation is fresh rather than showy. The orchestral playing and the sound are both first-rate. Because of its technical difficulties — intricate tempo relationships; and other problems — this music has been called a "conductor's trap," but the great Fritz came through with honors.

The Toscanini version is a marvelous example of "the Maestro's" clear-thinking powers, but the sound, so vital in this delicate music, is dessicated.

Munch is the right man for this music, but the French playing is rather pedestrian. [The coupling is with Albeniz's piquant treatment of *Iberia*.]

Fournet is straight-forward; not much subtlety nor imagination.

Bloomfield is sadly outclassed.

JEUX — POEME DANSE

Jeux was composed in 1912 for Diaghilev's PaPrisienne ballet seasons. The scenario is concerned with games of tennis and flirtation. This work is important Debussy, and is regarded by our contemporary "New Music" composers as a landmark in twentieth century experimentation in music.

* * * ANSERMET	Orch. Suisse Romande	LONDON STS (S) 15022 [Danse; Dukas]
* GOBERMAN	Vienna New Symphony Orch.	ODYSSEY (S) 31 26 0226 [Nocturnes; Prelude]
BAUDO	Czech Philharmonic	CROSSROADS (S) 22 16 0174 [Prelude; Premiere]

Ansermet is the right man for this translucent music. The sound is warm and clear. The *Stereo Record Guide* calls it "one of the finest Debussy discs in the catalogue." *High Fidelity* comments: "Ansermet's delicately precise yet glowing performance of *Jeux* easily outclasses the recorded competition."

Goberman, more at home in eighteenth century music, is just fair here. The playing is indifferent. The sound is fair.

Baudo and the Czechs though pleasant are unexciting.

LA MER

The Sea, completed in 1905, is Debussy's masterpiece in the orchestral form. There is no "program"; the music is an impressionistic and beautiful portrait of the sea and its subtly changing moods.

* * * TOSCANINI	NBC Symphony Orch.	VICTROLA VIC (M) 1246 [Iberia]
* * MUNCH	Boston Symphony Orch.	VICTROLA VIC (S) 1041 [Ravel, Rhapsodie Espagnole]
* LEINSDORF	Los Angeles Philharmonic	PICKWICK (S) 4015 [Ravel, Daphnis et Chloe Suite]
* DESORMIERE	Czech Philharmonic	PARLIAMENT (M) 110 [Nocturnes]
* FOURNET	Czech Philharmonic	CROSSROADS (M) 22 16 0091 (S) 22 16 0092 [Nocturnes]
* BARBIROLLI	Halle Orch.	VANGUARD (S) 177 [Ravel, Daphnis et Chloe Suite]
VAN BEINUM	Concertgebouw Orch.	PHILLIPS WS (S) 9097 [Nocturnes]

Toscanini's scintillating reading of this music is legendary. One of many tributes to this recording, paid by Edward Sackville-West and

Desmond Shawe-Taylor in *The Record Guide,* states: "One had thought it impossible that every detail should emerge quite so clearly, without to some extent impairing the sweep and surge and swell of this marvelous music." The sound is old and cramped, but after a few moments under Toscanini's spell, you forget its limitations.

Munch and the impeccable Boston Symphony offer both modern sonics and a fresh, sensuous performance.

High tension and taut control are offered on the Leinsdorf disc, but the orchestral playing leaves much to be desired.

Desormiere delivers a low-keyed, soft-focus reading, for those who like their sea becalmed.

The Fournet disc follows the Desormiere pattern.

The *Stereo Record Guide* found Barbirolli's version "a tremendously vivid and exciting musical experience, but undermodulated recording, that needs boosting up, gets in the way." I agree.

Van Beinum's version is ponderous, and is foggily "enhanced for stereo."

NOCTURNES (NUAGES, FETES, SIRENES)

Originally planned as a work in three parts for solo violin and orchestra, *Nocturnes* was begun in 1893. Debussy then revised his concept, and in 1899 he rewrote the work as three ensemble pieces. Here is Debussy's impressionistic vision of clouds, sea, festivals, etc.

* * MONTEUX	*Boston Symphony Orch.*	VICTROLA VIC (S) 1027 [Women's Chorus; Stravinsky, Firebird]
* GOBERMAN	*Vienna New Symphony Orch. and State Opera Woman's Chorus*	ODYSSEY (S) 32 16 0226 [Jeux—Poeme Danse; Prelude]
* DORATI	*Minneapolis Symphony Orch., Cecilian Singers*	MERCURY (M) 14029 (S) 18029 [Ravel, Pavane for a Dead Princess; La Valse]
VAN BEINUM	*Concertgebouw Orch., CollegiumMusicum Women's Chorus*	PHILLIPS WS (S) 9097 [La Mer]

Monteux wins by a mile. This conductor was one of Debussy's first interpreters, and one of the best who ever lived; his performance here is mellow and evocative. The sound is good.

Goberman is remarkably unconvincing. The sound is not bad.

Dorati comes up with a reading that is full of nervous energy, is hard-driven rather than gently impressionistic.

Van Beinum sounds curiously uninvolved. The sound is filmy.

PRELUDE A L'APRES-MIDI D'UN FAUNE

This, Debussy's most popular orchestral work, is one of the perfect short works of impressionism — sensuous, delicate, and shimmering. Inspired by Mallarme's poem of the same name, it was composed between 1892 and 1894.

* * PARAY	*Detroit Symphony Orch.*	MERCURY (S) 18078 [Petite Suite; Ravel, Tombeau; Valses]
* * MUNCH	*Boston Symphony Orch.*	VICTROLA VIC (S) 1323 [Ibert; Ravel, Bolero; La Valse]
* GOBERMAN	*Vienna New Symphony Orch.*	ODYSSEY 32 16 0226 [Jeux—Poeme Danse]
* PEDROTTI	*Czech Philharmonic*	PARLIAMENT (M) 157 [Khachaturian, Masquerade; Prokofiev, Classical Symphony]
* VAN REMOORTEL	*Vienna Symphony Orch.*	VOX (5) 11850 [Chabrier, Espana; Ravel, Bolero]
* BAUDO	*Czech Philharmonic*	CROSSROADS (S) 22 16 0174 [Jeux—Poeme Danse; Premiere]

The Paray record is excellent. Paray, sometimes underrated, is a master of French music. However, the Detroit Symphony does not match the glitter and sheen of the Boston Symphony.

Munch is also impressive; he has great empathy for "la gloire" of French music. The sound is clean. *Stereo Record Guide* was less enthusiastic: "Disappointing. . . . Somehow lacking in subtlety."

A disappointing, slipshod reading is offered by Goberman. The sound is only so-so.

Pedrotti is competent, and his program is fine.

Van Remoortel is pleasant, little more.

Baudo is much outclassed, and the sound is undefined.

THREE IMAGES POUR ORCHESTRE

Gigues, Iberia, and *Rondes des Printemps* make up the symphonic tryptich that Debussy wrote under the title *Images Pour Orchestre,* a work which occupied him from 1906 until 1911. Debussy himself conducted the premiere of *Rondes de Printemps* in Paris in 1910. Ten days earlier, *Iberia* had received its first performance with Gabriel Pierne conducting. Defending his music after its indifferent reception by the critics, Debussy wrote, "More and more I am convinced that music cannot be poured into any tight, traditional, frozen form. It consists of colors and rhythmic beats. . . ."

* * ARGENTA   *Orch. Suisse Romande*   LONDON STS (S) 15020

Argenta's imaginative reading has long been admired as the classic performance of the complete *Images*. The recording is pleasant.

CHAMBER MUSIC Although Debussy wrote little chamber music, what he did write is of the highest quality, and should be investigated by all lovers of this extraordinary, elusive composer.

PREMIERE RAPSODIE FOR CLARINET

The *Clarinet Rhapsody,* completed in 1910 as an exercise for students of the clarinet, is a slight work with pleasing, exotic passages.

* BOUTARD, BAUDO   *Czech Philharmonic*   CROSSROADS (S) 22 16 0174
                                              [Jeux—Poeme Danse; Pre-
                                              lude]

Andre Boutard is a good clarinetist, and does what he can with this eccentric score. The orchestral support is strong. The sound is pretty good.

QUARTET IN G (Opus 10)

This was one of the first works of Debussy that was publicly performed (1893). Critics were baffled; one called him "rotten with talent." Today, the *Quartet* is regarded as one of the few quartet masterpieces since Beethoven. If you love chamber music, get to know this work. If it sounds strange at first, "just let it all ooze around you a few times," to quote one young friend who is a convert to Debussy.

This work has been much recorded; string quartets love to play it, if just to show what they can do with music other than Beethoven and Mozart.

* * *	*Vlach Quartet*	7-ARTIA [Ravel, Quartet]	204
* *	*Fine Arts Quartet*	CONCERT DISC (M) (S) [Ravel, Quartet]	1253 253
*	*Stuyvesant Quartet*	NONESUCH (S) 71007 [Ravel, Quartet]	
*	*Loewenguth Quartet*	5-VOX [Ravel, Quartet]	12020

Of several good entries here, the palm goes to the burnished, highly colored version of the Vlach Quartet. *The Stereo Record Guide* comments: "This is unquestionably the finest performance of this elusive work in the present catalogues. . . . Indeed, the ensemble playing is outstanding, almost as if a hidden conductor was shaping the music." The sound is a little dry.

The Fine Arts Quartet delivers a highly atmospheric reading that one must admire. *Hi/Fi Stereo Review* comments: "Performance: satisfactory; reading: sonorous." *High Fidelity* agrees with: "Strong, forthright, polished reading."

The reissue of the Stuyvesant reading is also extremely good; *High Fidelity's* reviewer "welcomed it back with open arms." This is a full-blooded, urgent approach. The 1951 sound, although rather reverberant, is still fairly good.

The Loewenguth players must be respected for being indifferent to juicy tones and svelte vibratos; they play in a lean, wan style. The sound is rather dry.

SONATA NO. 1 IN D FOR CELLO AND PIANO

This tightly-knit work is the first of the three extraordinary sonatas which Debussy composed in his last tragic years.

* JANIGRO, DOYEN	WESTMINSTER (M) 9054 [Sonatas No. 2/3]

Janigro, sensitive and restrained, sounds right to me. The mono sound is acceptable. [The couplings are excellent.] Harold Schonberg (1955): "Janigro and Doyen make the music as interesting as limitations of the recording medium permit. The score, in all truth, is not one of Debussy's more interesting ones."

SONATA NO. 2 FOR FLUTE, VIOLA AND HARP

This intriguing late work is an evocation of eighteenth-century France.

* * SCHWEGLER, RUF, STORCK	TURNABOUT (S) 34161 [Ravel, Introduction and Allegro for Harp, String Quartet, Flute, and Clarinet; Roussel, Serenade, Opus 30]
* * WANAUSEK, WEISS, JELLINCK	WESTMINSTER (M) 9054 [Sonatas No. 1 and 3]

The Turnabout disc offers a well-played performance. [The record includes superb couplings of the same evocative nature by Ravel and

Roussel. Albert Roussel (1869-1937) was an officer in the French navy; he retired in 1894 to become a full-time composer. His music, delicate and fastidious, owes much to Debussy.]

The old mono Westminster which still sounds good, contains competent playing of the three important, late Debussy sonatas. Harold Schonberg (1955): "A heavy-sounding performance . . . without much imagination."

SONATA NO. 3 IN G FOR VIOLIN AND PIANO

This wonderful, intense, original sonata was written between 1916 and 1917, a period during which Debussy was operated on unsuccessfully for cancer. The composer was plied with morphia injections, and was in great fear for France which was in a life and death struggle with Germany. Edward Lockspeiser* movingly sketches Debussy at this time and his music: "Afflicted with cancer, he was aware that his end was near, yet he persisted in working continuously, indeed at that feverish pace that somehow takes possession of a dying man 'in order to give proof' as he put it 'that French thought will not be destroyed.' Usually hesitant in the gradual exteriorization of his ideas, he now announced a series of six sonatas for various combinations of instruments. On the handsome title page of his first, under the composer's name, appeared, as a natural assertion of pride during those war years, the words *Musicien Francais.*" Only three of the sonatas were completed: the *Cello Sonata,* the *Sonata for Flute, Viola, and Harp,* and the *Violin Sonata.* (The fourth sonata was to have been written for the unusual combination of oboe, horn, and harpsichord.)

*Lockspeiser, Edward, *Chamber Music,* Penguin Books.

* * FERRAS, BARBIZET	Everest	(M)	6140
		(S)	3140
[Faure, Sonata No. 2]			
* * FOURNIER, DOYEN	Westminster	(M)	9054
[Sonatas No. 1/2]			

Ferras and Barbizet love this music; their reading is refined. Ferras' tone is more opulent than usual. The piano accompaniment is sensitive and responsive. *Stereo Review* comments: "Performance: luscious; recording: excellent; stereo quality: fine."

A far leaner, more thoughtful version is to be had on a splendid old Westminster disc, with violinist Jean Fournier. [The couplings are the two other late, great Debussy sonatas: the *Cello Sonata,* and the *Sonata for Flute, Viola, and Harp.*] The sound is dry. Harold Schonberg: "Fournier is a good musician. . . . If you are interested in building up a Debussy collection, this disc belongs."

PIANO MUSIC   In his piano music we sense the most intimate Debussy. In these compositions, Debussy presents sonorities and colorations which composers had not discovered. Here is music of the highest importance.

Debussy can be called the Monet of music; nowhere is this appellation more appropriate than in his piano works.

CHILDREN'S CORNER SUITE

The endearing *Children's Corner Suite* was written between 1906 and 1908 for the composer's little daughter Couchou. English titles were used by Debussy both for the entire work, and for the individual movements (*Golliwoggs' Cakewalk*, etc.) to suggest a French child with an English nanny. The piece contains a short, caustic quotation from Wagner's *Tristan and Isolde*.

* * FRANKL	TURNABOUT	(S) 34166

Peter Frankl's version is brisk, lighthearted, and enjoyable.

CLAIR DE LUNE (from SUITE BERGAMASQUE)

In the *Suite Bergamasque,* (from Verlaine's phrase, "Masques et bergamasques) Debussy attempted to recapture the refinement of the French harpsichord composers of the sixteenth and seventeenth centuries, composers whom he adored. The third movement, an impressionistic sketch of night called *Clair de Lune,* is one of the most popular short pieces ever penned.

* * PRESTI AND LAGOYA		NONESUCH	(S) 71161
* * KLIEN		VOX STPL	(S) 511720
* * FRANKL		TURNABOUT	(S) 34166
* GOULD	*Morton Gould Orch.*	VICTROLA VIC	(S) 1174 [mixed Pops program]

The most evocative reading on low-priced records is to be heard on a two-guitar program by the gifted team of Presti and Lagoya. The sound is fine.

Both Klien and Frankl offer evocative readings in the original piano version.

Morton Gould, in an orchestral version, offers a pleasant though somewhat saccharine performance.

COMPLETE PIANO MUSIC: IMAGES (BOOKS 1 AND 2); CHILDREN'S CORNER; L'ISLE JOYEUSE; D'UN CAHIER D'ESQUISSES; ETUDES (BOOKS 1 AND 2); ARABESQUES, NO. 1 AND 2; LA PLUS QUE LENTE; PRELUDES (BOOKS 1 AND 2); POUR LE PIANO; SUITE BERGAMASQUE; REVERIE; NOCTURNE DANSE; BALLADE; MASQUES; DANSE BOHEMIENNE; ESTAMPES; VALSE ROMANTIQUE; MAZURKA; HOMMAGE A HAYDN; LE PETIT NERGE; BERCEUSE HEROIQUE

* HAAS   WORLD SERIES PHC 5012

Werner haas, a pupil of Gieseking, has taken on a gaint task here—nothing less than the complete piano music of Debussy. Haas is an intelligent pianist, but rather rigid at times. This monumental attempt must be chalked up as a noble failure. *Stereo Review's* appraisal is: "Performance: assertively Germanic; recording: good." *High Fidelity* also complains of a heavy approach: "Rather different from what Debussy had in mind."

PIANO WORKS: BOITE A JOUJOUX; BALLADE; DEUX ARABESQUES; DOUZE ETUDES; IMAGES (BOOK II); L'ISLE JOYEUSE; NOCTURNE, IN D-FLAT; LE PLUS QUE LENTE; PRELUDES (BOOK II); REVERIE

* * FRANKL   Vox   VBX   (S)   433

Peter Frankl uses an objective approach without the poetic intuition that a Gieseking brings to this music, yet he is entirely hearable. Critical opinion is divided on this album. *High Fidelity* comments: "Frankl is a superbly equipped technician, and conscientious musician," but *Stereo Review* says: "For all its fundamental competence and honesty, I find Frankl's playing frequently stiff." I myself find Frankl's interpretation most satisfying, if not soaring.

PRELUDES FOR PIANO, BOOKS 1 AND 2

The exquisite *Preludes* may be termed an intimate diary of Debussy's imaginative life. They are best enjoyed when heard individually, rather than by listening to these pieces in a series, one after the other. *Book One* was written in 1910; *Book Two* followed over the next three years.

* NOVAES   Vox   (M) 10180
                                            [Book 1]

Madame Novaes is subtle and atmospheric. The mono sound is dated.

TWO ARABESQUES

The two delicate arabesques of 1888, though poorly regarded by Debussy himself, are extremely popular today.

* * FRANKL   TURNABOUT   (S) 34166

Peter Frankl is sensitive and technically accomplished. *High Fidelity* finds his reading to be "a particular delight."

SONGS Debussy was one of the very best song writers of France. His songs (as well as his famous opera, *Pelleas et Melisande,* are not concerned with melodic line, as were the songs of the great German writers such as Schubert and Schumann. Instead, Debussy emphasizes fine shadings and poetic meanings, both in a free declamatory style.

PROMENOIR DES DEUX AMANTS (Song Cycle)

This song cycle—first-rate Debussy—was composed between 1904 and 1910.

* * BERNAC, POULENC   2-ODYSSEY (M) 32 26 0009

Pierre Bernac, along with Gerard Souzay, are the two greatest male interpreters of the elusive French song. Bernac is at his best here. The sound is poor, and rather harsh. This is a two-record album, given over chiefly to songs of Poulenc, who accompanies Bernac on the piano.

Delibes, Leo (1836-1891)

Delibes, a product of the Paris Conservatoire, held various opera and organ posts. He is best known in America as the composer of the popular ballets *Coppelia* and *Sylvia*. Few months elapse at the Opera-Comique in Paris without a performance of Delibes' opera *Lakme*. The English composer Elgar—of all people—declared that he had been influenced by the music of Delibes.

COPPELIA: SUITE

* * RIGNOLD	Paris Conservatory	Victrola VIC [Sylvia]	(S)	1130
* SEBASTIAN	RIAS Symphony Orch.	Everest [Sylvia]	(M) (S)	6116 3116
* SMETACEK	Czech Ensemble	Parliament		150

Rignold gives a graceful performance, by no means as sensuous as several noted high-priced recordings have been.

Sebastian and Smetacek both deliver competent, better-than-routine readings.

SYLVIA: SUITE

This felicitous and delicately scored ballet is firmly established in the classical ballet repertory. Tchaikovsky, who wrote great ballets himself, is said to have been influenced by the style of Delibes.

* * RIGNOLD	Paris Conservatoire Orch.	Victrola VIC [Coppelis Suite]	(S)	1130
* FISTOULARI	RIAS Symphony Orch.	Everest [Coppelia]	(M) (S)	6116 3116

Rignold is bright and zestful. The sound is clear.

Fistoulari, an old ballet hand, is agreeable here, but his players seem heavy-handed. They lack the elan of the Paris Conservatoire group on the Rignold disc.

Delius, Frederick (1862-1934)

Delius was the English-born son of a German wool merchant who had settled in England. In 1884, at the age of 22, Delius migrated to Florida as an orange-planter, but after a year he abandoned oranges for music. Returning to Europe, he studied in Leipzig, then settled permanently in France.

His music fits into no ready-made category. It is dreamy, exotic, rhapsodic, and Romantic with a capital R. At its worst, the music of Delius is unbearably vacuous; at its best it can be tenderly beautiful. In England, Delius is highly regarded, and the championing of his works by Sir Thomas Beecham has elevated Delius to the notable place he enjoys today.

VOCAL AND ORCHESTRAL MUSIC

The chief quality of this is a highly personal sweetness, an idyllic mood that, according to Sackville-West, "endears Delius especially to those who by birth or habit have acquired a taste for the unspectacular beauties of English landscape."

* BARBIROLLI	*Halle Orchestra*	VANGUARD EVERYMAN (M/S) SRV 240

This Delius miscellany is a pretty good sampler of the composer's music and style. Barbirolli, a Delius enthusiast, gives this music loving treatment. Individual works included are: *Idyll for Soprano, Baritone, and Orchestra, "Once I Passed Through a Populous City"; Irmelin: Prelude; On Hearing the First Cuckoo in Spring; Fennimore and Gerda: Intermezzo; The Walk to the Paradise Garden (Intermezzo from "A Village Romeo and Juliet").* Sound is rather vapid, but all right.

Demantius, Christoph *(1567-1643)*

Born in Bohemia, Demantius belongs to the generation of pre-Bach Lutheran composers who helped effect the transition from the Renaissance to the Baroque era in music. Demantius was a naturally inventive and original composer.

PROPHECY OF THE SUFFERING AND DEATH OF JESUS CHRIST; ST. JOHN PASSION

Both these works appeared in a single print in 1631, when Demantius was 64. They contain some bold chromatic harmonies and a strong sense of rhythm. However, the works are still comparatively uninteresting. Listeners with a special interest in the Renaissance-Baroque transition will find the great Praetorius more worth-while.

VOORBERG   *Hilversum Ensemble*   NONESUCH   (S) 71138

The performance strikes me as being on the dull side with neither intensity nor passion. The sound is clear.

Des Prez, Josquin (c. 1440-1521)

Born in Belgium, this musical genius of the 15th century was one of the most celebrated composers of his day. At first, he was a singer in the cathedral of Milan. About 1500, he entered the service of Louis XII in Paris. Here, Des Prez was hailed by all as "prince of musicians." He wrote more than 30 masses, 50 motets, and 70 chansons.

AVE CHRISTE

The four-voiced motet *Ave Christie, Immolate* is the first section of a longer composition. Probably a late work, there is no better example of Des Prez's magnificent art.

* * * HAHN, TRAEDER   *Kaufbeurer Martinsfinken,*   NONESUCH   (S) H 71084
Neidersaechsischer   [Di Lasso, Motets; H. Isaac,
Singkreis, Hannover   Missa Carminum]

The entire record is superb—a must for collectors of early music. The compositions of Henrich Isaac and Orlando di Lasso are also great. The sound and the singing are fine. This glowing recording originally derived from Camerata, a small but extremely good company in West Germany.

MASS: L'OMME ARME

The *Missa "L'Omme Arme" ("The Armed Man")* is a *cantus firmus* Mass—one with a "fixed melody." Josquin elaborated on the original melody, famous in his time. This is stark, innovative music of contrapuntal grandeur; you think you are standing in a medieval cathedral.

* VENHODA   *Prague Madrigal Singers*   CROSSROADS   (S) 22 16 0094
[Madrigals and Motets]

Venhoda is the foremost Czech interpreter of old music; his singers and players sound very much at home. The five short pieces that fill out the album provide a good sampling of Josquin's remarkable range. The sound seems boxed in.

SECULAR MUSIC AND MOTETS

The music of the fifteenth and sixteenth centuries is slowly coming into vogue among adventurous listeners who are surfeited with bland baroque and rococo music. One reason for the new interest in Renaissance music —to quote President Jac Holzman of Nonesuch Records—is "It cleans out your ears."

The secular pieces in this selection are fine "ear-cleaners" for those who care to hear the music of four hundred years ago. Here is charming, discreet gaiety, with variety and beauty.

* WEISS   *Collegium Musicum,*   EVEREST   (S)   3210
                   UCLA Madrigal Singers

The college singing is enthusiastic. The sound is spacious.

OTHER WORKS

Other excerpts of Des Prez are to be heard on the following commendable discs: *Chamber Music for Voices,* Mace (M) 9078; *Recorder Music of Six Centuries,* Classic Editions (M) 1018; *Anthology of Renaissance Music,* Dover (M) 5248. The last, a most admirable disc, features the New York Pro Musica Antiqua under the late Noah Greenberg. The sound on all three discs is dry.

Stereo recording of Des Prez excerpts are to be heard on two first-rate records released by Nonesuch: *Court and Ceremonial Music of the 16th Century,* Nonesuch 71012; and *Renaissance Vocal Music,* Nonesuch 71097. This last disc is most enjoyable, and includes secular songs of England, Italy, France, and Germany. The rich sonics are from Camerata of West Germany.

D'Indy, Vincent (1851-1931)

D'Indy, the most famous student of Cesar Franck, was a passionate Wagnerian and a determined opponent of Debussy's musical theories. Little of his work survives today in repertory.

SYMPHONY ON A FRENCH MOUNTAIN AIR
(Opus 25)

This symphony, with a solo piano part, was written in 1886, under Cesar Franck's influence. The work conveys a warm feeling for the French landscape.

* HENRIOT- SCHWEITZER, MUNCH	*Boston Symphony*	RCA Victor VIC (5) 1060 [French program]

The music is authoritatively played by two outstanding French musicians. The sound is good.

Dittersdorf, Karl (1739-1799)

A violinist as well as composer, Dittersdorf was one of the most prolific writers of his time. He held several posts as choirmaster or musical director to different bishops and princes, from one of whom he received a title of nobility. Dittersdorf frequently visited Vienna, where several of his comic operas were produced with notable success.

Altogether, he wrote about 115 symphonies, 44 operas, numerous cantatas and Masses, several oratorios, 35 concertos for different instruments, 47 sonatas, and much chamber music.

He was a friend of both Gluck and Haydn; much of his music resembles Haydn's in style. The concertos and chamber music are most widely sampled today.

CONCERTOS

The concertos available on low-priced records are: for *Double Bass and Orchestra, in E;* for *Harp and Orchestra, in A; Sinfonia Concertante for Double Bass, Viola, and Orchestra, in D.* The elephantine double bass is not the most facile instrument to serve as the solo voice for a concerto, and the good-humored *Double Bass Concerto* can be regarded as a musical curiosity. The neat *Harp Concerto* was transcribed by the composer from his own piano concerto. The urbane *Sinfonia Concertante* is the most pleasing of these three works.

* HOERTNAGEL, LEMMEN, STORCK, FAERBER	*Wuerttemberg Chamber Orch.*	TURNABOUT TV	(3) 4005

The playing of all three concertos is graceful. *High Fidelity* says: "Performances are highly competent." The sound is a little boomy, but not bad.

Donizetti, Gaetano (1797-1848)

Donizetti studied in Bologna, Italy. His first opera, *Enrico, Conte di Borgogna*, was performed at Venice in 1818. His early operas were influenced by Rossini. *Lucia di Lammermoor*, composed in 1835, made Donizetti famous. Near the end of his life, he was given to severe depressions and was confined in an insane asylum.

PLACE AND ACHIEVEMENT   Donizetti, a thorough craftsman, was content to accept the musical conventions of his day. He turned out operas with machine-like precision and regularity. Between 1822 until 1843, he would compose as many as three or four operas each year.

Donizetti wrote over 60 operas, most of them forgotten today. Glibness permeates much of his work. But the best of his operas, such as *Don Pasquale*, are marvelously light-hearted, skillful, well-turned works, which send the audience home whistling the neat melodies.

THE ESSENTIAL DONIZETTI
OPERAS: *Don Pasquale; Lucia di Lammermoor; L'Elisir d'Amore.*

OTHER WORKS
OPERAS: *Lucrezia Borgia; La Favorita; La Fille du Regiment; Il Campanello.*

BETLY

This mildly pleasant one-act jovial opera contains three or four tuneful arias that still appeal. The coloratura aria *In Questo Semplice* is sometimes heard in recitals, but the opera as a whole has vanished from the boards.

| TUCCARI, GENTILE, CATALANI, MORELLI | *Chorus and Orchestra of the Società del Quartetto, Rome* | DOVER HCR | 5218 |

This severely cut performance first appeared on the Period label in the early, dim days of long-play records—about 1949; Tuccari is a light-weight soprano, neat and agile. Gentile, in the laconic words of vocal expert Philip Miller, "is a tenor of the light Italian type, and has something of the lachrymose style not uncommon in his school." Catalani is smooth, but not much more. The chorus is poor, and the sound is just bearable.

DON PASQUALE

Most opera lovers regard *Don Pasquale* as Donizetti's masterpiece. Here are elegant charm and pointed wit. The pages still sound as fresh as they must have been when first heard in 1843. Perhaps the most perfect of all comic operas, *Don Pasquale* easily ranks with Rossini's *Barber of Seville*.

* * LA GATTA, LAZZARI, CORENA, POLI, LA ROSA PARODI	*La Scala Opera*	2-Vox OPBX	147
* BRUSCANTINI, VALLETTI, NONI, ROSSI		2-Everest-Cetra (S)	4042

The Vox set seems preferable to me. It has first-rate male singers—Corena is wonderful—and in *Don Pasquale,* it's the men who have the juicy roles. La Gatta goes shaky and shrill at times, but she has some good moments. The sound is only so-so.

The Cetra version, with the admirable Bruscantini, is rated "very pleasant and largely adequate" by Peter Gammond (*Opera on Record*). There is spirited pacing by conductor Rossi. The sound is fair.

L'ELISIR D'AMORE

First heard at the Paris Opera in 1832, *The Elixir of Love* is quite similar in style to the great *Don Pasquale.* Though the melodies are not so joyous and dazzling, the opera, as a whole, is a pretty piece and is fun. This work includes some juicy tenor arias, and used to be known at the Metropolitan as "Caruso's opera."

* * NONI, VALLETTI, POLI, BRUSCANTINI, GAVAZZENI		3-Everest/Cetra (S)	415/3
* CARRERI, TADDEI, ALVA, PANERAI, SERAFIN	*La Scala Orchestra and Chorus*	2-Seraphim (S)	6001

The Cetra performance is the more enjoyable, with assured singing and fine characterizations from the cast as a whole. Valletti has a pleasing voice, although he indulges in gulps and other emotional excesses. Soprano Noni is fresh and appealing. Veteran Poli slurs some of his arias, but is otherwise very good. Bruscantini blusters about with proper unction. The orchestra pacing is brisk, and the sound is decent. Peter Gammond commented in *Music on Record*: "The Cetra issue, old and sounding it, as is inevitable still contains enough good quality . . . . If the ultimate in sound is not needed, this is a really lively, clean performance which presents the work in an uncomplicated and altogether delightful way."

The Seraphim set has a first-rate, cultured soprano, and dependable singing from the rest of the cast. The tenor is good but not exceptional. Taddei sounds a bit tired, but the chorus is excellent. The sound is better than on the Cetra set. The English *Records and Recordings* found more virtue in the recording than I did, and said, "Conductor Serafin provides a fresh sensitive reading of the score that makes the utmost of Donizetti's sunny, elegant music." Serafin knows this music inside out; as far back as 1930, he conducted a famous performance at the Metropolitan with a cast headed by Benjamino Gigli and Ezio Pinza.

LA FAVORITA

The Favorite was a smash hit when it was first performed in Paris in 1840. Today, it is almost forgotten, and yet it contains some of Donizetti's gentlest and most tender pages.

| * * TAGLIABUE, BARBIERI, DI LELIO, RAIMONDI, NERI, MARIANO CARUSO, QUESTA | *Rome Studio Chorus and Orch.* | 3-EVEREST/CETRA | 405/3 |

The important roles receive first-rate handling from Raimondi and from the vital and fiery Barbieri. The playing is spirited and theatrical, in a stylish way.

There is an expensive rival to this recording on London, also recorded about 1956. Yet this Everest entry is in no way outclassed. In fact, Raimondi's youthful-sounding voice is far more agreeable than Gianni Poggi's is on the London disc. *Hi/Fi Stereo Review* comments: "While members of the Cetra cast set no high marks for *bel canto* excellence, they contribute to a very strong performance."

LA FIGLIA DEL REGGIMENTO

The Daughter of the Regiment is one of three operas that the unbelievably facile Donizetti completed in 1840—all for production in Paris where he was adored. Here is Gallic, perfumed elegance in a cheerful, tripping score, with bouncy—but not memorable—melodies.

| * PAGLIUGHI, BRUSCANTINI, CORSI, VALLETTI, CODA, ROSSI | *Rome Studio Chorus and Orch.* | 2-EVEREST/CETRA | 417/2 |

The Everest/Cetra entry is the only version extant in the American catalogue today. This opera stands or falls with its soprano; and Pagliughi, a famous coloratura in her day, is definitely not at her best in this recording. The rest of the cast is hearable; the ever-dependable Bruscantini is best of all. Italian sonics of 1951 are mediocre but acceptable. The knowledgeable George Jellinek commented in *Hi/Fi Stereo Review*: "Lina Pagliughi's tones reveal a touch of acid . . . but her singing is still colorful and lively. Bruscantini contributes a zesty and expertly sung Sulpizio, and Mario Rossi's leadership provides liveliness and authentic style."

LUCIA DI LAMMERMOOR

Lucia, written in 1835, is somber. Its famous "Mad Scene" is adored by sopranos, and the even more famous *Sextet* stands with the *Quartet* from *Rigoletto* as one of the most popular ensemble scenes in all of Italian opera.

Of the 67 operas that Donizetti wrote, *Lucia* is probably the best known and most popular. It is based on the novel *The Bride of Lammermoor* by Sir Walter Scott. Its action is set in a largely imaginary Scotland toward the end of the seventeenth century. Prima donnas revel in this role; some of the famous Lucias have included Adelina Patti, Marcella Sembrich, and Nellie Melba; Lily Pons sang it at her Metropolitan debut in 1931.

In the nineteenth century, *Lucia* was considered to be *the* romantic opera. In *Madame Bovary,* Flaubert describes the psychological reactions of Emma and her lover when they go to hear the opera in Rouen. In *Anna Karenina,* Tolstoy associates Lucia with the turbulant emotions of Anna and Vronsky.

* * * CALLAS, DI STEFANO, GOBBI, SERAFIN	*Florence Festival Orch.*	2-SERAPHIM	6032
* * SCOTTO, DI STEFANO, BESTIANINI, VINCO, SANZOGNO	*La Scala Opera*	2-EVEREST	(S) 439/2
PETERS, PEERCE, * TOZZI, MAERO, LEINSDORF	*Rome Opera Orch.*	2-VICTROLA VIC	(S) 6001

Callas was only 30, and at the top of her phenomenal powers, when she made this set. She recorded the opera again, later. The earlier disc now on Seraphim is much more secure, and invested with that special intensity that was Callas in her brief great years, before the wobble came into her voice. This set has been out of print for some years, supplanted by the later version in stereo. I welcome it back with open arms—here is another proof of the blessings bestowed upon us by the "low-priced record revolution." The sound though quite good is not spectacular. In reviewing this record the *New York Times* raved: "This Lucia is back, sounding better than ever. . . . It will serve as a loud rebuke to those who judge only by Callas' later recordings. . . . Here is the voice that made Callas a legend: huge, limitless in color, unrivaled in flexibility, guided by an artistic intellect that bordered on genius."

The performance with Renata Scotto is a very fine recording that has been unfortunately overshadowed by the Callas recording. But, unless you demand the ultimate in glamorous names, Scotto's is a first-class set. The master was originally taped by Ricordi, Italy, in true stereo; for a while, this *Lucia* was on the American market under the Mercury label. The sound is excellent and spacious. *High Fidelity* comments on the reissue: "Renata Scotto's intense yet delightfully musical interpretation of the mad heroine makes this set a very attractive contender—it is certainly far preferable to the other budget entry on Victrola."

I find the *Lucia* of Roberta Peters on Victrola lacking distinction. The singing is routine. Miss Peters has a pleasant voice, but it goes wiry in her high notes. Jan Peerce is expert, but the rest of the cast is unremarkable. Leinsdorf's conducting is uneventful—even plodding at times. The sound is early-era stereo of indifferent quality.

Dowland, John (1562-1626)

Dowland, born in Dublin in an age that loved the lute above all other instruments, was a famous lutanist as well as a composer. From 1580 to 1584, he was in the service of the English ambassador in Paris where he became a Roman Catholic. Denied a place at the English court on account of his religion, he traveled extensively on the Continent.

AYRES (3 Books)

Dowland's *Books of Ayres* are the most prized English contribution to the literature of song with lute accompaniment. Dowland, a melancholy by nature, signed himself "ever Dowland, ever doleful"; but to modern ears this bittersweet quality is most pleasing.

* * CAPE	*Brussels Pro Musica Antiqua*	DOVER	(M) 5220
* LEPPARD	*Ensemble*	NONESUCH	(S) 71167
*	*Golden Age Singers*	WESTMINSTER [Dances for Lute]	(M) 9619
	The Field-Hyde Singers	2-WESTMINSTER	9602/3

Stafford Cape and the Pro Musica Antiqua have a superb gift for making old music come alive. This accomplishment is evident in their recording of the *First Book of Ayres*. The mono sound is pleasant.

The Raymond Leppard Ensemble offers a good performance with clean stereo sound. Critic Harold Schonberg of the *New York Times* called the ingratiating voice of Janet Baker "the best British import since wool."

The Golden Age Singers are a bit too mournful for my ears. The lute accompaniment is by Julian Bream, the distinguished guitarist. The mono sound is all right. [Bream also plays the *Dances for Lute* on the reverse of the disc.]

The Field-Hyde Singers are competent, but they are outclassed by the other recordings.

Dufay, Guillaume (c. 1400-1474)

The Flemish composer Dufay, the most important composer of his period, was one of the supreme musical geniuses of all time. Along with Josquin des Prez, he was one of the most gifted composers before Palestrina. Dufay, famous throughout Europe, had friends and admirers at all the leading courts.

A master of both church music and warmhearted secular pieces, Dufay's highly personal music is striking; there is no better introduction to the vocal glories of the Renaissance. To quote authority Denis Stevens: "Dufay's music has relatively simple harmonies, clear texture, and instantaneous appeal deriving from melodic charm and beauty. . . . The warmth of Dufay's personality radiates from every page of his music."

HYMNS, CHORUSES AND SONGS

This is a worthy anthology of early music of various composers.

* *	*Zurich Ancient Instrument Ensemble*	ODYSSEY	(S) 32 16 0178

The music is tastefully sung on this disc, and the piquant sounds of the ancient instruments are doleful. The sonics are good.

LAMENTATIO SANCTAE MATRIS ECCLESIAE CONSTANTINOPOLITANAE; VERGINE BELLA

The Burgundian court, under four Valois dukes, held a dominant position in the musical world of the fifteenth century. This "Music from the Court of Burgundy," is fresh and lovely. Simplicity and soft elegance establish the mood.

* * BLANCHARD	*Roger Blanchard Vocal and Instrumental Ensemble; Pierre Poulteau Recorder Trio*	NONESUCH H	(S) 71058

Performed with both assurance and devotion, with warm sound from Club Francais du Disque, Paris. These two pieces are choice Dufay. [The other compositions are charming ballades and rondeaux, mostly from the reign of Philippe le Bon. Specific works included are: Binchois, *Files a Marier; Je Loe Amours; Magnificat Primi Toni;* Busnois, *Bel Acueil; In Hydraulis;* Fontaine, *Pastourelle en un Vergier;* Ghizeghem, *Allez Regretz,* Grenon, *La Plus Belle et Doulce Figure;* Mortoni, *Le Perontina;* Mureau, *Grace Attendant;* Anon.; *J'ay Prins Amour a ma Devise.*

Niclos Grenon (? - c.1450) belonged to an earlier generation than most of the composers heard on this record; he was associated with the Burgundian court as early as 1385. Pierre Fontaine (c.1385-1450) entered the Burgundian court briefly in 1404, and spent from 1420-1427 at the Papal Chapel.

We know almost nothing of Gilles Mureau (? -1512) except that he seems to have been associated with Chartres Cathedral for much of his life. Robert Morton (? -1475) was an Englishman who became a singer at the Burgundian court in 1457. Hayne Van Ghizeghem (? -1472) entered Philippe le Bon's service in 1457, and last appeared as a military man in 1472, at the seige of Beauvais—a disaster for the Burgundians.]

MASTERPIECES OF THE EARLY FRENCH AND ITALIAN RENAISSANCE: DONNES L'ASSAULT A LA FORTERESSE; LES DOLEURS DONT NE SENS

These delightful chansons are concerned mostly with love. Anyone who thinks early music is a bore can disabuse himself of that notion by hearing these works.

* * * Singers and Instrumentalists of Societe de La Musique d'Autrefois   NONESUCH H   (S) 71010

Here is one of the best records of its kind ever made. Don't miss it! The singing is vivid, appealing, and first-rate. The sound is luscious. [A note on the couplings: Gilles Binchois (c. 1400-1460) was a French soldier, then priest, and chaplain to Philip, Duke of Burgundy. Antoine Busnois (? -1492), a pupil of Ockeghem, was attached to the court of Charles the Bold of Burgundy. Loyset Compere (? -1518), also a pupil of Ockeghem, became Chancellor of St. Quentin Cathedral. Bartollommeo Tromboncino (dates unknown) was born at Verona in the late fifteenth century, and was attached to various courts at Mantua and Venice.]

SECULAR AND SACRED MUSIC

Here are 11 choice selections from Dufay, including some ravishing drinking songs and love songs.

* * STEVENS   Ambrosian Singers   DOVER   (M) 5261

The vivid singing by the English Ambrosian Singers is impeccable. Igor Kipnis called this "a notable record—stylistically admirable."

Dukas, Paul (1865-1935)

Dukas, a native of France, taught at the Paris Conservatoire. He was also a noted critic. The music of Dukas was much influenced by Impressionism, as well as by Cesar Franck and by the Wagnerians. He published comparatively little, rejecting a good deal of his work as unworthy. His dark-hued opera, *Ariane et Barbe-Bleue* (Ariadne and Blue-Beard), is much admired in France, though it is rarely played elsewhere. Dukas is the composer of the evergreen favorite, *The Sorcerer's Apprentice.*

LA PERI

La Péri is a ballet, or "poémes dansés," as Dukas preferred to title it. This is sparkling, uncomplicated, impressionistic music, written in 1912.

* ANSERMET	*Orchestre de La Suisse Romande*	STEREO TREASURY STS 15022 [Debussy, Jeux; Debussy-Ravel, Danse]

Ansermet is famous for his readings of French music; he is at his fastidious and colorful best here. *High Fidelity* comments: "Ansermet's *La Péri* . . . revels in sensuous melody and fragrant orchestral sonorities . . . a warm, clean recording." The 1959 English Decca sound is better than that on many masters just recently recorded.

THE SORCERER'S APPRENTICE

An "orchestral scherzo" of 1897, this music reached heights of fame as the climax of Walt Disney's film *Fantasia*. This is outright program music, based on a ballad by Goethe, *Der Zauberlehrling.*

* * SOLTI	*Israel Philharmonic*	LONDON STS (S) 15005 [Respighi, Boutique Fantastique]
* * MUNCH	*Boston Symphony Orch.*	VICTROLA VIC (S) 1060 [mixed program]
* * TOSCANINI	*NBC Symphony Orch.*	VICTROLA VIC (M) 1267 [Berlioz, Romeo and Juliet —Queen Mab Scherzo; R. Strauss, Don Juan; Till Eulenspiegel]
* VAN REMOORTEL	*Vienna Symphony Orch.*	VOX (5) 11850 [Chabrier, Espana Rhapsody; Debussy, Prelude; Ravel, Bolero]
DANON	*Czech Philharmonic*	PARLIAMENT (M) 150 [mixed program]

Solti's version is charged with the proper spookiness. [The reverse side holds the delightful ballet *La Boutique Fantastique,* which Respighi fashioned after the music of Rossini.]

Munch and the Boston Orchestra deliver a reading with incisiveness, humor, and orchestral virtuosity. The sound is clear. [The reverse includes an all-French collection.]

Toscanini's version is still thrilling, but the mono sound is wiry and thin.

Van Remoortel's performance is quite acceptable, but outclassed by the first-rate performances listed above.

Against the competition, Danon and the Czechs offer nothing outstanding.

Dunstable, John (c. 1370-1453)

Born some thirty years before the great Dufay, Dunstable was one of the most important composers of the early fifteenth century. He was English, but he also enjoyed a considerable reputation on the Continent, where most of his manuscripts have been found.

Hailed by music lovers in his day as "the fount and origin" of music, Dunstable was one of the great seminal forces of his day.

It was in the fifteenth century that choral music, in the modern sense of the term, came into being. Dunstable was one of the pioneers of this genre; his influence on later greats, such as Dufay, is unmistakable. His art is marked by clarity of design and by strongly molded melody.

AVE REGINA COELORUM

Ave Regina Coelorum is a fervent motet.

* *	**The Prague Madrigal Singers**	CROSSROADS (S) 22 16 0144

The singing is devotional and of the highest standard. [The album is called "Old English Vocal Music," and contains music of fourteen masters, including Byrd, Tallis, and Dowland. Only one Dunstable motet is included.]

SACRED AND SECULAR MUSIC

This varied collection provides a good opportunity to hear Dunstable's strikingly original voice.

* BURGESS	**Purcell Consort of Voices**	TURNABOUT	(3) 4058

The Purcell Consort, one of the most knowledgeable and enjoyable ensembles that specialize in early music, provides good singing by four voices.

Dvorak, Antonin (1841-1904)

The son of a butcher and innkeeper, Dvorak studied at the Organ School in Prague from 1857 to 1859. He became a professional string player, and played viola in the orchestra of the National Theatre, Prague, between 1862 and 1873. During these years, he also composed extensively. In 1875, he received a government grant on the recommendation of Brahms and Hanslick. Brahms continued to encourage Dvorak and help him get his works published. Dvorak visited England several times and composed much music for English societies.

In 1878, Dvorak achieved his first success as a composer with his *Slavonic Dances*. His reputation spread throughout Europe. In 1892, he came to the United States to become director of the National Conservatory of Music in New York. Here, he wrote some of his most celebrated music. After returning to Prague, he served as director of the Prague Conservatory from 1901 to 1904.

PLACE AND ACHIEVEMENT   Dvorak's music is universally loved. He had the gift of being able to write fresh, spontaneous melodies that at once touch the heart. This is a gift not often granted: Mozart, Schubert, Schumann, and Tchaikovsky come to mind as some of the few who shared this blessing.

Dvorak's music is cheerfully extroverted. He was hugely productive, almost compulsively so. Sackville-West has written that Dvorak's ever-flowing stream reminds him at times "of what happens when a tap comes unscrewed and the water has to be contained by main force until the plumber comes to the rescue."

Dvorak himself was aware that he wrote too much; near the end of his life he told Sibelius that he regretted having written so profusely. But if his work does not shake us with its profundity nor dazzle us with its brilliance, his music nevertheless has qualities which insure for it an affectionate place among music lovers. Sweet sadness, robust vitality, direct, uncomplicated musical expression—these are the qualities which we prize in Dvorak, and in which he succeeded as well as any other composer.

THE ESSENTIAL DVORAK

ORCHESTRAL MUSIC: *Symphonies No. 7, 8, 9, "From the New World"; Concerto in B Minor, for Cello and Orchestra; Slavonic Dances.*

CHAMBER MUSIC: *Quartet in F, "American"; Quintet in E-Flat; Trio in E Minor, "Dumky."*

OTHER WORKS

OPERA: *Russalka.*

CHORAL MUSIC: *Requiem.*

ORCHESTRAL MUSIC: *Symphonies No. 1, 2, 3, 4, 5, 6; 3 Slavonic Rhapsodies; Violin Concerto; Carnival, Concert Overture; Serenade for Strings.*
PIANO MUSIC: *Humoresques.*

SYMPHONIES   The symphonies are Dvorak's most enduring works. The greatest of them, such as the *"New World,"* are solidly built, straightforward pieces with Dvorak's special quality of gentle romantic sadness.

SYMPHONY NO. 5 IN F (Opus 76) (old No. 3)

This is a lyrical, atmospheric symphony. First heard in 1879, Dvorak revised it eight years later. It is rarely performed today.

The numbering of Dvorak's symphonies has lately been revised to make them conform more closely to their order of composition. Dvorak's publisher seems to have been a rather commercial type to put it mildly; among his several antics was his habit of giving the composer's works late opus numbers—thus suggesting works of maturity, hence more valuable merchandise.

* ROWICKI	*London Symphony Orch.*	PHILIPS WS (S) 908 [Carnival Overture]	
* SEJNA	*Czech Philharmonic*	ARTIA 171 [Othello Overture]	

The Polish conductor Rowicki is slow-paced, almost stately. The sound is clear.

Sejna's version is jauntier. The sound is thin. [The seldom-heard filler, *Othello,* is the third part of a *Triple Overture,* conveying, according to Dvorak, "the three great creative forces of the Universe—Nature, Life, and Love."]

SYMPHONY NO. 6 IN D (Opus 60) (old No. 1)

This is a cheerful symphony of 1880, untouched by any hint of melancholy. The structure is uncomplicated.

* * ROWICKI	*London Symphony Orch.*	PHILLIPS WX (M/S) 9008
* ANCERL	*Czech Philharmonic*	CROSSROADS (S) 22 16 0140

Rowicki plays this symphony most deliberately, stressing the architectural elements rather than taking the usual folksy approach to Dvorak. The result, in the words of *High Fidelity,* is "triumphant." The sound is pretty good.

The playing on the Ancerl disc is fresh and youthful-sounding, but the sonics are indifferent.

SYMPHONY NO. 7 IN D MINOR (Opus 70) (old No. 2)

This symphony, after some 50 years of neglect, has slowly found a place in the romantic repertory. A moody work influenced by Brahms, this opus is unlike most of Dvorak's nationalistic pieces. Some musicians regard this symphony as Dvorak's finest, even above his *"New World"* *Symphony.*

* * MONTEUX	*London Symphony Orch.*	VICTORIA	VIC (S)	1310
* * KOSLER	*Czech Philharmonic*	CROSSROADS	(M) 22 16 0097 (S) 22 16 0098	
* SEJNA	*Czech Philharmonic*	ARTIA [Devil Overture]		177

Papa Monteux glows in a reading that *Stereo Review* called "a magnificent, passionate, performance . . . first rate stereo quality."

Kosler and the Czechs are lyrical, very much in tune with the brooding, tragic lines of this work. *Stereo Review* comments: "Recording good, stereo quality good enough." *High Fidelity* was more impressed, and included this disc in a best-records-of-the-year list, commenting: "Kosler has produced a remarkably pointed and lucid account of Dvorak's great symphony." The sound is attractive.

The Sejna disc is hearable, but is much outclassed.

SYMPHONY NO. 8 IN G (Opus 88) (old No. 4)

Symphony No. 8 was composed in 1889. For a while it was known as Dvorak's "English" symphony because the composer quarreled with his former publisher, Simrock of Germany, and the new work was brought out by Novello of London. This is not a profound work, but rather a lyric, simple flow of melody, rather cozy and provincial. Following the *"New World" Symphony,* this is Dvorak's most popular work.

* * BARBIROLLI	*Halle Orch.*	VANGUARD (S) [Scherzo Capriccioso]		133
* * TALICH	*Czech Philharmonic*	ARTIA [Midday Witch]		178
* DORATI	*London Symphony*	MERCURY (S) [Carnival Overture]		18080

Barbirolli is most impressive, in a pastoral, tension-lacking performance. The sound is thin in the upper registers. When this one was released, Martin Bookspan went all out in *Stereo Review*: "Barbirolli's interpretation takes precedence over all others . . . a giant among contemporary conductors." [The coupling is with a pleasant short piece in the form of a

Czech country dance, *Scherzo Capriccioso*.]

Talich's mono reading remains one of the best to be heard; the English critic Sackville-West called it "far and away the most enjoyable performance." The sound is acceptable. [The coupling is with *The Midday Witch*, a rather lurid folklorish symphonic poem of slight interest.]

Dorati presents a pleasantly relaxed performance. The stereo sound is all right, but hardly the last word. [The coupling is with the popular and lively *Carnival Overture*, one of Dvorak's most frequently played orchestral pieces.]

SYMPHONY NO. 9 IN E MINOR—"NEW WORLD" (Opus 95) (old No. 5)

This is the most famous and most frequently played of Dvorak's works. It was written while Dvorak was in America (he came in 1892) as head of the National Conservatory of Music in New York. American folk melodies are incorporated, and the much-loved slow movement features the Negro spiritual *Goin' Home*. As befits one of the world's most widely played symphonies, the *"New World"* has hardly been neglected on recordings. Some 30 readings are in the current catalogue.

* * * TOSCANINI	*NBC Symphony Orch.*	VICTROLA	VIC	1249
		[Schumann, Manfred Overture]		
* * FRICSAY	*Berlin Philharmonic*	HELIODOR	(S)	25083
* * GIULINI	*Philharmonic Orch.*	SERAPHIM	(S)	60045
		[Carnival Overture]		
* * GOLSCHMANN	*Vienna State Opera Orch.*	VANGUARD	(S)	208
* * HOLLREISER	*Bamberg Symphony Orch.*	VOX	(M)	10810
			(S)	510810
* * KUBELIK	*Vienna Philharmonic*	LONDON STS	(S)	15007
* KUBELIK	*Chicago Symphony Orch.*	MERCURY	(M)	14021
			(S)	18021
* ANCERL	*Czech Philharmonic*	PARLIAMENT	(S)	170
* BARBIROLLI	*Halle Orch.*	VANGUARD	(S)	182
LEINSDORF	*Los Angeles Philharmonic*	PICKWICK	(S)	4005
LUDWIG	*London Symphony Orch.*	EVEREST	(M)	6056
			(S)	3056
RIGNOLD	*London Philharmonic*	SOMERSET St.Fi.		13100

The renowned Toscanini recording remains a miracle of translucency. Martin Bookspan, in his 1968 updating of the basic repertory, (the musical mausoleum of which our great orchestras are the curators) calls the Toscanini disc "A thrilling, vital account." Unmauled by souped-up stereo affectation, the mono sound is not bad; it is one of the best of the Toscanini series. The recording was made in 1953 at Carnegie Hall, not the notorious NBC Studio 8-H, praise be!

Fricsay's reading is warm and lyrical and it has much of the electric charge of the Toscanini disc. The Berlin Philharmonic is at its sonorous best here. The 1962 Deutsche Grammophon sound (this disc is originally from the DGG catalogue) is excellent. *High Fidelity* said: "There may be more personal statements of this symphony in the catalogue, but Fricsay's reading is the one to live with."

Giulini's reading, one of the best of the stereo versions available to us, is far more gentle and relaxed than Toscanini's tight-reined, bristling performance. In the words of *High Fidelity*, this record is "unusually fresh, expressive, and distinguished." The sound is good.

Golschmann is direct, hard-driving, and exciting. This is a top-notch record, with ample sound.

Another top-drawer reading is to be had from Hollreiser on Vox—a pleasing, cheerfully extroverted interpretation. The sound is pretty good.

The romantic, easy-going Kubelik-Vienna reading was a sonic wonder in the primeval days of stereo. It's a little plummy now, but this remains a vivid, highly lyrical performance.

Kubelik's Chicago performance has somewhat sharper sonics, but lacks a certain mellowness.

A gentle, non-sensational, and satisfying interpretation is to be heard from Ancerl and the Czech Philharmonic. I have persuaded myself that Ancerl's reading is in the true Czech idiom and is presented as it should be, quite unlike the tired warhorse that the *"New World"* Symphony has become in the hands of most conductors.

Barbirolli disappoints; his is a listless, unambitious performance. However, in fairness, I must add that the Barbirolli reading is highly regarded by many other critics.

A capable but uneventful reading is turned in by Leinsdorf.

Ludwig is okay, but not outstanding.

Rignold's version is unremarkable.

ORCHESTRAL MUSIC Dvorak wrote very many colorful works for orchestra, but most of them have perished. The *Slavonic Dances,* however, are still hugely popular, and the *Overtures* and *Seranades* are very much alive.

CARNIVAL OVERTURE (Opus 92)

This is the middle unit of a *Triple Overture* Dvorak composed to express "Nature, Life, and Love." Carnival is one of Dvorak's most popular orchestral pieces, probably because the violins are directed to "whirl into a Bohemian revel."

* DORATI	*London Symphony Orch.*	MERCURY (S) 18080 [Symphony No. 8]
* GIULINI	*Philharmonic Orch.*	SERAPHIM (S) 60045 [Symphony No. 9]
* ROWICKI	*London Symphony Orch.*	PHILLIPS WS (S) 9088 [Symphony No. 5]

All three readings are colorful and expert, and serve as fillers to longer works. The choice of the couplings should influence your decision.

CONCERTO IN B MINOR FOR CELLO (Opus 104)

This inspired work is the greatest romantic concerto for cello, the crowning achievement of Dvorak's copious, warm-hearted genius. "Why hasn't anyone shown me before that one can write a concerto for cello as fine as this?" asked Johannes Brahms after reading the manuscript copy for this cello concerto.

* * * ROSTROPOVICH, KHAIKIN	*Moscow Radio Orch.*	MONITOR (S) 2090 [Saint-Saens, Cello Concerto]
* JANIGRO, DIXON	*Vienna State Opera Orch.*	WESTMINSTER (M) 9716
* CASSADO, PERLEA	*Pro Musica Symphony Orch.*	VOX (M) 9630 [Tchaikovsky, Variations on a Rococo Theme]
* ROSTROPOVICH, RACHLIN	*USSR Radio Orch.*	PERIOD SHO ST-2 334 [Schumann, Concerto]
* ROSTROPOVICH, TALICH	*Czech Philharmonic*	PARLIAMENT (M) 139

The high-water mark has been set by the superb Russian cellist Rostropovich, and he can be heard on three low-priced discs in this concerto. Easily the best of three Iron Curtain discs is the reading on Monitor, a performance of rich romantic concentration. The sound is good.

Janigro's is highly poetic, but outclassed. The sound is mono.

Cassado is okay on a mono disc, but inferior to the great Russian.

The other Rostropovich versions are indifferently recorded.

CONCERTO IN G MINOR FOR PIANO (Opus 33)

The composer's only piano concerto, written in 1876, is rather monotonous and uninventive. It is seldom played.

* RICHTER, KONDRASHIN	*Moscow Radio Orch.*	PERIOD ˙ SHO (ST-2) 341 [Schumann, Concerto]
MAXIAN, TALICH	*Czech Philharmonic*	ARTIA (M) 179

The formidable Russian pianist Richter makes much more out of this music than one would believe possible. The sound is only so-so.

Maxian is nothing special. The disc is best summed up by *Music on Records* as "clean and competent."

CONCERTO IN A MINOR FOR VIOLIN (Opus 53)

Dvorak's *Violin Concerto* has never been a very popular piece with audiences. Except for a lovely slow movement, most of it is wearisome and conventional, far below this composer's best.

Joachim, the great violinist, and godfather to several romantic concertos including that of Brahms, was Dvorak's editorial adviser on this piece. Dvorak completed his first version of the concerto in 1879, and revised it again in 1882. A certain fragile charm keeps this concerto, however insecurely, within the modern repertory.

* SUK, ANCERL	*Czech Philharmonic*	ARTIA (S) 193 [Romance for Violin and Orchestra]
* GIMPEL, REINHARDT	*SW German Radio Orch.*	VOX 10290 [Goldmark, Concerto for Violin and Orchestra]

Joseph Suk, a descendant of Dvorak's son-in-law, plays with conviction, in a lyric, small-toned style. [On the reverse side, the *Romance for Violin and Orchestra* (Opus 11) is an inconsequential early piece, fulsome and romantic.]

Gimpel's reading is unremarkable. The English critic Peter Gammond dismissed it in *Music on Record* as being "not of very good quality, and a rather matter-of-fact performance." [The coupling is with the seldom-heard, timidly romantic concerto of Karl Goldmark.]

SERENADE IN D MINOR (Opus 44)

This rustic serenade, for wind instruments, cello, and bass, was written in 14 days in 1878. Clarity of line and nice organization marks the composition, parts of which are reminiscent of Mozart's writing for winds.

* * SCHMIDT-ISSERSTED	*Hamburg Radio Symphony Orch.*	HELIODOR (S) 25066
* TURNOVSKY	*Prague Chamber Harmony Orch.*	CROSSROADS (S) 22 16 0170 [Serenade]

The Hamburgers are polished, and warmhearted. [The coupling is excellent.]

The wind playing of the Czechs is persuasive. The sound is all right.

SERENADE IN E FOR STRINGS (Opus 22)

First heard in 1876, the *Serenade for Strings* was written in 11 days. It is a popular early work.

* * SCHMIDT-ISSERSTEDT	*Hamburg Radio Symphony Orch.*	HELIODOR [Serenade]	(S) 25066
* VLACH	*Czech Chamber Orch.*	CROSSROADS [Serenade]	22 16 0170

Schmidt-Isserstedt is fresh and relaxed in an effective reading. At times, unfortunately, the "electronically enhanced" sound is rather boomy.

The Czechs under Vlach are lyrical and appealing. The sound is acceptable. [The coupling is apt and good.]

SLAVONIC DANCES (Opus 46, Opus 72)

Dvorak's first set of *Slavonic Dances,* published in 1878, made him an international figure. "Like Byron, he awoke to find himself world-famous," wrote W. H. Hadow, in rather ecstatic prose, "and to look back upon the times of darkness and disappointment as a man looks back upon his dreams." Brahms had given the younger Dvorak a boost by praising him to the publisher Simrock.

The dances are still piquant, fresh, and highly enjoyable, and much admired for their folklorist style.

The composer originally set the *Slavonic Dances* for two pianos, the most highly salable version in his day; later, he wrote an orchestral version.

* * BRENDEL AND KLIEN		TURNABOUT (3) [Opus 46; 72]	4064
* * REINER	*Vienna Philharmonic*	LONDON STS [Opus 46: 1, 3, 8; 72: 1, 2; Brahms, Hungarian Dances]	15009
* * ROSSI	*Vienna State Opera Orch.*	VANGUARD (S)	189
* TALICH	*Czech Philharmonic*	2-PARLIAMENT [Opus 46; 72]	121
* HAGEN	*Austrian Symphony Orch.*	EVEREST (M) (S) [Opus 46; Smetana, The Moldau]	6104 3104

* DORATI	*Minneapolis Symphony Orch.*	MERCURY [Opus 46; 72]	18082
* MARTINON	*London Symphony Orch.*	VICTROLA VIC (S) 1054 [Opus 46; 72/7]	
SEJNA	*Czech Philharmonic*	2 ARTIA (S) 186/7 [Opus 46; 72; Smetana, Bartered Bride: Dances]	

Brendel and Klien offer a scintillating performance in a two-piano version.

Fritz Reiner, that old Magyar sorcerer, gives a rousing, all-out performance. The sound is brilliant.

Mario Rossi's performance on Vanguard is spirited and polished. This disc offers 12 of the 16 *Slavonic Dances*. The sound, as is the case with most Vanguard-Everyman discs, is clear, well-defined stereo.

The two-record set by the Czech Philharmonic under Talich goes back to the earliest era of LP. Irving Kolodin then hailed this record as "one of the glories of the post-war catalog." The performance still stands as the model of what can be done with this piece, but the sound is not so hot.

Four excerpts are neatly played on the Everest disc.

Dorati performs with brio. The sound is boxed in.

Martinon is acceptable, not outstanding.

Sejna's interpretation is plodding, but the playing is good, and the stereo sound surprisingly effective.

RUSALKA

This long, overwritten opera, based on the fairy tale *Ondine,* has been called by Conrad L. Osborne "one of the most lovable and touching operas in the repertory — or rather, out of the repertory." There are sudden flashes of inspired writing along with wearisome stretches and much melodic richness. If the length doesn't bother you, *Rusalka* is a fine opera to persue at home at leisure.

* * CHALABALA	*Prague National Theatre Orch.*	4-ARTIA	(S) 89D
FRICK, TROETSCHEL, KEILBERTH	*Saxon State Orch. and Chorus*	3-URANIA	(M) 219/3 (S) 5219/3

The Czech cast is full-voiced, and the conducting is properly sweeping and dramatic. The recording is decidedly clear.

The older Urania set, sung in German, has weak singers in several roles, as well as indifferent conducting. The sound is foggy.

STABAT MATER (Opus 58)

This deeply moving work was composed in 1876-77 in memory of Dvorak's eldest daughter who had just passed away. The alert listener will be startled by many stylish resemblances to Verdi's stunning *Requiem*, first performed in 1874.

TALICH	*Czech Philharmonic and Chorus*	2-ARTIA	182/3
REICHERT	*Ricklinghausen Chorus, Westphalian Symphony Orch.*	2-Vox SVUX	(S) 52020

Neither offering is commendable. The Czechs under Talich have an excellent chorus, good male singers, and poor female soloists. The sound is poor.

The Vox offering seems to be a provincial performance with undisciplined conducting. *High Fidelity* comments: "The weakness of the score is accentuated by the very stolidity of the performance."

CHAMBER MUSIC   Lovers of the orchestral music of Dvorak should not overlook the composer's many works of chamber music. Some of his finest and most melodious pieces were composed for small ensembles.

There is utter confusion in the cataloguing of Dvorak's 14 string quartets; some pieces blithely pop up with other opus numbers than those named here. I'll try to sort out the bewilderment: *Quartets 2, 3, 4,* and *6* were never published during Dvorak's lifetime. *No. 8 in E Major* was published as *Opus 80* by good old publisher Simrock when it was, in truth, an early work. The musical pundits of Prague have just begun to re-catalogue Dvorak's chamber music.

QUARTET IN E (Opus 27)

This is middle-period Dvorak — lyric and easy to hear, but unmemorable.

*	*Dvorak Quartet*	CROSSROADS (S) 22 16 0090 [Waltzes]

The Dvorak *Quartet,* though accomplished, throws too much sonic spotlight on the first viola. [The coupling is with two light-weight pieces from a cycle of piano works that Dvorak wrote in 1879-90.]

QUARTET NO. 2 IN D MINOR (Opus 34)

This spontaneous-sounding quartet, written in 1878, was dedicated to Brahms who strongly criticized it and urged revisions which the grateful Dvorak made.

| * | Smetana Quartet | Artia | (S) 717 |
| | | [Martinu, Quartet No. 4] | |

The Smetana Quartet's reading is relaxed — even mild-mannered — and not exactly stimulating. [The coupling is with a harmless, eclectic piece by Martinu.]

QUARTETS FOR STRINGS: IN A (Opus 2); NO. 6, IN F (Opus 96) ("American"); NO. 7, IN A FLAT (Opus 105); NO. 8, IN G (Opus 106)

The "American" Quartet is the attraction here. Opus 105 and 106, the other quartets, are also solid works, written within a few months after Dvorak happily sailed home to Prague after his three-year stay in America. The quartet Opus 2, No. 6, is a harmless, pleasant piece written when the composer was twenty-one.

The "American" Quartet is the most popular of Dvorak's string quartets. As with the "New World" Symphony, it was long believed that this work is permeated with Negro and American Indian folk music. It is true that an Indian tribe did entertain at Spillville during Dvorak's visit, but the main reason for this opinion is because Dvorak employed the pentatonic scale, a scale which has only five notes and lacks semitone intervals. Negro melodies of this period were often pentatonic, but so was much of Dvorak's own intensely Slovak music, long before Mrs. Thurber ever lured him to direct her "National Conservatory of Music" in America. In any case, the "American" Quartet is one of Dvorak's most beguiling works and was composed in America.

| Kohon Quartet | Vox SVBX | 550 |

The playing of the Kohon Quartet is more than good, with fine, sharp stereo separation between the instruments. High Fidelity comments: "Performance here is of a high caliber: rhythmically alive, accurate, and colorful." The Stereo Record Guide chimes in: "Warm-hearted playing, with a strong accent on lyricism."

QUARTETS FOR STRINGS: 1 IN A MINOR (Opus 16); 2 IN D MINOR (Opus 34); 3 IN E FLAT (Opus 51); 4 IN C (Opus 61); 5 IN E (Opus 80)

These middle-period quartets (written between 1874 and 1881) will appeal to all lovers of Dvorak's music. They are winsome, spontaneous-sounding, and technically proficient.

| * * | Kohon Quartet | Vox SVBX | 5498 |

The admirable Kohon Quartet, of New York University, plays with polish and spirit. However, the leader of the quartet — if I may offer an inconsequential quibble — seems to dominate his colleagues.

QUINTET IN G (Opus 77) (Orig. Opus 18)

This is really an early work, *Opus 18;* Dvorak's quixotic publisher, Simrock, blithely labeled it *Opus 77* in order to sell it as "mature Dvorak." Written in 1875 when Dvorak was thirty-four, this is a somewhat labored work, not as lyrical as most of Dvorak's music.

| * GRODNER | Berkshire Quartet, | 3-Vox SVBX | (S) | 551 |

The playing is affectionate. Irving Kolodin of the *Saturday Review* remarks that "the performance profits from open, resonant reproduction which is especially advantageous to the sound of the double bass."

QUINTET IN A FOR PIANO AND STRINGS (Opus 81)

This very popular work is filled with colorful scoring, vital rhythm, and bursting melody.

* * SANDOR	Berkshire Quartet	TURNABOUT (3) 4075 [Trio, Opus 90]
* SANDOR	Berkshire Quartet	3-Vox SVBX (S) 551 [Quintets, Quartets]
* GLAZER	Fine Arts Quartet	CONCERT-DISC M1251/S251
FARNADI	Barylli Quartet	WESTMINSTER 9025 [Quartet No. 7]

A warm, expansive reading by pianist Sandor and the Berkshire Quartet leads the field. The sound is pleasant. The piece can be obtained either as a single disc, or as part of a good three-record Vox box.

Glazer and the Fine Arts Quartet are expert, but they do not approach the ingratiating mood of the top entry.

The old Westminister mono disc is adequate but little more.

QUINTET FOR STRINGS NO. 3 IN E-FLAT (Opus 97)

This music was written in 1894, in the little Iowa town of Spillville, a Bohemian settlement that Dvorak visited during his stay in America. This is a bright, rhythmic work.

* *	*Dvorak Quartet, Kodousek*	CROSSROADS	(M) 22 16 0081 (S) 22 16 0082 ["Cypresses" Quartet]

The Dvorak Quartet are first-rate chamber music players, and this is one of the best of the Dvorak records from the Czech Supraphon catalogue. The sound is rather dry; the stereo balance, good. [The coupling is with the slight and inoffensive *Cypresses* for string quartet.]

TRIO IN E MINOR "DUMKA" (Opus 90)

The Dumka, a Ukrainian folk ballad, is marked by sudden swoops of gaiety, followed by passages of Slavic melancholy. Dvorak was attracted to this form, and used it in several works. This trio is an amiable, rather endearing work that just occasionally dips into banality.

* * *	FOURNIER, JANIGRO, BADURA-SKODA	WESTMINSTER (M) 9024 [Trio in F]	
* *	OISTRAKH, KNUSLEVITSKY, OBERIN	MONITOR (S) 2070 [Smetana, Trio in G]	
*	*Dumka Trio*	TURNABOUT (3) 4075 [Quintet, Opus 81]	
*	*Dumka Trio*	3-Vox SVBX (S) 571 [Bagatelles; Piano Quartets, Opus 23, 87; Piano Trio, Opus 21]	

The old mono recording by the youthful Fournier, Janigro, and Badura-Skoda has an insouciance and personal projection that have rarely been matched in recordings of this music. [The coupling is with an enjoyable, impulsively romantic *Trio, Opus 26.*]

Suave playing and fine team-work are to be heard from the Russians on the Monitor disc. The sound is all right. [The coupling is with Smetana's dark-hued *Trio,* composed in memory of the composer's daughter who had died at the age of five.]

The Dumka Trio (who play the "Dumka" Trio) are forthright and unexceptional; *High Fidelity* complains of a "lack of rhythmic vitality and variety." Although the sound is clear and the stereo effect well spaced, the violin is inclined to be shrill, and the piano to be tubby.

TRIOS FOR VIOLIN, CELLO, AND PIANO: NO. 1, IN B-FLAT (Opus 21); NO. 4, IN E MINOR (Opus 90) (DUMKA). QUARTETS FOR PIANO AND STRINGS: NO. 1, IN D (Opus 23); NO. 2 IN E-FLAT (Opus 87); BAGATELLES FOR HARMONIUM AND STRINGS (Opus 47)

This collection contains four good works for piano and strings, plus an oddity in which the harmonium replaces the piano. The works range from Dvorak's early maturity to his last years.

* GERHART,   *Dumka Trio*   Vox SVBX   (S)   571
WILLISON

The performances in this three-record Vox Box are unexceptional, commendable only if you really want that much Dvorak chamber music. If you do, the Vox Box recorded by the Kohon Quartet (reviewed previously in this section) is far more worthy.

Elgar, Edward (1857-1934)

Elgar was a wonder. He never enjoyed formal training in music, and yet he became one of the masters of orchestration, surpassed during his lifetime only by Richard Strauss. It is not at all easy to sum him up today. A romantic, from beginning to end, he was also the unabashed, self-satisfied apostle of Edwardian England. A strain of flashy brilliance, and what must be termed robust, blatant imperialism, have discouraged many music lovers from discovering the more profound Elgar. At his best, in the *Violin Concerto,* the *Cello Concerto,* the *Introduction* and *Allegro,* and the *Enigma Variations,* he is a mystical, poetic composer of astonishing technical brilliance.

CONCERTO FOR CELLO   (Opus 85)

This concerto is first-rate music, with little of Elgar's "Banner of St. George" brassy vulgarity. Dating from 1919, this pensive, yet rhapsodic writing, will probably outlive the bulk of Elgar's work. This concerto is not simply a showcase for a virtuoso, and is exteremely difficult to play convincingly.

* PINI, VAN BIENUM	*London Philharmonic*	EVEREST	(M)	6141
			(S)	3141

Pini handles this composition beautifully. However, it is an old disc that was recorded off-balance.

If you love this music, Jacqueline Du Pre is the girl to hear on a high-priced Angel. She has made the concerto one of Elgar's most highly-rated pieces today.

ENIGMA VARIATIONS   (Opus 36)

With the exception of the *Pomp and Circumstance March,* the *Enigma Variations* was Elgars most popular piece during his lifetime. The *Variations* are good music; each variation is a portrait of one of the composer's friends.

* * TOSCANINI	*NBC Orch.*	VICTROLA VIC	(S)	1344
		[Respighi, Feste Romane]		
* * BARBIROLLI	*Philharmonic Orch.*	VANGUARD	(S)	184
		[Vaughan Williams, Symphony No. 8]		
* * MONTEUX	*London Symphony Orch.*	VICTROLA VIC	(S)	1107
		[Brahms, Haydn Variations]		

Toscanini usually looked with disfavor upon "new" (1899) music;

Elgar's *Enigma Variations* was one of the few pieces that attracted him. Toscanini's reading is noble, and the NBC Orchestra handles the virtuoso parts with aplomb. [The coupling, nothing more than a flashy display piece for the orchestra, comes off agreeably.]

Barbirolli's reading has splendor, warmth, and eloquence. This disc dates from 1958, but is vastly preferable to his more recent version on Angel.

Monteux is eloquent, more direct, and restrained. The disc is well recorded. All three readings are good, and your preference for the various couplings may decide here.

POMP AND CIRCUMSTANCE MARCHES (Opus 39)

Only a few years ago, the trio section of *March No. 1, "Land of Hope and Glory,"* sent a shiver through all patriotic Englishmen, leaving a lump in the throat. To our ears, these robust marches are pleasant, and inconsequential.

BRAITHWAITE	*London Symphony Orch.*	RICHMOND [Collection]	(M) 19029

The music is stirringly played, but this music cries out for stereo, rather than the mono available on the Richmond.

STRING QUARTET IN E MINOR   (Opus 83)

This is discursive, post-Brahmsian, fairly interesting writing, dating from 1918.

Claremont Quartet	NONSSUCH	H 71140
		H 1140
	[Sibelius, String Quartet in D Minor, Opus 56, ("Voces Intimae")]	

The Claremont Quartet provides playing that is mildly tasteful, but pallid.

SYMPHONY NO. 1 IN A-FLAT

The astute critic, W. J. Turner, contemptuously dismissed this work as a "Salvation Army symphony." It's hard to disagree. This large-scale, complex composition is not one of Elgar's best.

BARBIROLLI	*Philharmonic Orch.*	SERAPHIM	(S) 60068

The work is authoritatively played by Sir John. The sound, however, is faded.

Enesco, Georges *(1881-1955)*

Roumanian born, Enesco entered the Vienna Conservatorium at the age of seven. He became a composer, conductor, violinist, and teacher. Yehudi Menuhin was one of his pupils. Enesco worked in a folklorist idiom which he successfully integrated with traditional classical music.

ROUMANIAN RHAPSODY NO. 1 *(Opus 11)*

This work, composed in 1901, is spiritually kin to Liszt's *Hungarian Rhapsody No. 2,* with which it is often coupled on records. It is flamboyant music of Pops program status.

* * GOLSCHMANN	*Vienna State Opera Orch.*	VANGUARD ·(S) 160 [Roumanian Rhapsodie No. 2; Liszt, Hungarian Rhapsody]	
* PERLEA	*Bamberg Symphony Orch.*	VOX (S) 9500 [Dvorak, Scherzo Capriccioso; Kodaly, Galanta Dances; Smetana, Moldau]	

Golschmann gives a full-bodied, straight forward interpretation. The sound is excellent. [Besides the two Enesco Rhapsodies, the Vanguard disc conttains the Liszt *Rhapsody,* nicely performed.]

Perlea gives a colorful performance in a mixed Pops program.

ROUMANIAN RHAPSODY NO. 2 *(Opus 11)*

Written in 1911, the *Roumanian Rhapsody No. 2,* though more lyrical, is less exuberant than the more famous *No. 1.*

GOLSCHMANN	*Vienna State Opera Orch.*	VANGUARD (S) 160 [Liszt, Hungarian Rhapsody No. 5]
SILVESTRI	*Czech Philharmonic Orch.*	PARLIAMENT (M) 137 [Rhapsody No. 1]

Golschmann is preferred, for a well-placed, flamboyant reading.

The Silvestri disc is fuzzily recorded.

SONATA NO. 3 IN A FOR VIOLIN AND PIANO *(Opus 25)*

A sonata in the popular Roumanian style, and, in the words of Yehudi Menuhin, "a remarkable and haunting work." This sonata has been heard by millions who are only vaguely aware that they are listening to Enesco, a Roumanian, and who may possibly believe that they are listening to Indian music. The piece is recorded on the flip side of the famous Menuhin-Ravi Shankar "West Meets East" recording.

* DRUIAN, SIMMS	PHILIPS WS (S) 9084 [Janacek, Sonata]
* FERRAS, BARBIZET	MACE (S) 9045 [Debussy, Sonata]

Druian gives a convincing interpretation, although after hearing Menuhin play the piece on the expensive Angel disc, it's hard to be satisfied with anyone else. The sound is fine and intimate. [The Janacek sonata, on the reverse side, is of interest.]

Ferras seems overly reserved in his interpretation, but he nevertheless presents an excellent program.

Fálla, Manuel de (1876-1946)

De Falla, a pianist, was the oustanding Spanish composer of his time. He lived in Paris; then moved back to Spain where he remained until the Civil War, and then moved to Argentina.

When young, his acquaintance with Debussy veered him toward impressionism and an obvious nationalism, but his later works are austerely neo-classical. He will probably be remembered for his earlier, intensely Spanish works: *El Amor Brujo, Nights in the Gardens of Spain,* and *The Three Cornered Hat.*

Here is Spain in all her passion, her pride, her violence. De Falla published very little, although he lived to be seventy. During his last two decades, he wrote nothing of consequence.

EL AMOR BRUJO   (Sung in Spanish)

Love the Magician is an Andalusian gypsy ballet which dates from 1915. Here are Spanish fury and color, including the great Pops favorite, the *Ritual Fire Dance.*

* * GABARAIN, ANSERMET	*Orchestra Suisse Romande*	LONDON STS	(S) 15014
* MADEIRA, VAN REMOORTEL	*Vienna Symphony Orch.*	Vox	(5) 11910
RIVAS, BENZI	*Paris Opera Orch.*	PHILLIPS WS	(M/S) 9054

Ansermet gives the best performance, with proper fire. Ansermet's soloist is "off-stage," as the composer instructed.

Van Remoortel's version is more restrained; but his soloist bellows on stage. This disc provides the best sound.

Benzi is pallid, and his soloist sounds sleepy.

For a really thrilling experience, listen to Grace Bumbry and Lorin Maazel charge through this work on a high-priced DGG disc.

CONCERTO FOR HARPSICHORD, FLUTE, OBOE, CLARINET, VIOLIN AND CELLO

This is a fairly interesting concerto, in de Falla's later, neo-classical style, and shows the influence of Stravinsky.

* RICHARD, LARDE, MAISONNEUVE, DEPLUS, ALES, LAMY, RAVIER	*Valois Instrumental Ensemble*	NONESUCH H [Piano Works]	(S) 71135

The music is competently played, and this record is definitely worthwhile. The sound is listenable. [We also have all the original keyboard music of de Falla on this record, (except for some juvenilia)—rugged, ascetic, Spanish music. Perhaps the most outstanding piece is the *Fantasia Baetica,* powerful music commissioned by Artur Rubinstein.]

NIGHTS IN THE GARDENS OF SPAIN (1909-1915)

This sensuous, highly colored score, containing symphonic impressions for piano and orchestra, is all that its title suggests.

* PANENKA, PEDROTTI	*Czech Philharmonic*	CROSSROADS (S) 22 16 0190	
* NOVAES, SWAROWSKY	*Vienna Pro Musica*	VOX (5) 8520 [Grieg, Concerto]	

An evocative reading, with surprisingly good sound, is offered by the Czechs on Crossroads.

Novaes is poetic, but Swarowsky is not subtle enough for this delicate music. The sound is dated.

THE THREE CORNERED HAT   (Ballet)

The Three Cornered Hat was originally a 1919 ballet written for Diaghilev with costumes and scenery by Picasso, and choreography by Massine. The text is based on a racy tale—the same used by Hugo Wolf for his opera *Der Corregidor.* A soprano voice off-stage is heard twice in the course of the action.

* HOWITT, JORDA	*London Symphony Orch.*	EVEREST	(M) 6057 (S) 3057
* DANCO, ANSERMET	*Suisse Romande*	RICHMOND	19100
* MADEIRA, VAN REMOORTEL	*Vienna Symphony Orch.*	VOX	(M) 11920 (S) 511920

The spirited Jorda reading appeals to me. The sound is vivid.

Ansermet's performance is brilliant. The sound of this old disc is still quite hearable. Danco is easily the best of the soloists.

Van Remootel is meticulous, and fairly exciting.

THE THREE CORNERED HAT   (Dance)

These are selected dance numbers from the ballet.

* * RODZINSKI	*Royal Philharmonic Orch.*	SERAPHIM [Collection]	(S) 60021

| * VAN REMOORTEL | *Vienna Symphony* | Vox   (5) 11910
[De Falla, El Amor Brujo;
Chabrier, Espana Rapsody] |
| * MACKERRAS | *Pro Arte Orch.* | Vanguard   (S)   178
[Mixed program] |

Rodzinski does well in a crisp, lean style. The stereo sound is pleasant. [This excellent record is called "Music of Spanish Masters"; besides the complete dances from the *Hat Granados,* it contains:. *Andaluza* (from *Danzas Espangnolas*); *Albeniz, Navarra,* and *El Corpus en Sevilla* (the latter from *Iberia*). The *Ritual Fire Dance* from *El Amor Brujo* provides a stirring filler.]

Van Remoortel delivers a vigorous reading. [The couplings are spirited and colorful.]

Mackerras is crisp and the sound is clean.

Fasch, Johann Friedrich (1688-1758)

A student at Leipzig University, Fasch was a contemporary of J. S. Bach. Fasch's undying fame in music is circumstantial, rather than musical: he was offered the cantorate at Leipzig before it was offered to Bach, but he turned it down. If Bach had not received the church appointment which demanded so much written-to-order music from him every week, his compositions would certainly have been different than they are. Bach admired Fasch, and even copied five of the latters orchestral suites.

CONCERTO FOR TRUMPET IN D

This sprightly, unpretentiuos trumpet music is outdoorsy, German, and harmless.

* ZICKLER, KEHR	*Mainz Chamber Orch.*	TURNABOUT TV 34090 [Hertel; Biber; Stoelzel: Trumpet concerti]

We hear good trumpeting from Heinz Zickler. Sound is fine and wide-sounding. [A note on the couplings: Gottfried Stoelzel (1690-1749) was Kapellmeister to the Duke at Gotha. He composed 22 operas, 14 oratorios, several masses, and other works; he is here represented by a rowdy concerto for six trumpets. Heinrich Biber (1644-1704) was in the service of the Archbishop of Salzburg; he wrote music that is technically accomplished, but dull.]

SYMPHONY IN G

The Fasch symphony is dull and pedestrian.

HOFMAN, MANNHEIMER SOLISTEN	NONESUCH 1123 [J. C. Bach, Sinfonietta in C; Haydn, Sinfonia "La Vera Constanca"; Trio in C, for Flute, Oboe and Cello, in C]

The sound is agreeable, and the playing is uneventful. [The J. C. Bach work is listenable, and the Haydn Trio is a delight.]

Faure, Gabriel (1845-1924)

A pupil of Saint-Saëns, Fauré was a composer, an organist, and a teacher. He was Director of the Paris Conservatoire between 1905 and 1920. The last two decades of his life were plagued by deafness; in the end, he was unable to hear his own music. He had a remarkable influence on his pupils, who included Nadia Boulanger and Maurice Ravel. Fauré's music is refined and civilized, and possesses a cool beauty.

BALLADE FOR PIANO AND ORCHESTRA (Opus 19);
PELLEAS ET MELISANDE
(Suite from the Incidental Music) (Opus 80)

The *Ballade* is rapturous music, with Chopinesque piano writing, and many evocative pages. The incidental music to *Pelléas* was written for a production of Maeterlinck's play, in London in 1898. Fauré was not particularly interested in orchestral writing *per se,* and he often disdained to do his own scoring. This sensuous *Ballade* was orchestrated by Fauré's pupil, Koechlin.

    * DEVETZI, BAUDO   NONESUCH H   71178

The music is colorfully and delicately played. In the *Ballade,* the Greek pianist Vasso Devetzi gives a very sensitive reading.

PIANO MUSIC (Completed)

Chopin seems to be the model for Fauré's piano music. The collection of his complete works will not be everyone's cup of tea—especially in a long six-record set. But for those who dote on Fauré, this collection offers the full range of the composer's development, from his early romanticism to the ascetic chromaticism of his later years.

    * CROCHET   VOX   SVBX 5423/24

The music is elegantly played in a kinetic, mercurial style typical of Paris Conservatoire musicians. Evelyn Crochet, a pupil of Edwin Fischer and Rudolph Serkin, is an excellent pianist—small-scaled, but possessed, nevertheless, of formidable technique. *High Fidelity's* piano critic Harris Goldsmith, who knows pianists as do few reviewers, said: "I am still astonished by the ravishing excellence of Miss Crochet's work on these discs and could hardly conceive of these interpretations being bettered." The selections included are: *Theme and Variations, Opus 73; Barcarolles (13);*

Valse-Caprices (4); *Pièces Brèves, Opus 84*; *Preludes, Opus 103*; *Nocturnes (13Q*; *Songs Without Words, Opus 17*; *Mazurka, Opus 32*. The sound is a bit dry, but acceptable.

REQUIEM (Opus 48)

Sublime music! There is no other verdict. Written in 1887, when Fauré was organist at the Madeleine Church in Paris, this *Requiem* is recommended to music lovers who shy away from booming, large-scaled religious works. Here is intimate, soft-spoken music, with the serene quality of the stained-glass window of a cathedral.

* * CHAMONIN, ABDOUN, MARTINI	*Chorale des Jeunesses Musicales de France; Orchestra des Concerts Colonne*	TURNABOUT TV	34147
* * BLANZAT, MOFFET, GUILLOU, MARTIN	*Chorus and Orchestra of the Church of St.-Eustache, Paris*	NONESUCH H	71158

Both discs are welcome. Fauré's *Requiem* lends itself extremely well to recording and both these entries are enjoyable.

The Turnabout version, however, has sweet, chaste-sounding singers who seem just right for Fauré's delicate tones. The sound is clear.

The Nonesuch disc is not to be slighted. Martin, of the Church of St. Eustache, Paris, is an authority on choral singing, and has given us many wonderful discs. This performance is dedicated and entirely agreeable; I just happen to prefer the lyric quality of the Turnabout version.

SONATA NO. 1 IN A FOR VIOLIN (Opus 13)

This lovely sonata was composed in 1876.

* FOURNIER, DOYEN	WESTMINSTER (M) 9072 [Sonata No. 2]	

It is poetically played. The mono sound is serviceable.

SONATA NO. 2 IN E MINOR FOR VIOLIN (Opus 108)

The two French artists are poetic here. The mono sound is serviceable. This sonata, written in 1917, when Fauré was a tremendously different composer than he had been in 1876, is music of refinement and elegance.

* FOURNIER, DOYEN	WESTMINSTER (M) 9072 [Sonata No. 1]	

* MANDEL, KOENIG	BAROQUE	(M)	1845
		(S)	2845
	[Franck, Sonata]		
FERRAS, BARBIZET	EVEREST	(M)	6140
		(S)	3140
	[Debussy, Sonata]		

Although sometimes tense and scratchy, Fournier's chaste reading is preferable.

The Mandel-Koenig interpretation will be agreeable to those who insist on a stereo recording.

The Ferras-Barbizet version is heavy-handed. I find the tremulous violin vibrato disturbing.

Flotow, Friedrich Von (1812-1883)

The son of a German nobleman, Flotow spent much of his life in Paris, but moved to Vienna in his later years. He wrote 18 operas in several languages. Most of his operas were popular in their day, but only one, *Martha*, has survived in repertory.

MARTHA

Until recently, *Martha* was quite frequently performed in Central Europe. This light-weight opera is uneven; as an entire work, it is of interest primarily to specialists.

One famous tenor aria is a concert favorite and often appears on recorded recitals by famous singers.

BERGER, ANDERS, GREINDL, ROTHER	*Berlin Radio Symphony Orch. and Civic Opera Chorus (Sung in German)*	3-URANIA	(M)	217
			(S)	5217
TASSINARI, TAGLIAVINI MOLINARI-PRADELLI	*(Sung in Italian)*	2-EVEREST/CETRA	(S)	406/2

Erna Berger is fine, but Peter Anders is rather unsteady in this German performance. The sound is extremely old.

The Everest/Cetra Italian version, more sentimental than sprightly, is well sung. The stereo sound is of indifferent quality.

Franck, Cesar (1822-1890)

The son of a Flemish bank clerk, Franck showed musical talent at an early age. When Franck was 14, Cherubini admitted him to the Paris Conservatoire. Cherubini even granted a special award to Franck, who at his entrance examination, not only composed a fugue on a given theme, but transposed it. Later, however, Cherubini refused Franck permission to compete for the *Prix de Rome* because Franck was a Belgian.

At 26, Franck married a French actress, and settled in Paris. He earned a living as organist and teacher at the Paris Conservatoire, and composed his own music between the hours of five and seven in the morning.

During his lifetime, he received no public recognition. Some of his dedicated pupils, led by D'Indy, organized a Franck festival in 1887, but the critics treated his music with derision. Gounod described the *D Minor Symphony* as "the affirmation of incompetence pushed to dogmatic length." Today, this work is held to be the one glorious symphony in French musical literature.

Shortly after the first public performance of his string quartet, Franck was struck by an omnibus; he died shortly afterward.

PLACE AND ACHIEVEMENT   Looking back from the mid-twentieth century, Franck seems more German than French in style. His work displays not a shred of the sensuousness typical of the French music of his day. Liszt seems to have had a pervasive influence on him; it may even be said that Franck achieved that quality of mystic, exalted contemplation that Liszt himself sought but almost always failed to achieve.

Franck's pupils—and they were many—adored him, but he nevertheless left only a slight mark on the pages of musical history. He is best seen as a composer of impassioned eloquence and purity, inspired by a deep religious nature.

THE ESSENTIAL FRANCK

ORCHESTRAL MUSIC: *Symphony in D Minor; Symphonic Variations, for Piano and Orchestra.*

CHAMBER MUSIC: *Quintet in F Minor, for Piano and Strings; Quartet in D Major; Sonata in A Major, for Violin and Piano.*

OTHER WORKS

ORATORIO: *Les Beatitudes.*

SYMPHONIC POEMS: *Le Chasseur Maudit, Les Eolides; Les Djinns; Psyche.*

CHURCH MUSIC: *Mass in A for 3 Violes.*

PIANO MUSIC: *Prelude, Chorale, and Fugue; Prelude, Aria and Fugue.*

ORGAN MUSIC: *53 "Pieces"; Three Chorales.*

GRAND PIECE SYMPHONIQUE; FANTASIE IN A MAJOR; PASTORALE

For many listeners, the true César Franck is to be found in his organ music. These are meditative, spiritual pieces; here Franck stands before us in mystical purity.

* * DUPRÉ   WORLD SERIES   (S)   9077

Marcel Dupré, heard playing the organ in the Church of Saint-Sulpice in Paris, is the ideal interpreter for this music. The sound is spacious. I should add that some critics find Dupré doddering (he is over 80), and detest Franck's organ music. I like both.

PSYCHE   (Complete)   (Sung in French)

This symphonic poem in four parts was written at approximately the same time as the *Symphony*. For many lovers of nineteenth-century music, *Psyche*, with its Wagnerian chromaticism is Franck's major orchestral work, rather than the more frequently played *Symphony in D Minor*. *Psyche* was originally scored as a symphony with chorus. Franck revised the score after a rather cool reception of the first performance in Paris in 1888. He extracted and condensed four orchestral movements into the form of a suite.

* FOURNET   *Prague Symphony Orch.*   CROSSROADS (M) 22 16 0117
                    Czech Philharmonic   (S) 22 16 0118
                    Chorus

The Czech players are quite all right. Jean Fournet handles the orchestra and chorus with delicacy. This recording is hardly the definitive performance, but it is enjoyable. The stereo sound is effective.

PSYCHE   (Excerpts)

Here are selections from the symphonic poem of 1887-88.

* * TOSCANINI   *NBC Symphony Orch.*   VICTROLA VIC   1246
                                                [Debussy, Iberia; La Mer]

The Toscanini reading is refined and atmospheric. This disc was recorded in Carnegie Hall in 1952, and the sound is thin.

QUINTET FOR PIANO AND STRINGS, IN F MINOR

This has been called erotic music; if so, it escape my ears. Nevertheless, it is one of Franck's most satisfying works, and it marked his return to chamber music after more than 35 years. It is satisfying, romantic music.

* BERNATHOVA	*Janacek Quartet*	ARTIA ALP	(M)	702
* RICHTER	*Quartet of the Bolshoi Theatre Orch.*	MONITOR MC		2036

The music on the Artia record is passionately played, and the sound is agreeable.

Richter's interpretation, to me, seems overly emotional, and too rambling.

SONATA IN A MAJOR FOR PIANO AND VIOLIN

This is one of the most popular of all romantic violin sonatas.

* NADIEN, HANCOCK	MONITOR MC (S) 2017 [Debussy, Sonata No. 3 in G Minor for Violin and Piano; Ravel, Piece en Forme de Habanera; Faure, Berceuse]

The music is sweetly played by violinist David Nadien, accompanied by pianist David Hancock. It is well recorded. [A well-selected French program fills out the disc.]

SYMPHONIC VARIATIONS FOR PIANO AND ORCHESTRA

Unorthodox in form, this is the closest Franck came to writing a piano concerto. This is a fairly popular concert piece.

* KATIN, GOOSSENS	*London Symphony Orch.*	EVEREST	(M)	6036
			(S)	3036
		[Schumann, Concerto]		

Katin's full-blooded playing has plenty of temperament, but not much poetry or refinement.

SYMPHONY IN D

Completed in 1888, the *Symphony in D* belongs to the last group of Franck's works, which includes as well the *Quartet* and the *Three Chorales for Organ*. This is an extremely popular symphony; indeed, it is a staple of the concert repertoire. The form Franck used here is "*cyclical*"—themes from one movement are used in another movement. Over-exposure sometimes makes the work sound hackneyed, but this symphony is a noble work from the pen of a deeply religious man.

* * * MUNCH	*Boston Symphony Orch.*	VICTROLA VIC	(S) 1034
* MUNCH	*Paris Conservatory Orch.*	RICHMOND [Symphony Variations]	(M) 19022
* BARBIROLLI	*Czech Philharmonic Orch.*	CROSSROADS	(M) 22 16 0127 (S) 22 16 0128
* BEECHAM	*Orch. National RTF*	SERAPHIM	(S) 60012
* VAN REMOORTEL	*Vienna Pro Musica Symphony Orch.*	VOX [Symphonic Variations]	(5) 12290
* GOLSCHMANN	*St. Louis Symphony Orch.*	PICKWICK	(S) 4012

Charles Munch was an acknowledged specialist of this score. Munch and the Boston Symphony are eloquent, well served by the acoustics of Symphony Hall.

The Munch Paris recording is much older. Badly recorded, it is issued in mono only; but you get the *Symphonic Variations* as a bonus.

Barbirolli takes a no-nonsense approach, with little of the *misterioso* that conductors since Mengelberg have emphasized in this work. Barbirolli's reading is too cut and dried.

Beecham's performance is disappointing; the RTF Orchestra provides only scrappy playing.

Van Remoortel is unexceptional, and so are his players.

Golschmann's interpretation is adequate, hearable, and unremarkable.

Fux, Johann Joseph *(1660-1741)*

A Viennese composer, Fux was also a formidable theorist. He composed over 400 works, including 50 masses and a quantity of other church music, 18 operas, 10 oratorios, 29 partitas and overtures, etc. His treatise on counterpoint, *Gradus ad Parnassum*, was for many generations the textbook that students struggled with at music conservatories in many nations and in many languages. The book was used by Haydn and Mozart.

Fux's music is formal, seldom noticeably inspired.

CONSTANZA E FORTEZZA   *(Orchestral Suite)*

The orchestral suite is a modern edition of extracts of Fux's opera, which was written to celebrate the coronation of the Emperor Charles VI as King of Bohemia in 1723. The music is inoffensive but unexciting.

Prague Chamber Orch.	CROSSROADS 22 16 0158 [Corelli, Concerto Grosso, Opus 6/8]

The Prague players come through with a workman-like, earnest performance—hardly more.

Gabrieli, Andrea (c. 1520-1586)

Andrea Gabrieli was born in Venice, and was second organist at St. Mark's in that city. The madrigals, motets, and other compositions of his youth are conservative; but his later works, employing involved double choirs, are exceptional for their bold harmonies and rich textures.

RICERCAR

This short instrumental piece just barely hints at the fine innovative spirit of the composer; but it is one of the very few of Gabrieli's works available.

* VENHODA · *The Prague Madrigal Singers and Musica Antiqua of Vienna*   CROSSROADS (S) 22 16 0044 [Giovanni Gabrieli, Two Motets; Monteverdi, Missa A Capella]

Out-of-tune, lugubrious sounds from ancient instruments do not offer me much enjoyment, but this wheezing might please devotees of these instruments. [Most of the works on this record are vocal. The singing is joyous and quite pleasing.]

Gabrieli, Giovanni (1551-1612)

Giovanni, a nephew and pupil of Andrea Gabrieli, turned out to be the more talented member of the family.

In 1968, he was catapulted into new fame as a result of Columbia's extraordinary new recordings of his work made at St. Mark's in Venice. These recordings took advantage of the antiphonal *cori spezzati* (double choirs) to achieve new stereophonic glories. Gabrieli, following his uncle's early experimentations, is best remebered for his polychoric music (music written for two or more complete choirs of voices) and for his antiphonal effects achieved by placing various choirs in different parts of the church. Since such effects are the delight of stereo fans, a swift rise in Giovanni Gabrieli's popularity can be expected.

CANZONI FOR BRASS CHOIRS

This is vivid, stimulating music. Much of it was composed to be played on ceremonial occasions at Saint Mark's Square in Venice.

* BARON	N. Y. *Brass Ensemble*	PERIOD	(S)	734
*	*Schuman Brass Choir*	PERIOD		526
		[Pezel]		

American expertise is evident on this agreeable Period disc, but little more.

The Schuman Brass Group is sonorous but the deeper glories of this music remain unrevealed.

MAGNIFICAT (Benedixisti Domine; O Quam Suavis; Beata Es Virgo Maria; Exaudi Deus; Cantate Domino; Ego Dixi Domine; Inclina Domine; Miserere Mei Deus; O Magnum Mysterium; Sancta Maria; Domine Exudi Orationem Meam)

These pieces, most of them motets, comprise an excellent collection of Gabrieli's brilliant and highly sonorous style. Here is lusty choral writing —in great contrast to the ethereal, rather over-awed quality of many English and American choruses.

* D'ALESSI	*Treviso Cathedral Choir*	VOX	(M)	8830

Msgr. d'Alessi coaxes some solid singing from this antiphonal group. You hear two separate choruses—each at different ends of the hall—as was the custom in Venice in Gabrieli's time. The boys sing their heads off, and the dynamics rarely drop below forte. Yet this music cries out for stereo treatment. But with so few recordings of Gabrieli available at low cost, this album is recommended for those who want to become acquainted with this music.

MOTETS

The motets of Giovanni Gabrieli are daring and striking inventions; they had a tremendous influence on seventeenth-century musicians through-out Europe.

* * VENHODA	*Vienna Musica Antiqua, Prague Madrigal Singers*	CROSSROADS (M) 22160043 (S) 22160044 [A. Gabrieli; Monteverdi, Missa]

The works are sung with fervor, but rather on the overly-solemn side. The stereo balance is good.

ORGAN MUSIC RECITAL

Gabrieli's organ music, composed in a modal idiom, is complex. The toccatas, ricercares, fantasias, and fugues are quite involved.

* DE DONA	Vox	(M) 8470

Though De Dona plays with clarity, more force and assertion would be welcome. The mono sound is clean.

PROCESSIONAL AND CEREMONIAL MUSIC (*O Jesu Mi Dulcissime; Hodie Completi Sunt; O Domine Jesu Christe; O Magnum Mysterium; Angelus Ad Pastorem; Nunc Dimittis; Canzona Quarti Toni; Inclina Domine; Exaude Deus; Sancta Et Immaculata Virginitas*)

These selections well illustrate Gabrieli's fascination with the variety of colors obtainable with different choral combinations, and his expertise in handling such combinations. Of special interest is the stirring *Exaudi Deus* for a seven-part chorus of male voices, and the moving motet for Christmas, *O Jesu Mi Dulcissime*. The latter is scored for two four-part choruses, each subdivided into sopranos, altos, tenors, and basses.

* * * APPIA	*Choirs and Orchestra of the Gabrieli Festival* VANGUARD	(S) 281

This is a stunning disc, and one of the best representations we have of the glory of Gabrieli's art. The chorus is flexible and pliant, and sings with a lovely tone. To reinforce the sonority, Appia introduces modern instruments that Gabrieli never dreamed of, but this is done in a discreet manner. Each work is preceded by a short "intonation" or prelude, well done by Anton Heiller. This is a fine record. The stereo is ringing and open.

SYMPHONIAE SACRAE (Canzone Quarti Toni; Canzone Septemi Toni, Nos. 1 and 2; Canzone Duodecimi Toni; Sonata Pian' E Forte; Sonata Octavi Toni)

These antiphonal works for brass ensemble are most worthwhile. Outstanding is the haunting, solemn *Sonata pian' e forte,* and the vivacious, bouncing *Canzone Septimi Toni, No. 2.* This is fine music, indeed. In stereo, Gabrieli stands revealed as a most rewarding composer.

* * STONE	*Brass Ensemble of the Vienna State Opera Orch.*	WESTMINSTER	(S) 1008

Sayard Stone is a youngish American conductor who loves and understands this period. He has at his disposal an expert Viennese ensemble which includes a marvelous tuba player, and he makes the most of them. These are eloquent performances. The stereo is true, and has been resonantly recorded.

Gaburo, Kenneth (1926-   )

Gaburo taught composition at the University of Illinois — (a hotbed of New Music. He is now on the faculty at the University of California at San Diego.

ANTIPHONY III; ANTIPHONY IV; THE WASTING OF LUCRECETZIA; FAT MILLE'S LAMENT

This collection is a little of everything in New Music. Some is purely electronic, two other numbers manipulate voices, instruments, and electronic gear with live performances. The long shadows of John Cage and Milton Babbitt clearly fall over most of this music, but Gaburo nevertheless produces strong, imposing effects.

* GABURO	*New Music Choral Ensemble; Members of the University of Illinois Contemporary Chamber Players*	NONESUCH	(S) H 71199S

This execution seems adept, and was performed by students of the composer at the University of Illinois. But is it music? Or rather, what is it? I cannot tell you.

Gay, John (1685-1732)
and
Pepusch, John Christopher (1667-1752)

John Gay wrote *The Beggar's Opera* in 1728. It was a burlesque of the mid-seventeenth-century puritan bans that forbade production of all plays, and that denounced all stage players as "rogues."

The tone of Gay's devastating musical mockery is much like that of Hogarth's engravings; Hogarth himself did a display poster of *The Beggar's Opera*. In the opera, pimps, beggars, and whores abound, as well as the highwayman MacHeath.

The music consists of no less than 69 English street and tavern airs, collected by Johann (later called John) Pepusch, a German violinist who settled in London and who played in the Drury Lane Orchestra.

THE BEGGAR'S OPERA

If you lover the Weill-Brecht *Three Penny Opera*—they simply updated the material to Berlin of the 1920's—you will enjoy the original version of some 200 years ago. In fact, some devotees are convinced that the earlier score is even more mordant than that of Weill.

* * * MORISON, SINCLAIR, SHACKLOCK, POLLAK, CAMERON, WALLACE, BRANNIGAN, YOUND, SARGENT	*Members of the Old Vic Company* *Pro Arte Orch. and Chorus*	SERAPHIM	SIB 6023
* FOBERMAN	*A double cast of actors and singers*	2-EVEREST	(M) 6127/2 (S) 3127/2

In 1920, Frederick Austin polished this score to put on a famous production in Hammersmith, England; the late Sir Malcolm Sargent did the orchestration. Though I had rather some of the spoken dialogue were dispensed with, the singing is refreshing and delightful. *Hi/Fi Stereo Review* called this release "incomparable," saying: "It is as though a proclamation had gone out summoning the most suitable talents in the British Isles to the microphones by royal decree." The sound is very good, indeed.

A very good show is also to be heard on Everest. Here the Pepusch score is untampered. Foberman provides rather more bite than Austin, and the singing is spirited. Though this disc is pleasant, it is definitely outclassed by the Seraphim set.

Geminiani, Francesco (c. 1679-1762)

Geminiani was born in Italy, studied with Corelli and with Alessandro Scarlatti in Rome, and then spent the rest of his life, after 1714, in London, Dublin, and Paris. He wrote several sets of concerti grossi and other compositions, as well as a number of important theoretical works. His "Opus 9," *The Art of Playing On The Violin,* written in English, seems to be the first violin method book ever published.

CONCERTO GROSSO, IN D MINOR (Opus 2, No. 3)

This is workmanlike music, somewhat in the style of Corelli.

* ROTH, TILNEY	*London Soloists Ensemble*	NONESUCH	H 71052

[A. Scarlatti, Concerto No. 3 in F Major; Telemann, Violin Concerto in A Minor; Vivaldi, Concerto Grosso, in D Minor, Opus 3, No. 11]

The music is played with verve and enthusiasm. The sound is somewhat undefined. [The other pieces on the disc are agreeable and particularly of interest to Baroque specialists.]

CONCERTI GROSSI (Opus 3, No. 2)

Geminiani's *Concerti Grossi* are "agreeable examples of musical deportment," in the English critic Sackville-West's neat phrase.

* MAINARDI	*Vienna State Folk Opera Orch.*	MACE	(S) 9077

[Boccherini, Cello Concerto in B Flat; Vivaldi, Concerto for Orchestra]

* DE STOUTZ	*Zurich Chamber Orch.*	VANGUARD	(S) 212

[Albinoni; Locatelli; Tartini]

Mainardi has the better collection, featuring a selection of Baroque cello works. The sound is all right.

De Stoutz is rather too efficient and fussy for my taste. But otherwise, this is a pleasant disc.

CONCERTI GROSSI (Opus 3: No. 2 in G Minor; No. 3 in E Minor; No. 6 in E Minor)

Here are different selections from the Opus 3—the *Concerti Grossi*—described above. These pieces, too, are pleasant, but hardly more.

* LINDE, HOELLER, BAUMGARTNER	*Lucerne Festival Strings*	HELIODOR	(S) 25050

Flues; Woodcock, Flute Concerto; Baston, Flue Concerto]

The music is handsomely played. The sound is impeccable—this disc was orginally on Archive. [This Heliodor record also offers three harmless, inconsequential flute concertos, by composers so obscure that one can only marvel at the fantastic choice of music made available to us on long-playing records. Michael Festing (c. 1700-1752) was a pupil of Geminiani in London. Robert Woodcock (dates unknown) seems to have been a flutist; he also published twelve concertos for flute and strings. John Baston (dates unknown) wrote a set of six concertos for flute. These *galant* writers of flute music are modest and ineffective composers.]

FOUR CONCERTI GROSSI
(Opus 2, Nos. 3, 4, 5, 6)

This is conservative, uneventful, unimportant writing, modeled after Corelli.

 * BIFFOLI, GIUSTO, *Gli Accademici di Milano* Dover   (M) 5231
  ECKERTSEN

The works are played with conviction and warmth. Sound is decent.

FOUR CONCERTI GROSSI (Opus 2, Nos. 1 and 2;
Opus 4, Nos. 1 and 2)

These works are very similar to those listed just above.

 * BIFFOLI, GIUSTO, *Gli Accademici di Milano* Dover   (M) 5232
  ECKERTSEN

Again, we hear effective performances from violinists Renata Biffoli and Pio Giusto, and from Eckertsen's instrumental ensemble. Sound is satisfactory.

CONCERTI GROSSI (Opus 7, No. 1/3, 5 and 6)

This music, too, is much like that listed above.

 * *   *I Musici*   Phillips WS (M/S) 9010

The marvelous I Musici Ensemble makes the music sound truly important. Phillips provides admirable sound.

THE ENCHANTED FOREST

Geminiani's lost instrumental collection, *The Enchanted Forest,* is slight music to accompany a spectacular choreographic work. Written for performance in Paris, it is essentially French in style. After completing this composition, Geminiani devoted himself entirely to writing theoretical books and essays.

* JENKINS   *Angelicum Orch. (Milan)*   NONESUCH   H 71151
[Locatelli, Il Pianto D'Ari-
anna]

The admirable Newell Jenkins plays the music with verve. The sound
is pleasantly intimate. [Locatelli was another student of Corelli, and his
The Plaint of Arianna is an apt coupling. Though the *Plaint* is not in a
class with Locatelli's stunning violin concertos, it is successful as an
experimental theatrical interlude for strings.]

Gershwin, George (1898-1937)

Born in Brooklyn, New York, Gershwin, who studied with Rubin Goldmark and then worked as a song-plugger, wrote his first successful song as well as his first musical comedy score in 1919. His *Rhapsody in Blue,* commissioned and introduced in 1924 by Paul Whiteman, made him world-famous. Gershwin divided his talents between popular and serious music, and was successful and respected in both fields. He died in Hollywood at the age of thirty-nine.

PLACE AND ACHIEVEMENT   George Gershwin holds a unique place in the annals of twentieth-century music. In the 1920's, many serious composers attempted to fuse jazz into the classical stream. Ravel mildly succeeded, and in an artificial way, so did Milhaud and Honegger. But most such works were merely parodies of jazz. George Gershwin, coming from a background of popular rather than classical music, combined the jazz beat with the classical form. Since then, nothing in classical music has caught the jazz spirit as well as *Rhapsody in Blue* and *Porgy and Bess.*

If you were to ask a normal European music-lover to name the greatest American composer, he would probably answer, "George Gershwin." No other American composer has been so loved and so played throughout the world. The critical argument as to what to call his music is still raging. Is it "popular" music or "serious" music? The public, however, hasn't bothered with this sort of dialectic; the public just loves Gershwin, and can't get enough of him.

THE ESSENTIAL GERSHWIN

ORCHESTRAL MUSIC: *Rhapsody in Blue; Concerto in F, for Piano and Orchestra; An American in Paris.*
OPERA: *Porgy and Bess.*
PIANO MUSIC: *Preludes.*
SONGS: [*There are too many to list.*]

OTHER WORKS

ORCHESTRAL MUSIC: *Second Rhapsody; Cuban Overture, for Orchestra; Variations on "I Got Rhythm," for Piano and Orchestra.*

AMERICAN IN PARIS (1928)

This dates from 1928 when Gershwin was in Paris, living it up at the Hotel Majestic. The score reflects a tourist's impressions of Paris, and his homesickness. This music, though it does not carry the stunning impact of the *Rhapsody in Blue,* nevertheless is good-spirited and unpretentious.

* * LEGRAND	*Grand Symphony Orch.*	MERCURY WING SRW (S) 18089 [Rhapsody in Blue]	
* STEINBERG	*Pittsburgh Symphony Orch.*	EVEREST (M) 6067 (S) 3067 [Porgy and Bess]	

Michel Legrand, extremely poetic and even lyrical, carries off the jazzy parts beautifully. This is really a first-rate performance.

Steinberg and the men of Pittsburgh sound overly cautious in the jazzy parts.

PORGY AND BESS (Folk Opera)

This was Gershwin's last work, and remains a masterpiece of American music. Critics still debate as to whether it is opera or musical comedy; but whatever it is, nearly everybody loves *Porgy and Bess* (Black nationalists today boycott it for alleged "Uncle Tom" attitudes.) The music is set to a good play by DuBose Heyward that the Theatre Guild had produced. Ira Gershwin, the composer's brother, wrote the strong libretto. The rich color, the drama, and the powerful writing are unsurpassed by any American score.

* * * WILLIAMS, MATTHEWS, LONG, WINTERS, ENGEL	*Orch. and Chorus*	3-ODYSSEY (S) 32 36 0018

This lovely re-created production, admired for both its musical and sonic splendor, was a stunner when it was released in 1951. Musically, it is still fresh and winning, and the rechanneled stereo is quite good. *Saturday Review's* Irving Kolodin comments: "To my taste, *Porgy and Bess* has not previously had such vitality, richness, and variety as it does in this creation."

PORGY AND BESS (Highlights)

* WINTERS, LUCAS, ELLINGTON, ELSY, STEVENS, ALWYN	*Chorus and Orch.*	HELIODOR H/HS 25052

The singing, in this presentable version of selections from Gershwin's lovable, vital, great folk opera, is spirited. The sound is acceptable. The entire effect, however, is by no means as authentic as that of the complete version listed above.

RHAPSODY IN BLUE (1924)

This is the daring piece that shook everything up, and began the inevitable marriage of jazz and concert music. Paul Whiteman and his orchestra introduced the *Rhapsody* in 1924, at a concert at New York's Aeolian Hall. After all these years, it is still the most successful piece of symphonic jazz. When played brilliantly, the music holds up well.

* * LEGRAND	*Grand Symphony Orch.*	MERCURY WING SRW (S) 18089 [American in Paris]
* SANROMA, STEINBERG	*Pittsburgh Symphony Orch.*	EVEREST (M) 6067 (S) 3067 [American in Paris]
* ATWELL, HEATH	*Ted Heath Orch.*	RICHMOND (M) 20037 [Music of Gershwin]
HAINES	*Hamburg Philharmonic Orch.*	Somerset ST/FI 1800

Michel Legrand, the popular French film composer and writer of the hit *Love is Blue,* runs away with the honors. His Gershwin is poetic and imaginative. The French orchestra successfully swings, as most American symphony orchestras are unable to do.

Jesus Maria Sanroma, who has played this music hundreds of times with the Boston Pops, is kinetic, although not exactly glittering. The disc is pleasurably hearable.

Atwell-Health, a British combination, plays affectionately and agreeably.

The Haines disc features spirited piano work but offers a rather stilted interpretation.

For those who wish to splurge: Bernstein, playing and conducting on Columbia, is supreme in a free and sweeping interpretation.

Gesualdo, Don Carlo (c. 1560-1613)

Gesualdo, the second son of a prince of Venosa, is famous in music history for having murdered his unfaithful wife, in 1590. Apart from this intriguing personal footnote, he is a remarkable composer. In his madrigals, he surpassed all of his contemporaries in his attempt to give complete expression to the varying moods of the text. Some of his chromatic harmonies and abrupt modulations sound startlingly modern even to twentieth-century ears. He published six books of madrigals, two books of motets, and other works.

MADRIGALS, VOLUME 1

This is wonderful music—extremely daring, poignant, and bizarre. It is a must for lovers of Renaissance music, and for all music students.

* * * CRAFT	*Soloists and Ensemble*	ODYSSEY	(M) 32 16 0107
* LITTLE	*Montreal Petit Ensemble*	Vox [Azzaiolo]	(500) 900

Robert Craft's exciting set is famous. He has recorded four albums of Gesualdo's music. Twelve five-part madrigals are included here, all searching pieces preoccupied with sorrow and death. Two six-voice Latin responses are also included, with two missing voice parts "recomposed" or filled in by the fervent Gesualdo admirer, Igor Stravinsky. The sound is quite satisfactory.

The Vox set is also good, but it does not convey the sense of dedication so apparent in the extraordinary Craft set.

Gibbons, Orlando *(1583-1625)*

Gibbons was organist of Westminster Abbey from 1623 to 1625. He composed a large number of anthems, keyboard pieces, madrigals, and other works. Gibbons wrote music in the tradition of Byrd and Dowland.

MADRIGALS AND LUTE SONGS

Here is a distinguished collection of songs and madrigals.

* * GREENBERG   *New York Pro Musica*   ODYSSEY   32 16 0171

The New York group plays and sings with impeccable style and with fresh exuberance. The sound is dry. [The recording, entitled "Elizabethan Verse and Its Music," also contatins works by Weelkes, Jones, Willbye, Ferrabotco, Morley, Kirbye, Dowland, Ward, and Tomkins.]

O GOD, THE KING OF GLORY; GREAT LORD OF LORDS; LORD SALISBURY'S PAVAN

These Gibbons pieces give a good indication of his reserved, even austere style, something uncommon among the madrigalists of his day.

* * PRESTON,   *Purcell Consort; Jaye*   TURNABOUT TV   (S) 34017
    BURGESS   *Consort of Violins*

The singing is exemplary. The sound is spacious. This record, entitled "Music of the High Renaissance in England" provides an intelligently selected program, tastefully blending solo, ensemble, and instrumental pieces. Altogether, the disc gives an ample and representative selection of the golden age of English music—around 1600. [Other selections on the record include: Ferrabosco II, *Dovehouse Pavan;* Byrd, *O Lord, How Vain; Lord Salisbury's Pavan; Elegy on the Death of Thomas Tallis; In Nomine a 5;* Weelkes, *As Vestas Was from Latmos Hill Descending;* Morley, *Hard by a Crystal Fountain;* Bull, *Prelude; In Nomine;* Tomkins, *Lady Folliott's Galliard.* Alfonso Ferrabosco (d. 1628) was in the service of James I and Charles I, and wrote music for several of Ben Jonson's masques. Another composer of the same name lived in the sixteenth century; hence, Alfonso is called "Ferrabosco II."]

[Gibbons is also well represented on two albums discussed elsewhere in this book: "Old English Vocal Music" (Crossroads 22 16 0144) and "English Madrigals from the Courts of Elizabeth I and James I" (Turnabout 34 202).]

Ginastera, Alberto (1916-   )

Ginastera is the leading contemporary Argentinian composer. He studied in his native country, and at eighteen came into contact with the music of Stravinsky and Bartok. Under Bartok's influence he began working toward a musical style which he terms "objective nationalism"—a national style that combines new techniques with indigenous themes. Ginastera's later style has veered more and more toward atonality. In 1968, his sex-laden opera *Bomarzo,* performed in New York, was a *succes de scandale.*

ESTANCIA

Estancia, commissioned by an American ballet company, depicts "scenes of Argentine rural life." This is South American folk material of the most obvious sort.

GOOSSENS   *London Symphony Orch.*   EVEREST   LPBR-6013
                                                          SDBR-3013
                                           [Antheil, Symphony No. 4]

The playing is spirited, and the sound is satisfactory. [George Antheil's *Symphony No. 4* is wearisome, a diluted version of Shostakovitch's style.]

PANAMBI

Ginastera wrote his one-act ballet *Panambi* at age twenty. The suite was compiled from the ballet four years later, in 1940. Based on a tale of the Indians of northern Argentina, it again emphasizes national identity. This is clever, provincial music, but little more. *Panambi* does not reflect the mature development of Ginastera's style. The atonal, highly expressive, and intensely personal style that rocked New York in the 1968 production of *Bomarzo* did not develop until two decades after the composition of *Panambi.*

* GOOSSENS   *London Symphony Orch.*   EVEREST   SDBR-3003
                                             [Antill, Corroboree]

Goossens delivers his usual energetic, clear-cut performance. The sound is pleasant.

Giordano, Umberto (1867-1948)

Giordano studied in Naples, and made his name with the "veristic" (realistic) type of opera popular in Italy in his day. *Verismo* was an artistic movement which aimed at a vivid and realistic representation of contemporary life—even some of its more sordid aspects.

ANDREA CHENIER

First performed in 1896—the same year as Puccini's *La Boheme—Andrea Chénier* is still popular in Italy. Although it is Giordano's most famous work, it never really caught on outside of Italy. It contains much lusty, beautiful music, and blood-and-thunder scenes.

* * CANIGLIA, GIGLI, BECHI, de FABRITIIS	*Chorus and Orchestra of Scala, Milan*	SERAPHIM IB	(M)	60
* TEBALDI, SOLER, SAVARESE, COLASANTI, BASILE	*Rome Radio Orch.*	EVEREST/CETRA	(S) 412/2	

Gigli is near perfect in the Seraphim set. This hot-blooded performance, recorded when he was still in his prime, was one of his best. As vocal critic Philip Miller wrote, "His aria *Improvviso* would bring down any house." The somber-voiced Caniglia is great, and the rest of the cast is fine. Admirers of Gino Bechi, the great Italian basso, regard this as one of his very finest recordings. The sound is not bad at all, considering that it dates from 1941.

The old Cetra set is not as well sung as the Seraphim recording; nevertheless, these discs have some melting moments of limpid vocal beauty from the young Renata Tebaldi.

FEDORA

This is Giordano's other successful opera; it is still a strong crowd-pleaser in Italy. It appeared two years after *Andrea Chénier* but never achieved the other opera's popularity. Here is more *verismo,* concerning the nihilist uprisings in Russia at the end of the last century. The lyrical writing offers fine opportunities for stand-up, gutsy singers.

* CANIGLIA, PRANDELLI, COLOMBO, BERTOCCI, ROSSI	*Rome Radio Orch.*	EVEREST/CETRA	(S) 452/2

This set offers a competent cast, although Caniglia is well past her best years. The sound is better than on most Everest/Cetra reconstructions (or resurrections) of old productions—adequate but hardly spectacular.

Glinka, Mikhail (1804-1857)

Glinka was the son of a wealthy Russian landowner. Until 1828, he worked in the Ministry of Communications while studying music privately. He then resigned his position in order to devote himself to music.

Glinka is usually regarded as the father of Russian music. His second opera *Russlan and Lurmila* (1842) created a Russian nationalistic style of music. That work included the exotic and oriental elements later embraced so enthusiastically by Russian composers. Glinka profoundly influenced Borodin, Mussorgsky, and Rimsky-Korsakov.

Although Glinka never reached a first-rate level of professional technique, his natural gifts imbued his music with a lyrical, singing quality.

KAMARINSKAYA

This colorful "orchestral fantasy" is now performed more often on Pops program than at serious concerts.

* TOSCANINI	*NBC Symphony Orch.*	VICTROLA VIC 1245 [Liadov, Kikimora; Sibelius, Finlandia; Smetana, Moldau; Tchaikovsky, Romeo and Juliet Overture]

Toscanini conducts the work with drama and polish. [A note on the couplings: Anatol Liadov (1855-1914) was a minor Russian composer who spent years studying and collecting Russian folk songs. His *Kikimora* is a "legend for orchestra," somewhat in the style of Liadov's teacher, Rimsky-Korsakov.]

RUSSLAN & LUDMILA: OVERTURE

Glinka's second opera is now seldom played. The short and sparkling overture, however, is very much alive.

* * REINER	*Chicago Symphony*	VICTROLA VIC (S) 1068
* ANCERL	*Czech Philharmonic Orch.*	CROSSROADS (M) 22 16 0085 (S) 22 16 0086 [Borodin, In the Steppes of Central Asia; Tchaikovsky, Capriccio, Overture]
SORKIN	*Musical Arts Symphony*	EVEREST (M) 6122 (S) 3122 [mixed program]

Reiner does the piece to a crisp in a vivid "Festival of Russian Music." Ancerl's interpretation comes off fairly well, but has little of the color and excitement of the Reiner performance.

The Sorkin disc is humdrum and hardly captivating.

TRIO PATHETIQUE

This slight—almost romantic—music of 1827 was originally scored for piano, clarinet, and bassoon.

* DAVID OISTRAKH,
KNUSHEVITZKY,
OBORIN

MONITOR   (S) 2068
[Taneyev, Trio, Opus 22]

The music is fervently played. David Oistrakh plays the violin; Sviatoslav Knushevitzky, the cello; and Lev Oborin, the piano. With such fine performers, one hardly minds the substitution of instruments for those in the original scoring. The sound is adequate.

Gluck, Christoph Willibald (1714-1787)

In 1736, at age 22, Gluck went to Vienna where he won the patronage of Prince Lobkowitz. Later, he studied for four years in Italy with Sammartini, and then proceeded to write several successful operas. He was then appointed Kapellmeister to the Empress Marie Theresa, a post he maintained for ten years.

When 34, he wrote *Orfeo*, his masterpiece, but his style aroused violent opposition. In 1773, he moved to Paris where, despite more cabals, he was successful. His last years saw Gluck back in Vienna as a rich and famous composer.

PLACE AND ACHIEVEMENT   Gluck is honored as a bold pioneer. He liberated opera from the tiresome conventions of the mid-eighteenth century, and proposed a more lofty conception of lyrical drama. What passed for Italian grand opera in his day contained stilted characters and bloodless music; opera at the time was little more than a showplace for the vocal techniques of castrati (eunuch singers).

Gluck discarded the old techniques; he tried—and succeeded—in achieving a poetic unity between text and music. The virtuoso became secondary to the glory of the song and the meaning of the drama. What we know and love as grand opera owes as much to Gluck as it does to any other composer.

THE ESSENTIAL GLUCK
OPERA: *Orfeo ed Euridice.*
ORCHESTRAL MUSIC: *Overtures to Iphigénie en Aulide, Alceste.*

OTHER WORKS
OPERAS: *Iphigénie en Aulide, Iphigénie en Tauride, Alceste.*
ORCHESTRAL MUSIC: *Concerto for Flute and Orchestra.*

CONCERTO IN G FOR FLUTE
This is a winsome concerto.

* * WANAUSEK, GIELEM	*Vienna Pro Musica*	Vox (M) 9440 [Pergolesi; Boccherini]	

The playing is fine and cool. The mono sound is clear. [The couplings are excellent.]

ORFEO ED EURIDICE

Orfeo is a moving work which has the distinction of being the oldest opera in the enduring repertory. It was the first opera that successfully attempted to create a unity of music and text. This milestone in opera has been well served on records; the extract with Kathleen Ferrier (on an expensive London) first brought Gluck to the attention of millions.

| * * * SIMONEAU, DANCO, ROSBAUD, BLANCHARD | *Roger Blanchard Vocal Ensemble, Concerts Lamoureux Orch.* | 2-PHILLIPS PHC | (S) 2-012 |
| BERGER, STREICH, KLOSE, ROTHER | *Berlin Civic Opera Orch. and Chorus* | 3-URANIA | (5) 223-3 |

A bulls-eye! This is dream music sung by a dream cast. Leopold Simoneau and Suzanne Danco are lyrical and sweetly musical. Rosbaud's pacing is just about perfect. The choral work, too, deserves special honors for the very French, very refined Blanchard ensemble. The sound is warm. The Phillips recording of *Orphée* uses the original French version, scored for a tenor in the role of Orpheus. The French version was made for a performance of the opera given at the Academie Royale de Musique in Paris in 1774. The opera had originally been performed in Vienna in 1762 in Italian with a male contralto (or castrato) singing the role of Orpheus.

The German cast, led by the velvet-voiced Klose, is distinguished; but after Rosbaud's triumph, this set is hard to accept. The sound is antiquated.

ORFEO ED EURIDICE: BALLET SUITE

This ingratiating ballet suite was made up from both the Vienna and Paris versions of the opera.

| * MACKERRAS | *London Symphony Orch.* | PHILLIPS WS (M/S) 9002 [Rameau, Castor et Pollux: Ballet] |

The classical atmosphere of this great opera is well suggested. The sound is good, though a bit darkish. [The Rameau work, a ballet suite from a typical "tragedie lyrique" of the Paris Opera of 1737, makes a nice coupling.]

Gounod, Charles (1810-1893)

Gounod studied at the Paris Conservatoire, and won the *Prix de Rome* in 1839. He was primarily a composer of opera in a lyrical style. His work is incredibly uneven; his masterpiece, *Faust,* was so far superior to his other operas that Paris heard the rumor that *Faust* was written by another hand.

FAUST (BALLET MUSIC)

For many years, Faust was perhaps the most popular opera in the world. Its tasteful and charming ballet music contributed greatly to its success.

* * GIBSON	*Royal Opera House Orch.*	VICTROLA VIC (S) 1108 [Bizet, Carmen Suite]	
* FISTOULARI	*Paris Conservatoire Orch.*	RICHMOND (M) 19046 [Mixed Program]	
* GOLSCHMANN	*St. Louis Syphony Orch.*	PICKWICK (S) 4020 [Bizet, Carmen Suite]	

Gibson's is the prettiest offering. The sound is all right. [The coupling will also please ballet lovers.]

Fistoulari's reading is most polished, but the sound is faded mono.

Golschmann's version is competent, and quite hearable.

PETITE SYMPHONIE FOR WIND INSTRUMENTS

This is refined music for woodwinds. The work was written for Paul Taffanel, a flutist and a friend of Gounod. The *Petite Symphonie* is scored for two flutes, two oboes, two clarinets, two horns, and two bassoons. Though inventive, it is music of little consequence.

BROTT	*Northern Sinfonia*	MACE (S) 9065 [Dvorak, Serenade in D Minor, Opus 44, for Winds, Cello, and Double Bass]	

The work is nicely played, but the sound is thin and filmy. [The Dvorak work is similarly pleasant but insignificant music.]

Grieg, Edvard (1843-1907)

Born in Bergen, Norway, Grieg began composing at the age of nine. In 1858, his parents were persuaded by Ole Bull, the famous Norwegian violinist, to send him to study in Leipzig. Here one of his fellow students was Arthur Sullivan of Gilbert and Sullivan fame. Grieg entered the Leipzig Conservatorium, but was forced to return home in 1860 to recuperate from a severe case of pleurisy.

But he returned to Leipzig, and after his graduation he settled in Copenhagen. Richard Nordraak, the first nationalist Norwegian composer, fired Grieg's imagination—he was then 21—and led the young man to the evolvement of his characteristic style. Tt 24, Grieg became a conductor and teacher in Norway's capital. Thereafter, his prestige steadily increased. He became the first Scandinavian composer to attain a worldwide audience.

Grieg's life was sunny, as composers' lives go, marred chiefly by grief for the loss of his only daughter when she was a baby. His honors were many. He was awarded a pension from the Norwegian government, and received accolades and degrees from many countries. Cambridge made him a Doctor of Music, at the same time it bestowed similar honors on Tchaikovsky, Saint-Saens, and Bruch. Grieg died in his sleep at 64, his end was as undramatic as his life.

PLACE AND ACHIEVEMENT Grieg's music derives its inspiration from the folk songs of Norway. Basically his is superficial music by a superficial composer. Nothing illustrates this better than the immortal tinklings Grieg composed for Ibsen's *Peer Gynt*.

Once hugely admired, Grieg is not considered of much account today by the musical world. Debussy — a first-rate critic — laid him low with the quip, "Grieg's music is a pink fondant stuffed with snow."

Grieg's music is mildly emotional, gently sad, never bombastic, never pretentious. His compositions resemble water-colors that are beautifully toned, pretty sketches that one is annoyed with oneself for keeping, but which are endowed with a sentimental appeal that forever prevents one from throwing them away.

ESSENTIAL GRIEG

ORCHESTRAL MUSIC: *Concerto in A Minor, for Piano and Orchestra; Peer Gynt, Suites No. 1 and 2.*

OTHER WORKS

ORCHESTRAL MUSIC: *Lyric Suite; Two Elegiac Melodies; Norwegian Dance, No. 2.*

PIANO MUSIC: *Ballade in G Minor; Lyric Pieces; Holberg Suite (also for string orchestra); 3 Sonatas for Violin and Piano.*

SONGS: [Grieg wrote many, including *I Love You.*]

CONCERTO IN A MINOR FOR PIANO (Opus 6)

One of the most popular piano concertos ever written, this composition if buoyant, engaging, easy to hear, and above all, highly romantic. Grieg wrote the piece in 1868 when he was 25.

* * * SOLOMON MENGES	*Philharmonic Orch.*	PICKWICK (S) 4034 [Schumann, Piano Concerto]	
* * * BACHAUER, WELDON	*Royal Philharmonic*	SERAPHIM (S) 60032 [Lyric Suite; Norwegian Dances]	
* * NOVAES, SWAROWSKY	*Vienna Pro Musica*	VOX (5) 8520 [Falla, Nights in the Gardens of Spain]	
* * LIPATTI, GALLIERA	*Philharmonic Orch.*	ODYSSEY (M) 32 16 0141 [Schumann, Piano Concerto]	
* * BAEKKELUND, GRUENER-HEGGE	*Oslo Philharmonic*	VICTROLA VIC (S) 1067 [Peer Gynt Suite]	
* JENNER, GRUENER-HEGGE	*Bavarian Radio Orch.*	MACE (3) 9064 [Elegiac Melodies]	
* BOUKOFF, RODZINSKI	*London Philharmonic*	WESTMINSTER (M) 18231 [Peer Gynt Suite]	
KATIN, DAVIS	*London Philharmonic*	RICHMOND (M) 19061 (S) 29061	
BLUMENTAL, SWAROSKI	*Vienna Pro Musica*	VOX (5) 11780 [Schumann, Piano Concerto]	

Among all this wealth my preference is for the poetic, patrician reading of Solomon.

Gina Bachauer is powerful and most dramatic. The sound is excellent. [This record also contains the pleasant little *Lyric Suite* and the Norwegian Dances.]

Novaes, as always, is beautiful. The sound is just fair and so is the orchestral accompanyment.

Lipatti's performance is splendid and much praised, but the dim sound is frustrating.

The young Scandinavian pianist Kjell Baekkelund renders a sweeping performance. [The disc includes warmly played excerpts from the Peer Gynt Suites.]

Jenner gives an acceptable, unremarkable reading. [The record includes two sweet *Elegiac Melodies for String Orchestra.*]

Boukoff is technically accomplished, and little more.

Peter Katin is rather brittle, and plays here without warmth.

PEER GYNT SUITES NO. 1 AND 2 (Opus 46, 55)

This incidental music to Ibsen's drama was commissioned by the playwright in 1874. Hugely popular and universally loved, this romantic music is not what one would term cerebral.

* * BARBIROLLI	*Halle Orch.*	VANGUARD (S) 222 [Symphonic Dances; Two Elegiac Melodies]
* * SPOORENBERG, VAN OTTERLOO	*Hague Philharmonic*	MERCURY (M) 14043 (S) 18043
* ABRAVANEL	*Utah Symphony Orch.*	WESTMINSTER (M) 18825 (S) 14057 [Piano Concerto]
* PERLEA	*Bamberg Symphony*	VOX (5) 12410 [Bizet, L'Arlesienne Suite]
RODZINSKI	*London Philharmonic*	WESTMINSTER 18231 [Piano Concerto]
DE CROSS	*Paris National Symphony Orch.*	PERIOD SHO 314 [Piano Concerto]

Barbirolli is best. He eloquently plays the *First* (and better) *Suite,* the *Two Elegiac Melodies,* and the rather sugary *Symphonic Dances.* The sound is adequate.

A more straightforward version — but with superior sound — is to be had from Van Otterloo (who plays both suites).

Abravanel is extremely lyric, and entirely hearable.

The Perlea reading is colorless, just adequate.

The old Rodzinski performance is meticulous, and little more.

De Cross is much outclassed.

SONGS   Grieg's lieder can hardly be compared to those composed by the great masters. Grieg produced simple, romantic songs of obvious appeal.

* FLAGSTAD		SERAPHIM (M) 60046 [Brahms, Songs; Wagner, Wesendonck]

Kirsten Flagstad, the great Norwegian soprano, never convincing in lieder, seems comfortably at home in the music of her compatriot. This is a pleasant disc, hardly an important one.

Handel, George Frideric *(1685-1759)*

Handel, an organist in Halle, Germany, became a member of the opera orchestra in Hamburg where his first opera was composed and performed. In 1710, he became Kapellmeister at Hanover. In 1711, he visited England; and in 1712, he settled there permanently and became a pre-eminent musical figure. Handel turned from opera to oratorio; and his influence on English music was enormous. He is buried in the Poets' Corner in Westminster Abbey.

PLACE AND ACHIEVEMENT   Handel is hailed as one of the greatest of the masters, and yet his music is played infrequently. He was a great German composer who somehow threw a long, towering shadow on English music. Though he wrote more than 45 Italian-styled operas, these have been quite forgotten; the Handel that survives is the safe-and-sound, rock-ribbed Handel of the sublime oratorio, *The Messiah*.

How to sum up this paradox? Why did Mozart and Beethoven revere Handel as the greatest of composers, while we rarely delight in his music? Our present adulation of Handel's contemporary Bach, cherished today as never before, certainly has much to do with Handel's lesser appraisal. The serious music lover, with access via records to all of Handel, can explore the creations of this widely neglected genius, and decide for himself whether Handel deserves a more exalted station.

THE ESSENTIAL HANDEL

CHORAL MUSIC: *Messiah, Israel in Egypt.*

ORCHESTRAL AND VOCAL MUSIC: *12 Concerti Grossi, Opus 6; Water Music; Chandos Anthems.*

OTHER WORKS

ORATORIOS: *Saul; Semele; Samson; Ode for St. Cecilia's Day; Judas Maccabaeus; various cantatas.*

MASQUE: *Acis and Galatea.*

ORCHESTRAL MUSIC: *Fireworks Music; Concertos for Organ; Concertos for Various Instruments and Orchestra; Sonatas for Violin, for Viola, for Oboe, etc.*

CHAMBER MUSIC: *String Trios.*

KEYBOARD MUSIC: *Suites; Chaconnes; Fugues, etc.*

ORATORIOS   Except for the hugely popular *Messiah,* Handel's oratorios are little played today. Taken out of dusty bins around Christmastime, some are momentarily admired as shamefully neglected masterpieces, and then forgotten again. The difficulty is that pages of sturdy power and beauty alternate all too often with tedious, tiresome, and uninspired stretches. Nevertheless, the passionate lover of choral music will find much to enjoy here. All the oratorios, except *Theodora,* are based on Old Testament texts.

Handel generally presented his oratorios in theaters—not churches—and we may regard these compositions as non-theatrical drama. The chorus is all-important, setting the mood and taking the place of scenery and action. Handel would hardly have recognized the customary amateur chorus of mixed voices with which his oratorios are performed today. *His* choruses were small groups of selected professionals. The soprano parts were sung by boys; the alto parts, by men.

BELSHAZZAR (Oratorio)

Belshazzar is a grandiose, somewhat stilted work of 1744. Belshazzar, like all Handel oratorios except *Theodora,* is based on a Jewish theme, and is drawn from sacred texts.

* * STAHLMAN, RAAB, RILLING	*Stuttgart Kirchenmusiktage* (*Sung in English*)	3-Vox	SVBX-5209
* GRISCHKAT	*Orchestra and Chorus* (*Sung in German*)	2-Period	1052

Rilling is the right man for this music; his chorus is powerful and brilliant.

The old Grischkat set is aided by excellent soloists. The score is extensively cut. The sound is filmy in many of the choral passages.

ISRAEL IN EGYPT (Oratorio) (Sung in English)

The chorus carries most of the weight in this full-bodied oratorio of 1738. The music is a vastly extended anthem, and there are many stirring pages.

* BURTON, ALLEN, CHABAY, BOEPPLE, DESSOFF	*Dessoff Chorus Symphony*	2-Vox	SVUX-52019

Though mutilated later editions are often used in performing this piece, the Vox recording is based on the original score. The singing, if not exactly polished, is clean. This is Americanized Handel without the usual hearty British *pomposo.* The English critic Peter Grammond (*Music on Record*) comments: "The orchestral part is very good indeed, the chorus less so, and the soloists not particularly impressive; but it is stylishly performed and decently recorded and is certainly the version to have." The *Stereo Record Guide* waspishly reports: "The soloists are barely adequate, and the two ladies warble away with little real sense of style."

MESSIAH (Oratorio)

The Messiah is perhaps the greatest oratorio ever written. Handel, unlike Bach, not a God-intoxicated man, was nevertheless in a state of exaltation throughout the feverish composition of this masterpiece. "I did think I did see all Heaven before me, and the great God himself," he exclaimed at its completion; and this compelling fervor is to be heard on every page of this transcendent opus.

* * BRANNIGAN, PROCTER, VYVYAN, MARAN, BOULT	*London Philharmonic Orchestra and Chorus*	3-RICHMOND	(M) 43002

Boult's version, well-paced, and moving, boasts England's best chorus, the London Philharmonic Choir. They are extraordinary. The soloists, led by Norma Proctor, the contralto, are satisfying. The sound is plummy mono. A rechanneled stereo version is expected, which may be an improvement. Vocal expert Philip Miller comments: "A great healthiness, admirably in keeping with the spirit of the work, and a mastery finish in every detail."

For those who want a first-rate stereo *Messiah* now, I recommend the expensive versions of either Beecham or Davis. Both are admirable. Davis is recorded with modern sonics. If you don't mind waiting, the solid and lively performance under Sargent—now on an expensive Angel—is due soon to drop to the low-priced Seraphim label. Reason: Angel also carries a glittering star-studded version conducted by Klemperer.

RESURREZIONE (Oratorio) (Sung in Italian)

This oratorio is a product of the young Handel's three-and-a-half-year study in Italy. An unremarkable work, it is nevertheless written with assurance and skill.

* EWERHART	*Santini Chamber Orchestra & Chorus, Muenster*	2-VOX	SVUX-52012

Ewerhart conducts like a sound Handelian, and the recording is pleasingly resonant. The soloists are attractive.

SAMSON (Oratorio)

Samson is a shamefully neglected masterpiece of Handel's maturity. First played in London in 1743 at Covent Garden Theatre as a concert work, *Samson* was a vastly popular oratorio in Handel's day, and a favorite of solemn massed-chorus festivals in Victorian Britain. This is a long work with 64 numbers, more than any other of his oratorios.

    * WEISSENBORN   *Hannover NDR Orchestra,*   3-EVEREST   (S) 3125/3
                                  Chorus

    This is a long-faced performance with strongly sung choruses. The soloists are competent. The sound is agreeable.

    For those who desire an exceptional recording, the performance by Abravanel on an expensive Bach Guild is recommended.

OPERAS   It was as a gifted composer of Italian opera that Handel first met the British public.

    Clarity of construction, and a dignified nobility are the hallmarks of his operatic style. Handel made no bold innovations; he took the standards as he found them, and left them unchanged.

    His 46 Italian operas are almost unplayed. Their dramatic style is weak. A story from classical history or mythology is gravely unfolded through a long series of static arias—a development not acceptable by today's public. (Most of Handel's heroic roles were written for castrati—male sopranos who had been castrated to preserve the purity and range of their boyish voices.)

JULIUS CAESAR

This rather stimulating opera, dating from 1724, contains many noteworthy passages. The love song—Cleopatra's seduction music—*V'adore pupile*—is often given at recitals.

    * SWAROWSKY   *Orchestra and Soloists*   2-Vox   SVUX-52011
                            (Sung in Italian)

    The serviceable Swarowsky set dates from 1953. Most of the recitatives are cut, and this has caused some rather bumpy key transitions. Peter Grammond comments: "The singing is a little brash at times . . . the recording is thin and sharp."

    The best performance is on a high-priced Victor set, performed by the New York City Opera company. It was this stunning revival, featuring the lissome voice of soprano Beverly Sills, that brought this opera back into American repertory.

MISCELLANEOUS VOCAL MUSIC   Most of Handel's vocal works are rarely heard in today's concert hall, but they are well worth investigating for home listening.

ARIAS: NINE GERMAN SONGS (NEUN DEUTSCHE ARIEN)

These nine arias are set to religious texts, and contain rich, complex melodies and counterpoint reminiscent of the Bach cantatas.

* MATHIS	*Ensemble of Baroque Instruments*	SERAPHIM	(S) 60015

Edith Mathis is a young Swiss soprano with a voice of remarkable purity and freshness. The stereo sound is clean.

ARIAS: FROM JUDAS MACCABAEUS, ALEXANDER'S FEAST, SAMSON, ACIS AND GALATAEA, JEPHTHA, JOSHUA AND SEMELE

These stately, noble arias span 30 years.

* LEWIS, SARGENT	*London Symphony Orchestra*	SERAPHIM	(S) 60028

Richard Lewis is a specialist in concert arias, oratorios, etc., and to my lights conveys an authentic feeling for this music. But *High Fidelity* disagrees: "Richard Lewis is a fine singer with many notable recorded achievements to his credit; this collection, unfortunately, is not one of them.

CHANDOS ANTHEMS

In 1717, Handel became composer-in-residence to the Duke of Chandos. The concerts held at "Cannons," the stately house of the Duke, featured from 24 to 30 singers, and a whole entourage of musical notables including Pepusch of *Beggar's Opera* fame; a cousin of Bach; Francesco Scarlatti, brother of Alessandro; etc. Most of this music is three-part choruses set to the words of six English psalms, supported by a three-part string orchestra.

This intimate, moving music will come as a welcome surprise to those who know Handel only through grandiose productions of *The Messiah*.

* * * BOATWRIGHT,   *Rutgers University*   3-VANGUARD   (S) 227/9
    BRESSLER, HELD,   *Collegium Musicum*
    MILLER, MANN

The *Gramophone* magazine of London, the respected doyen of record criticism, called this set "a model of how Handel should be done. . . . A triumphant success." The sound is fine, and the four soloists, led by the admirable and cultured singer Helen Boatwright, are very good. This set, I believe, originally appeared under the late, lamented "Cantate" label of Germany.

DETTINGEN TE DEUM

This music was written to celebrate the great victory during the war of the Austrian Succession.

This *pomposo* Handel, a stirring piece, will remind many listeners of *The Messiah*.

* WHEELER,   *Telemann Society Festival*   NONESUCH H (S) 71003
   LAURENCE,   *Chorus and Orchestra*
   PAVLIDES,
   FERRANTE,
   DENNISON,
   SCHULZE

This performance is entirely pedestrian.

LUCREZIA; ARMIDA ABBANDONARA

Here are four mildly interesting baroque cantatas or "pocket operas" — dramatic scenes that can be sung without scenery or costume.

* DAVRATH   *Vienna Soloisten*   VANGUARD C (S) 100-28
                                       [A. Scarlatti, Su le sponde del Tebro; Fiocco, Lamentatio secunda]

Natania Davrath's dignified voice comes off very well. The sound is splendid. [Joseph Hector Fiocco (1703-1741), born in Brussels, was an outstanding harpsichordist.]

ODE FOR ST. CECILIA'S DAY

The text, by John Dryden, praises the patron saint of music. Handel completed the score in only nine days, but this fact is never betrayed in this serene music.

The work contains some exciting choral and solo writing.

| * STICH-RANDALL,
YOUNG, BERNARD | Orchestra,
London Chorus Singers | Music Guild | (S) | 101 |
| HOFFMAN, LUDWIG,
ROTHER | Radio Berlin Symphony
Orchestra, Lamy Chorus | Urania | (M)
(S) | 702
5702 |

The *Ode* is well served by the cultivated American-European singer Teresa Stich-Randall. The sound is acceptable.

The Urania set is sung in German. The tone is distorted.

ORCHESTRAL AND INSTRUMENTAL MUSIC In recent years, more and more of Handel's music in this genre has been rescued from obscurity. Most of it consists of vigorous, sturdy, solidly constructed pieces rather reminiscent of J. S. Bach.

CONCERTOS FOR OBOE AND ORCHESTRA

Stendhal's aphorism, "All art is romantic in its own day," is appropriate to Handel. Handel's colorful, varied music excited *his* audience — but we tend to think of that audience as composed of staid, bewigged gentlemen.

| * * CASIER, BERNARD | Cento Soli Orchestra | Nonesuch | (S) 71013 |
| DE STOUTZ,
PAROLARI | Zurich Orchestra | [Concerti Grossi, Opus 3]
Mace   (S) 9063
[Concerto Grosso, Opus 6] | |

Casier is an elegant oboist. The entire record is blessed with staunch Handelian style.

De Stoutz is listenable, but not exactly sweeping.

CONCERTO GROSSI (Opus 3: No. 2, in B-Flat; No. 4 in F; No. 5 in D Minor; CONCERTO GROSSO, in G Minor)

Less known than the *Concerti Grossi* of *Opus 6*, these are still very sturdy, worthwhile pieces.

| * * CASIER, BERNARD | Orchestra of the
Cento Soli | Nonesuch | H(S) 1013 |

This fresh sounding disc features well-paced playing, with neat work by the oboist.

TWELVE CONCERTI GROSSI (Opus 6)

Handel composed his twelve *Concerti Grossi* at white heat — in the incredibly short period of one month in 1739. They are forceful, often noble works which rank among Handel's most popular compositions.

* * SCHERCHEN	*English Baroque Orchestra*	4-WESTMINSTER	9703/6
*	*Mozart Society Players*	BAROQUE (M) 1860 (S) 2860 [No. 5; Telemann, 3 Oboe Concertos]	
*	*Telemann Society*	VOX (M) 16250 (S) 516250 [No. 1; Sonata No. 11 in F; Oboe Concerto]	
BERNARD	*Dresden Ensemble*	BAROQUE (M) 1820 (S) 2820 [No. 6; Haydn, Cassations; Stamitz, Quartet]	
DE STOUTZ	*Zurich Orchestra*	MACE (S) 9063 [No. 4, 5; Oboe Concerto]	

The authoritative Hermann Scherchen is supreme in this complete version, available on four separate records. The sound is very good, but mono.

For those who seek a good mixed program, the Mozart Society Players give a vigorous reading of *No. 11*.

The Telemann Society is smooth in *No. 1*. The disc has an attractive sound.

The Dresden Ensemble, though rather ponderous, is enjoyable.

The Zurich group is competent but unremarkable.

LOVE IN BATH

This engaging "balletic entertainment," was compiled for a ballet entitled "The Great Elopement." Sir Thomas Beecham conducted this in 1945; and wrote the scenario himself. Most of the 20 separate movements are taken from the arias, the choruses, and the dances of Handel's operas.

* * BEECHAM, HOLLWEG	*Royal Philharmonic Orchestra*	SERAPHIM	(S) 60039

This successful pastiche is played with the usual Beecham verve and finesse. The sound is satisfactory.

ROYAL FIREWORKS MUSIC

Written in 1748 to celebrate the peace of Aix-la-Chapelle, this music
when first performed employed 24 oboes, 12 bassoons, a large brass
section, etc. Vigorous and entertaining, it is much like the *Water Music*
with which it is almost invariably coupled.

* APPIA	*Vienna State Opera Orchestra*	VANGUARD (S) 209 [Water Music Suite]
* SCHULZE	*Telemann Society Wind and Percussion Band*	VOX (500) 750
VAN BEINUM	*Concertgebouw*	RICHMOND (M) 19101 [Water Music Suite]

Appia is lively, but the reading is neither polished nor stylish.

Schulze's performance, though less than magical, is pleasant and
inoffensive.

Van Beinum disappoints with a stodgy reading on faded mono.

[The *Water Music* suites listed on the reverse sides are excerpts from
the complete work.]

SONATAS (Opus 1) FOR FLUTE; THREE SONATAS FOR FLUTE, "HALLE"

The *Opus 1* Sonatas have the vague indication, "Fifteen Solos for a
German Flute, Oboe, or Violin, and Continuo." These pieces are the
favorites of flute players who can come through with a cool Baroque
style.

* * * WUMMER, VALENTI	WESTMINSTER (M) 18583/4
* DEBOST, IVALDI	7-NONESUCH 1164 [Opus 1, No. 9, 11; "Halle" No. 2; Harp Concerto; Terpsichore, Ballet Suite]
* DUSCHENES, JONES	5 VOX 16340 [Opus 1/1, 2, 5; Oboe Sonata]
* TEMIANKA, HAMILTON	2-EVEREST (M) 6143 (S) 3143 [Opus 1; Oboe Sonata; Violin Sonata]
* OLEVSKY, VALENTI	3-WESTMINSTER 9064/6 [Opus 1; Oboe Sonata; Violin Sonata]

The Wummer-Valenti set is superb, although the sound is mono. Harold

Schonberg comments: "Wummer's leisurely playing is as good as we are going to get in this day and age."

Except for a quavery sound here and there, flutist Debost is good. [The rest of the program is middleweight Handel, but includes the attractive Harp Concerto and the stately ballet suite *Terpsichore*.]

Flutist Duschenes, though skillful and round-toned, is outclassed.

Temianka offers a well-played violin version.

Olevsky is studious, and has firm support from Valenti. The mono sound is good.

WATER MUSIC (Complete)

The celebrated *Water Music,* published around 1732, has been the subject of one of the most popular myths in music history — all about an angry King George I forgiving a penitent Handel at a royal water-party — a myth, however, that has been since exploded. However, the celebrated *Water Music* is splendid, vital, warmhearted Handel, universally admired.

* * * BOULEZ	*Hague Philharmonic*	NONESUCH	(M)	1127
			(S)	71127
* * VAN BEINUM	*Concertgebouw Orchestra*	PHILLIPS WS	(M/S)	9016
* SCHERCHEN	*Vienna State Opera*	WESTMINISTER	(M)	18961
			(S)	14142

Boulez is excellent. Here is an incisive, no-nonsense version that merits high praise. *High Fidelity* included this disc in a selection of "Year's Best Recordings."

Van Beinum is first-rate in a full-bodied reading, which is lovingly recorded. The only objection is that the orchestra Van Beinum uses is large and lush, more suited for Wagner than for Baroque.

Scherchen is effective and imaginative. As always, he presents some startling tempos, as well as huge crescendos untypical of Handel.

Haydn, Franz Joseph (1732-1809)

Haydn was born of peasant stock, the second of twelve children. At five, he went to live with a relative who taught him music. From his eighth to his seventeenth year, he was enrolled at the Vienna Choir School and lived in incredible poverty. When he left school, his belongings consisted of two second-hand books on harmony, a shabby coat, two shirts, and a pair of trousers.

In 1761, he began his long period of service in the household of the wealthy and cultured Count Esterhazy. Haydn wrote, rehearsed, and produced all the Esterhazy musical entertainments for nearly 30 years. The greater part of each year was spent at the country estate of Esterhazy, where Haydn wrote most of his compositions. His friendship with Mozart began in 1781.

On the death of Prince Nicolaus in 1790, the musical ensemble at Esterhazy was disbanded, but Haydn retained his title and salary, without any duties attaching to his post. In 1791, he left for London with a contract to write an opera, six new symphonies, and 20 other pieces. He stayed in England for more than a year. His music was received with great excitement, and he was nominated as an honorary Doctor of Music at Oxford. He returned to Austria, and remained there quietly until his death at seventy-seven.

PLACE AND ACHIEVEMENT   Only in our own day has Haydn been elevated to a high place in the musical hierarchy. In the later nineteenth century, Haydn was regarded as something of a porcelain piece, very dainty and amusing, the neat composer of harmless symphonies with cute subtitles such as "Clock," "Hen," "Farewell," etc. The tremendous new interest in eighteenth-century music, which began in America in the 1940's, was in large measure a passion for the serene compositions of Franz Joseph Haydn.

Haydn breathed life into certain musical forms. He was responsible for the creative, inquiring nature of the symphony and the string quartet. Craftsmanship is evident in every bar he ever wrote. Here is lucid music, "a daylit vision of natural beauty," to quote C. G. Burke. In our speed-crazed age of jets and computers, the sane, reasonable music of Haydn strikes a chord within all who long for a more ordered, more dignified world.

THE ESSENTIAL HAYDN

ORCHESTRAL MUSIC: Symphonies, No. 82-87 ("Paris"), 88, 92, 93-104 ("London Symphonies"); Concerto in D Major, for Cello and Orchestra; *Concerto in D Major, Opus 21, for Harpsichord and Orchestra; Concerto in E-Flat for Trumpet and Orchestra; Sinfonia Concertante in B-Flat.*

CHAMBER MUSIC: *Six String Quartets, Opus 33; Six String Quartets, Opus 76.*

CHORAL MUSIC: *The Creation, Oratorio; "Lord Nelson" Mass; "Mass in Time of War."*

OTHER WORKS

ORCHESTRAL MUSIC: *107 Symphonies; Overtures; Concertos for Various Instruments and Orchestra.*

ORATORIO: *The Seasons, and other oratorios.*

OPERA: *Orfeo ed Euridice; and 12 other operas; 4 marionette operas.*

CHURCH MUSIC: *Masses, cantantas, etc.*

CHAMBER MUSIC: *About 56 string trios, 84 string quartets, etc.*

KEYBOARD MUSIC: *Sonatas, variations, etc.*

SONGS: [*Haydn also wrote many short songs.*]

SYMPHONIES When Haydn undertook the cataloguing of his symphonies in his old age, he could not remember them all. He had written 107 or thereabouts. Along with his quartets, these symphonies are his supreme achievement.

The greatest of Haydn's symphonies are the so-called "London Symphonies," the last twelve—*No. 93-104.* However, his early symphonies, too, are pleasant; they are basically inventive little orchestral suites often with a prominent part for a solo instrument.

For years, there have been many dubious recordings of Haydn on the market. These began in the early 1950's with a flood of releases by shoestring record companies. Many of these discs derived from Vienna, from what was in fact a bunch of the boys recruited from a musician's cafe along the *Ringstrasse,* who were blithely touted on records as the "Austrian Symphony," and the "Vienna State Philharmonia," or the "Vienna State Opera Orchestra," or "Pro Musica," or by some other grandiose title. Even the august name "Vienna State Opera Orchestra" can be deceptive.

Austria subsidizes two operas in Vienna: the *Staatsoper* and the *Volksoper.* The *Staatsoper* (the National Opera) orchestra is the Vienna Philharmonic Orchestra. The *Volksoper* (the People's Opera) has an orchestra by that name. Any other designation generally indicates that the disc has been recorded by a pick-up group hired for a particular recording date.

The late conductor Max Goberman was engaged in recording all the Haydn symphonies. These are now available on the Odyssey label, a subsidiary of CBS. Goberman was an unusually gifted conductor of eighteenth-century music, and his performances are invariably sparkling. The sound is usually quite good, but not up to recent standards.

C. G. Burke's *Collector's Guide to Haydn*, published by Keystone Books, is recommended to anyone who wishes to study Haydn in depth with a literate and perceptive critic.

SYMPHONY NO. 4 IN D; SYMPHONY NO. 5 IN A; SYMPHONY NO. 6 IN D ("LE MATIN")

No. 4 is a lively jewel. *No. 5* opens with an *Adagio* that is one of Haydn's best. *No. 6* is a courtly evocation of "days without trial" at Esterhazy. These works constitute an excellent sampler of the young Haydn.

* * GOBERMAN	*Vienna State Opera Orch.*	ODYSSEY	(M) 32 16 0033
			(S) 32 16 0034

This disc illustrates the special qualities of conductor Max Goberman. *High Fidelity* sums it up perfectly: "Goberman's accustomed exuberance and splendid musicianship couldn't be more welcome."

SYMPHONY NO. 6 IN D ("LE MATIN")

This was composed when Haydn was twenty-nine, and under contract to Prince Esterhazy. *Symphonies 6, 7, and 8,* respectively entitled *"Morning," "Noon,"* and *"Night,"* were the first works he wrote for his new orchestra at Esterhazy in 1761. Haydn's scripts bristle with new ideas.

* * RISTENPART	*Saar Chamber Orch.*	NONESUCH	(S) 1015
		[Symphonies No. 7, 8]	
* GOBERMAN	*Vienna State Opera Orch.*	ODYSSEY	(M) 32 16 0033
			(S) 32 16 0034
		[Symphonies No. 4, 5]	
* BOETTCHER	*Vienna Festival Chamber Orch.*	TURNABOUT	(S) 34150
		[Symphonies No. 7, 8]	

The late Karl Ristenpart offers a sparkling record. Eric Salzman singled out this disc for a "Bouquet of Rococo Recordings" in *Stereo Review.* The sound is clear but there could be much more dynamic range.

The Goberman disc is pleasing.

Boettcher is adequate, little more.

SYMPHONIES NO. 9 IN C; NO. 10 IN D; NO. 11 IN E-FLAT

These are lightweight, uneventful pieces which will appeal only to addicted lovers of Haydn.

* GOBERMAN	Vienna State Opera Orch.	ODYSSEY	(M) 32 16 0081
			(S) 32 16 0082

The playing is excellent. The sound is only pretty good.

SYMPHONY NO. 13 IN D ("JUPITER")

Sometimes referred to as *Jupiter,* Haydn's finale is very similar in theme to the finale of Mozart's last symphony called *Jupiter.* This is one of the most vivacious of the early symphonies.

* * GOBERMAN	Vienna State Opera Orch.	ODYSSEY	(M) 32 16 0115
			(S) 32 16 0116
		[Symphonies No. 12, 14]	
* JONES	London Little Orch.	NONESUCH (S) (7) 1121	
		[Symphonies 29, 64]	
* PEDROTTI	Bolzano Orch.	TURNABOUT (3) 4128	
		[Symphonies No. 1, 28]	

Goberman, spirited as always, is best.
Jones is straight-forward, rather cut-and-dried.
Pedrotti is well-paced but not outstanding.

SYMPHONY NO. 31 IN D ("HORNSIGNAL")

Four horns yodel away in a fun symphony.

* * RILLING	Stuttgart Bach Collegium	TURNABOUT (S) 34104	
		[Symphony No. 59]	
* JONES	London Little Orch.	NONESUCH (S) 71031	
		[Symphonies No. 19, 45]	
* SWAROWSKY	Vienna State Opera Orch.	VANGUARD C (S) 10021	
		[Symphony No. 30]	

Rilling has the best sonics, and this is a litting reading.
The Jones version is pleasant; the sound is good.
Swarowsky is also hearable, but unremarkable.

SYMPHONY NO. 44 IN E MINOR ("TRAUER")

The *"Mourning"* or *"Trauer" Symphony* has been rather fancifully compared to Beethoven's *Eroica* by the impeccable Haydn authority Robert C. Marsh. As with the *Eroica*, there is a proudly moving slow movement of funereal dignity, and indeed, Haydn instructed that this music be played at his funeral.

* * JONES	*Lnodon Little Orch.*	NONESUCH (7) 1032 [Overture 14, Symphony 49]
* * SCHERCHEN	*Vienna State Opera Orch.*	WESTMINSTER (M) 18613 [Symphony No. 49]

Jones delivers a firm, resounding performance that *High Fidelity* calls "The finest stereo version of the "Trauer" we have." [The coupling is the strong, intense No. 49. The disc also includes the attractive curtain-raiser to Haydn's opera *Armida*.]

Scherchen's famous reading was beloved almost a generation ago; his reading remains the more profound. The sound is boxed-in.

SYMPHONY NO. 45 IN F-SHARP MINOR ("FAREWELL")

A seldom-played, harmless symphony, famous because of the goings-on in the finale. In this movement, pair by pair, the musicians snuff out their candles and slip away. This, it is reported, was Haydn's hint to his patron that the definitely non-union orchestra players at Esterhazy had been away from their families too long.

* SCHERCHEN	*Vienna State Opera Orch.*	WESTMINSTER (M) 14044 [Symphony No. 100]
* JONES	*London Little Orch.*	NONESUCH (S) 71031 [Symphonies No. 19, 31]

Scherchen gives a lilting mono performance.

The Jones version is also engaging, but the sound has not many highs or lows.

SYMPHONY NO. 48 IN C ("MARIA THERESIA")

Brilliant pomp is heard in this stately, ceremonial symphony written for the visit to Esterhazy of Holy Roman Empress Maria Theresia.

* RISTENPART	*Saar Chamber Orch.*	NONESUCH (S) 71101 [Symphonies No. 21, 82]

Ristenpart plays with appropriate pageantry.

SYMPHONY NO. 49 IN F MINOR
("LA PASSIONE")

The "Passion" of Jesus Christ is devotional, even tormented, music.

* * SCHERCHEN	*Vienna State Opera Orch.*	WESTMINSTER (M) 18613 [Symphony No. 44]
* JONES	*London Little Orch.*	NONESUCH (S) 71032 [Overture No. 14, Symphony No. 44]

Scherchen's intense interpretation is unmatched, but the mono sound is rather faded.

The Jones record, not as high-powered as the Scherchen, offers stereo.

SYMPHONY NO. 59 IN A ("FIRE")

This is one of Haydn's lesser works, quite undistinguished.

* RILLING	*Stuttgart Bach Collegium*	TURNABOUT (S) 34104 [Symphony No. 31]

The playing is zestful, in Haydnesque style. The sound is clean.

SYMPHONY NO. 73 IN D ("HUNT")

Hunting horns, hounds, and all you might expect of a work entitled *La Chasse,* this is one of Haydn's more jovial pieces, but certainly not remarkable.

*	*Prague Chamber Orch.*	CROSSROADS (M) 22 16 0031 (S) 22 16 0032 [Symphony No. 96]

The Praguers perform with plump playing and appropriately high spirits.

SYMPHONIES NO. 82, 83, 84, 85, 86, 87
("PARIS")

These are vintage Haydn, but not as great as the final series known as the *"London"* symphonies (No. 93-104).

JONES	*London Little Orch.*	3-NONESUCH (S) 73011

Jones, a usually reliable man, is both listless and heavy-handed.

SYMPHONY NO. 82 IN C ("L'OURS")

"The Bear" is an airy, felicitous work, one of the six commissioned by Les Concerts de la Loge Olympique of Paris. Here is skillful, high-level Haydn.

* * WAND	*Cologne Symphony Orch.*	NONESUCH	(S) 71101
		[Symphonies No. 21, 48]	

Wand is ingratiating. The sound is clear.

SYMPHONY NO. 83 IN G MINOR ("POULE")

This virile work is not quite first-rank among Haydn's work. *"The Hen"* is so named because of the oboe and string cacklings in the opening movement. The finale, based on Italian folk style, gives us—as the irrepressible Lloyd Moss delights to inform on his "Listening to Music" program of New York's WQXR—chicken cacciatore.

* JONES	*London Little Orch.*	NONESUCH	(S) 71083
		[Symphonies No. 12, 26]	

Jones's interpretation is heavy-handed. The sound is warm.

SYMPHONY NO. 85 IN B-FLAT ("LA REINE")

This is a melodious near-masterpiece. "La Reine" was Marie Antoinette of France who admired the music of Haydn.

* JOCHUM	*Nordwestdeutsche Philharmonic*	MONITOR	(S) 2122
		[Cello Concerto Opus 101]	

The playing is meticulous and pleasant. The sound is good.

SYMPHONY NO. 88 IN G

This lovable masterwork is perhaps the most highly rated of Haydn's first 88 symphonies. It has had countless recordings.

* * FURTWAENGLER	*Berlin Philharmonic*	HELIODOR	25073
		[Schumann, Symphony No. 4]	
* SCHERCHEN	*Vienna State Opera Orch.*	WESTMINSTER	(S) 14616
		[Symphony No. 92]	

Furtwaengler, a celebrated conductor, gives a reading that puts him in first place. It is slow, episodic, and fascinating. However, the sound, even when this disc was on the vaunted DGG label, was burdened with "sturdy but rather dark sonics without bite or distinctness of timbre," according to critic C. G. Burke (*A Collector's Guide to Haydn*).

Scherchen, a superb and always stimulating interpreter of Haydn, is as incisive as ever. The sound, however, is rather strident.

SYMPHONY NO. 90 IN C

This is small beer for Haydn—fun and games with trumpets and drums in the last movement.

* JONES	*London Little Orch.*	NONESUCH (S) 71191 [Symphony No. 91]	

The Jones performance, though a bit stolid, passes muster.

SYMPHONY NO. 92 IN G ("OXFORD")

This vivacious top-of-the-list symphony was Haydn's acknowledgment to Oxford for conferring a degree upon him in 1791. This was not a new Haydn work, and had been composed two or three years earlier. Haydn, in fact, had brought along a new symphony, but the orchestra had insufficient time to rehearse it.

* SCHERCHEN	*Vienna State Opera Orch.*	WESTMINSTER (M) 18616 [Symphony No. 88]	

Scherchen is vivid and exciting. The mono sound is agreeable.

SYMPHONY NO. 94 IN G ("SURPRISE")

Here is a cheerful and sunny work, top-drawer Haydn. The surprise, as always explained by program annotators, is the big bang of the second movement, preceded by pianissimo passages. Haydn allegedly wrote this resounding boom to wake up the ladies.

I believe this was the first of Haydn's symphonies to be recorded. There have been many versions since.

* * DORATI	*Hungarian Philharmonic*	MERCURY (S) 18077 [Symphony No. 103]	
* TOSCANINI	*NBC Symphony Orch.*	VICTROLA VIC (M) 1261 [Symphony No. 101]	
TURNOVSKY	*Prague Symphony Orch.*	PARLIAMENT (S) 609 [Symphony No. 101]	
ALBERT	*Mannheimer National Symphony*	PERIOD SHO (ST-2) 321 [Symphony No. 100]	

The best here is the crisp Dorati reading, with good sonics and couplings.

Toscanini's reading is not what our purist ears expect today in a Haydn performance. *High Fidelity* found the reissue "a downright failure: tense, overhasty, and impersonal." The sound is from NBC's notorious radio Studio of 1946-47—which means woody strings and shrill brass.

Turnovsky is quite unremarkable.

Albert is much outclassed, with dim sonics.

A splendid, entirely gracious reading is to be heard from Giulini on a high-priced Angel disc.

SYMPHONY NO. 96 IN D ("MIRACLE")

"Miracle!" cried one and all when the London audience at the first performance of this symphony left their seats to crowd around Haydn and thus escaped injury from a vast chandelier that suddenly dropped from the ceiling upon their vacated seats.

If not the very best of Haydn, this is nevertheless fine music.

*	*Prague Chamber Orch.*	CROSSROADS (M) 22 16 0031
		(S) 22 16 0032
		[Symphony No. 73]

Both a delicate and forceful reading is to be had from the Czechs. The sound is pretty good.

SYMPHONY NO. 99 IN E-FLAT

This is one of Haydn's noblest and richest works in the symphonic form. Haydn wrote: "There was no one about me to confuse and torment me, and I was compelled to become original."

* SCHERCHEN	*Vienna State Opera Orch.*	WESTMINSTER (M) 18325
		[Symphony No. 100]
* WOELDIKE	*Vienna State Opera Orch.*	VANGUARD (S) 211
		[Symphony No. 102]

Scherchen stands supreme in a robust performance. However, the mono sound is just barely serviceable.

That endearing classicist, Woeldike, races through the haunting *Adagio,* for reasons only to himself, marring its loveliness, and down-grading this reading.

SYMPHONY NO. 100 IN G ("MILITARY")

This is a symphony of military bearing with a battery of big drums, cymbals, kettledrums and triangle. Although popular, it is one of the lesser of Haydn's last symphonies.

* * SCHERCHEN	*Vienna State Opera Orch.*	WESTMINSTER (S) 14044 [Symphony No. 45]	
* * WOELDIKE	*Vienna State Opera Orch.*	VANGUARD (S) 187 [Symphony No. 101]	
* SCHERCHEN	*Vienna Symphony Orch.*	WESTMINSTER (M) 18325 [Symphony No. 99]	

Scherchen's recording of this work with the Vienna Symphony Orchestra in 1950 was a revelation to record collectors; it set off violent controversy among the righteous as to the orthodoxy of his slam-bang all-out approach. It also put the then fledgling Westminster company on the map. This esteemed old mono disc has aged badly, but Scherchen recorded the piece again for Westminster with the better Vienna State Opera Orchestra. This second version is available with fair stereo.

Woeldike offers a first-rate reading.

SYHPHONY NO. 101 IN D ("CLOCK")

This is the one with the tick-tock *Andante*. Nevertheless, this is late, sparkling, vintage Haydn, and a must for the Haydn collector.

* * WOELDIKE	*Vienna State Opera Orch.*	VANGUARD (S) 187 [Symphony No. 100]	
* TOSCANINI	*NBC Symphony Orch.*	VICTROLA VIC (M) 1262 [Symphony No. 94]	
DORATI	*London Symphony Orch.*	MERCURY (M/S) 18064 [Mozart, Symphony No. 36]	

Woeldike gives an unpolished, unmannered reading that is first-rate. The sound is good.

Toscanini is tense and hard-driven, hardly Haydnesque.

Dorati, though more polished, is not elegant. This is a superficial performance.

THE "LONDON" SYMPHONIES No. 93-104 These symphonies were written during Haydn's two visits to England, 1791-1792 and 1794-1795. The composer, liberated after 30 bucolic years at Esterhazy, was revered in England as a genius and a man of art, rather than taken for granted as he had been at Esterhazy. The *London Symphonies*—his last—are the crown of Haydn's symphonic output.

SYMPHONY NO. 102 IN B-FLAT

This is a mature product of the late Haydn.

* * WOELDIKE	Vienna State Opera Orch.	VANGUARD	(S)	211
		[Symphony No. 99]		
* SCHERCHEN	Vienna Symphony Orch.	WESTMINSTER	(M)	18326
		[Symphony No. 101]		

Woeldike is authoritative, decisive, and altogether impressive.
Scherchen is more eccentric than usual, less convincing than Woeldike.

SYMPHONY NO. 103 IN E-FLAT ("DRUM ROLL")

This is a magnificent symphony. The sobriquet derives from the long rumbling opening with kettle drum. Don't miss this one—it's a beauty!

* * * WOELDIKE	Vienna State Opera Orch.	VANGUARD	(S)	166
		[Symphony No. 104]		
* SCHERCHEN	Vienna Symphony Orch.	WESTMINSTER	(M)	18327
		[Symphony No. 104]		
* WAND	Cologne Philharmonic	COUNTERPOINT	(S)	5615
		[Symphony No. 82]		

C. G. Burke's comments on the Woeldike disc fully express my sentiments. "It is a comfort to lean on the reliable Mogens Woeldike, strong and upright, not brilliant but authoritative."
Scherchen is finely-chiseled and deliberate. The mono sound is all right.
Wand is commendable but outclassed.

SYMPHONY NO. 104 IN D ("LONDON")

The last of the 12 "London Symphonies" was Haydn's last symphony. It is one of his very best. "So ends the beguiling procession of Haydn's symphonies, in healthy, full-throated glory," writes C. G. Burke.

* * * WOELDIKE	Vienna State Opera Orch.	VANGUARD		(S)	166
* HORENSTEIN	Pro Musica Symphony	VOX	(S)	(5)	9330
		[Symphony No. 101]			
* SCHERCHEN	Vienna Symphony Orch.	WESTMINSTER		(S)	18327
		[Symphony No. 103]			

Woeldike overshadows all competition at any price, with a joyous record that Robert Marsh hears as "conveying a kind of eighteenth-century splendor unrivaled on records." Martin Bookspan, in his 1968 "Annual Updating of the Basic Repertory" in *Stereo Review,* lists this as *the* performance: "Woeldike's is one of the most electrifying of all Haydn symphony recordings—and he employs corrected texts."

Horenstein, though acceptable, is much outclassed.

Scherchen takes third place, defaulted by poor sonics.

CONCERTOS   With all the musical goings-on at Estherhazy, the remarkable thing is that Haydn did not write far more concertos than he did in his nearly 30 years as music director. One has the impression that he was not enamoured of the form. These concertos are agreeable and correct, but most of them lack the heart and the depth of Mozart's.

Musical archaeologists tread warily amidst Haydn concertos; many ascribed to him, though good music, are spurious. In the nineteenth century, a manscript could be published at a profit if the hallowed name of Haydn was attached to it. A crayoned signature "Haydn" was enough proof for even some august publishing houses to bring out an edition, which it was hoped would sell briskly. The numbering of the various concertos is also sticky. Musicologists hesitate to sort out and label the keyboard concertos until the paternity of several of these has been properly authenticated.

CONCERTO FOR CELLO, IN C

Here is a "new" concerto by Haydn that lay buried for 200 years in a pile of yellowing mauscripts in Prague. It was found in the library of an old Bohemian castle, the former seat of an aristocratic family that in better days had employed some of the same musicians who worked with Haydn at Esterhazy. This is a vigorous and forthright work and gives the virtuoso cellist plenty to do. This concerto has become the personal property of the young, beautiful, and gifted cellist Jacqueline du Pre, who can be heard on an expensive Angel.

| * SADLO, KLIMA | *Prague Radio Symphony* | ARTIA | (M) | 206 |
| | | | (S) | 7206 |

[Boccherini, Concerto in B-Flat]

From the evidence here, Milos Sadlo is an exrtemely talented cellist with a bold romantic style.

CONCERTO FOR CELLO, IN D (Opus 101)

The musical archaeologists are still wondering whether Haydn wrote, helped to write, or never wrote this concerto, but it nevertheless stands as Haydn's best known work for cello. This is a fairly conventional concerto of deceptive simplicity. Under the bow of a master cellist, this music is superb.

* * * NAVARRA, PAUMGARTNER	*Salzburg Camerata*	NONESUCH (S) 71071 [Boccherini, Concerto]	
* * HOELSCHER, JOCHUM	*Nordwestdeutsche Philharmonic*	MONITOR (S) 2122 [Symphony No. 85]	
* JANIGRO, PROHASKA	*Vienna State Opera Orch.*	WESTMINSTER (M) 18406 [Boccherini, Concerto in B-Flat]	
* CASSADO, PERLEA	*Bamberg Symphony Orch.*	VOX (5) 10790 [Boccherini, Concerto; Vivaldi, Concerto]	

The singing tone of Navarra is outstanding. This is one of his most poised and vital discs, and with the endearing Boccherini concerto on the back, this is a solid buy, even though the sound is rather gritty here and there.

Ludwig Hoelscher, a superb German cellist barely known to America, offers a fine, expansive performance.

Janigro is a sensitive artist, but the sound on this disc is thin.

Cassado is much too romantic for Haydn.

CONCERTO FOR FLUTE

There is no evidence that Haydn composed this work, and strong indications that he did not. However that may be, the music is entirely pleasing.

* LINDE	*Collegium Aureum*	VICTROLA VIC (S) 1324 [Horn Concerto No. 1]	
* NOACK, LEHAN	*Consortium Musicum*	MACE (S) 9039 [Horn Concerto No. 2; Trumpet Concerto]	
* WANAUSEK, ADLER	*Vienna Pro Musica*	VOX (M) 10150 [Leclair; Pergolesi]	

Linde offers a gracious reading that is somewhat pallid. The New York *Times* sensed more merit in this disc, and said: "The orchestra's playing is broad and firm and the Haydn style is in its bones. But best of all [on the reverse side] is the wonderful, open sound of the horn." [The Victrola disc is backed with the acrobatic, diverting *Concerto for Hunting Horn*.]

The Mace version is good, but not exceptional.
The mono Vox disc features first-rate flute playing. The sound is wan.

CONCERTO FOR HARPSICHORD, IN D (Opus 21)

I gladly yield to the urbane C. G. Burke *(Collector's Guide to Haydn)*
for an appraisal of this concerto: "This marvel is an apotheosis of form,
and it is customary to sneer at it for not aspiring higher. It aspires to
bubble. Its impetuous *Galanterie* wears like iron, and has won a wide
public love duplicated only by the trumpet and cello concertos."

* * VEYRON-LACROIX, HORVAT	*Vienna State Opera Orch.*	WESTMINSTER (M) 9707 [Concerto in C, G]	
* * BRENDEL, ANGERER	*Vienna Chamber Orch.*	TURNABOUT (M) 4073 (S) 34073 [Hummel, Concerto in B]	
* * BRENDEL, ANGERER	*Vienna Chamber Orch.*	VOX (M) 12170 (S) 512170 [Mozart, Concerto No. 22]	
* HEILLER, LITSCHAUER	*Vienna State Opera Orch.*	VANGUARD (S) 454 [Trumpet Concerto]	
* GILELS, BARSHAI	*Moscow Chamber Orch.*	ARTIA (S) 159 [Mozart, Piano Concerto No. 21]	

The best version is easily that of Veyron-Lacroix on mono Westminster.
This is a polished and dynamic reading. The sound is resonant. [The disc
contains two other persuasive Haydn concertos for keyboard.]

If you care for this music played on a piano (Haydn specified "keyboard"), the Brendel discs are first-rate. [This Turnabout recording offers
a rare chance to hear the extremely pleasing music of Hummel. Johann
Nepomuk Hummel (1778-1837) was a pupil of Mozart, and Kapellmeister to Prince Esterhazy; his music is remarkably refreshing. Some
of his piano music sounds faintly like Chopin.]

Mme. Heiller is far more delicate than her boldly driving conductor,
yet this is a presentable reading.

The deft piano playing of Gilels is marred by wavery sound.

CONCERTO FOR OBOE AND ORCHESTRA IN C

This modest, amenable concerto is now only "attributed" to Haydn.
Musicologists are convinced that he didn't write it, but they can't figure
out who did. The sensational music detective Robbins Landon suggests
that Beethoven may have written the pieces; others attribute it to Mozart.
At any rate, pseudo-Haydn or not, the work has comfortably survived.

* * HANTAK, NEWSTONE	*Prague Symphony Orch.*	7-Artia 203 [Harpsichord Concerto in C]
* * HUCHE, LEHAN	*Consortium Musicum*	Mace (S) 9040 [Sinfonia Concertante] *
* * PONGRACZ, SANDOR	*Hungarian Radio and TV Symphony Orch.*	Dover (M) 5283 (S) 7283 [Purcell, Fantasies]
* MILDE, REINHARDT	*Stuttgart Pro Musica Orch.*	Vox (M) 14300 (S) 514300 [Telemann, Concerto for Oboe]
* MILDE, REINHARDT	*Stuttgart Pro Musica Orch.*	3-Turnabout 4031 [Horn Concerto No. 2; Trumpet Concerto]

Hantak is a first-rate oboist. The sound is good.

Mace offers a warm, skillful reading with dependable Electrola sound. [Mace offers Haydn's felicitous *Sinfonia Concertante* as a coupling.]

The Dover record features sensitive Hungarian artists, and includes three exhilarating Purcell *Fantasies* for string trio.

Milde is rigid and ungracious—not a very appealing soloist.

CONCERTO FOR TRUMPET AND ORCHESTRA, IN E-FLAT

Today, this is perhaps the most popular piece of all Haydn's output. A famous 78-rpm recording of this jovial concerto sparked off the Haydn renaissance in the 1940's which is going stronger than ever. Haydn was fascinated with a contraption that Court Trumpeter Anton Weidenger had been struggling with—a trumpet with keys. The result was this scintillating work "for Weidlinger's clarion," as it was then termed. No work serves a better introduction to Haydn.

* * ESKDALE, LITSCHAUER	*Vienna State Opera Orhc.*	Vanguard 454 [Harpsichord Orchestra in D]
* SCHNEIDEWIND, LEHAN	*Consortium Musicum*	Mace (S) 9039 [Flute Concerto; Horn Concerto No. 2]
GLEISLE, REINHARDT	*Stuttgart Pro Musica*	Vox (500) 480 [Horn Concerto No. 2]
HOLLER, SWAROWSKY	*Vienna Philharmusica Orch.*	5-Urania 129 [Overture; Sinfonia Concertante]

Eskdale is the best buy. C. G. Burke, a Haydn authority, praises "the splendid timbre of the solo trumpet, and the strength of the orchestral projection." [The backing is top-drawer Haydn.]

Mace offers three concertos with competent soloists. The sound from Electrola is spacious. [The reverse contains the *Horn Concerto No. 2*, a lively work of disputed authorship.]

The Vox compilation, with trumpeter Gleisle, is a so-so affair with indifferent soloists.

Holler is stiff. The sound is uninviting.

CONCERTO FOR VIOLIN, NO. 1 IN C
(Hob. VIIa, No. 1)

This conventional but spirited piece is Haydn's most popular violin concerto. Fiddlers love to show off in the *Adagio*.

* * GOTKOVSKY, AURIACOMBE	*Toulouse Chamber Orch.*	NONESUCH (S) 71185 [Concerto No. 3]
* * KREBBERS, RIEU	*Amsterdam Chamber Orch.*	CROSSROADS (S) 22 16 0206 [Concerto No. 2]

Gotkovsky's reading is agreeably subdued and proper. The sound is boomy. [The reverse is *Concerto in A*, referred to as the "Melk" concerto. Most of the instrumental parts to this concerto vanished for nearly 200 years, but turned up at Melk in Lower Austria. What we hear can be considered a reconstruction; it is charming music.]

The extremely gracious reading by Krebbers is backed with the pleasant *Concerto in G*. The sound is a bit metallic.

FIVE CONCERTI FOR TWO LIRAS

The *Lira Organizzata* was a weird contraption rather like a hurdy-gurdy. The performer turned a crank with one hand and played on a keyboard with his other. Haydn wrote five concertos for two of these instruments to please the eccentric King of Naples who played the lira himself. These concerti are quite diverting, and are more than mere curiosity pieces.

* * RAMPAL, PIERLOT, DOUATTE	*Paris Collegium Musicum*	MUSIC GUILD (S) 116 [No. 2/4]
* * RAMPAL, PIERLOT, DOUATTE	*Paris Collegium Musicum*	NONESUCH (S) 71067 [No. 1/5]
* RUF, LAUTENBACHER, NIELEN, BEYER BERNDT		TURNABOUT (S) (3) 4055 [No. 1, 3, 5]

Music Guild and Nonesuch both offer the music transcribed for flute and oboe, played by two of the best men in the business. The vivacious rapport they achieve on the Music Guild disc has to be heard to be believed.

Turnabout offers a lively reading, well recorded.

SINFONIA CONCERTANTE IN B-FLAT (Opus 84)

This delightful "Concert-Symphony" for violin, cello, oboe, bassoon, and orchestra is an established favorite in which the symphony orchestra can show off the virtuosity of its first-desk players. The work is a masterpiece of Haydn's late London years.

* * * RISTENPART	*Saar Chamber Orch.*	NONESUCH (S) 71024 [Nocturni; Organ Concerto]	
* * MARKEVITCH	*Lamoureux Orch.*	HELIODOR (S) 25015 [Boccherini, Cello Concerto in B-Flat]	
* LEHAN	*Consortium Musicum*	MACE (S) 9040 [Oboe Concerto]	
* FAERBER	*Wuerttemberg Chamber Orch.*	VOX (M) 14180 (S) 514180 [Mozart, Sinfonie K. Anh. 9]	
WALTHER	*Hamburg Chamber Orch.*	URANIA (M) 129 (S) 5129 [Trumpet Concerto]	

Nonesuch offers a strong, handsomely played record. The sound from the Club Francais du Disque is as warm and right as is the playing. [The backing is an early, enjoyable *Organ Concerto,* vividly played.]

The Heliodor is also worthy, though less expansive in approach. [It features the first-rate Boccherini cello concerto on the reverse.]

Mace has a carefully elaborated performance with fine sound from Electrola. [It is backed with a graceful performance of the *Oboe Concerto.*]

The Faerber version offers rather pedestrian playing.

Walther is much outclassed.

STRING QUARTETS The current tremendous revival of interest in chamber music, as well as the advent of the long play record, has made Haydn's string quartets extremely popular.

For many music lovers, the string quartets are Haydn's most rewarding compositions. In the words of Sackville-West, "Never before — and seldom since — has a composer contrived to embody such varieties of thought and feeling, and to explore so thoroughly the intricacies of musical procedure in so economical a form."

The string quartet form had already existed when Haydn appeared on the scene—mostly divertimentos and little suites in which a violin was merely accompanied by the other strings. Haydn welded these into the superb form of four integrated string voices that constitute classical chamber music.

Tip on how to listen to Haydn and Mozart quartets: Forget about these great masterpieces being "good for you." This is fun music, not written with any MESSAGE—music written for amateur players. In the eighteenth century, composers wrote music that was primarily intended to be engaging and not too demanding upon the players. Such music was to be played for the enjoyment of the participants, and even played in a room where other people might be chatting or playing cards.

Beethoven changed all that. Beethoven wrote weighty chamber music for an *audience,* rather than agreeable music for dilettante performers. That is why Haydn was able to write some 84 quartets, and Beethoven only 16. Music was never the same after Beethoven; from his day on, content was all. Result: Brahms wrote only three string quartets, and destroyed most of his compositions rather than have published what he considered were inferior works.

So when you hear Haydn—relax and enjoy!

EIGHTY-TWO QUARTETS (Complete)

* *	*Dekany Quartet*	3-Vox (S) SVBX 555 [Opus 1/1,2; Opus 20]
* *	*Dekany Quartet*	3-Vox (S) SVBX 556 [Opus 1/3: Opus 33/6]
* *	*Dekany Quartet*	3-Vox (S) SVBX 559 [Opus 42, 54, 55]
* *	*Dekany Quartet*	3-Vox (S) SVBX 561 [Opus 17, 77]
* *	*Dekany Quartet*	3-Vox (S) SVBX 562 [Opus 2/1-4; Opus 71]
* *	*Dekany Quartet*	3-Vox (S) SVBX 563 [Opus 9; Seven Last Words of Christ]
*	*Fine Arts Quartet*	3-Vox (S) SVBX 595 [Opus 50, 103]

The Dekany Quartet, according to Vox, are young Hungarians living in Holland. This group was organized around 1964 expressly for this stupendous project. The playing, though on the impetuous side, is admirable. A winning air of spontaneous performance pervades these readings; here are four chamber-music lovers enjoying themselves and conveying their delight to the listener. *High Fidelity* threw a bouquet to the

Dekany Quartet, saying: "You have an album in which the elements of performance, engineering, musical discovery, and even bargain price are combined to appeal to a very wide and (I trust) grateful audience. To the Vox people who planned this project, a low bow."

The Fine Arts Quartet is quite fussy. The sound is dry.

QUARTET (Opus 20, No. 4), IN D

This is one of a group known as the "Sun" Quartets, so named because of an illustration on the title page of an early edition. This is adventurous, explorative music, not at all routine.

*	*Prague City Quartet*	CROSSROADS	
		(M) 22 16 0099	
		(S) 22 16 0100	
		[Quartets 76/4]	
*	*Fine Arts Quartet*	CONCERT DISC (M) 1228	
		(S) 228	
		[Quartet No. 76/2]	

The playing of the Czechs is refined. The sound is pleasant.

The Fine Arts Quartet are good, but somewhat less graceful than the top-ranked performers.

QUARTET (Opus 33, No. 2), IN E-FLAT ("JOKE")

The "Joke" refers to some musical fun in the *Finale*. This is a cheerful and lively quartet with only the *Largo* as a serious movement.

*	*Hungarian Quartet*	TURNABOUT (M) 4062	
		(S) 34062	
		[Quartet Opus 33/3, 64/5]	

The playing is engaging and on the smooth side.

QUARTET (Opus 33, No. 3), IN C ("BIRD")

Bird calls and cuckoo clucks account for the sobriquet. This is a charming quartet.

*	*Hungarian Quartet*	TURNABOUT (M) 4062	
		(S) 34062	
		[Quartet Opus 33/2; 64/5]	

The playing, though graceful, is rather pallid.

QUARTET (Opus 55, No. 2), IN F MINOR

This is an easy-to-like, diverting quartet.

* *	*The Stuyvesant String Quartet*	NONESUCH (M) 1114 (S) 71114 [Tartini, Quartet No. 1 in D Major; Purcell, Chacony in G Minor; Dittersdorf, Quartet in D Major]

The playing is spirited, and quite infectious. [The coupling with three other good pieces makes this a tempting disc.]

QUARTET (Opus 64, No. 5), IN D ("LARK")

This lyrical composition is perhaps the most often played of all Haydn's quartets.

* *	*Hungarian Quartet*	3-TURNABOUT (5) 34062 [Quartet Opus 33/2, 3]
* *	*Hungarian Quartet*	3-TURNABOUT (S) 34251/3 [Quartet Opus 76/2; Mozart, Quartet No. 17, 19; Schubert, Quartet No. 14]
*	*Hungarian Quartet*	VOX (S) 512080 [Quartet Opus 77/2]

The Hungarian Quartet is trim and graceful. The sound is clear.

QUARTET (Opus 76, No. 2), IN D MINOR ("QUINTEN")

This quartet has been called "a perfect little model of contrapuntal resourcefulness." I commend it highly.

* *	*Fine Arts Quartet*	CONCERT DISC (M) 1228 (S) 228 [Quartet Opus 20/4]
* *	*Hungarian Quartet*	TURNABOUT (M) 4012 (S) 34012 [Quartet Opus 76, No. 5]

The Fine Arts Quartet are crisp and assured. The sound is acceptable. The Hungarian Quartet are much more suave. But so is the sound.

QUARTET (Opus 76, No. 4), IN B-FLAT

A musing, contemplative *Adagio* is the essence of this top-drawer quartet.

| * * | **Prague City Quartet** | CROSSROADS (M) 22 16 0099 (S) 22 16 0100 [Quartet No. 20/4] |

The playing is exemplary. The sound is clear. [The backing is with an almost entirely gay work of an earlier period, regarded in Haydn's own lifetime as one of the "Great Quartets," so clearly did it transcend others of the period.]

QUARTET IN D MAJOR (Opus 76, No. 5)

With a long, serene slow movement almost as long as all three of the other movements, this quartet is a special favorite.

| * * | **Vienna Konzerthaus Quartet** | WESTMINSTER   (M)   9032 [Quartet in E-Flat Major] |

This disc is one of the best records the Vienna players have ever made, and they've made many good recordings. [*No. 6*, on the back, is repetitive, and of less inspiration.]

QUARTET IN B-FLAT (Opus 103) ("UNFINISHED")

This unfinished work, still incomplete three years after Haydn began writing it in his seventies, was sent to his publisher in 1806 with the poignant note quoting his own song, "Gone is all my strength. Old and weak am I." But the music is anything but weak — dark-hued and even philosophical.

| * * * * | **Amadeus Quartet** | WESTMINSTER   (M)   9033 [Quartet Opus 3/5; Trios] |

This is an early disc of the Amadeus Quartet, one of the world's top string quartets today. The playing is serious and satisfying. The sound is over-amplified but you get used to it.

SIX QUARTETS (Opus 50)

These were dedicated to Frederick William II who played the cello, and who succeeded his uncle Frederick the Great, the flute-player. Hence, these quartets are termed "The Prussian Quartets." They are urbane, much admired, and seldom played.

*   *Barchet Quartet*   Vox   (M) 7580
[No. 1, 2]

This mono performance is good, but on the rigid side. The sound is only so-so.

SIX QUARTETS (Opus 64) (Complete)

These are mature, first-rate Haydn quartets, and include the popular "*Lark Quartet.*"

*   *Vienna Konzerthaus*   3-WESTMINSTER
      Quartet   (M) 18603/5

The playing is rather heavy and humorless, as is the case with most Vienna Konzerthaus Quartet records. The once-admired reverberating Westminster sound that made this group sound larger than a string quartet today makes this group sound as though they were playing on electric violins.

MISCELLANEOUS CHAMBER MUSIC   Haydn wrote many pleasant divertimenti, cassations, piano trios, etc.

DIVERTIMENTI FOR BARYTON, VIOLA AND CELLO, NO. 45, IN D; NO. 49, IN G; NO. 60, IN A; NO. 64, IN D; NO. 113, IN D

Haydn wrote some 180 pieces using the melancholy baryton, since his employer, Prince Nicolaus Esterhazy, was a nimble player of this now vanished instrument. This music has a simple charm. The baryton was somewhat like a bass viola da gamba with six fretted strings.

* SCHWAMBERGER   *Salzburger Baryton Trio*   NONESUCH   (M/S) 71049

The playing is accomplished. The sound is good.

DUO IN B-FLAT

"Music for Two Violins" is a form of music not often heard these days. The Haydn *Duo* is written in the composer's most mature style.

* * D. OISTRAKH,   MONITOR   (M/S) 2058
  I. OISTRAKH   [Honegger, Sonatina; Prokofiev, Sonata for Two
Violins; Spohr, Duetto No.
2, in D]

The playing by father and son is smooth, and little short of superb. The sound, from the Paris studios of 1962, is first-rate. [Spohr's *Duetto* is surprisingly impressive, and both modern works sound like good, thought-out music. What the Oistrakhs make of the Prokofiev is dazzling.]

"SEVEN LAST WORDS OF CHRIST"

This deeply moving work consists of nine slow movements of a rather programmatic nature; each movement is prefaced with a line from The New Testament. (Sometimes only seven movements are played.) Four different versions exist: piano, vocal, orchestra, and string quartet.

* *	*Dekany Quartet*	3-Vox [Quartets]	SVBX	563
* * JONES	*London Little Orch.*	NONESUCH	(S) 71154	
* *	*Amadeus Quartet*	WESTMINSTER	9029	

The Dekany Quartet give an intense, concentrated performance. An eloquent orchestral reading is offered by Jones. The sound is warm. The Amadeus recording, hailed as a "lesser classic of the LP era" by *High Fidelity,* has good mono which in this case is no drawback.

SONATAS FOR FLUTE AND PIANO: IN C (Opus 87; IN G (Opus 90)

Both of these pieces are Haydn string quartets transcribed by another hand for flute and piano. The result is just barely adequate.

RAMPAL, VEYRON-LACROIX	7-NONESUCH	(S)	1045

The celebrated prowess of flutist Rampal is not too much in evidence on this one.

TRIOS FOR PIANO, VIOLIN AND CELLO

The Haydn trios are imaginative, diverting pieces, much favored by chamber music players ever since the days they were written. The piano part is usually the most interesting, so much so that when Ignaz Pleyel, who had been Haydn's prize pupil, published these works he labeled them "Collection Complette des Sonatates d'Haydn pour Piano-Forte."

* * KOGAN, ROSTROPOVICH, GILELS	MONITOR [No. 30 in D; Brahms, Trio, Opus 40]	(S)	2066

* * DAVID OISTRAKH	*Oistrakh Trio*	MONITOR (S) 2071 [Dvorak, Trio]
* * FOURNIER, JANIGRO, BADURA-SKODA		3-WESTMINSTER (M) 9026/8 [10 Trios]

The vital Kogan-Rostropovitch-Gilels interpretation is outstanding. [This disc is backed with the great *Horn Trio* of Brahms, and if a vibrato-laden French horn doesn't bother you too much, this is a solid buy.]

The Oistrakh version is rather romantically played by one of the great violinists of this century. [The coupling is good.]

Westminister offers an exhilarating, youthful reading. The sound, however, is thinnish.

PIANO MUSIC Haydn's piano music is quite uneven. Many of his fifty-odd sonatas and partitas were written for his pupils, to exercise them in technical problems of piano playing. With a few exceptions, they are not on a level with Mozart's works for piano. But there are many sudden flashes of inspiration that break through the rather bland patterns.

SONATAS FOR PIANO

* * * REISENBERG	MONITOR (S) 2097 [No. 50, 52]
* * BACKHAUS	LONDON STS (S) 15041 [No. 52, 48, 34]
* * KYRIAKOU	3-Vox SVBX (S) 574 [Vol. 2, No. 21/6, 33, 40/3, 51, 48]
* * KLIEN	3-Vox SVBX (S) 575 [Vol. 3, No. 20, 34/39, 44/46, 52]
GALLING	3-Vox SVBX (S) 576 [Vol. 4, No. 19, 27/32, 49/50; Variations No. 5, 6; Fantasia No. 4]
GALLING	NONESUCH (S) 71143 [No. 20, 23, 52]
NEUMEYER	3-Vox SVBX (S) 573 [Vol. 1, Sonatas 1/14, 18; 2 Sonatas in E-Flat for clavier and piano]

The best record is to be had from Nadia Reisenberg, who provides vigorous yet sensitive playing, and good selections. In 1955 *High Fidelity* commented: "No other Haydn record of the solo piano strikes the memory as comparable to this one."

Backhaus is robustily romantic and sparkling. The sound is fine.

Vox has no less than four volumes of Haydn keyboard sonatas, and each album is played by a different interpreter.

Vox's Volume Two features the admirable and elegant pianism of Rena Kyriakou; this is easily the best playing of the four. *High Fidelity* comments: "Mlle. Kyriakou, a marvelously accomplished and natural pianist, brought a wealth of delicacy and finesse to her assignment."

Vox's Volume Three is also good, with assured, bright readings by Walter Klien.

Vox's Volume Four, played academically by Galling, is of less interest.

The Galling performance on Nonesuch is correct and rather lifeless. Volume One offers 20 early works played on the harpsichord, the clavichord, and the hammerfluegel by Fritz Neumeyer; the set is of slight interest except to students and musicologists.

VOCAL MUSIC   There are profundities of Haydn revealed only in his religious vocal writings, especially in *The Oratorio, The Creation,* and in the late Masses. Haydn prayed to God and to the Virgin Mary every morning that he might be blessed with a successful day of composing. In the Masses and oratorios, his craft reached its heights. To quote Robbins Landon: "But there is no doubt that all Haydn's late Masses, in their steadfast unity of purpose and greatness of expression, are indeed a transfiguration of his style, and it is right and proper that they should close the long half-century of his artistic life."

CREATION (Oratorio)

One of Haydn's later works, *The Creation* is a glorious creation, one of the few oratorios that rival the vocal splendor of Bach. It was composed in 1797-98 as a result of Haydn's visit to London, at which time he had a chance to study carefully the oratorios of Handel. The text derives from Milton's *Paradise Lost* and from the Bible's first book *Genesis.*

To quote the felicitous C. G. Burke, *"The Creation* has the obviousness of the very earth, the sweetness of the south wind, the happiness of sunlight . . . it is cherubic, and cannot be doubted. It makes one believe in God, and even for a while in man."

* * VAN DIJCK,   *Cologne Guerzenich Orch.*   2-VANGUARD   (S) 238/9
SCHREIER, ADAM,   *and Chorus*
WAND

* STICH-RANDALL, DERMOTA, FELBERMAYER, WOELDIKE	*Vienna State Opera Orch. and Chorus*	2-VANGUARD	(M) 130/1
* WENGLOR, UNGER, ADAM, KOCH	*Berlin Radio Orch. and Chorus*	2-HELIODOR	(S) 25028-2
* COERTSE, PATZAK, ERNSTER, HORENSTEIN	*Vienna Volksoper Orch. and Musikfreunde Gesellschaft Singverein*	TURNABOUT	(S) 34184/5

Wand gives a most satisfactory performance which I fully enjoy. *High Fidelity* raves: "It is remarkable how close to eloquence this performance sometimes comes," but *Stereo Review* is less impressed: "Performance good, recording good, stereo okay." The sound is fair to good.

The Woeldike reading, much more dignified and less lovely, has better soloists than the top-rated record. The mono sound is still clear and good.

The Heliodor set is agreeable.

The Turnabout set is pleasant, although the soloists have their ups and downs. I find conductor Horenstein too impetuous for this music.

MASS NO. 5 IN B-FLAT ("LITTLE ORGAN")

This short, popular Mass, with a radiant part of the soprano, is middle-period Haydn, probably written in 1775. Though enjoyable, it is not in a class with his final great Masses. Robbins Landon remarks that this Mass "shines with the same affectionate innocence of a baroque carved angel at the side of the altar."

* KATONOSAKA, HASELBOECK, GILLESBERGER	*Vienna Volksoper Orch. and Chamber Chorus*	TURNABOUT (S) 34132 [Mozart, Missa K. 259]

Gillesberger made several noted and exciting recordings of Haydn Masses back in the salad days of the Haydn Society, the 1950's. I cannot trace the genealogy of the master tape used here, but it is on the whole rewarding. The sound is all right. [The Mozart coupling is a modest piece.]

MASS NO. 7 MISSA IN TEMPORE BELLI ("PAUKENMESSE")

This mass "In Time of War," a lament for the dead, is late, great Haydn, written in 1796 when the Imperial armies in Italy were being routed by the French forces.

** DAVRATH, ROESSL-MAIDAN, DERMOTA, BERRY, WOELDIKE	*Vienna State Opera Orch.*	VANGUARD	(S)	153
* THOMANN, JAHN, WING, KAWAMURA, GILLESBERGER	*Vienna Symphony Orch. and Chorus*	3-TURNABOUT	(S)	4138

Vanguard owns a winning performance with excellent soloists led by the somber-voiced Natania Davrath. The sound is agreeable.

Gillesberger, whose old recording of this work was famous on the old and venerated Haydn Society label, recorded it again for Vox, but with inferior soloists. If my ears do not betray me, this is the same performance transmogrified here on the Turnabout entry.

MASS NO. 9 IN D MINOR, MISSA SOLEMNIS ("NELSON MASS")

The greatest of Haydn's Masses (1798), this composition gives thanks for Nelson's annihilation of the French fleet at the Bay of Aboukir. The *Nelson Mass* is a lofty work that stands out not very far below Beethoven's *Missa Solemnis* and Verdi's *Requiem*.

** STICH-RANDALL, CASEI, EQUILUZ, SIMKOWSKY, SWAROWSKY	*Vienna State Opera Orch. and Chorus*	NONESUCH	(S)	71173
* STICH-RANDALL, HOENGEN, DERMOTA, GUTHRIE, ROSSI	*Vienna State Opera Orch.*	VANGUARD	(M)	470

The first-rate Swarowsky reading brings out all the drama and magnificence of this score. The soloists are good. The sound is excellent and spacious.

Rossi offers an impassioned performance. The sound is old but hearable.

MASS NO. 11 IN B-FLAT ("CREATION")

The eminent Haydn authority H. C. Robbins Landon is responsible, as much as anyone, for the great Haydn revival in our time. Landon dusted Haydn off and built him a new pedestal. Commenting on *Mass No. 11*, Landon said, "Choosing a favorite among the last six Haydn Masses presents the same dilemma as making a choice from Mozart's last six piano concertos." To me it seems that most people prefer the *Nelson Mass* because of its particular urgency and power; but I deem the Mass *In Time of War* and the *Heiligmesse,* and the *Schoepfungsmesse ("Creation" Mass)* equally as great.

| * * THOMANN, ZOTTL-HOLMSTAEDT, GILLESBERGER | *Vienna Volksoper Orch. and Chorus* | Vox | (S) | (50) 1020 |

Gillesberger delivers a taut, well-recorded reading with good soloists.

THE SEASONS (Oratorio) (Sung in German)

The Seasons was finished in 1801, three years after *The Creation.* Spring, summer, fall, and winter are represented along with all that you expect in a pastoral work. This composition is far less inspired than the noble *Creation.*

| * STICH-RANDALL, KRETSCHMAR, WENK, GOEHR | *North German Radio...... Symphony Orch. and Chorus* | 3-NONESUCH | (S) 73009 |

This warm reading is competent but hardly distinguished. The singing is just so-so.

SALVE REGINA NO. 3 IN G MINOR

Not great Haydn, this is nevertheless a restrained and lovely religious work.

| * * BUCKEL, LEHANE, VAN VROOMAN, WOLLETZ, REINHARDT | *Colleguim Aureum* | VICTROLA VIC   (S) 1270 [Mozart, Litaniae, K. 109] |

Here is a thoroughly prepared performance under Rolf Reinhardt, a conductor who knows his way in Haydn. The singing is exemplary. A small quibble: the soloists are at times recorded top-heavy against the choir and orchestra. This is not a very serious complaint, especially since Victrola has given us the only version of this music in the catalogue. The sound is excellent. [The coupling is with some lyrical church music by the young Mozart.]

CANTATA, "MISERI NOI, MISERA PATRIA (Excerpts) ARMIDAS RECITATIVE, "BARBARO! E ARDISCI ANCOR..." AND ARIA, "AH DEL SUO AMORE I FREGI"; CONCERT ARIA, "SOLO E PENSOSO"

This is pleasant, comparatively unimportant music for soprano and small orchestra.

* * BEARDSLEE, BOLLE   *The Musica Viva Ensemble*

MONITOR   MCS 2124 [Pergolesi, Adriano in Siria: Aria, "Lieto Cosi Talvolta"; Storace, The Pirates: Song, "Peaceful Slumb'ring on the Ocean"]

Both the singing and the style are good. If you like short vocal pieces, this disc is commendable.

Hindemith, Paul (1895-1963)

Born in Hanau, Germany, Hindemith studied at the Hoch Conservatory in Frankfurt. In 1915, he became concertmaster of the Frankfurt Opera; and in 1923, he became conductor of that group. He also founded and played in the Amar String Quartet which specialized in concerts of modern music. Hindemith was one of the important figures in the Donaueschingen Festivals of contemporary music (1921-26), and taught at the Berlin Hochschule from 1927 to 1935.

In 1934, a proposed performance of his opera *Mathis der Maler* was forbidden by the Nazis. After spending some time in Ankara as musical adviser to the Turkish Government, Hindemith emigrated to America in 1939. In 1942, he became professor of theory at Yale. Later he taught at Zurich University in Switzerland.

PLACE AND ACHIEVEMENT   A generation ago, Hindemith was considered one of the very greatest of living composers. With the exception of Stravinsky, no other contemporary composer was more esteemed or more influential. His music had character and strength, and it was hearable.

Today, Hindemith seems to have been by-passed. The line of succession of significant influence in music now seems to have led through the disciples of Schoenberg and even further — to even more revolutionary musicians who now cry, as did Boulez in a famous phrase, "Schoenberg est mort!"

Yet Hindemith may outlast many other writers of music who have zoomed to popularity and fame since World War I. Hindemith is a composer's composer; every bar demonstrates his supreme technical proficiency. Though he was a bold innovator, his feet were firmly on the ground, and he had a deep love and respect for both the classical and the romantic schools. The music of Paul Hindemith, while as free and experimental as any other music of his day, continues the grand line of classical composition, logically and inevitably. His twentieth-century music has permanence.

THE ESSENTIAL HINDEMITH

ORCHESTRAL MUSIC: *Mathis der Maler, Symphony; Symphonic Metamorphoses on Themes by Carl Maria von Weber; Symphony in E-Flat; Symphonia Serena; Konzertmusic, for String Orchestra and Brass Instruments (Opus 50); Noblissima Visione; Der Schwanendreher, Concerto for Viola and Orchestra; Concerto for Violin and Orchestra.*

SONGS: *Das Marienleben, Song Cycle.*

CHAMBER MUSIC: *Kleine Kammermusik, for Wind Quintet.*

OPERA: *Mathis der Maler.*

OTHER WORKS

ORCHESTRAL MUSIC: *Philharmonic Concerto, Theme and Variations According to the Four Temperaments; Die Harmonie der Welten; Concerto for Cello and Orchestra; Concerto for Piano and Orchestra; String Quartet No. 3; String Quartet No. 5, in E-flat.*

SONATAS: *Hindemith wrote sonatas for violin, for flute, for oboe, for bassoon, for English horn, for trombone, and for piano.*

CHAMBER MUSIC: *Quartet for Violin, Clarinet, Cello, and Piano.*

OPERAS: *Cardillac; Neues vom Tage.*

BALLET: *Saint Francis.*

ORATORIO: *Die Unaufhoerliche.*

CHORAL MUSIC: *Requiem for Those We Love.*

SONGS: *Die Junge Magd, Song Cycle.*

PIANO MUSIC: *Ludus Tonalis.*

CONCERT MUSIC FOR STRINGS AND BRASS; SYMPHONY IN B FLAT FOR CONCERT BAND

Hindemith's credo was based on *"gebrauchsmusik:"* music ordered, composed, packed, and delivered to meet the needs of a particular audience. The *Symphony in B-Flat* is a 20-minute piece written for the U. S. Army Band in 1951. It is an ingenious exercise, involving alto saxophones, cornet, and other brass instruments.

The *Concert Music* is far more substantial—a brilliant technical accomplishment. The possibilities of clashing antiphony of strings and brass are utilized here by a modern master of the orchestra. The work leads up to a dazzling, fugally designed finale. The presence of deeper values in this work, beyond its success as a mere showy *tour de force* is still a matter of debate among thoughtful musicologists.

* HINDEMITH   *Philharmonic Orch.*   SERAPHIM   (S) 60047

The work is efficiently conducted by the composer himself. The sound is fair.

CONCERTO FOR VIOLIN AND ORCHESTRA (1940)

This surprisingly romantic and melodious concerto dates from 1939.

* * * FUCHS, GOOSSENS   *London Symphony Orch.*   EVEREST   (M) 6040
                                                                         (S) 3040
                                                          [Mozart, Concerto No. 3]

This disc is well worth investigating by lovers of the violin concerto who are bored with the standard showpieces. This is a first-rate concerto, and is brilliantly played by Fuchs. The sound is excellent.

DAS MARIENLEBEN   (Opus 27)
(New Version, 1948)

This enormous cycle of 15 songs comprises a setting of Rilke's poems on the life of the Virgin Mary. The work was first composed in 1922; in 1948, after seven more years of labor, Hindemith drastically revised his *Life of Mary*. This is impressive music, but hideously difficult to sing. The cycle (at least the early version) has been called "one of the great examples of lieder." The audience for this work is limited.

    * LAMMERS, PUCHELT   2-NONESUCH HB (S) 73007

The soprano Gerda Lammers navigates her way through this tortuous music—not without some difficulty. She goes breathless here and there, but I dare say most other singers would, too.

DIE SERENADEN   (Opus 35); DUET FOR VIOLA
AND CELLO; SONATA FOR VIOLIN SOLO
(Opus 31, No. 1); MARTINSLIED   (Opus 45, No. 5)

Here are several good examples of Hindemith's early, stimulating *Gebrauchsmusik* period—roughly from 1924 to 1934. *Die Serenaden,* one of Hindemith's most attractive pieces, is an intimate cantata set for soprano, oboe, violin, and cello.

    * ADDISON,   *New York Chamber*   NONESUCH   (S) H 71149
      BRESSLER,   *Soloists*
      KAPLAN, TARACK,
      LYNCH, KOUGUELL,
      FULLER

These artists are technically admirable and also musically sensitive—with a full sympathy for Hindemith's music.

KLEINE KAMMERMUSIK   (Opus 24, No. 2)

This music of 1922 is charming and ironic—absolutely first-rate. This *Little Chamber Music,* scored for the usually staid combination of woodwind quintet (flute, clarinet, oboe, horn, and bassoon, with a piccolo substituted for the flute in the second movement), is one of the most widely accepted works of chamber music written in our time. George Grosz's savage cartoons of 1920's Germany seem to set the mood of this work. As Arthur Cohn puts it, "Some of the passages must have been written with acid."

* * * **New York Woodwind Quintet** CONCERT DISC (M) 1205
                                                    (S)   205
[Danzi, Quintets for Wood-
wind, Opus 67]

* **Haifa Wind Quintet** MACE   (S) 9053
[Beethoven, Trio Opus 87;
Danzi, Quintet for Wood-
winds, Opus 56]

The music is played with incisive bite by the New Yorkers. The
stereo sound is good.

The Haifa players, though spirited, are outclassed.

[For couplings, both ensembles feature wind music of Franz Danzi
(1763-1826). Danzi, the son of a German family of Italian origin, established himself in Munich. He wrote opera, church music, and other works,
but is remembered today primarily for his mildly engaging wind music.
The Haifa disc also contains the unimportant Beethoven *Wind Trio in C
Major (Opus 87)* and a slight, polished work by Jaques Ibert, called *Trois
Pieces Breves.*]

SYMPHONY MATHIS DER MALER";
SYMPHONIC METAMORPHOSES

"Mathis der Maler," a masterpiece, is Hindemith's most widely accepted
work. The symphonic arrangement is an orchestral triptych taken from
Hindemith's opera about the life of the painter Matthias Grünewald. Here
is eloquent, soaring music.

The *Symphonic Metamophoses,* based on themes by Weber, is an
engaging work. The romantic themes are worked over with Hindemith's
noteworthy virtuosity and contrapuntal spinning.

* HORVAT   **Zagreb Philharmonic
                Orch.**
                                      TURNABOUT TV (S) 34215
* KONDRASHIN   **Moscow Philharmonic
                Orch.**

On both sides of the record, the playing is skillful and intense. The
sound is agreeable. This is an acceptable, but not remarkable disc.

SONATAS FOR PIANO: NOS. 1 and 3

These two sonatas are highly regarded "underground" works. Like the
admirable violin concerto, they have strong reputations and are widely
discussed among musicians, but seldom played in public. At this writing,
these two remarkable sonatas of 1936 are available on only one record
at any price.

The *Sonata No. 1* is a large-scale five-movement compostion of linear design; the *Sonata No. 3* ends with a dazzling double fugue that requires the performer to have intellect as well as nimble fingers. The respected critic and authority, Alfred Frankenstein, was totally enthusiastic about this music. "The sonatas are among the loftiest . . . which Hindemith has to his credit; their scope, depth and richness of content place them in a direct line of descent from Beethoven's last sonatas."

* * BADURA-SKODA   Westminster XWN
                                         (M) 18200

Badura-Skoda gives a fine performance. Alfred Frankenstein, as enthusiastic about the performance as about the works themselves, commented: "Badura-Skoda presents a wonderfully plastic and vivid interpretation. To my knowledge, a finer registration of piano tone does not exist; its entire range of color and shading is presented with something very close to perfection."

Holst, Gustav *(1874-1934)*

Holst, born in England of mixed Swedish and English descent, was a solitary figure in modern music—mystic and aloof. Almost none of his works, save the highly popular *The Planets,* is currently in the active repertory. Along with Vaughan Williams, he may be remembered more for his influence upon the younger generation of English composers who are working today, than for his own work.

PLANETS, OPUS 32

This medley of picturesque music and brilliant orchestration, written in 1914-16, is scored for huge orchestra—including alto flute, bass, oboe, six-part female offstage chorus, etc., practically *ad infinitum.* The subtitle of each movement specifies the poetic mood of a planet, e.g. "Mars, the Bringer of War." Holst was bitter about the tremendous success of *The Planets,* compared to the utter neglect of what he believed to be his more significant pieces.

* SARGENT	*London Symphony Orch.*	RICHMOND	(M) 19095
BOULT	*Vienna State Opera Orch.*	WESTMINSTER	(M) 18919
			(S) 14067

Sargent's interpretation is more imaginative, but it is available only on old mono, whereas this music demands stereo.

Boult's reading disappoints. Although he knew this music intimately, the playing is indifferent.

The near-ideal version is to be found on a high-priced Capitol disc featuring Stowkowski.

Honegger, Arthur (1892-1955)

A Swiss composer, Honegger studied at the Paris Conservatoire. In 1916, together with Satie, Milhaud, and Jean Cocteau, he formed the group *Les Nouveaux Jeunes,* which later became the famous group, *Les Six.* Honegger was an extremely prolific composer, and is best remembered for two moving oratorios: *King David* and *Joan of Arc at the Stake.*

PACIFIC 231; PASTORALE D'ETE; CHANT DE JOIE; SYMPHONY NO. FIVE

Pacific 231 is all about a locomotive of the same name. It is rarely heard these days, but in the 1920's it was a sensation that provoked much shaking of critical heads and reams of columns asking "Whitther-is-music-drifting." Today it is a pleasantly dated period piece. The *Song of Joy* is sonorous Honegger, and very good music. The *Pastoral* is gentle sketching for woodwinds, horn, and strings. The *Symphony No. Five,* written in 1951, is a still-debated work. Some call it tired Prokofiev; others, including myself, regard it as a lean, incisive work.

* * BAUDO   *Czech Philharmonic Orch.*   CROSSROADS   (S) 2216-0078

This disc provides a good sampler of Honegger's craft. The playing is fresh-sounding and the sonics are quite clear.

Hovhaness, Alan (1911-   )

Hovhaness, born in Massachusetts of Armenian and Scottish parents, studied at the Boston Conservatory. His style delves deeply into musical styles and systems of the Orient, both near and far, and attempts to fuse them with the traditional forms of Western music. More than any other American composer, Hovhaness has identified himself completely with Eastern, especially Armenian, music, and the surprising thing is that his music is so widely played. People like it. Picturesque ideas, traces of Gregorian chant, esoteric Syrian modes, reiterated figures, etc. saturate the music of this unique composer.

Critical opinion of Hovhaness is divided. He has been dismissed as making use of contrived and self-conscious Orientalism—"rather like eating an egg buried for a hundred years."* On the other hand, the perceptive Virgil Thomson, a supreme critic and himself a composer, has written, "Hovhaness' work is not hard for everyone to like . . . each piece is like a long roll of hand-made wallpaper." The adventurous listener is urged to sample Mr. Hovhaness for himself.

"LOUSADZAK," CONCERTO NO. 1 FOR PIANO AND STRINGS; CONCERTO NO. 2 FOR VIOLIN AND STRINGS

Arthur Cohn calls Hovhaness' *Concerto No. 1* "Doubtless the most unusual concerto ever written for the piano." "Lousadzak," the Armenian sub-title, means "The Coming of Light." The piano imitates a number of Armenian instruments: the *rar*, the *Kanoon*, the *oud*, and others. The string orchestra mysteriously strums and plucks and it is all very exotic.

The violin concerto uses the solo violin as an instrument to sound like the human voice—with unearthly glissandos from the string orchestra. The total effect is beguiling.

* MARO AJEMIAN,   *String Orch.*   HELIODOR   HS 25040
ANAHID AJEMIAN,
SURINACH

The players themselves seem quite entranced with the work. Both the playing and the sound are quite effective.

*Arthur Cohn, *Twentieth Century Music in the Western Hemisphere.*

"LOUSADZAK," CONCERTO NO. 1 FOR PIANO AND STRINGS; CONCERTO NO. 2 FOR VIOLIN AND STRINGS

Arthur Cohn calls Hovhaness' *Concerto No. 1* "Doubtless the most unusual concerto ever written for the piano." "Lousadzak," the Armenian sub-title, means "The Coming of Light." The piano imitates a number of Armenian instruments: the *rar*, the *Kanoon*, the *oud*, and others. The string orchestra mysteriously strums and plucks and it is all very exotic.

The violin concerto uses the solo violin as an instrument to sound like the human voice—with unearthly glissandos from the string orchestra. The total effect is beguiling.

* MARO AJEMIAN, ANAHID AJEMIAN, SURINACH	*String Orch.*	HELIODOR	HS 25040

The players themselves seem quite entranced with the work. Both the playing and the sound are quite effective.

Ibert, Jacques (1890-1962)

Trained at the Paris Conservatoire, Ibert became Director of the Academie de France in Rome in 1937, and became Director of the Paris Opera in 1955. Ibert's music is very French and very droll; it may remind the listener of the deadpan of the old Rene Claire films. His works include music for the theater and for films, orchestral and chamber music, and pieces for piano and organ.

CONCERTINO DA CAMERA

This "little chamber concerto," dating from 1935, arranged for saxophone and 11 instruments, is a slight piece, brilliantly orchestrated. It is unpretentious, and fun.

* ABATO, SCHULMAN	*Chamber Orch.*	NONESUCH H 71030 [Glazounov, Concerto for Saxaphone; Villa-Lobos, Bachianas No. 6; Quintette]

The music is well played and recorded. [The other items on the disc are agreeable.]

CONCERTO FOR FLUTE

This slight work, dating from 1934, is more a small, amusing piece, than a full-scale concerto.

RAMPAL, FROMENT, LAMOUREUX	*Orchestra*	MUSIC GUILD (S) 141 [Jolivet; Rivier]

Rampal plays impeccably. The sound is pleasant.

DIVERTISSEMENT

This work, originally written as incidental music to a continental farce called *The Italian Straw Hat,* contains witty musical references to Mendelssohn's *Wedding March,* and a number of other humorous touches.

* * FIEDLER	*Boston Pops Orch.*	VICTROLA VIC (S) 1053 [Respighi, Boutique Fantasque]
* DESOMIERE	*Paris Conservatoire Orch.*	RICHMOND (M) 19028 [Chopin, Sylphides]

Fiedler does well, but in rather four-square fashion—without the French cabaret atmosphere that other conductors have evoked. The sound is excellent. [The coupling is with another successful fun piece, Respighi's *Ballet after Rosseni*.]

Desomière seems to capture more of the theatrical atmosphere—but the sound is mono.

ESCALES (PORTS OF CALL)

Ports of Call, an early work (1922), impressionistic in the vein of Debussy and Ravel, is not as droll as Ibert's later pieces, but it is nevertheless his most popular composition. The "ports of call" are Rome, Palermo, Tunis, and the music conveys predictable impressions of these places.

* * MUNCH	*Boston Symphony Orch.*	VICTROLA VIC (S) 1323 [Debussy, Prelude; Ravel, Bolero; Pavane; Valse]
* PARAY	*Detroit Symphony*	MERCURY 18030 [Ravel Program]

Munch gives a suave interpretation; the Boston orchestra plays brilliantly and is wonderfully recorded.

Paray version is colorful, but not in a class with the Boston recording.

Isaac, Heinrich *(c. 1450-1517)*

Isaac, probably a Netherlander (although the Italians called him "Arrigo tedesco"—Harry the German) entered the service of Lorenzo de Medici in Florence in 1480. There he was singer, composer, and probably music instructor to Lorenzo's sons. Isaac was an extraordinary composer. His music conveys a sweetness, a grace that at once touches the listener. When he is well played, he is never dull. He was a contemporary of Josquin de Prez, and ranks with him as one of the great masters of the Renaissance.

MISSA CARMINUM

This small-scaled mass, in the Lydian mode, contains much genial beauty.

* * * TRAEDER	*Niedersaechsischer Singkreis (Hannover)*	NONESUCH H 71084 [Des Prez, Ave Christe; Lasso, Motets]

This is a lovely record, on all counts—well performed and well recorded. [It also contains Lasso's striking dramatic two-part motet for six voices, and a fine work by Des Prez. All in all, here is a first-class selection of music by three great Dutch masters of the fifteenth and sixteenth centuries.]

VIRGO PRUDENTISSIMA; SECULAR WORKS

Isaac's music is part of a stunning two-record set called "The Triumph of Maximilian I." Maximilian was a great patron of the arts; his court included not only the composer Isaac, but the great painter Durer as well. This composer's *Virgo Prudentissima* for six voices is one of the glories of Renaissance vocal music.

* *	*London Ambrosian Singers*	2-NONESUCH 73016

The works are splendidly sung and recorded. There is a vibrant yet somber ambiance about this performance that is quite remarkable.

Ives, Charles (1874-1954)

Ives was born in Danbury, Connecticut. His father, a Civil War band-master, was a remarkably original musician. Ives, Sr. began the musical education of his talented son. Later, Charles went on to study under Horatio Parker at Yale. He played the organ professionally and was a member of various theater orchestras. Most of his adult life was spent in New York City where he was one of the directors of an extremely success-ful insurance firm. In 1947, he was awarded the Pulitzer Prize for his *Third Symphony,* which he had composed back in 1911.

PLACE AND ACHIEVEMENT   There has been no more incredible figure in American music than this solitary, elusive, long-ignored composer, Charles Ives. Although he was an "amateur composer" (the comparison with Grandma Moses in art is inevitably made) we have not seen, even in the 1960's, any more advanced and truly adventurous American writer. Today, he is overpraised, over-discussed, and hailed as a genius—and all this, of course, is a kind of critical penance for his long neglect. The knowledgeable Arthur Cohn has summed up Charles Ives: "Ives has come into his own.... It was part of Ives' method to be a finger painter, one who drew with original strength and the individuality of the primitive, yet lapsed into doodling from time to time . . . . This man was a creative cross-breed—a Joycean as well as a Proustian composer, with elements of the folk singer, the mountaineer, the revivalist.... He combined with seeming casualness all know compositional techniques, from four-part elementary harmony to a partial employment of the twelve-tone system, use of micro-tones, double orchestras, . . . and all other 'isms.' Yet he was no musical pirate. All these techniques were natural to him, were so years before Messrs. Schoenberg, Stravinsky, Haba, Stockhausen and the like 'discov-ered' them! . . . He was one of the most daring and original of visionaries, a composer who ran far in front of the pack."*

*Arthur Cohn, *The Collectors 20th Century Music in the Western Hemisphere,* Keystone Books, 1961.

THE ESSENTIAL IVES

ORCHESTRAL MUSIC: *General William Booth Enters into Heaven; Circus Band; Serenity, Psalms 24, 67, 90, 100, 150; New River; December; Three Places in New England; Unanswered Question; Washington's Birthday.*

CHAMBER MUSIC: *Largo for Violin, Clarinet and Piano; Quartets No. 1 and 2; 4 Sonatas for Violin and Piano.*

PIANO MUSIC: *Sonata No. 1 for Piano.*

SYMPHONIES: *No. 2, 3, 4; Holidays.*

OTHER WORKS

ORCHESTRAL MUSIC: *Anti-Abolitionist Riots; Some Southpaw Pitching; 3 Protests; Theatre Set: In the Inn; Browning Overture; Central Park in the Dark; Circus Band March; Harvest Home Chorales.*

PIANO MUSIC: *Three-Page Sonata for Piano; Three Quartertone Piano Pieces.*

FOUR SONATAS FOR VIOLIN AND PIANO

Composed between 1908 and 1914, Ives' four violin sonatas are top-drawer music. They contain a fantastic range of devices, including the predictable Ives Americana backdrops and musical horseplay. These sonatas may be summed up as fantastic musical murals, with images of remembered child-hood—much as Marc Chagall uses images and devices in his paintings.

* * DRUIAN, SIMMS
2-WORLD SERIES PHC 2-002
[Bartok, Sonata for Violin and Piano, No. 2]

The players here are splendid—Rafael Druian on violin and John Simms on piano. Arthur Cohn commented on this set: "The performance of any Ives duo-sonata is a test for a fiddler and a pianist. Druian's insight and Simm's fabulous knowledge combine in a performance that is as rare as snow in summer."* The sound is clean. [The Bartok filler is first-rate.]

*Arthur Cohn, *Twentieth Century Music in the Western Hemisphere,* Lippincott.

"HOLIDAYS" SYMPHONY

This is a four-movement symphony, with each movement representing both an American holiday—Washington's Birthday, Fourth of July, etc.— and a season. There are many evocative quotations, and all the Ivesian trademarks: a brass band, firecracker explosions, barn dance, and so on.

* JOHANOS   *Dallas Symphony Orch.*   TURNABOUT TV (S) 34146

The performance and sound are both agreeable. This disc is a good in-troduction for anyone who wants to find out what all the clamor about Ives is about.

QUARTETS FOR STRINGS: No. 1 ("A Revival Service"); No. 2

The *First Quartet,* written in 1869, consists almost entirely of hymn tunes. It is conservative writing in a manner suggestive of Brahms and Dvorak, of comparatively little interest today.

The *Second Quartet* (1907-13) is described by Ives on the score as a "String Quartet for four men who converse, discuss, argue (politics), fight, shake hands, shut up, then walk up the mountain to view the firmament." This is a fascinating quartet. Here we find Charles Ives writing with intensity and fervor, and using tools — atonalism, polyrhythm, and linear counterpoint—that became common property of all composers only decades later, in our own time. This is remarkable music.

*   *Kohon Quartet*   Turnabout   (S) 34157

The Kohon Quartet plays with enthusiasm; they manage the complex polyphony with expertness. When this record was in its pristine, mono state on the Vox label, Alan Rich commented on the sonics: "I am not charmed, however, by the shrillness of the sound in loud passages, for which the engineers are more at fault than the players." The stereo rechanneling has helped somewhat.

ROBERT BROWNING OVERTURE FOR LARGE ORCHESTRA; THE CIRCUS BAND MARCH; SET FOR THEATRE ORCHESTRA; THE UNANSWERED QUESTION

These orchestral works provide a good introduction to this "naive" composer who discovered, decades ahead of the others, almost every "way-out" technique employed in way-out music of the 1960's. *The Unanswered Question,* the worthiest piece here, is a philosophical essay in music. The subject is "the perennial question of existence." According to the composer, this piece is *not* to be played with exactitude. Tempi and meters are in opposition to one another.

* * FARBERMAN   *Royal Philharmonic Orch.*   Cardinal   (S) 10013

Farberman is loyal and literal. The sound is clean.

SONATA FOR PIANO, NO. 1

This is a tangled, kinetic sonata of great vitality. Ives wrote seven movements originally, in 1909, but two became lost due to his eccentric ways with his manuscripts.

As in most of Ives' music, much turn-of-the-century Americana is woven in. The composer himself described the work: "One movement is partly from an organ piece played in an organ recital in Center Church, New Haven, in 1897. The *Sonata* is in a way a kind of impression, remembrance, and reflection of the country life in some of the Connecticut villages in the 1880's and 1890's." However, the work is not as bucolic sounding as Ives' comment lead one to expect. Extremely difficult music, the *Sonata* lends itself extremely well to different kinds of interpretation.

<table>
<tr><td>* * MASSELOS</td><td>ODYSSEY   (M) 32 16 0059</td></tr>
<tr><td>* * LEE</td><td>NONESUCH H   (S) 71169</td></tr>
</table>

Masselos is astringent, even brittle, in his interpretation of the music. I prefer this version. The sound is clean.

Lee, in a very different kind of interpretation, is gentle and impressionistic. The sound is good.

SYMPHONIES: NOS. 1-4; HALLOWE'EN

This is a mixed bag. The symphonies are discursive and uneven. The primitivistic side of Ives predominates. There is considerable confusion just in sorting out what music was originally where; for example, the *Second Symphony* is in five movements. With the exception of the second of these, all were originally part of, or the complete scores of, different works—organ pieces, sonatas, string quartets, etc. The *Third Symphony* has a middle movement originally written for string quartet and organ.

The *Fourth Symphony* rates very high in the Ives iconology.

* FARBERMAN	*New Philharmonic Orch.;*	3-CARDINAL VCS (S)
	Ambrosian Singers	10032/34
	(in Symphony No. 4)	

Farbermann handles his forces efficiently with a literal, low-pressure approach. The sound is resonant. A sensational performance of the *Fourth Symphony* is to be heard with Stokowski and the American Symphony Orchestra on a high-priced Columbia disc. In this volatile music, it is highly arguable whether a strict reading (such as Farberman's) is to be preferred to the more idiosyncratic styles of Stokowski or Bernstein, available on high-priced discs.

UNANSWERED QUESTION

This work is extremely complicated to perform: the strings play offstage, while a wind group plus solo trumpet on stage propound "the unanswered question." The two instrumental groups are separate entities.

* * FOSS	*Zimbler Sinfonietta*	TURNABOUT TV (S) 34154 [Skalkottas, Little Suite for Strings; Milhaud, String Symphony No. 4; Bartok, Divertimento]

Foss copes with competence with all the technical problems of this work. For those who wish only one Ives piece on a mixed program, this record can be recommended. This disc started its commercial life, on mono, on the now defunct Unicorn label.

Janacek, Leos (1854-1928)

Janacek is an original and important composer. During most of his life, he was a teacher in Brno and Prague. The worth of his music was not generally recognized until after the performance of his opera *Jenufa* in Vienna in 1928. He composed nine other operas, choral works, chamber music, and other music—the bulk of it as yet little known. But slowly his music seems to be emerging from the obscurity in which it has been enshrouded for so long. The *Glagolitic Mass,* his operas *Jenufa* and *The Makropoulos Affair are* highly original, impressive works.

CONCERTINO FOR PIANO AND CHAMBER ORCHESTRA

This astringent work dates from 1925. A weird arrangement for piano and seven instrumentalists, and opening movements that utilize only two instruments, make this work intriguing.

* * PALENICEK	*Ensemble*	CROSSROADS (M) 22 16 0073 (S) 22 16 0074 [Sonata for Piano; Bartok, Sonata for Two Pianos and Percussion]
* * KLIEN, SANDOR, REINHARD	*Orchestra of the Southwest German Radio Ensemble*	TURNABOUT (3) 4130 [Bartok, Rhapsody for Piano and Orchestra; Honegger, Concertino for Piano; Stravinsky, Capriccio for Piano]

The Crossroads disc is stunningly recorded—one of their best. [With the Bartok *Sonata* on the reverse, this is a strong record.]

Turnabout presents a valuable pocket-sized survey of twentieth-century music. The works are exuberantly played and recorded.

DIARY OF ONE WHO VANISHED (Sung in Czech)

I am advised that if you know Czech, this is a shattering listening experience. Even without knowing Czech, the piece leaves a powerful impression. This cycle of 21 songs is all about a village youth seduced by a gypsy girl, and is regarded as one of the outstanding masterpieces of twentieth-century vocal music.

* KUHN	*Czech Women's Chorus Ensemble*	ARTIA	102

I find this singing inaccessible. The sound is fair.

For a taste of the raw passion in this music, a stunning performance is available from Haeflinger and Kubelik on an expensive DGG.

JENUFA

This opera is probably Janacek's masterpiece—but we won't know for sure until all ten of his operas are widely known and available. Couched in the composer's unique declamatory style, this work is dramatic in the great tradition of nineteenth-century opera; and yet this opera seems enveiled in a dreamlike quality that suggests Debussy's *Pelleas and Melisande*. The plot involves lust, jealousy, and infanticide, and all these build to first-rate musical theatre. The Prague National Theatre has mounted *Jenufa* more than 200 times, and it is slowly inching its way into the international modern operatic repertory.

* * VOGEL	3-ARTIA	80

Though this is a somewhat frenzied recording, the style seems appropriate to the work. The singing is strong. Even though one doesn't understand Czech, the listener senses the power of this intense, declamatory performance. The sound is agreeable.

LACHIAN DANCES; THE FIDDLER'S CHILD; JEALOUSY; THE BALLAD OF BLANIK HILL; THE ETERNAL GOSPEL; LORD, HAVE MERCY UPON US; THERE UPON THE MOUNTAIN

This collection of mainly earlier works by Janacek is vapid. Written chiefly around the turn of the century, these pieces contain little of the arresting power of his last tremendous years.

* WALDHANS, PINKAS, VESELKA	Brno State Philharmonic Orchestra, Czech Philharmonic Chorus, Prague Symphony Orchestra	2-CROSSROADS (S) 22 26 0016

The playing is agreeable, although rather slack. *Stereo Review* comments: "Performance: warm and convincing; recording: good; stereo quality: excellent." This disc was on *Saturday Review's* list of "Best Recordings of 1968."

SLAVONIC MASS (MISSA GLAGOLSKAJA) (Glagolitic Mass) (1927)

This is a highly charged folk song mass, not intended for traditional liturgical performance. "God is gone up with a shout," Janacek wrote on the top of the score. Yet this is intensely religious music: "In every creature there is a spark of God," the composer wrote on another manuscript, only months before his death. This is fist-shaking, bold, eccentric music; some critics hold it to be one of the outstanding pieces of our century. *Stereo Review* commented: "Janacek's Mass is strange and powerfully magical. There is nothing at all elsewhere in music closely akin to this extraordinary masterpiece."

* * DOMANINSKA, SOUKUPOVA, BLACHUT, HAKEN, ANCERL	*Czech Philharmonic Orchestra and Chorus*	PARLIAMENT	(S)	617

Here is a fine Czech performance; Ancerl seems to know this music inside out. The solo parts sound excruciatingly difficult, but they are done very well. The chorus and the brilliant organ part are also well performed. The sound, although harsh in places, is acceptable.

SONATA FOR VIOLIN AND PIANO

This somewhat primitive work will remind the alert listener of the chamber pieces of Charles Ives. Here are fascinating folk rhythms, and an attempt to make the violin and piano seem to combine into one instrumental sound.

* * DRUIAN, SIMMS		PHILLIPS WS (S) 9084 [Enesco, Sonata No. 3]		

This is rich, assured violin playing. The sound is extremely good and warm. [The Enesco *Sonata,* of interest in a folkish way, makes an appropriate coupling.]

STRING QUARTET NO. 2 (1923); QUARTET NO. 3

The *First String Quartet*—striking, mature music—was composed in 1923, and was inspired by Tolstoy's short story, *The Kreutzer Sonata.* Janacek wrote this quartet in an incredibly short period of nine days. The *Second Quartet* has the subtitle *Intimate Pages.* It was written in 1928, the year of the composer's death. He was 74, but this is still a passionate work, concerning the composer's love affair with a woman 40 years younger than himself.

* *	*Janacek Quartet*	CROSSROADS (M) 22 16 0013 (S) 22 16 0014		
*	*Smetana Quartet*	PARLIAMENT	(S)	626

The music is intensely played by the Janacek Quartet, and well recorded. This disc was a prize-winner in Paris.

The work of the Smetana Quartet is competent, but rather flaccid in comparison to the Janacek Quartet.

Khachaturian, Aram (1903-   )

Khachaturian is an Armenian who seems to have escaped the censorship and censure that have been allotted to most other Soviet composers. Hearing his music, one understands why. This is open, rhapsodic music that exploits Caucasian folk melodies to the hilt. This clever composer knows his orchestra inside out. His music has an immediate, even vulgar appeal.

CONCERTO FOR PIANO AND ORCHESTRA (1936)

This brash and banal piece is highly popular.

* * KATZ, BOULT	*London Philharmonic*	VANGUARD (S) 185 [Prokofiev, Concerto No. 1]	
* OBORIN, KHACHATURIAN	*St. Radio Orch.*	MONITOR (S) 2079 [Rachmaninoff, Rhapsody on a Theme by Paganini]	
KATIN, RIGNOLD	*London Symphony Orch.*	EVEREST (M) 6055 (S) 3055	

Katz's performance is flamboyant, in a late romantic style. Katz even puts in more than the work deserves. The sound is excellent. [So is the coupling.]

Oborin is kinetic and at times brilliant. The composer himself conducts.

Katin's performance is all right, technically accomplished, but the listener is not exactly carried away.

CONCERTO FOR VIOLIN AND ORCHESTRA (1940)

This glittering showpiece, dating from 1940, is saturated with Armenian and Georgian folk idioms. Most critics turn up their noses at Khachaturian, but few romantic violinists can resist this great opportunity to display their wares .

* * KOGAN, MONTEUX	*Boston Symphony Orch.*	VICTRO'A VIC (S) 1153 [Saint-Saens, Havanaise]	
* OISTRAKH, FRIEDMAN	*Moscow Radio Orch.*	PERIOD (M) 739 [Prokofiev, Concerto No. 1]	
BERNARD, KHACHATURIAN	*Bucharest Symphony Orch.*	PHILLIPS WS (M/S) 9046 [Prokofiev, Concerto No. 1]	

Kogan gives a luminous, lyrical reading. The sound is spacious.

The Oistrakh Period disc is poorly recorded.

Bernard's style of playing is much too effeminate.

GAYNE, BALLET-SUITE NO. 1

This suite contains the famous Sabre Dance. It is garish, theatrical music.

* GOLSCHMANN	*Vienna State Opera Orch.*	VANGUARD (S) 207 [Kabalevsky, The Comedians]

Golschmann charges through the piece with elan. The sound is boisterous.

MASQUERADE: SUITE (1944)

This suite, written in 1944, is very similar in character to the *Gayne* suite, but not as catchy.

* ROZHDESTVENSKY	*Moscow Philharmonic Orch.*	MONITOR (S) 2078 [Kabalevsky, Romeo and Juliet]
KHACHATURIAN	*Prague Radio Symphony Orch.*	PARLIAMENT (M) 157 [Prokoviev, Classical Symphony in D]

Rozhdestvensky gives a high-spirited reading, excellently recorded.

Surprisingly, the composer's is the weaker performance. The sound is filmy.

Kodaly, Zoltan (1882-1967)

Kodaly was an intimate friend of Bartok, and is best known to us for his collaboration with his fellow Hungarian in the collecting and studying of Hungarian folk songs. His music is not as bold as Bartok's, but more in the traditional pattern, with no striking break from the past. One feels a passionate sincerity in his music. Because of this sincerity and his preoccupation with folk elements, Kodaly has been often compared to the Englishman Vaughan Williams.

GALANTA DANCES

This is highly pleasant, rhapsodic music, dating from 1933.

* PERLEA	*Bamberg Symphony Orch.*	Vox (S) 9500 [Dvorak, Scherzo Capriccioso; Enesco, Roumanian Rhapsody No. 1; Smetana, Moldau]
* RODZINSKI	*London Philharmonic Orch.*	WESTMINISTER (M) 18775 [Hary Jano; Marosszek]

Perlea plays pleasantly on a good mixed, sure-fire program. The sound is agreeable.

Rodzinski is also ship-shape, and the mono sound is fair.

HARY JANOS: SUITE (1926)

Hary Janos is a popular figure in Hungarian folklore, an old soldier whose vivid imagination conjures up the most improbable adventures. Kodaly's suite is replete with the spirit of Hungarian songs and dances.

* FRICSAY	*Berlin Radio Symphony Orch.*	HELIODOR (S) 25069 [Von Einem, Ballade for Orchestra; Stravinsky, Movements for Piano and Orchestra; Dances from Galanta]
RODZINSKI	*London Philharmonic Orch.*	WESTMINSTER (M) 18775 [Galanta Dances; Marosszek Dances]

Fricsay, a fellow Hungarian, conducts this piece with gusto and sharply defined contrasts. The sound is acceptable. [Von Einem is a contemporary composer (1918-   ) of mild interest, and his piece is easily comprehensible. The Stravinsky *Movements* show the composer edging towards the tonal world of Schoenberg and Webern, but is otherwise not of special importance.]

The Rodzinski performance is properly spirited. Rodzinski was always dependable in this sort of thing. The music is brightly recorded on old mono. [The Marosszek dances are slight.]

PSALMUS HUNGARICUS   (Opus 13)

Composed in 1923 for the fiftieth anniversary of the union of the cities of Buda and Pest, this is one of the best choral pieces of the century. Stirring music throughout, it calls for an adult choir, a children's choir, and a tenor soloist.

* * NILSSON, FERENCSIK	*London Philharmonic Chorus and Orch.*	EVEREST	(M)	6022
			(S)	3022
		[Bartok, Dance Suite]		
KODALY	*Hungarian Orchestra and Chorus*	ARTIA [Te Deum]		152

The performance on Everest is sturdy; the sound is strikingly good.

Kodaly's own version, though a historical document, is badly sung; the tenor soloist is unacceptable.

TE DEUM

This large-scale setting of the *Te Deum*, dating from 1936, features Kodaly's unique Hungarian colorations.

* JURINAC, WAGNER, CHRIST, POELL, SWOBODA	*Vienna Chorus and Symphony Orch.*	WESTMINISTER [Theatre Overture]	(M)	18455
KODALY	*Hungarian Orchestra and Chorus*	ARTIA [Psalmus Hungaricus]	(M)	152

The Swoboda album contains good choral singing. The quartet is powerful; and Jurinac is a fine singer. The sound is old but decent.

The singing on Kodaly's own recording is disappointing. Both the soloists and the sound are unacceptable.

Lalo, Edouard (1823-1892)

Lalo, a Frenchman of Spanish origin, studied at the Paris Conservatoire. He wrote several operas, concertos, songs, and other works, some of which surface from time to time in France. His *Symphony Espagnole* assures him an enduring niche in the romantic repertory.

CONCERTO FOR CELLO AND ORCHESTRA, IN D MINOR

Here is a melodious, grateful composition for the cello and orchestra. Not a first-rate concerto, it is nevertheless enjoyable.

* CASSADO, PERLEA	*Bamberg Symphony Orch.*	Vox	(5) (S) 10920	[Saint-Saëns, Concerto for Cello and Orchestra No. 1, in A minor, Opus 33; Fauré, Elegie for Cello and Orchestra, Opus 24]

The Spanish cellist Caspar Cassado is a sensitive player, and this recording displays his talent to best advantage. The sound is only so-so. [The couplings provide a sampling of the best works of French cello music, all written between 1873 and 1833. The Saint-Saëns concerto is lovely, and the short Fauré piece is ravishing.]

SYMPHONY ESPAGNOLE FOR VIOLIN AND ORCHESTRA (Opus 21)

This romantic, lively concerto was written for the dazzling virtuoso Sarasate and first played by him in 1875. Although composed by a Frenchman —as was *Carmen*—this concerto is the definitive Spanish-gypsy violin piece.

* * * SZERYNG, HENDL	*Chicago Symphony Orch.*	Victrola VIC	(S) 1064	
* OISTRAKH	*Moscow State Orch.*	Period	SHO 312	[Mendelssohn, Concerto]
HAENDEL, ANCERL	*Czech Philharmonic*	Parliament	(S) 620	[Ravel, Tzigane]

The remarkable Szeryng is dazzling, far better than any other entry. The sound is splendid.

The tone and sonics of the Oistrakh disc preclude favor.

Haendel's interpretation is not bad, but the violin tone is small.

Lassus, Orlando (Roland De) (1532-1594)

The most famous of Palestrina's contemporaries, Lassus was likewise a wonderful composer. A choirmaster at St. John Lateran in Rome, he later joined the chapel of the Duke of Bavaria at Munich, and directed the ducal chapel from 1560 until his death.

Lassus was a remarkably prolific composer; his style embraced every technique of sixteenth-century choral writing. Only a portion of his music has ever been printed; masses, motets, magnificats, French chansons, and other works await resurrection in a projected 60-volume edition of his music.

His music is extraordinary. He was the outstanding composer of the Flemish contrapuntal school. Here is deeply expressive music.

* * * HAHN   *Kaufbeurer Martinsfinken*   NONESUCH   H (S) 71084
[Depres, Ave Christe; Isaac, Missa Carminum]

The music is simply and beautifully sung. This vibrant record is one of the best offerings of Renaissance music that I have ever heard. [The other works on this program are splendid.]

"AGNUS DEI" FROM THE MASS "IN DIE TRIBULATIONIS"

This is grave, fervent music.

* * REHMANN   *Aachen Cathedral Chorus*   MACE   (M) 9030

This excerpt is in a collection called "Sacred Music of the Masters." As is the wont of Joe Zerga of Mace Records, 17 composers—from Lassus to Mozart—are flung together here; and the fast shifts take a bit of getting used to on the part of the listener. Nevertheless, this disc is an excellent sampler of the choral art. To heighten the sacred focus of the record, even cathedral sounds from the Kaiserdom at Aachen are thrown in. The sound is resonant.

MADRIGALS AND MOTETS

Here is sixteenth-century choral music at the summit of its perfection—17 lovely excerpts of compositions colored by the intense personality that was Lassus.

* GRISCHKAT   *The Swabian Chorale*   DOVER   (S) 7269

The Swabian singers provide earnest singing. The sound is rather dry.

MISSA "ECCE NUNC BENEDICITE DOMINUM"; PROPHETIAE SIBYLLARUM

This mass, apparently written before Lassus was 20, is intensely emotional music within a severely constricted form. The composition contains bold, chromatic harmonies that even intrigue the modern ear.

* * VENHODA   *Prague Madrigal Choir*   NONESUCH   H (S) 71053

The work is well performed in a devotional style. Nathan Broder comments: "Singing . . . is flexible and sensitive." The sound is well balanced.

ST. MATTHEW PASSION

This is noble, affecting music.

* GRISCHKAT   *Swabian Chorale*   DOVER   (S) 7286

The work is gravely sung. The sound seems overly boxed-in.

Le Jeune, Claude (1528-1600)

Little is known of this appealing French composer. Some of his songs were printed in Louvain in 1554; in 1570, he became the court composer for the Duke of Anjou, brother of Henry III. He published very little music, and is remembered chiefly for his motets and madrigals.

CHANTS DE LA RENAISSANCE

Here are 14 songs for four to eight voices, many of them settings of love poems. These are light, graceful, airy pieces with much charm.

* *   *Jean-Paul Kreder Ensemble* NONESUCH   (M) 1001
                                                                    (S) 71001

The singing is fine, but the sound is rather boxed in. This disc was Nonesuch's famous first release, an instant success which is still going briskly.

Leoncavallo, Ruggiero (1858-1919)

With his 1892 opera, *Pagliacci,* Leoncavallo rose from an obscure job as a cafe pianist to world fame. He composed 15 other operas, but only one was even mildly successful. With the exception of one or two short songs, *Pagliacci* is the only one of his works still in favor.

I PAGLIACCI (Sung in Italian)

This is gripping, theatrical music. This opera is especially popular at the Metropolitan Opera's Saturday matinees, at which time it is inexorably linked with Mascagni's *Cavalleria Rusticana* to become "Cav" and "Pag", the best twin bill on the operatic boards.

* * GIGLI, PACETTI, BASIOLA, NESSI, PACCI, GHIONE	*La Scala Chorus and Orch.*	2-SERAPHIM (M) 6009 [Italian Songs]	
* DEL MONACO PETRELLA, PROTTI, EREDE	*Chorus and Orch. of the Accademia de Santa Cecilia, Rome*	2-RICHMOND 62009	
GAVAZZI, BERGONZI, TAGLIABUE, SIMONETTO		EVEREST/CETRA (S) 411/2	

The Gigli set is historic, in the best sense of this term. The golden tenor is at the top of his form; in *Pagliacci,* even his self-pitying gulps seem appropriate. Pacetti is rather stolid, and the rest of the cast ranges from good to fair. The sound is about as good as can be expected from a 1934 recording. On the fourth record side, Gigli sweetly sings a program of Italian songs, including *O Sole Mio* and *Non ti Scordar di Me.*

On the Del Monaco set, the sound is far more modern. Del Monaco is also a great voice, with a stand-up-and-belt-it-out style that is emotionally powerful. However, he is off-pitch now and then, and the choral parts seem foggy in spots. Clara Petrella, the best soprano of the three entries, gives a fine, fiery performance.

The old Cetra set, murkily rechanneled for stereo, is pedestrian and heavy-handed. I find nothing on this record to commend.

Liszt, Franz (1811-1886)

Born in Raiding, Hungary, Liszt studied under both Czerny and Salieri in Vienna, where he met Beethoven and Schubert. From 1823 to 1835, Liszt lived in Paris, became famous as a pianist, and was a friend of Chopin, Berlioz, and Paganini, and just about every figure on the artistic scene.

In 1835, Liszt eloped with the Countess d'Agoult; their daughter Cosima was born at Como in 1837. (Cosima was to become the wife of conductor Hans von Bülow, and later wife of Richard Wagner.)

Liszt, recognized as the greatest virtuoso of his day, gave concerts throughout Europe. From 1848-1861, he was director of music at the court at Weimar. From 1861 to 1869, he lived in Rome and took minor orders in the Church. From 1869 until his death, Liszt lived in Rome, Budapest, and Weimar. His pupils included many who became famous pianists themselves.

PLACE AND ACHIEVEMENT   Why this constant preoccupation with Liszt? We argue about him, read about him, are more aware of him than of a dozen better composers. We seem never to tire of the "Liszt dilemma": of proving him either shamefully neglected, or the most tremendous musical failure of the nineteenth century.

Eighty-one years after his death, the Liszt legend—and what a legend it is—survives. He is properly enshrined up there on his pedestal, perched shakily between Berlioz and Wagner. Every year or two, someone takes a pot-shot at the bust, but no one ever quite knocks him over once and for all.

There he is, the old charlatan, wens and all: the circus-rider, the gypsy, the great ham, the showman who could have given Barnum tips on free publicity, the near-alcoholic, the womanizer, the dirty old man— and we regard him with affection. Most of us shrug off his music as being embarrassingly second-rate. Yet we all smile indulgently at his famous antics, his lifelong role as Don Juan, his shocking musical vulgarity; and we hesitate burying both him and his staggering output in what Philip Hale once called "'that great graveyard of forgotten fantasias, masses, and symphonies.'"

We keep him around because historically, he is irremovable. He runs like an indispensable thread across the grand design of nineteenth-century music. Liszt was born when Beethoven was 41; he died when Richard Strauss was 22. Meanwhile, as Chopin put it, "Liszt had his hand in everything." He championed the cause of Weber, Schubert, Schumann,

Borodin, Berlioz, Chopin, Grieg, and Wagner at times when they were not august bodies but controversial figures. At one time or another he was intimate with Heine, Delacroix, Ingres, George Sand, Baudelaire, Berlioz, Chopin, Paganini, Rossini, Joachim, and Borodin. He grasped at once every new musical trend. He had a nose for genius; there was hardly a struggling composer of talent whom he did not help with performances or cold cash.

His name is inseparable from the lives of the greatest conductor of the century, Hans von Bülow, and of Richard Wagner—the two husbands, in turn, of Liszt's daughter Cosima. Liszt's gifts as a piano performer had never been equaled. He was the first pianist ever to give a complete recital by himself. Clara Schumann wrote, "What we pianists despair of ever playing properly, Liszt reads at sight." Chopin grumbled, "I would like to steal from Liszt the secret of how he plays my *Etudes*." Anton Rubenstein remarked, "If you have heard Liszt you have heard the greatest pianist of them all." Liszt invented the virtuoso pianist and all that went with it—a hundred candles lighting an elegant salon; beautiful, white-shouldered, and predatory countesses panting away; and the Great Artist crouched at the piano, dazzling one and all with his poetic profile and hypnotic eye, tossing his long flowing hair back over his noble forehead as he churned up a storm of lightning arpeggios and thunderous chords. In sum, Liszt, together with Chopin, was Romanticism incarnate.

When we come to the bewildering corpus of his compositions, we can only retreat. He wrote more music than almost any other man who ever lived: his works number nearly 1,400.

THE ESSENTIAL LISZT
ORCHESTRAL MUSIC: *Les Preludes, Mazeppa, Tone Poems; Concertos No. 1 and 2 for Piano and Orchestra; Hungarian Fantasy, for Piano and Orchestra; Mephisto Waltz.*
PIANO MUSIC: *Hungarian Rhapsodies; Liebestraum; Sonata in B Minor; Annees de Pelerinage.*

OTHER WORKS
ORCHESTRAL MUSIC: *Faust Symphony; Dante Symphony; Totentanz, for Piano and Orchestra; Transcendental Etudes; Funerailles; Transcriptions of Music by Bach, Mozart, Schubert, Schumann, Wagner, etc.*
PIANO MUSIC: *Ballades, Elegies, Etudes, Legends, etc.*
ORCHESTRAL MUSIC Some of Liszt's pieces—the two piano concertos, the *Hungarian Rhapsody No. 2*—are among the most popular music ever composed. But the vast bulk of his work is held in low repute by serious musicians.

CONCERTO NO. 1 IN E-FLAT FOR
PIANO AND ORCHESTRA

This very popular, very tempestuous concerto was first performed at Weimar, in 1855, with Liszt as soloist and Berlioz conducting.

* * BOLET	*Symphony of the Air*	EVEREST	(M) 6062
			(S) 3062
		[Hungarian Fantasia; Mephisto Waltz]	
* * BRENDEL, GIELEN	*Vienna Pro Musica*	VOX	(5) 10420
		[Concerto No. 2]	
* * PENNARIO, GOLSCHMANN	*Concert Arts Symphony*	PICKWICK	(S) 4025
		[Chopin, Concerto No. 2]	
* * BOUKOFF, SOMOGYI	*Vienna Symphony Orch.*	MERCURY	(M) 14066
			(S) 18066
		[Concerto No. 2]	
* KEMPFF, FISTOULARI	*London Symphony Orch.*	RICHMOND	(M) 19023
		[Concerto No. 2]	

Jorge Bolet is all sweep and glitter. [His recording includes the *Hungarian Fantasia* for piano and orchestra—Liszt's own arrangement of his fourteenth *Hungarian Rhapsody*—a showcase piece.]

Brendel is extremely poetic and romantic.

Pennario, also dashing, is a formidable technician. The stereo sound is very good.

Boukoff, a stormy pianist of impressive power, is recorded with the best sound.

Kempff (mono only) is ponderous, and not the man for this concerto.

CONCERTO NO. 2 IN A FOR PIANO AND ORCHESTRA

This popular, romantic work was a product of Liszt's fertile Weimar years (1863) in which most of his best music was written. It requires powerhouse technique.

* * BRENDEL, GIELEN	*Vienna Pro Musica*	VOX	(M) 10420
			(S) 510420
		[Concerto No. 1]	
* * BOUKOFF, SOMOGYI	*Vienna Symphony Orch.*	MERCURY	(M) 14066
			(S) 18066
		[Concerto No. 1]	
* * PENNARIO, LEIBOWITZ	*London Symphony Orch.*	VICTROLA	LM/LSC 2690
		[Concerto No. 2]	
FARNADI, BOULT	*Vienna State Opera Orch.*	WESTMINSTER	(S) 14125
		[Concerto No. 1]	
RAUCH, SMETACEK	*Prague Smphony Orch.*	PARLIAMENT	(S) 628
		[Chopin, Concerto No. 2]	

Brendel leads here with a poetic, eloquent, and entirely musical performance.

Boukoff gives a bravura reading, vividly recorded.

Pennario, all nerved up, offers a brilliant virtuoso rendition. The stereo is first-rate.

Farnadi is hearable, but quite unremarkable.

Rauch is quite outclassed.

FAUST SYMPHONY

This bombastic, repetitious work was composed, except for its final chorus, in 1854 under the watchful and approving eye of the princess with whom Liszt lived. Romantic, "big-thinking" music at its worst, this piece is almost never played today.

BEECHAM	*Royal Philharmonic, Beecham Chorus Society*	2-SERAPHIM (S) 6017 [Orpheus, Symphonic Poem]
KOCH, HORENSTEIN	*Southwest German Symphony Orch.*	2 Vox SVUX (S) 52029 [Mephisto Waltz]

Beecham, the old magician, does his exciting best, but even he cannot pump life into this work. Here is nice choral singing. The early-era stereo sound is pleasant. [The fourth side filler is a cogent performance of Liszt's symphonic poem, *Orpheus*. This one, at least, is mercifully short.] *High Fidelity* comments: "Thoroughly vital . . . and smoothly played . . . excellently remastered discs."

Horenstein excels at these outsized monsters, but the scratchy playing is no competition for Sir Thomas.

SIX HUNGARIAN RHAPSODIES (Orchestra Versions)

The *Hungarian Rhapsodies,* as arranged for orchestra by Liszt (but numbered differently from the original keyboard versions) are perhaps his most satisfying music.

* * FISTOULARI	*Vienna State Opera Orch.*	VANGUARD (S) 164 [No. 1-4]
* * FISTOULARI	*Vienna State Opera Orch.*	VANGUARD (S) 160 [No. 5, 6; Enesco, Rumanian Rhapsodies]
* LEHEL	*Hungarian Radio Symphony Orch.*	PARLIAMENT (S) 135 [Hungarian Fantasie; Brahms, Hungarian Dances]

Fistoulari delivers a rousing, colorful recording of the first four, on Vanguard 164, with well balanced sound.

On Vanguard 160, Fistoulari is even more convincingly *zigeuner,* in a reading of two different *Rhapsodies.* The sound is excellent. [Golschmann is equally good conducting the refreshing Enesco *Rumanian Rhapsodies* on the reverse.]

Lehel is spirited on a mixed program of Pops appeal.

MAZEPPA, SYMPHONIC POEM NO. 6

According to Liszt's biographer Sitwell, "flat and shallow" music characterizes this piece.

| NEMETH | *Hungarian Orch.* | MACE   (S) 9009 [Viski, "Enigma" (Tone-Poem)] |
| SCHERCHEN | *Vienna Symphony Orch.* | WESTMINSTER   (M) 14101 [Hungarian Rhapsodies 2, 3, 6] |

The Hungarian Players under Nemeth are not bad. The sound is right, although boomy. [The reverse side holds a tone-poem by Janos Viski (1906-1961) who was a pupil of Kodaly. It is folklorish in Kodaly's style, and of little interest.]

Scherchen is not convincing here.

MEPHISTO WALTZ

Liszt toyed with the "Faust" legend all his life; this *Waltz,* once considered the last romantic word, is now a Pops staple.

* * * REINER	*Chicago Symphony Orch.*	VICTROLA VIC (S) 1025 [Debussy, Iberia; Tchaikovsky, Overture 1812]
* * * BOLET		EVEREST (M) 6062 (S) 3062 [Concerto No. 1; Hungarian Fantasy]
* HORENSTEIN	*Southwest German Radio Symphony Orch.*	2-Vox VUX (M) 2029 (S) 52029 [Faust Symphony]

Reiner performs the work with icy glitter, as a filler to his superb *Iberia* and *1812 Overture.* The sound is fine.

An excellent piano version—Liszt wrote four Mephisto-Waltzes in all as well as a Mephisto-Polka—is heard from Bolet. This pianist has plenty of sweep and temperament, both welcome here. This is an outstanding disc.

Horenstein, as usual in romantic music, is passionate and convincing. The sound is rather boxed in.

LES PRELUDES, SYMPHONIC POEM NO. 3

Les Preludes was composed in 1848 as an introduction to a choral work entitled Les Quatre Elements, which was never published. "What is our life but a series of preludes to that unknown song of which the first solemn note is sounded by death?" Liszt wrote on the score. Les Preludes is the only one of Liszt's twelve symphonic poems that is entrenched in the concert repertory.

* * ANCERL	Czech Philharmonic	CROSSROADS (M) 22 16 0105 (S) 22 16 0106 [Berlioz, Overture; Rimsky-Korsakov, Capriccio; Weber, Invitation to the Dance]
KONWITSCHNY	Leipzig Orch.	PARLIAMENT (S) 126 [Tasso]
STERN	London Philharmonic	SOMERSET St.Fi. 1500 [mixed program]

Ancerl seems to have enthusiasm for this project, and the Czechs play very well, as they do on the other Pops-program staples on this record. The sound is pleasant.

The Leipzig players are competent but unexciting. [The dull Tasso, a symphonic poem based on a work by Goethe, was originally a work for piano. Biographer Sacheverell Sitwell, a passionate defender of Liszt, admits that Tasso "suffers from those faults of obviousness that were the bane of all Liszt's orchestral writings where he was not inspired and carried away by his subject."]

The Stern version is just adequate.

PIANO MUSIC: If there is a certain revival of interest in the music of Liszt, it is because of the pianists now playing these compositions. They point to his neglected later piano works as worthier than we would believe. David Bar-Ilan and Sergio Fiorentino, among other devout Lisztians, claim profound qualities for these compositions. The greatest of all Liszt's piano music, it is agreed, is the Sonata in B.

ANNEES DE PELERINAGE (Complete); PREMIERE ANNEE-SUISSE

These Swiss travel momentos (Chapelle de Guillaume Tell, etc.) are highly agreeable.

* FIORENTINO	DOVER (S) 7009

The Italian pianist, Sergio Fiorentino, is a studious-sounding Liszt specialist. The recording quality is chaste and dry.

THE CHRISTMAS TREE *(Complete)*

Wrtten between 1874 and 1876 for Liszt's eldest granddaughter, *The Christmas Tree* is a cycle containing traditional Christmas carols. Debussy, and even Bartok, are foreshadowed in this subtle concise music that doesn't sound at all like the crowd-pleasing Liszt we know too well.

* SZEGEDI	MACE	(M) 9006

This is an effective reading, at times poetic. *High Fidelity* comments: "A fine grasp of the cycle's lyricism and tender strength."

NINETEEN HUNGARIAN RHAPSODIES FOR PIANO

This splashing piano writing demands nimble fingers. If you are in the mood, you'll find the piano versions of the *Rhapsodies* stirring, though they hardly make demands upon the intellect.

* * BRENDEL	CARDINAL VCS (S) 10035 [No. 2, 3, 8, 13, 15, and 17; Csardas obstine]
* * VAZSONYI	VOX (M) 12340 (S) 512340 [2/3, 5/6, 11, 13, 15, 18]
* * JANIS	2-EVEREST (M) 6128/2 (S) 3128/2 [6 in collection]
FERRANTE & TEICHER (No. 2)	URANIA (M) 8011 (S) 58011 [Enesco; Roumanian Rhapsody, No. 1; Gershwin, Rhapsody]

Brendel comes off first with truly brllliant playing, and impeccable recording. This man Brendel, it appears, can play *any* composer well. *High Fidelity* comments: "Brendel offers a unique combination of musical-intellectual probity and blazing virtuosity."

Vazsonyi is an elegant pianist with a ravishing tone. The sound is warm.

Byron Janis is all glittering virtuosity. His mixed program is well recorded.

The two-piano version by Ferrante and Teicher is but mildly effective.

"LATE PIANO MUSIC OF LISZT": NUAGES GRIS; LA LUGUBRE GONDOLA, NO. 1; R.W., VENEZIA; VIER KLEINE KLAVIERSTUECKE; ELEGY NO. 2; SCHLAFLOS, FRAGE UND ANTWORT; DEM ANDENKEN PETOFIS; UNSTERN

Strong hints of music to come—Debussy, Bartok, and Stravinsky—are heard in this remarkable program. Barbaric dissonances, impressionism, progressions with ambiguous tonal focus, whole-tone scales—these are but a few of the characteristics of the late perceptiveness of Liszt. One feels in these pieces that Liszt is no longer writing music to show off his astounding resources, but is creating music for its own sake. *Nuages Gris* (1881) is an enigmatic piece, experimental, and of much interest. *La Lugubre Gondola,* and *R. W. Venezia* are two of a group of four pieces concerned with Richard Wagner, the composer's son-in-law. *Unstern* deals with misfortune and disaster, and is highly experimental, illustrating the enormous, sure-handed strides into modern dissonance of which Liszt was capable. The other pieces, though of lesser consequence, are also good.

* * FIORENTINO   Dover   (S) 7258

Fiorentino plays handsomely, with sweep and a sense of dedication. The sound is good, but dry.

Locatelli, Pietro (1695-1764)

Locatelli studied in Rome with Corelli, toured extensively as a violinist, and finally settled in Amsterdam where he became an impresario and produced concerts. He has left us much music: 12 concerti grossi, 12 violin concertos with 24 caprices to serve as cadenzas, and many other pieces for violin, for flute, and for chamber ensembles.

CONCERTI GROSSI (Opus 1)

These are a set of 12; eight are *concerti di chiesa* (for church performance), and four are *di camera* (for chamber performance). All are grave and pensive.

* *	I Musici	WORLD SERIES (S) PHC 9032

I Musici, a group of 11 strings and harpsichord, are so skillful and seductive that they make any music sound lovely. The disc is beautifully recorded.

CONCERTI NO. 11 and 12 FROM "L'ARTE DEL VIOLINO" (Opus 3)

The Art of the Violin is a set of 12 highly original violin concertos which contain pleasing melodies. What is most original about this music is that Locatelli deserts the traditional polyphonic style and explores the possibilities of melody and harmony. Written in 1733, *The Art of the Violin* not only suggests the modern violin cadenza, but also prepares the ground for Paganini and other virtuosos, by providing at least one *Capriccio* for solo violin in each concerto. This set, by a composer who was himself a noted violinist, catalogues technical aspects of the violin.

* LAUTENBACHER, KEHR	Mainz Chamber Orch.	TURNABOUT	TV 34047

This music, because of its technical difficulties, requires formidable playing. Suzanne Lautenbacher, a cultured musician, comes off impressively. The sound is agreeable.

NOTE: Vox-Turnabout offers *The Art of the Violin* in various sizes and weights, ranging up to a six-record Vox Box (SVBX 540/1).

Loeillet, Jean-Baptiste (1680-1730)

Loeillet was a minor French composer who went to London in 1705 and became a member of the King's Theatre orchestra. He was a noted flute and oboe player; the music of his that has been revived is played for the most part on these instruments. At its best, his music is pleasant and graceful.

SONATA IN C FOR FLUTE AND BASSO CONTINUO

This poised, graceful music is typical of Loeillet's work.

* LOLYA, EATON   MACE   (S) 9086

Gracieusement is the word for this well-played recording. This album of musical *galanterie* is called "The Rococo Flute"; it also contains works by Blavet, de Lavigne, and Naudot—all obscure composers and/or flute players themselves. Well-sounding disc.

TRIO SONATA IN C MINOR, NO. 5, FOR OBOE, RECORDER, AND HARPSICHORD; SONATE IN C MINOR *(Opus 2, No. 5)* FOR RECORDER AND HARPSICHORD; TRIO SONATA IN F MAJOR *(Opus 1, No. 1)*

This is polished music written to be played by talented amateurs such as the composer's noble patrons.

* POULTEAU,   MUSIC GUILD   (S)   113
  CHEVELET, SCHMIT

The music is nicely done. The sound is agreeable.

Lully, Jean-Baptiste (1632-1687)

Lully is an extremely important figure in the history of music, but his work communicates little to us today. He was court composer to Louis XIV, wrote music for the comedy-ballets of Molière (in which he also appeared as actor and dancer), and founded French opera, then called *Tragédie Lyrique.*

"DANCERIES" AT THE COURT OF VERSAILLES

This music sounds just as the title suggests. Here is grave, lovely writing.

* RAMPAL, BIRNBAUM	*Lamoureux Orchestra and Wind Ensemble*	PHILLIPS WS (M/S) 9036 [Lully, Blavet, Couperin, Rameau]

Rampal, of course, is the man for this music. The piece is nicely recorded. Two of Lully's gavottes, from his opera *Athys,* are included. [Michel Blavet (1700-1768) was a flutist and unoriginal composer who worked in Paris.]

LE TRIOMPHE DE L'AMOUR, BALLET SUITE

Louis was passionately fond of ballets, and Lully wrote at least 30 for him. *Le Triomphe* is lucid music of the elegant French court, but seems tedious today.

* BEAUCAMP	*Rouen Chamber Orch.*	PHILLIPS WS (M/S) 9045 [Purcell, Corelli, W. F. Bach]

The performances are adequate. This is a good record—if you like Lully. [The couplings are fine.]

Lutoslawski, Witold (1913-   )

This contemporary Polish composer is gradually becoming known in America. During World War II, Lutoslawski supported himself in Warsaw by being half of a two-piano team in a night club. His eclectic music, which often employs folk themes, is not particularly "difficult."

VARIATIONS ON A THEME OF PAGANINI

This is attractive, highly assured writing for two pianos.

* VRONSKY AND BABIN	SERAPHIM (S) 60053 [Rachmaninoff, Symphonic Dances; Bizet, Jeux d'Enfants]

Vronsky and Babin are old hands at two-piano partnership, and confidently suave. Most duo-pianos sound like musical ping-pong, but this team sounds like a team. [The other pieces on this disc are also good examples of this precarious medium.]

MacDowell, Edward (1861-1908)

MacDowell studied piano in New York and Paris, and composition in Frankfurt under Joachim Raff. Franz Liszt encouraged him to compose. In 1896, he became director of the newly founded Department of Music at Columbia University. He fell mentally ill in 1904.

MacDowell's best works are for piano. He was America's first major composer; once praised to the skies, his music has now fallen into near-oblivion.

CONCERTO NO. 1 IN A FOR PIANO (Opus 15)

The listener who enjoys Schumann and Rachmaninoff might care for MacDowell's melodic concertos.

　　* RIVKIN, DIXON　　*Vienna State Opera Orch.*　WESTMINSTER　(M)　9715
　　　　　　　　　　　　　　　　　　　　　　[Concerto No. 2]

The playing is warm and affectionate. The old mono recording is serviceable.

Machaut, Guillaume de (c. 1300-1377)

Machaut, a poet, was the dominant French composer of the 14th century.

NOTRE DAME MASS; GREGORIAN PROPER FOR THE MASS OF THE FEAST OF THE ASSUMPTION

The *Notre Dame Mass* is historically distinctive: it is the oldest complete Mass setting that we can attribute to a single composer. This is jagged, awkward writing, but fascinating to anyone interested in hearing Western music "creeping out of its cocoon." The chanted *Proper* makes a pointed contrast.

* * McCARTHY	*The London Ambrosian Singers, Vienna Renaissance Players*	NONESUCH	(S) H 71184

The performance is intense and earnest. The stereo sound is excellent.

Mahler, Gustav (1860-1911)

Born in Kalischt, Bohemia, Mahler studied at the Vienna Conservatory, then filled several minor posts as conductor. After a striking performance of Mendelssohn's *St. Paul* in Leipzig in 1885, he was appointed conductor at the Prague Opera. Later success in Budapest and at the Vienna Opera led to his reputation as one of the greatest conductors of his time. Mahler combined his conductorial engagements with composing. In 1908 he became conductor at the Metropolitan Opera House in New York; and in 1909, he was appointed conductor of the New York Philharmonic. Hard work and harsh opposition undermined his health. He collapsed from overwork inNew York, and was taken back to Vienna, where he died.

PLACE AND ACHIEVEMENT   Mahler is just about the only composer who has been admitted, in our time, to the pantheon of "greats" that make up the standard bill-of-fare of our symphony orchestras. "His time has come," in the words of Leonard Bernstein, and it seems true that Mahler's vast, chaotic, neurotic musical canvases strike a chord of reponse today although they went unanswered a generation ago.

A nervous energy and cosmic longing, together with a Dostoyevskyan pessimism and self-laceration, are the keynotes of his music. There are many shortcomings to his style—as is painfully apparent to any casual concert-goer who has been trapped in a seat while one of the more expansive Mahler works was being performed. Mahler can be bombastic, self-pitying, and almost hysterically raving. But it seems that it is these very neurotic features, together with his peaks of great eloquence and nobility, that have made him one of the most popular composers today.

THE ESSENTIAL MAHLER

ORCHESTRAL MUSIC: *Symphonies No. 1, 2, 4, 5, 8 and 9; Das Lied von der Erde, Song Cycle, for Tenor, Alto, and Orchestra.*
SONG CYCLES: *Kindertotenlieder; Lieder eines Fahrenden Gesellen.*

OTHER WORKS

ORCHESTRAL MUSIC: *Symphonies No. 3, 6, 7.*
SONGS: *Das Klagende Lied; Des Knaben Wunderhorn; Ruckert Lieder; many songs.*

ORCHESTRAL WORKS

Mahler's forte was in big-scaled works, and it is in this genre that his fame is based.

DAS LIED VON DER ERDE

This is the supreme Mahler achievement; few works of music possess the transcendental quality of his *Song of the Earth*. Mahler was haunted by the fear that his ninth symphony would be his last, as it was with Beethoven and Bruckner. For this reason he almost called this Opus his "Ninth Symphony," to get that dreaded number behind him. The last section of this work is an elegiac, deeply affecting farewell to this world and its beauty.

This music was the great singer Kathleen Ferrier's own farewell when she recorded it with Bruno Walter on high-priced London label. She was already stricken with cancer when she walked into the studio, and everyone there knew it. Any other performance must be compared to hers, which can only be described as imbued with a seraphic resignation.

* HOFFMAN, MELCHERT, ROSBAUD	*SW German Radio Symphony Orchestra*	TURNABOUT	34220
* MERRIMAN, HAEFLIGER, VAN BEINUM	*Concertgebouw Orchestra*	2-PHILLIPS WS PHC 2-011 [Songs of a Wayfarer]	
* CAVELTI, DERMOTA, KLEMPERER	*Vienna Symphony Orchestra*	3-Vox VBX	115

Rosbaud is efficient, and the soloist Grace Hoffman is surprisingly good —approaching the immortal Kathleen at times. However, the nasal Germanic tenor pains me.

Van Beinum is disappointing, with sluggish support from his soloists. The sound—"electronically enhanced"—is soggy. *High Fidelity* comments: "After the agonized introspection of Bernstein's *Das Lied*, Van Beinum's Mahler-without-tears approach may be either a disappointment or a refreshing antidote—depending on how strong a dose of Mahlerian *Angst* you fancy . . . The whole performance has a rather easygoing, uncommited nonchalance that I do not find particularly appropriate." The mono set is much better. The great *Wayfarer Songs* are the filler on this two-record set.

The old Klemperer set is very rushed (probably to get it onto one record, as it was made in the days when such accomplishments were a triumph of engineering). It features a fine tenor in Dermota, but an inexcusable female soloist. The sound is harsh.

SYMPHONY NO. 1 IN D

Mahler's first symphony was completed in 1888, the year of his appointment to the Budapest Opera. The *First*, together with the *Fourth*, are the most popular of Mahler's symphonies: they possess none of the wearisome, unending Teutonic stretches, sometimes found in his other works, that throw off the non-indoctrinated listener.

* * BARBIROLLI	*Halle Orchestra*	Vanguard	(S)	233
* HORENSTEIN	*Vienna Pro Musica Orchestra*	3-Vox VBX [Kindertotenlieder; Symphony No. 9]		116
* KUBELIK	*Vienna Philharmonic*	Richmond	(M)	19109
* SCHERCHEN	*London Philharmonic*	Westminster	(M)	18014
* ANCERL	*Czech Philharmonic*	Crossroads (M) 22 16 0011 (S) 22 16 0012		
* BRIEFF	*New Haven Symphony*	Odyssey		32160286

Barbirolli leads, with a poetic, even fervent reading. The sound is good.

The Horenstein version is something of a legend among gramophiles. This conductor is barely known in this country, the players are scrappy, the sound is impossible—and yet this is *it*. This Vox set was included in a list of "indispensible mono records" made up in 1968 by *High Fidelity*. The ineffable Bernard Jacobson comments: "a Horenstein set . . . contains my favorite versions of both the *First* and *Ninth Symphonies* as well as a good *Kindertotenlieder*."

Kubelik is finely shaded, but the sound is thin.

Scherchen is too hard-driving, even brutish.

Ancerl's reading disappoints.

A cleanly played but badly recorded disc, which includes a movement of the symphony that Mahler wrote and then discarded, is to be had from the New Haven Symphony. *Stereo Review* comments: "Performance: spirited; recording: brilliant; stereo quality: good."

SYMPHONY NO. 2 IN C MINOR ("RESURRECTION")

This is a gigantic, sprawling work, finished in 1864. The orchestra includes ten horns, six trumpets, and a warehouse of percussion instruments, including three ominous, Day-of-Judgment bells that are employed only on the last pages of the score.

* * * SILLS, KOPLEFF, ABRAVANEL	*Utah University Civic Chorus Utah Symphony Orchestra*	2 Vanguard C (S) 10003/4
* STEINGRUBER, ROESSL-MAJDAN, KLEMPERER		3-Vox VBX 115 [Das Lied von der Erde]

All praise to Abravanel and his Utah forces: here is playing and singing of the highest order. One doesn't expect things this good from Utah, but here it is, a performance to rank with most from the European Mahler-tradition ensembles. A special salute to Beverly Sills (the pride of New York's State Opera Company), and Florence Kopleff. The sound is staggeringly successful.

The old Klemperer set is famous; now that Bruno Walter has gone, Klemperer is our best Mahler interpreter. This is a superb, authentic reading, marred by ancient sound and some off-pitch singing. Soloist Hilda Roessl-Majdan, though, is great.

SYMPHONY NO. 3 IN D MINOR

Here is another out-sized, sprawling work—a huge symphony canvas and probably a masterpiece, written in 1895. The opening movement is a monumental march that lasts over half an hour by itself, so you know what to expect.

| * * FORRESTER, HAITINK | *Concertgebouw Orchestra Amsterdam Women's and St. Willibrord Boys' Chorus* | 2-PHILLIPS PHM (M) 2-596
PHS (S) 2-996 |

Haitink's forces are well-drilled, in a powerful and convincing reading. Haitink conveys the demonic Mahler quality that the score demands. Soloist Maureen Forrester is soaring. The disc features spacious, exciting sound from Phillips engineers—this must have been a heroic task for them.

SYMPHONY NO. 4 IN G

The *Fourth* is the gentlest of Mahler's orchestral works, and in many ways the most satisfying. Dating from 1900, it is lighter in character than most of its companions, bearing the same relation to them as the "Pastorale" Symphony bears to the rest of Beethoven's. There is a central idea, made explicit in the last movement, behind the music: the work is intended to evoke a child's idea of Heaven. Here, in verses taken from a famous anthology of German folk-poetry, a soprano voice describes the Paradise. The composer's setting of these verses is so apt and so charming that one readily understands the appeal that Mahler holds as a composer of songs—perhaps more as a song writer than as a creator of massive symphonic works.

| * * * HALBAN, WALTER | *New York Philharmonic* | ODYSSEY | 6 | (S) 32 16 002 |
| * RITCHIE, VAN BEINUM | *Concertgebouw Orchestra* | RICHMOND | | (M) 19104 |

Bruno Walter was Mahler's friend, disciple, and his leading interpreter. This famous reading has a devoted, affectionate quality, as well as highly acceptable re-channeled sound. *Stereo Review* went overboard on this one: "One of the greatest performances in the history of music."

The Van Beinum disc is much more straightforward, far less "singing." Another bad mark is nervous, tense singing by Margaret Ritchie in the finale.

SYMPHONY NO. 5 IN C-SHARP MINOR

Written in 1902, this is tempestuous, triumphant Mahler, and a work rich in spiritual qualities. This work contains a famous Adagietto for strings and harp that is one of the most gentle, delicate movements ever written.

* * * WALTER	*New York Philharmonic*	2-ODYSSEY (S) 32 26 0016 [Kindertotenlieder]
* * NEUMANN	*Leipzig Gewandhaus Orchestra*	2-VANGUARD C (S) 10011/2 [Berg: Wozzeck]
* SCHWARZ	*London Symphony Orchestra*	2-EVEREST (M) 6014 (S) 3014

If any recording is historic, in the best sense of the term, it is Bruno Walter's exultant, singing reading of Mahler's *Fifth*. Canby comments in the *Saturday Review:* "A tremendous performance, unmatchable . . ." The re-channeled stereo is inoffensive, and hearable, but sonically is not to be compared with the brilliant Neumann recording listed below. *High Fidelity* comments: "One does miss the occasional wild flights of neurotic abandon that course through Bernstein's performance of the *Fifth*. But the music is large enough to encompass Walter's saner approach, and his statement of the Adagietto and Finale is quite magnificent." [Walter's album is rounded off with one side that is worth the price of admission alone: the great singing of Kathleen Ferrier in the *Kindertotenlieder* song cycle.]

Neumann's reading has a driving, single-minded strength, but he is less successful with the many gentle passages. In any case, this is a first-class performance—altogether, a solid buy. [The *Wozzeck* excerpts are first rate and done very well indeed.] The stereo sound is splendid.

Schwartz offers a fair and careful performance, but is much outclassed by Walter and Neumann.

SYMPHONY NO. 7 IN E MINOR

This 1905 work is for the faithful only—hectic, patch-work, blurry Mahler that is less than sublime.

| * * SCHERCHEN | *Vienna State Opera Orchestra* | 2-WESTMINSTER | (M/S) (2)221 |
| * ABRAVANEL | *Utah Symphony Orchestra* | | (M) 1141/2 (S) 71141/2 |

Scherchen comes off very well in a brooding 1953 performance, with fair sound.

Abravanel is competent; he achieves a conscientious, disciplined reading that, however, doesn't quite convince. The result is hardly on a level with his astonishing later job in the Mahler *Second*.

For the scholarly: the Vanguard set is the first recording to use the new Critical Edition, eliminating inaccuracies, and incorporating changes that

Mahler made after the first publication of his symphony.

SYMPHONY NO. 8 IN E-FLAT ("SYMPHONY OF A THOUSAND")

The *Eighth* is a colossal work even by Mahlerian standards. This 1907 composition uses augmented orchestra, three choirs, "brass band," organ and soloists. The first of the two stupendous movements is a setting of the hymn *Veni Creator*. For those who care, the movement is also in a precise sonata form which requires astute conducting to hold together. Mahler's *Eighth* is exalted, intoxicating, heaven-storming music, and it demands a marvelous performance.

| * * MITROPOULOS | *Vienna Festival Orchestra, Soloists and Chorus* | 2-EVEREST | (S) 3189 |
| * ABRAVANEL | *Utah Symphony Orchestra* | 2-VANGUARD | (M) 1120/1 (S) 71120/1 |

Mitropoulos gives a stirring reading, with the relentless Mitropoulos drive. The sound, however, appears to be from a private tape of dubious origin; it has festival coughs galore.

Abravanel's record has much better sound, even if he is too careful, and not abandoned enough for this mad, God-possessed music.

SYMPHONY NO. 9 IN D

The *Ninth*, written in 1909, was Mahler's noble swan-song. (The *Tenth Symphony* was never finished.) The *Ninth* is a rambling, death-haunted work. Ever since the loss of his five-year old daughter, Maria Anna, in 1907, Mahler had what would today be called a death-fixation.

| * * ANCERL | *Czech Philharmonic* | 2-CROSSROADS | (M) 22 26 0005 (S) 22 26 0006 |

| * HORENSTEIN | *Vienna Symphony* *Orchestra* | 3-Vox BVX (M) 116 [Kindertotenlieder; Symphony No. 1] |
| LUDWIG | *London Symphony* *Orchestra* | 2-EVEREST (M) 6050 (S) 3050-2 |

Ancerl does well here, with much drive and emotional urgency. But still, we do not feel the stamp of a master hand, as with a Klemperer or a Bernstein. The Czechs provide fine orchestral playing, except for some saxophonish-sounding French horn vibratos. The reliable *American Record Guide* comments: "Ancerl is inclined to skim over the surface; his effort is helped by some excellent articulation by the Prague musicians." The sound is satisfying — sonically, one of the best from Crossroads. The Ancerl reading has been on several recent "Best of the Year" lists.

The Horenstein version is famous, and hotly disputed. A superb English critic, Edward Sackville-West, calls it politely "a most unfortunate issue," whereas *High Fidelity's* Mahler critic calls it "sublime." The sound, however, is most unserviceable.

The Ludwig performance is wooden and inadequate.

SONG CYCLES (WITH ORCHESTRA)

For many music lovers, these gems for voice and orchestra are the supreme Mahler.

KINDERTOTENLIEDER

Here is a great setting of sentimental, tearful poetry by the German Romantic Johann Michael (1902). If you are a parent, *Songs on the Death of Children* can be almost unbearably painful.

| * * * FERRIER, WALTER | *Vienna Philharmonic* | 2-ODYSSEY (S) 32 26 0016 [Symphony 5] |
| * * LUDWIG, VANDERNOOT | *Philharmonic Orchestra* | SERAPHIM (S) 60026 [Songs of a Wayfarer] |

The haunting voice of Kathleen Ferrier lives forever on this splendid disc. The English journal, *The Gramophone:* "Kathleen Ferrier, under Bruno Walter's inspired direction, sings these songs as, one feels, Mahler must have imagined them . . . an outstandingly beautiful performance." *High Fidelity* comments: "Ferrier's *Kindertotenlieder* is just about the definitive statement from a female throat on this music; may it never leave the catalogue." The dark-hued, rechanneled sound is satisfactory.

Christina Ludwig is an admirable, meticulous singer, who matches vocal and verbal colors remarkably.

Dietrich Fischer-Dieskau provides a great, virile performance of these songs on Deutsche Grammophone.

SONGS OF A WAYFARER

Mahler himself wrote the words to this haunting and most lovely song-cycle.

* * LUDWIG, BOULT	*Philharmonic Orchestra*	SERAPHIM (S) 60026 [Kindertotenlieder]
* MERRIMAN, VAN BEINUM	*Concertgebouw Orchestra*	2-PHILLIPS WD PHC 2-011S [The Song of the Earth]

Ludwig is warmly admired for her Mahler lieder, and this is one of her best discs.

Nan Merriman is an intelligent singer with a gravely dark voice that lends itself well to Mahler's music. Her *Wayfarer Songs* are one side of an unmoving reading of Mahler's supreme work, *The Song of the Earth*.

YOUTH'S MAGIC HORN

Mahler set these songs to a famous collection of German folk-poetry in 1888. This is exciting, highly imaginative writing. *Youth's Magic Horn* is an exuberant song cycle, not Mahler's greatest, but a must for all lovers of Mahler's music.

* * FORRESTEH, REHFUSS PROHASKKA	*Symphony Orchestra of the Vienna Festival*	VANGUARD SRV (S) 285
* * LUDWIG	*(in recital)*	SERAPHIM (S) 60070 [Mahler Lieder]
* SYDNEY, POELL, PROHASKA	*Vienna State Opera Orchestra*	VANGUARD (M) 478

The warm, Mother-Earth voice of Maureen Forrester lends itself splendidly to Mahler; her singing here alone makes this album worthwhile. *Stereo Review* comments: "Performance: first-rate; recording: excellent; stereo quality: excellent."

Ludwig is also outstanding, and her record contains other excellent Mahler vocal material as well. Her seemingly effortless handling of the song *"Ich ging mit Lust"* here is in itself worth the price of the record. The sound is agreeable.

Prohaska's reading is all that one desires here, on an old Vanguard set. Lorna Sydney is barely adequate, but Alfred Poell, the Viennese baritone, is superb. The sound is dated, but clear.

Marcello, Alessandro (c. 1684-c. 1750)

A Venetian nobleman, and brother to the more famous Benedetto, Alessandro Marcello was a philosopher, painter, mathematician, skilled orator, and singer as well as a composer. He published cantatas, solo sonatas, and concertos.

SIX CONCERTI FOR OBOE (OR FLUTE) AND VIOLIN ("La Cetra")

In gracious Renaissance fashion, Marcello held weekly concerts at his home, where he and his friends played works that he had composed. Only a mere handful of Marcello's output has survived to our day. These concertos are light-weight music, but luminous and gracious.

* * I MUSICI	PHILIPS	(S) WS 9085

"I Musici"—literally "The Musicians"—are magicians as well. On any recording by this ensemble, you are assured of the highest musicianship. The sound is spacious.

CONCERTO FOR OBOE

This concerto, with its haunting second movement, is one of the loveliest oboe concertos in the literature.

It is uncertain whether Alessandro Marcello really wrote this piece: it has been attributed to Benedetto Marcello, again to Alessandro, and in the 19th century to Vivaldi. Taking no chances, some scholars attribute it to "Anonymous—18th century Venetian."

* * * I MUSICI		PHILIPS (S) WS 9085 [Concerto, "La Cetra"]
* * ROTHWELL BARBIROLLI	London Pro Arte Orch.	VANGUARD (S) 191 [Albinoni, Concerto (Opus 7)]
* * HOLLIGER, AUBERSON	Geneva Baroque Orch.	MONITOR (S) 2088 [C. P. E. Bach, Oboe Concerto in E flat major; J. S. Bach, Concerto for Oboe and Violin in D minor; Bellini, Oboe Concerto in E flat major]
* PIERLOT, RISTENPART		COUNTERPOINT (5) 608 [Hasse, Quantz; Vivaldi program]

The first three listings are all worth-while records; in making a choice among them, probably the other items on the backs of these discs should be the decisive factor.

As usual, I Musici produce a superior record, with great ensemble playing. The oboe tone is warm, and the sound is resonant.

Evelyn Rothwell is an expert oboist, and offers a good, varied program.

Holliger is also outstanding. He offers a solid program that includes a great Bach concerto.

Pierlot is a first-rate musician, but offers a less interesting program.

Marcello, Benedetto (1686-1739)

Benedetto Marcello, the brother of Alessandro Marcello, was a lawyer, composer, librettist, and writer on musical subjects. A nobleman, he signed himself, after his name, "nobile Veneto dilettante di contrapunto" ("noble Venetian dilettante in counterpoint").

SONATAS FOR FLUTE AND CEMBALO

This is light, pleasing music, written for performance by dilettantes.

* WATSON, KAPP	MONITOR (S) 2120 [mixed program]
BORIOLI (harmonica), MIGLIORANZI- BORIOLI	EVEREST (S) 3172 [mixed program]

William Watson is stylishly pleasing. [The Watson album contains only one sonato by Marcello, among an interesting, wide-ranging program of other works. Other items include J. S. Bach's *Sonata in E Major,* De Falla's *Five Spanish Songs,* and Frank Martin's *Ballade.* The Martin *Ballade* is an imaginative piece by an austere and respected Swiss composer of our own day.]

Borioli's harmonica version is for those who enjoy harmonica versions.

SONATA NO. 2 IN E MINOR FOR CELLO AND CONTINUO

* * COLLEGIUM MUSICIAM Saarensis	NONESUCH (H) 71119

This album is labeled "Masters of the High Baroque"; I recommend it. It features some fine, brisk playing, and good, dry, uncluttered sound from Club Francais du Disque, Paris. The Marcello work is well performed, with spirit as well as elegance.

[The other items in the album include Buxtehude: *Sonate in D for Violin, Viola da gamba, and Continuo* (Opus 2, No. 2); *Sonata in E Minor for Violin, Viola da gamba, and Continuo* (Opus 1, No. 7); Leclair: *Sonata in D for Violin, Viola, and Continuo* (Opus 2, No. 8); Pergolesi: *Sinfonia in F for Cello and Continuo;* Telemann: *Trio in F for Recorder, Viola da gamba, and Continuo.* These works are pleasing — particularly the two Buxtehude pieces. Here is a good chance to sample a composition of Jean-Marie Leclair (1697-1764), a lively Baroque musician of the French school who was ignored for two hundred years but is now being rediscovered and admired. Generally, though, one should beware of albums pompously labeled "Masters of the . . . ." These are often pretentious wrap-up titles covering all the short, odd tapes lying around the studio that nobody could figure out how to package. Some examples: "Early Works of 17th-Century Masters," "Masters of Fanfares and Organ Works of the North German School," etc. The most hilarious usage of this catch-all is on the Mace label: "Orchestral Music of the Classical and Baroque Periods."]

Martinu, Bohuslav (1890-1959)

Martinu continued the Czech national school of music that was founded by the composers Smetana and Dvorak. Nevertheless, Martinu was an extremely cosmopolitan composer, and also came under the influence of Stravinsky and Hindemith. After a short stay in Portugal, Martinu came to the United States, where he composed most of his music.

CONCERTO FOR TWO STRING ORCHESTRAS, PIANO, AND TYMPANI

This is one of Martinu's more impressive works; if you want to include but one Martinu in your record collection, this should be it. Utilizing breathless, motorized sounds and rhythms with cross accents and asymmetrical phrasings, this effective, skillful composition shows the influence of Stravinsky's *Sacre du Printemps*.

The Martinu composition on the reverse side of the record, the *Three Frescoes of Piera della Francesca*, was inspired by the 15th-century painter whose art the composer admired on visits to the Church of San Francisco at Arezzo. To quote the knowledgeable and succinct Arthur Cohn, this music is "Czechized Respighi, without brass orgy, gramophone nightingales, and overcelebrated orchestration."

* SEJNA	*Czech Philharmonic*	ARTIA [Three Frescoes]	(S)	135

The music is played with conviction. The sound is acceptable.

OBOE CONCERTO

A lyric, high-spirited piece, with a poignant slow movement, this piece is extremely well suited to the tone and range of the oboe. Oboists tell me that this 1955 concerto is one of the best modern compositions for the instrument.

* HANTAK, TURNOVSKY	*Brno State Philharmonic Orch.*	PARLIAMENT [R. Strauss, Oboe Concerto]	(S)	606

The oboe playing is excellent, but fiercely recorded—much too close to the microphone. [The disc also includes the Strauss concerto, a florid work in Strauss' singing style.]

PIANO CONCERTO NO. 3 AND VIOLIN CONCERTO

This is facile writing in what may be termed the conservative international style of the 1940's. Mischa Elman commissioned the lyrical violin concerto; the lively piano concerto was commissioned by Rudolph Firkusny.

* PALENICEK (piano), ANCERL	*Czech Philharmonic Orch.*		
* BELCIK (violin), NEUMANN	*Prague Symphony Orch.*	ARTIA	(S) 7 205

The playing of both the works is pleasantly clear and decisive. The sonics are fair.

Mascagni, Pietro (1863-1945)

Mascagni, the son of a poor Italian baker, was an obscure opera conductor and mall-town music teacher when his one-act thriller *Cavalleria Rusticana* won first prize in an opera competition in 1889. Overnight, Mascagni found world-wide fame.

Mascagni continued to write operas until his death at eighty-two. However, none of his later operas equalled his one early success.

CAVALLERIA RUSTICANA

This earthy tale of rural passions has been a favorite ever since its first production. Mascagni originally wrote this opera in two acts, but he revised the score in order to conform to the rules of the competition. To avoid disqualification, he left the curtain up throughout the opera, and filled in the time break with the now-famous *Intermezzo*.

Today, the opera is nearly always performed on a double bill with that other short work of Italian *verismo (realism) Pagliacci*. The paire are familiarly referred to as "Cav and Pag."

* * DEL MONACO, NICOLAI, PROTTI, GHIONE	*Chorus and Orch.*	2-RICHMOND RS (M) 62008
SIMIONATO, CADONI, TAGLIABUE, BASILE	*Rome Radio Orch.*	2-EVEREST/CETRA (S) 410-2
GIGLI, RASA, SIMIONATO, BECHI, MASCAGNI	*La Scala Chorus and Orch.*	2-SERAPHIM IB (M) 6008

The Richmond set is by far the best of the three. Del Monaco, in his rip-roaring unmodulated style, is most successful. Nicolai could be steadier, but the conducting is well paced and exciting. The chorus is clear and sonorous. The sound is good.

The singers on the Cetra-Everest set are not much. Braschi is thin; Tagliabue's Alfio is shaky; and Simionato has too much vibrato for most tastes.

The unhappy Seraphim version presents the performance conducted in 1940 by the composer, and includes a spoken introduction by Mascagni. However, it was recorded too late in Mascagni's lifetime, as well as in Gigli's and Bruna Rosa's, to do justice to their talents. [Side 4 of the Seraphim set includes Italian songs—among the *Anima e Core* and Fedri's *Ninna Ninna*—sung by Gigli.]

L'AMICO FRITZ

This work, composed in 1891, and Mascagni's one successful comic opera, contains much tuneful, engaging music.

* * TAGLIAVINI,   2-Everest/Ceta (S) 429/2
TASSINARI, PINI,
MASCAGNI

This excellent performance was conducted by the composer himself. Tagliavini is silver-voiced, and the admirable Tassinari could hardly be bettered. This hoary set is still quite hearable. Philip Miller (in *Guide to Vocal Records):* "Probably destined to stand as the definite performance."

Massenet, Jules (1842-1912)

Massenet studied composition under Ambroise Thomas at the Paris Conservatoire.. From 1878-1896, Massenet held a professorship in that institution.

From 1878-1896, Massenet held a professorship in that institution.

Massenet was an extremely successful opera composer. Today, his operas seem to suffer from lack of dramatic conviction; and he is sometimes dismissed as an "inferior Gounod." His tear-jerking opera *Thais* has been written off by WQXR's Lloyd Moss as "Sadie Thompson in the desert"; Peter Grammond acidly comments: "His music might have been specially commissioned by Mantovani, who has recorded it."

But Massenet, I believe, may be in for a quasi-camp revival. Fair winds are blowing in his direction since the New York City Opera's stunning production of his opera *Manon*. In any case, his music is suavely melodious—even voluptuous; and Massenet knew how to write arias that singers could sing effectively. His unadventurous but polished skill keeps at least *Manon*, his masterpiece, very much alive today.

DON QUICHOTTE (DON QUIXOTE)

Written for the great basso Chaliapin, this opera was first performed at Monte Carlo in 1910. This is one of Massenet's 30 operas (including those unperformed or unpublished) that have now vanished entirely from repertory. But *Don Quichotte* contains suave melodies, and strong economical writing.

| * CHANGALOVICH, KALEF, KORESHETZ, DANON | 2-Everest/Cetra (S) 400/2 |

This is an earthy performance from Belgrade. The Yugoslavs have presented this opera all across Europe to high praise. The *American Record Guide* comments: "These Belgrade performers are inspired." The sound is rather dry.

LE CID

This ballet suite is a favorite light-classical piece. An abundance of Spanish colors and rhythms are heard.

| * * MARTINON | *Israel Philharmonic* | London   LTS 15051 [Meyerbeer, Les Patineurs] |

Buoyance and elan are both heard. The *Stereo Record Guide*: "Martinon gives sparkling performance and the orchestra displays utmost virtuosity." The sound does not reach sonic splendor, but it is good. [Giacomo Meyerbeer (1791-1864) was born Jakob Liebermann Beer, and enjoyed a tremendous vogue with his operas. Wagner, for a while tremendously influenced by Meyerbeer, repaid him with a notorious anti-semitic attack, "Die Juden in Musik." In any case, *Les Patineurs,* which pictures a skating scene, is a lilting and popular ballet number.]

NOTE: Three melodious Massenet arias, from *Herodiade, Thais,* and *Le Jongleur de Notre Dame,* may be heard on a remarkable record called *The Great Mary Garden,* Odyssey 32 16 0079. Even this scratchy relic conveys her dramatic talent. Mary Garden (1874-1967) was a legend in an age of legendary singers. The sound is terrible, but Thais is a role forever associated with Mary Garden, and her charisma comes through even today; so that one understands how Debussy, when merely hearing her *speak,* cried, "Voila ma Melisande!"

SCENES PITTORESQUES; SCENES ALSACIENNES

Here are pleasant melodies, arranged in predictable, unenterprising orchestration.

* WOLFF   *Paris Conservatoire Orch.*   LONDON   STS 15033

The playing is colorful and energetic; the sound is lively.

THAIS

This 1894 opera concerns the famous fourteenth-century courtesan who tried to seduce a saintly monk.

* SEBASTIAN   *Paris Opera Orch.*   3-URANIA   (M)   227
                                                              (S) 5227

The set is uneven in quality. The soloist, Geori-Boue, better known to us from Beecham's striking album of Gounod's *Faust,* is a first-rate "presence," but has a tendency to go shrill. The rest of the cast is undistinguished, but stylish in an appropriately Gallic, world-weary way. The sound is poor.

WERTHER

This opera still holds the boards in France, but never caught on outside of that country. Although inspired by Goethe, the opera is rather monotonous.

* TASSINARI, TAGLIAVINI, MOLINARI-PRADELLI	3-Everest/Cetra	(S) 436/3
JUYOL, LEGER, BOURDIN, SEBASTIAN	3-Urania	(M) 233-3 (S) 5233-3

The Everest/Cetra set has a few annoying hisse during what seem to be tape slices. On the whole, however, it is a decent production, despite the close-to-the-mike, booming voices. Tassinari and Tagliavini are solid Italian singers. They sing in French, but the performance still sounds passionately Italian.

The old Urania set is more truly French in style; the cast is from the Opera Comique. George Sebastian conducts authoritatively and knowledgeably. The singers have flair and temperament, but are not outstanding. The sound is just adequate.

Mendelssohn, Felix *(1809-1847)*

The son of a Hamburg banker, and the grandson of a great Jewish scholar, Mendelssohn gave his first piano concert at nine. At the age of 17, he embarked on a career as a composer; he soon attained great popularity throughout Europe.

In 1829, Mendelssohn conducted a performance of J. S. Bach's *St. Matthew Passion* in Berlin—the first performance of the work since Bach's day. This production brought the then-ignored Bach to world fame. In 1833, Mendelssohn became music director in Dusseldorf, and in 1835, he became conductor of the Leipzig Gewandhaus Orchestra. Eight years later, with Schumann, he was one of the founders of the Leipzig Conservatory of Music. Dividing his time among conducting, teaching, and composing, he overworked himself to a state of physical collapse.

PLACE AND ACHIEVEMENT Mendelssohn's popularity diminished in our time—a reaction against the taste of mid-Victorian times when both he and his music were revered as the epitome of virtue. He was one of the first great Romantics, but we no longer care for his style of Romanticism. It is rather bland—overly neat and bloodless. But he was a consummate workman. His best works have a cheerful, effortless appeal. We can forgive him for being a gentleman composer and avoiding the violent emotional storms and stresses of a Liszt or a Wagner; he also avoided their self-pity.

THE ESSENTIAL MENDELSSOHN

ORCHESTRAL MUSIC: *Symphony No. 3 ("Scotch"); Symphony No. 4 ("Italian"); Symphony No. 5 ("Reformation"); Concerto in E Minor, for Violin and Orchestra; A Midsummer Night's Dream, Suite; Fingal's Cave (Hebrides) Overture; Ruy Blas Overture.*

CHAMBER MUSIC: *Octet in E-Flat Major; 2 Piano Trios.*

CHORAL MUSIC: *Elijah, Oratorio.*

PIANO MUSIC: *Songs Without Words; Rondo Capriccioso; Variations Serieuses.*

OTHER WORKS

CHORAL MUSIC: *St. Paul, Oratorio.*

ORCHESTRAL MUSIC: *Concerto in E Minor, for Piano and Orchestra; Capriccio Brilliant, for Piano and Orchestra; Incidental Music to "Athalie."*

CHAMBER MUSIC: *Quartet No. 1, in E-Flat Major; Quartet No. 6, in F Miror.*

PIANO MUSIC: *Capriccios, Variations, and Preludes and Fugues, for Piano; Piano Sonatas.*

CHAMBER MUSIC: TRIO NO. 1 FOR PIANO, VIOLIN, AND CELLO (Opus 49)

The concert season of 1839-40 was a brilliant one at the Leipzig Gewandhaus. Schubert's *Ninth Symphony* was played no less than three times; one concert included Beethoven's four *Fidelio Overtures,* and the visiting soloists included the legendary Franz Liszt—who caused a scandal by charging unheard-of prices for his appearance. Among the novelties of the season was a new piano trio by the distinguished conductor of the orchestra—Herr Mendelssohn himself. This trio was played on February 10, 1840. The composer was at the piano, and his good friend, the great Ferdinand David, played the violin part.

The reviews of the Mendelssohn *Trio* were favorable, and Robert Schumann was all but carried away. In his all-out, impetuous style, he declared that the trio was the greatest since those of Beethoven. The *Trio* has since become the more popular work of Mendelssohn's chamber music.

How Mendelssohn found time to compose, with his exciting and fatiguing schedule as conductor and soloist, is a mystery. But he was a glutton for work—his musical day began at seven in the morning and ended long after midnight. This year—1840—was one of the sunniest periods in Mendelssohn's life. He was thirty; he had been married for two years to a beautiful young woman with whom he was idyllically happy; he was a famous composer and pianist; and he was at the helm of the renowned Gewandhaus concerts in Leipzig.

Mendelssohn's mania for perfection affected the publication of the *Trio.* He insisted on revising it after the piece was already on the market; for a while, there were two versions on the piano racks of the best homes in Europe. The revised edition is usually heard today.

* *	*Beaux Arts Trio*	PHILLIPS WS (S) 9082	
		[Trio No. 2]	
* *	*Suk Trio*	CROSSROADS (S) 22 16 0178	
		[Brahms, Trio No. 3]	

Two really first-rate readings are available to us. Both provide admirable interpretations and fine sound. The couplings may help you decide. The Beaux Arts disc has also the second Mendelssohn trio, another felicitous contribution to the romantic library. The Suk Trio is backed by the somber Brahms *Piano Trio No. 3.*

CONCERTO NO. 1 IN G FOR PIANO *(Opus 25)*

This is a pleasant concerto—not Mendelssohn at his best, but elegant.

* PRESSLER, SWAROWSKY	*Vienna State Opera Orch.*	MONITOR [Chopin, Concerto No. 2]	(S) 2117

The *First Concerto* is played with romantic dash by Menachem Pressler, the gifted pianist of the Beaux Arts Trio. The sound is agreeable. [The backing is with the romantic Chopin *Concerto No. 2,* artfully executed.]

CONCERTO IN A-FLAT FOR TWO PIANOS AND ORCHESTRA; OVERTURE "THE FAIR MELUSINA" *(Opus 32)*

This "newly-discovered" concerto was composed shortly before Mendelssohn turned sixteen. It is a precocious work, if not a profound one. This work was part of a large collection of Mendelssohn manuscripts, in 44 volumes, long buried in the State Library of Berlin.

* BILLARD, AZAIS, RISTENPART	*Chamber Orchestra of the Saar*	NONESUCH H	71099

The work is nicely played. The sound is clean.

CONCERTO IN E MINOR FOR VIOLIN *(Opus 64)*

This is gentle, singing, endearing music—one of the most popular concertos ever written. It is also an expertly "violinistic" concerto. Every bar lies well and sounds well, and for this we must thank Ferdinand David, the famous Concertmaster of the Gewandhaus Orchestra in Leipzig, whom the composer constantly consulted during the composition of this work.

* * * MILSTEIN, STEINBERG		PICKWICK [Bruch]	(S) 4023
* * LAREDO, MUNCH	*Boston Syhphony Orch.*	VICTROLA VIC [Bruch, Concerto No. 1]	(S) 1033
* CAMPOLI, BOULT	*London Philharmonic*	LONDON STS [Bruch, Scottish Fantasy for Violin and Orchestra, Opus 46]	(S) 15015
* CAMPOLI, VAN BEINUM	*London Philharmonic*	RICHMOND [Bruch, Concerto No. 1]	(M) 19021
OISTRAKH		PERIOD SHO [Lalo, Symphonie Espagnole]	(S) 312

Milstein gives a splendid, vibrant performance. The sound is fine.

The Bolivian-born violinist Jaime Laredo is remarkably gifted, and his is a youthful, impetuous reading.

Campoli, while not so striking, gives a neat, sweet interpretation.

The blurry Oistrakh tapes are both to be avoided, unless you don't mind percolated sound. If you must have Oistrakh—whose reading of this work is world-famous—invest in the high-priced Columbia disc. The Columbia record provides an exquisitely played Mozart concerto as well.

MIDSUMMER NIGHT'S DREAM, INCIDENTAL MUSIC (Opus 21 and 61)

This, the best-loved of all Mendelssohn's works, is a double miracle: first, that he wrote the incredible overture at 17; and second, that he recaptured that infectious spirit when, at twice that age, he was commissioned to provide additional incidental music for Shakespeare's play.

* * * MONTEUX	*Vienna Philharmonic*	VICTROLA VIC (S) 1023 [Schubert, Rosamunde]
* * KEMPE	*Royal Philharmonic*	SERAPHIM (S) 60056 [Humperdinck, Hansel & Gretel Suite]
* VAN BEINUM	*Concertgebouw Orch.*	RICHMOND (M) 19035 [Schubert, Rosamunde]
* PARAY	*Detroit Symphony Orch.*	MERCURY (M/S) 18067 [Symphony No. 5]
* GOLSCHMANN	*Vienna Opera Orch.*	VANGUARD (S) 161 [Symphony No. 4]

Monteux's version is one of his best recordings. A safe rule of thumb in low-priced record selections is to take Pierre Monteux, whenever you see him; the sound is usually highly acceptable and the performances are of the highest standard.

Kempe's interpretation is both expressive and precise. The stereo sound is only so-so. [The disc also contains an attractive reading of the *Hansel and Gretel Suite*.]

Van Beinum's reading comes off very well, with sonorous playing by the Holland orchestra. The mono sound is well recorded.

Paray's recording is also enjoyable, headstrong rather than polished.

Golschmann's reading is adequate, but outclassed by the other performances listed.

OCTET IN E FLAT FOR STRINGS (Opus 20)

Written when Mendelssohn was all of sixteen, this is masterly instrumental
writing for four violins, two violas, and two cellos.

* *	*Fine Arts Ensemble*	CONCERT DISC	(M)	1261
			(S)	261
*	*Janacek and Smetana Quartets*	WESTMINSTER	(M)	18856
			(S)	14082

The Fine Arts Group is youthful and exuberant, drily recorded.
The Janacek combination has less verve, but better sound.

OVERTURES

These are vivacious, highly colored descriptive pieces, with solid orchestration.

* BBECHAM	*Royal Philharmonic*	PICKWICK [Berlioz; Rossini]	(S)	4036

Sir Thomas Beecham was an imaginative interpreter of Mendelssohn's
works. On the Pickwick disc are the overtures to *Midsummer Night's
Dream* and *Fair Melusine,* as well as brilliantly played Berlioz and Rossini
overtures. At this writing, no other commendable performance of
Mendelssohn overtures is available on low-cost records, but others will
certainly appear.

SYMPHONY NO. 3 IN A (Opus 56) ("Scotch")

The *"Scotch" Symphony* was written in 1842, as an act of homage to
Queen Victoria, to whom it is dedicated.

* * DORATI	*London Symphony Orch.*	MERCURY [Hebrides Overture]	(M)	14056
			(S)	18056
* KLEMPERER	*Vienna Symphony Orch.*	VOX	(M)	11840
* VAN REMOORTEL	*SW German Radio Orch.*	VOX [Midsummer Night's Dream]	(5)	11310

Dorati's version is sonorous, and even over-recorded in a lush way.
The antiquated Klemperer disc offers us a picturesque interpretation
that is most attractive, although the sound is dated mono.
Van Remoortel's performance is agreeable.

SYMPHONY NO. 4 IN A (Opus 90) ("Italian")

"I have entered Italy at last," Felix Mendelssohn wrote to his teacher in 1830. "My family will tell you of the exhilarating impression made on me by the first sight of the plains of Italy. I hurry from one enjoyment to another, hour by hour, and constantly see something novel and fresh." Later he reported, "I have once more begun to compose with fresh vigor, and the 'Italian' Symphony makes rapid progress. It will be the most mature thing I have ever done."

Very little of the music was written down on paper, however. Felix had an odd system of working: he resisted writing black notes on white paper in final score, for he was a perpetual reviser and polisher and was never satisfied. For this reason, he carried his unfinished symphony about with him in his head, only partially sketched in his notebook. He had an extraordinarily vivid memory for every dettail.

Even after the introduction of the symphony in London in 1833, he postponed publication for four more years, while planning even further revisions. It was not performed in the final version, that we know, until after his death.

* * * STEINBERG	*Pittsburgh Symphony*	PICKWICK (S) 4027 [Tchaikovsky, Capriccio Italien; Wolf, Italian Serenade]
* * GOLSCHMANN	*Vienna State Opera Orch.*	VANGUARD (S) 161 [Midsummer Night's Dream]
* KLEMPERER	*Vienna Symphony*	VOX (M) 11880 [Schubert, Symphony No. 4]
* CANTELLI	*Philharmonic Orch.*	SERAPHIM (M) 60002 [Schubert, Symphony No. 8]
* SOLTI	*Israel Philharmonic*	LONDON STS 15008 [Schubert, Symphony No. 5]
* VAN REMOORTEL	*Vienna Musikgesellschaft Orch.*	VOX (3) (S) 11210 [Tchaikovsky, Capriccio Italien]

Steinberg conducts a glowing performance, with excellent couplings.

Golschmann's version is light and spirited. [The disc contains the attraction of the *Midsummer Night's Dream* as well.]

Klemperer's interpretation is the sunniest of all, but it has thin, dated sound.

Cantelli's version is appealing and graceful. The mono sound is fair.

The Solti disc is grim; it lacks charm.

Van Remoortel's reading is shipshape and quite hearable.

SYMPHONY NO. 5 IN D (Opus 107
("Reformation")

This symphony comprises a Lutheran confession of faith, complete with the melody of *Ein Feste Burg Ist Unser Gott* as its climax.

* PARAY   *Detroit Symphony Orch.*   MERCURY   (M/S) 18067
                                                   [Midsummer Night's Dream;
                                                   Incidental music]

Paray's version is satisfactory, although several high-priced records offer more sensitive interpretations of this music. The sound is sonorous.

Messiaen, Oliver (1908-   )

A pupil of Dukas and an accomplished organist, Messiaen is also a devout Catholic and a singular musical voice. His work includes symphonic poems, as well as vocal, piano, and organ music. Messiaen claims that his music had been strongly influenced by (a) bird-song; particularly calls of the nightingale, lark, and thrush; and (b) the 120 Indian folk rhythms collected by Charnagadeva in the 13th century.

Some critics hail him as great; but Harold Schonberg of the New York *Times* finds his work (at least in *Le Banquet Celeste*) "pretentious and tiresome." Messiaen has been extremely influential as a teacher of avant-garde composers.

QUATUOR POUR LA FIN DU TEMPS

Recorded under the composer's supervision, this work was "conceived and written during my captivity. *The Quartet for the End of Time* was given its first performance in Stalag VIII-A, on January 15, 1941, in Silesia, in atrocious cold. . . ." The work includes sonorous, strange sounds, and fanciful imagery ("God's Presence in Himself," etc.). This is mystic, overloaded romantic stuff which will remind some listeners of Scriabin.

* FERNANDEZ, DEPLUS, NEILZ, PETIT	Music Guild	(S)	150

The music is somberly played. I can only presume that they are doing what they should be doing.

THREE LITURGIES

Here are more theological settings written in 1945. The electronic "Onde Martenot" — an electronic instrument which produces musical waves by means of a wire stretched over a keyboard — is used. According to Messiaen, "The opening and closing sections represent all things: the planets, flowers, birds. . . ." I do not know what to make of this music.

Y. LORIOD, J. LORIOD, COURAUD	*Chorus*	Music Guild	(S)	142

The work is enthusiastically played by accomplished musicians. The sound is splendid.

MERLE NOIR, FOR FLUTE AND PIANO

Subtitled *The Blackbird,* this work contains unaccompanied flute passages which, I presume, are intended to be birdlike. To quote Arthur Cohn: "One cannot quarrel with Messiaen's devotion to bird-song interpretation. It is a kind of 'my bird music, right or wrong, but my bird music.'" Three recordings of this odd piece are listed in Schwann's catalogue.

* BRUDERHANS   ARTIA   (S)   715
                                                [Bach, Flute Sonata;
                                                Haydn, Flute-Sonata; Hin-
                                                demith, Flute Sonata]

The flutist is fluent. (The balance of this disc is devoted to worthwhile flute sonatas.) The sound is clean.

OISEAUX EXOTIQUES; LA BOUSCARLE; REVEIL DES OISEAUX

More bird-song.

LORIOD, NEUMANN   *Czech Philharmonic Orch.*   CANDIDE CE   (S) 31002

I cannot tell you about the playing, because I haven't the faintest idea of how this music is supposed to sound. I yield to the equally uneasy reviewer for *High Fidelity:* "This latest addition to the growing Messiaen discography is devoted entirely to one aspect of the composer's work, the *style oiseau.*"

Milhaud, Darius (1892-   )

Milhaud is the most famous member of the group called "Les Six," the name given by Henri Collet in 1920 to a group of six young French composers who were influenced by the artistic principles of Jean Cocteau and by Erik Satie's ideal of simplicity. The others of the group—who soon were no longer six—were Louis Durey, George Auric, Arthur Honnegger, Francis Poulenc, and Germaine Tailleferre.

Milhaud, a sophisticated composer in the French tradition, is strongly eclectic; he seems to have absorbed every musical idea of the century. A remarkably facile composer, he has tried his hand at everything from opera to chamber music—over 400 works, in all.

CREATION DU MONDE

La Creation, a ballet, has some historical importance as one of the first serious pieces to make use of the American jazz idiom. In La Creation, Milhaud also successfully uses his innovation of polyphony—a simultaneous combination of different keys. Today, this work, once famed as iconoclastic and revolutionary, merely sounds like a nostalgic French period piece of 1923.

* * MILHAUD	Orchestra of Theatre des Champs Elysees	NONESUCH (S) 71122 [La Boeuf Sur le Toit]
* CAREWE	London Symphony Orchestra Chamber Group	EVEREST (M) 6017 (S) 3017 [Stravinsky, L'Histoire Du Soldat]

Milhaud conducts his own music with *esprit* and with unique authority. The sound is dry and brisk. [The reverse side contains another Milhaud ballet, Le Boeuf Sur le Toit (English Title: The "Do-Nothing Bar"). This work was meant to be a "cinema symphony" to accompany silent movie comedy. It provides good, low-down fun, with Brazilian tangos, sambas, and a farcical jaunty tune repeated fifteen times.]

The Carewe reading is effective, and is backed by a truly great piece—Stravinsky's skeletal L'Histoire Du Soldat.

SCARAMOUCHE SUITE (Opus 165b)

The title Scaramouche means buffoon, or scamp; the suite is one of the most successful two-piano works extant.

* GIERTH, LOHMEYER	MACE	9023
* STECHER, N. HOROWITZ	EVEREST	(M) 6147 (S) 3147 [Brahms, Haydn Variations]

The Mace disc is brashly played, as suits the music. This jazzy score even includes, believe it or not, the old radio refrain, *We Want Cantor*. The Everest team is breezy and efficient. The stereo sound is acceptable.

SYMPHONY NO. 4 FOR STRINGS

This work, commissioned to celebrate the 1848 Revolution, is a cold, linear piece, of cerebral rather than emotional appeal.

* * FOSS   *Zimbler Sinfonietta*   TURNABOUT TV   34154
[Ives, Unanswered Question; Skalkottas, Little Suite; Bartok, Divertimento]

Lucas Foss, a composer himself, is an excellent interpreter of modern music, and this album is a fine example of his abilities. [The other items on the disc provide a commendable survey of modern music: The Bartok demands dazzling technique, and comes off very well indeed; the use of a small orchestra provides a succinctness not often attained. The Ives composition is one of his most popular pieces.]

Montemezzi, Italo (1875-1952)

Although he was twice rejected by the Milan Conservatorio, the talented Montemezzi nevertheless became a successful Italian operatic composer. His most popular and enduring work is *The Love of Three Kings.*

L'AMORE DEI TRE RE (The Love of Three Kings)

This opera is one of the few resounding successes by an Italian composer who lived after Puccini. This is melodic, expressive, very satisfying music. The opera provides four striking roles for singers who have formidable acting ability. The part of King Archibaldo is a terrific role for a basso; the part of Princess Fiora provides high-voltage sex.

* BRUSCANTINI, CAPECCHI, PETRELLA, BERTOCCI, BASILE	*Rome Radio Orch.*	EVEREST/CETRA (S) 447-2

After the appetite-whetting introduction above, I must unfortunately report that the singing is only fairly good, led by the fiery Clara Petrella who was much admired in her day. Petrella provides vocal charisma, but not vocal polish. Bruscantini is the best of the three kings. The sonic balance is better than is usual on old Cetra sets, even though the listener is aware that the singers are each in turn hugging the mike, as was the custom in 1952, when this performance was first recorded.

High Fidelity comments on this disc: "The old Cetra recording is hardly adequate."

Monteverdi, Claudio *(1567-1643)*

Born in Cremona, Italy, Monteverdi was the eldest son of a doctor. He studied with Ingegneri. In 1583, he published his first work, a book of madrigals. In 1589, he became violist in the orchestra of the Duke of Mantua. In 1601, Monteverdi became *maestro di capella*. Later, he became absorbed with opera, producing his masterpiece *Orfeo* in 1607. In 1613, Monteverdi left Mantua to accept the post of choirmaster at St. Mark's Cathedral in Venice.

PLACE AND ACHIEVEMENT   Monteverdi looms large in the history of music. One of the greatest composers before Bach, he was a genius who adapted the ideas of the Renaissance revolutionists who had just preceded him.

The earlier composers—Palestrina, Byrd, and Victoria—had all sought perfection in music by weaving unaccompanied voices in polyphony. The revolutionary Florentine composers just before Monteverdi, had written vocal music accompanied by instrumental playing. In such compositions, the singer might declaim the words of a poem against a musicl background. The road toward opera had been broken. Monteverdi shrewdly combined the new recitative with the best elements of the old style, and his *Orfeo* (1607) is opera's first masterpiece. Monteverdi also wrote the first operatic duet.

Monteverdi's music is plaintive, and filled with grave emotion. We are aware of a restless intellect at work. His madrigals convey a passionate sadness. When his music is well sung, it can still grip us.

THE ESSENTIAL MONTEVERDI
OPERA: *Orfeo; Ballo delle Ingrate; Combattimento di Tancredi e Clorinda; Lagrime d'Amante; Lamento d'Arianna.*

OTHER WORKS
OPERA: *Incoronazione di Poppea;* [*Monteverdi wrote at least 12 other operas, of which only three survive complete.*]
CHURCH MUSIC: *Magnificat for Six Voices; Three Masses, Vespers, Magnificats, Motets.*
SECULAR MUSIC: *Madrigals.*

IL BALLO DELLE INGRATE, MADRIGALS

Some of this music was included in the celebrated album of Monteverdi pieces that Nadia Boulanger made back in 1937. When these discs were first heard by music lovers, they revealed the beauty of Monteverdi's work to an utterly astonished audience.

Il Ballo delle Ingrate (The Ballet of the Ungrateful Woman) is a semi-topical stage piece. It was first performed in 1608, with choreography, as part of the festivities for the marriage of the son of the Duke of Mantua.

| * * LOEHRER | Vocal and Instrumental Soloists of Societa Cameristica (Lugano) | NONESUCH | (S) H 71092 |

The music is splendidly sung by the Lugano ensemble. *Il Ballo* is backed with *Madrigali Amorosi,* madrigals on love themes, which contains some of the most lyrical pages in Monteverdi's entire body of work. Individual madrigals included are: *Dolcissimo Uscignolo;* and *Lamento Della Ninfa ("Non Havea Febo Ancora").* Cynus of Paris produced the fine, intimate sound.

IL COMBATTIMENTO DI TANCREDI E CLORINCA

This somewhat heavy-going work is from Monteverdi's eighth and last published collection, *Madrigals of War and Love,* published in 1838.

| * SPEISER, MALACARNE, MALAGUTI, KEHR | Mainz Chamber Orch. | TURNABOUT [3 Madrigals] | (3) 4018 |
| * LOEHRER | Vocal and Instrumental Soloists of Societa Cameristica (Lugano) | NONESUCH   H 71090 [Madrigals, Altri Canti di Marte; Gira il Nemico Insidioso; Hor Ch'el Chiel e la Terra; Perche t'en Fuggi, o Fillide] | |

The music is intensely sung on the Turnabout set; the sound is agreeable.

The Nonesuch performance is on the lugubrious side—a little too mournful for my taste. The sound is clean.

INCORONAZIONE DI POPPEA

The Coronation of Poppea is a tedious opera, with little of the gripping power of *Orfeo.*

| * ULRICH-MIELSCH, BUCKEL, EWERHART | Chamber Orch. | 3-Vox SOPBX | (S) 5113 |

Here is chaste, tasteful singing. The sound is all right.

LAGRIME D'AMANTE (*from Madrigals, Book VI*)

Lagrime D'Amante (Tears of a Lover at a Beloved's Tomb) was inspired, we are told, by the death of Monteverdi's beautiful pupil Caterina Martinelli, who died in 1608 at the age of 18.

* * * GREENBERG	*New York Pro Musica*	ODYSSEY (M) 32 16 0087 [Madrigals]	
* * GIANI	*Nuovo Madrigaletto Italiano*	NONESUCH (S) 71021 [Madrigals]	
* RANDOLPH	*The Choral Singers*	WESTMINSTER 9622	

The Odyssey set is superbly sung by New York's renowned Pro Musica Ensemble. Leading specialists in Renaissance music. Their disc, cryptically entitled "Monteverdi," is a choice selection of the master's madrigals. With Russell Oberlin as countertenor, this fine record is zestful and vital. The sound is dry but hearable. This disc was on a select list of "best-ever monos" made up by *High Fidelity:* "Noah Greenberg's tremendous enthusiasm made everything he touched catch fire.

The Nonesuch disc is excellent—with voices not so fine as the Pro Musica, but with a poetic impoct the other versions do not possess. The stereo sound is good.

The knowledgeable David Randolph gives an outstanding performance, although his singers are of lesser quality. The mono sound is filmy. [His disc is backed with five striking examples of Double Choruses by Schuetz, Lotti, Allegri, and Lassus—music employing a small "echo" chorus that repeats what the large chorus has sung, a half-bar later.]

LAMENTO D'ARIANNA

This still affecting *Lament* is all that survives from the opera *Arianna*. This music was once extremely popular; contemporary sources tell us that "every house that harbored a harpsichord or a flute was filled with the plaintive accents of *Arianna* sung by trembling voice."

* *	*Montreal Ensemble*	VOX (M) 910 (S) 500910 [Madrigal Collection]
* GIANI	*Nuovo Madrigaletto Italiano*	NONESUCH (S) 71021 [Ecco Silvio; Lagrime d'Amante al Sepolcro dell' Amata ("Incenerite Spoglie' O)]

The Montreal Ensemble sings intensely, yet pleasingly. The sound is warm. The Nonesuch version is also appealing, but not so intense. The sound is all right.

MADRIGALI GUERRIERI ET AMOROSI

This passionate music is as affecting today as it was in Venice in the early seventeenth century.

* * * VENHODA   *Prague Madrigal Singers*   CROSSROADS (M) 22 16 0023
    (S) 22 16 0024
    [Lassus, Madrigals]

The Prague musicians provide fervent singing. This is a good selection of Monteverdi's secular music. A *bravo* to Crossroads for this handsome product. The sound is good. [Lassus, on the reverse side, had few equals in the art of madrigal-writing.]

MAGNIFICAT A 6 VOCI

This is powerful music. Written for six-part chorus and keyboard accompaniment, it was published as part of a collection of scared works in 1610, three years before Monteverdi took over the post of choirmaster at San Marco in Venice. This amazingly forward-looking music is not at all wearsome.

* * * KAHLHOEFER   *Soloists, Kantorei*   NONESUCH (S) 71134
    Barmen-Gemarke   [Schuetz, Deutsches Magnificat; Psalm 2; "Saul, Saul"]

* * RILLING   *Spandauer Kantorei*   TURNABOUT (M) 4099
    (S) 34099
    [Schuetz, Deutsches Magnificat]

The Nonesuch set is lovely; the thrilling soprano of Maria Friesenhausen raises this record above any competition. The sound is excellent.

The Turnabout set with the redoubtable Rilling is also fine. The sound is commendable.

[Both the Nonesuch and Turnabout discs include the stark Schuetz work on the reverse.]

MISSA A CAPELLA

This mass, for six voices, is a good example of Monteverdi's striking polyphonic writing. It does not display Monteverdi the revolutionary, but rather Monteverdi the master using traditional material.

* VENHODA   *Prague Madrigal Singers,*   CROSSROADS (M) 22 16 0043
    Vodrazka   (S) 22 16 0044

The work is reverently sung by the admirable Prague Madrigal singers. The sound is good, although it seems slightly boxed in.

IL RITORNO D'ULISSE IN PATRIA

This long Monteverdi opera is not on a par with the monumental *Orfeo*. But genius is genius, and there are lovely melodies here, too—although not enough to make the whole work satisfying. Even on three records, this set contains only excerpts of this very long work; some seven roles are entirely missing.

FAHBERG, BENCE, EWERHART	*Santini Chamber Orch., Soloists*	Vox	(5)	211

The music is gravely sung. The sound is adequate.

SE I LANGUIDI MIEI SEGUARDI

Monteverdi described *Se I Languidi* as a "Love Letter for Solo Voice in Theatrical Style." It is, in effect, a miniature unstaged opera scene, with a passion that carries well across more than three centuries.

* * CUENOD, PINKHAM		Music Guild	(S) 109
		[other Monteverdi selections]	

If you like Monteverdi, don't miss this one. The album is vaguely titled "Monteverdi: Secular Vocal Works," and it is a beauty. Cuenod has the ideal pure voice for this music, and is a thorough musician. The sound is thin but pleasant.

VESPRO DELLA BEATA VERGINE

This somber church music is magnificent.

* * CONNORS, SAMS, MINTY, ROGERS, FYSON, NOBLE, KEYTE, STEVENS	*Accademic Monteverdiana Orch., Ambrosian Singers*	2-Vanguard	C10001/2
* GRISCHKAT	*Stuttgart Bach Orch., Swabian Choral Singers*	2-Vox VUX	2004

Dennis Stevens, who knows his way in this period as do few conductors, achieves a striking performance in the Vanguard set. The sound is splendid.
The Grischkat interpretation is much too stolid.

Moore, Douglas *(1893-   )*

Moore, born in New York State, studied with Ernest Bloch and Vincent d'Indy. He has won many awards, and is now a professor of music at Columbia University. He has written in many forms, and has come as close as anyone (with the probable exception of Gershwin's folk opera *Porgy and Bess*) to composing a good, indigenous American opera that people enjoy hearing. The operas *The Devil and Daniel Webster* (1938) and *The Ballad of Baby Doe* (1965) are his successes.

THE BALLAD OF BABY DOE *(Sung in English)*

Don't overlook this one—an enjoyable work of Americana— as American as *Bonnie and Clyde*. The drily amusing book is by John Latouche, and deals with love in the Colorado silver mines.

* * SILLS, CASSEL   3-Heliodor   (M/S) 25035
   BIBLE, BUCKLEY

These admirable singers are the same who offered the New York City Opera Company's engaging production some years back; their performances on this record are equally successful. The balance between the orchestra and the singers is not ideal, but the record is still entirely hearable.

Morley, Thomas (1557-1602)

Morley was English,, a pupil of the great Byrd, and organist at St. Paul's Cathedral. In his forties he published *A Plaine and Easy Introduction to Practical Musicke,* a manual of technique, which includes some delightful music. He was also granted a royal license to print music and music-paper.

Morley is a master of the apparently artless (but actually intensely artful) madrigal; his music has wit and spontaneity. He published some nine volumes of songs and instrumental music; these have placed him in the front rank of the Elizabethan madrigalists.

CANZONETS; FIRST BOOKE OF BALLETS IN FIVE VOYCES; MADRIGALLS TO FOURE VOYCES OTHER WORKS

This a good sampler of Morley in his light-hearted "fa-la-la" style.

* *	*Deller Consort*	Vanguard (S) 157 [Wilbye, Madrigals]	

I am quite dotty about Alfred Deller, a supreme musician, and the world's greatest counter-tenor (the highest male voice, in an alto range). This is a good chance to hear him and his six-voice Deller Consort, who are unmatched in this sort of thing. The sound is pleasant. [John Wilbye (1574-1638), another madrigalist, is on the reverse side. His works, not as great as Morley's are technically more sophitiscated.]

OTHER WORKS

Sweet madrigals and other pieces by Morley can be found on a superb album, Everyman (S) 147, entitled *Album of Beloved Songs,* with the Deller Consort, and featuring the haunting voice and supreme musicianship of Alfred Deller.

The record, Dover 5248, *Anthology of Renaissance Music,* contains two excerpts of sacred music by Morley, as well as noble music from Des Prez, Lassus, Vitcoria, and Palestrina. Some utterly unknown music by Jaquet of Mantua (ca. 1495-1559) is included, as well as a lovely short prayer found at Bologna, and an exuberant Christmas motet by a pupil of Josquin des Prez, one Jean Mouton (ca. 1475-1522). The singers are the New York Pro Musica under Noah Greenberg. The disc is well recorded. This record should not be missed by lovers of Renaissance music.

An excellent album, *English Madrigals from the Courts of Elizabeth I and James I,* features charming, outdoorsy madrigals by Morley, Wilbye, Orlando Gibbons, and Byrd. This music concerning nymphs, love, and melancholy, was composed by such musical poetasters of the period as John Bennet, Thomas Weelkes, Giles Fanaby, George Kirbye, Richard Alison, John Ward, Thomas Tomkins, Thomas Bateson, Thomas Vautor, and Thomas Greaves. This unpretentious, gallant music, stylishly sung by the "Purcell Consort of Voices" under Grayston Burgess, is heard on Turnabout (S/M) 34202. The sound is highly agreeable.

Mozart, Leopold (1719-1787)

The father of the great Wolfgang Amadeus Mozart, Leopold, was a thoroughly proficient musician and composer.

He wrote an instruction manual for the violin which survives as a treasurehouse of information on the musical practices and customs of his day. His music is correct, accomplished, and unoriginal.

CONCERTO IN D FOR TRUMPET

This is an amiable, vigorous concerto, with bold high solo writing for trumpet.

* * ANDRE, BEAUCAMP		PHILIPS WS (M/S) 9049 [Albinoni; Telemann, Concerto; Vivaldi, Trumpet-Violin Concerto]
* * SCHERBAUM, RISTENPART	Saarbruecken Radio Chamber Orch.	HELIODOR (S) 25056 [J. Christian Bach, Bassoon Concerto; M. Haydn]

Both André and Scherbaum are world-famous virtuosos. European conductors always select one or the other when recording a formidable solo trumpet part such as Bach's *Brandenburg Concerto No. 2*. André plays this piece in a very French, very lyrical, and very refined style. However, what really sways me toward this disc is that it contains three other vivacious eighteenth-century trumpet concertos. They are unimportant works, but will please those who dote on Baroque concertos.

Some years ago, trumpeter Adolph Scherbaum rated a write-up in *Time* magazine. His playing is far more ebullient and sturdier than André's, but the rest of the record is of milder interest.

Mozart, Wolfgang Amadeus

Mozart was born in Salzburg, Austria, the son of a violinist and composer. He showed early signs of musical talent (playing violin, harpsichord, and organ) and began to compose at five. At six he played in Munich and Vienna. In 1763, together with his father and his sister Maria Anna, he embarked on a long tour of Germany, Belgium, Paris, London, and Holland. By the time the boy Mozart returned home to Salzburg, he had already written his first three symphonies and some thirty other works.

In 1777, in the company of his mother, Mozart set out to conquer Paris. He met with indifferent success. Later, his father's efforts to secure him a court position at Vienna failed. Mozart worked at Salzburg, composing prolifically, and was attached to the Archibishop's household. He was literally booted out from that post in 1771, and the following years in Vienna and in other cities saw a series of disappointments despite some popular success with his operas. Acute financial worries continued to the end of his life, and he was reduced time and again to scribbling begging letters to friends, asking for a loan. He died of malignant typhus in Vienna; where his body lies buried is unknown.

PLACE AND ACHIEVEMENT   These lines are being written on the day of the death of the great theologian Karl Barth. Nothing could sum up better our feelings today about Mozart than Barth's "Letter of Thanks to Mozart." "I have only a hazy feeling about the music played there where you now dwell. I once formulated my surmise about that as follows: whether the angels play only Bach in praising God I am not quite sure; I am sure, however, that *en famille* they play Mozart and that then also the Lord God is especially delighted to listen to them."

Music flowed from Mozart's pen unceasingly. His habit was to compose complete movements in his mind before writing them down on paper. (The great overture to *Don Giovanni* was written two nights before the opera's premiere.) He was influenced all his life by the music of others—Johann Christian Bach, Handel, Haydn, and Gluck, among others—yet he had the genius to extract what he needed from another man's style and to incorporate it in his own clear, unmistakable voice.

"There is only one Mozart," Rossini wrote, and the world agrees with him. Like Johann Sebastian Bach and Richard Wagner, he is a musical universe of his own. The more intimate one becomes with Mozart's music, the more one is struck with his extraordinary range and powers. Certainly no composer ever had such a range of moods and expression. Joy, profound sorrow, pure musical pleasure, and laughter—these are the qualities of that profound artist and aristocratic craftsman we know and love as Mozart.

As short a time as seventy years ago Mozart's image was that of a rather sweet, rather cute eighteenth-century drawing room composer. He was not much played. It seems incredible to us today, with our passionate love of Mozart's operas, that the Metropolitan Opera House saw no reason, with Mozart out of fashion, to stage *Don Giovanni* from 1907 until the early 1930's. Today, perhaps no other composer has the universal appeal Mozart has. You can listen to his music when the heroics of Beethoven become wearisome, when Tchaikovsky seems too pathetic, when Wagner becomes detestable, and even when the great Bach seems to be "a celestial sewing machine," in Colette's phrase. Mozart never lets you down. He is the composer for all moods, all seasons.

THE ESSENTIAL MOZART

OPERAS: *The Marriage of Figaro; Don Giovanni; The Magic Flute; Cosi Fan Tutte.*

ORCHESTRAL MUSIC: *Symphony No. 35, in D major "Haffner"; Symphony No. 39, in E-flat major; Symphony No. 40, in G minor; Symphony No. 41, in C major, "Jupiter"; Eine kleine Nachtmusik, for strings.*

CONCERTOS: *Concerto No. 20, in D Minor (K.466), for piano and orchestra; Concerto No. 24 in C minor (K.491), for piano and orchestra; Concerto No. 27, in B-flat major, for piano and orchestra; Concerto No. 4, in D major (K.218), for violin and orchestra; Concerto No. 5, in A major (K.219), for violin and orchestra; Concerto in A for Clarinet, (K.622); Sinfonia Concertante in E-flat for Oboe, Clarinet, Bassoon, Horn and Strings, K.Anh.9 (297b); Sinfonia Concertante in E flat for Violin and Viola (K.364).*

CHORAL MUSIC: *Requiem; Mass in C (K.427), ("The Great"); Mass in C (K.317) ("Coronation").*

CHAMBER MUSIC: *"Haydn" quartets; 2 piano quartets; Quintet in A major, for clarinet and strings; Quintet in G minor, for strings; Quintet in D, (K.593) for strings; Sonatas in C major (K.296), G major (K.301), E minor (K.304), D major (K.306), F major (K.377), B-flat major (K.378), B-flat major (K.454), A major (K.526), for violin and piano.*

PIANO MUSIC: *Sonata in A major (K.331); Fantasia and Sonata in C minor (K.475 and K.457); Sonata in D major (K.576); Sonta in F major (K.497), for four hands.*

OTHER WORKS:

Mozart wrote many other operas, masses, symphonies, concertos, chamber music works, piano sonatas, etc.

A note about the "K" numbers which follow each piece of Mozart's music: These numbers were given to Mozart's compositions by Ludwig Alios Friedrich Ritter von Köchel (1800-1877), an Austrian Imeperial Councillor. Köchel devoted his years of retirement to the cataloguing of Mozart's huge and bewildering output. Though much revised since then, Köchel's catalogue numbers invariably follow Mozart's pieces.

SYMPHONIES   Mozart wrote 41 symphonies. They are a "barometer of his musical growth," to use John Burk's nice phrase, and they stand with the composer's string quartets as a striking phenomenon of musical evolution. Mozart composed his first symphony when he was eight years old. After writing some 24 pleasant, youthful, exuberant symphonies — of no great importance to us — he suddenly found his true voice, which is first heard in his *Symphony No. 25 (K. 183)*. It must be remembered that the models for a "symphony" that the adolescent Mozart was expected to draw upon were little more than short pieces in three parts, often connected. This form of symphony was casually regarded as a vehicle for diverting, entertaining music, and little more. The form was held to be a lightweight one, similar to the old-fashioned "Italian overtures" of the period.

To my ears, the mature Mozart masterpieces begin with *No. 34 (K. 338)*. The style has been perfected; the musical thought grows deeper and deeper, and culminates gloriously in the last three symphonies *(No. 39-41)* which were all composed in two months during the summer of 1788.

SYMPHONIES (41) (Complete)

* KEHR	*Mainz Chamber Orch.*	3-Vox SVBX (S) 5119 [1, 4, 5, 6, 7, 8, 9, 10, & K. 45a, 45b, 75, 76]
* KEHR	*Mainz Chamber Orch.*	3-Vox SVBX (S) 5118 [18, 19, 20, 21, 22, 23, 24, 25 & K. 161, 163]
* LEINSDORF	*Philharmonic Symphony of London*	3-WESTMINSTER (S) 1001 [1/13]
* LEINSDORF	*Philharmonic Symphony of London*	WESTMINSTER (M) 18864 (S) 14078 [14, 15, 16, 17]
* LEINSDORF	*Philharmonic Symphony of London*	WESTMINSTER (S) 14039 [18, 21]
* LEINSDORF	*Philharmonic Symphony of London*	WESTMINSTER (M) 18782 (S) 14097 [18, 19, 20]

* LEINSDORF	*Philharmonic Symphony of London*	WESTMINSTER [21, 22, 23, 24]	(S) 14756
* LEINSDORF	*Philharmonic Symphony of London*	WESTMINSTER [25, 26, 27, 28]	(S) 14675
* LEINSDORF	*Philharmonic Symphony of London*	WESTMINSTER [29, 30, 31, 32]	(S) 14216
* LEINSDORF	*Philharmonic Symphony of London*	WESTMINSTER [33, 34]	(M) 18186 (S) 14186
* LEINSDORF	*Philharmonic Symphony of London*	WESTMINSTER [35, 36, 37]	(M) 18146
* LEINSDORF	*Philharmonic Symphony of London*	WESTMINSTER [38, 39]	(S) 14980
* LEINSDORF	*Philharmonic Symphony of London*	WESTMINSTER [40, 41]	(S) 14527

Neither of the staggering and gallant undertakings from Kehr is remarkable. Volume One of the series contains nine symphonies which Mozart wrote in his middle teens. Volume Two has twelve works which he wrote at an even tenderer age, including three that he composed when he was eight or nine. The conducting and playing are straightforward, and now and then one hears considerable vitality and grace. Nathan Broder comments in *High Fidelity*: "The Mainz Chamber Orchestra may not be the most polished band in the world, and as recorded here the sound of the violins is not likely to deceive you into thinking you're in Carnegie Hall."

The complete recording of the Mozart symphonies by Leinsdorf is well-turned-out, in a tailor-made fashion, and is faithful to Mozart. The orchestral playing is good and full-bodied, with English woodwinds that sing out sweetly and clearly. The sound is adequate, but not acceptable for those who expect true high fidelity. In sum, this worthy attempt is serviceable; it provides honest Mozart, but not outstanding Mozart.

SYMPHONY NO. 23 IN D (K. 181)

No. 23 was written in 1773. It has a dramatic *Allegro* and a poignant *Andantino* which features a solo oboe. This is a lovely, unpretentious work.

| * * MUELLER-BRUEHL | *Mainz Chamber Orch.* | NONESUCH (S) 71055 [Symphonies 29, 30] |
| * KEHR | *Mainz Chamber Orch.* | TURNABOUT (M) 4002 (S) 34002 [Symphonies 20, 25] |

Mueller-Bruehl comes up with a warm, entirely Mozartean-sounding disc — not the easiest of tasks. You hear all of the instruments in their various lines, an accomplishment not often heard on records. *Stereo Record Guide* comments: "Playing: stylish; recording: excellent. . . . A good bargain. . . . One of the very best discs in the Nonesuch series."

Kehr is hardly inspired, but this is a cleanly played, graceful disc.

SYMPHONY NO. 25 IN G MINOR (K. 183)

No. 25 was composed in 1773. This is one of the best of the "early" Mozart symphonies — a grave, somber work with a scintillating *Finale*. Only twice in his life did Mozart compose a symphony in the minor mode — here in *No. 25* and in the famous *Symphony No. 40*. Both are in G minor, a key that seems to have held a special significance for Mozart. *Symphonies 20* and *23*, also on this disc, are smoothly worked pieces, with considerable charm.

* KEHR	*Mainz Chamber Orch.*	TURNABOUT	(M) 4002
			(S) 34002
		[Symphonies 20, 23]	
KLEMPERER	*Pro Musica*	VOX	11820
		[Symphony 36]	

Kehr offers a bright, light reading that is quite acceptable. I cannot recommend the Klemperer disc, which is badly aged. For those who seek Klemperer's serious Mozart, however, he has done this symphony in recent years on high-priced Angel records.

SYMPHONY NO. 29 IN A (K. 201)

Mozart was 18 when he wrote this unpretentious, unceremonious work which is a delight to the ear. Really a string piece, with graceful colorations by horns and oboes, it is one of the most popular of Mozart's earlier symphonies.

* * * BARSHAI	*Moscow Chamber Orch.*	ARTIA	(S) 185
		[Boccherini, Symphony]	
* * DAVIS	*London Sinfonia*	VICTROLA VIC	(S) 1378
		[Symphony 39]	
* MUELLER-BRUEHL	*Cologne Soloists Ensemble*	NONESUCH	71055
		[Symphonies 23, 30]	
* KEHR	*Mainz Chamber Orch.*	3-VOX	SVBX-5120
		[Symphony 26/8, 30/4]	
BARBIROLLI	*Halle Orch.*	VANGUARD	S-180
		[Symphony 41]	
TURNOVSKY	*Czech Philharmonic*	CROSSROADS	(M) 22 16 0041
			(S) 22 16 0042
		[Symphony 40]	

The Barshai performance is a knockout. This is an utterly spontaneous-sounding performance, and the playing is alive and sensitive.

Colin Davis, a conductor who is a red-hot favorite these days, is crisp and poised.

Mueller-Bruehl is highly polished — a bit lacking in drive, but pleasing nonetheless.

Kehr has at his disposal "an ensemble that is not first-grade, but it tries very hard," to quote Nathan Broder. The Mainz players are smallish-sounding, but this is a neat record.

Barbirolli is stodgy and pretentious, a disaster in this music that cries out for wings.

Turnovsky's version is clearly directed, unsubtle, and unexceptional.

SYMPHONY NO. 31 IN D (K. 297) ("PARIS")

When Mozart was in Paris longing for an opera commission, he turned out this smoothly crafted symphony to show the hard-to-please Frenchmen what he could do. It is urbane, fashionable music, with a delicate and lovely slow movement for strings only. In this work, Mozart uses clarinets for the first time; he had been listening to the astonishing, way-out orchestra at Mannheim, and this was his chance to employ the new technical skills he had learned.

* LEITNER	*Bavarian Radio Symphony*	HELIODOR .(S) 25034 [Symphony 36]	
* KEHR	*Mainz Chamber Orch.*	TURNABOUT 34240 [Symphonies 32, 34]	

Leitner is festive and bustling — a good mood for this work. The playing is agreeable.

Kehr obtains a graceful reading, but one which could have had more niceties of shadings.

SYMPHONY NO. 33 IN B-FLAT (K. 319)

This lovely symphony deserves far more performances than it has received. The only orchestral colors, besides strings, are oboes, horns, and bassoons — all Mozart had at his disposal with the Salzburg ensemble for which this music was composed. Nevertheless, the winds are handled expertly and prominently.

* * WAND	*Cologne Philharmonic*	COUNTERPOINT 5613 [Symphony 41]	
* KEHR	*Mainz Chamber Orch.*	3-VOX SVBX-5120 [Symphonies 26/32, 34]	

Wand has a gracious feeling for eighteenth-century style; it is pleasantly evident on this performance.

Kehr is spirited rather than polished. The playing is agreeable.

SYMPHONY NO. 34 IN C (K. 338)

No. 34 is Mozart's first symphony of important stature and it shows a more fully developed style than any that preceded it. It is not one of his most popular, but it is a buoyant work that no Mozart lover should miss.

* * KEHR	*Mainz Chamber Orch.*	TURNABOUT [Symphonies 31, 32]	(S) 34240

This is one of Kehr's best jobs in his Mozart series. He is vital and incisive—and the players are right there with him.

SYMPHONY NO. 35 IN D (K. 385) ("HAFFNER")

This is party music. In 1782, when Siegmund Haffner of Salzburg needed a seranade for a special occasion, he spoke to Mozart's father, who promptly wrote to his son in Vienna, urging him to supply the music. Wolfgang obliged, and two years later reworked it into the version we know now.

* * * BEECHAM	*Royal Philharmonic*	3-ODYSSEY	(M) 3236 0009
* * WAND	*Cologne Symphony*	NONESUCH [Symphony 38]	(S) 71079
* KRIPS	*Israel Philharmonic*	LONDON STS [Symphony 41]	(S) 15058

The Beecham performance is available only in a three-record album of great Mozart symphonies. These are great readings indeed, historic performances that will be studied as long as people listen to Mozart. Beecham's way with Mozart is crisp, vital, intensely alive, and, when called for, superbly genial. This is personalized, at times eccentric, Mozart; we are as much aware of Sir Thomas as we are of Wolfgang Amadeus. A minority report from *High Fidelity's* knowledgeable Peter Davis: ". . . Beecham's performance sounds stuffy and overfed . . . that special Beecham charm, but the rest is pure John Bull." The mono sound has faded and will not do for hi-fi addicts.

Guenter Wand is very good, providing a reading that is detailed, balanced, and well-poised. The sound is resonant.

The Krips reading, as always, is handsomely tailored and correctly fitted. The trouble is that one yearns for sparkle, flair, a sense of drama—and these Herr Krips does not provide. For those who want this symphony with its coupling of the great *"Jupiter"* Symphony, however, this disc will do.

Those who don't mind spending more can get a dazzling supersonic *"Haffner"* Symphony on Angel Records by Daniel Barenboim, the musical darling of the day.

SYMPHONY NO. 36 IN C (K. 425) ("LINZ")

This symphony represents a milestone in the artistic development of Mozart. It was written in Linz in 1783. Mozart had been asked to supply a symphony for a concert; having neglected to bring one with him, he conceived, put on paper, copied, rehearsed, and performed this lovely work—all within the space of four days!

* * DORATI	*London Symphony Orch.*	MERCURY (M/S) 18064 [Haydn, Symphony 101]	
* * WAND	*Cologne Guerzenich Symphony*	VANGUARD (S) 255 [Symphony 39]	
* LEITNER	*Bavarian Radio Symphony Orch.*	HELIODOR (S) 25034 [Symphony 31; Petits Riens: Overture]	

Dorati, usually noted for more spectacular music, presents a first-rate reading of classifical proportions. The sound is good.

Wand's players are clean; they supply delightful nuances. Wand himself seems to be a first-rate Mozart man.

Leitner is solid, but somewhat earnest and humorless.

SYMPHONY NO. 38 IN D (K. 504) ("PRAGUE")

The *"Prague"* Symphony was composed in 1786. This is no longer Mozart the young wonder, but the mature and profound artist. His players must have been bowled over with his unheard-of-technical demands; Mozart well knew that they couldn't possibly play this "new music" with the agility and expertise he called for. However, he was writing music of creative genius, whether his players could cope with it or not.

* * * BEECHAM	*Royal Philharmonic Orch.*	ODYSSEY (M) 3216 0023 [Symphony 41]	
* * WAND	*Cologne Symphony Orch.*	NONESUCH 71079 [Symphony 35]	
* KUBELIK	*Chicago Symphony Orch.*	PICKWICK (S) 4042	

The Beecham reading is long-celebrated, magnificent, and available on fair mono only. Sackville-West comments: "A performance to convince one that this is Mozart's greatest symphony."

Wand is vital and his phrasings are tasteful. The sound is warm.

Kubelik, hardly the ideal Mozartean, is all nervous energy, with little geniality, let alone depth of feeling.

SYMPHONY NO. 39 IN E-FLAT MAJOR (K. 543)

This first of Mozart's great final trio of symphonies is mostly a joyous, lighthearted score—this, despite adverse circumstances. On June 27, 1788, the day after he finished the work, he wrote a letter to his friend and fellow Mason, the amateur musician Michael Puchberg, asking for money. In it he said, "I have worked more during the ten days I have lived here than in two months in my former apartment; and if dismal thoughts did not so often intrude (which I strive forcibly to dismiss), I should be very well off here, for I live agreeably, comfortably, and above all, cheaply."

* * FURTWAENGLER	*Berlin Philharmonic Orch.*	HELIODOR (S) 25079 [Eine Kleine Nachtmusik; Marriage of Figaro Over- ture; Abduction from the Seraglio Overture]
* * DAVIS	*London Sinfonia*	VICTROLA VIC (S) 1378 [Symphony 29]
* * MAAG	*Japan Philharmonic Orch.*	CROSSROADS (M) 22 16 0125 (S) 22 16 0126 [Symphony 41]
* * TOSCANINI	*NBC Symphony Orch.*	VICTROLA VIC (S) 1330 [Symphony 40]
* * WAND	*Cologne Guerzenich Symphony*	VANGUARD (S) 255 [Symphony 36]

Furtwaengler delivers a romantic, sonorous reading that may not be everyone's Mozart, but is certainly a striking and historical statement. Together with the attractive couplings, this is a most worthwhile disc. All these items were originally on the Deutsche Grammophon label, recorded between 1938 and 1944. Admirers of Furtwaengler will be grateful to Heliodor for the couplings as well.

"Eine Kleine Nachtmusik" sings and trips as light as a feather. The reprocessed sound is just barely acceptable.

Davis produces a reading of "great finesse and vigor," according to *Stereo Record Guide*. I must agree, and also praise the splendidly Mozartean winds and strings of the London Symphony. The sound is warm.

Maag is the soul of elegance and finesse. The sound, however, is harsh.

Toscanini is noble. This is a classic disc for those who favor the Maetro's disciplined, polished Mozart. The sound, however, is dim.

Wand is admirable, with an utterly different, far more direct approach than the studied version by Furtwaengler; no hint of mannerism or idiosyncrasy intrudes. The playing is fresh-sounding.

SYMPHONY NO. 40 IN G MINOR (K. 550)

This symphony and the *"Jupiter"* that follows it are the most popular of Mozart's 41 efforts in this form. *No. 40* is a poignant piece of music. There are noble pages of the highest order, without a trace of gloom. Wagner described the *Andante* as "the tender murmuring of angels' voices."

* * PROHASKA	*Vienna State Opera Orch.*	VANGUARD [Serenade, K. 525]	(S)	162
* * STEINBERG	*Pittsburg Symphony Orch.*	PICKWICK [Schubert, Symphony 8]	(S)	4001
* * TOSCANINI	*NBC Symphony Orch.*	VICTROLA VIC [Symphony 39]	(S)	1330
* * WAND	*Cologne Symphony Orch.*	NONESUCH [Serenade 9]	(S)	71047
* LUDWIG	*London Symphony Orch.*	EVEREST [Schubert, Symphony 8]	(S)	3046

The Prohaska disc is first-rate. This man works wonders with Mozart (and Bach)—always with convincing flair. Although he uses a small-sized, eighteenth-century ensemble, he makes the music sound important. A bit more sweep and passion would have made this a great disc; it nevertheless stands as a remarkably successful performance. [The coupling is a favorite Mozart piece, *Serenade: A Little Night Music.*] The sound is clean.

The Steinberg disc uses larger forces and is handsomely played. This is a warm, direct reading.

The Toscanini reading is historic, perfect, and inhumanly cold. The sound is dim.

Wand is vital and intense; he commands one's respect. [The coupling is with a well-played version of the lilting *"Posthorn" Serenade.*]

Ludwig is precise, even meticulous, and I find a lack of warmth and poetry.

SYMPHONY NO. 41 IN C (K. 551) ("JUPITER")

The *"Jupiter"* is the last, and for many, the greatest Mozart symphony. The sobriquet, it is believed by some, applies to the Jovian, noble first movement. The symphony was written in about 14 days—somewhat beyond belief since this is one of the most profound symphonies ever

434   MOZART, W.

penned. One striking feature of this work, the capstone of Mozart's symphonic effort, is the great fugue that closes the symphony. There is a towering finality about it, an absolute supremacy, that even Mozart himself had never equalled.

* * PROHASKA	*Vienna State Opera Orch.*	VANGUARD (S) 167 [Overtures: Don Giovanni; Le Nozze di Figaro; Die Zauberfloete]
* * BEECHAM	*Royal Philharmonic Orch.*	ODYSSEY (M) 3216 0023 [Symphony 38]
* MAAG	*Japan Philharmonic Orch.*	CROSSROADS (M) 2216 0125 (S) 2216 0126 [Symphony 39]
* LUDWIG	*NDR Orch.*	VOX (M) 12510 (S) 512510 [Haydn, Symphony 94]
* KRIPS	*Israel Philharmonic Orch.*	LONDON STS-15058 [Symphony 35]
* BARBIROLLI	*Halle Orch.*	VANGUARD (S) 180 [Symphony 29]

The 1960 Phohaska disc is not world-shaking—maybe that's what I like about it. The music sings, and we are with Mozart. *High Fidelity,* discussing this reissue: "It was a bargain then, and it is a bargain now, for the clarity and definition of the sound—and its fidelity to reality—remains unimpared and comparable to the best in more recent recordings."

Beecham's historic statement remains a virtuoso performance of stature. The sound is not as good as on the Prohaska—but you can't have everything.

Peter Maag has made a considerable reputation as a Mozart-Haydn man, and this is a neat, rather than forceful, disc. The sound, however, is harsh and metallic.

Ludwig is well-paced and energetic, with few surprises.

Krips is *gemutlich* to the point of boredom, and the winds of the Israel Philharmonic are not exactly brilliant here.

Barbirolli is dull, even disinterested.

PIANO CONCERTOS Mozart wrote more masterpieces in the piano concerto form than any other composer. They are rich, buoyant, and delicate, and an endless joy to the lover of Mozart.

The piano concerto played a vital role in Mozart's life, just as the piano sonatas did in Beethoven's. Mozart often supported himself by giving concerts and playing the solo piano part himself in his new concertos. Most of them were written after he was 21; they are mature works. As Mozart authority Nathan Broder put it, "Of all the numerous categories of music to which Mozart contributed voluminously, that of the piano concerto assays highest in percentage of gold to ore."

A note on performances of these concertos on low-priced records: We live in an age that loves Mozart as no generation has before. One result of this is a bumper crop of mostly young, intelligent dynamic pianists who love to play Mozart, and who present us year after year with recordings that rival any in the catalogue.

The following pages are star-studded with an extraordinary list of really first-rate Mozart interpreters. Almost any disc with such artists as Haskil, Kraus, Engel, Klien, Frankl, Brendel, Matthews, Haebler, and Badura-Skoda insures pure listening pleasure and true Mozart style. The sonics, of course, vary widely.

CONCERTI FOR PIANO AND ORCHESTRA (K. 107) (ARRANGED FROM THREE SONATAS BY J. CHRISTIAN BACH)

These "extraordinarily primitive" little concertos, according to musicologist Alfred Einstein, were written by Mozart when he was 13 and still billed as "the greatest prodigy that Europe, or that even human nature had to boast of." Each is based upon a clavier sonata by J. C. Bach.

* * ENGEL, KOPPENBURG	*Frankfurt Chamber Orch.*	ODYSSEY (S) 3216 0164 [Symphony 1; J. C. Bach, Symphony 4]	
* VEYRON-LACROIX, RISTENPART	*Saar Radio Chamber Orch.*	MUSIC GUILD (S) 133 [Concerto 8]	

The Odyssey disc is entitled "Mozart in London" and is well worth having for the superbly Mozartian playing of Karl Engel. Loving attention is lavished on modest music, and the result is a delight. This is playing of the highest order, and if the pieces on the reverse side were of more interest, this would be a solid three-star disc. [The slight *Symphony No. 1* was written in London to pass the time when Mozart's father was ill and the child was forbidden to practice. J. C. Bach, ("The English Bach") was a son of the great Johann Sebastian, and had a most profound influence on the young Mozart when the child came to London. The Bach *Sinfonia* is amenable, not more.]

Veyron-Lacroix, a gifted and classical musician, gives an agreeable performance.

PIANO CONCERTO NO. 9 IN E-FLAT (K. 271)

Written in 1777, when Mozart was 21, this concerto reveals a great advance over those that preceded it; Mozart strikes out boldly, with new eloquence. This work still shines for us, while the vast bulk of piano concertos written at the same time by others seem today to be mere musical gallantry.

* * KRAUS, DESARZENS	*Vienna State Orch.*	MONITOR [Sonata 11]	(S) 2105
* NOVAES, SWAROWSKY	*Vienna Pro Musica*	VOX [Concerto 20]	(M) 8430

Lili Kraus is one of our most intelligent and sensitive Mozart players. The sound is good.

Madame Novaes is poetic; her silvery touch makes this a disc of interest to piano-lovers. The orchestra is barely adequate, and the mono sound is less than good.

PIANO CONCERTO NO. 11 IN F (K. 413)

This is really a showpiece for the pianist, with lightly sketched accompaniment. It is not a very stimulating work. Mozart wrote it in 1782 for his concerts in Vienna.

* * FRANKL, FAERBER	*Wuerttemberg Chamber Orch.*	TURNABOUT [Concerto 15]	(3) 4027

Frankl is one of the most exemplary Mozart players I know; he is trim and musical here.

PIANO CONCERTO NO. 12 IN A (K. 414)

This is a cheerful, attractive concerto, written in Vienna in 1782.

* * ENGEL, BOETTCHER	*Vienna Symphony Orch.*	MACE [Concerto 14]	(S) 9048

Engel is very good, and has Mozart in his bones. Only a certain absence of absolute assurance and brilliance could be noted here by the quibbler.

CONCERT RONDO FOR PIANO (K. 386)

This *Rondo* is held to be an alternate finale for the *Concerto in A (K. 414)*. Why Mozart wrote an alternative finale—very similar to the first version—remains a mystery. In any case, this graceful *Rondo* is the perfect filler for piano recordings with a few minutes to use up.

| * * A. FISCHER, FRICSAY | *Bavarian State Orch.* | HELIODOR   (S) 25001 [Rondo K. 382; Beethoven, Concerto 3] |

Annie Fischer is one of the most sympathetic Mozart pianists we have; here she is all she should be. [The coupling, Beethoven's *Third Concerto,* is handsomely played.]

PIANO CONCERTO NO. 14 IN E-FLAT (K. 449)

"Had I to mention three or four Mozart concertos whose neglect was unjustified," wrote Arthur Hutchings in his *Companion to Mozart's Piano Concertos,* "I should head my list with *K. 449,* the first of Mozart's mature series." This is not a display piece, but it demands musicianly understanding.

| * * * KLIEN, ANGERER | *Vienna Pro Musica* | Vox   (5) 11650 [Concerto 16] |
| * * ENGEL, BOETTCHER | *Vienna Symphony Orch.* | MACE   (S) 9048 [Concerto 12] |

Klien is a complete delight. This vivid reading is one of the best available.
The highly gifted Karl Engel's playing here is also a joy—a never-dull, thoughtful, persuasive performance.

PIANO CONCERTO NO. 15 IN B-FLAT (K. 450)

Mozart wrote that this concerto was "bound to make the performer sweat." It calls for much brilliance, but this is neither one of the greatest nor one of the most popular Mozart concertos.

| * * * FRANKL, FAERBER | *Wuerttember Chamber Orch.* | TURNABOUT (3) (S) 4027 [Concerto 11] |

The young Hungarian Frankl plays with a wonderfully buoyant rhythm, and the clean fingerwork is a delight. The supreme Mozart authority, Nathan Broder, comments: "It is a pleasure to be able to say that the Turnabout disc is good enough to take a place with rivals that cost twice as much. Indeed, I am not sure that this version of the charming *K. 450* is not the best available."

PIANO CONCERTO NO. 16 IN D (K. 451)

This is a spontaneous-sounding concerto, written within seven days in 1784. Much of it is show-off music, designed to please a socialite audience. It is carefully developed Mozart, nevertheless.

* * KLIEN, ANGERER	Vienna Volksoper Orch.	TURNABOUT [Concerto 23]	(S) 34286

Klien is light and graceful. The sound is pretty good.

PIANO CONCERTO NO. 17 IN G (K. 453)

"The G Major Concerto holds a special place in the hearts of all Mozarteans," wrote that admirable Mozartean, John N. Burk. "There is an astonishing variety of moods . . . and the concerto never tries to dazzle with virtuosity." This music is pure joy from start to finish.

* * BRENDEL, ANGERER	Vienna Volksoper Orch.	TURNABOUT (S) (3) [Concerto 19]	4080
* RICHTER-HAASER, KERTESZ	Philharmonic Orch.	EVEREST [Concerto 26]	(S) 3161

Brendel is a first-rate Mozart interpreter. His is a beautifully poised reading.

Richter-Haaser "offers restrained elegance and tends to under-value the power of Mozart's writing," according to the alert ears of *Stereo Record Guide*. I myself find it chaste Mozart, admirable in its way.

PIANO CONCERTO NO. 18 IN B-FLAT (K. 456)

This concerto moved Leopold Mozart, the composer's father—and a hard-to-please critic—to tears of delight when he heard it when visiting Vienna in 1785.

* VON SCHILHAWSKY, ALBERT	Radio Bavaria Orch.	NONESUCH [Concerto 24]	(S) 71059

The Nonesuch disc is, on the whole, a satisfactory reading, although a certain rhythmic rigidity and a lack of strong individuality bother me. The sound is clear.

PIANO CONCERTO NO. 19 IN F (K. 459)

In this concerto, Mozart weaves his musical fantasy, with subtle interplay between piano and orchestra. As John Burk remarks, "This concerto is the choice for a performer who loves Mozart at least as much as his own prowess in glittering cascades."

* * * BRENDEL, BOETTCHER	*Vienna Volksoper Orch.*	TURNABOUT [Concerto 17]	(3) 4080
* * * KRAUS, RIVOLI	*Amsterdam Philharmonic Society Orch.*	MONITOR [Concerto 26]	(S) 2809
* * HASKIL, FRICSAY	*Berlin Philharmonic Orch.*	HELIODOR [Concerto 27]	(S) 25042
* HAEBLER, MELLES	*Vienna Symphony Orch.*	VOX [Concerto 20]	(S) 11010
* BADURA-SKODA	*Vienna State Opera Orch.*	WESTMINSTER [Concerto 24]	(M) 18662

If you haven't discovered pianist Brendel yet, you should. This man plays Mozart as well as he plays Chopin, a feat unheard of in this age of musical specialization. His recording here is poetic and individual, and marked with exquisite workmanship.

Lili Kraus loves Mozart—and I love Lili Kraus ever since I was bowled over by the set of Mozart violin-piano sonatas she made with Szymon Goldberg (now out of print). Skill, insight, and a born feeling for Mozart are all to be heard. The sound is warm.

Another great lady, the late Clara Haskil, delivers a penetrating, even trenchant reading that is a source of fascination for Mozrt lovers. Haskil was one of the best European pianists of a generation ago; her playing is always unshowy and deeply reasoned. Fricsay's accompaniment is unusually sympathetic. The sound is satisfactory. [The coupling is with the greatest of all Mozart piano concertos.]

Haebler is another lady we must respect. Her playing is alive and graceful.

Badura-Skoda's old mono recording is sensitive, but the sound is quite thin.

PIANO CONCERTO NO. 20 IN D MINOR (K. 466)

This, for most music lovers, is Mozart's greatest concerto. It is the first of his two concertos in the minor mode, the other being *No. 24*. Both these works have a special brooding, contemplative quality.

No. 20 is a deceptively simple concerto, with the solo piano part often naked and exposed. A simple melodic line, such as Mozart writes here, demands far more from a pianist than technique: it demands heart.

* * * BRENDEL, BOETTCHER	*Vienna Volksoper Orch.*	TURNABOUT	(M) 4095 (S) 34095 [Beethoven, Rondo in B-Flat]

* * MATTHEWS, SWAROWSKY	*Vienna State Opera Orch.*	VANGUARD [Concerto 24]	(S)	142
* * HASKIL, SWOBODA	*Winterthur Symphony*	WESTMINSTER [Concerto 19]	(M)	18380
* HAEBLER, MELLES	*Vienna Symphony Orch.*	VOX [Concerto 19]	(M) 11010 (S) 511010	
* DE LA BRUCHOLLERIE, PAUMGARTNER	*Salzburg Mozarteum*	NONESUCH [Concerto 23]	(M) 1072 (S) 71072	
* NOVAES, SWAROWSKY	*Vienna Pro Musica*	VOX [Concerto 9]	(M)	8430
* BADURA-SKODA, HORVAT	*Vienna State Opera Orch.*	WESTMINSTER [Concerto 23]	(M)	18225

Brendel plays with soul, and with a beautifully limpid tone.

Matthews beguiles the ear and has the musical maturity demanded here. [His disc is backed with the other great Mozart concerto in the minor mode.]

Clara Haskil, on so-so mono, is concerned, intense, and very fine indeed.

Haebler, an expert Mozartean, is poised and vivacious, but less striking than the artists mentioned above.

De la Bruchollerie is very romantic—not my type of Mozart.

Novaes is delicate, but her disc has poor orchestra work, and the mono sound is sadly aged.

Badura-Skoda, in what is one of his best performances, is strikingly good. However, he has indifferent accompaniment, and the mono disc is badly aged.

PIANO CONCERTO NO. 21 IN C (K. 467)

This is the concerto "made famous" by the film *Elvira Madigan,* which uses the striking performance by Geza Anda on high-priced DGG records. This is really a happy work, even carefree. It is blessed with an enchanting slow movement (used in the film) that is magic itself. It is hopeless to convey the appeal of this movement in mere words, but Sackville-West tries: "The dream-like *Andante* of this concerto, with its muted strings, endless cantilena, and gently lapping accompaniment in twelve-eight time, ranks among the most lovely things in music, and therefore in all music."

* * GILELS, BARSHAI	*Moscow Chamber Orch.*	ARTIA [Haydn, Concerto in D]	(M)	159
* TIPO, PERLEA	*Vienna Pro Musica Orch.*	VOX [Vivaldi, Concerto]	STPL-513010	

Gilels is shimmering and dedicated. The sound is wavery in places, however, at least on my copy.

Tipo is imbued with musical feeling, but his disc is not otherwise remarkable.

For those who crave this music there are several striking performances on high-priced discs. The old Schnabel performance on Angel stands alone; Anda on DGG and Casadesus on Columbia are both sonically good and intensely poetic.

PIANO CONCERTO NO. 22 IN E-FLAT (K. 482)

In 1785 Mozart interrupted his work on *The Marriage of Figaro* to write this concerto and two others. This is a highly melodic concerto with a brilliant piano part.

* * BRENDEL, ANGERER	*Vienna Chamber Orch.*	Vox (S) (5) 12170 [Haydn, Concerto Opus 21]	
* BADURA-SKODA	*Vienna Konzerthaus Orch.*	WESTMINSTER (M) 1866 [Concerto 14]	

Brendel, that unimpeachable Mozartian, is all elegance and feeling. Badura-Skoda is very enjoyable, on a still-hearable mono disc.

PIANO CONCERTO NO. 23 IN A (K. 488)

Written in 1786, this is a "relatively simple" Mozart concerto—unpretentious, with a most eloquent slow movement. It is one of the most popular of the Mozart piano concertos.

* * * KLIEN, MAAG	*Vienna Volksoper Orch.*	TURNABOUT (S) 34286 [Concerto 16]	
* DE LA BRUCHOLLERIE, PAUMGARTNER	*Salzburg Mozarteum*	NONESUCH (S) 71072 [Concerto 20]	
* BADURA-SKODA, HORVAT	*Vienna State Opera Orch.*	WESTMINSTER (M) 18225 [Concerto 20]	

Klien and Maag provide an unassailable team of Mozart purveyors. Klien is fresh and lyrical. The work between soloist and orchestra is especially well-knit. The orchestra playing is exuberantly alive, spirited rather than polished.

De la Bruchollerie delivers a romantic reading. The sound is clear.

Badura-Skoda, one of the most widely hailed Mozart interpreters of the 1950's, is trenchant and enjoyable, on a mono disc with thinnish sound.

PIANO CONCERTO NO. 24 IN C MINOR (K. 491)

This concerto is superb music; it should not be missed by any Mozart lover. It was written in 1786, five weeks before the production of *The Marriage of Figaro.* Mozart utterly ignored the pleasant flipperies that his audience really wanted; instead, to quote the great Mozart biographer Alfred Einstein, "Mozart evidently needed to indulge in an explosion of dark, tragic, passionate emotion."

* * * MATTHEWS, SWAROWSKY	Vienna Symphony Orch.	VANGUARD [Concerto 20]	(S)	142
* * KLIEN, MAAG	Vienna Volksoper Orch.	TURNABOUT [Fant. K. 475; Piano Sonata 14]	(S)	34178
* VON SCHILHAWSKY, ALBERT	Radio Bavaria Orch.	NONESUCH [Concerto 18]	(S) (7)	1059
* BADURA-SKODA, PROHASKA	Vienna Symphony Orch.	WESTMINSTER [Concerto 27]	(M)	18267

Matthews has sweep, dramatic passion, and virile beauty of phrasing. This is one of the best existing readings of this concerto.

Klien is extremely good, with all the virtues ascribed to him in the other write-ups on these pages. The vibrant orchestral work is admirable.

The Von Schilhawsky reading is most lyrical, but is outclassed. However, this is a perfectly acceptable disc with good sound.

The Badura-Skoda disc, well-played, is old and stiff-sounding.

PIANO CONCERTO NO. 25 IN C (K. 503)

This lovely, serene concerto was written in 1786 for public performance in Vienna.

| * * * BRENDEL, ANGERER | Vienna Pro Musica Orch. | TURNABOUT [Concerto 27] | (M) 4129 (S) 34129 |

Brendel provides a model of clarity—no easy task. The playing is penetrating and crystal-clear. This reading has been highly praised; it is one of the best to be had at any price. *Stereo Record Guide* comments: "Altogether delightful Mozartean charm and the character of Brendel's playing are matched by an orchestral contribution with a strong personality of its own." To my ears, the orchestral playing is less than refined, but this disc is a joy.

PIANO CONCERTO NO. 26 IN D (K. 537)
("CORONATION")

This is a longish concerto—a full half hour; it was perhaps the most popular Mozart piano concerto of the nineteenth century. The grand subtitle, "Coronation," is due not to any regality of the work but to the fact that Mozart performed it in Frankfurt during the coronation festivities of Leopold II, in 1790. This work does not stand as one of the supreme Mozart concertos. As John Burk remarks, "Its place is lower on the slopes of Parnassus."

But there is much melodic charm and a spell-binding slow movement in what remains a formal, even rhetorical concerto.

* * * KLIEN, MAAG	*Vienna Volksoper Orch.*	TURNABOUT	34194
		[Fant. K. 397; Piano Sonata 17]	
* * KRAUS, RIVOLI	*Amsterdam Ensemble*	TURNABOUT	(S) 34194
		[Concerto 19]	
* RICHTER-HAASER, KERTESZ	*Vienna Ensemble*	EVEREST	(S) 3161
		[Concerto 17]	

Klien and Maag win here, with a warm-blooded, delectable reading as good as any on records.

The great Lili Kraus is always authoritative in Mozart; she is beautifully poised. This is also an outstanding disc, just a shade outclassed by the ensemble work of Klien-Maag.

Richter-Haaser is quite restrained and almost bloodless, despite sturdy, lively accompaniment from Kertesz. *Stereo Record Guide:* "At times the pianist almost goes out of his way to secure an effect of tinselled elegance."

PIANO CONCERTO NO. 27 IN B-FLAT (K. 595)

Composed at the beginning of Mozart's last year, 1791, this is often termed his "farewell" to the great series of piano concertos. It is an even-flowing work, appealing rather than overwhelming.

* * * BRENDEL, ANGERER	*Vienna Volksoper Orch.*	TURNABOUT (S) (3)	4129
		[Concerto 25]	
* * * HASKIL, FRICSAY	*Bavarian State Orch.*	HELIODOR	(S) 25042
		[Concerto 19]	
* BACKHAUS, BOEHM	*Vienna Philharmonic Orch.*	LONDON	(S) STS-15062
		[Piano Sonata 11]	

Brendel wins here, with highest marks for intelligence, sympathy, and musicianship.

Clara Haskil's Mozart was classic, and needs no extra praise from me. This is a probing, searching, intense Mozart, and Fricsay delivers dynamic accompaniment. The sound is agreeable, but not vivid.

Backhaus is ponderous but highly enjoyable—he was one of the German giants of the keyboard before World War II. However, *Stereo Record Guide* disagrees somewhat and says: "Backhaus is magisterial, but rhythmically rather uneven, and the performance does not always flow as smoothly as one might wish." The sound is rather dry.

CONCERTOS FOR TWO OR MORE PIANOS These are winning pieces —not very profound—but highly enjoyable, which sound particularly good in stereo.

PIANO CONCERTO (THREE PIANOS), IN F (K. 242)

This is tasteful music, written for an aristocratic amateur lady pianist, Contessa Lodron, and her two daughters. As John Burk remarks, "The three ladies in flowing satins can be imagined as a captivating sight . . . . There are no fast tempos, nothing to dismay amateur fingers, except perhaps the cadenzas. It is amiable music, easy to play, and could not have exerted from its composer much more than his ready facility."

This work is much favored by famous musical families that want to show off their progeny—as an example, recordings by the Casadesus and Menuhin clans.

* * HEPHZIBAH, YALTAH, JEREMY, AND YEHUDI MENUHIN	*London Philharmonic Orch.*	SERAPHIM [2-Piano Concerto 10]	(S) 60072
* * SANCAN, POMMIER, SILEIE		NONESUCH [Concerto 10]	(S) 71028

Seraphim offers a scintillating disc. The Menuhin clan is presented *en famille* in Mozart music-making. Yehudi Menuhin presides beamingly from the podium; son Jeremy and his aunts Hephzibah and Yaltah (Yehudi Menuhin's sisters) perform this bubbly concerto. [On the reverse, son-in-law Fou Ts'ong, a first-rate and sensitive pianist, joins Yaltah in another fine concerto.]

The Nonesuch entry is also very good, and the tasteful soloists are beautifully together in style. A bit more of the Menuhins' lightness and aplomb would have been in order, but this is an entirely commendable disc.

CONCERTO NO. 10 FOR TWO PIANOS, IN E-FLAT
(K. 365)

This is a *gemutlich*, homey concerto, without bravura; it does not make great technical demands upon the players. Mozart supposedly wrote it in 1779 for performance with his sister.

* * * BRENDEL, KLIEN	3-Vox Turnabout [Sonata K. 448]	VBX-66 (3) 4064
* * * H. MENUHIN, FOU TS'ONG, Y. MENUHIN	Seraphim [3-Piano Concerto K. 242]	(S) 60072
* * SANCAN, POMMIER, SILEIE	Nonesuch [3-Piona Concerto]	(S) 71028
* * GILELS, ZAK	Monitor [Saint-Saens, Carnival of the Animals]	(M) 2006
* * BADURA-SKODA, GIANOLI	Westminster [Concerto 7]	(M) 18546

Miraculously, all of these five entires afford felicitous Mozart style, and happy listening.

The Brendel-Klien version is sparkle itself, and my favorite. I should comment here that Mozart wrote beautifully for modern stereo — neat, balanced, alternating melodies.

The extremely delicate style of Fou Ts'ong and Yaltah Menuhin stands out on a winning disc.

Sancan and Pommier do not use Mozart's cadenzas—which wouldn't bother Mozart at all, and shouldn't bother you. The two are zestful, and very much together.

Gilels and Zak are superb on decent mono.

Badura-Skoda and Gianoli are also good on fair mono.

CONCERTOS FOR SOLO WIND INSTRUMENT AND ORCHESTRA

Many eighteenth-century composers (Vivaldi and Telemann, for example) wrote far more solo concertos for wind instruments than did Mozart, but no composer ever came close to Mozart's natural grace and expertise in writing for winds. To quote Edward Greenfield, "His music seems to go right to the heart of the instrument he is writing for, and reveals in glowing fashion every facet of its personality."

Mozart composed his wind concertos in each case with a specific player in mind—a friend, or a *musikant* (amateur), or a virtuoso. What is remarkable is that almost none of these works are merely curiosity pieces today—the fate that has befallen most writing for solo horn or clarinet, etc. They are, instead, extremely popular. The lovely, great clarinet concerto, the four exuberant horn concertos, the shimmering flute concertos, the elegant concerto for flute and harp, and the *Sinfonia Concertante* for four solo winds and orchestra—these are fully developed works by a master. Mozart had an intimate understanding of each wind instrument—which register was the easiest for the player, which tones brought out certain colors, which other instruments blended best with it, and so on.

The reader may perhaps assume that *any* composer who sets out to write, say, a concerto for horn and orchestra, knows the technical side of the instrument upside down. As a horn player myself, I can assure you that most composers simply write melodies they feel would sound agreeable when played by a French horn—and hope that the horn player can cope with it. This is why almost no horn concertos survive—Mozart's four are the major exception—or reach our concert halls regularly.

CONCERTO FOR BASSOON IN B-FLAT (K. 191)

This is the best bassoon concerto ever written. The slow movement is an amazingly successful attempt to draw out grace and a sense of tragic burlesque from that brusque instrument.

* * ZUKERMAN, FAERBER	*Wuerttemberg Chamber Orch.*	TURNABOUT (S) 4039 [Weber, Andante; Bassoon Concerto]
* * ZUKERMAN, FAEBER	*Wuerttemberg Chamber Orch.*	4-TURNABOUT (S) 34188/91 [Clarinet Concerto; Flute Concerto 1, 2; Flute-Harp Concerto; Horn Concerto; Sinfonia Concertante K. 297b]
* * BIDLO, SMETACEK	*Prague Symphony Orch.*	CROSSROADS (S) 2216 0168 [Flute-Harp Concerto]
* BIDLO, ANCERL	*Czech Philharmonic Orch.*	PARLIAMENT (M) 104 [Violin Concerto 4]
* KLEPAC, MAERZENDORFER	*Mozarteum Orch.*	HELIODOR (S) 25002 [Flute Concerto 1]

In its first and final movement this wry concerto bubbles over with good humor, and this is best caught by Zukerman. His reading is available on a single disc or in a very good four-record compilation of wind music by Mozart.

Bidlo sounds like a prize bassoonist; he gets zestful assistance from the sturdy Czechs under Smetacek.

Bidlo's performance with Ancerl is limited by barely acceptable mono sound.

Klepac also sounds like a virtuoso of the singular bassoon. *High Fidelity*: "Unfortunately, the plodding accompaniment militates against the fine solo work."

CONCERTO FOR CLARINET IN A (K. 622)

This is Mozart's last concerto for any instrument. It is certainly his greatest in the wind category, and the most popular clarinet concerto ever written. With the sole exception of the haunting *Clarinet Quintet* by Brahms, no other work by any composer has so caught the dulcet and pensive beauty of the clarinet. There is a radiant and especially poignant coloration to all of Mozart's music written in his final year—such as this *Clarinet Concerto*, the *Piano Concerto No. 27*, and the *Requiem* itself.

* * * GEUSER, FRICSAY	*Berlin Radio Symphony Orch.*	HELIODOR (S) 25017 [Violin Concerto 5]	
* * * DOERR, LEITNER	*Bamberg Symphony*	NONESUCH (S) 71074 [Sinfonia K. 364]	
* * * PRINZ, MUENCHINGER	*Vienna Philharmonic Orch.*	LONDON (S) STS-15071 [Flute-Harp Concerto]	
* * GOODMAN, MUNCH	*Boston Symphony Orch.*	VICTOR VICS (S) 1402 [Clarinet Quintet]	
* * MICHAELS, REICHERT	*Westphalian Symphony Orch.*	VOX (5) 11110 [Clarinet Quintet]	
* * MICHAELS, REICHERT	*Westphalian Symphony Orch.*	4-TURNABONT (S) 34188/91 [Bassoon Concerto; Flute Concerto 1, 2; Flute-Harp Concerto; Horn Concerto; Sinfonia Concertante K. 297b]	
* LANCELOT, PAILLARD	*Paillard Ensemble*	MUSIC GUILD (S) 136 [Flute-Harp Concerto]	
WLACH, RODZINSKI	*Vienna State Opera Orch.*	WESTMINSTER (M) 18287 [Bassoon Concerto]	

The playing of Heinrich Geuser is top-notch. This splendid, sensitive performance has only recently been released in this country, which proves again the many efficacies of low-priced record merchandising. *High Fidelity:* "Heliodor has come up with a beauty. . . . Geuser is a marvelous musician with an excellent technique and creamy tone." Conductor Fricsay provides solid support. [The coupling is with a lovely violin concerto played to the romantic hilt by Oistrakh.]

Nonesuch is also a winner, with a buoyant performance by Doerr, a clarinetist with strong musical personality. The sound is good. [The coupling is first-rate.]

Prinz is an elegant player, with a singing style. [The coupling is superb.]

Benny Goodman is careful, studious, and pleasant. He receives powerful support from the Boston Symphony. The sound is resonant.

Michaels is another gratifying player. His performance is also available in Turnabout's four-record box of goodies—Mozart wind music, Turnabout 34199/91. [The coupling is with another great Mozart work for clarinet, the *Clarinet Quintet.*]

Lancelot is clean and competent; the sound is fair. [The coupling is lovely music, handsomely played.]

Wlach's performance is dull.

CONCERTO FOR FLUTE, NO. 1 IN G (K. 313)

Mozart, who claimed to dislike the flute (or rather, bad flute players), composed a set of "short and easy" flute concertos and quartets in 1778 for a dilettane named de Jean. Mozart was supposed to get 200 gulden— but he only got half that sum. And, as usual, he was hard-pressed for cash.

In this concerto Mozart exploits the limpid colors and winged quality of the flute.

* * BARWAHSER, PRITCHARD	*Vienna Symphony Orch.*	PHILIPS WS [Concerto 2]	(M/S) 9011
* * WANAUSEK, SWAROWSKY	*Vienna Pro Musica*	VOX [Concerto 2]	(M) 8130
* TASSINARI, PAUMGARTNER	*Camerata Academy*	HELIODOR [Bassoon Concerto]	(S) 25002

A rather rigid, but valid reading comes from Barwahser. *Stereo Record Guide* comments: "This is cool playing, very beautiful in timbre and phrasing . . . at the same time rather detached." The rechanneled sound is decent, an improvement over the booming bass and wiry treble of the original mono disc.

The old mono Wanausek disc is the most lyrical of all and still highly enjoyable.

Tassinari plays efficiently, without much grace. [The coupling is excellent.]

CONCERTO FOR FLUTE, NO. 2 IN D (K. 314)

This concerto is spirited and rather carefree. In the finale, Mozart uses a theme that appears three years later in his opera, *The.Abduction from the Seraglio.*

This concerto is held to be a rearrangement of an oboe concerto which Mozart wrote in Salzburg the year before, and which is now lost.

* * * WANAUSEK, SWAROWSKY	*Vienna Pro Musica*	Vox [Concerto 1]	(M) 8130
* * RAMPAL, GOLDSCHMIDT	*Lamoureux Orch.*	7-EVEREST	(S) 3194
* LINDE, FAERBER	*Wuerttemberg Charmber Orch., Heilbronn*	4-TURNABOUT [other Mozart Wind Concertos]	34188/91
* BARWAHSER, PRITCHARD	*Vienna Symphony Orch.*	PHILIPS WS [Concerto 1]	(M/S) 9011
* MARION, RISTENPART		NONESUCH [Concerto 1]	(S) 71126

The best performance remains captured on clean mono, played by the remarkable Camillo Wanausek. A panagyric from the crack English critic Shawe-Taylor: "We have no hesitation in describing Wanausek . . . simply on recorded evidence, as great. He is a peerless Mozartean stylist, the shaping and coloring of whose phrases is hauntingly beautiful. If this is not Mozartean perfection, then such perfection is unattainable in this world."

Rampal is impeccable as always, if you want to buy seven records of flute music.

Linde comes off well, with a vivacious reading, available in an attractive four-record album of Mozart music for wind soloists.

Barwahser is cool and limpid; his disc takes some getting used to. But this is a good performance, with solid rather than amiable orchestral support.

Marion is sprightly and quite hearable.

CONCERTO FOR FLUTE AND HARP, IN C (K. 299)

Here is "music for the two blissful innocents of the orchestra," to quote Edward Greenfield. "These essentially delicate and ethereal instruments combine here to produce sonorities that sometimes seem to have no business on this prosaic earth of ours."

This is irresistible "salon" Mozart. The combination of flute and harp is refined and aristocratic—grace itself. The harp part is rather primitive, as the instrument at that time lacked the mechanical devices of the modern harp we know. Don't overlook this concerto, if Wolfgang Amadeus is your man.

* * * PATERO, STORCK, FAERBER	*Wuerttemberg Chamber Orch.*	TURNABOUT [Adagio K. 617a; Fantasia K. 608]	(S) 34087
* * * RAMPAL, LASKINE	*Paillard Ensemble*	MUSIC GUILD [Clarinet Concerto]	(S) 136

450   MOZART, W.

* * * TRIPP, JELLINEK, MUENCHINGER	*Vienna Philharmonic Orch.*	LONDON (S) STS-15071 [Clarinet Concerto]
* * WANAUSEK, JELLINEK	*Vienna Pro Musica*	VOX (M) 8550 [Adagio K. 617; Andante K. 315]
* NOVAK, PATRAS, PESEK	*Prague Symphony Orch.*	CROSSROADS (S) 2216-0168 [Bassoon Concerto]

The imaginative, impeccably played Patero-Storck version is outstanding, a model of sympathetic Mozart playing. *Stereo Record Guide* raves: "Here is a disc not to be missed by any true Mozartean. The performance of the *Flute and Harp Concerto* is possibly the best available. [The coupling is unusual, pleasant, slight music of curious interest: A *Fantasia for Mechanical Organ* (played on a regular organ) and the most delicate *Adagio for Glass Harmonica*.]

On the Rampal-Laskine disc you get not only the great Rampal but the stately French harp playing of Lily Laskine, perhaps the most famous harpist of a generation ago. Even Toscanini, usually above such things, agreed to conduct a harp concerto when the admirable Lily was soloist. The sound is a bit undefined. [The backing is with a lively reading of the great *Clarinet Concerto*.]

Tripp and Jellinek also provide a most gracious disc, firmly supported by one of the best Mozart conductors in the business, Karl Muenchinger. *Stereo Record Guide:* "The listener is completely carried away by the refined beauty of phrase and phrasing. Muenchinger and the Vienna Philharmonic must also have been moved, for they play with rare insight and feeling throughout both scores." [Backing is with a pure reading of the great *Clarinet Concerto*.]

The old Vox mono disc, featuring the superb flutist Wanausek, is still worthy and most hearable.

Novak and Patras offer cut-and-dried, unimaginative Mozart, still sympathetic but not as poetic as the entries mentioned above. [The coupling is with a first-rate performance of the worthwhile *Bassoon Concerto*.]

CONCERTI FOR HORN (K. 412, 417, 447, 495)

The four horn concerti are delightful, lighthearted pieces. They are also first-rate Mozart. They were written for Mozart's crony, Ignatz Leitgeb, an erstwhile horn player in the Kapelle Orchestra in Salzburg.

* * * BRAIN, KARAJAN	*Philharmonia Orch.*	SERAPHIM (M) 60040 [Horn Program]
* * LINDER, SWAROWSKY	*Vienna Orch.*	VANGUARD (S) 173

* BARBOTEU, DOUATTE	*Paris Coll. Mus.*	MONITOR (S) 2118
STEFEK, ANCERL	*Czech Philharmonic Orch.*	CROSSROADS (M) 2216 0035 (S) 2216 0036 [No. 3; Sinfonia Concerto K. Anh. 9]
MUEHLBACHER, BAUER-THEUSSL	*Vienna Volksoper Orch.*	4-TURNABOUT (S) 34188/91 [Bassoon Concerto; Clarinet Concerto; Flute Concerto 1, 2; Flute-Harp Concerto; Sinfonia Concertante K. 297b]

Dennis Brain was a world-famous virtuoso of the French horn—the only one to ever reach such heights. He died in 1957 at the age of 36. His playing conveys a range of timbre, a personality and elegance yet to be heard from another hornist on discs. If you fall in love with this record, you'll be interested in Brain's classic disc of all four of Mozart's horn concertos, which has been an amazing best-seller over the years on expensive Angel. The mono sound here is decent.

Linder has a fine singing sound—effective, but miles away from the great Dennis Brain.

Barboteu is technically brilliant, but I cannot stand that wah-wah vibrato that French French hornists dote upon. (Brain and Linder, listed above, play in the German, classical tradition of horn players. The "French" horn has nothing to do with France; it developed from the old hunting horn.)

Stefek is pretty good, but also has a vibrato that throws me off completely.

Muehlbacher is quite undistinguished. *High Fidelity:* "He has some excellent moments, and never really comes a cropper. . . . But one worries constantly that he might."

VIOLIN CONCERTOS Mozart wrote his five authenticated violin concertos between April and December, 1775. At least three of them are masterpieces—small-sized, gentle works written with consummate skill and lasting freshness.

They are anything but bravura, showcase pieces. As John Burk, that eminent Mozartean, remarks, "The violin concertos of Mozart, or at least the best of them, have a firm and enduring place in the heart of every violinist who puts music as an art above music as a personal opportunity."

We always think of Mozart as a pianist, and it comes as a shock to remember that he was also a talented violinist. Sometimes he earned his living by the violin; he did so in 1775, the year of the incredible five violin concertos. After much dickering, Mozart wrangled an appointment as concertmaster of the Salzburg court orchestra. This was not a congenial post nor an easy one; Mozart was expected to act both as first violinist and as leader of the orchestra, and also to appear as soloist. And his duties as composer were staggering. In a typical week, quite as a matter of course, he would dash off music for a patriotic holiday, for a grandson's birthday, and for a sudden wedding announcement. And there was always a piece to be written immediately in honor of an unexpected but very distinguished visitor to court.

VIOLIN CONCERTO NO. 3 IN G (K. 216)

This lovely violin concerto shows a miraculous development over *No. 2*, which Mozart had written just three months before. To quote John Burk: "The spectacle of Mozart, aged nineteen, growing in musical stature from month to month in the succession of violin concertos, becomes miraculous in his *Third*. The orchestra takes on a new inner life, while the soloist has a constant, pliant singing line."

* * * MAKANOWITZKY, RISTENPART	*Saar Chamber Orch.*	NONESUCH [Concerto 4]	(S)	71056
* * KOGAN, SANDERLING	*National Philharmonic*	BAROQUE [Khrennikov]	(M) (S)	1866 2866
* * FUCHS, GOOSSENS	*London Symphony Orch.*	EVEREST [Hindemith, Concerto]	(S)	3040
* OISTRAKH, BARSHAI	*National Philharmonic*	ARTIA [Szymanowski]	(M)	156
* LAREDO, MITCHELL	*National Symphony Orch.*	VICTROLA VIC [Bach, Concerto 1]	(S)	1129

Leading a very good field is Makanowitzky, in a marvelously dew-fresh, exhilarating, intimate reading. I have nothing but praise for this exciting musician, whose style is diametrically opposed to the cool, classical poise of a Heifetz.

The admirable Russian violinist Kogan presents an uncluttered, rather intense reading that is first-rate. This man has a gently singing tone ideal for Mozart. The sound is just so-so.

Fuchs is extremely good; he plays with effortless art. This is a reading worthy of our respect. *Stereo Record Guide* comments: "Among the very best Mozart stereo discs. . . . Fuchs' style is less bland than Oistrakh's and less polished too. But this performance is so spontaneous-sounding throughout and the playing so affectionate in the slow movement (both from orchestra and soloist) that one can enjoy it equally, if in a different way." [The coupling is fine if you want a seldom-played modern masterpiece.]

The great David Oistrakh is warm and endearing, and he has firm support. The mono sound is of indifferent quality.

The young Bolivian violinist Jamie Laredo is agreeable in an intimate, small-scaled reading without much charm.

VIOLIN CONCERTO NO. 4 IN D (K. 218)

Here is more solid gold. This bright, inventive concerto rivals Mozart's *Fifth Concerto* in popularity. The *Fourth* seems to have been the violin concerto preferred by Mozart himself.

* * * MAKANOWITZKY, RISTENPART	*Saar Chamber Orch.*	NONESUCH [Concerto 3]	(S) 71056
* * PAUK, FAERBER	*Wuerttemberg Chamber Orch.*	TURNABOUT [Concerto 5]	(S) 34186
* NOVAK, TALICH	*Czech Philharmonic Orch.*	PARLIAMENT [Bassoon Concerto]	(M) 104

Makanowitzky delivers an amazingly fresh, appealing reading that is pure joy. Mozart would have loved this violinist. The coupling is fine; and so is the sound.

Pauk plays with verve; this is a sophisticated reading. [The coupling is excellent.]

On fair mono, Novak is agreeable, little more.

VIOLIN CONCERTO NO. 5 IN A (K. 219)

The *Fifth* is another violin masterpiece from that incredibly productive year, 1775. Mozart tossed off this brilliant concerto in December, two months after he wrote his *Fourth*.

* * * MILSTEIN, BLECH	*Festival Orch.*	PICKWICK [Bach, Concerto 1]	(S) 4013
* * OISTRAKH, KONWITSCHNY	*Saxon State Orch.*	HELIODOR [Clarinet Concerto]	(S) 25017
* PAUK, FAERBER	*Wuerttemberg Chamber Orch.*	TURNABOUT [Concerto 4]	(S) 34186

Milstein plays with a fine conception of classical poise and purity that quite outclasses all other readings in our category; this disc can stand with any rival edition. The coupling is excellent; the sound is good.

David Oistrakh delivers his usual smooth and musical performance. This is a rather swollen, romanticized reading which is not to my personal taste. However, Oistrakh's admirers will delight in this colorful version. The violinist gets plodding support from Konwitschny. A dissenting opinion from *High Fidelity* reads: "Oistrakh gives a polished account, comparable to the readings of Menuhin, Milstein, and Stern, his most formidable competition."

Pauk is sympathetic in a well-knit, lively performance, but he is outclassed by his lofty rivals.

CHAMBER MUSIC FEATURING WIND INSTRUMENTS Some of Mozart's most endearing and most popular works are to be found here. The melting Clarinet Quintet, the polished Oboe Quartet are masterpieces of the genre, unsurpassed by any other composer.

QUARTETS FOR FLUTE AND STRINGS (K. 285, 285a, 285b, 298)

The Flute Quartets are early, slight pieces of much delicacy and lightness.

* * * NICOLET	*Drolc Quartet*	MACE	(S)	9029
		[Brahms, Clarinet Quintet]		
* BARON	*Fine Arts Quartet Members*	CONCERTO-DISC	(S)	215
* WANAUSEK	*Europa Quartet Members*	VOX	(500)	830
* WANAUSEK	*Europa Quartet Members*	3-VOX	(S) SVBX-548	
		[Various Mozart works]		

Shimmering flute playing is provided by Nicolet. [The coupling is superb music, handsomely played.]

Baron is a fine flutist. The sound is rather dry.

The ordinarily fine playing of Wanausek is lost on the Vox discs. To quote *Stereo Record Review:* "The extremely sensitive flutist Wanausek is burdened here with boxed-in sound, to say nothing of the slithery, schmaltzy sound of the first violinist."

QUARTET FOR OBOE AND STRINGS, IN F (K. 370)

This is a debonair little gem which was written for Friedrich Ramm of Munich, the best oboist of Mozart's day.

* * * HOLLIGER	*Pascal Quartet*	MONITOR	(S)	2115
		[Quintet K. 581]		
* SOUS, ENDRES, RUF, SCHMIDT		TURNABOUT	(S) (3)	4035
		[Quintet K. 407; Trio, K. 498]		
* SOUS, ENDRES, RUF, SCHMIDT		VOX	(S) (50)	1000
		[Horn Quintet]		
* SOUS, ENDRES, RUF, SCHMIDT		3-VOX	(S) SVBX-548	
		[Various Mozart works]		

Holliger is superb and the Pascal Quartet provides fine string work. This is one of the best performances available today. [The coupling is excellent.]

The unimpressive Sous performance is available in no less than three combinations with other works. Dissenting opinion from *Stereo Record Guide* which finds it "a good performance, well recorded." Nathan Broder in *High Fidelity,* 1965, was far less enthusiastic: "Sous plays at a practically unyielding mezzo-forte throughout. This is one of the less appealing versions of this music on records."

QUINTET FOR CLARINET AND STRINGS, IN A (K. 581)

This is one of the beloved flowers of the entire chamber music repertory. As with the great Clarinet Concerto, it was written for the clarinetist Anton Stadler. This masterpiece is Mozart's greatest chamber music for a solo wind instrument. It was written in 1789, a ripe year in Mozart's musical maturity. Mozart loved the clarinet and had been bowled over when he heard them in the famous Mannheim Orchestra. He wrote wistfully to his father, "If only we had clarinets in our orchestra! What wonderful things one can do with them. . . ."

This is a serious quintet in the true sense, not just a display piece for clarinet with harmless string accompaniment. The Quintet was highly progressive music when first written. A string quartet and a clarinet were matched and blended in a manner that no one before Mozart had conceived of. The felicitous Sackville-West, speaking of Mozart's *Clarinet Quintet,* must be quoted here: "Many people have been led to explore the world of chamber music through this gate; It is difficult to imagine a listener who could remain deaf to a flow of melody so limpid and serene. The charms of the clarinet—its incomparably gentle legato, its agility, its sudden plunges down two octaves into a deep, brown pool—all are exhibited by Mozart as though he had just fallen in love with the instrument."

* * GEUSER	*Drolc Quartet*	MACE (S) 9028 [Weber, Quintet]	
* KELL	*Fine Arts Quartet*	CONCERT-DISC 203	
* MICHAELS	*Endres Quartet*	VOX (5) 11110 [Clarinet Concerto]	
* MICHAELS	*Endres Quartet*	3-VOX SVBX-548 [Flute Quartets, Quintet K. 407, 452; Quartet K. 370; Trio K. 498]	
* WLACH	*Vienna Konzerthaus Quartet*	WESTMINSTER 18269	

| SIMENLAUER | *Pascal Quartet* | MONITOR   (S) 2115 |
| | | [Oboe Quartet] |

A thoughtful reading is provided by Geuser, with firm support from the Drolc Quartet. [The coupling is excellent.]

This reading with the famous clarinetist Reginald Kell is first-rate, and Kell has nuances that few clarinets can achieve. There is no coupling, however, which makes this an expensive buy.

The Michaels reading, available also in a Vox box of three discs, is competent.

The old Wlach reading on mono is still entirely enjoyable. Harold Schonberg, in 1955: "Wlach is a graceful clarinetist with style and tradition."

Simenlauer is also serious, and musically intelligent. The Pascal Quartet is fine. [The coupling is first-rate Mozart.]

Superb readings of this great *Clarinet Quintet* are to be had on expensive discs from Boskovsky on London and DePeyer on Angel.

QUINTET FOR HORN AND STRINGS, IN E-FLAT (K. 407)

This plump and unpretentious work written in 1782 preceded the horn concertos that Mozart wrote for his friend Leitgeb. This is pleasant, simple Mozart.

* * BARROWS	*Fine Arts Quartet*	CONCERT-DISC 204
		[Oboe Quartet]
* SPETH	*Pascal Quartet*	MONITOR (S) 2114
		[Quintet K. 46]
* HUBER	*Endres Quartet*	VOX (50) 1000
		[Oboe Quartet]
* HUBER	*Endres Quartet*	TURNABOUT (3) 4035
		[Various Mozart pieces]
* HUBER	*Endres Quartet*	3-VOX SVBX-548
		[Various Mozart pieces]

The felicitous hornist John Barrows is excellent here; the Fine Arts Quartet provide neat teamwork. [The coupling is good.]

Speth is enjoyable. [The coupling is with a spurious but entertaining transcription of a Mozart Serenade for winds.]

Huber provides a competent, unexciting reading that *Stereo Record Guide* found to be "a good performance, well recorded." But I definitely agree with *High Fidelity's* Nathan Broder who found that "the sound of the horn is sepulchral and blurry." [The Huber performance is available on three different couplings.]

QUINTET FOR PIANO AND WINDS IN E-FLAT
(K. 452)

This work is a masterpiece scored for piano, oboe, clarinet, horn, and bassoon.

After the first performance in Vienna in 1784, Mozart wrote to his father, "I consider it to be the best work I have ever composed."

* * BRENDEL	*Hungarian Quintet Members*	Vox (S) (5) 11520 [Beethoven, Quintet]
* * BRENDEL	*Hungarian Quintet Members*	3-Vox (S) SVBX-548 [Various Mozart works]
* * GLAZER	*N. Y. Woodwind Quintet Members*	CONCERT-DISC (S) 213 [Beethoven, Quintet]
* L. BRAIN, WATERS, D. BRAIN, JAMES, HORSLEY		SERAPHIM (M) 60073 [Berkeley]

Brendel and the Hungarians play with finesse. This is a pleasing disc. Glazer and the New York Winds are robust and enjoyable.

The Seraphim disc is called "The Art of Dennis Brain" and displays that great hornest's incomparable virtues. The reading, however, is pallid. [The backing is a mild, conservative Trio, written to show off Brain's assured range and silver tone.] The 1953 sound is just fair, rather metallic.

TRIO IN E-FLAT FOR CLARINET, VIOLA, PIANO
(K. 498)

This is a gentle piece from 1786 in which the three instruments are beautifully matched.

* TRIEBSKORN, LEMMEN, LUDWIG	TURNABOUT (S) 4035 [Quartet K. 370; Quintet K. 407]
* TRIEBSKORN, LEMMEN, LUDWIG	3-Vox (S) SVBX-568 [Piano Trios]
* TRIEBSKORN, LEMMEN, LUDWIG	3-Vox (S) SVBX-548 [Various Mozart pieces]

The Triebskorn reading is bland, boring and unattractive. The same performance is available from Vox in no less than three various couplings.

STRING QUARTETS   By the age of seventeen Mozart had composed about a dozen indifferent string quartets. During the next ten years he was profoundly influenced by Haydn's string quartets; once he became aware of the great potentiality of the form, he took to quartets like a duck to water. His finest are the six masterpieces Nos. 14 through 19. These shining jewels were published by Mozart with a renowned dedication to his friend and admirer, Joseph Haydn.

COMPLETE RECORDINGS OF MOZART STRING QUARTETS

*	Barchet Quartet (Vol. 1, Nos. 1-10)	3-Vox	(M) VBX112
*	Barchet Quartet (Vol. 2, Nos. 11-17)	3-Vox	(M) VBX-13
*	Barchet Quartet (Vol. 3, Nos. 18-23)	3-Vox	(M) VBX-14

The earth-bound Barchet Quartet is inclined to efficient, hard-driven performances that have little of Mozart's singing, spontaneous character. Harold Schonberg in *Guide to Chamber Music*, 1955: "Dependable, but essentially routine playing. One would like to hear a greater degree of grace and volatility. There is something stolid about the way the Barchet Quartet shapes a phrase." The sound is usually acceptable.

MOZART STRING QUARTETS IN ALBUM

* * *	Fine Arts Quartet	3-Concert-Disc (S) 504 [No. 15, 16, 19, 21, 22, 23]

The trenchant Fine Arts Quartet is widely admired as one of the very best American string quartets. They are utterly musical and play in a lean, intense style. This highly praised collection consists of three quartets of the six which Mozart dedicated to Haydn, plus the last three quartets Mozart wrote. Nathan Broder in *High Fidelity*, 1965: "The Fine Arts Quartet displays its fine qualities. . . . Every man is an artist as well as a skilled musician. The sound is first-rate throughout, with good stereo directionality."

STRING QUARTET NO. 15 IN D (K. 421)

Mozart biographer John Burk: "Mozart's only quartet in a minor key (among the last ten quartets) is not only outstanding, it is one of his most sharply arresting and ferociously earnest works."

* * *	Yale Quartet	Vanguard (S) C-10019 [Quartet 21]

* *   *Fine Arts Quartet*   Concert-Disc   (S)   227
                                                    [Quartet 19]

The Yale Quartet is passionate and turbulent in this most "un-Mozartean" quartet. *Stereo Review* joins in: "Performance: taut and intense; recording: splendid; stereo quality: excellent." The sound is superb.

The Fine Arts ensemble is rewarding and eminent, but the special ambiance of sound that Vanguard captured for the Yale Quartet walks away with the honors here.

STRING QUARTET NO. 17 IN B-FLAT (K. 458) ("HUNTING")

This is one of Mozart's most loved quartets, with a rollicking "Hunt" theme in the first movement.

*   *Hungarian Quartet*   Vox   (S) (5) 12130
                                                    [Quartet 19]

*   *Hungarian Quartet*   3-Turnabout   (S) 3451/3
                                                    [with various Haydn and
                                                    Schubert Quartets]

The Hungarian Quartet is a smooth ensemble, and this is a neat performance. My complaint about this group is a lack of incisiveness and of body. This reading is available on one record or as part of a three-disc album.

STRING QUARTET NO. 19 IN C (K. 465) ("DISSONANT")

This is a great quartet, the last of the six which Mozart dedicated in 1785 to his "very celebrated and most dear friend, Joseph Haydn." The poignant first twenty-one bars of the piece caused no end of bewilderment when they were first heard; hence, the "Dissonant" Quartet.

* * *   *Fine Arts Quartet*   Concert-Disc   (S)   227
                                                    [Quartet 15]

*   *Hungarian Quartet*   Vox   (S) (5) 12130
                                                    [Quartet 17]

*   *Hungarian Quartet*   3-Turnabout   (S) 3451/3
                                                    [also Haydn and Schubert
                                                    Quartets]

*   *Barchet Quartet*   Dover   (M)   5200
                                                    [Quartet 18]

The Hungarian Quartet is well-recorded, but their bland, innocuous

Mozart is not for me. Their toothless version is available on a single disc or in a three-disc album.

The Barchet Quartet is competent here, little more.

STRING QUARTET NO. 20 IN D (K. 499)

This is a rather conventional quartet, probably deliberately written "conservatively" to please the publisher Hoffmeister in 1786.

Stuyvesant Quartet	NONESUCH [Quartet 21]	71035

Spirited playing by the Stuyvesant Quartet is messed up by fake pseudo-stereo electronics. *Stereo Review:* "Even with its low price tag, the Nonesuch disc is hardly very attractive."

STRING QUARTETS NOS. 21-23

The quartets Nos. 21, 22, and 23 were composed by Mozart with the hope of a dedication to King William of Prussia. The king was a cellist, and Mozart lovingly favors the cello in these quartets of supreme craftsmanship.

Roth Quartet	2-PHILLIPS WS (M/S) PHC-2-008	

The now-defunct Roth Quartet play intelligently, but the "re-processed" sound is harsh. Harold Schonberg in 1955: "Some nice things can be said about details of the Roth performance, but on the whole it is tonally rough and not absolutely secure in intonation." The luscious cello part is lyrically handled by the famous cellist Janos Starker.

STRING QUARTET NO. 21 IN D (K. 575)

This is an uncomplicated quartet of 1789, with a few of Haydn's light-hearted touches.

* * *	*Yale Quartet*	VANGUARD [Quartet 15]	C-10019
* * *	*Fine Arts Quartet*	CONCERT-DISC. [Quartet 16]	258
*	*Stuyvesant Quartet*	NONESUCH [Quartet 20]	71035

The Yale Quartet, in a stunning disc, are supreme here. *High Fidelity,* 1968: "The music is bathed in a sunny ambiance, high in grace and ingenuousness." [The coupling is excellent.]

The Fine Arts Quartet are also excellent — and a solid buy.

The recording of the Stuyvesant Quartet was originally on a small label called Philharmonic (owned by the Shulman brothers — two members of the Stuyvesant Quartet). The playing is incisive. *Stereo Review* on the unconvincing sound: "But I think it was a mistake for Nonesuch to give this 1952 tape the pseudo-stereo treatment, and to use the echo-chamber effect at that. The result is helpful neither to Mozart nor to the performers."

STRING QUARTET NO. 22 IN B-FLAT (K. 589)

This quartet of 1790, the second of the quartets for the King of Prussia, is smoothly flowing and highly agreeable.

* *	*Fine Arts Quartet*	CONCERT-DISC (S) 259 [Quartet 23]	

The Fine Arts Quartet let the music sing here. The ensemble work, as usual with this group, is excellent.

STRING QUARTET NO. 23 IN F (K. 590)

This absorbing music is Mozart's last quartet, and in biographer John Burk's words "it makes an exciting culmination to them all, in Mozart's most mature handling of the style. . . . The composer ends his adventures in the string quartet at the very top of his bent."

* * *	*Fine Arts Quartet*	CONCERT-DISC (S) 259 [Quartet 22]	
* * MORINI, GALIMIR, TRAMPLER, VARGA		WESTMINSTER (M) 9074 [Beethoven, Quartet 4]	

The Fine Arts Quartet are sinewy and dedicated and this is a first-class disc. [The coupling is excellent.]

The old once-prized Westminster disc is more subdued, more poetic, and still cherishable. The mono sound is still entirely hearable.

STRING QUINTETS Except for the early quintet, K. 174, these statements are products of Mozart's deepest maturity. They rank with the very finest music he has left us. They are more profound than the string quartets; in a sense, they are Mozart's final consummation. As Harold Schonberg once wrote: "Into the string quintets Mozart poured everything he knew about music and life. An exaggerated statement? Wait until you become familiar with the music!"

The scoring of the *Quintets* is for the usual string quartet form—first violin, second violin, viola, and cello—plus a second viola. This addition lends a more somber coloration to the music.

If you want to sample only one of Mozart's string quintets, try the one that Tchaikovsky loved above all else: the *Quintet in G Minor, K. 516.*

COMPLETE STRING QUINTETS
(K. 174, 406, 515, 516, 593, 614)

* * * GRAF	*Heutling Quartet*	3-SERAPHIM	(S) 6028
* * GERHARD	*Pascal Quartet*	3-MONITOR	(S) 2111/3
* KESSINGER	*Barchet Quartet*	3-VOX	(S) SVBX-5003

The beautifully recorded, stunningly played album by the Heutling Quartet with Graf has been ecstatically received by every music critic, including the New York *Times, High Fidelity,* and *Stereo Review.* This is an accomplishment of the highest order, with deep musical intelligence shining from every page. This set is a solid buy, great Mozart, and will afford endless pleasure and satisfaction.

The Pascal Quartet, never to be slighted, here produce a version that "does honor to the composer" in the words of the New York *Times'* Harold Schonberg in 1955. (Schonberg also prefers Pascal to the expensive Budapest Quartet recordings.) This is a rugged, powerful reading that does not aim for mere elegance. The sound is a bit rough-edged in places, but acceptable.

The Barchet Quartet is Mozartean, rather earth-bound and rigid, but entirely hearable.

STRING QUINTETS (K. 515 INC)

This is one of the great quintets. For the most part, it is in a serene mood. There is an *Andante* here that is really a lovely duo for first violin and first viola.

* * * PRIMROSE	*Griller Quartet*	VANGUARD	(S) 158
		[Quintet 516]	

The performance by the English Griller Quartet, with William Primrose, the famous violist, is vivid and extremely enjoyable.

STRING QUINTET (K. 516 in G)

For many music lovers, this is the greatest thing Mozart ever penned. Tchaikovsky, who worshipped Mozart, wrote to his "Beloved Friend" Madame von Meck: "In his chamber music Mozart charms me by his purity and distinction of style and his exquisite handling of the parts. Here too are things which can bring tears to our eyes. I will only mention the Adagio of the D minor [G minor] String Quintet. No one else has ever known as well how to interpret so exquisitely in music the sense of resigned and unconsolable sorrow."

The reader who cares about Mozart, or about chamber music, is directed, nay, ordered, to hear this heavenly music without delay.

* * * PRIMROSE	*Griller Quartet*	VANGUARD [Quintet 515]	(S)	158

The Grillers with Primrose well capture the passionate melancholy of this music, one of the most personal, most moving statements we have from Mozart. Igor Kipnis in *Stereo Review*, 1965: "At the time these two performances were first released, they were hailed for their sensitivity and depth. Time has not changed this stimate for me. This rendition of the *G Minor Quintet* is one of the most moving I have heard on records — the playing captures perfectly the restlessness of the score, but without the nervousness that so often permeates modern interpretations . . . Vanguard's stereo reproduction is warm and vibrant."

STRING QUINTET (K. 593 in D)

* * PRIMROSE	*Griller Quartet*	VANGUARD [Quintet 614]	(S)	194

This is a masterly quintet, with a mystic, profound slow movement that is one of Mozart's most moving accomplishments. The Grillers are manly and powerful.

STRING QUINTET (K. 614 in E-Flat)

This is essentially a gentle piece, and it is Mozart's farewell to chamber music for strings. It was written in the last year of his life.

* * * PRIMROSE	*Griller Quartet*	VANGUARD [Quintet 593]	S)	194
* STANGLER	*Vienna Konzerthaus Quartet*	WESTMINSTER [Quintet 516]	(M)	9036

The Grillers are warm and persuasive here. [The coupling is excellent.] The old Vienna reading is more romantically conceived and is quite hearable.

VARIOUS CHAMBER MUSIC PIECES   Anyone dealing with the mass of Mozart's chamber music is hard put to classify its bewildering assortment. Suffice it to say here that Mozart wrote prolifically for many small combinations of instruments. Most of this output is music of the highest order. The pieces dating from Kochel 200 upward are seldom disappointing.

Eric Blom is worth quoting from *Mozart's Chamber Music:* "What domestic music making would be like without Mozart's chamber music is hard to imagine. . . . We would miss our most perfect felicities."

Thus, those who love the spirit of Mozart silently treasure—along with Wolfgang Amadeus himself—The King of Prussia who played the cello, the cheesemonger Leitgeb who played the horn, and all the other undying worthies who prompted Mozart, in one way or another, to write his chamber music masterpieces.

ADAGIO IN C, RONDO IN C FOR GLASS HARMONICA, FLUTE, OBOE, VIOLA AND CELLO (K. 617)

This amazing ethereal trifle, a product of Mozart's last unhappy year, can bring tears to anyone who reflects on Mozart demeaning himself, for a small fee, with a composition for an inane instrument (invented by Benjamin Franklin, by the by) that was nothing more than glass bowls with water in them. And yet Mozart wrote a masterpiece of miniature music. The great musicologist Alfred Einstein calls the piece "one of Mozart's heavenly works . . . filled with unearthly beauty." A writer in the *London Observer* once devoted a column to this music's "strange, rarified, and almost painful beauty . . . a somewhat inhuman beauty, angelic and deathly, which keeps creeping into Mozart's music in his last year."

* * SWOBODA	*Vienna Pro Musica*	Vox (M) 8550 [Andante; Concerto for Flute and Harp]
* PETER MAAG	*Vienna Soloists, Vienna Ensemble*	2-TURNABOUT (S) 34213/4

Swoboda uses a celeste instead of a glass harmonica, and this is a delicate performance. The old sound is still quite clean.

Peter Maag also uses a celeste, in a nice performance.

ADAGIO AND FUGUE IN C (K. 546)

This great, serious music contains some of Mozart's most daring, quite astonishing harmonic progressions. It is also highly expressive writing. It can be played either by a string quartet or a string orchestra.

| * VALCH | *Czech Philharmonic Orch.* | PARLIAMENT (S) 163 [Divertimento, K. 136; Serenade K. 525] |

An incisive reading is to be had from Vlach and his string ensemble, fairly well recorded.

DIVERTIMENTO IN E-FLAT FOR STRING TRIO (K. 563)

This lovely, sensitive music was a thank you note to Mozart's loyal friend and benefactor, Michael Puchberg. Puchberg was besieged by Mozart with begging letters and desperate appeals for loans. He usually came through.

* * *	*Pasquier Trio*	MHS 623 (Musical Heritage Society) (S)
* * *	*Trio a Cordes Francais*	NONESUCH (S) 71102
* * * POUGNET, RIDDLE, PINI		WESTMINSTER (M) 9068

We have no less than three superb readings available here. A classic reading by the veteran Pasquier Trio is a joy. Nathan Broder says in *High Fidelity:* "The performance has a polished vigor, where vigor is needed; elsewhere it is elegant and sensitive. There is complete unanimity, and a pliancy that never pulls a phrase out of shape." The sound from Erato, France, is hard in a few places, but not bad. The stereo separation is particularly good. This disc is available by mail order only from Musical Heritage Society ($2.50); see address in the listing at the beginning of this book.

The Trio a Cordes Francais is first-rate, both flexible and precise. The stereo separation is handsomely done.

Pougnet, Riddle, and Pina are also dizzily rewarding. Harold Schonberg commented in 1955: "Completely assured playing, buttressed by first-class musicianship. You can't go wrong with it." The 1944 sound is still clean.

DUOS FOR VIOLIN AND VIOLA (K. 423/4)

These spirited, ingenious pieces were written to help out Michael Haydn, (according to two of Haydn's pupils), who was sick and unable to complete the commission he had received for this music. Mozart obliged his friend and allowed Haydn to pass them off as his own. This music is extremely vivacious—by no means little trifles. Mozart wrings amazing results out of this spare combination.

* * SUK, SKAMPA (No. 2)		CROSSROADS (M) 22 16 0015 (S) 22 16 0016 [Sinfonia Concertante, K. 364]
* * NOVAK, SKAMPA (No. 1)		CROSSROADS (M) 22 16 0079 (S) 22 16 0080 [Brahms, Quintet, Opus 115]

Suk and Skampa seem thoroughly at home in this music. The sound is agreeable.

Novak and Skampa are also Mozartean, but a bit less polished than the Suk-Skampa team.

QUARTETS FOR PIANO AND STRINGS: NO. 1, IN G MINOR (K. 478); NO. 2, IN E FLAT (K. 493)

In Mozart's day the combination of piano and strings was an unknown form. Mozart agreed by contract to write three piano quartets. When the first was published, very few copies were sold because the public found it difficult to perform. The project was abandoned. The two he completed are both marvelous Mozart, and in musicologist Alfred Einstein's phrase, "full of manly jubilation."

* * * SZELL	*Budapest Quartet Members*	ODYSSEY	(M) 3216 0139
* * HANCOCK	*New Art Trio*	TURNABOUT	(S) 34192

The superbly poised reading of George Szell and the Budapest Quartet is a joy here. George Szell is, of course, the famous conductor of the Cleveland Orchestra and stands revealed here as a superb Mozart pianist. (He started out as a would-be concert pianist.) *High Fidelity,* on this reissue: Snap up this classic before it disappears again—definitely a cornerstone for any chamber music collection. The remastering has been most expertly handled." The 1946 sound is wiry.

A smart, stylish reading is heard from pianist David Hancock and the New Art String Trio. This record was on *Saturday Review's* list of "Best Recordings of 1968."

SONATAS FOR VIOLIN AND PIANO

The violin sonatas are delightful and heartwarming pieces that should not be missed by any Mozart lover. This is intimate, rewarding music of the highest order. Superb workmanship is here, and sheer beauty. "The intimacy of feeling expressible through the subtleties of a team of combined solo players"—so writes scholar H. C. Colles on chamber music. Nowhere is this treasurable "intimacy of feeling" more apparent than in Mozart's blessed sonatas for violin and piano.

K. 296, 301, 302, 304, 305, 306, 377, 380
* * * SZIGETI,   3-VANGUARD   (S) 262/4
HORSZOWSKI

K. 303, 376, 378, 379, 454, 481, 526
* * * SZIGETI,   3-VANGUARD   (S) 265/7
HORSZOWSKI

Sonatas for Violin and Piano (Complete)
* * PAUK, FRANKL   6-Vox   (S) SVBX-546/7

K. 376 in F
* KOGAN, GINSBURG   MONITOR   (M)   2011
                                  [Beethoven, Sonata 7]

K. 454 in B-Flat
* * OISTRAKH,   MONITOR   (M)   2005
YAMPOLSKY   [Bach, Two Violin Sonatas;
                                  Beethoven, Piano Trio 7]

A great classic performance is rendered by Szigeti and Horszowski. This is fine music making indeed. These discs were made by Columbia in the 1950's and were never released; they have now appeared on Vanguard's low-priced "Everyman" label. All chamber music lovers owe a debt of gratitude to Vanguard for ferreting these golden discs out of Columbia's vaults. Szigeti's violin playing is angular, lean, and entirely convincing. These releases are a must and are available on two separate three-record albums. The artificial stereo is harmless.

Pauk and Frankl also present all of Mozart's violin sonatas, except those he wrote as a child, and throw in for good measure two sets of variations for violin and piano. The artists are highly skillful Mozarteans and this is a worthy venture, but the exhilaration provided from Szigeti and Horszowski is lacking.

In one Mozart sonata Oistrakh is lyric and appealing. [The couplings are superb.] The mono sound is good.

Kogan delivers a strong, no-nonsense reading of one sonata. The mono sound here is fair.

TRIOS FOR PIANO, VIOLIN, AND CELLO
(K. 254, 442, 496, 502, 542, 548, 564)

These are tasteful salon pieces, yet filled with Mozart's exquisite workmanship. The piano is predominant as soloist in most of them.

* * * FOURNIER, JANIGRO, BADURA-SKODA (NOS. 1, 3/7)	2-WESTMINISTER (M) 9056/7	
* *	*Mannheim Trio* (Nos. 1, 3/7)	3-Vox (S) SVBX-568 [Trio K. 498]

On perfectly good 1950's mono, the youthful, vibrant quality of Fournier, Janigro, and Badura-Skoda is a joy to the ear and a solace to the soul.

The Mannheim Trio are thorough musicians and their offering here is rewarding. The sound is pleasant throughout.

SERENADES   This is Mozart's "party music" *(unterhaltungsmusik)*. The serenades, as well as the divertimentos, were designed for performance in ballrooms or banquet halls. In the summer, this party or "night music" would be played in a garden or under the patron's window. Much of it is extremely worthwhile — filled with elegance and good humor.

A fact that is generally overlooked is that a considerable amount of Mozart's total output is "entertainment music." His age was crazy about refined musical entertainment, and Mozart happily produced it. The sharp cleavage made today between "serious music" and "table entertainments" was unknown in the days of Haydn and Mozart. Music was music, usually *written to order,* and it had to please the patrons, or else. (Contemporary composers take note.) Beethoven later came along and changed all that with his dramatic musical pronouncements, and the "age of the awed and glum listener" was ushered in. Mozart was expected, at all times, to dish up any and all music that might be requested — from a solemn Mass to a breezy stage piece, or even pop dance music for ballrooms. He cheerfully obliged.

SERENADE NO. 4 IN D (K. 203)

This is a light, tuneful serenade, written for a grand social affair in Salzburg in 1774. The first *Andante* of this work could well be the slow movement of a full-sized violin concerto.

* RISTENPART	*Saar Chamber Orch.*	NONESUCH [Dances]	(S) 71194

This is a stylish reading, with a touch of harshness here and there in the recording. [The coupling is a very slight work by Mozart.]

SERENADE NO. 6 IN D (K. 239) ("SERENATA NOTTURNA")

In *Serenade No. 6*, Mozart divided his musicians into two separate groups to give novelty and striking effect to the musical interplay.

* * * DAVIS	*Philharmonic Orch.*	SERAPHIM	(S) 60057	
		[Serenade K. 525]		
* BOETTCHER	*Vienna Festival Orch.*	TURNABOUT	(3) 4056	
		[Serenade 9]		
* REMOORTEL	*Pro Musica*	DOVER	5202	
		[Serenade 9]		

Davis and his players enter completely into the spirit of this winsome serenade.

Boettcher and his group are competent, and quite hearable.

Remoortel's version is just serviceable, with indifferent playing.

SERENADE NO. 7 IN D (K. 250) ("HAFFNER")

This is a long serenade, written by Mozart for Siegmund Haffner, a merchant of means who ordered the work for the wedding of his daughter Elisabeth. There is almost enough featured solo violin to make up a full-length violin concerto, but the leisurely movements become repetitious. The over-all result of this piece, however, is witty and poetic wedding music.

* LEITNER	*Wuerttemberg State Orch.*	TURNABOUT	(M) 4013
			(S) 34013

The playing is attractive and light, but the direction is not as imaginative as it might be. Suzanne Lautenbacher's violin solos are a standout.

SERENADE NO. 9 IN D (K. 320) ("POSTHORN SERENADE")

This is a lovely serenade, with a humorous musical quotation of the four natural notes of the then-familiar posthorn.

* * WAND	*Cologne Symphony Orch.*	NONESUCH	(S) 71047
		[Symphony 40]	
* BOETTCHER	*Vienna Festival Orch.*	TURNABOUT	(M) 4056
			(S) 34056

* REMOORTEL	*Pro Musica*	DOVER	5202
		[Serenade 6]	

Wand is relaxed and his players are dexterous. This is good Mozart. Boettcher is unremarkable and rather heavy-handed. Remoortel's version is hearable, but little more.

SERENADE NO. 10 IN B-FLAT FOR 13 WIND INSTRUMENTS (K. 361)

The year 1781 was an eventful one for Mozart. It saw the production of his first great opera, *Idomeneo;* a visit to Vienna in the retinue of the Prince Archbishop of Salzburg; his dismissal by his exalted employer, emphasized by the boot of the Archbishop's steward; his engagement to Constanze Weber; and the composition of several major works, including the *Serenade, (K. 361).* The earliest surviving mention of a performance of this work appears in the *Wiener Blaettchen* for March 20, 1784, announcing a benefit concert for the clarinetist Anton Stadler in the Nationaltheater which would include a "big wind piece of quite an exceptional kind composed by Herr Mozart."

This great serenade is a gem of variety, and is much more than "mere entertainment." Mozart here is absorbed with the challenge of producing a dazzling variety of color combinations from his thirteen wind instruments. During the music's course, each instrument often plays a solo part on its own.

* PESEK	*Prague Winds*	CROSSROADS (M) 22 16 0019
		(S) 22 16 0020

Here are rather rigid, unjoyous results. *Stereo Record Guide:* "It is a pity that the direction is not as imaginative as the playing."

SERENADE NO. 11 IN E-FLAT (K. 375)

"At 11 o'clock last night I was serenaded by two clarinets, two bassoons, and two horns playing my own music," writes Mozart on November 3, 1781, referring to the *Serenade* which was to become *K. 375.* This new work had been played all over Vienna on Saint Teresa's Night to the profit of the performers, and now they were coming to show their gratitude. "The six musicians are poor wretches who play quite nicely, all the same. . . ." This is one of the great *Serenades,* full of variety of invention and sheer *joie de vivre.*

* * WINOGRAD	*Wind Ensemble*	HELIODOR	(S) 25013
* * JENKINS	*Woodwind Octet*	EVEREST	3042

*   *Vienna Philharmonic*   Westminster   18134
                Winds

Arthur Winograd's reading is airy and joyous, and the playing is polished Mozart. This is an excellent disc. The late, great Mozart authority, Nathan Broder, commented in 1959: "Winograd gives the alert but at the same time relaxed, easy treatment required but seldom received by this type of music."

Jenkins is vivid; here, too, is good Mozartean style.

The Vienna band is a bit portentious. The old sound is quite good.

SERENADE NO. 12 IN C MINOR (K. 388)

This fine serenade is in a somber mood and a minor key. It was probably written for Mozart's musician friends in Vienna rather than for sociable entertainment.

This is possibly Mozart's greatest music for winds. The carefree quality of his earlier *Serenades* has almost entirely vanished; instead, there are poignant oboe lines, and fierce harmonic clashes. The great *Trio* of this work is a contrapuntal *tour de force*.

* * WINOGRAD   *Wind Ensemble*   Heliodor   (S) 25013
                                             [Serenade 11]

Winograd is excellent and the players are expressive.

SERENADE IN G (K. 525) ("EINE KLEINE NACHTMUSIK")

This much-loved, delightful miniature music is probably Mozart's most popular piece. It carries the ambiance of soft Salzburg evenings — all grace and suavity. It was written in 1787, in that great year that also produced *Don Giovanni*.

* * * DAVIS   *Philharmonic Orch.*   Seraphim   (S) 60057
                                          [Serenade 6]

* * PROHASKA   *Vienna State Opera Orch.*   Vanguard   (S)   162
                                          [Symphony 40]

* * STEINBERG   *Pittsburg Symphony Orch.*   Pickwick   (S)   4003
                                          [Handel, Water Music]

* KLEMPERER   *Pro Musica*   Vox   11870
                                          [Beethoven, Symphony 5]

* BOULT   *Vienna State Opera Orch.*   Westminster   (M) 18942
                                                      (S) 14126

* REINHARDT	*Stuttgart Pro Musica*	Vox 9780
		[Musical Joke; Haydn, Toy Symphony]
* FURTWAENGLER	*Berlin Philharmonic Orch.*	HELIODOR (S) 25079
		[Symphony 39]

Colin Davis wins hands down with a miraculously light and sensitive reading. *Stereo Record Guide:* "Played with stylish skill. . . . Relaxed yet entirely convincing. . . . The stereo perfectly adds another dimension."

Prohaska is ebullient, and anything but mannered. This is a good, unvarnished reading. The playing is also spirited and unrefined. Irving Kolodin (1955): "Prohaska's ensemble plays beautifully . . . his fault is a weaker sense of balance than this music requires."

Steinberg is also enjoyable, and the playing is first-rate. This reading could have had more Mozartean charm.

Of Klemperer, Irving Kolodin says in *Guide to Orchestral Records,* 1955: "Anyone interested in my conception of a classical version of this work can hear it in the Klemperer performance. . . . But it is definitely limited in sound." I quite agree; Klemperer is superb, but the sound on this ancient disc in tinny.

Boult is forthright and entirely hearable.

Reinhardt is lively, and the program is pleasant. The sound is adequate.

Furtwaengler's Mozart here is much admired by many critics, but I find it downright stentorian. The old sound is metallic.

DIVERTIMENTOS FOR WIND INSTRUMENTS As the intrepid musicologist H. C. Robbins Landon once remarked, to the fury of pious Baroque lovers, "Minor baroque music is music to eat by." This fact is generally forgotten, so enshrined are the light *Tafelmusik* (table music) pieces of Mozart, Vivaldi, Telemann, etc. For example, the five *Divertimentos* designated *K. 213, K. 240, K. 252, K. 253,* and *K. 270* were composed between 1773 and 1776 to be played at the dinners of the Prince Archbishop of Salzburg. They are all written for two oboes, two bassoons, and two horns. It is nonsense to treat this music — and the other slight doodlings and light pieces of Vivaldi, etc. — with the reverent awe usually reserved for the Dead Sea Scrolls. All these eighteenth-century trifles (as well as the bulk of that century's *ten thousand* symphonies, for that matter) were well-carpentered entertainment pieces — by composers who sometimes were undying geniuses.

DIVERTIMENTO NO. 1 IN E-FLAT (K. 113)

This pleasant little piece was written in Milan in 1771, after the production of Mozart's opera, *Ascanio in Alba.* Mozart was fifteen at the time.

* *	*Vienna Octet Members*	LONDON STS-15053 [Beethoven, Quintet Opus 16]
* * MACKERRAS	*London Pro Arte*	VANGUARD (S) 186 [German Dances; Petit Riens]

The Vienna group is superb is this trifle. The sound is clean.
Mackerras also rovides some fresh-sounding Mozart.

DIVERTIMENTO NO. 10 IN F (K. 247)

This attractive *Divertimento* was written for a party given by the Countess Lodron in 1776.

* *	*Collegium Aureum*	VICTROLA VIC (S) 1335 [Divertimento 11]

Meticulous playing and spirited tempos are to be heard from our sole entry here. The sound is spacious.

DIVERTIMENTO NO. 11 IN D (K. 251)

This is really a septet for string quartet, with two horns and an oboe solo. It is a sparkling piece; Mozart may have written it in 1776 for his sister Nannerl's 25th birthday.

* * MUENCHINGER	*Stuttgart Chamber Orch.*	LONDON STS-15035 [Schubert, German Dances; Minuets]
*	*Collegium Aureum*	VICTROLA VIC (S) 1335 [Divertimento 10]

Muenchinger is first-rate in this sort of thing. This is a singing, impeccable reading. [The coupling is with slight, enjoyable pieces.]
The Collegium Aureum is highly agreeable, but outclassed.

DIVERTIMENTO NO. 15 IN B-FLAT (K. 287)

Mozart was fond of the combination of strings and two horns; he wrote four *Divertimentos* for this grouping. *No. 15* is one of the most popular and contains much expressive music and fine detail.

* MARTIN	*Paris Orch. Soloists*	NONESUCH 71046

The Paris group is neither very impressive nor well-drilled. This is rather mundane Mozart.

DIVERTIMENTO NO. 17 IN D (K. 334)

This is a gem of a *Divertimento*, almost with the solidity of a string quartet. It was composed for Mozart's special friend, Sigmund von Robinig, in 1779. The scoring is for strings and two horns.

* * SANDERLING	*Leningrad Philharmonic*	MONITOR	(S)	2067
*	*Vienna Konzerthaus Ensemble*	WESTMINSTER		9069

The Russian ensemble comes through with a vivid, elegant reading that is thoroughly Mozartean. The sound is good.

The old Vienna performance is rather stolid.

MISCELLANEOUS WORKS   Mozart wrote many short pieces for orchestra. These are very much alive today and provide agreeable listening.

CONCERTONE FOR TWO VIOLINS, OBOE AND CELLO (K. 190)

This odd title may have been coined by Mozart himself. The piece is really like a sinfonia concertante with two "principals" dividing themselves from the orchestral body. The composition contains a long and lovely slow movement. This engaging work is little played, for reasons unknown to me. It would be highly enjoyed by any Mozart lover.

* * MAKANOWITZKY, HENDEL, RISTENPART	*Saar Chamber Orch.*	NONESUCH (S) (5) 71068 [Sinfonia Concertante K. Anh. 9]	
* * LAUTENBACHER, KELTSCH, RILLING	*Stuttgart Bach Kollegium*	TURNABOUT (S) (3) 4098 [Sinfonia Concertante K. 364]	

Makanowitzky is fresh and vivid. The sound and couplings are first-rate.

Also attractive is the group with the ever-dependable Suzanne Lautenbacher, which provide an attractive performance. This is a cultured, highly Mozartean reading, with an excellent coupling.

DIVERTIMENTO IN F (K. 522) ("MUSICAL JOKE")

Mozart here lampoons a fumbling would-be composer. The harmonies are incorrect, the opening theme ends a bar too soon, and other things go wrong. This parody was written by Mozart in June, 1787, as a relaxation from his work on *Don Giovanni*. He had just finished his profound *G Minor Quintet* — and in August would compose *Eine Kleine Nachtmusik*.

* * SPACH, ROTH, KEHR, BARTELS, SICHERMANN, GRAESER		TURNABOUT (3) 4134 [Haydn, Toy Symphony; L. Mozart]	
* REINHARDT	*Stuttgart Pro Musica*	Vox 9780 [Serenade K. 525; Haydn, Toy Symphony]	

Spach *et al* are spirited and offhand. The sound is fair.
Reinhardt is too sober for this piece.

GERMAN DANCES

Mozart wrote most of these dances from 1787 through 1791, for performance at balls. They are unimportant, tuneful pieces, bubbling with vitality. Although they are not often performed at concerts, they make for enjoyable home listening. The delightful set listed as *K. 509* belongs to the stunning year of 1787, which saw the composition of *Don Giovanni* and the great string quartets.

* * * DAVIS	*Philharmonic Orch.*	SERAPHIM	(S) 60057
* * MACKERRAS	*London Pro Arte Orch.*	VANGUARD	(S) 186
*	*Prague Chamber Orch.*	CROSSROADS	22 16 0202
* WAGNER	*Innsbruck Symphony Orch.*	TURNABOUT	(3) 4011

A good rule of thumb these days is: grab Colin Davis recordings of Mozart. Here, as always, he is zestful and stimulating.

Mackerras is another comparatively new name on the podium scene. This conductor's Mozart readings are crisp and entirely convincing.

The Prague players are appealing; the Czechs have a light touch in Mozart. The sound is dry.

The Wagner disc is indifferently played. The sound is hazy.

OVERTURES

The short overtures to Mozart's great operas *(Don Giovanni, Marriage of Figaro, The Magic Flute, Abduction from the Seraglio, Cosi fan Tutte)* are sparkling gems. They are complete musical entities in themselves; besides being performed as curtain-raisers to the respective operas, they are very often given as the opening numbers in orchestral concerts.

* * * DAVIS	*Royal Philharmonic Orch.*	SERAPHIM	(S) 60037 [mixed program of overtures]

* * KRIPS	*London Symphony Orch.*	EVEREST 3199 [mixed program of overtures]	
* * PROHASKA	*Vienna State Opera Orch.*	VANGUARD (S) 167 [mixed program of overtures]	
* FURTWAENGLER	*Berlin Philharmonic Orch.*	HELIODOR (S) 25079 [mixed program of overtures]	
* ANCERL	*Czech Philharmonic Orch.*	PARLIAMENT (S) 167 (S) 622 [mixed program of overtures]	

Colin Davis is a young English conductor who is red-hot these days; he is often mentioned as a possible successor to Leonard Bernstein with the New York Philharmonic. His Mozart is widely respected for its finesse, wit, and secure sense of style. All are to be heard here. The reading is both refreshing and penetrating, and the tempos sound precisely right. This is a remarkable disc. The sound is clear.

SINFONIA CONCERTANTE IN E-FLAT FOR OBOE, CLARINET, BASSOON, HORN AND STRINGS (K. Anh. 9(297b)

Like the *Symphonia Concertante for Violin and Viola,* this work is broadly expansive and "symphonic." The quartet of soloists are set off as a unified group against the orchestra itself. No music for wind soloists is more satisfying than this exhilarating piece. Mozart wrote it in Paris in 1778. The score disappeared, without performance. It seems that Mozart wrote it again, from memory, since a score was later found in the State Library in Berlin.

* * * RISTENPART	*Saar Orch.*	NONESUCH (S) 71068 [Concertone]	
* * FAERBER	*Wuerttemberg Chamber Orch.*	VOX (M) 14180 (S) 514180 [Haydn, Sinfonia]	
* * FAERBER	*Wuerttemberg Chamber Orch.*	4-TURNABOUT (S) 34188/91 [Bassoon Concerto; Clarinet Concerto; Flute Concerto 1, 2; Flute-Harp Concerto; Horn Concerto]	
SMETACEK	*Czech Philharmonic Orch.*	CROSSROADS (M) 2216 0035 (S) 2216 0036 [Horn Concerto No. 2]	

The exciting Nonesuch disc under Ristenpart is a beauty. This is one of the most cherishable performances of wind music that I have heard. The edition used here does some juggling around—a flute plays what is customarily the oboe part—but it all comes off handsomely. This playing possesses a sweep and crisp assurance that are rarely heard in wind recordings, which tend to be phlegmatic. The stereo sound is excellent.

Bubbly playing and good Mozart are also to be had from Faerber's band. *High Fidelity* comments: "Faerber is after a *galant* style, crisp, witty, lyric, but with pulse and meter firmly defined under an evenly flowing legato line." The Faerber performance is available on either Vox or Turnabout, with choice of couplings. [The coupling on Vox is first-rate; Haydn's piece for wind soloists is one of the rare other works in the literature that stands close to Mozart's.]

The Czechs under Smetacek are quite unexceptional. [The horn playing on the reverse is awful.]

SINFONIA CONCERTANTE IN E-FLAT FOR VIOLIN AND VIOLA (K. 364)

This is a glorious, richly developed work that subtly contrasts the solo violin and viola against each other and against the orchestra. It is supreme Mozart. The pre-eminent musicologist Alfred Einstein has called this score "Mozart's crowning achievement in the field of the violin concerto." It was written in 1779, the year that also saw the *"Posthorn" Serenade*, the *Concerto for Two Pianos*, and the *Symphony No. 33*.

* * * LAUTENBACHER, KOCH, KERTESZ	*Bamberg Sympony Orch.*	NONESUCH [Clarinet Concerto]	71074
* * LAUTENBACHER, RILLING	*Stuttgart Bach Kollegium*	TURNABOUT (3) [Concertone]	4098
* OISTRAKH, BARSHAI	*Moscow Ensemble*	ARTIA (M) [Bach, Violin Concerto 1]	165
* BARCHET, KIRCHNER, SEEGELKEN	*Stuttgart Pro Musica*	VOX (M) 11830 [Sinfonia Concertante K. Anh. 9]	
* SUK, SKAMPA, REDEL	*Czech Philharmonic Orch.*	CROSSROADS (M) 22 16 0015 (S) 22 16 0016 [Duos]	

The distinguished, entirely Mozartean Suzanne Lautenbacher leads off here with violist Koch in a joyous, sunny reading for which I have nothing but praise. Kertesz is right there with her, and the disc has excellent overall balance. [The coupling is with a fine reading of the great *Clarinet Concerto*.]

The Lautenbacher-Rilling reading displays excellent teamwork. It is somewhat reserved. [The coupling is with some pleasant, little-heard Mozart duos.]

Another lovely, extremely violinistic reading is to be had from Oistrakh and Barshai, on old mono. Oistrakh's view of Mozart is somewhat romantic.

Barchet and Kirchner provide a rather rigid, German reading that is also extremely musical, on fair mono.

Suk and Skampa offer lightweight, lyrical Mozart that is quite outclassed by the top entry here. As usual, I find Suk eminently satisfying in chamber music, but he does not have enough bite for really rewarding solo playing.

PIANO SONATAS   Mozart's piano sonatas are often underrated or even dismissed as trivia because generations of children have been forced to master them at an early age. The best of the sonatas are fine pieces, thoroughly worked out; they are much, much more than "pretty pieces."

Mozart's piano music is spontaneous-sounding, yet perfectly finished. Grace, felicity, charm, lucidity — all that we call "Mozartean" shines in these pages. Mozart biographer John Burk clearly sums up Mozart's piano music: "The music for piano solo was the most direct, the most sensitive of all to his tonal thoughts. The keyboard was his closest confidant. It responded as instantaneously to his fingertips as his fingers responded to the animation of his tonal moods. There was no barrier whatever between thought and deed, there were no clumsy performers, rehearsals, copyists, audience ceremony, money-minded publishers. The sonatas ar an immediate, a personal emanation. Their style is the utter simplicity of melody lightly supported."

COMPLETE PIANO SONATAS

VOLUME I (K. 279, 280, 281, 282, 283, 284, 309, 310, 311, 330)

* KLIEN	Vox SVBX	(S) 5428
	(three discs)	
	Vox VBX	(S) 428

VOLUME II (K. 331, 332, 333, 457, 533, 570, 576, 545, RONDO (K. 494), FANTASY (K. 475)

* KLIEN	Vov SVBX	(S) 5429
	(three discs)	
	Vox VBX	(S) 429

Walter Klien, a pupil of the famous Italian pianist Michelangeli, is an uncluttered, thoroughly Mozartean pianist whose readings are always faithful — and sometimes exhilarating. Igor Kipnis in *Stereo Review*, 1965: "The general impression one receives is that of a well-trained pianist executing a large body of music to a set pattern. Mozart, I think, might refer to Klien, as he did once to Clementi, as a *mechanicus*: everything seems a little too pat and too calculated — even the sentiment. On the other hand, one could not call these performances poor. Vox's piano sound is excellent."

PIANO SONATA NO. 8 IN A (K. 310)

This reflective, personal sonata, unintended for public performance, was written by Mozart in Paris in 1778. It earned him a scolding letter from his father, who told him not to waste his time on "unprofitable" pieces.

* * * MATTHEWS	VANGUARD (S) 196 [Fantasia K. 475; Sonatas 13 and 14]
* BRENDEL	VANGUARD C-10043 [Fantasia K. 396; Rondo K. 511]

Matthews is both singing and disciplined; this is Mozart playing of the highest order. [The couplings are excellent.]

Brendel is thoroughly competent. *High Fidelity:* "There is something unpleasantly Prussian about the way Brendel pecks at every downbeat." The sound is harsh.

PIANO SONATA NO. 10 IN C (K. 330)

This is a gay, melodic sonata, written in Paris in 1778.

* * HASKIL	PHILLIPS WS (S) 9076 [Schubert, Sonata D. 960]

The late, great Clara Haskil's Mozart is intense and penetrating, and quite unlike anyone else's Mozart. There is little joyous quality about it; rather, an intellectual quality. This is impressive Mozart that probes rather than sings. The 1954 sound is decent.

PIANO SONATA NO. 11 IN A (K. 331)

This famous sonata has a rondo "Alla Turca," which is nothing more than an irresistible "Turkish" march that has delighted beginning piano students down the generations.

* * KRAUS	MONITOR (S) 2105 [Piano Concerto 9]

* NOVAES   Vox   (M) 9080
[Sonatas 5, 15; Rondo K. 511]

Kraus is personal and romantic — and highly enjoyable. Harold Schonberg in 1955: "A typical Kraus performance; broad design, occasional sparkle, many mannerisms."
Novaes is musically mature, as always. The mono sound is pallid.

PIANO SONATA NO. 13 IN B-FLAT (K. 333)

Mozart wrote this quiet, unpretentious sonata in Paris in 1778. It was probably intended for private performance among his friends, rather than for a glittering public concert.

* * * MATTHEWS   VANGUARD   (S) 196
[Fantasia K. 475; Sonatas 8, 14]

Matthews achieves warmth without romanticizing. This is a most impressive disc.

PIANO SONATA NO. 14 IN C (K. 457)

Mozart himself coupled this powerful sonata with his *Fantasia for Piano in C Minor, K. 475.* They must be regarded as one musical entity. Mozart biographer John Burk: "The Sonata and the Fantasy introductory stand apart from all Mozart's piano works. . . . They have no trace of the gaiety of style which was Mozart's heritage, and his custom throughout his life. . . . No other music of Mozart so unmistakably points the way to Beethoven, and no other music proves that if Mozart had lived only a few years longer, he could have become an artistic companion to Beethoven."

* * * MATTHEWS   VANGUARD   (S) 196
[Fantasia K. 475; Sonatas 8, 14]

* * KLIEN   TURNABOUT   (S) 34178
[Fantasia K. 475; Piano Concerto 24]

The Denis Matthews reading is a triumph of *legato,* musically flowing Mozart. Herbert Glass, in *Stereo Review,* 1967, rates this as one of the best piano discs ever made by anybody.
Klien is also first-rate and entirely Mozartean. His is a refreshing disc.

PIANO SONATA NO. 15 IN C (K. 545)

This "Sonatina" of 1788 is a simple piece, clearly intended for an unsophisticated pianist. Nevertheless, there is crystalline Mozart magic here. This is a very popular work.

* * GULDA

MACE   (S) 9060
[Bach, Italian Concerto;
Chopin, Andante; Schubert,
Scherzos]

* NOVAES

Vox   (M) 9080
[Sonata 5, 11; Rondo]

Gulda is a tasteful, simple, and lucid Mozartean pianist, and this is an enjoyable performance. [The couplings are excellent.]
Novaes is refined. The mono sound is poor.

PIANO SONATA NO. 17 IN D (K. 576)

This sonata, which Mozart marked as being "for beginners," was the only one composed in an intended set of six for the Princess Friedericke of Prussia. Despite its simplicity, this crystal-clear sonata is fine and appealing music.

* * * KLIEN

TURNABOUT   (S) 34194
[Fantasia K. 397; Piano
Concerto 26]

Klien is absorbing and a first-rate Mozart pianist. There is nothing more difficult to play then nakedly "simple" pieces of Mozart such as this. Everything is exposed; there are no fireworks to cover up with. You have to have "Mozart soul power."

FANTASIAS FOR PIANO   Mozart was expected to provide improvizations at every piano concert. Fantasias were a popular form of piano improvization.

FANTASIA IN C (K. 396)

This is "free," inventive Mozart, not concerned with form but with "musical play."

* * * MATTHEWS

VANGUARD   (S)   196
[Piano Sonatas 8, 13, 14]

* * BRENDEL

VANGUARD   (S) C-10043
[Rondo K. 511; Piano Sonata 8]

* * KLIEN   3-Vox   (S) SVBX-5406

Matthews is extremely rewarding on this renowned disc. [The coup-
lings are fine.] So is the sound.
Brendel is more disciplined than poetic, but his is also a very good
Klien is bristling here, with fluent finger work. *High Fidelity*, 1968:
"Klien presses forward with a fidgety pseudo-volatility that spells Vienna
in capital letters to anyone who knows his ABC's of performance style."

FANTASIA IN C (K. 475)

This is great Mozart of 1785—an inexorable, powerful work.

* * KLIEN   TURNABOUT   34178
                                 [Piano Concerto 24; Sonata
                                 14]

Klien delivers a splendid, light-fingered performance. [The couplings
are excellent.]

FANTASIA IN D (K. 397)

This melodic Fantasy was composed in Vienna in 1782.

* * KLIEN   TURNABOUT   (S) 34194
                                 [with various Mozart piano
                                 pieces]
* * KLIEN   3-Vox   (S) SVBX-5407

Klien is lucid and direct, if rather inflexible.
Klien's version is also available in a three-record album.

MISCELLANEOUS PIANO PIECES Mozart wrote much lovely and
striking music for the piano in addition to his more formal piano pieces.

MISCELLANEOUS PIECES FOR PIANO

This compilation is a mixed bag of six records, from juvenilia up to the
mature Mozart. Some very popular pieces are included.

KLÍEN   Vox SVBX   5406/07
                                (each 3-disc set)

Klien plays with his usual assured, assertive style that is always enjoyable, if not inspiring.

SONATAS FOR PIANO, 4 HANDS
(K. 497, 521)

These two delightful sonatas for two players at one piano—four hands—are among Mozart's finest works. They are direct, melodic, and filled with strength and vitality. They were obviously written for a modest parlor that did not afford two pianos, but this did not bother Mozart in the least. These works are superbly worked out and are models of musical clarity.

* BADURA-SKODA, DEMUS	WESTMINISTER (M) 18813

The delicately turned Viennese team of Badura-Skoda and Demus is enjoyable here. The 1950's mono sound is clean, but of course two-piano music comes across far better on stereo.

SONATA FOR TWO PIANOS, IN D (K. 448)

This very popular music is gay and delightful throughout. It is one of the most freely expressive of Mozart's piano works.

* * * BRENDEL, KLIEN	TURNABOUT (S) (3) 4064 [Fugue in C, K. 426; Concerto K. 365]
* LUBOSHUTZ, NEMENOFF	EVEREST (M) 6076 (S) 3076 [Chopin, Rondo; J. Strauss, Fledermaus excerpts]

Brendel and Klien are singing and superb on this famous disc. *Stereo Review* in 1967 included this record on a short list of the best piano recordings ever made.

The veteran team of Luboshutz and Nemenoff romanticize this music in an unconvincing manner. Harold Schonberg: "Their interpretation does not have much sparkle, and some of their tempos are over-deliberate."

OPERAS Opera was Mozart's main ambition and his dearest delight. This is made plain in his letters. Handed a new opera text, he plunged into work with joy and zeal. This contagious enthusiasm can be heard in his great operas: *Don Giovanni, The Marriage of Figaro, The Magic Flute, Cosi fan Tutte,* and *The Abduction from the Seraglio.*

Opera brought out the passionate best in Mozart. His vocal melodies in the operas are superb and brim with sheer *élan*. The orchestral writing is brilliant with inner wealth. Listening to his operas, we feel that Mozart was really a man of the theatre; he loved its excitement, its promise of fame. Mozart was always yearning to write a *schlager*—a hit opera that would send them home whistling his hit tunes.

Of the thousands of operas written in the last two hundred years, a bare handful survive. Nothing is more perishable and more subject to change in fashion. There are several composers of the nineteenth century whose operas are in the permanent repertory: Verdi, Wagner, Puccini, Rossini, Bellini, Donizetti. But there is only one eighteenth-century composer whose operas still delight us today: Mozart.

THE ABDUCTION FROM THE SERAGLIO (DIE ENTFUEHRUNG AUS DEM SERAIL) (K. 384) (Complete) (Sung in German)

Written in 1781-82, this was Mozart's first full opera in the German language. The tale, set in the Orient, has two Turkish characters—the pasha and his overseer—but the heroine is a sturdy German *Fräulein*. This is a charming, innocent opera, lightweight and without the persuasive appeal of such Mozart masterpieces as *The Marriage of Figaro* and *Don Giovanni*.

* ROTHENBERGER, POPP, GEDDA, UNGER, FRICK, RUDOLF, KRIPS	*Vienna Philharmonic Orch.*, 2-SERAPHIM *Chorus of the Vienna State Opera*	(S)	6025

The Krips set on Seraphim is serviceable, but an up-and-down affair. As with most Krips recordings, the conducting is honest, thoroughly rehearsed, and blighted with a dullish mood. One yearns to hear sparkle in Mozart opera, and Herr Krips does not provide it. As for the singing: Rothenberger is an outstanding Constanza, and Unger sings the Petrillo really beautifully. Gedda is lackluster, and the fine basso Gottlob Frick disappoints here with a wobbly, vocally insecure performance.

THE ABDUCTION FROM THE SERAGLIO (DIE ENTFUEHRUNG AUS DEM SERAIL) (K. 384) (Excerpts) (Sung in German)

Here are excerpts from the opera.

* * * WUNDERLICH, LEAR, HOTTER, JOCHUM	*Berlin Philharmonic Orch.*	HELIODOR [Excerpts from The Magic Flute]	(S) 25075

The excerpts on Heliodor are taken from first-rate complete recordings of *Seraglio* and the *Flute*. This is a lovely record, with conductor Jochum delivering a brisk, warm, affectionate, thoroughly Mozartean performance. [Conductor Boehm does as well on the reverse side.] There is some great singing on this record, principally the warm, beautiful voice of the late Fritz Wunderlich, who died in 1966 at the age of 36, some weeks before he was to make his debut at the Met. The American soprano Evelyn Lear is excellent, and even the formidably gifted voices of James King and Martti Talvela are to be heard in bit roles. This disc is a solid buy for those who like opera highlights—or for those who wish a memento of the late, great Fritz. [There is an equally good performance of *The Magic Flute* on the reverse side.]

Those who wish a superb complete performance of *Seraglio* are referred to the Sir Thomas Beecham set on high-priced Angel.

BASTIEN UND BASTIENNE (K. 50)
(Sung in German)

This is really a one-act operetta that Mozart composed in Vienna in 1768, when he was twelve years old. The story of *Bastien* is a simple French romance of a shepherd and shepherdess who are jealous, quarrel, then patch up their differences. This is a mildly charming little piece, with spoken dialogue interspersed. It is more than a curiosity, and yet less than a fully satisfying opus.

* HOLLWEG, KMENTT, BERRY, PRITCHARD	*Vienna Symphony Orch.*	PHILIPS WS	(M/S)	9024
* DUESKE, COERTSE, GUENTER, EBERT	*Hamburg Symphony Orch.*	TURNABOUT	(M) (S)	4053 34053

John Pritchard, the English conductor on the Philips World Series disc, has made a name for himself with Mozart. The singing is good and the pace is lively. The rechanneled stereo doesn't get in the way, because you can't hear it. This record was on the American Columbia label, in the early 1950's. The sound is agreeable.

The Turnabout entry has a first-rate Bastienne in Mimi Coertse. This reading uses a soprano rather than a tenor for the role of Bastien (both ways have historical precedent), and the stereo engineering is hectic.

CLEMENZA DI TITO (K. 621) (Spng in Italian)

This opera was written in 18 days in 1791, just after Mozart had written *Cosi fan Tutte* and before he finished *The Magic Flute*. In fact, he put aside the urgent completion of *The Magic Flute* to get this assignment out of the way; he likewise neglected the pressing commission to write the *Requiem*, which had just been ordered from him.

La Clemenza di Tito was written for the Prague ceremonies cerebrating the coronation of Leopold II. A nice story has it that Mozart hurriedly dashed off most of the score in a coach en route from Vienna to Prague.

This opera is almost never presented these days, despite our great love for Mozart; the music is simply not up to his own standard. The plot is lifeless, and even though there is a certain amount of beautiful music (especially the strong first-act finale and some lovely arias), this opus must be regretfully written off as an arid failure.

NENTWIG, SAILER, PLUEMACHER, MANGOLD, WEIKENMEIER, MUELLER, LUND	*Swabian Choral Society,* *Tonstudio Orch., Stuttgart*	3-DOVER	(S) 5251/53

Dover is recirculating a venerable set I first heard when it was on the Period label—about 1955. This opera calls for only two male singers and four women—originally, all sopranos—and the cast here is just fair. The Titus is often painfully flat, and only mezzo Hetty Pluemacher delivers two arias with style and some beauty of tone. The conductor has a nice sense of pace and movement. All things considered, I would say that this opera can be skipped by all except the Mozart faithful who wish to become familiar with every dramatic work he composed.

COSI FAN TUTTE (K. 588) (Sung in Italian)

This *opera buffa* (comic opera) was composed in Vienna in 1789-1790. The ironic text (the English translation of the title is *So Do They All*) is by Lorenzo Da Ponte, the great librettist of Mozart's *Don Giovanni*. Two love-stricken young men are infuriated by a bachelor who claims that no women are to be trusted. A wager is made; the two men pretend to go to war, return disguised, and each woos the beloved of the other. The women eventually yield. Both men are bitterly disillusioned, but they are advised by the worldly bachelor to marry their girls anyway and not to expect too much from fickle women.

Much has been written about Mozart's and Da Ponte's real intentions in the text. The moral seems to be not that the two women are false in their declarations of true love to their betrothed; rather, it is that a woman, poor creature, is perfectly capable of sincerely falling in love with another man who shows up at the right time. As the sage Conrad L. Osborne has philosophized on the mocking message of *Cosi:* "Things may be rough today, but tomorrow the world will still be here, and so will you, making a damned fool of yourself again."

Cosi is a great opera, but a few rungs below Mozart's towering trio: *Don Giovanni, The Magic Flute,* and *The Marriage of Figaro. Cosi* contains few solidly popular arias, which explains its lesser popular success. Nevertheless, it is a beautifully conceived work, with pages of inspired writing and great vocal ensembles. The collaboration between composer and librettist is ideal. Anyone who has enjoyed the top three Mozart operas should give himself the pleasure of another Mozart masterpiece. The excellent English critic Sackville-West sums up *Cosi* in his *Record Guide:* "For many years *Cosi Fan Tutte* was the Cinderella of Mozartean opera, but it is now firmly established in public esteem. Though less richly human than *Don Giovanni* or *Figaro,* it is an even purer work of art than either; over the burlesque passions of Da Ponte's characters and the chessboard complications of the plot Mozart has shed his own celestial radiance. . . . and poured into it much of his loveliest music."

* * DELLA CASA, LUDWIG, LOOSE, DERMOTA, KUNZ, SCHOEFFLER, BOEHM	*Vienna Philharmonic Orch. and Chorus*	3-RICHMOND	(M) 63008 (S) 63508
* * SOUEZ, HELLETSGRUEBER, EISINGER, NASH, DOMGRAF-FASSBAENDER, BROWNLEE, BUSCH	*Glyndebourne Festival Orch. and Chorus*	3-TURNABOUT	(M) 4120/2
STICH-RANDALL, SCIUTTI, MALANIUK, KMENTT, BERRY, ERNSTER, MORALT	*Vienna Symhony Orch. and State Opera Chorus*	3-PHILIPS WS	(M/S)-PHC-3-005

The Boehm recording is very good, if hardly electrifying. The conducting at times is a little slack for this sparkling fun-piece, but the performance contains solid virtues. Lisa della Casa is a fresh-voiced, delicious soprano; Christa Ludwig achieves a playful quality (yet vocally steady) that fits perfectly. The rest of the cast is good, except for Paul Schoeffler's rather stilted, even gruff Don Alfonso. This version has some drastic cuts, probably in order to keep it a three-record package. The sound is warm and clear.

The Turnabout set is a very famous, historic recording of the 1930's. It is a must for all Mozart lovers, but because of its antiquated sound, it certainly should not be the only *Cosi* for anybody. (Nevertheless, the sound is surprisingly lively, once one accepts its limits.) The men, led by John Brownlee, are first-rate, and the women all have a sure sense of style. This is undoubtedly due to conductor Fritz Busch, who is the real hero of this performance. His Mozart is always sparkling, affectionate, and vivid. Philip Miller comments: "Brownlee in his prime does a fine job of characterization. . . . But chief honors go to Fritz Busch, who molded and held the spirited performance together." These records are a treasure for anyone who cares about Mozart.

The Moralt recording is simply unattractive. The only interest here is soprano Teresa Stich-Randall's Fiordiligi, which is polished and rather cool, sung in her usual impersonal style. The other singers range from uninteresting to unpleasant. The conducting is plodding and bad Mozart.

Those who are ready to buy an expensive four-record album in order to obtain up-to-date stereo (but not a better performance than the two recommended here) are directed to the recording on Angel, also under Karl Boehm, which features Elisabeth Schwarzkopf.

DON GIOVANNI (K. 527) (Complete)
(Sung in Italian)

Don Giovanni is regarded by many, myself included, as the greatest opera ever written; it ranks as one of the two or three greatest on any critic's list. Completed in Prague in 1787, the opera was written on order for an impresario in Prague whose cash-box was overflowing— from sold-out performances of Mozart's *Marriage of Figaro*.

As with *Figaro*, Mozart's librettist was the fascinating Lorenzo da Ponte. Da Ponte was an adventurer who had been banished from Venice for immoral conduct. A Venetian Jew, born Emmanuele Conegliano, he had taken Christian orders at the age of 14. When Mozart approached him with the Prague commission, Da Ponte came up at once with the subject of Don Juan, the Spanish libertine who is piously punished after a life of hell-raising. The libretto is a marvel of characterization; many musicologists believe that Casanova, a friend of Da Ponte and Mozart, and an expert on love, also had a hand in sketching the masterly plot.

For the opera lover, *Don Giovanni* is an endless source of joy. It is perfect—a total experience in art. There is infinite variety as well as superb melodies and dazzling vocal ensembles. There is something super-human about it. Few experts agree on how it should be performed. The opera has fascinated people like the philosopher Kierkegaard, who was obsessed with the music and who wrote endlessly about Don Giovanni. Bernard Shaw was also mad about the opera. Mozarteans never tire of the side issues surrounding the opus: What happened later to Donna Anna (whom Don Giovanni woos at the beginning of the opera), did he really make love to her, and such fine points as the differences between Da Ponte's characterization of Elvira and Mozart's own.

But what fascinates everyone above all else is how Mozart achieved such vital, Shakespearean power with economical and haphazard eighteenth-century orchestral equipment. The English opera buff Robin May has caught this in his volume *Operamania: "Don Giovanni* provides a glimpse of naked genius, all the more baffling because of all great opera composers Mozart the man seems most elusive. . . . There is little doubt that Shakespeare would have been amazed if he could know the sheer amount of argument that the character of Hamlet has provided down the ages. He simply wrote a play. That is what I feel about Mozart and *Don Giovanni* . . . my obsession with it will never end."

For those unconcerned with poetic philosophizings about great music, *Don Giovanni* is a warm, powerful, bittersweet work with heaven-sent melodies—that makes one humble before the sublime genius of Mozart.

* * * SOUEZ, HELLETSGRUBER, MILDMAY, VON PATAKY, BROWNLEE, BACCALONI, BUSCH	*Glyndebourne Orch.*	3-TURNABOUT	(M) 4117/9
* * CURTIS VERNA, VALLETTI, TAJO, TADDEI, RUDOLF	*Radio Italiana Orch.*	3-EVEREST/CETRA	(S) 403/3
ZADEK, JURINAC, SIMONEAU, LONDON, BERRY, WEBER, MORALT	*Vienna Symphony Orch.*	3-PHILIPS WS PHC	(S) 3-009

The Turnabout set is more than thirty years old and is world-famous. Busch's achievement here ranks with Beecham's *Magic Flute* as a pinnacle of Mozart opera conducting by which all others must be measured. Fritz Busch was the brother of Adolph Busch, by the way, of the legendary Busch Quartet—Adolph is also known to music lovers as the father-in-law of Rudolph Serkin, who is the father of Peter Serkin—quite a family. The name of Fritz Busch is barely known in this country, but he was revered in Europe as a Mozart conductor of genius. His *Don* here is pure champagne; when you have heard his tempi it is almost impossible to accept any other. They sound exactly *right*. The Australian-born John Brownlee is nothing less than magnificent; you can see the Don; you are swept away. Salvatore Baccaloni was Toscanini's favorite *buffo*, and his lecherous portrait of Leporello remains a marvel. Pataky is a silver tenor. The women are good, and Aubrey Mildmay's Zerlina is first-rate. She was Mrs. John Christie, incidentally, wife of the founder of the famous Glyndebourne Festival in England. The Christies brought in Fritz Busch (and a bright youngster named Rudolph Bing) to launch the to-hell-with-the-cost Glyndebourne Festival. All Mozart lovers, by edict, should be compelled to hear this set. Philip Miller: "Chief among its virtues is the guidance of Fritz Busch, who gets a remarkably integrated performance from his international cast." This set was on a "great mono records" list compiled by *High Fidelity* in 1968. The sound is thin, but lively.

The old Cetra set, recirculated by Everest, is notable for some good singing by such dependable artists as Giuseppe Taddei and Caesare Valletti, except that Taddei's Don goes shaky now and then. Tajo provides a fine, luridly sketched Leporello. The women are poor. The conducting—always the vital factor in Mozart opera—is exciting and well-paced. The sound is indifferent.

The Moralt set is plodding and unforgivably dull. The conducting is abominably heavy. George London has the authority for the Don, but his thickish voice just doesn't come across here. The only virtues are a liquid Elvira from Sena Jurinac, and a superbly lyric Ottavio from Leopold Simoneau. It is a pity they are wasted because of conductor Moralt. It seems that Mozart conductors are born, not made, and when a real one appears, there must be rejoicing in the heavens.

DON GIOVANNI (K. 527) (Excerpts)

Here are selections from the opera.

* * HILLEBRECHT, WUNDERLICH, PREY, WIEMANN, KOHN, ZANOTELLI	*(Sung in German)*	Turnabout	(M) 4030 (S) 34030
* * STICH-RANDALL, DANCO, MOFFO, GEDDA, CAMPO, ROSBAUD	*(Sung in Italian)*	Vox	(M) 15110

The Turnabout excerpts are sung in German and were recorded around 1960 by Electrola Records of Germany. The women are fair; the men are excellent. Hermann Prey is first-rate and dashing as the Don. Fritz Wunderlich, although not as moving and liquid-toned as he was on later recordings, is still excellent. The conducting is brisk, even driving.

The Rosbaud excerpts, on mono only, are taken from an open-air performance given at Aix-en-Provence in 1956. The singers are excellent. Anna Moffo is a delightful Zerlina; Teresa Stich-Randall's Donna Anna, after a shaky start, is fiery and original. The conducting is gracious and sure-handed, and the sound is decent.

NOTE: The Mozart record buff who likes hunting can still track down complete *Don Giovanni* and *Figaro* by Hans Rosbaud and Aix-en-Provence ensembles in some record stores. Both were first imported to this country on the Oleon label, and later pressed here in 1964 on the low-priced Vox label. They are collectors' items, and exhilarating Mozart.

IL RE PASTORE (K. 208)

This one, termed a "dramatic Festival Opera," was composed in Salzburg in April, 1775, for a reception of the Archduke Maximilian. It is a pastoral tale of the love of a shepherd and his shepherdess, with many struggles between love and duty. As in most of the youthful Mozart operas, there is occasionally much beauty and distinction, but not enough to elevate the work into the category of outstanding Mozart—or even worthwhile Mozart.

| GIEBEL, NENTWIG, PLUEMACHER, HOHMANN, LUND | 2-Everest-Cetra (S) 449-2 |

This old Cetra set is barely adequate, both musically and sonically, but it will fulfill a need for die-hard Mozarteans, as no other performance is listed in the catalogue. One must be grateful to Everest for providing battered sets such as these, if only for the use of students and musicians. Philip Miller charitably remarks: "The singers, with their sweet and modest voices, are not equal to the music's demands."

LA FINTA GIARDINIERA (Sung in German)

The Lady Disguised as a Gardener is an *opera buffa* (comic opera in a farcical style), composed between 1774-75. Jealousy and unrequited love are the themes, and the story wheels into complete confusion. The final curtain falls on a happy settlement that finds all the lovers properly matched.

This is youthful Mozart, with many flashes of inspiration—the first clear sign of Mozart's operatic genius. Many of the arias are jewels. Of all the unfamiliar Mozart operas, this one will most please the curious listener.

| * GUILLAUME, PLUEMACHER, HOHMANN, NEIDLINGER, REINHARDT | *Stuttgart Orch.* | 3-Everest   (S) 444/3 |

The Everest edition offers singing that is just fair, conducting that is unremarkable. The sound is so-so.

THE MAGIC FLUTE (DIE ZAUBERFLOETE) (K. 620) (Complete) (Sung in German)

The Magic Flute was composed in Vienna between July and September,

1791. Mozart's last opera, it was written for a suburban theatre near Vienna. The plot is a mish-mash about the Temple and Sacred Grove of Isis and Osiris, with a young hero undergoing the test of virtue, etc. The opera is a curious mixture of allegory and fantasy, with concealed references to Freemasonry. This work takes some time to ingratiate itself upon the listener. Many Mozart lovers, who fall in love at first hearing with *Don Giovanni, Figaro,* and *Cosi fan Tutte,* remain detached, respectful, and admiring in the presence of *The Magic Flute.* This is a marvelous score. No greater vocal ensembles have even been penned, and one needs only a few repeated hearings to be introduced to the beauties of the heavenly *Magic Flute.*

* * * LEMNITZ, BERGER, BEILKE, ROSWAENGE, STRIENZ, HUESCH, TESSMER, GROSSMANN, BEECHAM	*Berlin Philharmonic Orch. and Chorus*	3-TURNABOUT	(M) 4111/3
* * * STADER, STREICH, HAEFLIGER, FISCHER-DIESKAU, GREINDL, FRICSAY	*RIAS Orch. and Chorus*	3-HELIODOR	(M) 25057-3
* GUEDEN, LIPP, SIMONEAU, BERRY, BOEHME, BOEHM	*Vienna Philharmonic Orch. and State Opera Chorus*	3-RICHMOND	(M) 63007 (S) 63507

Place of honor, without any hesitation, goes to the great 1937 recording under the inimitable baton of Sir Thomas Beecham. I don't know whether Mozart singers are born or whipped into shape by an iron conductor, but I have yet to hear a more joyous, *right*-sounding conception of Mozart than is to be heard here from such remarkable interpreters as Huesch, Roswaenge, and, above all, Tiana Lemnitz. But the propelling force, the master hand, is Sir Thomas. His work is intoxicating—never leaden, never dull, always inspired and sure. This set is a must for the Mozart devotee. This famous set was on *High Fidelity's* "indispensible mono recordings" list of 1968. Sound — well, 1937. But it's not bad at all.

For those not enchanted with recordings of the 1930's, I can strongly recommend the fine Heliódor set. Ideally, all good Mozarteans should have this Heliodor set *and* the classic Beecham version—they make for fascinating comparisons. Fricsay is poised, the orchestra plays beautifully, and the sound is highly agreeable, if not sumptuous. (The recording was made in 1956.) The singers are a joy—Fischer-Dieskau is fine as Papageno, Rita Streich is brilliant as the Queen of the Night, and Maria Stader offers a sensitive, delicate Pamina. Conductor Fricsay's approach is direct, simple, and human, without the clouds of pomposity that often hang over the *Magic Flute*.

The Boehm version is good, but not as good as the two sets just discussed. Boehm is a first-rate Mozart conductor—clear, meticulous, and unmannered. But in this set he is simply uninspired—not pedestrian, but neither elevated nor elevating. Simoneau is a full-voiced Tamino, Hilda Gueden is lovely, and Walter Berry is just about competent as Papageno. But a pall hangs over this earth-bound set. The sound is satisfactory. NOTE: This set is not to be confused with a later, better Boehm recording on high-priced D.G.G. records.

THE MAGIC FLUTE (DIE ZAUBERFLOETE) (K. 620) (Complete) (Sung in German)

Here are selections from the opera.

* * * WUNDERLICH, BOEHM	*Berlin Philharmonic Orch.*	HELIODOR [Excerpts from Entfuehrung]	(S) 25075
* * KOETH, GRUEMMER, PREY, FRICK	*Berlin Philharmonic Orch., Berlin Symphony Orch., Chorus*	TURNABOUT	(M) 4072 (S) 34072

The admirable one-record Heliodor disc of excerpts consists of one side of *The Magic Flute*, backed by *Seraglio* excerpts. It is a joy, and well worth buying for the singing of the late Fritz Wunderlich alone. For more detailed remarks on this disc, see comments under Mozart's opera *Abduction from the Seraglio*.

Turnabout also offers a good disc, with solid Mozart singers (Hermann Prey is outstanding) and firm conducting.

THE MARRIAGE OF FIGARO (K. 492) (Complete)

This *opera buffa* (comic opera) is perhaps the very greatest ever written in this difficult genre. Of all comic operas, only Rossini's *The Barber of Seville,* and Donizetti's *Don Pasquale* are in the same exalted class. The text is the work of Lorenzo da Ponte, Mozart's crony and incomparable librettist. The story is simply that of a young husband whose ardor for his wife has cooled; and we behold the fun and games of extramarital inclinations on a single "mad day." Rossini's *Barber of Seville,* set to an earlier play by the same author, is concerned with the same characters three years earlier, when the husband, then a dashing lover, woos his wife.

The music is gay, the ensembles are heavenly, and the characterizations are marvelously sketched in music. In a word, *Figaro* is irresistible. It was completed in Prague in 1787.

* * * ROTHENBERGER, GUEDEN, MATHIS, PREY, BERRY, SUITNER	*Dresden State Opera Orch.* *(Sung in German)*	3-SERAPHIM	(S) 6002
* GATTI, TAJO, CORENA, PREVITALI	*Radio Italiana Orch.* *(Sung in Italian)*	3-EVEREST/CETRA	(S) 424/3
* MILDMAY, HELLETSGRUEBER, RAUTAVAARA, WILLIS, DOMGRAF-FASSBAENDER, HENDERSON, TAJO, BUSCH	*Glyndebourne Festival Orch.* *(Sung in Italian)*	3-TURNABOUT	(M) 4114/6

The Seraphim set is a masterpiece of the gramophone art. This is a chamber performance, really; the orchestra sounds like a smallish group, the harpsichord continuations between the arias are prominently featured, and there is an intimacy, a sense of spontanaeity about the performance which, to my ears, no other version approaches. In a word, I love it dearly. This is a first-rate German cast, and they sing in German, which will disturb a few people, as *Figaro* is usually done in Italian— but the ear gets used to it. Hilde Gueden is a cool, imperious Countess; Edith Mathis is ravishing as Cherubino. Hermann Prey is an elegant, lyrical Count, and Walter Berry delivers a fine characterization—not overdone—of Figaro. The real hero is conductor Otmar Suitner, who has presented us with a firm-paced, effervescent Mozart performance that will certainly become a classic.

I must add that this set—sung in German—would probably never had been released on the American market at all at the usual high prices. The revolution in low-priced records has not only brought us cheaper goodies, but has opened the doors to many wonderful performances that otherwise would never have come our way at all. The sound here is fine.

Fernando Previtali, a veteran conductor of *opera buffa,* delivers a lively, crisp, enthusiastic show that has little nuance or shadings. But this is certainly preferable to some of the cloddish Mozart reviewed elsewhere in these pages. Gatti's Countess is just so-so; the men, Tajo and Corena, have rich, creamy voices and sure Italianate style. The sound is hearable, if not exactly a delight to the ear.

The Fritz Busch reading is widely famous. It was the first *Figaro* on records (78 rpm). But apart from sentiment, the singing, by standards we have become accustomed to from many first-rate operatic recordings, is poor. The women are dull; the Figaro is cloddish, even snarling. The only virtue that remains—for eyes undimmed by nostalgia for original Glyndebourne casts—is Fritz Busch's vivid conducting. Even here Busch's work cannot compare to his miraculous *Don Giovanni,* also discussed in these pages. The sound is shallow, but lively.

THE MARRIAGE OF FIGARO (K. 492) (Excerpts) (Sung in Italian)

Here are selections from the opera.

> * * STICH-RANDALL,   *Aix Festival Orch.*   Vox   (M) 15120
> STREICH, REHFUSS,
> ROSBAUD

The one-record mono selection on Vox is put together from a complete performance, recorded on mono, at the Aix Festival in France in 1955. Live performances, when they are good, have a heady, impulsive quality that the best of studio versions rarely obtain—and this on-the-spot recording is first-rate. The chorus is rather hectic, the sound just passable, but everything moves—and vividly.

RELIGIOUS VOCAL MUSIC Mozart wrote almost all of his church music for performance in Salzburg. It is anything but dry, routine music-to-order; it is music of a composer of unshaken faith, as Mozart's letters clearly show. It is also usually joyous, exultant music, without a trace of glumness. This has caused many listeners to regard it as suspect, or as irreligious. For a comment on this, I gladly yield to the urbane C. G. Burke: "Hard treatment awaits liturgical music that does not whimper. . . . Invective has been pointed at [Mozart's Coronation Mass] for being spirited, elegant, and sensuous. . . . This is to suppose that neither health nor manners can befit a church. . . . The observant critic in church sees that the customary Mass there induces sleep, and concludes from this that sleep is the desirable and admirable result expected from a Mass. No one sleeps during a Mozart Mass, and so it must be an unholy thing."

AVE, VERUM CORPUS (K. 618)

Mozart wrote this exquisite motet for a school chorus at Baden, near Vienna, where he was a welcome visitor. This is simple, deeply moving music of the highest order. It is vastly popular.

> *Vienna Volkoper Ensemble*   2-Turnabout   (S) 34213/4

The Vienna Ensemble sings with unadorned style; this is an adequate performance.

(LA) BETULIA LIBERTA (Oratorio) (K. 118)
(Sung in Italian)

This oratorio was set to a sacred text and sung in concert form during Lent, when opera performances were forbidden. Judith exhorts the Israelites to have faith in their God and not yield to the Assyrians. She leaves the besieged city of Bethulia and returns with the head of Holofernes, the enemy of her people. This work has 15 arias and choruses. It was written in 1771, when Mozart was fifteen. While dealing with this bloodcurdling story, he was scribbling letters to his mother, "I kiss Mama's fingers a thousand times."

This is certainly not great Mozart, but able, gifted work on the part of the ambitious fledgling composer. Many graceful arias and impressive choruses are heard—all bearing the unmistakable stamp of Mozart.

* CUNDARI, LONDI, LAZZARINI, MUNTEANU, WASHINGTON, CILLARIO	*Milan Angelicum Orch. and Polyphonic Chorus*	3-VICTROLA VIC (S) 6112

The three women in the cast are all good, and so is the bass with the startling name of Paolo Washington. The conducting is on the ponderous side, and the recitatives go on and on in the dullest way. With all my love of Mozart, I really cannot urge anyone to buy this opera. This is a remarkable student work, pointing to great accomplishments to be; the performance, while decent, is not extraordinary. The *Saturday Review's* Irving Kolodin, taking off in purplish prose: ". . . But the flight into the empyrean that draws us upward on its wings rises with almost frightening power, an assurance in the command of musical materials that baffles the understanding. The concluding chorus reaches heights of rejoicing that Mozart himself rarely surpassed." The more earth-bound report of *High Fidelity* holds: "This recording has its uses . . . . A marked shortcoming of this recording is the excessive reverberation; the recording must have been made in the lions' dungeon beneath the Colosseum."

EXSULTATE, JUBILATE (K. 165)

Mozart wrote this ravishing music at seventeen for Venanzio Rauzzini, the castrato singer who had been featured in Mozart's opera *Lucio Silla* in Milano. The work is in three joyous movements. Sopranos have adopted the last movement, a setting of the word *Alleluia,* to show off their coloratura charms. (Remember Deanna Durbin in the film *100*

Men and a Girl, with Stokowski, when she comes into the hall where the Great Maestro is conducting?)

| * * * SCHWARZKOPF, SUSSKIND | *Philharmonic Orch.* | SERAPHIM   (M) 60013 [Bach, Cantata 51] |
| * LAVERGNE, GROSSMANN | *Pro Musica Orch.* | TURNABOUT   (M) 4029 (S) 34029 [Benedictus K. 117; Vivaldi, Gloria] |

Elisabeth Schwarzkopf has just about owned this music since she made this glorious disc in the 1950's, and she still keeps her title. This is a vivid, bravura, famous disc; [there is another dazzling piece for soprano on the reverse side]. The mono sound, never good to begin with, is quite thin—but never mind.

Lavergne is quite hearable, but quite outclassed. [If you're after Vivaldi's soaring choral piece *Gloria* on the reverse, it's a good buy.]

LITANIAE DE B. M. V. (LAURETANAE) (K. 109)

Mozart's litanies were intended for private performance as well as for church services. They are constructed as concert works, intended to please. This one is likeable, but not great for Mozart. He was all of fifteen when he wrote it in 1771.

| * BUCKEL, LEHANE, VAN VROOMAN WOLLITZ, REINHARDT | *Collegium Aureum Ensemble, Children's Chorus* | VICTROLA VIC   (S) 1270 [Haydn, Salve Regina] |

The Collegium Aureum Ensemble is expert. The sound is clean.

LITANIAE LAURETANAE IN D (K. 195)

This Litany of 1774 is rather formal and ceremonial, but contains a tender and expressive solo section, *Agnus Dei.* This is not an important Mozart work.

| * BAUER | *Soloists, Orch. and Chorus of Dresden Cathedral* | EVEREST   (S) 3233 |

The amateur soloists are effective, and the nonprofessional air about this performance is something of an asset—as often happens in church music. The sound is resonant.

MASS IN C (K. 317) ("CORONATION")

This is a brilliant, joyous, often operatic Mass, composed in 1779 for an annual service of a church near Salzburg to celebrate the coronation of the Virgin. Mozart was twenty-three.

* * * STICH-RANDALL, CASONI, BOTTAZZO, LITTASY, RISTENPART		NONESUCH 71041 [Vesperae solennes de Con- fessore, in C, K. 339]
* LIPP, LUDWIG, DICKIE, HORENSTEIN	*Vienna Pro Musica Chorus*	TURNABOUT (3) 4063 [Vesperae solennes de Con- fessore, in C, K. 339]

The choral work on the Ristenpart set is clean and well-balanced. Teresa Stich-Randall's cool, limpid voice is a stand-out in this *Mass*. *Stereo Record Guide:* "Stich-Randall's soaring simplicity of phrase is like a lark: it moves me greatly."

Horenstein achieves good rapport among his talented soloists, but the tempos seem driven, with the kind of nervous twitch that makes this conductor's Mahler so famous, but is inappropriate in Mozart.

MASS IN C MINOR (K. 427) ("THE GREAT")

This glorious *Mass* was written in Vienna, in the season of 1782-83. Mozart was twenty-two at the time and a devoutly religious young man. He put some heavenly soprano solos in the work so that he could show off the soprano voice of his bride, Constanze, when the couple made their first visit to Mozart's family in Salzburg. This is very great music indeed, and not a few Mozarteans prefer it to Mozart's great *Requiem* itself.

It is not generally realized that Wolfgang Mozart was a deeply religious man. Mozart was commissioned from time to time to write a piece for the Church but in Vienna, he had no official connection with the Church. He was a free-lance composer who occupied himself with whatever offers came his way—serenades, piano concertos, operas.

But Mozart's religious feeling remained strong and demanded fulfill-ment. And so in the summer of 1782, he began to write a new Mass. He said that this was a vow he had made, in his heart of hearts, when he had brought his young wife Constanze to Salzburg. The Mass was to be Mozart's humble thanks to God for his good fortune.

"I have the score done for half of the Mass," Mozart wrote. "It's still lying here waiting to be finished—which is the best proof that I really made the vow." But the Mass waited in vain for completion. The reasons for this are obscure. We have only the first half-dozen movements—a magnificent torso.

There are few pages more profound in all music. This *Mass* represents his personal coming to terms with God and with his art. This composition remains perhaps the only religious creation in music on a par with Bach's *Mass* and the *Mass* of Beethoven.

* * * LIPP, LUDWIG, DICKIE, BERRY, GROSSMANN	*Pro Musica Orch., Vienna Oratorio Chorus*	TURNABOUT	(S) 34174
* STADER, CASEI, KMENTT, REHFUSS, AUBERSON	*Vienna State Opera Orch. and Chorus*	2-VANGUARD	(S) 258/9

An elevated, often soaring reading is to be had from veteran conductor Grossmann and his admirably blended soloists.

The two-record Vanguard version is an enlarged version of the *C Minor Mass,* in essence due to Alois Schmitt, Court Music Director of Dresden, and first performed in 1901. With the assistance of prominent Mozart scholars, Schmitt took over sections from earlier Mozart Masses and worked out sketches by the master in order to fill out the missing sections of the *Credo* and other movements. However, I am uncomfortable with this fleshing-out of Mozart. The singing is earnest. Soloist Maria Stader has an almost ideal voice for Mozart's Masses.

MISSA BREVIS IN C (K. 220) ("SPATZENMESSE")

This is a short, uncomplicated mass of no great appeal. It seems that Mozart was deliberately simple here, writing with untutored singers in mind.

* GROSSMANN	*Vienna Symphony Orch.*	Vox [Missa K. 194]	(M) 7060

Grossmann is unpretentious; the mono sound is fair.

MISSA BREVIS IN C (K. 259)

This is a short, undeveloped mass of 1776, consisting largely of alternate choral and solo quartet passages.

* GILLESBERGER	*Vienna Volksoper Orch. and Chamber Chorus*	TURNABOUT (S) [Haydn, Mass 5]	(3) 4132

The veteran conductor Gillesberger is an old hand with Mozart church music and is competent in this piece.

REQUIEM (K. 626)

Very great Mozart, and very great music indeed—this is Mozart's only *Requiem Mass*. It is also the last music he wrote, and death prevented him from finishing it. Much mystery is connected with this piece, centering on just how much of this music Mozart actually wrote and how much was finished by lesser hands.

To begin with, the true "mysterious stranger" tale beloved of annotators of record jackets: In 1791 Mozart was surprised one day by the entrance of a stranger who brought him an unsigned letter ordering a Requiem. Mozart accepted the engagement; but he was a dying man and never finished it. It later came to light that the anonymous patron, Count Walsegg, had ordered it secretly to be performed privately in memory of his wife; Walsegg wished to pass it off as his own composition.

Mozart's widow, anxious to collect the promised fee (half had been paid in advance), engaged a pupil of Mozart's named Suessmayr to finish off the *Requiem*. How much Suessmayr actually wrote is still disputed to this day. In any case, this is wonderful, pensive, resigned music. One curious note: Mozart banished flutes, oboes, clarinets, and horns from the score and limited his woodwinds to bassoons and a pair of basset-horns—the latter being a little-used type of tenor clarinet. Mozart loved the basset-horn, and so did George Bernard Shaw, who wrote of this instrument as possessing a "peculiar watery melancholy and the total absence of any richness or passion in its tone, just the thing for a funeral."

* * * SEEFRIED, PITZINGER, HOLM, BORG, JOCHUM	*Vienna Symphony Orch. and State Opera Chorus*	HELIODOR	(S) 25000
* * GRUMMER, FRICK, KEMPE	*Berlin Philharmonic, St. Hedwigs Chorus*	PICKWICK	(S) 4039

Anyone who knows Jochum's authoritative work in Bach's *B-Minor Mass* would expect a superlative reading of Mozart's *Requiem* from this gifted conductor. That expectation is entirely fulfilled in a soaring, yet gentle performance. The singing has both warmth and earnestness, and there are some sensational climaxes. The soloists and chorus are excellent. In sum, here is one of the best Mozart *Requiem* available today, regardless of price. One sour note comes from Peter Gammond in *Music on Record:* "Weighty but pedestrian."

Kempe's pure reading has been highly praised for its chaste ambiance.

The soloists are really wonderful, particularly soprano Grummer and basso Frick. The chorus is fine; I like its untheatricality. Peter Gammond in *Music on Record:* "Kempe is inclined to moon over the whole thing and to be a bit over-religious."

VESPERAE SOLENNES (K. 339)

This is a light-hued piece of 1780, with a gentle soprano aria, *Laudate Dominum,* which is one of the loveliest melodies in all church music.

* * * STICH-RANDALL, CASONI, BOTTAZZO, LITTASY, RISTENPART	*Sarre Orch. and Chorus*	NONESUCH [Mass K. 317]	71041
* HORENSTEIN	*Vienna Pro Musica Symphony Orchestra and Chorus*	TURNABOUT [Mass K. 317]	(3) 4063

Strong, unhurried direction makes Ristenpart's version impressive. He is also blessed with the moving Stich-Randall.

By comparison, the Horenstein version is tense and impatient.

VARIOUS VOCAL WORKS Like his musical contemporaries, Mozart wrote music by the yard, to order. A fee was a fee. In the last sad year of his life he was so hard up for cash that he even accepted a commission to write some soporific tootlings for a glass harmonica. It is not surprising, then, that he wrote much vocal music, for just about every conceivable purpose—weddings, funerals, parties, birthdays, etc.

CANONS, COMIC ENSEMBLES, AND ARIAS

This is a collection of low-comedy pieces by Mozart, some of it scatalogical. It all doesn't add up to much, unless you're fascinated by the idea of the Master bothering to write such bawdy distractions.

KOETH, SCHREIER, PREY, BERRY, MEYER, KELLER	*Vienna Akademie Kammerchor, Convivium Musicum of Munich*	SERAPHIM	(S) 60050

Some fine singers, especially Hermann Prey and Walter Berry, are wasted in this trivia.

CANTATA: EINE KLEINE FREIMAURER (K. 623)

This seldom-played cantata was written in 1791, just after Mozart had finished his opera, *The Magic Flute.* The cantata contains some of that opera's sonorousness, but little of its charm.

* CUENOD, GIRAUDEAU, SOUZAY, MEYER	*Vienna Pro Musica Orch., Mulhouse Oratorio Chorus*	3-TURNABOUT	4111/3
	Vienna Volksoper Orch. and Soloists	2-TURNABOUT	34213/4

Cuenod and Souzay are splendid soloists and the male chorus is good. The Vienna Volksoper ensemble is rough. The sound is poor.

MASONIC MUSIC (Complete)

Mozart was an enthusiastic Mason (so were Goethe, Lessing, and Schiller). This not particularly interesting music was connected with Masonic ceremonials such as services for deceased members. The famous and beautiful motet *Ave Verum Corpus* is also included in this collection, although I still haven't figured out what (if anything) it had to do with Masonic rites.

PETER MAAG	*Vienna Volksoper Orch., Soloists, and Wind Quintet*	2-TURNABOUT	34213/4

These recordings stem from a 1966 jubilee concert of the Masonic Grand Lodge Mozart in Vienna. The orchestra is ragged. There is a semi-professional air about the proceedings that gets in the way.

Mussorgsky, Modest (1839-1881)

Born in Karevo, Russia, Mussorgsky was educated in the Military School for Ensigns. After becoming an officer, he decided to abandon his military career for music. Balakirev and Borodin inflamed him with ardor and with the idea of writing nationalistic music. Under these two mentors, he began to compose.

Although largely self-taught, Mussorgsky is perhaps the most original musical genius Russia ever produced. In his later life, he suffered from neglect and poverty and he died at age 42 on a lonely death-bed in a soldiers' hospital.

PLACE AND ACHIEVEMENT   The most intensely Russian of composers, Mussorgsky flung away the trite conventions that saturated the music of his day. He based his work, for the most part, on Russian folk song and even on the inflections of Russian speech.

His greatest achievements were in opera and in song. His masterpiece, *Boris Godounov,* is outstanding for its dramatic power and splendid color. The opera presents the towering figure of Boris — perhaps the most dramatic characterization in music.

THE ESSENTIAL MUSSORGSKY
OPERA: *Boris Godounov.*

ORCHESTRAL MUSIC: *A Night on Bald Mountain (completed and orchestrated by Rimsky-Korsakov); Pictures at an Exhibition (orchestrated by Ravel).*

VOCAL MUSIC: *Song of the Flea; Songs and Dances of Death. [There are about 70 others, too numerous to mention.]*

OTHER WORKS
OPERAS: *The Fair at Sorochinsk; Khovantschina.*

PIANO MUSIC: *[There are many assorted short pieces.]*

BORIS GODOUNOV (sung in Russian)

This raw, massive Slavic masterpiece, written in 1874, is one of the greatest operas ever written. The characterization of Boris is almost Shakespearian in its depth and power; Boris is often termed "the Russian Macbeth." Rimsky-Korsakov revised the unmanageable mass of manuscript that Mussorgsky left at his death; and the tidied-up version is the one almost always used today, except at London's Covent Garden. Whether Rimsky-Korsakov improved or mutilated the opera is still a matter of hot dispute, but there is no question that his ruthless editing was responsible for its world-wide fame.

* GOLOVANOV   *Bolshoi Theatre Orch.*   3-PERIOD   (M) 1033

Pirogov, a great Russian bass, is featured. His singing is very convincing and very Slavic, but at times is vocally unsteady. This set cannot compare in any way with the great performances available by Boris Christoff and George London on high-priced records. Nevertheless, Pirogov's characterization is much admired. In this record, the entire, unedited opera (not Rimsky-Korsakov's version) is used. The sound is not very good.

This recording appears to have been made from one of the "mystery tapes" that frequently turned up from behind the Iron Curtain during the early days of LP recordings. Often, an enterprising soul flew to Vienna or Budapest, turned on his radio and his portable tape recorder, and flew back to America with a "new recording." All was quite legal, as Russia has no copyright agreements with the West.

BORIS GODOUNOV (Selections)

* * REIZEN   *Chorus and Orchestra of*   MACE   (M) 2016
                the Bolshoi Theatre

The basso, Mark Reizen, sings with sweeping force; he is one of the best of the many great Russian basses. The mono sound, dating from 1958, is all right.

MUSSORGSKY SONG RECITAL: SONGS AND DANCES OF DEATH; KING SAUL, GOPAK; THE WINDS ARE HOWLING; THE SONG OF THE FLEA

Lovers of the vocal art—or of the Russian soul—should not miss hearing this music. Mussorgsky achieved great artistic success as a composer of songs—far more than did Tchaikovsky or any other Russian. In the song form, Mussorgsky seems untroubled by the problems of orchestral technique which always plagued him.

* * CHRISTOFF,   *Orchestra National*   SERAPHIM   (M) 60008
    TZIPINE   *de la RTF*

Boris Christoff has both voice and perception; at times he sounds amazingly like the great Chaliapin of earlier decades. Christoff has said that his admiration for Mussorgsky made him decide to give up a law career and to become a singer. The mono sound is fine and full.

The excerpts from *Songs and Dances of Death* are part of a special four-record issue by Angel Records—a project of love.

NIGHT ON BALD MOUNTAIN

This fine descriptive music, written in 1867, was "completed"—or rather entirely rewritten—by Rimsky-Korsakov. *Night on Bald Mountain* is a musical impression of a Witches' Sabbath, traditionally held on Midsummer's Eve in the Harz Mountains of Germany. The composer worked on this short orchestral piece all his life, but was never quite satisfied with it. Rimsky-Korsakov revised and re-orchestrated it, and today *Night on Bald Mountain* is one of the most popular descriptive orchestral works in the repertory.

* * * REINER	*Chicago Symphony Orch.*	VICTROLA VIC (S) 1068 [Russian Program]	
* * SARGENT	*London Symphony Orch.*	EVEREST (M) 6053 (S) 3053 [Pictures at an Exhibition]	
* HOLLREISER	*Vienna Symphony Orch.*	VOX (5) (S) 11690 [Russian Program]	
* GOLSCHMAN		VANGUARD (S) 210 [Pictures at an Exhibition]	
* ANSERMET	*Paris Conservatoire Orch.*	RICHMOND (M) 19087 [Russian Pops Program]	
* CHALABALA	*Czech Philharmonic*	PARLIAMENT (S) 151 [Mixed Program]	

Reiner gives the finest interpretation available on low-priced records. His recording features a well-selected program and striking sound.

Sargent also provides a colorful reading. The sound is ageeable.

Hollreiser delivers a vivid, competent performance.

Golschman's reading is lively and well-recorded.

Ansermet's interpretation is precise and finicky. The sound is only fair.

Chalabala's performance is winning and appealing, but the sound is murky.

PICTURES AT AN EXHIBITION *(Orchestra)*

This work is much more famous in its orchestral version; few works are so firmly established in the concert repertory. In its orchestral form, three men were responsible for its success: Mussorgsky, who originally wrote the marvelous piece for piano; Maurice Ravel, who did the brilliant orchestration; and Serge Koussevitsky, who in 1921 asked his friend Maurice Ravel to arrange the work for orchestra, and who then conducted the first performance at a "Koussevitsky Concert" in Paris.

* * * TOSCANINI	*NBC Symphony Orch.*	VICTROLA VIC (M) 1273 [Ravel, Daphnis and Chloe Suite No. 2]	

* * KUBELIK	Chicago Symphony Orch.	MERCURY	(M) 14028
			(S) 18028
* * ANSERMET	Suisse Romande Orch.	RICHMOND	(M) 19073
		[Ravel, La Valse]	
* GOLSCHMAN		VANGUARD	(S) 210
		[Night on Bald Mountain]	
SARGENT	London Symphony Orch.	EVEREST	(M) 6053
			(S) 3053
		[Night on Bald Mountain]	

This piece was a Toscanini favorite, and this recording is one of the Maestro's very best. Toscanini pays marvelous attention to detail. The sound is all right. [The coupling is first-rate Ravel.]

Kubelik offers a solid, high-tension stereo version, extremely well recorded.

Ansermet is crisp and colorful; less hard-driven. The sound is only mono.

Golschman's interpretation is hearable, but hardly outstanding.

The playing of the London Symphony Orchestra is too pedestrian for this spectacular virtuoso piece.

PICTURES AT AN EXHIBITION (Piano)

Victor Hartmann, painter and close friend of Mussorgsky, died in 1873, at the age of 39. After attending a memorial exhibition of Hartmann's paintings, Mussorgsky set ten of the artist's pictures to music, as a tribute to his departed friend. Mussorgsky wrote the pieces for the piano.

The original piano version of the Pictures has always been a great testing ground for the virtuoso pianist.

Several of the short sketches that make up the Pictures are masterpieces of character portrayal in music—the gesticulating Jewish peddlers, the market women, the scampering children in the Tuileries, etc. This is highly descriptive music at its very best. This music demands subtle color, high imagination, and fiery technique of a performer.

| * * * RICHTER | ARTIA | (M)   154 |
| | [Prokofiev, Sonata No. 7] | |

Richter plays with fiery imagination and stupendous technique. The sound is all right. [A great Prokofiev sonata is included on the back of the disc.]

There have been many recorded versions of the Pictures, but today, the catalogue lists only two: the famous Horowitz recording (a high-priced disc) and that of Richter. All others have vanished in the face of this awesome competition.

Nardini, Pietro (1722-1793)

Nardini was a violinist, as were so many Italian 18th-century composers. He studied under Tartini, and in 1771 was appointed musical director at the court in Florence. Leopold Mozart (the great Mozart's father) praised Nardini's violin playing.

CONCERTO FOR VIOLIN IN G; CONCERTO FOR VIOLIN IN E MINOR

This is pleasant uneventful music of the period.

* * TOMASOV   *Vienna State Opera*   Vanguard   (S)   154
              Chamber Orch.   [Tartini, Concerto in D]

The works are nicely played; the soloist possesses a singing violin tone.

Nicolai, Otto *(1810-1849)*

Nicolai, a German, wrote some operas in Italian style, and founded the Vienna Philharmonic. His masterpiece, *The Merry Wives of Windsor,* was produced only two months before his untimely death at the age of 39.

THE MERRY WIVES OF WINDSOR *(sung in German)*

Verdi's *Falstaff,* based on similar Shakespearean material, has overshadowed this work in popularity. Nevertheless, Nicolai's opera remains a pleasing blend of German and Italian inspiration. This opera is an institution in Germany; the overture is often played elsewhere.

STRIENZ, LUDWIG,   3-Urania   (5) (M) 214-3
ROTHER

The incomparable Wilhelm Strienz is superb as Falstaff. Unfortunately, that is all I can recommend about this venerable set. The sound is old.

Nielsen, Carl (1865-1931)

Twenty years ago the name of Carl Nielsen was known only to a small band of followers in America. Unlike almost every other twentieth-century composer of major or minor importance, Nielsen was shamefully neglected during his lifetime. He had some reputation within his native Denmark, and a few scattered admirers abroad, and that was all. He died bitter, cynical, and in despair over the musical life. In 1950, a Danish orchestra played Nielsen's bold *Fifth Symphony* at the Edinburgh Festival. It was a sensation, as were the orchestra's Nielsen programs the following year in London. Nielsen's popularity became widespread.

Nielsen's major works are his six symphonies. His music has occasionally been linked with that of his contemporary Sibelius, but there is really little in common between the two distinguished Scandinavians. Sibelius always strikes one as a brooding mystic, stirred by the northern landscape rather than by humanity. Nielsen is a humanist—warm, engaging and serene.

CONCERTO FOR VIOLIN AND ORCHESTRA (Opus 33)

This, the first of Nielsen's concertos, was first performed in 1912. Despite the commonly held opinion that Nielsen was neglected and then suddenly discovered (and *ipso facto* therefore a genius), I am not convinced that this is a good concerto.

VARGA, SEMKOW   *Royal Danish Orch.*   TURNABOUT TV   (M)   4043
                                                                                      (S) 34043

Varga seems to grapple successfully with the very difficult solo part. The sound is decent.

STRING QUARTET NO. 3 IN E-FLAT (Opus 14); SERENATA IN VANO

The interesting *Quartet No. 3,* for which Brahms seems to have been the inspiration, displays much technical skill, particularly in a tightly-woven first movement. The *Serenata,* a wind piece, is a good example of Nielsen's "modern" technique that still retains traditional tonal principles.

  *   *Copenhagen String Quartet* TURNABOUT TV   (S) 34109

Both pieces receive sensitive and dedicated playing. The sound is clean.

SYMPHONY NO. 2 ("Four Temperaments")

This basically good-humored symphony was inspired by the composer's visit to a village tavern in Zealand. On the wall of the inn, a print drolly illustrated the four human temperaments: choleric, phlegmatic, melancholic, and sanguine. The composer mused over his glass of beer, and then went home to produce the four musical pictures which make up this work.

Even when well played and recorded, however, this inoffensive music is not of a quality comparable to Nielsen's *Fourth* and *Fifth Symphonies.*

* GARAGULY	*Tivoli Concert Symphony Orch.*	TURNABOUT	(3)	4049

The performance and the sonics are both quite acceptable. When this performance was on the Vox label, the English *Stereo Guide* commented: "The performance here is generally an excellent one, its vivacity compensating for any occasional lack of discipline. The recording is perhaps a little dry, but it is clear and undistorted. Recommended."

SYMPHONY NO. 4 (Opus 29) ("The Inextinguishable")

This is a violent, passionate work, reminiscent of Mahler and the early Schoenberg, and curiously, of Vaughan Williams. The title refers to the "elementary will to life." This work was written during the First World War when, as the composer wrote, "the whole world is disintegrating . . . National feeling . . . has become like a spiritual syphilis that has devoured the brains, and it grins out through the empty eye-sockets with moronic hate."

* * MARKEVITCH	*Royal Danish Orch.*	TURNABOUT TV	(M)	4050
			(S)	34050

Markevitch gives a tempestuous performance, brimming with nervous energy. The recording is brilliant. *Hi/Fi Stereo Review* commented: "This high-voltage reading of Nielsen's heaven-storming piece adds up to a real humdinger of a record, as well as a best buy at the price."

SYMPHONY NO. 6 ("Sinfonia Semplice")

Compared to Nielsen's other compositions, this is a bitter, negative work. He wrote it when *angina pectoris,* the disease that killed him, had already destroyed the solid health he had always enjoyed. Nielsen at this time was a frustrated, bewildered man, unable to understand why the outside world adored Sibelius and passed him by. This is not a very good piece; its interest is primarily for confirmed admirers of Nielsen.

LANDAU   *Westchester Symphony*   TURNABOUT   (S) 34182
                      Orch.   [Sibelius, Humoresques]

The playing is hardly of high standard, but it will do for Nielsen fans who want this music. [The Sibelius filler piece is slight.]

Ockeghem, Johannes (c. 1425-1495)

Ockeghem taught Josquin Des Prez; both composers were founding fathers of Western music, and they were the first two in a long succession of famous Flemish composers.

MOTETS, INSTRUMENTAL AND VOCAL

These works display little of Dufay's or Des Prez' strange and gripping beauty, but Ockeghem's music is nevertheless excellent, and a priceless heritage.

* * BLANCHARD	*Ensemble*	MUSIC GUILD (S) 134 [Des Prez, Missa Hercules]

This disc provides impeccable playing and singing under the direction of Roger Blanchard, a man to reckon with in Renaissance music. The sound is clean, but a bit dry. Records of Ockeghem are hard to find. Coupled with music by the great Des Prez, this record is of the highest interest for the music lover who desires to trace the beginnings of the art.

Offenbach, Jacques (1819-1880)

The son of a Jewish cantor of Cologne, Offenbach studied at the Paris Conservatory. In 1849, he became conductor at the Comedie Francaise. In 1855, he leased his own theater, and enjoyed tremendous success both as an impresario and as a composer of comic opera.

Gay, irresistible melodies made Offenbach the darling of the pleasure-loving Second Empire. During a career of 25 years, he produced some 90 comic operas. His serious opera-comique, *The Tales of Hoffmann,* was presented a year after his death. Many of his brilliant light operas are still popular in France. Few composers can rival Offenbach for clever, sparkling music.

GAITE PARISIENNE

In 1938, the French composer Manuel Rosenthal raided the vast treasure-house of Offenbach melodies and came up with this delicious ballet score.

* * FIEDLER	*Boston Pops Orch.*	Victrola	VIC (S) 1012
* LEIBOWITZ	*London Philharmonic*	1-Parliament	(S) 177
MONTIEL	*Ballet Orch.*	Somerset St. Fi.	(S) 11100

Arthur Fiedler and the Boston Pops play this piece with sparkle and elan. The sound is striking.

Leibowitz does not begin to suggest the raciness of this score.

The Montiel disc is outclassed.

LA BELLE HELENE (Sung in French)

This first-rate operetta never caught on in America, but still trots the boards in Europe as *Die Schoene Helena.* The intoxicating music and satirical libretto still amuse. Wicked Paris of 1864 is spread before us by a master of *opera bouffe.*

* LEIBOWITZ	*Paris Philharmonic*	2-Renaissance	SX 206

Andre Dran is perfect as Paris, and the rest of the cast is good. A reviewer of *Hi/Fi Stereo Review* commented: "My ears tell me that this performance, while entertaining enough, isn't the last word in style." The sound is decent, but dry.

ORPHEUS IN HADES (Sung in French)

Here are Can-Can ensembles, and all that you expect to go with this bubbly music. Bernard Shaw, who loved *Orpheus*, wrote: "Offenbach's music is wicked; it is abandoned stuff—every accent in it is a snap of the fingers in the face of moral responsibility." The crackling gaity of the score has hardly dimmed since 1858. As with *Gaîté Parisienne*, Offenbach has fared very well at the hands of his editors; the celebrated overture to this work was composed by one Carl Binder, using the melodies of the opera.

| * COLLART, MOLLIEN, DRAN, DEMIGNY, LEIBOWITZ | *Paris Philharmonic Orch. and Chorus* | 2-EVEREST | S-438/2 |

The singers here are only so-so; the real star is the spirited conductor, Rene Leibowitz. The sound is clean but dated.

OVERTURES: ORPHEUS IN THE UNDERWORLD; THE GRAND DUCHESS OF GEROLSTEIN; LA BELLE HELENE; BLUEBEARD; LE MARIAGE AUX LANTERNES

These overtures are sparkling and vivacious.

| * MARTINON | *The London Philharmonic Orch.* | RICHMOND | (M) B 19098 |

Under the zestful baton of this admirable Offenbach conductor, the music is played with brio and high style. This once-famous mono Decca FFRR disc, still has an enjoyable acoustical flair.

TALES OF HOFFMANN (Sung in German)

As the old saying goes, in every comedian there lurks the soul of a Hamlet, and Offenbach was no exeception. Rossini called him the "Mozart of the Champs-Elysees"; Offenbach played to full, spellbound houses, night after night. With his gay umbrellas and violently colored clothes, he had grown into a living legend. Yet, Offenbach yearned to write a serious opera.

How *Hoffmann* was born is obscure. In 1851, a play written by Jules Barbier and Michel Carre entitled *Les Contes Fantastiques d'Hoffmann* had been produced at the Odeon in Paris. This play dealt with a group of tales culled from the printed works of Ernst Theodor Amadeus Hoffmann (1776-1822), a German author-composer who was one of the founding fathers of the Romantic movement, and who had a genuine penchant for things bizarre.

When Offenbach first realized that Hoffmann's tales might serve as a serious libretto, he was up to his eyebrows in the comic theatre. Not until 25 years later did he begin to write music for a libretto that Barbier had fashioned from the earlier play. In its final form, the opera differs materially from the play.

ANDERS, BERGER,   2-Urania   (5) 114/2
STREICH,
MUELLER,
ROTHER

This one available set at a low price is sung in an abridged version, in stolid German; it is not at all the kind of recording we expect today. Peter Anders is shaky, but Erna Berger delivers some lilting arias. The sound is badly dated.

Orff, Carl (1895-   )

This German composer studied in Munich, conducted opera in Munich and Darmstadt, and has been a teacher in Munich since 1950. His compositions comprise stage works of three types: cantatas with optional action and dance (*Carmina Burana*, 1937); *Trionfo di Afrodite*, 1953); operas (*Der Mond*, 1945); and plays with music (*Die Bernauerin*, 1947; *Antigonae*, 1949).

Carl Orff is perhaps the most popular of contemporary composers. Stratvinsky, of course, is much more known and famous, but most of the Stravinsky music that listeners enjoy was composed as early as 1910. The music that Stravinsky writes today has not yet been accepted by most cultured ears.

The music of Orff captivates the listener at once with its emotional, primitive appeal. It would be safe to say that many of the people who enjoy Carl Orff are indifferent to most other modern composers. Orff goes his own way, independent, ignoring all fashions and trends. He is a medievalist in the twentieth century. Yet he is extremely listenable; the first time you hear one of his "scenic cantatas," the music bowls you over. However, once his tricks become familiar, the effect is somewhat less. But in any case, Orff ranks as an original, highly talented composer.

CARMINA BURANA

American record companies "discovered" Carl Orff. Even before his music was widely performed in this country, his *Carmina Burana* became a best-seller in the record shops. So much for instant fame via the phenomenon of the record mass-market industry.

Sex is the theme of this Rabelaisian text—profane love, even a section on the delight of deflowering virgins.

* SMETACEK	*Czech Philharmonic*	PARLIAMENT	(S)	161
* VULPIUS, ROTZSCH, REHM, HUEBENTHAL, KEGEL	*Leipzig Children's Choir, Radio Leipzig Chorus and Orch.*	HELIODOR	(M/S)	25004

The Czech disc is less than fiery, which won't do.

The Heliodor recording comes from East Germany, and if you're wondering what's going on there, musically speaking, the answer seems to be—not much. The solos are pleasant, but the total effect is bucolic, and not a red-hot rendition which this driving primitivistic score demands. The sound is all right.

The best available version is Ormandy's, on a high-priced Columbia.

CATULLI CARMINA

Catulli Carmina, dating from 1943, is a complete piece in itself. It is also the second part of a trilogy, entitled *Trionfi,* the first part of which is the sensational *Carmina Burana.*

Love poems of the Roman poet Catullus are the text of *Catulli Carmina,* and after 2000 years, they are still audacious. Much of the Latin text is unprintable in English, as you will see if you glance at the liner notes. This is vivid, frenzied music.

The composer suppressed two earlier, presumably more erotic, versions.

* * ROON, LOEFFLER,   *Vienna Chamber Chorus*   TURNABOUT (3)   (S) 4061
      HOLLREISER

* TATTERMUSCHOVA,   *Prague Symphony Orch.*   CROSSROADS
    ZIDEK, SMETACEK   (M) 22 16 0003
                                                            (S) 22 16 0004

Hollreiser is convincing and exciting. The sound is realistic.

The Czechs have not wrung passion from this score. The instrumentation alone should provide a violent experience—four pianos, four tympani, and about 12 other percussion instruments, including maracas and stone sounds—but little of Orff's emotional upheaval gets across on this disc.

Paganini, Niccolo (1782-1840)

Born in Genoa, Paganini is remembered as the most famous violinist the world has ever seen. He made his first concert tour at thirteen. From 1805 to 1813, he was music director at the court of the Princess of Lucca. In 1828, he began his celebrated tour of Vienna, Germany, Paris, and London.

He is held to have been the greatest of all violinists in technical accomplishment. He was also a performer of extraordinary fascination—even magnetism—rousing his listeners to a hysteria similar to the furore caused by the pianist Franz Liszt.

He left two violin concertos, nine sets of variations, and other pieces for the violin. His flashy *Concerto No. 1* is still favored by romantic fiddlers, and his 24 *Caprices* are a must for the student violinist.

SONATA CONCERT AT A FOR VIOLIN AND GUITAR; SONATA A OPUS POSTHUMOUS FOR VIOLIN AND GUITAR; GRAND SONATA FOR GUITAR WITH VIOLIN ACCOMPANIMENT

These are irresistible compositions; light and fanciful music.

* * * BAUML, KLASINC   MACE   (M) 9024

This is an utterly charming record. Guitarist Marga Bauml and violinist Walter Klasinc provide assured and lovely playing. The beautiful, warm sound is from Electrola.

Paisiello, Giovanni (1740-1816)

This Italian began as a composer of church music, but found his true métier in *opera buffa*. He wrote more than a hundred light operas, and was director of music in Napoleon's chapel in 1802-03. A writer of sharp opera characterizations, Paisiello is believed to have influenced Mozart.

THE BARBER OF SEVILLE

Once upon a time, the title "The Barber" meant to opera-lovers that tremendous hit by Paisiello, not the now-famous opera by Rossini. In fact, Paisiello's 1781 treatment of the Beaumarchais play was so revered that his partisans were infuriated when, in 1816, the young Rossini had the impudence to use the same material for *his* opera. Paisiello's opera is witty and neat and contains pleasant melodies, but contains little that is memorable.

* * SCIUTTI,   EVEREST   (S) 443/2
  CAPECCHI, PETRI,
  RANERAI, FASANO

The Everest set, with true stereo recorded by Ricordi of Italy, has very clear sound. The score is severely cut to fit on a two-record set, but there is a winsome eighteenth-century appeal to this work that is brought out by the incisive conducting of Renato Fasano. The singing is highly professional, with Graziella Sciutti a stand-out. *High Fidelity* comments: "The performance is a superb one with stylish singing . . . and affectionate leadership."

Palestrina, Giovanni Pierluigi Da
(1525-1594)

Born in Palestrina, near Rome, Giovanni became a chorister at Santa Maria Maggiore in Rome in 1537; he later became organist and choirmaster at Palestrina Cathedral. In 1555, Pope Julius II made him a member of the Papal Choir. He was dismissed, probably because he married, but he nevertheless succeeded Lassus as musical director at St. John Lateran. Upon his wife's death in 1580, Palestrina resolved to become a priest, and actually took the tonsure; but some months later, he married a wealthy widow.

PLACE AND ACHIEVEMENT Sir Donal Tovey has remarked that Palestrina, like Spinoza, was a God-intoxicated man. For him his music was an act of faith. Like the work of his great Spanish contemporary, Victoria, his art burns with an intense religious fervor. This mellifluous music of the Catholic rite must first be accepted for what it was if its full beauty is to become evident. His is the pure voice of the Roman church.

Palestrina was the greatest composer of the sixteenth century. His noble, sonorous music was a reaction against the overly complex counterpoint that had become an obsession of the composers who had preceded him.

THE ESSENTIAL PALESTRINA
CHURCH MUSIC: *Christmas Mass; Magnificat; Motets; Masses: Ascendo ad Patrem; In Festis Apostolorum; Missa Papae Marcelli; Missa Sine Nomine.*

OTHER WORKS
CHURCH MUSIC: [*Palestrina wrote more than 90 Masses, 500 Motets, Magnificats, Hymns, etc.*]
SECULAR MUSIC: [*Palestrina wrote 4 Books of Madrigals, etc.*]

MISSA PAPAE MARCELLI

This is perhaps the greatest of Palestrina's masses, and definitely the best-known. As explained by musicologist Alfred Einstein, this mass is the result of a homily on music delivered by Pope Marcellus II on April 12, 1555 to the Sistine Choir of which Palestrina was a member. *Missa Papae Marcelli* was hailed by the stern Council of Trent as being "a model of purified writing, containing nothing lascivious nor impure." This warm, tender work pleases those who find much of Palestrina's music rather cold and forbidding.

| * THEURING | *Akademie Kammerchor* | WESTMINSTER | (M) | 9605 |
| * VESELKA | *Czech Philharmonic* | PARLIAMENT [Motets] | (S) | 612 |

The Theuring recording is well sung. The mono sound is acceptable.
The Czech disc is reverent, but suffers from fuzzy recording.

THE SONG OF SONGS

These motets are set to erotic verses from the Old Testament which,
after dedicating the work to Pope Gregory, Palestrina palmed off as "an
allegorical expression of the love of Christ for his Church."

| * DOBRODINSKY | *The Slovak Philharmonic Chorus* | CROSSROADS DT | 22 16 0186 |

This is indifferent, glum singing, and poor recording quality as well—
a pity.

Pasquini, Bernardo (1637-1710)

Born approximately a half century before Bach, Pasquini worked in Rome, and was harpsichordist of the opera orchestra in which Corelli was first violinist. His pupils included Domenico Scarlatti.

FIFTEEN SONATAS FOR TWO ORGANS AND TWO HARPSICHORDS

This is terse, vigorous music.

* * ALAIN, TAGLIAVINI   Music Guild   (S)   139

Marie Claire Alain and Luigi Tagliavini are impeccable musicians. This is a rewarding record, recommended to Baroque lovers who are weary of Vivaldi et alia. The sound is clean.

Penderecki, Krzysztof (1933-   )

It's pronounced Pen-de-RETS-ki and this is a name to remember—Penderecki is Poland's leading contemporary composer. With his extremely impressive *Passion*, he has jetted full-blown onto the world's cultural scene, hailed by the critics as being little short of a musical Second Coming. His work holds immediate appeal for the sophisticated listener despite the use of such outlandish devices as wailings, the striking of the fiddle with the bow, and others equally as weird.

PASSION ACCORDING TO ST. LUKE

"No single piece of music emerging from Eastern Europe since . . . a decade ago has made a fraction of the impact of the *St. Luke Passion*," says English critic Peter Hayworth. The *Passion*, which had its world premiere in 1966, was commissioned by the West German Radio in Cologne for the 700th anniversary of the cathedral in Muenster.

There is much to admire in this large-scale, fervently religious music. The composer has not hesitated to use any device that seems to "play," as they say in the theater. There are passages suggestive of Gregorian chant, clusters of random sounds, a twelve-tone series, and a basic structure built on the notation order B*A*C*H (B flat, A B C)—the composer's homage to J. S. Bach. This is intense, overwhelming music of our time—a must for anyone who cares for modern music.

* * * WOYTOWICZ, LADYSZ, HIOLSKI, BARTSCH, CZYZ	*Cologne Radio Symphony Orch. and Chorus*	Victrola VIC (M/S) 6015

Fervently sung with utter conviction, this powerful recording is a tape of a historic cathedral performance at Muenster. The sound is first-rate.

THRENÓDY FOR THE VICTIMS OF HIROSHIMA

Written in 1960, this powerful piece is one of the more famous works of the so-called "New Music." The *Threnody* gives us a totally new panorama of sound. The over-all effect is no less than shattering.

* * MADERNA	*Rome Symphony Members*	Victrola VIC (S) 1239 [Brown; Bousseur; Stockhausen]

The enormously dedicated playing, and the excruciating use of the highest possible sound of stringed instruments, yield both a fascinating and a disturbing experience.

Pergolesi, Giovanni Battista (1710-1736)

Pergolesi was an extremely gifted composer. His is gentle, somewhat facile music that appeals at once. Before he was struck down at the untimely age of 26, he was one of the significant figures in Neapolitan opera.

CONCERTINI NO. 2 IN G

This is pretty, ingratiating music. Its authorship has been "challenged," but is now generally attributed to Pergolesi.

* MAINARDI, NICOLET, DEMMLER, BAUMGARTNER, MARKEVITCH, LEHMANN	*Lucerne Festival Strings, Berlin Philharmonic, Bavarian State Orch.*	HELIODOR H (M/S) 25033 [Corelli, Concerto Grosso in D, Opus 6 No. 1; Vivaldi, Cello Concerto in G, P. 120; Cimarosa Concerto for 2 Flutes in G]

The music is smoothly and winningly played. The sound is darkish, but still all right. [The work is backed by other good concertos, especially a winsome *Concerto for Two Flutes* by Cimarosa.]

CONCERTO FOR FLUTE AND STRINGS IN G

Much of the writing formerly believed to be by Pergolesi is now challenged. At best, it is today "attributed" to him. A shroud of mystery surrounds the facts about what he really wrote. In any case, this is a charming concerto.

* * ADENEY, HAAS	*London Baroque Ensemble*	VANGUARD (S) 192 [Albinoni; A. Scarlatti; Tartini; Vivaldi]
* * WANAUSEK, ADLER	*Vienna Pro Musica*	VOX (M) 9440 [Gluck; Boccherini]

Adenay and the staunch players of the London Baroque Ensemble are polished and highly musical. The sound is pleasant.

Wanausek is very good on decent mono. This man is a superb artist, and makes the music sound more important than it really is.

LA SERVA PADRONA

If you love singing, don't miss this unpretentious piece that first brought the feel of everyday life into the pretentious world of opera. This gay little "one acter" became a mainstay of barnstorming singers who traveled throughout Italy with shoestring productions. Later, *La Serva Padrona* went to Paris and created a storm—running for 100 consecutive performances.

* * SCOTTO, BRUSCANTINI, FASANO	*Virtuosi di Roma*	EVEREST	(S) 445/1
* * ADANI, MONREALE, SPINELLI, GRACIS	*Pomeriggi Musicali of Teatro Nuovo, Milan*	NONESUCH	(S) H 71043
* ZEANI, ROSSI-LEMENI, SINGER	*Musica et Litera Chamber Orch.*	VOX OPX (50) (S) 380	

Bruscantini, on the Everest set, is a joy to hear. Set off against him are the delightful voice and style of Renata Scotto. *High Fidelity* rates this as "a performance that has yet to be bettered." This set, recorded in true stereo, in 1952, is from the Recordi Opera Catalogue; the sound is better than on the regular Everest/Cetra series.

The Nonesuch entry offers crisp sound, and spirited, assured singing. The *Stereo Record Guide* comments: "in the best opera-buffa tradition."

The Vox record is a stylish concert version. It does not approach the theatrical sense of the other versions, but it is enjoyable.

STABAT MATER (Sung in Latin)

This widely-loved music has a secure place in the repertory; it is Pergolesi at his most human. These are simple, warmly devotional pages.

* * KUESTER, KLAEMBT, SCHROEDER	*Cologne Bach Orch. and Madrigal Chorus*	MACE	(S) 9014
* STICH-RANDALL, HOENGEN, ROSSI	*Vienna State Opera Orch. and Chorus*	VANGUARD	(S) 195
SAILER, MUENCH, KEHR	*Mainz Chamber Orch.*	VOX	(M) 9960
GRISCHKAT	*Stuttgart Choral Society*	PERIOD	(M) 530

Mace leads, with nicely blended soloists, and fresh singing from the Cologne Chorus. German Electrola has provided excellent sonic techniques.

Rossi's disc features the wan, intelligent soprano of Stich-Randall, and attractive choral work.

The Vox set from Mainz contains good choral work, little more. The sound is just fair.

The old Grischkat recording on Period is lethargic.

Ponchielli, Amilcare (1834-1886)

This Italian composer studied at the Milan Conservatory, and soon after his graduation, wrote his first opera. He reached fame in opera before writing his masterpiece, *La Gioconda;* but today, he is remembered only for this one work alone. Toward the end of his life, he became *maestro di capella* at the Cathedral of Bergamo.

Though his music is dramatic, it lacks the bold vigor and authority found in the works of Verdi and others.

LA GIOCONDA   (Complete)

Even with its impossible libretto, *Gioconda* can be an exciting opera if you have six first-rate singers.

* * * CALLAS, BARBIERI, POGGI	*Radio Italiana Orch.*	3-EVEREST/CETRA	(S) 419/3
* * MILANOV, ELIAS, DI STEFANO, WARREN, PREVITALI	*St. Cecilia Accademy*	3-VICTROLA VIC	(M/S) 6101
* * CALLAS, COSSOTTO, COMPANEEZ, MIRANDA FERRARO, CAPPUCCILLI, VINCO, VOTTO	*La Scala*	3-SERAPHIM	(S) 6031

Everest/Cetra offers the young Maria Callas (who worked for less in her Radio Italiana days). The great prima donna exhibits fire and imagination and temperament galore. Barbieri is excellent, and the rest of the cast is uninhibited and unsubtle. The sound is fair. The set was La Divina's recording debut. *High Fidelity:* "Chock-full of bad singing, but it is bad in a big way . . . . But the performance has life and color, even in its worst moments."

The Victrola disc with Zinka Milanov and Leonard Warren offers a satisfying performance with still-thrilling moments. Zinka's best years were behind her when this set was made, but she still shows temperament and much to admire, including her seemingly floating B-flat in *"Enzo Adorato, Ah, come t'amo."* She would hold the note effortlessly as she crossed the stage when singing this role at the Met, and her fans would go wild. The rest of the cast passes muster, but Warren is shaky here and there. The conducting is routine. The sound is pleasant.

Seraphim offers a 1960 recording with Maria Callas, but "La Divina" is not in her best form. The sense of high tragedy that she conveys so well comes through, and there are impressive moments when she uses those chilling chest tones, but despite these moments, I do not hear much that can be called great singing. As for the rest of the cast, the less said the better. *High Fidelity:* "Pretty largely a dud because the leading singers do not bring to it a full measure of interpretative flair or vocal weight."

In sum, the earlier, free-wheeling Callas *Gioconda* on Everest is preferable—but you get much more modern sonics on Seraphim. Opera buffs will have a fine time analyzing the two performances.

LA GIOCONDA . (Excerpts)

* * CALLAS, BARBIERI, POGGI	*Radio Italiana Orch.*	EVEREST	(M)	6169
			(S)	3169
* * CALLAS, BARBIERI, POGGI, VOTTO	*Radio Televisione Italiana*	PICKWICK	(S)	4048

This disc is a one-record excerpt of the complete Callas-Barbieri performance evaluated above.

The Pickwick disc, too, is a cherishable, one-record extract of the early-Callas complete version on Everest/Cetra. The attraction, of course, is the theatrical sweep and curdling theatricality of "La Divina," and it is impossible not to be chilled, if not moved, in her *Suicido!* aria. Callas' somber chest tones are something to hear, even if she goes shrill now and then in the high register. The rehabilitated sound is rather metallic, but after you get used to it, it isn't annoying.

Poulenc, Francis (1899-1963)

A gifted pianist as well as composer, Poulenc was a member of the French coterie know as *Le Six*. (The others were Auric, Durey, Honegger, Millaud, and Tailleferre.) Poulenc composed ballets, chamber music, concertos, songs, piano music, and other works. His piquant style, combining Gallic clarity and satire, is much admired as witty and often elegant music. Poulenic, the theoretician of *Le Six,* produced music that epitomized, in the words of Jean Cocteau, "the sophistication of the graceful."

AUBADE, CHOREOGRAPHIC POEM FOR PIANO AND INSTRUMENTS; SONATA FOR CLARINET AND PIANO; SONATA FOR OBOE AND PIANO

I don't know what to make of this frivolous music. It is piquant, even charming, but after a few bars one longs for something more meaty. Friends who are Poulenc fans tell me that "his music is bound to be a bit unfathomable to those of us who listen with non-French ears." But no one ever said you needed German ears for Beethoven.

* BOUTARD, PIERLOT, FEVRIER, BAUDO	*Orchestra of the Lamoureux Concerts*	NONESUCH	(M/S) 71033

The playing is insouciant, and is crisply recorded.

LES MAMELLES DE TIRESIAS

This may be termed an *opera-bouffe,* based on a poem by Apollinaire.

* GIRAUDEAU, CLUYTENS	*Chorus and Orchestra of the Paris Opera-Comique*	SERAPHIM	(M) 60029

High Fidelity magazine found this performance "very French and very funny," and perhaps you will, too. With my limited French, the humor of this one eludes me. The mono sound is bright.

SONG CYCLES: BANALITES (1940); CALLIGRAMMES (1948); 4 POEMS DE GUILLAUME APOLLINAIRE (1931)

You don't have to know French to enjoy this, but it helps. This is happy music, full of fun, civilized and urbane. This composition supports Poulenc's reputation as the most remarkable French writer of songs since Debussy and Ravel.

* BERNAC	2-ODYSSEY	3226 0009

Many of these songs were written for Bernac, and he and composer Poulenc (a first rate pianist) handle them together with great assurance. The mono sound is agreeable. [Some attractive Debussy, Chabrier, Ravel and Satie fill out this two-record set.]

Praetorius, Michel (1571-1621)

Praetorius, Kapellmeister to the music-loving Saxon court, was a prolific composer in varied styles. He also was an important theorist; his *Syntagna Musicum* is indispensible even today to musicologists. His Christmas hymns are lovely, unadorned chorales; the *Dances* are zestful and elegant. Praetorius, who died 54 years before J. S. Bach was born, can be seen as an important forerunner of Bach. This is an extremely interesting composer.

DANCES FROM "TERPSICHORE"

Here is vivid, fresh-sounding music, especially recommended for those who dote on consorts of pommers, krummhorn, gambas, recorders, and other quaint instruments.

* * TRAEDER   *Ferdinand Conrad*   NONESUCH   (S) 71128
                     Instrumental Ensemble,   [Schein, 2 Suites from
                     Niedersaechsischer   "Banchetto Musicale"]
                     Singkreis Hannover

The performance is first-rate; and the conducting is both vital and enthusiastic. *High Fidelity* commented: "This unpretentious but lovely record should not be allowed to slip past without a warm welcome." The sound is exemplary.

Prokofiev, Serge   (1891-1953)

This Russian composer left his native land within months after the Bolshevik Revolution of 1917 and he lived chiefly in Paris. Het returned to Russia in 1933, and became closely identified with Soviet ideology, and even wrote a ballet, *The Age of Steel*. He was widely welcomed by the Soviets, and became one of the leading cultural figures within Russia. In 1948, without warning, he was attacked for his "calophonic music." He meekly wrote a hack work, "On Guard For Peace," which won him the Stalin Prize in 1951. Bitter and ill, he had recovered his pre-eminent position by the time of his death.

PLACE AND ACHIEVEMENT   In twentieth-century music Prokofiev holds a solitary place. It is difficult to label him neatly. His music is precise, formal, often cynical, and always cool and astringent. Much of it is entirely unaffecting, although one always admires the hand of the master craftsman at work. He does not touch our hearts, as do many lesser composers.

His lighter, less portentious efforts seem most likely to survive—*Peter and the Wolf, Lieutenant Kije,* as well as the mordant Violin Concertos.

THE ESSENTIAL PROKOFIEV

ORCHESTRAL MUSIC: *Classical Symphony; Symphony No. 5; Symphony No. 6; Concerto No. 3 for Piano and Orchestra; Concertos Nos. 1 and 2 for Violin and Orchestra; Peter and the Wolf; Romeo and Juliet, Ballet; Lieutenant Kije.*

CHORAL MUSIC: *Alexander Nevsky, cantata.*

PIANO MUSIC: *Sonata No. 7.*

OTHER WORKS

ORCHESTRAL MUSIC: *The Age of Steel, L'Enfant prodigue; Cinderella; Stone Flower; ballets. Symphonies No. 2, 3, 4, 7; Concertos Nos. 1, 2, 4, 5 for Piano and Orchestra; Concerto for Cello and Orchestra; Scythian Suite.*

VOCAL MUSIC: *The Love for Three Oranges; War and Peace; operas. On Guard for Peace; oratorio.*

CHAMBER MUSIC: *Overture on Hebrew Themes, for clarinet, string quartet, and piano; 3 sonatas for violin and piano; 2 string quartets.*

PIANO MUSIC: *Eight sonatas; Visions fugitives; Sarcasmes; Suggestion diabolique; Tales of an old grandmother.*

Some of Prokofiev's most enduring music is in his astringent, yet most lyrical concertos. His two violin concertos and his *Piano Concerto No. 3* rank with the best music of our century.

CONCERTO NO. 1 IN D FLAT FOR PIANO (Opus 10)

Prokofiev's *Concerto No. 1* was revolutionary work in 1911. Its performance by the composer the following year—Prokofiev was a first-rate pianist—was a sensation; it launched his reputation as a daring young man. This percussive work is in one continuous movement and is not very rewarding today.

* * KATZ, BOULT	*London Philharmonic Orch.*	VANGUARD	(S)	185
		[Khachaturian, Concerto No. 1]		
* RICHTER, ANCERL	*U.S.S.R. State Orch.*	ARTIA	(M)	123
		[Bach, Concerto No. 1]		

Mindro Katz is a first-rate Roumanian pianist and plays this music in a steely, convincing manner. The sound is crisp.

Richter is fine, but the sound is harsh.

CONCERTO NO. 2 IN G FOR PIANO (Opus 16)

Here are stormy, romantic pages utilizing Russian melodies. The work was hissed when first heard in 1913; Prokofiev rewrote it, and presented the new version (this one) in 1924, with Koussevitsky in Paris. By this time he was world-famous, and there were no more hisses.

* * BALOGHOVA, ANCERL	*Czech Philharmonic*	ARTIA	(S)	707
* * HENRIOT-SCHWEITZER, MUNCH	*Boston Symphony Orch.*	VICTROLA VIC	(S)	1971
		[Ravel, Concerto in G]		

Baloghova plays with impressive flair. The sound is decent. A drawback here is that the concerto is spread over two sides—no coupling.

Madame Henriot-Schweitzer is less forceful, but this is a good reading, and Munch and the Boston Symphony back her to the hilt. The coupling is superb.

CONCERTO NO. 3 IN C FOR PIANO (Opus 26)

One of the Russian composer's best and most popular works. Written in 1921, this is lyric music, more sentimental than most of Prokofiev's austere works.

* * GILELS, KONDRASHIN	*U.S.S.R. State Radio Orch.*	MONITOR	M/S	2061
		[Kabalevsky, Piano Concerto]		

* * GRAFFMAN, JORDA   *San Francisco Symphony*   VICTROLA   (S)   1105
                                                 [Classical Symphony]

Gilels is brilliant, and exciting. [The Kabalevsky "Youth" Concerto on the
back is Komsomol agit-prop music, and bad.]

Graffman is also perfectly at home in this concerto; he delivers a performance just a bit less convincing than that of Gilels. But the coupling
with the lovely 'Classical' symphony makes this an attractive, well-
sounding disc.

CONCERTO NO. 5 IN G FOR PIANO (Opus 55)

This is unappealing structural Soviet music, dating from 1932, in five
terse movements. There are some critics, however, who rank this music
as "among Prokofiev's finest achievements."

* BRENDEL,   *Vienna State Opera Orch.*   TURNABOUT   (S)   4160
  STERNBERG   [Romeo & Juliet, Excerpts]

The versatile Brendel makes the most of this uninteresting concerto.
The sound is shallow, with little sonority.

CONCERTO NO. 1 IN D FOR VIOLIN (Opus 19)

This is lyric, top-drawer Prokofiev. He worked eight years on this concerto (1912-1921), and it is an intriguing mixture of fine melodic writing
in his usual icy style. The sole violin part at times is deliberately unmelodic,
figurative.

* * OISTRAKH,   *State Radio Orch.*   MONITOR   (S)   2073
    KONDRASHIN   [Chausson, Poeme; Ravel,
                                            Tzigane]

    BERNARD,   *Bucharest Symphony Orch.* PHILLIPS WS   M/S 9046
    BUGEANU   [Khachaturian, Concerto]

Oistrakh is the ideal man to play this music. His work in the mocking,
sarcastic passages of the second movement, is superb. Monitor achieves
good sound on this Russian tape.

Christian Bernard is pallid, without the authority of Oistrakh.

CONCERTO NO. 2 IN G FOR VIOLIN (Opus 63)

This is an arresting, brilliant work, and a masterpiece.

* KOGAN,   *U.S.S.R. State Orch.*   MONITOR   2051 M
  KONDRASHIN   [Saint Saens, Havanaise]

Kogan is solid and secure, but with ten formidable recordings currently available on high-priced records, I cannot recommend this as outstanding. Wait until a better low-priced disc is available.

SYMPHONY-CONCERTO FOR CELLO AND ORCHESTRA

This rather uninteresting work was a disaster at its Moscow premiere, because the cellist had trouble with the formidably difficult solo part. It was drastically rewritten for the great cellist Rostropovitch in 1952. The work is seldom played, and is curiously unaffecting.

* ROSTROPOVICH, SANDERLING	*Leningrad Philharmonic*	MONITOR (M) 2021 [Shostakovitch, Concertine for 2 Pianos]
* NAVARRA, ANCERL	*Czech Philharmonic*	CROSSROADS (S) 22160200 [Respighi, Adagio for Cello and Orchestra]

Rostropovich offers bravura playing, and authenticity. [The coupling is brittle Shostakovitch.] The sound is decent mono.

Navarra is elegant, but less knowledgeable in this curious score. (The coupling is weakish, neoclassicist music.) The sound is pretty good.

CINDERELLA (Opus 87) (Ballet Excerpts)

This is in the great Tchaikowsky ballet tradition, without the sugar plums. Prokofiev's *Cinderella* is colorful, and without the fairy-tale whimsical quality of other ballet composers.

* * STOKOWSKI	*N. Y. Stadium Symphony Orch.*	EVEREST M6016/S3016 [Villa-Lobos, Bachianas No. 1; Uirapuru]
* RIGNOLD	*Royal Opera House Orch., Covent Garden; Suites 1, 2*	VICTROLA VIC (S) 1138
MEYLAN	*Prague Radio Symhony Orch.*	CROSSROADS 22160058S

Stokowski comes off best, with a dramatic reading.

Rignold is more ballet-conscious, and efficient.

The Prague entry is agreeable, with adequate sound.

LIEUTENANT KIJE SUITE (Opus 60)

This suite for orchestra was adapted by the composer from a film score he wrote in 1933. It's all a satire on Czarist stupidity and great fun. It is also delightful music, and enormously popular.

* * SARGENT	*London Symphony*	EVEREST (S) 3054 [Shostakovich, Symphony No. 9]
* * GOBERMAN	*Vienna New Symphony*	ODYSSEY (S) 32160084 [Classical Symphony; Love for Three Oranges; Suite (excerpts)]
* ROSSI	*Vienna State Opera Orch.*	VANGUARD (S) 174 [Peter and the Wolf]

Sargent has the right sardonic touch here. [The coupling is superb.] The sound is resonant.

Goberman is also sparkling. [The couplings are first-rate.] The sound is diffused. and just fair.

Rossi is entirely hearable, and you get the immortal "Peter and the Wolf" on the reverse side.

LOVE FOR THREE ORANGES (Opus 33)

This crisp, shrewdly made suite is from the opera by the same name that Prokofiev was commissioned to write by the Chicago Opera Company. The opera was a failure in Chicago in 1921, but was successfully revived by the New York City Opera in 1949.

| * * STEINBERG | *Pittsburgh Symphony* | PICKWICK (S) 4008 [Rimsky-Korsakof, Coq D'or Suite] |

Steinberg does well by this music, in an assured reading. The coupling is fine. The sound is bright.

PETER AND THE WOLF (Opus 67)

This is a fairy tale for symphony orchestra, and a narrator tells the story as the music illustrates it. The immortal Peter is a delight for all ages. To write concert music that children will love is not the easiest of tasks, and the successful attempts can be counted on one hand. In this gentle endearing music, Prokofiev wrote a masterpiece.

| * * NOHAIN, ETCHEVERRY | *Lamoreux Orch.* | MERCURY (S) 18092 [Saint-Saens, Carnival of Animals] |
| * * KARLOFF, ROSSI | *Vienna State Opera Orch.* | VANGUARD (S) 174 [Lieutenant Kije] |

* DE WILDE, SWAROWSKY	*Vienna Pro Musica*	VOX	(S) 9280 [Britten, Young Person's Guide]
* KEESHAN, STOKOWSKI	*Stadium Symphony Orch.*	EVEREST	S 3043

The Etchelerry version is crisp and droll, but the narration is in French, rather than in English.

I like Rossi's elegant light-hearted touch on Vanguard, backed by the entertaining *Lieutenant Kije*. Karloff is not too intrusive in the narration, and stereo sound is clean.

The Swarosky-Vienna version is also pleasant, and for children, offers a better coupling with Britten's *Young Person's Guide to the Orchestra*.

The Keeshan-Stokowski version is quite pleasant.

ROMEO AND JULIET (Excerpts)

This is ballet music written for the Kirov Theatre in Leningrad, 1940. Everything went wrong before the premiere; two weeks before opening night the orchestra players tried to have the performance canceled "to avoid a scandal." *Romeo* is delicate writing, almost chamber music for Shakespeare, but seems exactly right after repeated hearings. As Ulanova, the great Russian ballerina, said, "I cannot now conceive any other music for *Romeo and Juliet*."

* * * SKROWACZEWSKI	*Minneapolis Sympohny Orch.*	MERCURY	50315M/90315S
* * MITROPOULOS	*N. Y. Philharmonic*	ODYSSEY	32160037M 32160038S

Skrowaczewski gives us a disciplined reading, with virtuoso orchestral playing. I must applaud the fine horn-playing in particular.

Record Guides comment:

"The most distinguished selection in the present catalogue. The acoustics are crystal clear."

Mitropoulos is impetuously romantic, but not as satisfying as the Skrowaczewski performance.

SYMPHONY IN D (Opus 25) (CLASSICAL)

This was Prokofiev's first symphony, and a deliberate attempt on the part of the composer to write with eighteenth century grace and wit, much as Mozart did. The work is an unflawed masterpiece, and it is difficult not to fall in love with its serene beauty.

| * * GOBERMAN | *Vienna New Symphony* | ODYSSEY   (S) 32160084
[Kije Suite; Love for Three
Oranges (excerpts)] |
| * * JORDA | *San Francisco Symphony* | VICTOR VIC   (S)   1105
[Piano Concerto #3] |

Goberman delivers a sparkling performance that is hard to beat. The sound is just fair.

Jorda's version is poised, and a handsome performance of Prokofiev's Third Piano Concerto makes this an attractive disc. The sound is clear.

SYMPHONY NO. 5 (Opus 100)

This is pre-purge Prokofiev (1944), before the commissars were breathing down his neck. It is also a powerful, solidly constructed symphony that was already hugely popular during Prokofiev's lifetime.

* * MARTINON	*Paris Conservatoire Orch.*	VICTROLA VIC	(S) 1169
* * SARGENT	*London Symphony*	EVEREST	(S) 3034
* DORATI	*Minneapolis Symphony Orch.*	MERCURY	(S) 18081
SLOVAK	*Czech Philharmonic*	CROSSROADS	22160116 S

Martinon's reading is vivid, and "The French Orchestra gives just that glitter and hardness to Prokofiev's score that makes it truly convincing", in the words of the *Stereo Record Guide*. The sound is excellent.

Sargent also does well in a closely-knit, urgent performance.

The Dorati version has less impact, but is quite hearable.

The Czech entry is unremarkable.

SYMPHONY NO. 6 IN E FLAT (Opus 111)

The *Sixth* is an intriguing score, but it is weighted down with many flabby pages. This is basically cheerful Prokofiev probably written to pacify the cultural commissars (1949).

| MRAVINSKY | *Leningrad Philharmonic* | ARTIA | 158 M |

The Leningrad Philharmonic sounds like a good ensemble. Alfred Frankenstein's verdict: "Mravinsky makes a very good case for the work, and the recording is passable."

ALEXANDER NEVSKY (Opus 78)

This is a towering, full-blooded cantata for mezzo-soprano, chorus and orchestra. It was originally composed in 1938 as music for a film by Serge Eisenstein.

* * IRIARTE, ROSSI	*Vienna State Opera Orch.*	VANGUARD	(M)	451
* * SOUKUPOVA, ANCERL	*Czech Philharmonic*	TURNABOUT	(S)	34269

I prefer the old Vienna set, despite an echo and some dubious Russian. Iriarte has a deep compassionate voice and Rossi makes the orchestral parts the most significant. The Czech version boasts a splendid, deep-throated chorus, and the soloist is moving, if rather passionless. This is a lyrical rather than heroic reading, but a good one.

WAR AND PEACE (Complete Opera)
(Sung in Russian)

This is a sprawling, uneven work that Prokofiev labored on from 1941 until 1952. His setting of Tolstoy's huge novel is a gallant, even noble effort, but the composer himself was aware of the hopelessness of his task. For this reason, Prokofiev did not label his *"War and Peace"* an opera, but rather "lyric-dramatic scenes after Tolstoy's novel."

* VASOVIC-BOKACEVIC, CVEJIC, POPOVIC, JANSSEN	*Vienna State Opera Orch.* *Piano*	HELIODOR	S) 325039

This Belgrade-Vienna combination is hardly the Bolshoi Opera, but the singing is strong, if heavy-handed. The sound is resonant, and I enjoyed it all in all more than *High Fidelity's* bare nod, "A tolerable enough job."

MUSIC FOR PIANO—COMPLETE

* GYORGY SANDOR	*Piano*	3-Vox/SVBX	5408
		3-Vox/SVBX	5409

Sandor has the technical equipment and the understanding to grapple with all this, and on the whole he does an admirable job. But two albums and six records are a bit much; this is for specialists only. *Saturday Review* included Sandor's effort in their list of "Best Recordings of 1968", and commented ". . . . . . discovers the essential nature of the music successfully in probably nine cases out of ten—which is not a bad average for some five and a half hours of performance."

SONATA NO. 7 FOR PIANO (Opus 83)

Nothing pretty or pleasant here: primitive sounding patterns in a piano-percussive style. This is motorized, glass-walled music of our time.

* * RICHTER	ARTIA 154 M [Mussorgsky, Pictures at an Exhibition]

Richter gave the premiere of this work in 1943, and this is a strong performance, faithful to Prokofiev's steely, brutal style. As played by Richter, this music can be exciting, even hypnotic, if that is the word for all this hammers-and-anvils goings-on. The coupling is superb. The sound is fair.

Puccini, Giacomo (1858-1924)

Coming from a musical family, Puccini studied at the Milan Conservatory. His first opera was *Le Villi,* performed at the Theatre dal Verme in Milan in 1884. In 1893, with *Manon Lescaut,* Puccini achieved international sucess. In 1907, Puccini visited the United States for the American premiere of *Madame Butterfly.* The Metropolitan Opera House commissioned him to compose a work and the result was *The Girl of the Golden West,* based on a play by David Belasco. Puccini's last opera, *Turandot,* was completed by Franco Alfano.

PLACE AND ACHIEVEMENT Along with Verdi and Mozart, Puccini is one of the three best-loved and most often heard opera composers today. Nevertheless the critics find him too theatrical, too sentimental, and sometimes downright vulgar. Ironically, this was the estimate of Verdi some 40 years ago, but today, Verdi has been elevated to an exalted rank in the musical hierarchy.

Puccini was a genius of the musical theater. His greatest operas, *La Boheme, Madame Butterfly,* and *Tosca,* are endlessly played because they are dramatically effective. No composer was more careful in choosing librettos. Puccini believed in his stories and in his characters, and this conviction comes through in the opera house.

The brilliant critic Sackville-West has written: "'Without *Boheme, Tosca* and *Butterfly,* the balance-sheets of a good many establishments would look dismal indeed. Like *Carmen, Faust* and *Rigoletto,* they belong to that small group of operas which never fail to come off, however poor the musical or scenic resources of the company may be. . . . What captivated the world is the quality which has attracted generations of great singers: An ardent, soaring, spontaneous vocal line. Puccini's music is not profound, but it transmits abundant impressions of charm, tenderness, passion, pathos: in short, of humanity. His characters live."

THE ESSENTIAL PUCCINI

OPERAS: *La Boheme; Toscà; Madame Butterfly; Turandot.*

OTHER WORKS

OPERAS: *Manon Lescaut; The Girl of the Golden West; La Rondine; Gianni Schicchi; Il Tabarro; Suor Angelica.*

LA BOHEME (Complete) (Sung in Italian)

Written in 1896, this imperishable, greatly beloved opera, founded on Henri Muerger's charming *Scenes De La Vie De Boheme,* relates a naive, artist-in-garret story. Puccini was a master of theater, and the sentimentality in Boheme is never allowed to get in the way of the action.

* * * DE LOS ANGELES, AMARA, BJOERLING, TOZZI, MERRILL, REARDON, CORENA, BEECHAM		2-Seraphim	(M) 6000
* * ALBANESE, PEERCE, McKNIGHT, VALENTINO, TOSCANINI	NBC Symphony Orch.	2-Victrola VIC	(S) 6019
* TEBALDI, GUEDEN, PRANDELLI, EREDE		2-Richmond	(M) 62001
* CARTERI, TAGLIAVINI, SANTINNI, TADDEI, SIEPI		3-Everest/Cetra	(S) 402/2

The Beecham set is a joy, a vibrant performance. The sheer beauty of the gorgeous voices of de los Angeles and Bjoerling is unforgettable. *High Fidelity* comments: "This *Boheme* is still unchallenged as the most irresistible in the catalogue." The sound is good.

Toscanini conducted the world premiere of *La Boheme* just 50 years before he recorded this album; his authority asserts itself on every page. His tempi are incredibly fast—this set was made from a 1946 radio broadcast, in the days when the stop--watch ruled the recording companies and even Arturo Toscanini. (The Toscanini opera re-releases seem to be falling into a discernible pattern: the conducting by a genius, with singers who do not match our best talent of today, recorded on discs of inferior but still enjoyable sonic quality.) Philip Miller commented in 1955 *(Guide to Vocal Records)*: "Toscanini's performance has the familiar clean-cut precision, but is marred by inadequacies of reproduction . . . still, no rival can match the Maestro's credentials as a *Boheme* authority."

In the Richmond set, La Tebaldi is weighted down by pedestrian colleagues, and only Gueden stands out as Musetta. These two discs are on the disappointing side. The sound is fair.

On the three-record Everest/Certa entry, Carteri is appealing, and there is good ensemble work. The men, led by a fresh-voiced Tagliavini, are strong. Taddei and Siepi are staunch pillars, too. The sound is only so-so. Philip Miller: "Some good singing, and a nice spirit among the cast."

LA BOHEME (Excerpt) (Sung in Italian)

* TEBALDI, GUEDEN, PRANDELLI, EREDE	Richmond	(M) 23034

Here is a serviceable single disc for those unwilling to invest in the entire opera.

THE GIRL OF THE GOLDEN WEST (LA FANCIULLA DEL WEST) (Sung in Italian)

This opera, composed in 1910, is based on David Belasco's play about the California Gold Rush. Less inspired than Puccini's other works, this record will appeal mainly to Puccini devotees.

* GAVAZZI, SAVARESE, CAMPAGNANO, BERTOCCI, BASILE	EVEREST/CETRA (S) 453/3

The singing is lusty; the sound, acceptable, although the voices are on top of us. Philip Miller (1955) "There are several fine voices, but no outstanding vocalism."

MADAME BUTTERFLY (Complete) (Sung in Italian)

First produced in Milan, in 1904, this is one of Puccini's most powerful and enduring scores.

* * * TEBALDI, RANKIN, CAMPORA, EREDE		3-RICHMOND (M) 63001
* * MOFFO, ELIAS, VALLETTI, CORENA, LEINSDORF	Rome Opera Orch.	3-VICTROLA VIC (S) 6100
* PETRELLA, TAGLIAVINI, QUESTA		3-EVEREST/CETRA 421/3

In our time Renata Tebaldi owns this opera. Comparing this set on Richmond (the low-priced arm of London) with her later stereo version on the high-priced London, *High Fidelity* remarks: "Tebaldi was in really prime vocal estate when she [first] recorded it—her voice has never sounded more full-bodied and balanced. Moreover, she achieves a sense of involvement in the emotions of this part that is unusual in her work. Philip Miller adds, "Tebaldi . . . does much lovely singing . . . the work of a true artist."

The admirable Anna Moffo, offered on low-priced Victrola to make room for the higher-priced glittering Leontyne Price set, is not to be slighted. Moffo is a first-rate singer, and Leinsdorf is dramatic. The stereo of this disc is the best available for the opera.

The old Cetra set is notable for splendid singing by the young Tagliavini. The discs are serviceable.

MADAME BUTTERFLY (Excerpts) (Sung in Italian)

* * TEBALDI, RANKIN,   RICHMOND   (M) 23063
    CAMPORA, EREDE

Here is an admirable one-record selection.

MANION LESCAUT

Manon Lescaut, produced in 1893, was Puccini's first great success. The opera presents the tale of the Abbe Prevost—the same story used by Massenet in his Manon. This work does not compare with the great Puccini operas but the composer's youthful exuberance shines through.

* PETRELLA,   EVEREST/CETRA   (S) 461/3
   CAMPAGNANO,
   MELETTI, LATINUCCI,
   DEL CUPOLO

The singing is honest if unsensational, and the conducting is well-paced. The sound is decent.

TURANDOT (Complete) (Sung in Italian)

This melodrama, one of the best on the boards since 1900, is not music you can listen to day after day. However, there are few chilling moments in the entire range of opera equal to this opera's climax when Tosca surveys the murdered body of her would-be seducer and exclaims, "Before him all Rome trembled!"

* * MILANOV,   Rome Opera Orch.   2-VICTROLA VIC (S) 6000
    BJOERLING,
    WARREN, CORENA,
    LEINSDORF

* TEBALDI, CAMPORA, Santa Cecilia Orch.   2-RICHMOND   (M) 62002
   EREDE, FRAZZONI

* CANIGLIA, GIGLI,   Rome Opera Orch.   2-SERAPHIM   (M) 6027
   BARGIOLI,
   DE FABRITIS

Victrola provides a formidable entry. The singers are very good, even though Milanov was past her best years when these records were made. This set was demoted to low-priced Victrola to make way for La Price on the higher-priced Victor. The sound is pleasant stereo.

The Frazzoni set is hearable, but there is no distinguished characterization. I suspect hanky-panky with inferior tapes. Tebaldi is splendid, and Campora is a first-rate Cavaradossi, but the total result is undistinguished. The sound is mono. *Stereo Review's* verdict: "I respond with undiminished fondness to its endearing values, but I am sufficiently aware of its dated sounded to refrain from recommending it as any listener's *only* recorded *Tosca*."

The Gigli-Caniglia set should have been great—but it's not. The indifferent sound precludes all but die-hard Gigli fans. *Saturday Review's* Irving Kolodin disagrees, and says: "Gigli's remarkable singing may rank as the best thing he ever did for the phonograph." However, Desmond Shawe-Taylor, perhaps England's best critic, leans to my response, and says: "This *Tosca* may be neglected by all but passionate Gilgi addicts."

TURANDOT (Complete) (Sung in Italian)

The master's last opera, completed by one Alfano, was produced in 1926. Turnodot is the beautiful Princess of China, and Puccini had intended this as a more serious" opera. There are lovely pages in this work, but this pretentious, unconvincing piece never really caught in the manner of his great operas.

* * CIGNA, MERLI, NERONI, POLI, GHIONE	*Rome Radio Orch.*	EVEREST/CETRA (S) 427/3

The Cetra set is quite listenable. Most Cetra records have a spontaneity and verve about them; they were made almost a generation ago in non-stop sessions on a shoestring budget, and with little rehearsal. Young artists would record for low fees. At the time Italy had such future stars as Tebaldi, Callas, Taddei, Bergonzi, and Simionato, then not too well-known; this was in the day's before Scala Milano and the New York Metropolitan beckoned to them. These stars with youthful voices, can be heard on these sets in a lusty abandon that disappeared when world ratings hung on every new recording. Cetra also affords the opportunity to hear lesser-known singers of worth. The Cetra *Turandot* offers the excellent Gina Cigna and Afro Poli. The sound has the drawback often encountered in Cetra sets which have been souped up and "rechannelled": foggy boom and annoying distortions. The old Cetra monos were perfectly acceptable before being mangled; this is the price we pay to find that magic word "stereo" on a record jacket.

Purcell, Henry (c. 1659-1695)

Purcell was English, and a boy chorister at the Chapel Royal. When his voice changed in 1673, he was appointed "keeper, maker, mender, repairer, and tuner" of the King's instruments. A pupil of John Blow, Purcell succeeded him as organist of Westminster Abbey.

Purcell was easily the most original and most talented English composer of his century. He is often referred to as "the father of English music." His opera, *Dido and Aeneas,* was the first great opera in English music. It is still the best to my ears. He was extremely active in many fields. Theater music, as well as church music, absorbed him. His rich intrumental *Fantasias* are inventive works that still fascinate.

Purcell wrote in a style that is clear-cut and brilliant, and stamped with his incisive personality.

4 SUITES FOR STRING ORCHESTRA

This was pit music for the Restoration stage, inserted because the audience loved it when a character in a play called to the pit musicians, "Pray oblige us with the last new song."

| * MAHLER | *Chamber Orchestra of the Hartford Symphony* | EVERYMAN SRV | 155 |

The playing is vivid; it conveys the Purcell style. The sound is clear.

MUSIC FOR THE FUNERAL OF QUEEN MARY

This thrilling music conjures up England in the late seventeenth century.

| * * * | *Jones Orchestra and Singers* | SERAPHIM   (M) 60001 [Bach, Magnificat] |

All praise to the Jones Ensemble; no one plays and sings this sort of thing with the same spirit as the English. For those who know and love Purcell's *Come Ye Sons of Art,* this record is a must. The mono sound is clear and entirely acceptable. [The Bach *Magnificat,* on the reverse, is great music, played superbly.]

SONATA FOR TRUMPET AND STRINGS; THE VIRTUOUS WIFE: SUITE; THE GORDIAN KNOT UNITED: SUITE; SUITE FOR HARPSICHORD

This is an amiable group of Purcell's stage works—not profound music, but solid.

| * GERLIN, DELMOTTE, | *Rhenish Chamber Orch.* | NONESUCH H | (M) | 1027 |
| KEHR | *of Cologne* | | (S) | 71027 |

The Nonesuch disc features deft trumpet work in the *Sonata,* and solid, skillful playing throughout. The music is clearly recorded.

THE INDIAN QUEEN

Purcell's operas were actually stage pieces, rather than full-fledged operas in the modern sense; they do not stand up well in performance. But for phonograph listening they are very good indeed; *The Indian Queen* has much in it to be recommended. The opera features brilliant writing, bold harmonies, and a certain quality that can only be called Englishness.

| * * BERNARD | *London Chamber Orch.* | MUSIC GUILD | (S) | 124 |

The opera is stylishly sung, with intimate sound.

THREE FANTASIAS A 3

"Fancies" they were called in Purcell's time. These are contrapuntal pieces to show off the composer's invention and poetic imagination, rather than his technical abilities.

| * * | *Hungarian String Trio* | DOVER | (S) | 7283 |

The works are skillfully played. The sound is clean.

TRIO SONATAS (FROM THE SECOND BOOK OF TEN)

This is virile music. The distinguished critic B. H. Haggin said this record will "appeal to anyone who likes the poetry of John Donne." That is an unusual way of summing it up; even if you don't know John Donne, you should listen to this pensive music.

* * CIOMPI,		DOVER	(M)	5224
TORKANOWSKY,				
KOUTZEN				

The playing is trenchant and convincing. The **mono** sound is agreeable.

Rachmaninoff, Sergei (1873-1943)

Rachmaninoff was born in Onega, in the Novgorod district of Russia. When Rachmaninoff was nine, his parents separated and his mother took him to St. Petersburg and enrolled him at the College of Music. Later, he entered the Moscow Conservatory where he became a protege and fervent disciple of Tchaikovsky.

His *First Piano Concerto* and *First Symphony* were abject failures, and for a miserable period he was utterly unable to compose. But he sought psychological help, and when he was himself again, he wrote his great *Piano Concerto No. 2.* This work marked Rachmaninoff's giant stride to success. He became conductor of opera at the Moscow Grand Theatre, and he was soon one of the most celebrated musicians in Moscow. His house became a favored gathering place for the leading intellects of Russia. The fame of the *Prelude in C-Sharp Minor* brought him invitations from all over the world to conduct and perform as a pianist.

In 1917, he left Russia and settled in America. He appeared widely on the concert stage during the rest of his life. He died in Beverly Hills, California, in 1943.

PLACE AND ACHIEVEMENT   Yearning, dark brooding and bitter pessimism are the dominant characteristics of Rachmaninoff—and everybody loves his music except the critics, who deem his work too obvious in its emotional appeal. Yet no other twentieth-century composer's piano concertos are as popular as those of Rachmaninoff.

Many critics declare that Rachmaninoff did not write great music. His symphonies are marred by relentless repetitious which downgrade the beauty they hold. Rachmaninoff was a nostalgic, unhappy master-pianist who was able to write lovely themes, but who often lacked the power to properly develop them. And yet—as with Schubert and Schumann, who also struggled uneasily with "big" forms, there is a direct emotional appeal in Rachmaninoff's music that wins loyal listeners.

THE ESSENTIAL RACHMANINOFF

ORCHESTRAL MUSIC: *Concerto No. 2, for Piano and Orchestra; Concerto No. 3, for Piano and Orchestra; Rhapsody on a Theme of Paganini, for Piano and Orchestra; Symphony No. 2; The Isle of the Dead, Tone Poem.*

PIANO MUSIC: *Prelude in C-Sharp Minor; Prelude in G Minor.*

OTHER WORKS

ORCHESTRAL MUSIC: *Symphonies No. 1 and 3; The Bells, Choral Sym-*

phony; Concertos No. 1 and 4, for Piano and Orchestra; Symphonic Dances.

PIANO MUSIC: *Moments Musicaux; Preludes; Etudes; Tableaux; 2 Sonatas for Piano; Lello Sonata.*

SONGS: *In the Silent Night; Lilacs; Vocalise; The Island;* and other songs.

CONCERTO NO. 1 IN F-SHARP MINOR FOR PIANO *(Opus 1)*

This concerto was written in 1890-91 when the composer was all of 18. Most of the familiar Rachmaninoff musical trademarks are present. But this concerto is hardly in the class of the towering *Second*.

* * JANIS, REINER	*Chicago Symphony Orch.*	VICTROLA VIC (S) 1101 [R. Strauss, Burlesque]
* RICHTER, SANDERLING	*Moscow State Symphony*	MONITOR (M) 2004 [Saint-Saens, Piano Concerto No. 5]
KAMENIKOVA, PINKAS	*Brno State Philharmonic Orch.*	CROSSROADS (S) 22 16 0716 [Rhapsody on a Theme by Paganini]

Byron Janis is a first-rate Rachmaninoff interpreter. Poetry, bravura, and flashing technique are present, and he avoids oversentimentalizing. The sound is excellent. [The Strauss coupling is a weakish piece.]

Richter is fine, but the sound is so-so mono. [The coupling is worthwhile for piano lovers.]

The Czech entry on Crossroads is just barely adequate, and the pianist is pedestrian.

CONCERTO NO. 2 IN C MINOR FOR PIANO *(Opus 18)*

This undisputed masterpiece is an indispensable concerto in the romantic pianist's arsenal. Record jacket annotators and radio intermission commentators never weary of telling the tale of its genesis. Rachmaninoff, in 1899, suffered from a pathological depression, and could not compose a line. A certain Dr. Dahl practiced auto-suggestion upon him daily for four months, repeating: "You will begin to write your concerto . . . . You *will* begin to write your concerto. . . ." Then *Voilà!* the great concerto is written and dedicated to Dr. Dahl. It is all true, even though it sounds like vintage satire by Mike Nichols and Elaine May.

* PENNARIO, GOLSCHMANN	*St. Louis Symphony Orch.*	PICKWICK (S) 4030

* DE GROOT, VAN OTTERLOO	*Hague Philharmonic Orch.*	MERCURY	(M) 14040 (S) 18040 [Tchaikovsky, Serenade in C for Strings (two movements only)]
* KATIN, DAVIS	*New Symphony Orch.*	RICHMOND	(M) 19050 (S) 29050
RICHTER, SANDERLING	*Leningrad Philharmonic Orch.*	PARLIAMENT	(M) 134
RICHTER		Vox (5)	(S) 16220 [Tchaikovsky, Concerto No. 1]
RICHTER, KONDRASHIN	*Moscow Symphony Orch.*	3-PERIOD	(M) 1163 [Bach, Concerto No. 1]
BRAILOWSKY, JORDA	*San Francisco Symphony Orch.*	VICTROLA VIC	(S) 1024 [Mendelssohn, Piano Concerto; Weber, Invitation to the Dance]
BLUMENTAL, GIELEN	*Wiener Musikgesellschaft*	Vox (5)	(S) 11500 [Tchaikovsky, Concerto No. 1]

Pennario is the best on stereo, but this is an extroverted, flashy reading.

The Dutch pianist Cor de Groot gives a refined performance that lacks imagination.

Katin's version has steel-fingered power, but little more.

Thin or tubby sound is the drawback on the three Richter entries.

Brailowsky is less worthy.

I am not really happy with any recording offered here. Get Richter on expensive DGG, Rubinstein on RCA, or Byron Janis on Mercury. All of them are splendid, well-recorded discs.

CONCERTO NO. 3 IN D MINOR FOR PIANO (Opus 30)

This formidable, slavic-romantic concerto, dating from 1909, was the composer's own favorite among his works.

* * * JANIS, MUNCH	*Boston Symphony Orch.*	VICTROLA VIC	(S) 1032
* * HOROWITZ, COATES	*London Symphony Orch.*	SERAPHIM	(M) 60063 [Haydn, Sonata for Piano, No. 52, in E-Flat]

Byron Janis is marvelous in the haunting first movement, and Munch is poetically with him throughout. The sound is excellent. Janis was a pupil of Vladimir Horowitz, and has much of his sorcery.

The Seraphim disc contains legendary readings of the utmost interest to piano-maniacs. The 1930 sound is adequate, all considered, and can be heard with comfort, if not exactly with the pleasure offered in modern recordings. The Rachmaninoff is a fiery, sweeping reading by the piano wizard Horowitz—even more glittering here than on the recording of the *Third Concerto* he did twenty years later.

PRELUDES FOR PIANO (Opus 23, Opus 32)

Rachmaninoff's solo piano music is rewarding. These musical schemes are less grandiose than those of Rachmaninoff's concertos and symphonies; one senses that the composer is speaking intimately to his instrument.

* * KEENE   2-PHILLIPS WS
                                                       (M/S) 2-006

Here is precise, yet sensitive playing, with many dazzling moments. Heady praise from none other than Artur Rubinstein: "I cannot imagine anyone, including Rachmaninoff himself, playing the *Preludes* more beautifully. I was flabbergasted. . . ." Two records are a bit much, though, for me. The stereo sound is commendable. Constance Keene is a pianist well worth knowing.

RHAPSODY ON A THEME OF PAGANINI
(Opus 43)

This magical work is admired even by those who detest Rachmaninoff. This is cool, poised, exhilarating music, dating from 1934, without the overblown quality of much of his other writing.

* * * ZAK,   *Moscow Philharmonic*   MONITOR   (S) 2079
      KONDRASHIN   [Khatchatourian, Piano
                                                 Concerto]

* KATCHEN, BOULT   RICHMOND   (M) 19076
                                                 [Dohnanyi, Variations on a
                                                 Nursery Theme]

    KAMENIKOVA,   *Brno State Philharmonic* CROSSROADS (S) 22 16 0176
    PINKAS   *Orch.*   [Piano Concerto No. 1]

Elegance, discipline, and high-strung rhythmic precision make the Zak disc a beauty.

Katchen is a fine pianist, but he does not bring here the steely, tight-spring energy this work demands.

Kamenikova gives a small-scale, diffident performance. The sound is only fair.

Rubinstein on an expensive Victor offers great playing and resonant sound.

SYMPHONY NO. 2 IN E MINOR (Opus 27)

This lush, emotional work, in the Tchaikovsky tradition, has been a world success ever since the composer himself conducted it in St. Petersburg in 1908. It is the best of his three symphonies. But do not expect an intellectually satisfying experience—this is heart-tugging music for those who have hearts that like to be tugged.

* * BOULT	*London Philharmonic Orch.*	VICTROLA VIC	(S) 1139
* SANDERLING	*Leningrad Philharmonic Orch.*	HELIODOR	(S) 25029

Boult strikes fire. The stereo sound is clean.

Sanderling is workmanlike but little more. The 1957 sound is dully recorded.

Rameau, Jean Philippe (1683-1764)

This French composer first studied music in a Jesuit school, then went to Italy. He became famous as a theorist. His successfully produced operas aroused much hostility in Paris. Partisans of Pergolesi's gay Italian style attacked Rameau's music as too cerebral.

Rameau, little heard today, looms in the history books as a forerunner of Gluck in the development of opera. He led opera away from the stereotyped patterns of the Italian composers of his day. For his period, his music contains striking harmonic originality, yet to our ears, it usually sounds dry and unremarkable.

LA GUIRLANDE

"A Pastoral Ballet With Vocal Music" is the sub-title of this sweet, gentle composition, in which the paintings of Boucher and Watteau seem to spring to life.

* SANEVA, LESUEUR, WAHL	*Versaille Chamber Orch., Brasseur Chorus*	NONESUCH	(7) 10023

The music is daintily sung. The sound is clear.

HIPPOLYTE ET ARICIE   (Selections)

This suite is from the ballet Rameau composed in 1735—elegant but somewhat tedious French baroque writing.

* COURAUD	*Lamoureux Orch.*	PHILLIPS WS [Surprises]	(S) 9062

The work is played with Gallic finesse. The sound is resonant.

PIECES DE CLAVECIN EN CONCERT

Here is enjoyable music from the court of Louis XV. These five "concertos" date from 1741.

* RAMPAL, VEYRON-LACROIX, NEILZ	NONESUCH	(7) 1063

This disc offers luscious playing by the flutist Mr. Rampal and his fellow musicians. The sound is warm. If you like the period, don't miss this one.

Ravel, Maurice (1875-1937)

Ravel was born in France near the Spanish frontier; his mother spoke Spanish all her life. When Ravel was twelve, he entered the Paris Conservatoire. His radical leanings kept him from winning the Grand Prix de Rome, although he made four attempts. Ravel had already written much remarkable music, and his failure to win the Grand Prix roused such controversy that Dubois, the director of the Conservatoire, was forced to resign.

Ravel banded together with several other composers in a group that called itself the "Societe Des Apaches." These musicians—who included Vines and Maurice Delage among its earliest members, and later Florent Schmitt, Manuel de Falla, and Stravinsky—adopted the name "Apaches" to proclaim their endorsement of innovation and experiment. They worshipped Debussy and championed the music of "The Russian Five" who were still unknown in Paris.

During World War I, Ravel interrupted his career to drive an ambulance. After a few months, he came back to Paris, his hair streaked with grey and his nerves shattered.

His ballet *Bolero* brought him world fame. In 1932, an automobile accident brought on a breakdown from which he never recovered. His memory was gone, and his creative power had suffered an irreparable blow. He remained in his villa at Montfort L'Amaury near Paris, until his death.

PLACE AND ACHIEVEMENT   Ravel was a man of culture and taste; his music is sophisticated and urbane. After Debussy, Ravel is the best French composer of our century. The harmonic discoveries of Liszt, the impressionism of Debussy, the early French classicists such as Couperin all influenced Ravel. He was not a prolific composer—he even provided double duty for many works by rewriting piano pieces for orchestra—but his dazzling best displays French refinement and sensitivity surpassed only by Debussy.

THE ESSENTIAL RAVEL

ORCHESTRAL MUSIC: *Rapsodie Espagnole; Daphnis et Chloe; Symphonic Fragments, two series; Mother Goose Suite (also for piano duet); La Valse; Bolero; Concerto for the Left Hand; Concerto in G Major, for Piano and Orchestra.*

PIANO MUSIC: *Pavane pour une Infante Defunte (also for orchestra); Valses Nobles et Sentimentales (also for orchestra); Le Tombeau de Couperin (also for orchestra); Gaspard de la Nuit.*

SONG CYCLE: *Sheherezade.*

OPERA: *L'Enfant et les Sortileges; L'Heure Espagnole.*
CHAMBER MUSIC: *Quartet in F Major; Trio in A; Introduction and Allegro.*

OTHER WORKS

ORCHESTRAL MUSIC: *Alboraoa del Gracioso; Tzigane, for violin and orchestra.*
SONGS: *Chansons Madecasses; Chants Populaires; Deux Melodies Hebraiques; and other songs.*
PIANO MUSIC: *Sonatina; Menuet Antique; Jeux D'Eau; and other works.*

BOLERO

This ballet music, written for Ida Rubinstein, a remarkable and exotic actress-dancer, is Ravel's most famous piece. Due to overexposure, *Bolero* is now often relegated to Pops programs. *Bolero,* emphasizing its repetitive point, can be a stunning work in the concert hall but can be wearisome for home listening. *Bolero,* for some reason, usually does not record well, or its booming crescendos seem to almost break the speakers.

* * * MUNCH	*Boston Symphony Orch.*	VICTROLA VIC [La Valse]	(S) 1323
* * PARAY	*Detroit Symphony Orch.*	MERCURY [Rimsky-Korsakov, Capriccio Espagnol]	(M) 14031 (S) 18031
* VAN REMOORTEL	*Vienna Symphony*	VOX [French Program]	(M) 11850 (S) 511850
* WALLENSTEIN	*Virtuoso Symphony*	AUDIO FIDELITY [Bizet, Carmen Suite]	500005
MUNCH	*Paris Conservatorie Orch.*	RICHMOND [Berlioz, Benvenuto Cellini Overture]	(M) 19001
DESOMIERE	*Czech Philharmonic*	PARLIAMENT [Rhapsody Espagnole]	(S) 114
GOOSSENS		PICKWICK [Mussorgsky, Pictures at an Exhibition]	(S) 4031
BAUDO	*Czech Philharmonic*	CROSSROADS [Alborada; Daphnis and Chloe I; La Valse]	(M) 22 16 0038 (S) 22 16 0040

Munch and the Boston lead the list. Here is verve and superlative solo work. This is a fine thoroughly French record. A minority report from

William Flannigan in *Stereo Review* reads: "I've never come away from a Munch-Ravel performance without the wish that this conductor would just lay off this composer."

Paray is glittering and spirited. The sound is excellent. There is a splendid coupling.

Van Remoortel is exciting in an entirely acceptable reading.

Wallenstein's version is less than hypnotic, but the sound is good.

Munch, on mono, is much less worthy than on his Boston disc. The orchestral playing is inferior.

Desomiere disappoints; his solo players are not up to the demands of the music.

Goossens is hurried. The contrived musical explosion does not convince.

Baudo is languid, and the piece indifferently recorded; his players are apathetic.

CONCERTO IN D FOR THE LEFT HAND

Written in 1930-31 for a determined, one-armed pianist, Paul Wittgenstein, this concerto has become a classic of twentieth-century piano literature.

* PERLEMUTER, HORENSTEIN	*Concert Colonne Orch.*	Vox (M) 9220 [Concerto in G]

Perlemuter plays it with taut distinction. The mono sound is metallic.

CONCERTO IN G FOR PIANO AND ORCHESTRA

Ravel called this 1930-1931 work "a concerto in the strict sense, written in the spirit of Mozart and Saint-Saens." Much of it deliberately jazzy, has the feel of the twenties, but the composition also contains a haunting slow movement that has not yet been surpassed in any other twentieth-century piano concerto.

* * HENRIOT-SCHWEITZER, MUNCH	*Boston Symphony Orch.*	VICTROLA VIC (S) 1071 [Prokofiev, Concerto No. 2]
* PERLEMUTER, HORENSTEIN	*Concert Colonne Orch.*	Vox (M) 9220 [Concerto in D; Pavane]
BERNATHOVA, SMETACEK	*Prague Symphony Orch.*	PARLIAMENT (S) 631 [Bartok, Concerto No. 3]

Henriot-Schweitzer leads with a convincing performance. The sound is satisfactory.

Perlemuter is competent and lyrical. The sound is mono.

Bernathova is just adequate, and the sound is blurry.

The superlative and sweeping reading by Bernstein on an expensive Columbia, remains the definitive yardstick.

DAPHNIS ET CHLOE (Complete Ballet)

We are indebted to the great ballet impressario Diaghilev for yet another masterpiece. Ravel composed this music (1909-1911) for the choreographer Fokine who worked for Diaghilev; Nijinsky and Karsavina danced the leading roles, and Pierre Monteux conducted the premiere in 1912.

Here is some of the most shimmering music of this century. The wordless chorus backgrounds have been stolen by Hollywood films over and again: a forest chase and a wild dance ends, according to the scenario, in "joyous tumult."

* * * MUNCH	*Boston Smphony Orch.*	Victrola VIC	(S)	1271
* ANSERMET	*Orchestra Suisse Romande*	Richmond		19094

Munch is supreme—among the very best readings to be found in the catalogue—as he is in most French orchestral music. The sound is gorgeous.

Ansermet's version is glittering, but the sound is mono and the Suisse Romande, with all respect, is not the Boston Symphony.

MOTHER GOOSE (MA MERE L'OYE)

Ravel was never happier than when in the company of the children of his friends. This enchanting suite is a direct outcome of his devotion to little Jean and Mimi Godensky with whom he spent hours playing games and telling them stories. As so often occurs in the compositions of Ravel, *Mother Goose* was orchestrated from a four-hand piano suite which he had written some years before in 1908. It bears the subtitle *Five Children's Pieces.* The first performance in this form took place in 1910; two years later, the ballet version was presented in Paris under the musical direction of Gabriel Grovlez. Ravel, inspired by tales of Perrault and others, wrote the charming libretto.

* * * K. KLIEN, B. KLIEN		Turnabout (S) 34235 [Debussy, Epigraphes; Milhaud, Scaramouche]
* * * CASADESUS		3-Odyssey (M) 32 36 0003 [Complete piano works of Ravel]
* * MUNCH	*Boston Symphony Orch.*	Victrola VIC (S) 1060 [Dukas, The Sorcerer's Apprentice; d'Indy, Symphony on a French Mountain Air]

* PEDROTTI	*Czech Philharmonic*	CROSSROADS (S) 22 16 0188 [Pavane Pour une Infante Defunte; Debussy, Iberia]

The Kliens offer a sparkling, zestful piano version. The program and the sound are both first-rate.

Casadesus is supremely authoritative, in a three-record album. The sound is brittle.

In the more popular orchestral version, Munch is suavely assured. [The couplings are highly pleasant.]

Pedrotti is quite hearable but outclassed.

PAVANE POUR UNE INFANTE DEFUNTE

This short, poignant work was the first piece to win success for Ravel. Even though *Pavane* became famous, Ravel thought little of it, asserting that he saw all of its faults and none of its virtues. Ravel wrote *Pavane* originally in 1899 for solo piano. He orchestrated the piece in 1910, insisting that the title was not programmatic. "It is not a funeral lament for a dead child," he said, "but rather an evocation of the pavane which could have been danced by such a little princess as painted by Vlasquez at the Spanish Court."

* * * CASADESUS		3-ODYSSEY (M) 3236 0003
* * REINER	*Chicago Symphony Orch.*	VICTROLA VIC (S) 1199 [Alborada del Gracioso; Valses Nobles et Sentimentales; Paven for a dead Princess; R. Strauss, Le Bourgeois Gentilhomme]
* W. HAAS		2-PHILLIPS WS (M/S) 2-001
* HORENSTEIN	*Concerts Colonne Orch.*	VOX (M) 9220 [Ravel program]
* DORATI	*Minneapolis Symphony Orch.*	MERCURY (M) 14029 (S) 18029 [La Valse; Debussy, Nocturnes]

The best reading of the original piano version is in the superb Casadesus album. The sound, however, is rather harsh.

A compelling performance of the orchestral version is to be heard on the Reiner disc. *High Fidelity* comments: "Reiner finds just the right intensity of hard glitter for the Ravel items, and the Chicagoans are again in top form." The 1959 sound is good, but not outstanding by today's standards. [The Reiner disc offers a distinguished program. Ravel's elegant *Valses Nobles et Sentimentales* is included; this also began life as a piano piece, and was later orchestrated for a ballet—called *Adelaide*. The *Alborada Del*

Gracioso is a stunning piano piece, not quite successful in its orchestral transcription.]

Werner Haas is correct but unimaginative.

Horenstein's direction is lively, but the playing is indifferent.

Dorati is hard-driven. The sound is just fair.

RAPSODIE ESPAGNOLE

This is an unusually lush score for the astringent Ravel. This 1907 work is sensuous and impressionistic, and is almost irresistibly seductive. It is one of Ravel's most popular pieces. Symphony players enjoy playing this piece, because they can show off.

* * * MUNCH	*Boston Symphony Orch.*	VICTROLA VIC (S) 1041 [Debussy, La Mer]	
* * PARAY	*Detroit Symphony Orch.*	MERCURY (M) 14030 (S) 18030 [Alborada del Gracioso; Ibert, Escales]	
* SILVESTRI	*Czech Philharmonic*	PARLIAMENT (M/S) 114 [Bolero]	
BLOOMFIELD	*Rochester Philharmonic*	EVEREST (M) 6060 (S) 3060 [La Valse; Debussy, Iberia]	

Munch and the Boston win with a glittering and evocative performance. [The coupling is excellent.]

Paray, quite colorful, is most worthy.

Silvestri is commendable. [The coupling is *Bolero*.] The sound, however, is only so-so.

Bloomfield is much outclassed.

LA VALSE

La Valse conjures up a Viennese ballroom, in the hey-day of Johann Strauss, as imagined by a great French musical impressionist.

* * * MUNCH	*Boston Symphony Orch.*	VICTROLA VIC (S) 1323 [Bolero; French program]
* * PARAY	*Detroit Symphony Orch.*	MERCURY (M) 14029 (S) 18029 [Pavane pour un enfant defunte; Debussy, Nocturnes]
* * BARBIROLLI	*Halle Orch.*	VANGUARD (S) 177 [Daphnis et Chloe; Debussy, La Mer]

| * ANSERMET | | RICHMOND   (M) 19073
[Mussorgsky, Pictures at an
Exhibition] |
| BLOOMFIELD | *Rochester Philharmonic* | EVEREST   (M) 6060
(S) 3060
[Rhapsody; French program] |

Charles Munch, Boston Symphony—what more could be desired for *La Valse?* The disc is sweeping and vivid, both in playing and in sound.

Paray is less dignified, even headstrong, which is how most conductors play *La Valse*—but this is a winning reading!

Barbirolli's disc is well-recorded, and there is a clean-cut, well-paced spirit in this performance.

Ansermet offers a good chiseled reading that never gets overblown. But his cool rendition is on mono, and the sound is faded.

Bloomfield is inadequate.

CHAMBER MUSIC   Ravel has left us many lovely pieces in this category. His poised, evocative chamber music ranks with the best produced in this century.

INTRODUCTION AND ALLEGRO FOR HARP, FLUTE, CLARINET AND STRING QUARTET

This is poetic, magical writing from the Ravel of 1905-06. It should not be missed by lovers of chamber music.

| * * | *Endres Ensemble* | TURNABOUT   (S) 34161
[Debussy, Sonata No. 2 for
Flute, Viola, and Harp] |

The Endres Ensemble sounds fresh and spontaneous; it takes polished ensemble players to achieve this fine effect. The sound is agreeable. [The Debussy on the reverse is good impressionistic music.]

Those who are ready to spend more are referred to the classic recording by the Hollywood Quartet on Capital—one of the best chamber music discs ever made.

QUARTET IN F

This is a chiseled, controlled piece which is a masterpiece.

* * *	*Vlach Quartet*	ARTIA [Debussy, Quartet]	(7) (S)	201
* *	*Stuyvesant Quartet*	NONESUCH [Debussy, Quartet]	(7) (S)	1007
* *	*Fine Arts Quartet*	CONCERT-DISC [Debussy, Quartet]	(M) (S)	1253 253

A superb example of chamber ensemble playing can be heard from the Vlach Quartet. *Stereo Record Guide:* "The true spirit of the music emerges with remarkable freshness." The sound is natural and clear.

The Stuyvesant Quartet manages Gallic poise and order. Virgil Thomas called this record "beautifully performed and engineered." Today, by modern sonic standards, however, the sound is quite dry.

The Fine Arts Quartet is not to be slighted; they are excellent players, less assertive here than usual. The sound is dry; in places, even gritty.

TRIO IN A (PIANO)

This masterpiece, composed at the beginning of World War I while Ravel was waiting to be called up for military service, is first-rate chamber music.

* *	PRESSLER, GUILET, *Beaux Arts* GREENHOUSE	PHILLIPS WS (M/S) [Schuman, Trio]	9053
* *	OISTRAKH, KNUSHEVITZKY, OBORIN	MONITOR (S) [Chopin, Trio]	2069

The Beaux Arts Trio—Pressler, Guilet, Greenhouse—is one of the best trios to be heard today. All of Ravel's musical irony and impressionistic style are conveyed handsomely.

The Oistrakh Trio is fine, but as against Oistrakh's suavity I prefer violinist Guilet's dry-wine tone, particularly so in the exotic "Pantoum," a Malayan poetic form, of the second movement. [The Chopin Trio on the reverse side is mildly interesting, not really a trio but more of a "baby piano concerto" in an apt phrase of Harold Schonberg.]

PIANO MUSIC   Ravel's piano music, less popular than his orchestral and chamber music, always evinces elegant style. Ravel developed techniques for producing new sonorities and color for the piano.

PIANO MUSIC (Complete)

Ravel's piano music is extremely difficult to play; it becomes a shambles in the hands of anyone who has less than formidable talent. These are not intimate sketches as are most of Debussy's piano music; Ravel's pieces are cold, glittering, and virtuistic—like fine hard jade.

* * * CASADESUS	3-Odyssey (M) 3236 0003
* * PERLEMUTER	3-Vox SVBX (S) 5410
* HAAS	2-Philips WS (M/S) 2-001

For all Ravel recordings, the shimmering touch of Robert Casadesus is just about tops. Casadesus has been hailed as the perfect interpreter of Gallic music. Though the sound is hardly high fidelity, the reading is true Ravel, as authentic as you can get. Casadesus was a friend of the composer. Harold Schonberg of the New York *Times* said of this set: "It is hard to think of a better man for this project."

Vlado Perlemuter, a gifted pianist, is admirable here, and his range of piano colorations is impressive. The reproduction is good.

Werner Haas of Stuttgart was Gieseking's foremost pupil. His playing is refined, though without the authority of Casadesus, nor the shadings of Perlemuter. The sound is dry and crisp.

GASPARD DE LA NUIT; JEUX D'EAU; LE TOMBEAU DE COUPERIN

This is icy, poised Ravel—great piano music! *The Tomb of Couperin,* written in 1917, is described by Ravel as "a tribute not so much to Couperin as to eighteenth-century French music in general."

* * WEBSTER	Dover HCR (M) 5213
	HCRST (S) 7000

Webster is very cool, very brisk. Some of the poetic delicacy of a Casadesus is missing, but Webster offers, nevertheless, an original and powerful version, which I commend to you. The sound is pleasant.

OPERA   There is an urbane, sophisticated tone to Ravel's vocal writing, with little of the sentimentality of other masters in this field.

L'ENFANT ET LES SORTILEGES

This sensitive, humorous opera, based on Colette's slight tale of the naughty boy whose toys come to life, teaches a lesson in love and tenderness. From the child's first temper tantrum to the animals' final benediction, the opera is enchanting. Some consider this composition as Ravel's supereme creation. The socer is a marvel of orchestration.

* * * DANCO, WEND,	*Motet Choir of Geneva;*	RICHMOND R	(M) 23086
CUENOD, ANSERMET	*Orchestre de la Suisse*	SR	(S) 33086
	Romande		

Here are suave, polished direction and singing. All in all, this reading is as authoritative as we are likely to get, and I commend it to you. The verdict of *Music On Record* (1963): "Ansermet's performance is oldish but idiomatic, although there is some lack of gusto." The 1954 stereo sound is a little plummy, but enjoyable.

Reger, Max (1873-1916)

Reger was born in Bavaria. A pianist and conductor as well as a composer, he held high teaching posts in various German cities, and conducted the Meiningen Court orchestra from 1911 to 1914.

A prolific composer, his opus numbers run up to 147, and his works include compositions for orchestra, organ, chamber ensembles, piano, and many other scorings. Reger was solidly schooled in Bach and Brahms. His music is harmonically complex, and somewhat ponderous and turgid. As a youth, Reger was held to be a dangerous revolutionary in his musical style, but today he is passed over as being too conservative. He still enjoys an impressive reputation in Germany.

SONATAS NO. 1, 3, 7 FOR UNACCOMPANIED VIOLIN

Reger adored Bach, and these sonatas resemble Bach's in many respects. They were probably inspired by Bach's great sonatas for unaccompanied violin. However, it is questionable whether the music itself is much more than a cerebral exercise.

* BRESS	Dover	(S) 7016

Bress is a fast-rising young Canadian violinist, and this music is just his meat. The sound is very good.

Respighi, Ottorino (1879-1936)

This Italian studied in St. Petersburg with Rimsky-Korsakov, and in Berlin with Max Bruch. In 1913, he was appointed professor at the Liceo Reale di St. Cecilia in Rome; in 1923, he became its principal. He tried to bring about "a symphonic renascence" in Italy, with a stream of noisy symphonic poems that still enjoy popularity. Despite its blatancy, this music has technical skill, vivid imagination, and a feeling for romantic beauty.

FESTE ROMANE (ROMAN FESTIVAL)

This was the third and last of Respighi's musical guided tours of Rome. It is a very noisy score, if there ever was one, with even the suggestion of the clamor of a crowd.

* * TOSCANINI	NBC Symphony	VICTROLA VIC (S) 1344 [Elgar, Enigma]	
* * PEDROTTI	Czech Philharmonic Orch.	PARLIAMENT (S) 155 [Fountains of Rome]	
* DORATI	Minneapolis Symphony Orch.	MERCURY (M) 14039 (S) 18039 [Vetrate di Chiesa]	
* GOOSSENS	London Symphony Orch.	EVEREST (M) 6150 (S) 3150	

Respighi was one of the few "modern" composers that the Maestro liked to conduct. This is an affectionate, bred-in-the-blood reading. The sound is fair. Irving Kolodin comments: "Comfortably beyond challenge." The coupling is most worthwhile.

Pedrotti is flamboyant and exciting. This is a good reading. The sound is crisp.

Dorati is exciting, but in a mechanical way. The sound is decent.

The Goossens interpretation is adequate, but unremarkable.

FOUNTAINS OF ROME

This is vivid, descriptive, traditional writing of 1917. It depicts four memorable Roman fountains at various times of day.

* * * TOSCANINI	NBC Symphony Orch.	VICTROLA VIC (M) 1244 [Pines of Rome; Berlioz, Overture; Saint-Saens, Danse Macabre]	
* * SARGENT	London Symphony Orch.	EVEREST (M) 6051 (S) 3051 [Pines of Rome]	

* * PEDROTTI	*Czech Philharmonic Orch.*	PARLIAMENT (S) 155 [Feste Roman]
* DORATI	*Minneapolis Symphony Orch.*	MERCURY (M) 14035 (S) 18035 [Pines of Rome]
QUADRI	*Vienna State Opera Orch.*	WESTMINSTER (M) 9713 [Pines of Rome]

Toscanini gives a superbly vital and colorful reading, but the sound is just fair. Martin Bookspan in *Stereo Review's* 1968 updating rates it the best buy, regardless of price.

Sargent plays with gusto and evokes the feeling of a spacious, outdoor atmosphere. The gushing of the Triton Fountain is spectacularly conceived.

Pedrotti's interpretation is full-blooded and hearable. This is a good reading. *Stereo Review:* "Quite satisfying, and excellent value."

Dorati's version is well-drilled and energetic; the sound is quite thin.

Quadri is imaginative, but the sound is boxed in.

PINES OF ROME

This is pleasant, evocative, flashy music, dating from 1924.

* * TOSCANINI	*NBC Symphony Orch.*	VICTROLA VIC (M) 1244 [Fountains of Rome: Berlioz, Overture; Saint-Saens, Danse Macabre]
* * PREVITALI	*Accademia St. Cecilia Orch., Rome*	LONDON STS 15024 [Casella, La Giara]
* * SARGENT	*London Symphony Orch.*	EVEREST (M) 6051 (S) 3051 [Fountains of Rome]
QUADRI	*Vienna State Opera Orch.*	WESTMINSTER (M) 9713 [Fountains of Rome]

The Toscanini reading is classic and exhilarating, but the sound is just adequate. In other words, this performance is the yardstick, but for modern sound we must seek elsewhere. Martin Bookspan, in his 1968 "Updating of the Basic Repertory" for *Stereo Review* rates the Toscanini disc as the best available at any price.

Previtali suggests with musical rhetoric the romantic atmosphere; the disc is well recorded. [Coupling is with the cheerful, pleasing *La Giara* by Alfredo Casella. Casella (1883-1947) was a noted Italian composer, conductor, pianist, and critic; his music is eclectic in style.]

Sargent is crisp and enjoyable, with a good sense of orchestral contrasts.

Quadri is good, on faded mono.

Rimsky-Korsakov, Nicholas *(1844-1908)*

Rimsky-Korsakov planned on a naval career; for six years he attended the Naval College in St. Petersburg. During this period, he studied music privately.

A meeting with the noted composer Balakirev in 1861 fired Rimsky-Korsakov's own dream of becoming a composer. He composed a symphony which Balakirev played in St. Petersberg in 1865.

In 1871, Rimsky-Korsakov became professor of composition at the St. Petersburg Conservatory. Two years later, he retired from the Navy, and for the rest of his life he was prominent as teacher, conductor and composer.

PLACE AND ACHIEVEMENT Rimsky-Korsakov's forte was brilliant orchestration; at that, he has rarely been surpassed.

The Russian soul and national identity absorbed him. His melodies are often in the spirit of Russian folk songs, and his harmonies are suggestive of the old scales of Russian church music.

His music is generally derided today by serious critics, with such comments as "Russian sugar and spice sprinkled with consummate skill" (David Hall), but his suave melodies, piquant rhythms, and blazing orchestral colors maintain Rimsky-Korsakov's position as a popular favorite.

THE ESSENTIAL RIMSKY-KORSAKOV
ORCHESTRAL MUSIC: *Scheherazade Suite; Capriccio Espagnol; Russian Easter Overture; Le Coq d'Or (The Golden Cockerel).*

OTHER MAJOR WORKS
OPERAS: *Sadko, Sniegurotchka (The Snow Maiden).*
ORCHESTRAL MUSIC: *Symphonies No. 1 and 3; Antar Symphony; Concerto for Piano and Orchestra; Dubinushka.*

CAPRICCIO ESPAGNOL *(Opus 34)*

Rimsky-Korsakov originally planned his *Capriccio Espagnol* as a fantasy for solo violin and orchestra, but he realized that in doing so he would have to sacrifice the virtuoso display of orchestration that he had in mind. As the composer points out in his autobiography, the *Capriccio* is a brilliant piece for the orchestra, "selecting melodic designs and figurations exactly adapted to each kind of instrument." Tchaikovsky himself wrote to his colleague: "I must tell you that your *Spanish Capriccio* is a colossal masterpiece of orchestration, and you may regard yourself as the greatest master of the present day."

Besides being colorful and melodic, this music can serve as a textbook on orchestration. Its lessons were not lost on Rimsky-Korsakov's student, Igor Stravinsky.

* * PARAY	*Detroit Symphony Orch.*	MERCURY	(M) 14031
			(S) 18031
		[Ravel, Bolero]	
* ANCERL	*Czech Philharmonic*	CROSSROADS	(M) 22160105
			(S) 22160106
* ROSSI	*Vienna State Opera Orch.*	VANGUARD	(M) 110
		[Tchaikovsky, Capriccio Italian; Overture "1812"]	
ANSERMET	*Orchestra Suisse Romande*	RICHMOND	(M) 19055
		[Coq d'Or]	

Paray gives an expert reading; the cadenzas by the various instruments are impeccably rendered. The sound is fine.

Ancerl's version is well-played, but hardly brilliant.

Rossi is entirely acceptable. The sound is good mono.

Ansermet gives a great performance, but the sound is mono—rather faded but still hearable. *Capriccio Espagnol* is a piece that especially demands stereo.

COQ D'OR: SUITE

This suite consists of colorful orchestral music from Rimsky-Korsakov's opera *Coq d'Or (The Golden Cockerel)*. This opera, his last stage work, brought to a close a tremendous 30-year period of Russian opera, which included the premieres of Mussorgsky's *Boris Godounov,* Tchaikovsky's *Eugene Onegin,* and Borodin's *Prince Igor.*

* * STEINBERG	*Pittsburgh Symphony*	PICKWICK	(S) 4008
		[Prokofiev, Love for Three Oranges]	
* * PARAY	*Detroit Symphony Orch.*	MERCURY	(M/S) 18070
		[Borodin, Prince Igor Polovetsian Dances]	
* ANSERMET	*Orchestra Suisse Romande*	RICHMOND	(M) 19055
		[Capriccio Espagnol]	

Steinberg and the Pittsburgh are outstanding, with fine orchestral work. The disc also includes the zestful and worth-while Prokofiev work, *Love for Three Oranges.*

Paray is very hearable, indeed. His is a colorful and dramatic interpretation. The sound is clear.

Ansermet, too, is satisfactory. The sound is decent mono.

SCHEHERAZADE (Opus 35)

The Thousand and One Nights are here set to music, with a brilliant score. Many critics condescend to *Scheherazade,* yet it is still thrilling music, if you don't hear it too often.

* * MONTEUX	*London Symphony Orch.*	VICTROLA VIC	(S)	1013
* * ANSERMET	*Paris Conservatoire Orch.*	RICHMOND	(M) (S)	19086 29086
* * STEINBERG	*Pittsburgh Symphony*	PICKWICK	(S)	4029
* ROSSI	*Vienna State Opera Orch.*	VANGUARD	(S)	163
DORATI	*Minneapolis Symphony Orch.*	MERCURY	(M) (S)	14008 18008
GOOSSENS	*London Symphony*	EVEREST	(M) (S)	6026 3026
CHALABALA	*Czech Philharmonic*	PARLIAMENT	(S)	103
PERLEA	*Bamberg Symphony Orch.*	VOX	(5)	10220
ROEHR	*ND Symphony Orch.*	SOMERSET ST. FI.		2600
QUADRI	*Vienna State Opera Orch.*	WESTMINSTER	(M)	9714

Monteux provides a lush, imaginative *Scheherezade* both delectable and colorful.

Ansermet's is a more fiery, sensuous, and exciting version.

Steinberg's vivid performance is also rewarding, with brilliant solos and enjoyable stereo.

The other listed low-priced performances are competent but not outstanding.

Those who long for the finest *Scheherazade,* both musically and sonically, should acquire the high-priced Stokowski disc, on the London label.

Rossini, Gioacchino (1792-1868)

Rossini's mother was an opera singer; his father, the town trumpeter. At ten, Rossini was a choirboy; and at 12, he became the cembalist at the local opera house.

His one-act opera, *La Cambiale di Matrimonio*, was produced in 1810. *Il Barbiere di Sevigila (The Barber of Seville)*, produced when he was 26, created a sensation. During the first half of his life, he traveled with his wife, Isabella, from one opera house to another, selling opera scores as fast as he wrote them. On his travels, he was drawn through the streets of towns by cheering admirers who harnessed themselves to his carriage.

In 1824, Rossini became director of the Theatre Italien in Paris. He was extremely well paid throughout his career. He put six months of concentrated labor into his opera *William Tell;* and his overwork resulted in insomnia, nervousness, and eyestrain. It was his last opera. Even after a long rest, he seemed to have no more drive to compose. He wrote only one big work after *Tell,* the superb religious piece, *Stabat Mater.*

When his wife died, Rossini remarried and settled in Paris, and his house became world-famous for great food, witty conversation, and the amusing little pieces Rossini wrote to entertain his guests.

Rossini's music combines an elegant and gay melodiousness with clarity of line, and with constant wit.

PLACE AND ACHIEVEMENT   Rossini was one of the most gifted melodists who ever lived. He burst upon the scene precisely when European audiences had tired of pompous Neopolitan opera, and were yearning for lighthearted musical entertainment an dfor tunes that they could go home whistling.

In Leigh Hunt's pharse: "Rossini, in music, is the genius of sheer animal spirits." Franz Werfel labeled him "The only creator of truly comic music." Yet there is still much of the ready hack in Rossini. Commonplaces and musical chatter fill tiresome pages of many of his operas—except for *The Barber* which remains the masterpiece of all comic musical creations. His other operas are ebullient—full of high vitality, and often of crude buffoonery. They are also uneven. But taken all in all, and when sung by sure Italian singers, Rossini provides delightful listening.

THE ESSENTIAL ROSSINI

OPERAS: *The Barber of Seville; William Tell; La Cenerentola.*
ORCHESTRAL MUSIC: *Overtures to L'Italiana in Algeri; Semiramide; La Gazza Ladra.*
RELIGIOUS MUSIC: *Stabat Mater.*

OTHER WORKS

OPERAS: *L'Italiana in Algeri; Semiramide; La Gazza Ladra.*
RELIGIOUS MUSIC: *Petite Messe Solennelle.*
PIANO MUSIC, SONGS, ETC.: *Sins of My Old Age.*

THE BARBER OF SEVILLE *(Complete)*
(Sung in Italian)

The Barber, the greatest comic opera ever written, contains shrewd characterizations; it bubbles with irresistible high spirits. Melodies abound—singers love to sing it—and audiences never seem to weary of *The Barber.*

* * SIMIONATO, TADDEI, INFANTIONO, PREVITALI	*Rome Radio Orch.*	EVEREST-CETRA	(S) 413/3
* D'ANGELO, MONTI, CAPECCHI, TADEO, CAVA, BARTOLETTI	*Chorus and Orch. of the Bavarian Radio*	HELIDOR HS	(S) 25072/3

I hold affection for the old Cetra set, now refurbished for stereo. Giulietta Simionato is a superlative Rosina, and her lyrical line is excellent. Giuseppe Taddei is a first-rate Figaro, virile-sounding and accomplished. Previtali keeps everything moving. All in all, there is a pleasant theatrical atmosphere to the set. The sound is decent.

The Heliodor set not long ago was on the prestigious Deutsche Grammophone label, but got clobbered in the competitive market by the glittering Callas-Gobbi version on Angel. Nevertheless, the Heliodor disc features a spirited and polished conducting job, with workmanlike singers. *High Fidelity* commented: "The modest joys of this performance have been accorded superbly naturalistic, well-balanced sonics."

LA CAMBIALE DI MATRIMONIO
(MARRIAGE BY PROMISSORY NOTE)
(Complete) (Sung in Italian)

Rossini's first opera, written when he was 18, contains not much musically, but drops intriguing hints of genius to come.

* SCOTTO, CAPECCHI, PETRI, FASANO	*Rome Radio Orch.*	EVEREST/CETRA	(S) 446/2

The disc provides polished singing all the way. The sound is good. This master tape was not originally part of the Cetra series, but came from Ricordi, the famous music publishing house of Italy, who made the recording in the late fifties. The stereo sound is true, not faked.

LA CENERENTOLA (Complete) (Sung in Italian)

This opera dates from the era when singers reigned supreme, dictating to composers how their parts should be written. Sparkle and elegance light up this work. It is hard to understand why *La Cenerentola* has been dropped from the boards—probably because it is next to impossible to find singers who can navigate the highly ornamented score. The soprano is all-important in this delightful *Cinderella* of Rossini. Opera buffs may recall that this was one of Conchita Supervia's great roles.

* * SIMIONATO, VALLETTI, ROSSI	*Rome Radio Orch.*	2-Everest-Cetra	432/2

Simionato, who sings with smoothly liquid tone, seems entirely sure of herself—a real mezzo-soprano in the best Italian tradition. The delicious ensembles are done well. The men are very good, especially the *buffo* Christiano Dalamangas. The sound goes harsh now and then, but is otherwise acceptable.

OVERTURES

These are supreme achievements, firmly placed in every repertory. There are as many as 40 recordings of Rossini's overtures in the Schwann catalogue—15 at low prices.

* * TOSCANINI	*NBC Symphony Orch.*	2-Victor VIC	(M) 1248/1274
* * GIULINI	*Philadelphia Orch.*	Seraphim	(S) 60058
* PREVITALI	*Accademia St. Cecilia Orch.*	2-Everest	(S) 3186
* MAAG	*Paris Conservatory Orch.*	London Sts	(S) 15030

Over the years, Toscanini recorded most of the Rossini overtures; we have two records from him on low-priced Victrola. Martin Bookspan commented, in *Hi/Fi Stereo Review*: "Get the Toscanini collections and forget all about the others." But it is not so simple. As Bookspan himself goes on to say: "This would be unfair to readers who insist upon, and are entitled to, high-quality reproduction. Despite mono sound and reproduction that sometimes is just barely adequate, these performances are among the greatest delights of recorded music."

For better sound, along with warm playing, we now have Giulini's

stereo recording of five Rossini overtures on Seraphim. Giulini is a
Rossini specialist, with sensitivity and skill.
been surpassed.

I also enjoy the two-record set of the Overtures by Previtali. The
reading is hard-driving, and somewhat undisciplined.

Maag delivers a more refined interpretation. The sound is vivid.

STABAT MATER

If you are only acquainted with the Rossini of *Barbiere,* there is a sur-
price. Maria Stader is in excellent voice, and so is that thorough musician
such as this, Rossini is irrepressible; gay melodies abound, and it's all
quite zestful rather than solemn.

* * * STADER, RADEV, HAEFLIGER, BORG, FRICSAY	*Berlin Radio Chorus* *and Orch.*	HELIODOR	(M/S) 250032

This is the best version of the *Stabat Mater* to be had—regardless of
price. Maria Stader is in excellent voice, and so is that thorrough musician
Ernst Haefliger, who manages to sound properly Italian. Fricsay keeps
everything moving with a dramatic hand, much as he does in his famous
reading of Verdi's *Requiem.* The mono sound is very good; the enhanced
stereo is darkish.

PETITE MESSE SOLENNELLE

Don't let the "solemn mass" of the title scare you off. This 1863 work
is operatic Rossini in style—and a joy!

* * SCOTTO, COSSOTTO, KRAUS, VINCO, VERGANTI, PRANZ, BENEDETTI, BERTOLA	*Polyphonic Chorus of* *Milan*	2-EVEREST	(S) 441/42

Renata Scotto is the best of a strong cast; her phrasing and musicianship are unusual. The original scoring for two pianos and harmonium is
used. Later, Rossini rescored the *Mass* for orchestra, "because somebody
else would be sure to do it after my death, and probably do it badly."
On the whole, the sound is very well transferred from the Italian Ricordi
catalogue. The stereo is true, not phoney.

IL SIGNOR BRUSCHINO (Complete)
(Sung in Italian)

This bouncy one-acter, written in 1813 when Rossini was 21, was hitherto known to us chiefly because its gay overture was one of Toscanini's favorites.

* RIBETTI,	*Ennio Gerelli, Orch. da*	TURNABOUT TV (S) 34158
PONTIGGIA,	*Camera di Milano*	
CAPECCHI,		
MAUGERI, VINCO		

The singers seem to be having a wonderful time, and it's all highly diverting. Dry sound, but listenable. The stereo is electronically mastered.

WILLIAM TELL (Complete) (Sung in Italian)

In 1829, after completing this work at age 38, Rossini abandoned his operatic activity. He composed *William Tell* for the French stage at a time when he was the most popular composer-musician in Paris. Although his acknowledged masterpiece, *William Tell* is almost never performed today. It contains rousing melodies and splendid opportunities for *bel canto* singing. However that may be, the opera never really caught on, even in Italy—perhaps because of its serious, elevated style and its earnest, almost intellectual quality. *William Tell* represents Rossini's most ambitious pages. If you love *The Barber*, you will probably like *William Tell*— but don't expect the same brand of fun.

* TADDEI, CARTERI,	*Rome Radio Orch.*	EVEREST/CETRA (S) 420/4
TOZZI, CORENA,		
ROSSI		

The ringing voice of Giuseppe Taddei is alone worth the price of the record. Corena is rather callow, with a powerful high register. Carteri is a graceful soprano with a smoothly flowing melodic line. There are stirring, all-out ensembles. The dramatic and splendid voice of Taddei is in its prime here. I do not know of another singer today who could turn in such a William Tell (Guillaume, to be accurate—historically the original libretto is French). The sound on mono was rather boxed in; the "stereo" facelift caused *High Fidelity's* Peter Davis, ordinarily a peaceable man, to write: "It gives the impression of something recorded on defective tape by an inexpensive transistor job at 1-⅞ ips. There can be no excuse for this sonic malfeasance. . . ."

Rubin, Andrew (1939-   )

This young composer was born in Philadelphia. He is also a filmmaker.

TRAGOEDIA

*
Moog electronic music synthesizer   NONESUCH   (S) H 71198S

This much-discussed work is a four-movement symphony, played by an electronic Moog synthesizer. It is an ambitious piece, with pretentious greek tragedy titles for the sections, and symphonic effects such as thundering brass climaxes, etc. It employs every conceivable electronic gimmick, including tones of fixed pitch. This is interesting music, if *music* is the right word.

Saint-Saens, Camille (1835-1921)

Saint-Saens gave his first concert in his native Paris at the age of ten. After 1848, he studied organ under Benoit, and composition under Halevy. In 1857, he was appointed organist at the Madeleine. A meeting with Liszt in 1852 turned him toward the symphonic poem and toward a "cyclic" design in his symphonies and concertos. His opera *Samson et Dalila* was first performed by Liszt at Weimar, Germany, in 1892.

Saint-Saens was an incredibly prolific composer. His opus numbers run to 169, and he composed music until the last year of his life.

PLACE AND ACHIEVEMENT Saint-Saens remarked once that he "composed music as naturally as a tree bears apples." His music is endowed with sure technique, even to the point of glibness; his works are models of French clarity and correctness.

Few of his nearly 200 works are performed today because most of them are superficial and commonplace. But his best work reveals a sensible, dependable craftsman at work, a composer who admittedly was not attempting to delve after man's deepest feelings.

THE ESSENTIAL SAINT-SAENS

ORCHESTRAL MUSIC: *Symphony 3, in C Minor; Danse Macabre, Tone Poem; The Carnival of Animals, Suit for Two Pianos and Orchestra; Concerto No. 2 in G Minor, for Piano and Orchestra; Concerto No. 3 in B Minor, for Violin and Orchestra; Concerto No. 1, in A Minor, for Cello and Orchestra; Introduction and Rondo Capriccioso, for Violin and Orchestra; Havanaise, for Violin and Orchestra.*

OPERA: *Samson et Dalila.*

OTHER MAJOR WORKS

ORCHESTRAL MUSIC: *Concerto No. 2, in A Minor, for Violin and Orchestra; Concertos Nos. 2, 4, and 5, for Piano and Orchestra; Le Rouet d'Omphale, Phaeton, La Jeunesse d'Hercule, Tone Poems; Jota Aragonese, Rapsodie Auvergne, Suite Algerienne, for Orchestra; Symphony No. 2 in A Minor.*

CHORAL MUSIC: *Christmas Oratorio; Requiem.*

CHAMBER MUSIC: *Two Sonatas for Violin and Piano; Two Sonatas for Cello and Piano; Two Piano Trios; Two String Quartets.*

KEYBOARD MUSIC: *Etudes, Valses, Fugues, etc., for Piano; Three Preludes and Fugues for Organ.*

CARNIVAL OF THE ANIMALS

A suite for two pianos and orchestra, this indestructible classic is subtitled "a grand zoological fantasy." Saint-Saens regarded this as private, family music, and would not allow it to be published nor publicly performed during his lifetime.

* GILELS, ZAK, ELIASBURG	*USSR State Orch.*	Monitor (M) 2006	[Mozart Concerto for Two Pianos, K. 365]

The playing is good-humored and the sound is pleasant.

A solid, thoughtful performance of Mozart is found on the reverse side of the disc.

CONCERTO IN A MINOR FOR CELLO AND ORCHESTRA (Opus 33)

Although Saint-Saens knew the cello thoroughly, and wrote highly professional cello music, this concerto does become rather tiresome.

* * ROSTROPOVICH, STOLYAROV	*Moscow Radio Orch.*	Monitor (S) 2090	[Dvorak, Concerto]

Rostropovich is superb. The sound is acceptable.

DANSE MACABRE (Opus 40)

Saint-Saens' graveyard concert may be the most successful work ever penned on a *totentanz* (dance of death) theme. When it was first played in London, critics pointed to it with disgust as "one of the many signs of the intense and coarse realism that is entering into much of the musical composition—so-called—of our day." Time has reduced its starkness to little more than a Halloween shiver, and the work is now one of the mainstays of Pops programs.

* * TOSCANINI	*NBC Symphony Orch.*	Victrola VIC 1244	[mixed program]
* ANSERMET	*Suisse Romande Orch.*	Richmond (M) 19097	[mixed program]

Toscanini is supremely efficient in a famous performance.

Ansermet is all glitter, with good mono sound.

HAVANAISE FOR VIOLIN AND ORCHESTRA

The *Havanaise* provides music supremely suited to the violin, written by a man who knew the instrument well.

* * KOGAN, MONTEUX	*Boston Symphony Orch.*	Victrola VIC (S) 1153	[Khachaturian, Violin Concerto]

| * * SZERYNG, LINDENBURG | *Orchestra National de Radio France* | EVEREST | (M) 6152 (S) 3152 |
| * ROSAND, REINHARDT | *South West German Radio Orch.* | VOX | (5) 10470 |

Kogan plays with an impressively lean musical style, with excellent support by the Boston Orchestra and the RCA engineers. In Russia, many music lovers rank Kogan above Oistrakh; upon hearing Kogan's performance of the *Havanaise,* one can understand why.

Szeryng gives a fine, romantic performance that is also admirable.

Rosand intellectualizes the music too much; it is, after all, primarily showpiece music for the violin and violinist.

INTRODUCTION AND RONDO CAPRICCIOSO (Opus 28)

This is beguiling music, even for critics who usually turn up their noses at salon classics. Because few other works show off the virtuoso so well, violinists love to play this music.

* * OISTRAKH, MUNCH	*Boston Symphony Orch.*	VICTROLA VIC [Chausson, Poeme]	(S) 1058
* KOGAN, GAUK	*State Radio Orch.*	MONITOR	(S) 2076
* SZERYNG, LINDENBURG	*Orchestra National Radio France*	EVEREST	(M) 6152 (S) 3152

Oistrakh leads here, with the additional benefit of Munch and the Boston Symphony sound.

Kogan is also excellent—passionate and warm.

Szeryng gives a clean, lyrical performance, but the disc is indifferently recorded.

SYMPHONY NO. 3 IN C MINOR ("ORGAN") (Opus 78)

Though not a truly great work, this symphony ranks well above Saint-Saens' other works, and shows his expertise at its best. It is curiously constructed in two long movements, each made up of sections utilizing a Lisztian *idée fixe* or theme. The forces of full orchestra, organ, and piano duet are employed.

| SWAROWSKY | *Vienna Philharmonica* | PARLIAMENT | (S) 174 |

Swarowsky is properly serious, but the "Vienna Philharmonica"—whatever that may be—would have benefited from a few more rehearsals. The sound is acceptable.

Sammartini, Giovanni Battista (1701-1775)

Giovanni Sammartini worked in Milan as *maestro di capella,* and taught Gluck from 1737-41. He was the most important Italian composer of symphonies in his day, but his music is little played today.

SYMPHONY NO. 5 IN D (Opus 107) (J.C.73); D MAJOR (J.C.15); G MAJOR (J.C.50); AND E-FLAT MAJOR (J.C.30)

Here are the endless melodic ideas, restless energy, and polish that comprise the musical make-up of Giovanni Sammartini—and you should hear his work. He is never pretentious; he seems to be having a fine time, composing for his own delight.

* * JENKINS	*Angelicum Orchestra of Milan*	NONESUCH H	(M) 1162 (S) 71162

Newell Jenkins, a Sammartini *aficionado,* has culled five choice symphonies from the master's 77 extant symphonic works. And when Sammartini says *spiritoso,* you should hear the *spiritoso* of Jenkins and his happy music-makers of Milan. This is altogether a sweet record, with excellent sound.

Sarasate, Pablo de (1844-1908)

One of the most phenomenal violinists who ever lived, Sarastate inspired many composers of his time. Among the works written for his fiery fingers were Lalo's *First Violin Concerto,* and Bruch's *Second Violin Concerto.* Sarasate's own pieces were great concert favorites 50 years ago, and still are very much part of the romantic fiddler's repertory.

CARMEN FANTASY (Opus 25)

This lush, colorful favorite of romantic violinists is based on themes from Bizet's opera.

* * KOGAN, NEBOLSIN	*Moscow Radio Orch.*	MONITOR (S) 2076 [Saint Saens, Introduction and Rondo Capriccioso]

Russia's No. 2 violinist provides firm, brilliant playing. The sound is respectable.

ZIGEUNERWEISEN (Opus 29, No. 1)

This Gypsy fantasy is an endearing souvenir of the romantic salon.

* ROSAND, SZOEKE	*South West German Radio Orch.*	Vox (M) 11600 (S) 511600

Rosand takes a rather careful, no-nonsense approach. There are few sparks.

Satie, Eric *(1866-1926)*

Satie's mother was a pianist and composer; his father was a music publisher in Paris. In 1883-84, he attended the Paris Conservatoire with disappointing results as he was not amenable to scholastic training. He began to compose piano pieces in his own extremely personal style. He is believed to have influenced Debussy, whom he met in 1890 while playing the piano in a Montmartre cabaret. Satie lived in poverty and obscurity, his music known only to a small circle of friends. But in 1910, he suddenly became a celebrity, as a group of young composers hailed him as their pioneering leader.

Satie composed three ballets, including *Parade* which was produced by Satie, Cocteau, Picasso, and Diaghilev in Paris in 1917. Satie also produced a symphonic drama named *Socrate,* as well as some other works of an original cast.

Satie was a loner who worked against the impressionist tide of his day.

PLACE AND ACHIEVEMENT Today, there is a Satie boomlet, and recordings of his piano music appear on *Billboard's* classical charts. The Satie vogue seems to be particularly strong among college people—it is easy to understand why.

Satie was definitely anti-materialism and anti-establishment—so much so that he achieved a reputation as a clown which was doubtlessly betted by the titles he bestowed on some of his pieces: *Genuine Flabby Preludes for a Dog, The Three Distinguished Waltzes of a Fop, Three Pieces in the Form of a Pear.*

Satie was way ahead of his time. Today, avant-garde audiences sit through unendurably long underground films showing people engaged in boring, repetitive acts. In 1920, Satie wrote a one-minute piece called *Vexations;* and he instructed that it was to be played 840 times in succession. It was. It took 14 hours.

Satie will never be a majority taste, of course, but his music is intriguing. Here is surrealism; the jumbling of familiar elements in unfamiliar combinations. The thought of what he might have done with a 1968 electronic Moog synthesizer makes one's mind boggle.

Little of Satie is available as yet on low-cost discs; but one of these days, the record companies will "discover" his with a vengance.

SOCRATE

Written in 1919, this "symphonic drama" is one of the most original works of this century. It is based on the *Dialogues* of Plato and Satie being Satie, all the music is sung in the soprano range.

For those who still regard Satie as a *farceur,* it is instructive to note that the wonderful opening bars of *Socrate* are preceded in Satie's notebooks by innumerable alternate and rejected versions of the short phrase.

There is classic calm—and restraint—in this strange music. In the death scene, the music does not rise in intensity, but disappears in a monotonous repetition of a bare fifth. The effect is overwhelming.

* * JOURNEAUX, LINDENFELDER, PREBORDES, CARPENTIER, LEIBOWITZ	*Paris Philharmonic*	COUNTERPOINT	(5)	510

The assured conducting of Rene Leibowitz stands out, and the women sing well. The sound is agreeable. (If your dealer never heard of the Counterpoint label, tell him it is issued by Everest.)

TROIS MELODIES

These "three melodies" are dada—deliberate nonsense—in music.

* BERNAC	2-ODYSSEY	3226 0009

Bernac is perhaps our best interpreter of 20th century French songs, and he understands this music to perfection. The sound is very good. [This album is primarily composed of Poulenc songs; the Satie is a filler.]

Scarlatti, Alessandro (1660-1725)

The greatest and most prolific of the composers of Italian opera in his time, Scarlatti wrote 115 operas (by his own estimate), 160 oratorios, some 600 cantatas, and many other works. They are all unplayed today; only fragments remain on records to remind us of the harsh verdicts of posterity. Nevertheless, Alessandro Scarlatti was a very important figure in the history of music; he founded the Neapolitan school of opera, and can be called one of the fathers of both grand opera and comic opera.

CANTATA PASTORALE PER LA NATIVITA DE NOSTRO SIGNORE GESU CHRISTO

This is worth-while music of intrinsic beauty.

* STOKLASSA, KEHR   *Mainz Chamber Orch.*   TURNABOUT TV   34180 [Haydn, Cantilena Pro Advento; Purcell, Behold, I Bring You Glad Tidings]

The singing is agreeable; the sound is pleasant.

CHAMBER CANTATA: "OH DI BETLEMME"

Some of Scarlatti's most intimate and original ideas are heard in his cantatas.

STOKLASSA, KEHR   *Mainz Chamber Orch.*   TURNABOUT   (S) 34180 [Haydn, Cantilena; Purcell, Verse]

This performance is too solemn—even lethargic.

CONCERTO NO. 3 IN F

The Viennese symphonic style of Haydn and Mozart is heard in embryo here. Otherwise, the work is of little interest, except for students of music history.

*   *London Soloists Ensemble*   NONESUCH H   71052 [Geminiani, Concerto Grosso in D Minor; Telemann, Concerto in A Minor for Violin]

The playing is vivid and as expressive as this staid music permits.

Scarlatti, Domenico *(1685-1750)*

The son of the famous Alessandro, Domenico Scarlatti was brought up in an atmosphere saturated with music.

He wrote a dozen large-scale operas, cantatas, organ works, etc., but found his own true style to be in miniature, jewel-like sonatas for the harpsichord. Well over 500 of these little masterpieces have been left to us, and they are wonderful.

Scarlatti fans are quite mad; they call each other at midnight, and play for each other, over the telephone, the latest tiny marvel they have just discovered in Domenico's inexhaustible jewel-box. But these sonatas were not written to be played one on top of the other, piggy-back: they are self-contained little morsels, and should be savored as such.

EIGHT SONATAS FOR VIOLIN AND HARPSICHORD

This is exhilarating music.

* * OLEVSKY,   WESTMINSTER   (M) 9046
    VALENTI

The sonatas are played with the robust, full-bodied style that Scarlatti demands. The sound is agreeable.

SIXTEEN SONATAS FOR HARPSICHORD

These small-scaled beauties often suggest a Spanish flavor. Ralph Kirkpatrick, who ought to know, reminds us in his valuable study of Scarlatti that when the composer entered the service of the Infanta of Portugal, he hispanized himself musically as well as personally. This remarkable metamorphosis took place after Scarlatti was fifty, for the most part, after his sixty-seventh year.

* * * SGRIZZI   NONESUCH   H-7109

This disc is a beauty. Sgrizzi is one of the best harpsichordists I have ever heard. His techniques is formidable. Every stroke has obviously been thought out by a sound musician. Sgrizzi does not hesitate to suggest the atmosphere of strumming guitars and Spanish dancing. The disc, from Cynus of Paris, is well recorded.

SONATAS FOR HARPSICHORD, VOL. 10

* * VALENTI   WESTMINSTER   (M) 9338

The inflammable, almost belligerent Valenti is most welcome. The sound was recorded a bit too close to the microphone, but one forgets this after a few bars.

SONATAS FOR HARPSICHORD, VOL. 11

* * VALENTI   WESTMINSTER   (M) 9341

Another first-class recording by Valenti. Don't let the mono bother you; no one who has all his marbles needs stereo for harpsichord music.

Note: I am advised by Westminster that 26 discs of Valenti playing Scarlatti are available. Not all of them are in stock at all times, but you can't go wrong on any of them. These are historic recordings—and wonderful.

SONATA IN D MAJOR (Longo No. 57), and SONATA IN G MAJOR (Longo Sup. No. 57)

These sonatas are among the bare handful that Scarlatti wrote especially for the organ with two keyboards. These are unexpecional compositions, and they make one impatient to get back to looking to The Master on harpsichord where he is definitely at his best.

* * * TAGLIAVINI   MUSIC GUILD   (S) 129
                                           [Scarlatti, Trabaci, Merula,
                                           Frescobaldi, Rossi, Pasquini,
                                           Zipoli]

This disc, entitled "Italian Organ Music of the 17th and 18th Centuries," is a marvelous record for organ lovers. This recording contains striking music by obscure composers such as Zipoli, Trabaci, etc.—composers who conjure up all of Musica Italia in the grand tradition. The Serassi organ of Berbambo, used here, is extremely beautiful; so is Signor Tagliavini's playing. All praise to him for resurrecting these works, many of which had heretofore been gathering dust in libraries.

SONATAS (Piano)

Here are Scarlatti's harpsichord works played on a piano.

* * GILELS   MONITOR   (M) 2060
                                           [Beethoven, Fantasy Opus
                                           80]

There are infidels who want to hear Scarlatti on a piano. For such, this record can be recommended. The sound is listenable. [On the back, Gilels gives a strong reading of the Beethoven *Fantasy*.]

ELEVEN SONATAS (Piano)

* * HASKIL   WESTMINSTER   (M) 9320

Clara Haskil makes an exquisite thing of Scarlatti on the piano. This is romantic, subdued Scarlatti, played by an artist who makes full use and great effect out of the piano's crescendo and diminuendo. (The cool harpsichord plays only piano or forte.) The sound is excellent.

SIXTY SONATAS

* * * KIRKPATRICK   2-ODYSSEY   (M) 3226 0007

There is nothing more fascinating for the music lover than comparing great artists in their renditions of the same music—Toscanini compared to Bruno Walter in the Beethoven *Symphonies,* Tebaldi building her *Madame Butterfly* differently than does Callas. Apart from the fun, such exercise sharpens your ears.

After you've heard Valenti and Sgrizzi and Haskil and Landowska, you are ready for Ralph Kirkpatrick. This is a classic, authoritative reading. Kirkpatrick is not only our leading authority on Domenico Scarlatti; he is perhaps the best harpsichord player in the world. The sound is fine.

SONATAS FOR HARPSICHORD

Here are more jewels from the master miniaturist—more bubbling originality. Harold Schonberg of the New York *Times* comments: "It is not necessary to dwell on Scarlatti's unique genius. Of the 500-odd sonatas he composed, none are repetitive. Constant flow and invention are ever present; the man was a magician."

* * * KIRKPATRICK   2-ODYSSEY   (M) 3226 0012
                                              [Vol. 2]

The distinguished Kirkpatrick plays another volume, if anything, even more flawlessly than his rendition of Volume One. In each shining gem, Kirkpatrick goes at once to the heart of the matter. These are two of the best harpsichord discs extant. Peter Davis of *High Fidelity* offers lyrical praise: "Kirkpatrick brings both thorough scholarship and a keen sense of enjoyment to his tasks—the performances are absolutely delightful."

SINFONIAS (3) FOR FLUTE, OBOE, STRINGS

These works are fairly interesting, but hardly more; in these pieces Scarlatti seems to be still under the influence of his father, and groping about to establish his own style.

| * RISTENPART | *Saar Chamber Orch.* | ODYSSEY | (M) 32 16 0015 |
| | | | (S) 32 16 0016 |

The music, played with grace, is recorded with room-sized sound.

Schoenberg, Arnold (1874-1951)

Born in Vienna, Schoenberg was practically self-taught. He composed short pieces for school friends with whom he played the violin. At 16, he decided to become a musician; he studied counterpoint with Zemlinsky in Vienna.

During World War I, Schoenberg was a soldier in the Austrian army. At this time he began experimenting with the technique of the twelve-tone system. He did not begin writing in this revolutionary mode until 1922, but from that time on, the system dominated his musical thinking. "I am a man possessed," he remarked.

From the end of World War I until the rise of the Nazis in Germany, Schoenberg divided his activities between Berlin and Vienna. In 1933, and moved to America and settled in California. Until his death, he remained a composer who aroused violent controversy.

His most distinguished pupils were Alban Berg, Anton von Webern, and Egon Wellesz. His *Harmonielehre* is one of the few important modern treatises on harmony.

PLACE AND ACHIEVEMENT   Few composers (or other people, for that matter) have been so attacked, maligned, and disputed, as was Arnold Schoenberg. People who have never heard a note of his music in their lives still passionately declare that Schoenberg was a madman.

Today he is seldom played, but we see him as a tremendous historical figure. It was Schoenberg who first faced up to the fact that tonality and key structure, the very basis of Western music, had been exhausted by the end of the nineteenth century. He set out to devise a new verbal grammar for music.

He was not at all the only one who felt that music after Wagner was on the brink of disintegration. Bartok, Stravinsky, and others were also desperately aware of the abyss, but tried to hang on with stop-gap innovations, such as neo-classicism, the use of folk music, etc.

Schoenberg alone had the will and courage to push on into the unknown, constructing a new basis "with twelve notes equal to each others." Schoenberg was a great revolutionary and a seminal force; "The New Music" that is upon us owes more to his thinking than to the influence of any other composer.

THE ESSENTIAL SCHOENBERG

ORCHESTRAL AND CHAMBER MUSIC: *Verklaerte Nacht (Transfigured Night), for String Orchestra; Theme and Variations for Orchestra; Pierrot Lunaire, Melodrama; Gurre-Lieder, for Soloists, Chorus and Orchestra; Five Pieces for Orchestra; 4 String Quartets.*

OPERA: *Moses and Aaron.*

OTHER WORKS

DRAMATIC WORKS: *Die Glueckliche Hand, Drama with Music; Von Heute auf Morgen, One-Act Opera; Erwartung, Monodrama; A Survivor from Warsaw, for Narrator, Men's Chorus, and Orchestra.*

ORCHESTRAL AND CHAMBER MUSIC: *Kammersymphonie; Concerto for String Quartet and Orchestra; Concerto for Violin and Orchestra; Concerto for Piano and Orchestra; Ode to Napoleon, for Recitation, Piano and String Orchestra.*

VOCAL MUSIC: *De Profundis, for Chorus a Cappella; Songs.*

CHORAL MUSIC

These pieces, for a cappella chorus, are not Schoenberg's most epochal works; they are of interest primarily to specialists. The specific works included are: *Friede auf Erden (Opus 13); Dreimal Tausend Jahre (Opus 50A); De Profundis (Opus 50B); Three Folk Songs (Opus 49); Three Folk Songs (1929).* A lot of this music is quite romantic, not at all forbidding. *Friede auf Erden* is a sonorous chromatic study and *De Profundis* is a version of Psalm 130 for a speaking and singing chorus.

*   *Gregg Smith Singers*   EVEREST   (S) 3182

Here is intense, assured singing by the dauntless Gregg Smith Singers, who move about with astonishing ease from Gabrielli to Schoenberg. Much of the master's unaccompanied choral music is here, all except for Opus 27, 28 and Opus 35. The sound is good.

CONCERTO FOR PIANO (Opus 42); CONCERTO FOR VIOLIN (Opus 36)

When Schoenberg's linear *Violin Concerto* came out in 1936, it was labeled "impossible, hysterical." Today, it is shrugged off by our young way-out composers as being "impossibly old-fashioned." "Schoenberg est mort!" cried Pierre Boulez, and there went whatever was left of 400 years of tradition.

The *Piano Concerto* dates from when Schoenberg was nearly seventy.

Both these concertos are incredibly complex, and loaded with severe technical problems for the players. These are works of great originality and power, and I detect some warmth of feeling, even romantic expression, in his atonal style.

* BRENDEL,   *Symphony Orch. of the*   TURNABOUT TV (S) 34051)
MARSCHNER,   *Southwest German Radio*
GIELEN

The players, especially Marschner, are most accomplished; they seem dedicated to their fearsome task. The sound is clean.

FIVE PIECES FOR ORCHESTRA (Opus 16)

Time has done strange things with this music since 1909. The casual listener, twirling his FM radio dial, might listen to it amenably, in the innocent belief that this music was certainly not composed by that lunatic Schoenberg. The *Five Pieces* belong to an early cluster of remarkable works with which Schoenberg ventured into the uncharted sea of "beyond tonality." This music is not yet dodecaphonic (twelve-tone); it is rather a stunning essay in orchestral pigmentation. Color changes via sound are achieved in a way that had never been attempted before 1909.

Schoenberg's music here makes me think of Freud's subterranean explorations into the dark recesses of the human soul—and we must always remember that Freud's *Mitteleuropa* was also Schoenberg's. This is important music.

* * WAND	*Cologne Guerzenich Symphony Orch.*	NONESUCH (S) H 91192 [Stravinsky, Dumbarton Oaks Concerto; Webern, Cantata No. 1]

The music is intelligently played, with a sense of dedication. Wand and his players are first-rate. [Stravinsky's *Dumbarton Oaks Concerto* has never seemed important to me; it is little more than a routine exercise of his fertile brain. The Webern is discussed separatly in this volume.]

FOUR QUARTETS (Complete)

In evaluating the significant chamber music of the first half of this century, Schoenberg's quartets hold a place next to Bartok's. The *First Quartet* is still in the classical mold; in the words of Arthur Cohn, this composition is "boiling and seething, an emotional unification of the classical era and the romantic school." At the same time, the piece gathers up all that Wagner and Strauss had done. The outer reaches of atonality are explored in the *Second Quartet,* a 1908 work. The *Third* is an early twelve-tone work, written in a mature disciplined style. The *Fourth* (1936) reaches the land of no return, a synthesis of tone rows and nineteenth-century designs.

This is extremely difficult music, both for the listener and for the players. The *Quartets* span thirty years of Schoenberg's uncompromising artistic life—from 1905 to 1936.

*	*Kohon Quartet*	3-Vox	SVBX (S) 590

The Kohon Quartet seems to do what is expected of them in this fiendish music. They wade fearlessly into the score, and their technical abilities are awesome. The sound is good.

ODE TO NAPOLEON BUONAPARTE, FOR STRING QUARTET, PIANO, AND RECITER (Opus 41)

The *Ode* is a curious work set to sarcastic, flaming verses—by Byron, of all people. Schoenberg's intent was to write an anti-Hitler theme. Written in 1943, this *Ode* is an odd mixture of tonality and atonality—as though backing up Schoenberg's statement—after he had embraced the twelve-tone technique—that "there is still plenty of good music to be written in C Major." This declamation is an odd business with notes, sharps, and flats, but no identifiable pitches—extremely difficult music to get into.

* NICKRENZ, JACOBSON	*Claremont Quartet*	NONESUCH (S) H 71186 [Webern, String Quartet, Opus 28; Stravinsky, Three Pieces for String Quartet and Concertino for String Quartet]

The players are less than convincing; the pretentious reciter is funny. [The Stravinsky pieces are of early vintage, and seem to be studies for larger things. The Webern is reviewed separately in this volume.]

PIERROT LUNAIRE

"Sharp daggers at white heat," is James Huneker's description of this music. This work is sick, sick, sick, yet one of the revolutionary landmarks of twentieth-century music. Technically, this is amazing music for 1912; Schoenberg here has reached a point of no return in totally organized chromaticism. The vocal soloist is required to recite the text in *Sprechstimme*—a half-sung, half-spoken articulation. The effect is gripping, and points the way to the experiments with voice and machines of our electronic composers of today.

Pierrot Lunaire is a setting of 21 poems by Albert Giraud for voice and eight instruments. A full half-century has passed since this composition shook up its first audience; listeners today are still disturbed by it. But repeated, attentive hearings reveal esoteric beauties that no other composer has evoked. The most secret of motions are flung out in words and music. This is German expressionism at its most paranoid, half-mad best.

* * PILARCZYK, BOULEZ	*Domaine Musical Ensemble*	EVEREST	(M) 6171 (S) 3171

Conductor Boulez started out as a composer who detested Schoenberg; he later was converted and became one of Schoenberg's adoring admirers. (He later reverted away.) Boulez, a knowledgeable mathematician, once said, "Music is a science as much as an art." His charted, programmed approach can be felt in this precise, distinguished reading. The work is well sung and well played. The sound is clean.

QUINTET FOR WINDS (Opus 26)

This is a rather friendly piece for Schoenberg, and unimportant music.

Danzi Quintet	WORLD SERIES PHC 9068

The Danzi Group is one of the best wind ensembles in Europe, but they seem to be picking their way across this music somewhat gingerly. The sound is resonant.

SERENADE (Opus 24)

The *Serenade* is all Viennese charm, even though the signature is Schoenberg. This is not an earth-shaking piece, but is nevertheless interesting. The off-beat ensemble—clarinet, bass clarinet, mandolin, guitar, and string trio—makes for very odd effects indeed, which Schoenberg exploits to the hilt. The fourth movement is a setting of a Petrarch sonnet for bass-baritone.

* RONDELEUX, BOULEZ	*Domaine Musicale Ensemble*	EVEREST SDBR (S) 3175

In an assured performance, Boulez approaches this score without qualms, and makes all sound reasonable. The sound is clean.

VERKLAERTE NACHT (Opus 4)

This is sick music, post-Wagner romanticism—and yet a triumph. This fervent, sensuous, *echt*-Wagnerian piece was the first usage of the symphonic poem form in chamber music. An early work by Schoenberg (1899), this program music is derived from a sentimental poem by Richard Dehmel, describing a moonlit meeting between lovers. The woman confesses that she is pregnant by another man. Time has filtered the once abhorrent *Verklaerte Nacht* into a pleasing, ultra-romantic work.

* * STOKOWSKI	*Boston Symphony Orch.*	SERAPHIM (S) 60080 [Loeffler, A Pagan Poem]
* BOULEZ	*Domaine Musicale Ensemble*	EVEREST (M) 6170 (S) 3170

*   *Ramor Quartet*   TURNABOUT (3) (S) 4032
                             [Berg, Lyric Suite]

My ear still quivers with the old Stokowski 78-rpm recording of this music, which was incomparably sensual, and which sparked Schoenberg's early fame in America. I am happy to report that this job by the Maestro is also intensely passionate; his recording is rightly termed by *High Fidelity* as "truly stupendous." The sound, from Capitol in 1959, is good. [The coupling is Loeffler's *A Pagan Poem.* Charles Martin Loeffler (1861-1935) was born in France, and was naturalized as an American citizen in Boston at the age of 26. He was a violinist, played with the Boston Symphony, and was deemed by many to be the outstanding "American composer" of this generation. This tone poem is heavily perfumed, atmospheric music of 1901-1906, in the style of D'Indy. Stokowski wrings every ounce out of it.]

The Boulez reading is forthright and clear, but compared to Stokowski, Boulez is quite pallid.

In the string quartet version, the Ramor Quartet is successful in a lush, but not overly sentimental reading. [The reverse disc records the important *Lyric Suite* by Alban Berg.]

Schubert, Franz (1797-1828)

Born in Vienna, Schubert was the twelfth child of a poor schoolmaster. At eight, he learned the violin from his father and the piano from his brother. Possessed of a beautiful voice, he won, at eleven, a fellowship at a Jesuit school where he remained for several years, singing in the Imperial choir. On leaving the school, he became a schoolmaster, partly to avoid military conscription, partly because his father wished it.

He taught in his father's school from 1814 to 1816. In 1818, he became piano teacher in the household of Count Johann Esterhazy. From 1819, he lived and composed in Vienna where he made very poor deals with his publishers. He was often penniless.

Schubert remained miserably poor throughout his life, existing most of the time on the generosity of his friends. In 1828, he arranged the first and only concert devoted to his works. He died that same year, of typhus, at the age of 31.

Schubert was extremely prolific. He composed his first song, *Hagar's Lament,* at 14; three quartets at 15; his first symphony and quartets No. 4, 5, and 6 at 16. In 1814, he completed his first opera, a Mass, two quartets, and many songs, including *Gretchen am Spinnrade.* In 1815, with an incredible rapidity which continued to the end of his life, he wrote four song cycles, two symphonies, his first piano sonata, and about 145 songs. He was all of 18 at this time.

Though involved in one or two love affairs, he never married. His devoted friends recognized his genius. He was a gentle, lovable man with no thought but music, no time for anything else. He wrote compulsively, and ceaselessly, as though an overwhelming force within him demanded him to write.

PLACE AND ACHIEVEMENT   "The most poetic of all musicians," was how Liszt summed up Schubert. The remark is still accurate. Schubert was a man possessed by melody. He was always obliged to struggle with the demanding techniques of counterpoint and orchestration. He longed to write a successful opera, but the organization of such a work was too much for him. Even his orchestral works and chamber music are instrumental song-fests, so to speak.

Schubert was barely recognized as a serious composer in his time; yet today, his very name signifies song and melody. We must be grateful for this overweening impulse within him; Schubert's gift for melody was inexhaustible, certainly the most outstanding in music. If his ventures into stricter forms were less than successful, Schubert—denied the intellect of a Beethoven or a Mozart—was certainly supreme in the realm of the song.

THE ESSENTIAL SCHUBERT

ORCHESTRAL MUSIC: *Symphony No. 5, in B-Flat; Symphony No. 8, in B Minor, "Unfinished"; Symphony No. 9, in C Major; Incidental Music to Rosamunde.*

CHAMBER MUSIC: *Quartet in A Minor; Quartet in D Minor, "Death and the Maiden"; Quintet in C Major, for Strings; Quintet in A Major, for Piano and Strings, "Die Forelle"; Trio in B-Flat Major, for Piano and Violin, and Cello; Trio in E-Flat Major, for Piano, Violin, and Cello.*

PIANO MUSIC: *Moments Musicaux; Impromptus; Sonata in C Minor, Sonata in A Major, Sonata in B-Flat Major (Posthumous).*

VOCAL MUSIC: *More than 600 songs, including Gretchen am Spinnrade, Erlkoenig, Hark, Hark, the Lark, Die Forelle, Der Tod und das Maedchen, Ave Maria, Staendchen, An die Music, and so forth.*

SONG CYCLES: *Die Schoene Muellerin, Die Winterreise, Schwanengesang; Mass No. 2 in G.*

OTHER WORKS

ORCHESTRAL MUSIC: *Symphonies No. 1, 2, 3, 4, 6, 7.*
VOCAL MUSIC: *Songs, Masses, etc.*
CHAMBER MUSIC: *Other String Quartets.*
PIANO MUSIC: *Sonatas.*

SYMPHONIES AND ORCHESTRAL PIECES "Schubert's symphonies seem near debaucheries of exquisitely musical thoughtlessness," Bernard Shaw wrote sourly; yet this is the general opinion about most of Schubert's larger works. With the exception of the very popular last two, Schubert's symphonies have generally been accounted wearisome.

Today, Schubert's symphonies are being "cleaned," much as art-restorers remove excess varnish and the retouchings of lesser hands from an old master. Dennis Vaughan, a gifted English conductor, has devoted himself to comparing the original manuscripts of Schubert's symphonies with the mangled published editions, and Vaughan has discovered thousands of errors and "improvements." Restored, they stand as much bolder and more interesting works. The performances recorded in recent years represent Schubert's symphonies in various stages of "restoration."

SYMPHONY NO. 2 IN B-FLAT (D. 125)

This is a frustrating, badly-organized piece, restored or unrestored.

* RISTENPART	*South German Philharmonic*	CHECKMATE	(S) 76005
		[Symphony No. 1]	
COURAUD	*Bamberg Symphony Orch.*	VOX	(M) 10240
			(S) 510240
		[Symphony No. 6]	

Ristenpart's performance is all right. The sound is fine.
Couraud's version is lackluster.

SYMPHONY NO. 3 IN D (D. 200)

Most of the melodious, unimportant *Third Symphony* was composed during one week in 1815, but it received no public performance until the 1880's.

* NEUMANN	*Czech Philharmonic*	CROSSROADS	22 16 0184
		[Symphony No. 8]	
G. L. JOCHUM	*North West German Philharmonic*	MONITOR	(S) 2121
		[Symphony No. 1]	

The Czechs give us a serious, but poorly-recorded job.
The Jochum disc is dry and lustrous. [The value of the reverse side contains Schubert's effort at age 16, the unplayable *First Symphony*.]

SYMPHONY NO. 4 IN C MINOR, "TRAGIC" (D. 417)

Schubert gave this work the appellation "Tragic"—which seems to refer in general to *Weltschmerz*, rather than to any personal tragedy in the composer's life. The 19-year-old already had three symphonies as well as eight operas and four masses under his belt when he wrote this work, and a marked improvement in orchestral handling can be easily noted by the attentive listener. This is good music, and not at all tragic to our ears. Often played in Europe, it has never caught on here.

* KLEMPERER	*Lamoureux Orch.*	VOX	11880
		[Mendelssohn, Symphony No. 4]	
* SACHER	*Vienna Symphony Orch.*	EVEREST	(M) 6102
			(S) 3102
		[Brahms, Hungarian Dances]	

The beautifully conceived Klemperer disc is ancient, to put it mildly, and was never well-recorded to begin with.

Sacher's performance is competent, and the sound is clean.

SYMPHONY NO. 5 IN B-FLAT (D. 485)

So much of Schubert's music has been lost, destroyed, altered, and discovered anew, that the story of the fate of the lovely *Fifth Symphony* can stand retelling here. Schubert never heard his *Fifth Symphony*. This music was shamefully neglected. (Despite the popular fancy that most composers are scandalously ignored during their lifetimes, this notion simply is not true, except in isolated cases such as Franz Schubert.) For 42 years, the score gathered dust in the archives of the Music Society in Graz, Austria. Schubert had submitted the work to them, but there is no evidence they ever played it. In 1860, a conductor of Vienna's Society of the Friends of Music, heard that there was an "undiscovered" Schubert symphony at Graz, dating back to the 1820's. The conductor does not seem to have been in a hurry to track it down, although there had been a revival of interest in Schubert's orchestral work, largely due to the efforts of Mendelssohn and Schumann. Another five years elapsed before the gentleman found time to journey to Graz. Then, realizing what a masterpiece he had discovered, the conductor went to it with a will, and the symphony was performed in Vienna in 1865.

| * * SOLTI | *Israel Philharmonic* | LONDON   STS-15008 [Mendelssohn, Symphony No. 4] |
| * TOSCANINI | *NBC Symphony Orch.* | VICTROLA VIC   (S) 1311 [Symphony No. 8] |

Solti's version is warm and human, yet firm. The sound is pleasant, but rather diffused.

There is little joy or poetry in the ominous Toscanini reading. Although everything is trim and beautifully shaped. It is classical, but it is not singing, heartfelt Schubert. The sound is thin and hard.

SYMPHONY NO. 6 IN C, "LITTLE" (D. 589)

This is an uneven work. Only a conductor of the caliber of Thomas Beecham was able to convince us that this is great music.

This is happy, puckish Schubert, and awaits a good reading on a low-priced label.

* COURAUD	*Bamberg Symphony Orch.*	Vox	(M) 10240
			(S) 510240
		[Symphony No. 2]	
* SCHERCHEN	*Vienna State Opera Orch.*	Parliament	141

Couraud is plodding, and without charm. The sound is fair.
The old Scherchen set is coarsely recorded.

SYMPHONY NO. 7 IN E (D. 729)

This symphony, orchestrated by the conductor Weingartner, was completed from a sketch that Schubert left. The piece is little more than a curiosity.

| * LISCHAUER | *Vienna State Opera Orch.* | Vanguard | (M) | 427 |

The playing is convincing, with much Viennese charm and warmth.

SYMPHONY NO. 8 IN B MINOR, "UNFINISHED" (D. 759)

The greatest "fragment" in music, this piece is beloved by millions who, generally speaking, don't go for the long-haired classical stuff. This masterwork was discovered by a determined conductor on the prowl for lost manuscripts. Upon his querying an aged, quavering musician, the oldster pointed to a batch of yellowing manuscripts and said," "Oh, I still have a lot of things by Schubert—help yourself." Thus was this great music restored to the world.

* * * MUNCH	*Boston Symphony Orch.*	Victrola VIC	(S)	1035
		[Beethoven, Symphony No. 5]		
* * PROHASKA	*Vienna State Opera Orch.*	Vanguard	(S)	203
		[Beethoven, Symphony No. 5]		
* * TOSCANINI	*NBC Symphony Orch.*	Victrola VIC	(S)	1311
		[Symphony No. 5]		
* GOBERMAN	*Vienna New Symphony Orch.*	Odyssey	(M) 3216 0009
			(S) 3216 0010
		[Magnificat; Overture]	
* STEINBERG	*Pittsburgh Symphony Orch.*	Pickwick	(S)	400
		[Mozart, Symphony No. 40]		
* LUDWIG	*London Symphony Orch.*	Everest	(M)	6046
			(S)	3046
		[Mozart, Symphony No. 40]		
* CANTELLI	*Philharmonic Orch.*	Seraphim	(M) 60002
		[Mendelssohn, Symphony No. 4]	

Munch turns in a noble performance, and it's hard to outplay the Boston Symphony. The sound is glowing.

Prohaska is artless, lets the music speak for itself, and his musicians are also affecting. Irving Kolodin was less approving: "Prohaska seems to be purveying a Vienna tradition of mysterious quiet and sudden outbursts."

Toscanini's version is beautifully shaped, even chiseled. The sound is adequate. Irving Kolodin: "Illuminating . . . . But I would not argue with anyone who deemed it somewhat tense."

Goberman is poetic, and the other Schubert couplings are fine. The sound is over-diffused.

Steinberg is meticulous, ship-shape, and the whole performance is curiously unmoving.

Ludwig is meticulous, careful, and little more.

The Cantelli version, much praised in some quarters, strikes me as over-dramatic and over-momentous.

SYMPHONY NO. 9 IN C, "THE GREAT" (D. 944)

"A more exasperatingly brainless composition was never put on paper," cried Bernard Shaw—a statement which illustrates how the sins of a music critic who writes well are condoned. The fact is that the Symphony No. 9 in C is one of Schubert's true masterpieces—a large-scaled, ambitious work, restless and impassioned, with more control and expertise than Schubert generally managed with the symphonic form.

* * FURTWAENGLER	*Berlin Philharmonic Orch.*	HELIDOR	(M) 25074
* * SKROWACZEWSKI	*Minneapolis Symphony Orch.*	PHILIPS WS	(M/S) 9044
* PERLEA	*Bamberg Symphony Orch.*	VOX	(M) 10200 (S) 510200
KONWITSCHNY	*Czech Philharmonic Orch.*	PARLIAMENT	(S) 173

The Furtwaengler rendition, lyrical and chiseled, has been famous for years. Martin Bookspan in *Stereo Review's* 1968 "Annual Updating of the Basic Repertory, lists this version as the very best available. "Furtwaengler's reading is extraordinary, informed throughout with a unique librancy and fluidity." The sound is ancient, metallic, but endurable.

Skrowaczewski's version is youthful, fresh, and quite dramatic. The sound is spacious.

Perlea's reading is fairly run-of-the-mill. The sound is cramped.

Konwitschny is downright dull.

ROSAMUNDE: INCIDENTAL MUSIC
(Opus 26, D. 797)

Schubert, stage-struck all his short life, yearned to write a smash opera. The closest he came, in repeated tries, was this charming incidental music to a feeble play which closed on the second night.

* * MONTEUX   *Vienna Philharmonic Orch.*   VICTROLA VIC   (S) 1023
                                               [Mendelssohn, Midsummer
                                               Night's Dream]

Papa Monteux is glowing here, and the orchestral work is genial and cleanly-phrased. The sound is not remarkable, but quite decent.

WANDERER FANTASY (FOR PIANO AND ORCHESTRA) (D. 760)

This is Liszt's rather opaque arrangement for solo piano and orchestra of the great *Wandered Fantasy* of Schubert.

* * BRENDEL, GIELEN   *Vienna Volksoper Orch.*   Vox STPL   514160
                                               [Beethoven, Choral Fantas-
                                               ia, Opus 80]

As has been remarked in these pages, that man Brendel can play anything, and play it well. In the Schubert he is sweeping, well-disciplined, and musicianly, all at once. The sound goes boomy in spots, but that is nothing serious. The reviewer of *Stereo Review* comments on this disc by saying: "The one convincing performance I have ever heard, on or off records, of this version of the Schubert work." [The Beethoven on back is first-rate music. It is cleanly played, but with no particular inspiration.]

CHAMBER MUSIC Some of Schubert's warmest, most moving pages are to be found in his melodious chamber music. He was far more successful in this intimate form than in orchestral music.

OCTET IN F FOR STRINGS AND WINDS (Opus 166, D. 803)

This is a masterpiece, and one of the best works for string quartet and assorted winds we possess. This is a melodious fun-piece—with no particular message for the world. One senses that Schubert and his pals are settling down for a night's good music-making, with plenty of beer and knockwurst within reach.

* * N. Y. WOODWIND QUARTET MEMBERS	*Fine Arts Quartet*	Concert Disc	(M) 1220
* * LANCELOT, HONGNE, COURSIER, LOGEROT	*Pascal Quartet*	Monitor	(S) 2110
* WLACH, OEHLBERGER, VON FRIEBERG, HERMANN	*Vienna Konzerthaus Quartet*	Westminister	(M) 9044

The Fine Arts Quartet is excellent, rather brisk, and the sound is clean.
The Pascal, also good, in a less lighthearted reading.
The Vienna group, as usual, sentimentalize too much.

QUARTET FOR FLUTE, GUITAR, VIOLA, AND CELLO (D. 96)

Schubert wrote only the cello part and Trio II of the *Minuetto;* the rest of this charming piece was composed by a celebrated guitarist Wenzel Matiegka.

* * BOURDIN, MEMBRADO, COLLOT, TOURNUS	World Series (M/S) 9025 [8 Minuets]	
* MESS, FAISS, KIRCHNER, S. BARCHET	Period (S) 730 [Quintet in A]	
* HECHTL, WALKER, GEISE, TACHEZI	Turnabout (S) 34171 [Haydn, Cassation in C]	

I like the poignancy of the World Series disc. The sound is room-sized, and good.
The Period release is old, but beautifully played.
The Turnabout offering is of lesser appeal, but is neatly done.

QUARTETS FOR STRINGS

Schubert's early, boyish string quartets are little played. Most of them were written as composition exercises, or to provide his friends with some music making. But nevertheless, even though Schubert himself regarded them as "not solemn enough" for this august form, there are soaring moments in most of them. The great quartets, from No. 12 upwards, are all masterpieces.

COMPLETE EDITIONS OF SCHUBERT QUARTETS

✶ ✶ ENDRES QUARTET

✶ VIENNA
KONZERTHAUS
QUARTET

9 Vox SVBX   (S) 5004/6

7-WESTMINSTER
(M) 9037-43

The Endres Quartet plays crisply, and they hold your interest. There is little of the Vienna group's warmheartedness—but also little of their annoying excesses. The sound is pretty good, constricted at times.

The Vienna performances have cheered a whole generation of record lovers. This is gemuetlich playing which gets lachrymose at times, but it has appeal.

NO. 12 IN C MINOR, "QUARTETSATZ" (D. 703)

This is a superb, single *Allegro* movement that Schubert clearly intended to be the first movement of a complete quartet. It is dark, profound music which is bound to staggering revelation to those who know only the sunny, lyric Schubert.

✶ ✶	*Pascal Quartet*	MONITOR (S) 2106 [Quintet in A]	
✶ ✶	*Smetana Quartet*	CROSSROADS (M) 22 16 0029 (S) 22 16 0030 [Quintet in A]	
✶	*Amadeus Quartet*	WESTMINSTER (M) 9019 [Brahms, Quartet No. 1]	

The Pascal Quartet is excellent, this is an intense, satisfying performance.

The Smetana quartet is also first-rate, with admirable ensemble playing.
The Amadeus reading is good, but less well recorded.

NO. 13 IN A MINOR (Opus 29, D. 804)

This piece should not be missed. Here is brooding, exultant Schubert, one of the most satisfying quartets in the repertory.

✶ ✶	*Janacek Quartet*	CROSSROADS (S) 22 16 0166
✶	*Vienna Konzerthaus Quartet*	WESTMINSTER (M) 9042

The Janacek Quartet gives us a fine reading. The sound is clean.

The Vienna players are overly mannered, and plagued by the over-amplified recording that makes them sound like a string orchestra.

NO. 14 IN D MINOR, "DEATH AND THE MAIDEN" (D. 810)

This is the most popular of Schubert's quartets, quite possibly because of the famous song on which the variations of the second movement are based. This is poignant, lovely Schubert.

* * *	*Smetana Quartet*	Artia	(M)	103
* *	*Koeckert Quartet*	Heliodor	(S)	25003
*	*Hungarian Quartet*	Vox	(M)	12520
			(S)	512520
*	*Fine Arts Quartet*	Concert-Disc	(M)	1212
			(S)	212

The performance by the Smetana Quartet is world-famous, and remains one of the most triumphant editions of this masterpiece. A rave from *High Fidelity:* (in 1959) "What a heavenly performance! The best 'Death and the Maiden' I have ever heard on or off records." The mono sound is warm and entirely enjoyable.

The Koeckert Quartet is impressive. They provide admirable musicianship as well as technical virtuosity.

The Hungarian Quartet is bland and smooth, rather than trenchant. This imaginative music demands more bite and conviction.

The excellent Fine Arts version is marred by unattractive, dry sound.

QUINTET IN C (Opus 163, D. 956, FOR STRINGS

This is music that will tear your heart out—a sublime masterpiece. I know of nothing else that grips the listener so profoundly. J. B. Priestly wrote that we should get down on our knees and thank the inventors of the long-playing record for the privilege of hearing this quintet in the solitude of our homes.

* *	*Endres Quartet, Kiskalt*	3-Vox [Quartets; Quintet]	VBX-6
*	*Vienna Konzerthaus Quartet, Weiss*	Westminster	(M) 18265

Neither entry here, alas! scales the sublime heights of this quintet. Endres Quartet is straight-forward, and does not do justice to the poetry of this music.

The Vienna players try hard, but they are erratic and overly sentimental.

Patience is counseled for the low-price buyer. If you must have this music—and I think you must—get the higher-priced Casals set, or that of the Budapest Quartet, both on high-priced Columbia.

PIANO QUINTET IN A   (Opus 114, "Trout," D. 667)

A blithe work, nicknamed because of the fact that the fourth movement is a set of variations on the melody of Schubert's song *The Trout*. A contrabass adds to the bucolic appeal. This music is tremendously popular, probably because it engages the listener at once with lilting melody.

* * WUEHRER	*Barchet Quartet* (*Members*)	DOVER HCR	(M)	5206
* * BADURA-SKODA	*Vienna Konzerthaus* (*Members*)	WESTMINSTER	(M)	18264
* * PERLEMUTER	*Pascal Quartet* (*Members*)	MONITOR [Quartet No. 12]	(S)	2106
* * RENTNER	*Hungarian Quartet* (*Members*)	TURNABOUT	(S)	34140
* * MATTHEWS	*Vienna Konzerthaus* (*Quartet Members*)	VANGUARD	(S)	151
PANENKA	*Czech Ensemble*	CROSSROADS [Quartet No. 12]	(M) (S)	22 16 0029 22 16 0030
GLAZER	*Fine Arts Quartet* (*Members*)	CONCERT-DISC	(M) (S)	1206 206

We are presented with several good choices here.

Wuehrer plays with authority, as always, and the strings are good. The sound is unattractive.

The Badura-Skoda version is light-hearted bracing. The old sound suffers from poor balance between piano and strings.

Perlemuter is another sound choice. This is a winning, sunny disc.

Kentner is genial and assured. The strings are on the bland side.

Matthews and the Vienna group have a cheerful buoyance that I admire.

Panenka and the Czechs are expert and efficient. The sound is first-rate. The Glazer version is pleasant, not outstanding.

SONATA FOR CELLO AND PIANO, IN A MINOR (Opus 36), "ARPEGGIONE"

Although long regarded as being a mere curiosity piece, this is ravishing music. Schubert "singing" for cello that is not to be missed.

The arpeggione was an odd-ball instrument invented in 1823; it resembled a cello but was designed with six strings and the fretted keyboard of a guitar. Today, arpeggione music is played on a cello.

* OLEFSKY, HAUTZIG	Vox	PL 12890
		STPL 512890
	[Grieg, Sonata for Cello]	

Olefsky is pleasing — this is warm lyrical, Schubert, not flashly. [The Grieg Sonata on the back is pleasant.]

But if you can lay your hands on the old Emmanuel Feurmann recording of this Schubert, don't ask questions — just grab it!

SONATAS FOR VIOLIN AND PIANO (Opus 137)

Here is gentle, lyric song from one of the world's great melodists.

* * GRUMIAUX, CASTAGNONE	PHILLIPS WORLD SERIES	(S) 9103
* * MARTZY, ANTONIETTI	2-MACE	(M) 9012/13
	[No. 1 in D; No. 2 in A minor, No. 3 in G minor, Sonata for Violin and Piano in A, Opus 162: ("Duo"); Rondo brillante, Opus 70]	

Grumiaux is intimate and sweet-sounding in this music, which suits the informal nature of this piece for amateurs. The rechanneled stereo is not bad.

Martzy is more assertive, less spontaneous, and also very satisfying.

TRIO NO. 1 IN B-FLAT (PIANO), (OPUS 99, D. 898)

"One glance at Schubert's Trio and the troubles of our human existence disappear, and all the world is fresh and bright again," wrote Robert Schumann. Today, this piece is one of the most popular in the chamber music library.

| * * * | *Suk Trio* | Crossroads (S) 22 16 0148 [Nocturne] |
| * * | *Beaux Arts Trio* | 2-Philips WS (M/S) 2-003 [Trio No. 2] |

All praise to the Suk Trio. This is an elegant, polished performance, more satisfying, more Schubertian, than any other I have ever heard. This Crossroads disc is a beauty. The filler is *Nocturne,* a stunning fragment. The sound is clean.

The Beaux Arts Trio are fine, indeed, and more volatile, but my heart was won by the Czechs on the Crossroads disc.

TRIO NO. 2 IN E-FLAT (PIANO) *(Opus 100, D. 929)*

Longer, and less endearing than the first piano trio, *Opus 100* is nevertheless beautiful music.

| * * | *Beaux Arts Trio* | 2-Philips WS (M/S) 2-003 [Trio No. 1] |
| * * FOURNIER, JANIGRO, BADURA-SKODA | | Westminster (M) 18482 |

The Beaux Arts Trio are dashing, vital, and play with sweep and strength, the sound is fine.

I hold great affection for the Westminster disc that I have lived with for years and which has never let me down. This is youthful, spirited music-making at its best. Harold Schonberg's view: "This is chamber music in the best sense—genial, unpretentious, and very musical.

PIANO MUSIC Schubert's piano music is still controversial. Some critics love its badly-organized "heavenly lengths"; others cry out in exasperation. In any case, Schubert's compositions are not expert pianistic writing, and are not comparable technically to the superb piano music of Chopin or Schumann. Schubert expressed his ideas, and let the pianist stumble after him. For that reason the greatest of Schubert's piano pieces are seldom played, for pianists prefer to show off their talents in more amenable music. Nevertheless, the great piano sonatas of Schubert have a pensive, gently probing, elusively haunting quality that is typically "Schubertian."

IMPROMPTUS *(Opus 90, D. 899 and Opus 142, D. 935)*

Here is glorious, deathless music — improvisations that go straight to the heart.

* * * KRAUS	CARDINAL	(M/S) 10031
* * * BRENDEL	VOX	(M) 12390
		(S) 512390
* * * RICHTER	MONITOR	2027
	[Opus 90/2, 142/2; Sonata Opus 42]	
* BADURA-SKODA	WESTMINISTER	18060

In this reading, Lil Kraus presents a seminar on *alte-schule* Middle-European piano playing; Schubert would have adored her. The sound is stunning. This Cardinal record lists at $3.50—just $1.00 above our budget —but this exceptional disc is worth it.

Alfred Brendel is amazing: simple and serene. Nothing is harder to achieve on a musical instrument than this "nakedness" that Schubert demands, and Brendel achieves this goal. The disc is well recorded.

Richter, of course, is tremendous—and the whirlwind *E-Flat Impromptu* has never been played better on records.

Bandura-Skoda is a first-rate pianist, and here he is very good indeed, but unimaginative.

MOMENTS MUSICAUX *(Opus 94, D. 780)*

Here is charm of the Vienna school, and very popular, very slight piano pieces.

* * BRENDEL	VOX	(M) 12140
		(S) 512140
* * BADURA-SKODA	WESTMINISTER	(M) 18161

Both Brendel and Badura-Skoda have what it takes to their fingertips. Take your pick.

SONATA IN A MINOR FOR PIANO *(Opus 42, D. 845)*

This is meditative, soul-searching music, to be heard not in the concert hall, but on your floor at two o'clock in the morning.

This intense Schubert is searchingly played by the most intense keyboard master of our time. Richter delivers a strong, authoritative reading that is hard to imagine better played. The sound is entirely acceptable.

SONATA ("GRAND DUO") IN C FOR PIANO, 4 HANDS (Opus 140, D. 812)

This is fairly interesting music, and there are those who rate the "Grand Duo" very highly indeed. Some musicians believe that this music is a four-hand reduction of Schubert's lost "Gastien" Symphony.

Brendel and Crochet are first-rate, although a bit *effete*.

Westminster provides good teamwork by two pianists who have the Schubertian style in their bones.

SONATA IN D FOR PIANO (Opus 53, D. 850)

Pianists keep away from this rough-hewn, jagged work, unless in addition to dazzling fingers they possess keen intellect.

Richter has what it takes: both intellect and technique. This is a forceful interpretation that brings out all the rugged quality of this sonata. The sound is agreeable.

SONATA IN B-FLAT FOR PIANO (Opus Posthumous, D. 960)

Schubert has left 21 piano sonatas for posterity: some finished, some unfinished. This is one of the greatest by Schubert, or by anyone else. The *Sonata in B-Flat* ranks with the terrifying *C Major String Quintet* as a composition that carries us quite beyond fine art — into sheer magic. In this piece Schubert finally solved the problem of pouring out his lyric utterances in a large-scale form. There is little in music that is as profound as this sonata.

* * HASKIL	PHILIPS WS 9076
	[Mozart, Sonata No. 10]
* BADURA-SKODA	WESTMINSTER (M) 9321
	[Sonata Opus 120]

The distinguished Clara Haskil had the depth to plumb the simple eloquence of this great sonata. This is an intellectual rather than spontaneous reading.

Badura-Skoda is good, somewhat lighter in treatment than Haskil. This old mono is very well recorded.

WANDERER FANTASIE FOR PIANO
(Opus 15, D. 760)

This is a colossal piece; lightning strikes the piano. Immensely dynamic piano writing.

* * * KUERTI	MONITOR (S) 2109
	[Piano Sonata Opus 78]
* * BRENDEL	VOX (M) 11610
	(S) 511610

Vienna-born Anton Kuerti is extraordinary. Hardly the strongest of pianists, he seems to get through these fiery pages by merit of sheer intellect and inrate musicality. *Stereo Review* raved "Kuerti's record contains some of the most sheerly beautiful piano playing I have heard in a long while." The sound is resonant.

The gifted Brendel is splendid. Poetic and convincing, the pianist pays strict adherence to the text.

The most esteemed version on records today is Richter's formidable delivery on a high-priced Angel. This reading also has the advantage of employing a new edition of the music by Badura-Skoda, which corrects about 200 errors and misprints which have crept into the score over the years.

SONGS Schubert wrote melodies as naturally as a bird sings. Nothing in music seems more effortless, more marvelous than Schubert's songs, of which he left over 600. With the miracle of the long playing record, the listener can explore this treasure for himself, properly, as these songs should be heard, in the intimacy of one's room.

DIE SCHOENE MUELLERIN

"The Miller's Beautiful Daughter" is a cycle of twenty songs, very beautiful, but without the gripping power of Schubert's "A Winter's Journey."

* WUNDERLICH, NONESUCH (S) 71211
STOLZE

This is an early attempt at lieder by the great Fritz Wunderlich (1957), and must be chalked up as a disappointment. The singing is cautious and Wunderlich seems rathrer overawed by his project.

Those who want Wunderlich's glowingly beautiful voice in this music are referred to his later, far more assured accomplishment on the expensive DGG label. However, the DGG version costs almost five times as much; if you are ready to settle for this great music adequately sung, this set is servicable. The rechanneled sound is vile.

DIE WINTERREISE (Opus 89)

The Winter's Journey was written in 1827, the year before Schubert died. A dark, despairing cycle of 24 songs set to banal poetry, these pieces are recognized as the greatest song-cycle ever penned. Fischer-Dieskau, the great lieder singer of our time, is sometimes assumed to have a monopoly on this score—this is not so.

* * PREY, ENGEL 2-Vox LDL 502
SLDL 5502

Prey has an intimate style that suggests these songs are being sung for you alone; I still haven't figured out how he conveys this feeling. Here is a young, beautiful voice. Prey's comprehension of the words is extraordinary; sometimes, he seems to be groping for the right musical phrase — but he always seems to find it. Which, of course, is Schubert's genius. The sound of this original Electrola record is excellent. The history of this disc proves that remarkable plums are to be had on low-cost records for implausable reasons. Electrola is the powerful German arm of English EMI, the great British cartel that owns and releases Capitol-Angel records in America. But Angel, doing very well, indeed, with its high-priced Fischer-Dieskau recording, is not interested in marketing a second *Winterreise* by a less glamorous name. So Vox-Turnabout picked up the American rights, and you are with a very fine recording in the low-priced field. The *Stereo Record Guide* was less enthusiastic: "Prey . . . is almost too careful and too consciously meaningful for basically simple songs."

SONG RECITALS Recitals of exclusively Schubert songs are hard to come by at low prices; the best Schubert offerings are scattered on recitals of the songs of various composers.

SONGS OF GREEK ANTIQUITY

These are out-of-the-way Schubert songs, each set to a text that portrays a scene or character from ancient Greece. This is esoteric Schubert, far, far from *Hark, Hark the Lark*. But they are lovely.

* * FISCHER-DIESKAU,   Heliodor   H 25062
    DEMUS   HS 25062

The noble voice of the great lieder singer Fischer-Dieskau is in top form.

CHORAL MUSIC Schubert's choral music, while lacking the architectural strength so necessary in this form, nevertheless holds up with its poignancy and sheerly musical appaal.

MASS NO. 6 IN E-FLAT (D. 950)

Written in the last year of Schubert's shabby life — age 31 — when advanced syphilis had made him bald, and he went around in a ludicrous wig. This music is sheer glory. Don't miss it if you like choral music.

MORALT   *Vienna Symphony Orch.*   Lyrichord   (M)   76

This performance is dignified.

Schumann, Robert (1810-1856)

Schumann was fortunate in having a father who was a writer and editor, and who encouraged his boyish interest in music and literature. In 1829, Schumann was a law student at Leipzig, and studied piano and harmony with Friedrich Wieck, his future father-in-law. At the end of the following year, he abandoned his university studies for music, and composed his *Opus 1.*

In 1832, tragedy struck. He suffered an injury to his right hand, caused by his having invented a contrivance for developing finger technique, and he was forced to give up his hope for a career as a concert pianist.

In 1833, he founded the *Neuse Zeitschrift Fuer Musik.* Schumann was a first-rate music critic.

In 1840 he married Clara Wieck, the daughter of his former teacher, despite the bitter opposition of her father. Clara became the leading interpreter of Schumann's piano music.

Marriage with Clara led to bursts of musical eloquence. During 1840, their first year as husband and wife, he composed 15 sets of songs, including the cycles *Myrten, Frauenliebe und Leben,* and *Dichterliebe,* comprising some 120 songs. In 1841, he wrote the *First Symphony,* the first movement of the *Piano Concerto* (then called *Phantasie in A Minor*), and began the *D Minor Symphony* (later *No. 4*). In 1842, he wrote the three *String Quartets,* the *Piano Quartet,* and the *Piano Quintet.*

The eldest of Schumann's five children was born in 1841, and he expressed his joy in the symphonic form. During the next year, he devoted himself to chamber music. When the Leipzig Conservatorium was founded in 1843, Schumann was appointed teacher of composition.

But the following year he suffered a severe nervous breakdown and moved to Dresden. His work began to be disturbed by periodic crises of mental exhaustion — black moods of depression accompanied by utter prostration. Brahms, whom the Schumanns loved and championed, tried to do what he could to help, but it was of no avail.

In 1850, Schumann moved to Duesseldorf to become a conductor there. His black moods deepened, and he felt himself a failure. In 1854, in a fit of despair, he threw himself into the Rhine, and was taken to a private sanatorium at Endenich, where he died two years later.

PLACE AND ACHIEVEMENT   Schumann was a great Romantic. Nineteenth-century poetry and literature fired his imagination. Like Schubert, melodies just poured out of him. His best tunes are fresh, simple, and poignant; but he was also a great writer of turbulent, tempestuous music.

Yet his large-scaled works contain serious shortcomings that prevent them from being regarded as unflawed masterpieces. His technique was not always equal to his ambitions. When stuck, he strung together unrelated fragments and hoped for the best. The symphonic and sonata forms overawed him; the shadow of Beethoven always hung over him. He spent much time pursuing "something big."

And yet, if we are never shattered by Schumann as we are with Beethoven, we are grateful for the poetic flashes and poetic moods that he conjures up. His is a voice we would not care to be without — the voice of romance.

THE ESSENTIAL SCHUMANN

PIANO MUSIC: *Etudes Symphoniques; Carnaval; Fantasiestuecke (Opus 12); Fantasie in C Major; Scenes from Childhood.*

ORCHESTRAL MUSIC: *4 Symphonies; Concerto in A Minor, for Piano and Orchestra; Concerto in A Minor, for Cello and Orchestra; Overture to Manfred.*

CHAMBER MUSIC: *Quintet in E-Flat Major, for Piano and Strings.*

VOCAL MUSIC: *Dichterliebe, Song Cycle; Frauenliebe und Leben, Song Cycle; Die Beiden Grenadiere, Die Lotosblume, Der Nussbaum, and many other songs.*

OTHER WORKS

OPERA: *Genoveva.*

CHAMBER MUSIC: *Quartet in E-Flat Major, for Piano and Strings; three Piano Trios; two Sonatas for Violin and Piano; three String Quartets.*

PIANO MUSIC: *Davidsbuendlertaenze; Toccata; Paganini Etudes; Kreisleriana; Romances; Novelletten; Arabeskes; Humoreskes; Albumblaetter; three Sonatas.*

SONG CYCLE: *Liederkreis; Album for the Young.*

CONCERTOS AND ORCHESTRAL MUSIC

Schumann's most popular works are to be found here, and they are highly romantic and stormily dramatic pieces.

CONCERTO IN A MINOR FOR CELLO AND ORCHESTRA (Opus 129)

This rather heavy and uninteresting concerto is the product of a period of Schumann's life when his gifts had sadly declined. I do not know why it still holds its place in the concert hall, except that there is a great scarcity of cello concertos that appeal to the public.

* * ROSTROPOVICH, SAMOSUD	*Moscow Philharmonic*	MONITOR [4-Horn Concerto]	2023
* CASALS	*Prades Festival Orch.*	ODYSSEY	32 16 0027
ROSTROPOVICH, RACHLIN	*U.S.S.R. Radio Orch.*	PERIOD SHO	(Sta-2) 334

Rostropovich is a magnificent cellist; he can fascinate simply by playing a C major scale. Yet too much of his playing here is heavy; and at times, a Slavic sentimentality streams down the pages. [This record is backed by Schumann's silly, impracticable *Concerto for Four Horns.*]

The Casals disc bewilders me; with all respect, the reading is odd and uncertain. The sound is thin and undefined.

Avoid the foggy Rostropovich reading on Period.

CONCERTO IN A MINOR FOR PIANO AND ORCHESTRA (Opus 54)

Clara Schumann played the piano solo at the premiere of her husband's concerto, and Felix Mendelssohn conducted. This was in 1846, and Clara continued to champion the work all through her long career. Curiously enough, it needed championing, for Robert Schumann was considered to be a "difficult" composer in his day. Our ears have no trouble hearing the beauties of this concerto which has become one of the mainstays of the piano repertory. It is also the only large-scale work by Schumann that critics agree is entirely successful.

* * * LIPATTI, KARAJAN	*Philharmonia Orch.*	ODYSSEY [Grieg, Concerto]	32 16 0141
* * NOVAES, SWAROWSKY	*Vienna Pro Musica Orch.*	VOX [Chopin, Concerto No. 2]	11380
* * HESS, SCHWARZ	*Philharmonia Orch.*	SERAPHIM	(M) 60009
* * SOLOMON, MENGES	*Philharmonia Orch.*	PICKWICK [Grieg, Concerto]	(S) 4034
* * RICHTER, GAUK	*State Radio Orch.*	MONITOR [Bach, Concerto No. 1]	(M) 2050
* KATIN, GOOSSENS	*London Symphony*	EVEREST	(S) 3036
* GULDA, ANDREAE	*Vienna Philharmonic*	LONDON [Weber, Konzertstueck]	STS-15026
BLUMENTHAL, SWAROWSKY	*Vienna Pro Musica Orch.*	VOX (5) [Grieg, Concerto]	11780

Dinu Lipatti was a wonderful Rumanian pianist who died in 1950 at the age of 33, struck down by leukemia. We can only echo the words of his godfather, George Enesco: "Adieu, cher Dinu. You were one of the chosen ones." His records are few but supreme, and this is one of his best. Despite aged sound, his warmly human touch and his poised, elegant style remain for us to admire. Martin Bookspan, in his 1968 "Annual Updating of the Basic Repertory," *Stereo Review,* ranks this record as the very best available on the market today, regardless of price, and adds: "Lipatti's Schumann will always retain a hold on my affections for its fleet-fingered authority and depth of perception."

Novaes is exciting, with a *bravura* approach.

Myra Hess, rather beyond her peak years here, is affectionate and feminine, in the good sense of the word. *High Fidelity* comments: "Her Schumann interpretations are poetic without degenerating into sentiment, comfortable without being cozy, and finely detailed without losing sight of a total design."

Solomon plays most sensitively, and with delicate fingerwork that is hard to match.

Richter is sweeping and brooding, and the sound is all right.

Katin's version is glittering but superficial.

Gulda's performance is quite pedestrian; he does not seem to enjoy this music.

Blumenthal is much outclassed.

INTRODUCTION AND ALLEGRO IN G— "KONZERTSTUECK" (Opus 92)

This is not top-drawer Schumann, but it still possesses the romantic appeal that keeps Schumann's music alive.

* BOUTRY, RISTENPART	*Saar Chamber Orch.*	NONESUCH	(M) 1044 (S) 71044
		[Concertstueck]	

Here is a good, if unexciting performance, with acceptable sound.

SYMPHONIES These four emotion-charged symphonies are all staples of our symphony orchestras.

SYMPHONY NO. 1 IN B-FLAT, "SPRING" (Opus 38)

No. 1 is the most ingenious of symphonies, and the happiest of Schumann's four. The work was highly revolutionary in 1841: the world had never before heard a composition in the classical sonata form that was nothing less (or nothing more) than sheer melody.

* * * KRIPS	*London Symphony Orch.*	LONDON STS-15019
		[Symphony No. 4]
* SWAROWSKY	*Vienna State Opera Orch.*	AUDIO FIDELITY (M) 30015
		(S) 50015
		[Piano Concerto]

Krips turns in a fine performance, a little more stern than his usual *Gemuetlichkeit,* but nevertheless glowing.

Swarowsky is bearable, but little more.

SYMPHONY NO. 2 IN C (Opus 61)

In December 1845, Schumann wrote the sketch of his *Second Symphony* within a few days. He postponed the orchestration because of ear trouble, one of the early symptoms of his later mental illness. Schumann finished the piece hurriedly, only shortly before the first performance was scheduled.

This symphony is one of Schumann's most important attempts at expanding and developing the traditional sonata form. Just how far he succeeded in this and in his other symphonies is still being argued by critics. The public, however, has accepted this symphony as a masterpiece.

| * PARAY | *Detroit Symphony Orch.* | MERCURY   (M/S) 18061 |

Paul Paray, a conductor whose work I admire, is disappointing. His usual flair is absent, and the result is a rather routine performance. One virtue of the record, however, is that Paray uses Schumann's original orchestration — most conductors feel compelled to improve on the composer's alleged deficiencies in scoring for orchestral instruments. The sound is good.

SYMPHONY NO. 3 IN E-FLAT, "RHENISH" (Opus 97)

This exhilarating symphony was composed on the Rhine and inspired by the legends and romance of that river. This is a broad, rough-hewn work that impresses from its opening bars.

* * * TOSCANINI	*N.B.C. Symphony Orch.*	VICTOR VIC (S) 1337
* * PARAY	*Detroit Symphony Orch.*	MERCURY (M) 14059
		(S) 18059
* WAND	*Cologne Symphony Orch.*	VANGUARD (S) 235
		[Symphony No. 4]

Toscanini's trenchant, partly poetic reading has a strength unmatched by other performances. The sound is fair, quite hearable.

Paray performs with zest and vitality. The sound is pleasant.

Wand's performance is competent but not outstanding.

SYMPHONY NO. 4 IN D MINOR (Opus 120)

"I see Robert bustling about," Clara Schumann noted in her diary, "and I hear D Minor sounding wildly from a distance, so I know in advance that another work will be fashioned in the depths of his soul." Madame Schumann's conjecture proved to be true, and the result was the *Symphony No. 4, Opus 120.* Schumann at this time, was at the peak of his erratic powers, floating on a wave of happiness, and the symphony is imbued with his profound love for Clara Schumann. He even made it a point to keep the *D Minor Symphony* from his wife until her birthday, when he presented it to her as a gift. Clara entered this touching remark in her diary: "Robert cannot be happier in the composition of such a work than I am when he shows it to me."

* * KRIPS	*London Symphony Orch.*	LONDON [Symphony No. 1]	STS-15019
* * WAND	*Cento Soli Orch.*	VANGUARD [Symphony No. 3]	(S) 235
* FURTWAENGLER	*Berlin Philharmonic*	HELIODOR [Haydn, Symphony No. 88]	(M) 25073
VAN REMOORTEL	*South West German Radio Symphony Orch.*	VOX [Symphony No. 3]	(M) 11270 (S) 511270

Krips leads with a splendid performance. We are never aware of "Krips' Schumann"; it is the composer who impresses. The sound is clean, but not outstanding.

Wand is forceful. [Vanguard offers a bargain coupling of two solid performances.]

Furtwaengler is ponderous, and often eloquent but his mannerisms saturate his reading. One hears Herr Furtwaengler hammering out (and distorting) "his" Schumann.

Van Remoortel brings up the rear.

CHAMBER MUSIC Poignant, throbbing, music of *sturm und drang* can sum up these works.

QUINTET IN E-FLAT FOR PIANO AND STRINGS (Opus 44)

One of the most popular pieces in the chamber music repertory, this is surging, ultra-romantic music — Schumann at his best.

| * DEMUS | *Barylli Quartet* | WESTMINSTER
[Piano Quartet] | 9045 |

This is rather a labored performance, on the pallid side. [The *Piano Quartet* is one of Schumann's lesser efforts, and far less interesting than the *Quintet*.]

THREE QUARTETS (Opus 41) (Complete)

Schumann's quartets have never been really popular chamber music. All contain striking pages, but as a whole, they do not satisfy. One is left with the impression that Schumann longed for the piano, and was not really comfortable in the quartet form.

| * | *Bulgarian Quartet* | CROSSROADS | (M) 2226
(S) 0014 |
| * | *Kohon Quartet* | 3-Vox
[Brahms, Quartets] | SVBX-542 |

The Bulgarians, whoever they may be, are highly impressive. The sound is resonant.

The Kohon Quartet is serious-sounding. [With the Brahms *Quartets* thrown in, the set is a bargain.]

TRIO NO. 1 AND 3

Here is dark, ominous Schumann.

| *Trio di Bolzano* | DOVER H CR (M) 5205 |

This is an interesting record, greatly marred by scraping tone and poor ensemble work.

PIANO MUSIC Schumann, a pianist, was terribly in love with another fine young pianist, Clara Wieck. So during the first ten years of his composing life, it hardly occurred to him to write for any other instrument. Of all Schumann's work, it is this early piano music that holds our affections today.

CARNAVAL (Opus 9)

Joyous romanticism of 1835, complete with references to a secret society of young Davids who were going to slay the Philistine, this first-rate piano music is Schumann's most popular solo piece.

| * * NOVAES | TURNABOUT   (S) 34164
[Kinderscenen; Papillons] |

Second to no one in her conception of this music, Guiomar Novaes offers delicate, womanly, romantic playing of the highest order. The sound, though a bit thin, will do.

KINDERSCENEN (Opus 15)

Scenes from Childhood, according to the composer, was meant for grown-ups, not children — a looking-back on childhood in maturity. The imperishable *Traumerei* is included here.

* * NOVAES	TURNABOUT (S) 34164 [Carnaval, Papillons]
* BADURA-SKODA	WESTMINSTER (M) 9342 [Symphonic Etudes]

Novaes leads in a stunning performance that is sheer poetry. The sound is decent. [The Novaes disc is backed with eight exquisite poetic miniatures called *Papillons*. Novaes is peerless.]

Badura-Skoda is entirely acceptable, but does not approach the poetry of Novaes.

KREISLERIANA (Opus 16); FANTASIA IN C MAJOR (Opus 17)

The Kreisleriana, Opus 16, though dedicated to Chopin, was really written for and inspired by Schumann's great love, Clara Wieck. It is a romantic fantasy in eight movements, remarkable for its extremes of contrasting emotions. The *Fantasia in C Major, Opus 17,* was written at a despairing moment in the lovers' difficult courtship when Clara's father forbade the pair to communicate. Famous for its difficulty, the *Fantasia* contains some of the most exalted love-music ever written. Schumann later wrote to Clara: "You will only be able to understand the *Fantasia* if you recall the unhappy summer of 1836 when I had to give you up."

* * PERLEMUTER	DOVER HCR (M) 5204

Here is virtuoso playing by a serious artist. This music grows upon the listener with repeated hearing. The recording quality is agreeable.

NOVELETTEN (Opus 21) (Complete)

Each section of the *Noveletten* was intended as a separate piano work and is played as such. But record companies like packages.

* * WEBSTER	DOVER HCRST 7002

Webster is extremely good, and the resonant sound is most successful. This is another outstanding disc — only $2.00 — by an enterprising little firm, hardly known to the average record buyer. Don't let the low price scare you; this disc was included in the 1966 edition of "Stereo-Year's Best Recording," issued by *High Fidelity* Magazine.

SYMPHONIC ETUDES (Opus 13)

One of Schumann's most-performed solo pieces, this music consists of a set of a dozen bold variations on a theme suggested by the Baron von Fricken, a wealthy amateur musician whose adopted daughter Ernestine captivated Schumann just before he met Clara. These are volatile miniatures, and were highly avant-garde in 1834.

* * NOVAES	Vox (M) 10170 [Fantasiestuecke, Opus 12]
* * HESS	Seraphim (M) 60009 [Piano Concerto]

Novaes is both brilliant and sweeping, with filigree-like finger work. The mono sound is fair.

Hess is also very good, but much more lady-like; assured rather than striking. The sound is decent.

SONGS Schumann poured his heart into his shorter piano pieces and into his songs. He is one of the four great masters of German lieder, on the same exalted plane with Schubert, Brahms, and Hugo Wolf. These are mostly love-songs composed for his own love story. In 1840, the year of his stormily opposed marriage to Clara Wieck, he furiously wrote no less than 132 songs, over half his efforts in this medium. In his piano accompaniments, Schumann has no superior. For a full decade before this vocal outburst, he had devoted himself exclusively to an intense study of the piano, and had developed a conception of accompaniment that was new to the world. Schumann's songs are lyrical and sensitively shaded. Here are the important song-cycles and a few admirable collections.

FRAUENLIEBE UND LEBEN (Opus 42)

Eight great songs of love, marriage, motherhood, and death. A triumph of the song-cycle form, *A Woman's Life and Love* has always been a favorite at recitals despite its mawkish poetry.

* * DELLA CASA	Turnabout 34125 [Richard Strauss, Songs]

Lisa Della Casa is lovely and intelligent, with a natural, unstrained voice. *High Fidelity* comments: "The lovely, natural quality of Lisa Della Casa's cool, flute-like soprano recommends this disc—few of the singer's other recordings show off her voice quite so ravishingly." The disc is well recorded, with 1963 sound. [The Strauss songs are discussed separately.]

DICHTERLIEBE (Opus 48)

"Oh Clara!" Robert wrote to his wife. "What bliss to write songs! Too long have I been a stranger to it." *The Poet's Love,* set to lyrics of Heine, is a product of Schumann's miraculous year of creative outburst. These are passionate songs, perhaps Schumann's finest contribution in this form.

* * HAEFLIGER	HELIODOR (S) 25048 [Beethoven, An die Ferne Geliebte]
* PREY	2-Vox LDL-(5) (S) 562 [Liederkreis, Opus 39; Poems]

Haefliger has an ardent tenor that pleases, and he does not overdramatize. This is a relatively subdued interpretation, and a fine one. *High Fidelity* comments: "The tenor's voice sounds so beautiful and the dramatic shadings so finely conceived and controlled that the mood of dreamy, sensuous languor never once threatens to degenerate into spineless romantic jelly."

Hermann Prey, generally a first-rate lieder singer, is strained and rather unsatisfying here. The disc is well-recorded. [His two-record set also includes the intense, most beautiful *Liederkreis* — a cycle of 12 songs, many of them masterpieces. Here Prey is much better. Every bar seems conscientiously thought out, and his voice is warm and properly impassioned.]

SONG COLLECTIONS

* * * HOTTER, MOORE	SERAPHIM (S) 60025

This beautifully sung record, entitled "Great German Songs," includes five wonderful pieces by Schumann. It should not be missed.

Schutz, Heinrich (1585-1672)

The German master Schutz studied in Venice under Giovanni Gabrieli, and was greatly influenced by Monteverdi. In 1615, he became Kapellmeister to the Elector of Saxony in Dresden. He held this post until his death.

Schutz was an incredibly prolific composer. He wrote steadily throughout his long life. His fame rests, for the most part, on his sacred music: the oratorios for Christmas, Passiontide, and Easter, the *Symphoniae Sacrae,* and the *Geistliche Koncerte.*

With Bach and Handel he is considered one of the three most significant composers for the Protestant Church. He has been often called, with much justification, the greatest German composer before Bach. In his striking works he achieved a wonderfully rich union between the German and Italian styles of his day; and at the same time he forged a distinctive, supremely imaginative, personal style of his own. His grave, intense, austere compositions are a must for anyone who cares about seventeenth-century music.

CHRISTMAS ORATORIO

Few large-scale oratorios can approach the intimate, stark beauty of Schutz's "The Story of the Joyful and Blessed Birth of God and Mary's Son" — to quote the original title. The master was almost eighty when he wrote it, and we must turn to great religious paintings to find such rare beauty as he achieves here.

* FLEBBE, EHMANN	*Westphalian Chorus*	VANGUARD	(S)	232
* GRISCHKAT	*Swabian Chorus*	TURNABOUT	(3)	4088

Decent choral work gives the Vanguard set the edge here. The soloists are just fair. The sound is agreeable. This set stems from the now defunct German "Cantate" label — which usually featured semi-professional singers.

The Turnabout set is well sung, especially by the tenor, and some wobbly trumpets and trombones seem to lend a not unattractive non-professional sound. The sound is wiry but adequate. *Music on Records* (1963): "This disc cannot be recommended except for strictly utilitarian purposes."

EASTER ORATORIO

This is lovely, tender music, and just the sort of thing our giant high-priced labels steer clear of; at the present writing, the indispensible Schwann catalogue lists these three low-priced versions and no others at all. Written in 1623, this work is a good example of how Schutz achieves moving music with the simplest of means.

* * WOLTERS	*North German Singkreis*	Heliodor	(S)	25055
* HINREINER	*Salzburg Mozarteum*	Music Guild	(S)	125
* GRISCHKAT	*Swabian Chorus*	Vox	(500)	970

Of three listenable recordings, I prefer Wolters. The Heliodor set, previously on the Archive label, features the respected Helmut Krebs as the Evangelist. Here is sensitive, expressive singing that brings out the subtle beauty of this lovely music.

The Music Guild performance, on the whole, is acceptable. The music is projected less vividly than on the Heliodor disc. Music Guild titles their record "The Resurrection" (closer to the German title) in case you have to hunt for it.

Grischkat gives a brisk, confident reading. The sound is adequate.

ITALIAN MADRIGALS (Opus 1)

What an *Opus 1* it is! Apparently written under the watchful eye of teacher Giovanni Gabrieli, these madrigals evidence apprentice Schuetz's coming-of-age. They are very sunny and Italian, with little of the stripped-down profundity of Schutz's old age.

* * RILLING	*Gaechinger Kantorei*	Nonesuch	(S) 71177

This music is most effectively sung and well recorded.

KLEINE GEISTLICHE KONZERTE

This is Schutz at the top of his form: stern music for one to five voices, with accompaniment.

* EHMANN	*Westphalian Ensemble* (Book 1)	2-Nonesuch	(7) 3012

Perhaps it is the solemn singing on this set that wearies my spirit; nevertheless, I feel that two records of *The Little Sacred Concertos* are a bit much. *Music on Records'* verdict, when this set was on the "Cantate" lael: "indifferently performed."

MOTETS

Schutz published forty sacred motets in 1625, not for Church use, but "for private use by Christians." They should not be missed by the lover of sacred music. I hasten to add that Schutz does not call these pieces "Motets," but rather "Cantiones Sacrae" or "Symphoniae Sacrae" or "Geistliche Chormusik." But Schwann's catalogue, which all of us lean on, lumps them together as "motets" to make life simpler; and so do I.

* * TRAEDER	*Hannover Niedersaechsischer Singkreis*	NONESUCH	(7)	1062
* * CAILLARD	*Vocal Ensemble*	WESTMINSTER	(M)	18898
			(S)	4090
		[Bach, Praetorius; Scheidt]		
* GROSSMANN	*Vienna Symphony Orchestra Strings*	LYRICHORD	(M)	91

Nonesuch offers 17 motets on this disc, and the weaving of voices in these four-part choruses is a joy.

The Caillard Ensemble, one of Europe's finest groups for vocal chamber music, is heard here in a program of various composers.

The Grossmann set is an honorable relic.

MOTETS (SYMPHONIAE SACRAE—SMALL SACRED CONCERTI)

These works are beauties. All lovers of this "prince of Protestant musicians" will respond enthusiastically to this extraordinary music. Schutz was 43 and Hofkapellmeister at the court of Dresden when he visited Venice for the second time and fell under the spell of the way-out music of worldly Monteverdi. The result was this delightful music which contains some very erotic bits derived from "The Song of Songs."

* * * RILLING	*Vocal and Instrumental Ensemble*	NONESUCH [Books 1-9]	(7)	1160
* * CUENOD, PINKHAM	*Vienna Ensemble*	WESTMINSTER	(M)	9607

Helmuth Rilling is superb. This vital young German conductor is a man to be reckoned with; and from what I've heard, we'll be hearing a good deal more from his. The Nonesuch disc is from Baerenreiter, a Swiss-German house with a formidable reputation in Europe both for authentic recordings and for knowing where to find the right men to play the music. The sound is warm and grateful.

Cuenod and his ensemble are good indeed. They seem to know and love this music.

MOTETS (SYMPHONIAE SACRAE)

These are "Vocal Concertos" from Book II of the *Symphoniae Sacrae,* published in 1647. Here is moving, grave, powerful music which appeals to the intellect as well as to the emotions.

* * * RILLING   *Vocal and Instrumental*   NONESUCH   (S) H 71196
                    Ensembles

This is an exhilarating disc. The musicians deserve every praise. *HiFi/ Stereo Review* comments: "The performances are quite stirring and the vocalists are all first-rate. . . . Performance: outstanding; recording: excellent; stereo quality: fine." However, *High Fidelity* points out: "The bass is distressingly boomy and it is hard to find an appropriate balance."

MUSIKALISCHE EXEQUIEN

This was written as funeral music for Prince Henry of Prussia who was so taken with the work that he ordered it played repeatedly while he was still alive. This is extraordinary music not to be missed by the lover of this period.

* * GILLESBERGER   *Vienna Chamber Chorus*   Vox (ST)   DL-(50) 1160

Fervent singing and good style make this a worthwhile performance of a forgotten masterpiece. The mono sound is entirely hearable.

ST. JOHN PASSION

This stark, compelling music was also written near the end of the master's life. The feeling conveyed is that of the Old Testament preacher murmuring, "Vanity of vanities, all is vanity." There are no arias, no chorales — and the impact is tremendous.

* STEMANN, BRUNO,   *Stuttgart Choral Society*   DOVER   5213
   GRISCHKAT

The music is played and sung with a rough-hewn sincerity. The sound is thin but acceptable. Philip Miller (*Guide to Vocal Records,* 1954): "The performance is not all it might be."

ST. MATTHEW PASSION

At the end of a long life, Schutz turned his back on the Italian influence of much of his earlier music, and used the framework of the Gregorian chant to achieve that stark, man-is-dust simplicity that still grips his listeners 300 years later.

* * STEMANN, GRISCHKAT	*Stuttgart Choral Society*	DOVER HCR	(M)	5242
* EQUILUZ, THEURING	*Vienna Akademie Kammerchor*	WESTMINSTER	(M)	9606

The Dover set is an ancient and honorable one; if I am not wrong, it was issued a dozen years ago on the Renaissance label. Grischkat has a gravity and at times a religious passion that is all Schutz. The Evangelist is excellent; Stemann sings this moving music with a stern simplicity that still holds me more than do the more gorgeous and sonically up-to-date versions. The sound is adequate. Philip Miller: "A painstaking and sincere presentation."

The Vienna players offer a rather over-dramatic verision, with sudden changes of tempi, as though the conductor is trying to pep things up a bit. The sound is decent.

Shostakovich, Dimitri (1906-   )

Shostakovich studied composition at St. Petersburg Conservatoire. At 13, he wrote a *Scherzo for Orchestra*. His *First Symphony* was performed in Leningrad in 1926. During the next years, his music alternated between the political as in the *Second Symphony* (1927) dedicated to the October Revolution of 1917, and the satirical as in the ballet *The Golden Age* (1930).

In 1936, he fell into official disfavor. His *Fourth Symphony* (1936) was withdrawn in rehearsal, and the *Fifth* (1937) which depicted "the re-education of the human mind . . . under the influence of new ideas" was characterized by Shostakovich as "a Soviet artist's practical reply to just criticism."

During World War II, he attempted three times to join the Red Army, but was turned down each time. So Shostakovich remained in Leningrad, and joined the fire-fighting brigade at the Conservatory, but his major activity was writing music that would express the meaning of the war for the Russians.

In 1956, on his fiftieth birthday, Shostakovich received the Order of Lenin. Today, he is universally admired as one of the pre-eminent composers of our time.

PLACE AND ACHIEVEMENT   Shostakovich is one of the most striking composers of our century. Hampered for many years by the political demands of Russia's cultural commissars, his elusive and deeply emotional music nevertheless has stature. He is a compoer given to crude humor, deliberately tawdry antics, even savagely raucous pages that puzzle us when they follow long eloquent. passages of extraordinary beauty. Desperately intense, Shostakovich's music at times sounds anguished. Here is a true voice of our time.

THE ESSENTIAL SHOSTAKOVICH

ORCHESTRAL MUSIC: *Symphony No. 1; Symphony No. 5; Symphony No. 6; Symphony No. 7; Symphony No. 9; Symphony No. 10; Symphony No. 13; Concerto for Piano, Trumpet, and String Orchestra; Concerto for Violin and Orchestra; Concerto for Cello and Orchestra.*
CHAMBER MUSIC: *Quinetet for Piano and Strings.*

OTHER WORKS

ORCHESTRAL MUSIC: *Other Symphonies.*
BALLET: *The Age of Gold.*
OPERA: *Katerina Ismailova.*

ORATORIO: *Song of the Forest.*

CHAMBER MUSIC: *10 String Quartets; Sonata for Cello Piano; Trio in E Minor.*

PIANO MUSIC: *2 Sonatas; 24 Preludes;* and *24 Preludes and Fugues for Piano.*

CONCERTO NO. 1 FOR PIANO, AND STRING ORCHESTRA (Opus 35)

Here are fun-and-games, Shostakovich style, composed in the early thirties. This concerto contains the usual wrenching mixture of comic and grim elements—and it holds up.

* LIST, WESENIGK, JOCHUM	*Berlin Opera Orch.*	WESTMINSTER	(M) 18960 (S) 14141
		[Concerto #2]	

The players are all right, but the sound is dry and boxed in.

CONCERTO FOR VIOLIN AND ORCHESTRA (Opus 77)

This 1948 composition is one of the finest violin concertos since Brahms. I have heard this concerto many times on records, and the work still grows on me. As with all of Shostakovich's music, there are exasperating moments when he plays the clown but we have come to accept this and overlook it.

* * OISTRAKH, MRAVINSKY	*Leningrad Philharmonic Orch.*	MONITOR	(M) 2014
OISTRAKH		PERIOD SHO (ST-2)	342

Oistrakh is supreme — in fact, the concerto was wrtiten for him — Mravinsky is Russia's best conductor. The sound is still good.

The sound on the Period version is unclear and in places quite foggy.

CONCERTO IN E-FLAT FOR CELLO (Opus 107)

This interesting, closely written concerto of 1959 is concentrated lyricism, notable for its folk material and complex polyphony.

* ROSTROPOVICH, KONDRASHIN	*Moscow State Orch.*	PERIOD SHO (ST-2)	337

Rostropovich is a superlative and deeply moving cellist. The sound is fair.

SYMPHONY NO. 1 IN F (Opus 10)

Written in 1924-25, when the composer was all of nineteen, this is one of the most stunning efforts ever penned by a young composer. When this piece burst upon the world in the 1920's, the impact was stunning: a new voice had been heard, the voice of a genius. This is a saucy, impudent score bursting with boyish exuberance. Shostakovich is poking fun at the Musical Establishment, and having a wonderful time doing it; and the listener enjoys the fun. Not bad for a "graduation exercise" which the student composer submitted to the Leningrad Conservatory in 1925.

* * ANCERL	*Czech Philharmonic Orch.*	ARTIA [Festive Overture]	(S)	710
* * MARTINON	*London Symphony Orch.*	VICTROLA VIC [The Age of Gold]	(S)	1184
* HORVAT	*Zagreber Philharmonic Orch.*	TURNABOUT [Symphony #9]	(S)	34223
* SILVESTRI	*Moscow State Orch.*	MONITOR [Khrennikov: Symphony #1]	(S)	2077
MITCHELL	*National Symphony Orch.*	WESTMINSTER [The Age of Gold]	(M)	18293

Ancerl gives us an energetic, even sparkling performance. The sound is excellent.

Martinon presents a zestful reading, full of high spirits. [The coupling is Shostakovich's enduring 1930 ballet, *The Age of Gold* — all about wicked capitalists, virtuous Soviet athletes, and love. Still good fun.]

Horvat is on the right track, but his players are not exactly virtuosos.

Silvestri is effective. The sound is good.

Mitchell is much outclassed.

SYMPHONY NO. 5 (Opus 47)

Many believe that this 1937 work is the best of Shostakovich's symphonies; it is certainly the most popular. No. 5, highly imaginative, is an authoritative statement made in a relatively uncomplicated score, as scores go these days.

* * * SKROWACZEWSKI	*Minneapolis Symphony Orch.*	PHILIPS WS	(S)	9081

* * STOKOWSKI	*New York Stadium*	EVEREST	(M)	6010
	Symphony Orch.		(S)	3010
* * ANCERL	*Czech Philharmonic Orch.*	PARLIAMENT	(S)	168
GOLSCHMANN	*St. Louis Symphony Orch.*	PICKWICK	(S)	4016

Skrowaczewski is extraordinary. Surely few other conductors have such a sure grip on the music of our time. This is a thoroughly-conceived, exciting reading. Said *Stereo Record Guide* in 1962: "Although this is a willful reading, it is also a consistently exciting one. The sound is astonishingly clear."

The spectacular Stokowski way with Shostakovich is famous, and is as good as ever here. The sound is clean. Merited praise in its day, but I prefer the later Skrowaczewski.

Ancerl gives a supple reading, very moving in the *Largo* which is the heart of the piece as it is in so much of Shostakovich. The sound is resonant.

To begin a list of querulous complaints, the Golschmann has cramped sound.

SYMPHONY NO. 6 (Opus 54)

I offer a minority report: this is one of the great musical masterpieces of our century. Tightly-knit, with a grave, passionate first movement, this symphony which has never caught on with popular taste, towers above most of Shostakovich's output.

* GAUK	*USSR State Radio Orch.*	ARTIA	(M)	167
* BOULT	*London Philharmonic*	EVEREST	(M)	6007
	Orch.		(S)	3007

Gauk and the Russian players are lyrical, but more bite would have been welcome.

Boult for me is less than gripping, but *Stereo Record Guide* says: "Boult secures some very good playing, and the recording is excellent."

SYMPHONY NO. 7 (Opus 60)

This famous *"Leningrad" Symphony* was written during the German invasion in World War II when the composer was a fire-fighter in Leningrad. It remains war-time music: the composer has given us a scenario describing the victory of the Children of Light over the Powers of Darkness.

| * ANCERL | *Czech Philharmonic Orch.* | 2-PARLIAMENT | (M) | 127 |

Ancerl is properly stirring, and tries valiantly to sustain interest in these often-flagging pages. The sound is decent.

SYMPHONY NO. 9 (Opus 70)

This lightweight score is very entertaining indeed: musical satire, savage trombone mockery, Shostakovich's grim-grotesque-gay slant on life are all displayed here.

* SARGENT	*London Symphony Orch.*	EVEREST	(M)	6054
			(S)	3054
		[Prokofiev: Lieutenant Kije]		
* GAUK	*USSR State Radio Orch.*	MONITOR	(M)	2015

The late Sir Malcolm Sargent was at his best in entertaining music such as this. The sound is good. [*Lieutenant Kije,* another enduring piece from Russia, makes an agreeable coupling.]

Gauk's interpretation is more intense and hard-driven, but I prefer Sargent's satirical approach.

SYMPHONY NO. 10 IN E MINOR (Opus 93)

This symphony, one of the best to come from this master's pen in the last 20 years, is a tight, forceful work, sans the dreary sections that turn us away from many of his earlier symphonies.

* * MITROPOULOS	*New York Philharmonic*	ODYSSEY	(M)	32160123

Mitropoulos was fond of this work; he gave the American premiere, and conducted the piece 20 times in one season. His feeling and his excitement are caught in this recording, and the Philharmonic goes right along with him. The sound is decent mono.

SYMPHONY NO. 13 (Opus 113)

Shostakovich's *"Babi Yar" Symphony* is a setting to music of five of Yevtu-shenko's controversial poems. The Commissars permitted performance of this work only after the author made revisions in the text to imply that non-Jews were also massacred by the Nazis at Babi Yar. In any case, this is much more than *agit prop* music; it is a powerful score.

* * GROMADSKY, KONDRASHIN	*Moscow Philharmonic Orch., Male Chorus*	EVEREST	(M)	6181
			(S)	3181

Kondrashin is all we might expect. Gromadsky is one of Russia's great bass voices. This disc was on *Saturday Review's* 1968 list of "Best Recordings of the Year." The sound is resonant.

STRING QUARTET NO. 4 (Opus 83); PIANO QUINTET IN G MINOR (Opus 57)

It is the *Piano Quintet* that is the attraction here. This steely score contains some of Shostakovich's finest pages — extraordinary variety with little of the composer's cliches that can be so wearisome.

* * BERNATHOVA   *Janacek Quartet*   ARTIA ALP   (S)   198

The Janacek Quartet really digs in here, and the pianist is up to the demanding part. The sound is clean.

PRELUDES AND FUGUES (Opus 87)

In 1950, Shostakovich visited Leipzig in commemoration of the 200th anniversary of Bach's death. This is a twentieth-century's composer's version of the *Well-Tempered Clavier* — an act of homage in the form of a true work of art. Serious and difficult, this music holds primary interest for pianists who will find much to study in these disciplining preludes and fugues.

* * GILELS   SERAPHIM   (M) 60010
[No. 1, 5, 24; Chopin: Sonata No. 2]

* SHOSTAKOVICH   SEREPHIM   (M) 60024
[No. 6/8, 20, 22, 24]

For those listeners for whom three excerpts are enough, the lyrical Gilels can be warmly recommended. The disc is well recorded. [The coupling offers a refined reading of the Chopin *Sonata*.]

The composer himself is more trenchant and less polished, but of course, extremely convincing.

SONATA IN F FOR CELLO AND PIANO (Opus 40)

This reflective music is a kind of private diary. No symphonic hi-jinks nor bombast here, but rather the intimacy of chamber music.

* SHAPIRO, ZAYDE   NONESUCH   (S) H-71050
[R. Strauss: Sonata, Opus 6]

The *Sonata* is well played, but the piano seems to be way off in another studio. [The Strauss work is early — a singing piece of mild interest.]

Sibelius, Jean (1865-1957)

The son of a regimental Finnish doctor, Sibelius was a sensitive child who revealed in books, music, and nature. In his fifth year, he started experimenting with harmonies at the piano. He composed his first piece when he was ten, a duet for violin and cello, entitled *Drops of Water*.

Until his second year at Helsingfors University, Sibelius expected to study law. When he decided to become a composer, he transferred to Helsingfors Conservatory, and later went to Berlin and to Vienna, where he studied under Robert Fuchs and Carl Goldmark.

He returned home when Finland was seething with revolt against the ruthless despotism of Czar Nicholas II. Sibelius produced many fervently patriotic works, and folklorist pieces which were his personal protest. His famous work, *Finlandia,* completed in 1899, remains one of the most explosively patriotic pieces of music ever written.

By 1897, Sibelius was world-famous, and revered to such a degree that the Finnish Senate voted him an annual grant, which allowed him to give up teaching and to devote himself to composition.

In 1908, he was struck with a malignant growth in his throat, and subsequently underwent 13 operations, and suffered terrible pain. Nevertheless, his great *First* and *Second Symphonies* were composed during this period.

He died at ninety-two, the Grand Old Man of Finland, a national idol, and a composer hailed world-wide as the greatest symphonist since Brahms.

Sibelius, a living legend in his own time, was a simple man, devoted to the Finnish countryside. He was a hard drinker, and an inveterate cigar smoker. There was also a vain side to him: the massive head that he kept shaved rather than reveal his baldness, the composer-recluse who emerged from his solitude only to visit his tailor, or to order shoes from abroad.

He seems to have entered a decline in the last 30 years of his life, and his last known work was completed before 1930.

PLACE AND ACHIEVEMENT   Sibelius is difficult to place among twentieth-century composers. He is inseparably bound to the wild and desolate countryside of Finland, and yet he is far more than a nationalistic tone-painter such as Borodin whom Sibelius often resembled in his early period. Silbelius is a profound and personal composer, attuned to nature as were few other writers. His music, with its suggestion of non-human forces, has a unique power.

He was a great romantic, working clearly within traditional forms. His music belongs more to the late nineteenth century than it does to our own period. His style is terse, sculptured, rough-hewn.

Thirty years ago, Sibelius was one of the two or three most popular classical composers for American and English audiences. However, outside of Scandanavia, he was always received indifferently in Europe. Today, his reputation has slumped sharply—no uncommon occurrence for a composer who was praised extravagantly by the previous generation.

THE ESSENTIAL SIBELIUS

ORCHESTRAL MUSIC: *Symphonies No. 1, 2, 4, 5, and 7; Concerto for Violin and Orchestra; En Saga; The Swan of Tuonela; Finlandia; Tapiola.*

OTHER WORKS

ORCHESTRAL MUSIC: *Symphonies No. 3 and 6; Pohjola's Daughter; Belshazzar's Feast; Valse Triste*

CHAMBER MUSIC: *Karelia Suite; Tone Poems; Voces Intimae*

PIANO MUSIC: [*He wrote many short pieces.*]

SONGS: [*There are a number of songs.*]

CONCERTO IN D MINOR FOR VIOLIN   (Opus 47)

This stunning piece is perhaps the best introduction to the Norse mysticism of Sibelius.

* * SPIVAKOVSKY, HANNIKAINEN	*London Symphony Orch.*	EVEREST	(M) (S)	6045 3045
SITKOVCKY, ANOSOV	*Czech Philharmonic Orch.*	PARLIAMENT	(M)	148

Spivakovsky is impressive, and the sound is pleasant.
The Czech interpretation is all right, but the sound is muddy.

FINLANDIA   (Opus 26)

Finlandia suffers from over-exposure; the world practically considers this the Finnish national anthem. The piece is so inflammatory that Czarist Russia at one time banned its performance. (The rebel Finns played it anyhow, and called it *Impromptu.*) Almost every conductor has a go at it sooner or later, but surprisingly, there are relatively few low-cost versions available.

* * TOSCANINI	*NBC Symphony Orch.*	VICTROLA VIC [Glinka, Kamarinskaya; Smetana, Moldau]	1245
* TUXEN	*Danish State Radio Symphony Orch.*	RICHMOND	(M) 19053

BOULT	*London Symphony Orch.*	VANGUARD	(M)	490
BLOOMFIELD	*Rochester Philharmonic*	EVEREST	(M)	6068
			(S)	3068

[Symponhy No. 5]

Toscanini's, a stirring reading, is the best.

Tuxen's performance, very dramatic, is the best-recorded disc of the lot.

Boult's version is meticulous and competent.

Bloomfield does not pass muster.

SYMPHONY NO. 1 IN E MINOR   (Opus 39)

This mercurial, Russian-sounding work—one of Sibelius' early pieces—evidences the hallmarks of this master: sweeping, dramatic statements; poignant melodies; and high emotion. It remains one of his most popular symphonies.

| * * COLLINS | *London Symphony Orch.* | RICHMOND | (M) | 19069 |
| * * BARBIROLLI | *Halle Orch.* | VANGUARD | (S) | 132 |

Collins is one of the best Sibelius interpreters we have, and I prefer his intense reading. The sound is satisfactory.

Sir John has been a passionate admirer of Sibelius since the thirties, and knows what to do with this music. His, too, is a fine performance. The sound is all right.

SYMPHONY NO. 2 IN D   (Opus 43)

This 1901 composition is perhaps the most popular Sibelius work. Theatrical, with climatic surges, this symphony packs strong emotional impact.

* * COLLINS	*London Symphony Orch.*	RICHMOND	(M)	19103
* PARAY	*Detroit Symphony Orch.*	MERCURY	(M)	14057
			(S)	18057
* DORATI	*Stockholm Philharmonic Orch.*	VICTROLA VIC	(S)	1318

Collins rates first, with a pulsating, heroic reading that must be near the top of anyone's list, regardless of price. The sound is spacious.

Paray and Dorati are both competent, but not as satisfying as the Richmond disc.

SYMPHONY NO. 5 IN E-FLAT   (Opus 82)

This heroic, full-bodied work is usually played on state occasions in Finland, and is often called "a Finnish prayer to God."

| * * BARBIROLLI | Halle Orch. | VANGUARD | (S) | 137 |

Barbirolli delivers what is probably the best version available at any price. This is eloquent and romantic conducting of the highest order. [*Pohjola's Daughter*, an engaging tone poem by Sibelius, fills up the Barbirolli disc.]

TAPIOLA   (Opus 112)

Tapiola, in Finnish mythology, represents the spirit of the northern forests. This is a haunting work. Many listeners find Sibelius more endearing in his short pieces, such as this one.

| * * BEECHAM | Royal Philharmonic | SERAPHIM | 60000 |
| | | [Faure, Pavane; Delius, A Summer Evening] | |

Beecham, a firm Sibelius enthusiast, is magical. [The rest of the program is also done to perfection.]

THE SWAN OF TUONELA (from "FOUR LEGENDS") (Opus 22)

Tuonela, the land of death, is surrounded by a broad river with rapid currents, on which the Swan of Tuonela floats majestically, singing. That is all you need to know—besides the fact that this is one of the composer's loveliest works.

| BOULT | London Symphony Orch. | VANGUARD | (M) | 489 |
| SMETACEK | Prague Symphony Orch. | PARLIAMENT | M) | 148 |

Boult's reading is all right, without much poetry.
Smetacek's version is poorly recorded.
Neither of the above elicits raptures from me. Have patience, until a better low-priced performance is released.

Smetana, Bedrich (1824-1884)

Born in Bohemia, Smetana studied in Prague, and became concert-master of the orchestra of the Emperor Ferdinand I of Austria. Smetana held posts in Sweden, and he then returned to Bohemia to divide his energies between composing, conducting, and teaching. His last years were bitterly tragic: he was struck with deafness, then with insanity, and died in an asylum near Prague.

Smetana, called the father of Bohemian music, rarely used folk songs in his work, though his operas and orchestral pieces are saturated with Czech atmosphere. His pleasant, melodic music has been overshadowed by the compositions of his more gifted younger compatriot, Dvorak.

THE BARTERED BRIDE

This masterpiece of comic opera is magnificent music. Entirely nationalistic in spirit, *The Bartered Bride* nevertheless possesses a universal quality that delights the cosmopolitan ear.

* * CHALABALA	*Czech Opera-Company* (Sung in Czech)	3-ARTIA	(S)	82
* RICHTER, BOEHME, STREICH	*Berlin Civic Opera Production* (Sung in German)	2-VOX		OPBX-148

The Artia set has zest, winsome appeal, and exciting singers who seem to know this music as if they learned in the cradle. The sound is just adequate, but hearable.

The German set sounds much better, but the intensely Czech flavor is diluted when *Prodana Nevesta* becomes *Die Verkaufte Braut*. The German singing, though pleasant, is rendered with a heavy hand.

MOLDAU (from MY FATHERLAND)

This romantic nationalistic music is the most popular excerpt from the great cycle *Ma Vlast*.

* * KUBELIK	*Chicago Symphony Orch.*	MERCURY	(M)	14026
			(S)	18026
* * TOSCANINI	*NBC Symphony Orch.*	VICTROLA		VIC-1245
* PERLEA	*Bamberg Symphony Orch.*	VOX	(M)	9500
HAGEN	*Austrian Symphony Orch.*	EVEREST		3104

Kubelik wins by a mile, with a sweeping, warm-hearted interpretation. The disc is nicely recorded.

The Toscanini disc is plagued by a taut approach to this mellow music, and by dead sound.

Perlea gives a serviceable, pleasant reading.

Hagen goes nowhere with the "Austrian Symphony"—whatever pickup ensemble that may be.

MY FATHERLAND (MA VLAST)

The Moldau (Vltava), the second of a set of six tone poems extolling Bohemia, is the most famous in the set. However, the entire cycle is worthy of the listener's attention. Here is rich, varied orchestral writing, which holds up well.

* * ANCERL	*Czech Philharmonic*	2-CROSSROADS (M) 22 26 0001 (S) 22 26 0002
* SARGENT	*Royal Philharmonic*	2-SERAPHIM (S) 6003 [Dvorak, Symphonic Variations]
TALICH	*Czech Philharmonic*	2-PARLIAMENT (M) 111

For Bohemian music we had best look to Czech conductors and Czech orchestras. Ancerl delivers a strong reading, and his players are excellent. The sound is remarkably clear. (If you hesitate to buy recorded-in-Czechoslovakia records, you might compare this Crossroads disc with the Seraphim recording; the sound on the Czechoslovakian disc is far more resonant and spacious.)

Sargent gives a rather unimaginative reading, and is outclassed by Ancerl's.

Talich, usually a reliable conductor, is disappointing.

QUARTET NO. 1 IN E MINOR, "FROM MY LIFE"

The First Quartet, a serene work, has a solid place in the repertory. There is a chilling moment in the finale where a screaming E in altissimo describes Smetana's nightmare of approaching deafness and the strange noises that plagued the composer.

*	*Smetana Quartet*	CROSSROADS (M) 22 16 0111 (S) 22 16 0112 [Quartet No. 2]
*	*Endres Quartet*	Vox (M) 10192 [Borodin, Quartet No. 2]

The Smetana Quartet players give a supple interpretation, marked with good musicianship, but the rendition, for all that, is not particularly moving. The sound is fine. [The coupling is the lesser known *Second Quartet*—more bittersweet music, describing the composer's struggle against unrelenting fate. The *Second Quartet* contains very advanced harmonic structure for its period.]

The Endres players give a satisfactory reading, although not remarkable. The sound is not as good as that of the Crossroads set. [The Endres performance is backed with the lush Borodin quartet.]

Soler, Padre Antonio (1729-1783)

A Spanish composer and monk, Soler wrote church music, sonatas for harpsichord, six quintets for strings and keyboard, and other works. He seems to have been greatly influenced by Domenico Scarlatti who lived in Spain between 1729 and 1754. He is an intriguing composer.

SIX CONCERTI FOR TWO KEYBOARD INSTRUMENTS (Organs and/or Harpsichords)

Padre Soler, long under the great shadow of Scarlatti, is very listenable. He is a strong musical personality. Soler spent his life in monkish severity, and it is doubtful whether he ever set foot outside his monastery at Montserrat; yet this is often wordly, sophisticated writing. The combination of organ and harpsichord seems startling, but it turns out to be a charming idea.

* PAYNE, NEWMAN   TURNABOUT   (S) 34136

Here are sensitive playing and good recording.

SONATAS FOR HARPSICHORD

These are stimulating, musically intriguing pieces, well worthwhile for the lover of eighteenth-century music.

* * VALENTI   WESTMINSTER   (M) 9322

Valenti is one of the most brilliant harpsichordists since Wanda Landowska. He obviously loves this music, and one can sense his affection in his playing. His charged approach may sometimes be too overpowering for the low-keyed music of the lonely friar of Montserrat, but I am not one to argue with such a dynamic musician as Fernando Valenti. The sound is robust.

Spontini, Gasparo (1774-1851)

Spontini studied in Naples, and was highly esteemed in his day for his sumptuous operas, which now are almost entirely forgotten. He settled in Paris in 1803, director of the Ittalian Opera in Paris.

LA VESTALE

La Vestale, Spontini's most famous and most successful opera, was composed in 1807; it is recalled by opera buffs as one of Rosa Ponselle's great vehicles. A product of the generation that came after Gluck, the opera is obviously influenced by that great master. The melodies are broad and noble, but quite lifeless today.

VITALE, GAVARINI,   EVEREST/CETRA   (S) 451/3
NICOLAI, PREVITALI

The singing is desiccated; the sound is thin. Better skip this one. Philip Miller in *Guide to Vocal Records* (1955): "This cast manages to convey an impression of the composer's music."

Stamitz, Johann Wenzl (1717-1757)

This Bohemian composer and violinist was the father of Karl Stamitz, also a composer. Johann's claim to fame is that he was invited to the court at Mannheim where he became leading violinist, and then chamber music director of this renowned ensemble. There were great goings-on at Mannheim around 1745; the music-intoxicated Elector Karl Theodor supported an orchestra of 50 men whose playing was the wonder of Europe. Pilgrims came from all over to listen and learn; one such visitor was Mozart.

ORCHESTRAL TRIOS

All music was new music at Mannheim, no sooner written by the house musicians than played. The place was a hothouse of new ideas and restless experimentation.

| * SVIHLIKOVA, MUNCLINGER | Members of the Czech Philharmonic Orch. | CROSSROADS | (M) 22 16 0005 (S) 22 16 0006 |

One catches some of the excitement on this well-played record. The recording quality is good.

SYMPHONY IN A

Stamitz wrote no less than 75 symphonies for the great Mannheim orchestra. This is one of the best of these symphonies, although to our ears, it does not possess much content. You will understand why Mozart's father wrote to his son, "I just heard symphonies by Stamitz . . . which are very much liked, as they are very noisy."

You will also hear the "New Mannheim ideas"—unexpected fortes, sudden silences, and the famous "Mannheim crescendo" that Stamitz has been generally credited with having introduced.

| * STADLMAIR | Munich Chamber Orch. | NONESUCH H   71076 [Mozart, Divertimento in D, K. 136] |

The playing is spirited and gracious. The sound by Eurodisc engineers, who are among the finest in Europe, is pleasant.

Stamitz, Karl (1745-1801)

Son of the composer Johann Stamitz, Karl became second violinist in the Mannheim Orchestra from 1762 to 1770. Later, as a famous violinist-composer, he traveled all over Europe. He put in some years in St. Petersburg to which Catherine the Great was luring Europe's top musicians in order to Westernize Russia's culture. As with Carl Philipp Emanuel Bach, Karl Philipp Stamitz in his day was much more famous than his illustrious father.

CONCERTO NO. 3 IN F-FLAT FOR CLARINET AND ORCHESTRA

Does Mozart sound like Stamitz? Or perhaps Stamitz sounds like Mozart? Stamitz was famous throughout Mozart's life, so there is every reason for the startling resemblance.

* * GLAZER, WAGNER	*Innsbruck Symphony Orch.*	TURNABOUT (M) 4093 (S) 74073 [Bassoon Concerto; Flute Concerto]
* * KLEIN, MUELLER-BRUEHL	*Cologne Soloists*	NONESUCH 71148 [Albinoni, Oboe Concerto; Telemann, Horn Concerto; Vivaldi, Flute Concerto]

Glazer plays expertly and with warm musicianship. [There are two other good Stamitz concertos here.]

Klein is also highly hearable, and this disc also has intriguing concertos by Baroque composers. Couplings may decide the choice here.

CONCERTO IN D FOR VIOLA AND ORCHESTRA (Opus 1); SINFONIA CONCERTANTE FOR VIOLIN AND VIOLA WITH ORCHESTRA

No one can miss the striking similarity of this composition to Mozart's early violin concertos. The "Mannheim sound" and expertise permeated Europe, and influenced many composers, and Mozart was bowled over by it. Karl Stamitz was himself famous as a viola player, and he knew how to write for the instrument. This is entertaining music, and little more—but that was all it pretended to be. New-fangled clarinets were employed in this work—but employed gingerly and only for harmonic doodlings—no melodies were assigned to the clarinet as yet. Later Stamitz went overboard and wrote many clarinet concertos.

* * LAUTENBACHER, WALLFISCH, FAERBER	*Wuerttemberg Chamber* *Orch., Stuttgart Soloists*	TURNABOUT	34221

Susanne Lautenbacher is widely respected on the continent as a sensitive violinist. In this record, she exhibits solid musicianship as well. The viola concerto is interesting, especially in its beautiful slow movement. The sound is clean.

DIVERTIMENTO FOR VIOLA D'AMORE, THEORBO AND BASSOON VIOLIN

These pleasantries offer no major message, just a happy musical evening for three musicians. A theorbo, a small bass lute, was used as a continuo —that is, an instrument that played the bass line of the work and kept the harmonies moving.

* HORAK, PITTER, POSTA	CROSSROADS	(M) 2216 0103 (S) 2216 0104

The music is agreeably played. The sound is fair.

QUARTETS FOR WINDS AND STRINGS (Opus 4, No. 3, in D; No. 6, in A; Opus 8, No. 1 in D; Nos. 3, in F)

If you played this music for ten knowledgeable music lovers, nine would say the piece was by Mozart—maybe that would be the verdict of all ten. Only one thing is missing in these quartets: Mozart's genius.

* RAMPAL, LANCELOT, PIERLOT, COURSIER	*Trio Cordes Francais*	NONESUCH	H (M) 1125 H (S) 71125

Here is polished playing by the best winds of France. The sound is room-sized and pleasant.

Strauss, Johann (1825-1899)

"The Viennese Waltz King" was the son of another famous composer of waltzes, Johann Strauss, Senior. The younger Strauss' first music lessons were taken secretly, since his father had forbidden a career in music for his son. In 1844, despite his father's earlier prohibitions, Strauss Junior embarked upon a musical career. He first appeared as a café bandleader. He was hugely successful—even adored—in Vienna. In 1872 he visited the United States as a conductor. *The Blue Danube* waltz and his light operetta, *Die Fledermaus,* are his enduring masterpieces.

Strauss was a composer of "popular" music, as was George Gershwin; in both cases the sheer gift of melodic writing elevated their work into the concert hall.

DIE FLEDERMAUS *(Sung in German)*

This operetta (*The Bat,* in English), Strauss' masterpiece, was first performed in Vienna in 1874. With the possible exception of Gilbert and Sullivan's *Mikado, Die Fledermaus* is certainly the greatest operetta ever written.

* * * GUEDEN, PATZAK, DERMOTA, LIPP, KRAUSS	*Vienna Philharmonic Orch.,* *Vienna State Opera Chorus*	2-RICHMOND	(M) 62006

The Clemens Krauss recording is famous for its heady, champagne lightness. If you love light opera, or just plain good singing, don't overlook this one. This famous set has been bravoed by one and all. Vocal authority Philip Miller (in *Guide to Vocal Records*): "One of the great modern recordings. A well nigh perfect cast attuned to the style of the music, and entering into the spirit of the comedy with rare good humor." The fine mono sound is entirely enjoyable.

SEKUNDEN POLKA; VIOLETTA POLKA; KLIPP-KLAPP GALOP; STUDENTEN POLKA; FREUT EUCH DES LEBENS WALTZ; DEMOLIERER POLKA

These are vivacious, carefree, short pieces.

* * PAULIK	*Vienna State Opera Orch.*	VANGUARD EVERYMAN SRV (M/S) 205 [Johann Strauss, Sr., Furioso Galop; Lehar, Merry Widow Waltz; Waltzes from "The Count of Luxembourg"; Waltzes from Eva]

This vivacious record features one of the best Strauss conductors in the business. Here is *gemuetliches,* likeable, and authentically Viennese playing. The sound is first-rate. [A note on the couplings: Franz Lehar (1870-1948) was Hungarian, and became famous as a composer of operettas. *The Merry Widow* was his *Schlager,* or hit operetta. Six romantic waltzes by Lehar can also be heard, lovingly played, on Victrola VIC (S) 1106.]

THE STRAUSS FAMILY

To sort out the various members of this family of composers:

Johann Strauss, Senior (1804-1849) was a self-taught musician. He served as assistant to Joseph Lanner when Lanner organized a dance orchestra; Strauss then launched his own orchestra in 1825. Famous almost at once, he soon became known as "The Waltz King," a title which passed to his son when Johann Junior formed his own rival orchestra. Johann Strauss, Senior, published some 250 waltzes.

Josef Strauss (1827-1880) and Edward Strauss (1835-1916), also sons of Johann Strauss, Senior, were also prolific composers. They were directors of the family orchestra which Johann Strauss, Junior, took over upon his father's death; he left it to his brother's care when he decided to devote his time to writing operettas. Edward finally disbanded the orchestra in 1902.

COLLECTIONS OF MUSIC
By VARIOUS STRAUSSES

* * * BARBIROLLI	*Halle Orch.*	EVERYMAN	(S)	237
* * * DORATI	*Minneapolis Symphony*	MERCURY WING		18000
* * * KRAUSS	*Vienna Philharmonic Orch.*	RICHMOND	B	19106
* * PAULIK	*Vienna State Opera Orch.*	EVERYMAN	(S)	202
* * DORATI	*Minneapolis Symphony*	MERCURY/WING		18065

The first record, called "Viennese Night with Barbirolli," features music of the two Johann Strausses, Junior and Senior, played to a fare-thee-well. This is one of the best Strauss records available regardless of price. The sound is highly enjoyable.

Four favorite waltzes are done to a crisp by Hungarian-born Dorati. The re-processed sound is pleasant.

The Richmond disc, "New Year Concert No. 2 (1953)," is the fourth of the now-legendary Strauss recordings by the late Clemens Krauss. (The earlier ones are Richmond 19066; 19089; and 19090.) No better performances of the music of Johann Strauss and his followers are to be heard on discs. Conductor and players both love and cherish this music; the delicate, subtle rhythms and bubbly nuances come through on this series as on few others. The Richmond disc and the others in its series were famous London FFRR records of 15 years ago; the sound is still entirely enjoyable. *High Fidelity* went all-out on this series: "An absolute must for every specialist in Viennese musical traditions. . . . [the sound] is still impressive today." Due to the public's slavish adoration of that term "stereo," these gems are being cut out of Richmond's catalogue; as this is being written, they may be had in cut-out bins in record stores for about one dollar.

The Everyman disc, entitled "The Strauss Dynasty of Vienna," includes music by Johann Junior, and Josef. This less familiar program is buoyantly played by a master of this type of music. The sound is warm and clear.

Johann Junior, Josef, and Edward Strauss are all represented in Dorati's "Strauss Family Album." All you need are *Sachertorte* and you're back in Vienna. The music is liltingly played. The sound is fair.

Strauss, Richard (1864-1949)

Born in Munich, Strauss wrote his first composition before he was 10 years old. In 1885 he became assistant conductor to the famous Hans von Buelow at Meiningen. He turned from the style of Brahms to that of Liszt and Wagner, and began the series of tone poems which brought him fame as the champion of program music.

Strauss won success without a struggle. He guest-conducted widely, and was a prolific composer. With his opera, *Elektra*, in 1909, Strauss began his collaboration with the Jewish writer Hugo von Hofmannsthal, which was to become a model relationship between composer and librettist. They wrote six operas together.

When the Nazis came to power, Strauss became a tacit follower of Hitler. He accepted the title of President of the Third Reich Music Chamber. He lent his name to the program of purging German music of Jewish or "unwholesome" influences. When Bruno Walter was removed from his post as musical director of the Leipzig Gewandhaus Orchestra, Strauss substituted for him. He conducted in Bayreuth when Toscanini refused to come.

But Strauss came into conflict with the Nazis when he insisted on collaborating with the Jewish author Stefan Zweig on the opera *Die Schweigsame Frau (The Silent Woman)*. He resigned his official position in 1935 and went into seclusion. During World War II he lived in Switzerland most of the time.

PLACE AND ACHIEVEMENT　Strauss, who died in 1949, was really a nineteenth-century composer. His best music was written before 1911. The mantle (and the controversy) of Liszt and Wagner fell upon him. He was really the last of the great writers of the romantic era; he was the end of the great tradition.

His finest music is warm and vital. His worst reveals a craving for sensationalism at any price. Even those who detest his music admit that Strauss was one of the greatest orchestrators that music has known and that his melodies are marvelous.

Strauss did not much change the course of music, and his vast fame during his lifetime seems to have vitiated his work. But his opera *Der Rosenkavalier*, his tone poems *Till Eulenspiegel* and *Don Juan*, and some haunting songs are unflawed masterpieces.

THE ESSENTIAL STRAUSS

ORCHESTRAL MUSIC: *Don Juan; Death and Transfiguration; Till Eulenspiegel's Merry Pranks; Thus Spake Zarathustra; Don Quixote; A Hero's Life.*

OPERAS: *Salome; Elektra; Der Rosenkavalier; Arabella.*
VOCAL MUSIC: *Four Last Songs; Allerseelen; Morgen; Wiegenlied; Traum Durch die Daemmerung; Staendchen.*

OTHER WORKS

OPERAS: *Ariadne auf Naxos; Capriccio; Die Frau ohne Schatten.*
ORCHESTRAL MUSIC: *Burleske, for Piano and Orchestra; Sinfonia Domestica; An Alpine Symphony; 2 Concertos for Horn and Orchestra; Concerto for Oboe and Orchestra; Bourgeois Gentilhomme Suite; Metamorphosen, for Twenty-Three Solo Strings.*

ORCHESTRAL MUSIC The tone poems are important works—products of the younger Strauss when he was busy with post-Wagnerian notions of how to convey ideas and intellectual images through music. "Telling a story" in music or presenting a philosophical music-message to the world is quite out-dated today, but the tone poems nevertheless contain some fine writing by Strauss. Many music lovers are fond of *Till Eulenspiegel* and *Don Juan,* but retreat before Strauss' somewhat abstruse operas. The novice is well-advised to begin with these tone poems, and to venture later into the vocal works.

ALSO SPRACH ZARATHUSTRA (Opus 30)

Here is Zarathustra on his mountaintop, as viewed by Friederich Nietzsche. Richard Strauss was greatly attracted to the writings and philosophy of Nietzsche. Man and Nature, Man and Superman, the idea of the artist dominating posterity by his works—all this the composer took very seriously. His tone poem *"Thus Spake Zarathustra"* suggests the lofty themes by which both Nietzsche and Richard Strauss were carried away. The work baffled its first hearers; many who had been enchanted with his early tone poems, *Don Juan* and *Till Eulenspiegel,* didn't know what to make of *Thus Spake Zarathustra.* I leave the modern listener to decide for himself whether the piece has weathered posterity's rocks and shoals since its premiere in 1896. (In case the opening "Sunrise" music here sounds familiar: it was used for the film, "2001: A Space Odyssey.")

* * REINER	*Chicago Symphony Orch.*	VICTROLA VIC	(S)	1265
* * KARAJAN	*Vienna Philharmonic*	LONDON STS	(S)	15083

This work is a Reiner specialty; he is sinewy and the orchestra is magnificent. The sound is very good, although there is too much reverberation in places. The *Stereo Record Guide's* verdict: "A tense, hard-driven, and certainly exciting reading."

The Karajan reading of the 1950's features first-rate orchestral playing, the tonal opulence of the Vienna ensemble, and a free-wheeling interpretation by Karajan that is far less tightly-knit than the Reiner version. The sound is still decidedly good. An amusing footnote to this performance: The producers of "2001: A Space Odyssey" insisted on this recording as background music. Only Karajan would do. London agreed, but insisted, for some reason, that the fact that Karajan's version was used would not be mentioned. Only after the huge success of the film did London hastily start publishing the fact that Karajan's was the "original performance."

DEATH AND TRANSFIGURATION (Opus 24)

Here is more murky philosophy in music, all about the mind of a sick man as he wanders through his childhood. This is over-ripe, post-romantic writing that is not my dish, although the piece is quite often played.

* * RODZINSKI	Philharmonic Orch.	SERAPHIM	(S)	60030
* * REINER	Vienna Philaharmonic Orch.	VICTROLA VIC	(S)	1004
* STEINBERG	Pittsburgh Symphony Orch.	PICKWICK	(S)	4028
HORENSTEIN	Bamberg Symphony Orch.	VOX	(M)	9060

Rodzinski delivers a stirring, brilliant reading that has received much praise. High Fidelity commented: "I know of no other version to match this one both for biting rhythmic clarity and healthy, heart-on-sleeve lyricism." The sound is pretty good.

Reiner comes through powerfully, as always in Strauss. The sonics are better here than on the Rodzinski disc.

Steinberg, a conductor who is always worthy of our respect, is also entirely hearable here, but hardly brilliant. The orchestral work and the sonics are both excellent.

Horenstein is overpassionate here and is quite outclassed.

DON JUAN (Opus 20)

This 1888 work is bursting with vitality. It is the piece that brought world fame to the youthful Strauss. This exultant work is still most impressive today.

* * * TOSCANINI	NBC Symphony Orch.	VICTROLA [Till Eulenspiegel]	VIC-1267
* * * REINER	Chicago Symphony	VICTOR (S) VIC-1392 [Salome Finale]	

* * JOCHUM	*Concertgebouw Orch.*	PHILIPS WS [Don Juan, Suite]	(S) 9106 Rosekavalier
* STOKOWSKI	*New York Stadium* *Symphony Orch.*	EVEREST	(M) 6023 (S) 3023
HORENSTEIN	*Bamberg Symphony Orch.*	VOX	(M) 9060

Toscanini's sweeping reading remains the classic one. *Stereo Review's* 1968 "Annual Updating of the Basic Repertory" listed this version above all others available regardless of price, and added, "It has an impetuoisity quite unmatched by any other performance." A sour report from *High Fidelity:* "Don Juan seems to have taken a vow of chastity." The sound is only adequate, but not bad after you get used to it.

Reiner is sardonic and superb. The sound is splendid.

Jochum delivers a warmhearted, exuberant reading. *Stereo Record Guide* commented: "The recording is dim and the exhilaration of the music fails to come through." The sonics are fair.

Stokowski is flamboyant here, which is all right, but the total effect is too lush for my taste. The sound is clear.

Horenstein is quite outclassed.

EINE ALPENSINFONIE (Opus 64)

Skip this weakish piece unless you're a die-hard Strauss fanatic.

* KEMPE	*Royal Philharmonic Orch.*	VICTROLA	(LM/LSC) 2923
* STRAUSS	*Bavarian State Orch.*	SERAPHIM	(M) 60006

Kempe plays with warmth. The sound is pleasant.

The Seraphim disc features the composer himself on the podium, but the Kempe version is far better recorded.

EIN HELDENLEBEN (Opus 40)

Strauss was 34 when he wrote this—the last and the largest of his tone poems. I never cared for this bombastic self-adulating music.

* * * BEECHAM	*Royal Philharmonic Orch.*	SERAPHIM	(S) 60041
* * * REINER	*Chicago Symphony Orch.*	VICTROLA VIC	(S) 1042
* DORATI	*Minneapolis Symphony* *Orch.*	PICKWICK	(S) 4041

Beecham's rousing way with this music is famous. He liked to tackle big-scaled, wide-screened musical epics, and this one certainly fits that category. *Stereo Record Guide* commented: "The reading is immensely vigorous, yet both tender and sensuous when the music calls for it." The sound is spacious and holds up very well.

Reiner's version has a sardonic quality to it, as all his Strauss does; this is a rich, satisfying job, and the "battle music" section of this piece comes across perfectly.

Dorati is crisp and meticulous, but much outclassed.

TILL EULENSPIEGEL (Opus 28)

This delightful tone poem, still incredibly brilliant, comprises a seminar on orchestration for budding composers. "Till" was a legendary rogue whose wit and bag of tricks triumphed over the establishment of his record.

* * * REINER	*Vienna Philharmonic Orch.*	VICTROLA VIC	(S) 1004 [Death and Transfiguration]
* * TOSCANINI	*NBC Symphony Orch.*	VICTROLA	VIC-1267
* DORATI	*Minneapolis Symphony Orch.*	MERCURY	(M/S) 18072 [Rosenkavalier Suite]
* * STEINBERG	*Pittsburgh Symphony Orch.*	PICKWICK	(S) 4028 [Death and Transfiguration]
* JOCHUM	*Concertgebouw Orch.*	PHILLIPS WS	(S) 9106 [Don Juan, Rosenkavalier Suite]
FURTAWAENGLER	*Berlin Philharmonic Orch.*	PERIOD	(M) 716 [Wagner, Meistersinger]
HORENSTEIN	*Bamberg Symphony Orch.*	VOX	(M) 9060 [Death and Transfiguration; Don Juan]
KONWITSCHNY	*Czech Philharmonic Orch.*	PARLIAMENT	(M) 115 [Rosenkavalier]

Fritz Reiner studied and worked under Strauss; his reading is alive and authentic. This is a cocky, crisp *Till,* and the orchestral parts run like a watch. The sound is splendid.

The Toscanini disc, long the classic reading, was rated the best to be had at any price by *Stereo Guide's* 1968 "Annual Updating of the Basic Repertory," which praised its "unbridled excitement." My own opinion is closer to *High Fidelity's* view, "Toscanini's Till Eulenspiegel goes about his pranks with teeth clenched and hardly a wink." The sound is just fair.

Dorati is also extremely vivid. The sound is a bit metallic.

Steinberg delivers a mellow rather than a prankish *Till,* which is entirely pleasant, if you like this interpretation.

Jochum is exciting and entirely enjoyable. However, the sound is filmy in many places.

The dim and faulty sound of the Furtwaengler disc precludes serious discussion.

Horenstein is pretty good, but the sound is indifferent.

Konwitschny is quite pallid here.

VOCAL MUSIC The operas and songs of Strauss have a sensuous, dramatic, and opulent quality that is quite remarkable. At his best, as in *Rosenkavalier,* lovely melodies abound, often half-hidden in the complex orchestration.

DER ROSENKAVALIER (Opus 59) (Sung in German)

This is a masterpiece, one of the greatest operas ever written. Strauss wanted to write a comic work in the vein of Mozart. Hofmannsthal, his collaborator, supplied him with a libretto that is unique in opera for its vivid portraits and profound knowledge of the human heart. It is perhaps the greatest musical book since da Ponte's *Don Giovanni* for Mozart. The music, too, is nothing less than sheer genius. It takes more than a mere singer to portray Strauss' aging, still lovely Marschallin—it takes a real woman. There are breath-taking moments in *Der Rosenkavalier.* From the first act, when the Marschallin contemplates her fading beauty in a mirror, to her last-curtain, whispered farewell to love, *"Ja Ja,"* this is musical revelation of character that any playwright might envy.

In sum, *Der Rosenkavalier,* at once sentimental and ironic, is the most sensuously beautiful of Strauss' music. It is also one of the very last operas written that claims a sure place in the international repertory.

* * * KLEINER, REINING, GUEDEN, JURINAC, WEBER	*Vienna State Opera Chorus, Vienna Philharmonic Orch.*	4-RICHMOND	(M) 64001
* BAEUMER, LEMNITZ RICHTER, BOEHME, KEMPE	*Dresden State Opera Chorus, Saxon State Orch.*	4-URANIA UR	(M) 201/4

High Fidelity magazine's critic Peter Davis, a man from whose lips superlatives are not easily wrung, calls the Kleiber set "one of the really great opera recordings of the past twenty years." I have little to add to this except that the sound is still entirely acceptable.

The Urania set is ancient; on the whole, it disappoints. But there are lovely things here, of interest to lovers of the vocal art; Kempe and his singers are veteran Strauss performers. Tiana Lemnitz is thrilling as Octavian, the young lover. (If you know her voice from Beecham's *Magic Flute* set, you know what to expect here.) The opening scene, in which mistress and young lover are almost, not quite, in bed, was a great *scandale* in 1910, and its audaciousness is suggested better here than on most performances.

NOTE: Lovers of Richard Strauss, and of singing, are directed, nay, commanded to listen to the two-record excerpts of *Rosenkavalier* with Lotte Lehmann and Richard Mayr on expensive Angel. This performance has never been equaled on records, and it offers the perfect introduction to this opera—two records instead of the complete four, far less wearisome for the uninitiated.

DER ROSENKAVALIER *(Selections)*

* * * LUDWIG, BERRY, HOLLREISER   *Berlin German Opera Orch. and Male Chorus Members*   VICTROLA VIC (S) 1269 [Scenes from Elektra and Die Frau ohne Schatten]

This superb disc offers a one-record sampler of what to expect in Strauss operas. The singing is opulent, and so is the sound. This offering was on *Saturday Review's* List of "Best Recordings of 1968."

DIE FRAU OHNE SCHATTEN
(Complete song in German)

"The Woman Without a Shadow" is not an easily digested work, but it is rated as perhaps the most profound of all of Strauss' operas. The composer himself thought so, and so did his famous librettist, Hofmannsthal. The theme here is the essential relationship between man and woman—a favorite subject of Richard Strauss.

* * * RYSANEK, GOLTZ, HOFF, SCHOEFFLER, BOEHM   *Vienna Philharmonic Orch.*   LONDON SRS RICHMOND SERIES   63509 [4 Records]

This is a very good, not sonically gorgeous, version that can be highly recommended. Rysanek is radiant-voiced, and very human. Boehm is very precise, organized, and lyrical.

This reading is far more satisfying than the one other entry in the catalogue—a taping of a live performance in Munich on the expensive DGG label. The 1956 sound has been improved, and is clean and resonant.

SALOME (OPUS 54) (Complete) (Sung in German)

Here is Oscar Wilde's play, with remarkably little rewriting. All of Strauss'
dramatic and carnal qualities are heard—a triumph of decadent poetry in
music.

* * GOLTZ, PATZAK, DERMOTA, KRAUSS	*Vienna Philharmonic Orch.*	2-RICHMOND	(M) 62007

The opera is expertly sung by people who understand this music.
Clemens Krauss was a master of Strauss' works, and once a collaborator
with Strauss himself. The sultry, intense voice of Goltz conveys all the
passionate evil of Salome. Patzak is fine as Herod; he is a first-rate singer-
actor. The mono sound is clear.

SALOME (Final Scene)

* * BORKH, REINER	*Chicago Symphony*	VICTOR [Don Juan]	(S) VIC 1392
* WELITSCH, REINER	*Metropolitan Opera Orch.*	ODYSSEY [Operatic Program]	(M) 32160077

Borkh is just fairly effective, but the shining stars here are Reiner and
his opulent orchestra.

The fiery Ljuba Welitsch and the unforgettable Fritz Reiner are heard
in the horrific final scene. Their collaboration in this opera set New York
on its ear in the Forties, and made people suddenly aware that a genius
called Reiner had been around for years. Ljuba is stirring, but shrill at
times. The sound is dry and frustrating.

SONGS: MORGEN; EINERLEI; WALDSELIGKEIT; HAT GESAGT; SEITDEM DEIN AUG; SCHLECHTES WETTER; BEFRETT

Richard Strauss is almost the only major composer who wrote masterpieces both in opera and in song. Yet, after writing some 150 songs in the
years before 1919, Strauss turned away from the *lied;* it was almost thirty
years later, just before his death, that he returned to the form.

* * * DELLA CASA, PESCHKO	TURNABOUT TV 34125 [Schumann: Frauenliebe und Leben, Opus 42]

Lisa Della Casa does lovely things in a choice selection of Strauss lieder.
She has admirable composure, freshness, and deep affection for this
music. The sound is clean. [The *Frauenliebe* is also distinguished.]

Stockhausen, Karlheinz (1928   )

This famous German composer, another pupil of Messiaen, wrote the first published score of electronic music (Electronic Studies, 1593-54). The acknowledged leader in this new branch of music, Stockhausen is the first composer to include among his academic credits, evidence of specialized knowledge in acoustical science and electronic instrumental techniques.

One cannot help but be fascinated by the range of his imagination. Here is radical music. We are in a new world of sound; and new corridors of musical experience are flung open. Stockhausen has certainly enlarged the musical vocabulary.

He lives in Cologne where he is the director of the Electronic-Music Studio, the first such studio to be established anywhere.

MOMENTE

This stunning work composed in 1963 and revised in 1965, is easily the most impressive piece of electronic music this listener has heard. It is written for soprano, four choral groups, and 13 instrumentalists.

I cannot begin to describe what is going on, but some explanation of Stockhausen's new vocabulary may be instructive.

parameters mathematically decided, serial considerations applied to the heights and depths of color and sound.

time fields visual depiction of sounds, rather than conventional notes.

sound objects electronic treatment of sounds not possible with conventional instruments.

* * * ARROYO, ALOYS   *Cologne Radio Symphony*   NONESUCH   (S) 71157
    & ALFONS   *and Chorus*
    KONTARSKY,
    STOCKHAUSEN

This wondrous record is quite an experience, although I am not at all sure what that experience is. The piece is highly recommended to the intrepid musical explorer. The sound is also out of this world.

PROZESSION FOR TAMTAM, VIOLA, ELECTRONIUM, PIANO MICROPHONE, AND POTENTIOMETERS

This music is extremely difficult to grasp, let alone to explain lucidly on paper. The score largely consists of indications for the performers of snatches and sections from Stockhausen's earlier works, *to be played from memory. Get it?* "Last Year in Marienbad" with an electronium, on tape, so to speak.

* * * ALINGS, GEHLHAAR, *Studio Ensemble*   CANDIDE CE   31001
FRITSCH, BOJE,
KONTARSKY,
STOCKHAUSEN

The playing is extremely accomplished. The pianist, the formidable Aloys Kontarsky, has recorded all of Stockhausen's piano music for Columbia. Which helps, as this score requires the pianist to know Stockhausen's piano music inside out. The composer himself conducts—if that is the word—and handles the potentiometers. Candide is Vox's new "intermediate price label." The sound is splendid.

NO. 5 ZEITMASSE

Composed in 1956, *Zeitmasse* is "musical atomization" for five woodwinds. Rhythms almost cease to have defined contours. *Zeitmasse* means "Tempi" and the disordered, deliberately disfigured tempi here introduce a new concept of relative, rather than absolute, rhythm. The composer gives one indication that may be a clue to the reader as to what to expect: "The tempi as slow as possible, are determined by the breath capacity of the woodwind player."

* * CRAFT   *Instrumental Group*   ODYSSEY   (S) 3216 0154
[Boulez: Le Marteau sans Maitre]

The playing is highly expert and sympathetic and this disc has been widely praised. [The coupling is an outstanding work of the New Music.] The sound is good.

Stravinsky, Igor Fedorovitch (1882-   )

Stravinsky intended to follow a career in law, but was guided to composing as a profession by Rimsky-Korsakov, who was both pleased and resentful of his protege's strikingly original work. A meeting with Diaghilev proved to be momentous; the great ballet impresario commissioned Stravinsky to arrange two pieces by Chopin for the ballet *Les Sylphides*. This led to a stunning series of ballets that have not been equaled in this century — *The Firebird* (1910), *Petrouchka, The Rite of Spring, The Song of the Nightingale,* and other works.

The Rite of Spring was an epoch-making work. Its first Paris performance, perhaps the most famous premiere of the century, literally resulted in a riot. Half of the audience stood up and cheered, while the other half screamed and booed.

During the war of 1914-18, Stravinsky's style entered a new phase marked by economy of medium. His works at this time included *The Soldier's Tale* for narrator and seven instruments, *Ragtime* for 11 instruments, and other works.

In 1925, when Stravinsky first visited the United States, he conducted the New York Philharmonic. On his return to Paris, he became a French citizen. When France fell in 1941, he applied for American citizenship and settled in California.

Stravinsky is undoubtedly the most famous composer of our time.

PLACE AND ACHIEVEMENT   Stravinsky is the Picasso of modern music. Both have been protean forces, enormously famous and influential, and both are the personification of modernity in art. They are both many-faceted creators, artists who have turned with consummate ease to a bewildering array of styles.

Stravinsky embraces a new world of sound. Whatever he comes up with is original, surprising, and challenging. He makes stern demands upon his listener. His music is often caustic, forbidding, and aloof. He has traversed so many brilliant periods that we cannot keep up with him. People today listen admiringly to *Petrouchka* and *Le Sacre Du Printemps* — works which were written a half century ago. I sincerely trust that the disconcerting music this genius has written in the 1960's will be acceptable to audiences within another half century.

THE ESSENTIAL STRAVINSKY

ORCHESTRAL MUSIC: *Ballet Music and Suites from the Firebird; Petrouchka; The Rite of Spring; Card Party; Symphony in Three Movements; Symphony of Psalms; Capriccio, for Piano and Orchestra. L'Histoire du Soldat.*

658   STRAVINSKY

CHORAL MUSIC: *Oedipus Rex, Opera-Oratorio; Symphony of Psalms; Les Noces.*

OTHER WORKS

OPERAS: *Mavra; The Rake's Progress.*
BALLETS: *Pulcinella; Apollon Musagete; The Fairy's Kiss; Perséphone; Orpheus; Agon.*
CHURCH MUSIC: *Mass.*
ORCHESTRAL MUSIC: *Symphonies of Wind Instruments; Symphony in C Major; Concerto for Piano and Orchestra; Dunbarton Oaks, Concerto; Concerto for Violin and Wind Instruments.*
PIANO MUSIC: *2 Concertos for Unaccompanied Piano; Sonata for Piano.*

APOLLO; RENARD

This is not the best of Stravinsky's music.

ANSERMET	Orchestra de la Suisse Romande, Soloists	STEREO TREASURY STS 15028

The veteran Ansermet does the ballet *Apollo* with meticulous flair; the barnyard humor of *Renard* may amuse you. The soloists are droll. The sound is spacious.

JEU DE CARTES

The 1931 violin concerto is a forbidding work but an important one. Here is Stravinsky's logical, exacting musical intellect on glittering display, in a neo-classical exercise. The *Duo Concertant* is more mid-career Stravinsky, and of less interest. The 1936 ballet *Jeu de Cartes,* or *Card-Game,* is a delightful piece. In the ballet, life is a card game, and a perfidious Joker upsets every hand — until he is laid low by a Royal Flush in Hearts.

* GITLIS, ZELKA, BYRNES, HOLLREISER	Concerts Colonne Orch., Bamberg Symphony	DOVER	(M) 5208

Gitlis is a dazzling violinist, and sounds exactly right in these cold, cerebral pages. The Bambergers play the *Card-Game* with unexpected panache and humor. The sound is decent.

FIREBIRD SUITE

The piece that brought Stravinsky's name before the world, *Firebird* was ordered by the fabulous ballet impresario, Serge Diaghilev, that Lorenzo the Magnificent of the early twentieth century. It would seem he commissioned about every second masterpiece we have that was written between 1910 and 1925. When the composer Liadov failed to make progress on the ballet Diaghilev had commissioned from him, the impresario withdrew the assignment and gave it in 1909 to the 27-year-old Igor Stravinsky. The young composer had just made a name for himself with his piece called *Fireworks*. Working strenuously on the score, Stravinsky delivered the music in 1910.

* * * GIULINI	*Philharmonic Orch.*	SERAPHIM	(S) 60022
* * * MONTEUX	*Paris Conservatoire Orch.*	VICTROLA VIC [Debussy, Nocturnes]	(S) 1027
* DORATI	*Minneapolis Symphony Orch.*	MERCURY [Borodin, Symphony No. 2]	(M) 14010 (S) 18010

It is not often in this book that we encounter two three-star discs for one piece of music, but these two records are really plums.

Carl Maria Giulini is highly respected for his warm-hearted opera conducting; it comes as a bit of a surprise to find him here in Stravinsky and French repertory. His is a first-rate disc, with radiant pellucid readings. Both the Philharmonia and the 1957 sound are lustrous.

Monteux really deserves to be given a place of honor here, if for no other reason than the fact that he introduced Stravinsky and fought for his works in the good old days. Monteux conducted the first performances of both *Rite of Spring* and *Petrouchka*. The sound is rather dry but well defined.

Dorati's version is over-driven and taut. The sound is not well defined.

LES NOCES; PRIBAUTKI; BERCEUSES DU CHAT; FOUR RUSSIAN SONGS; FOUR RUSSIAN PEASANT SONGS

Here is musical primitivism, from 1914-1919, when African art was shaking up Stravinsky as well as Picasso. *Les Noces* is a landmark of modern music; Carl Orff's *Carmina Burana* and a dozen other noted pieces owe homage to this key work for chorus, vocal soloists, four pianos, and percussion battery. In this music Stravinsky uses Russian folk-poetry to describe a peasant wedding. He invented his own form of theater, a ritual form in which singing, speech, mime, etc. are interconnected through music. There are no characters in this work, only types; the soloists and the chorus take whatever role happens to fit at the monent.

It works.

* * BOULEZ	*Various Ensembles*	NONESUCH H	(M)	1133
		H	(S)	71133

Boulez does not give us romantic or sensual Stravinsky, as Monteux or Anserment often do. his is mod, cold, linear, computerized Stravinsky. The sound is appropriately crisp.

PETROUCHKA *(Complete Ballet)*

Here is music that well appeal even to those who generally can't stand Stravinsky. This delightful ballet has held up firmly since its 1911 premiere.

As Stravinsky tells it in his autobiography, he originally conceived *Petrouchka* as a *konzertstueck* (concert piece) for piano and orchestra, but one with a literary program. "I had in mind a distinct picture of a puppet," he wrote, "suddenly endowed with life, exasperating the patience of the orchestra with a diabolic cascade of arpeggios." Eventually this idea became the ballet we know as *Petrouchka*. The work contains four scenes, and has been performed most notably with choreography by Michel Fokine.

* * ROSBAUD	*Concertgebouw Orch.*	PHILLIPS WS	(M/S)	9051
* * ANSERMET	*Orchestra Suisse Romande*	RICHMOND	(M)	19015
* * DORATI	*Minneapolis Symphony Orch.*	MERCURY	(M) (S)	14038 18038
* GOOSSENS	*London Symphony Orch.*	EVEREST	(M) (S)	6033 3033
RIGNOLD	*London Philharmonic Orch.*	SOMERSET ST. FI.		11800

Rosbaud is the best of all — a clear, exciting reading, especially in the tableau scene. The stereo sound is excellent.

The Ansermet disc was world-famous when it came out in 1950, and has been used by countless hi-fi buffs as a demonstration record to show off the wonders of the New Age. Ansermet's articulated, glittery show is still immensely satisfying. The mono sound is frustrating.

Dorati's reading is very good, even gripping.

Goossens is an old hand with this score — he even recorded it way back on 78's. He gives an affectionate performance.

Rignold plays it sentimentally, like a nineteenth-century ballet score.

LE SACRE DU PRINTEMPS (THE RITE OF SPRING)

Here is the astounding, beautiful, seminal work that set off fist-fights when it was first produced as a ballet at the Paris Champs-Elysees Theatre in 1913. Well, we've heard a few "modern" works since that day and *The Rite of Spring* now sounds downright respectable, and very much a part of the musical establishment. But before it was assimilated into our musical language, it must have been a staggering piece for listeners.

* * * BOULEZ	*Orchestra National*	NONESUCH [Etudes]	(S) 71093
* ANSERMET	*Orchestra Suisse Romande*	RICHMOND	(M) 19008
* GOOSSENS	*London Symphony Orch.*	EVEREST	(M) 6017 (S) 3407

Boulez is great; this is an original musician's re-thinking of Stravinsky's masterpiece. His is a vital performance. The stereo sound is clear.

Ansermet's version (in mono only) was highly respected when it first appeared; it is still the last word for the primitive approach to Stravinsky that most of us grew up on. The sound is still listenable.

Goossens is quite competent.

Subotnick, Morton (1933-   )

A Californian, Subotnick is connected with the Intermedia Program at the School of Arts at New York University.

SILVER APPLES OF THE MOON

SUBOTNICK   *Electronic Music Synthesizer* NONESUCH   (S) II 71174S

Nonesuch hails this record as a "signal event in the related history of music and the phonogrph: for the first time an original, full-scale composition has been created expressly for the record medium."

Which, of course, is what Leopold Stokowski, a genius whose role in the development of New Music has yet to be adequately recognized, has been urging composers to do asfar back as 1931. When the rest of the musical world was still using wind-up phonographs, Stoky was studying electro-magnetic waves and their application to recordings, at the Herz Institute in Berlin.

The *Silver Apples* has been a surprisingly popular success. I do not like it. I find it slick and almost commercial, and I would rather hear the Beatles or Ars Nova who are more alive and exciting and throw everything at you: electronics, jazz, raga, and renaissance music, rolled up in one bag. However, the sound is superb.

THE WILD BULL

* * SUBOTNICK   *Electronic Synthesizer*   NONESUCH   (S) H 71208

Like Subotnick's previous work, *Silver Apples of the Moon.* This piece was also written on commission for Nonesuch Records. It was composed on a modular electronic synthesizer built for Mr. Subotnick at the San Francisco Tape Music Center.

The *Wild Bull* is a short piece—18 minutes—and seems to me far more interesting than the *Silver Apples.* There are intriguing rhythms and a number of sound colors, and it really sounds like new, new music. For a sure sign of how electronic music is avoiding the large concert hall, it should be observed that this music was first heard at The Electric Circus, a far-out dance hall in New York. The *New York Times* commented: "With perhaps the best combination of electronic technique and musical ability since Varese, Mr. Subotnick exploits both pitched and un-pitched sounds, micro-tones, jazzy syncopations, obstinato devices and even fugue-like textures."

Suk, Josef *(1874-1935)*

Sulk, Dvorak's son-in-law, and a violinist, violist, and teacher of composition played in the Bohemian String Quartet. In 1930 he became Director of the Prague Conservatoire.

QUARTET FOR STRINGS, IN B-FLAT (Opus 11)
This is dullish, academic music.

    *   *Smetana Quartet*   CROSSROADS (M) 22 16 0047
    (S) 22 16 0048
[Novak, Quartet for Strings in G]

The playing is competent, but of no special interest. [Novak was a Czech composer of little or no originality.]

SERENADE IN E-FLAT FOR STRINGS (Opus 6)
This music, too, seems like watered-down Smetana and Dvorak.

    * WINOGRAD   *String Orch.*   HELIODOR   (S) 25026
[Brahms, Liebeslieder]

The playing is respectable, but not particularly striking.

Sweelinck, Jan *(1562-1621)*

Because many of his pupils held important organ posts throughout Europe, Sweelinck was affectionately known as the "maker of organists." For more than 40 years, he himself was the organist at the Aude Kerk (Old Church) in Amsterdam. Born a century before Bach, his pieces foreshadow Bach's great organ music.

FOUR ORGAN PIECES

This is not great music, but it is good music, and it will appeal to lovers of the organ. Sweelinck holds interest for those who wish to hear a famous composer of the period when the Netherlands was in the forefront of Europe's musical life.

* * CHAPELET   ODYSSEY   (S) 3216 0068
                                                        [Scheidt, Pasquini, etc.]

The delightful Compenius organ, designed in 1612 for court entertainment for the Danish royal family, is something to hear. Chapelet plays with ebullience and vitality. This disc includes the works of several fairly obscure composers, all of which are played on the Compenius. As one listens, the centuries seem to fall away. The sonics are beautiful. This record is of particular interest to lovers of organ music.

Szmanowski, Karol (1881-1937)

This Polish composer, who came from a very musical family, achieved a great reputation in his country. His music has been championed enthusiastically by Artur Rubenstein, the great Polish pianist. Szymanowski's music has really never caught on in the repertory, although he was internationally famous at the time of his death. His music, late romantic and sensuous, has some of the over-ripe ecstatic qualities of Scriabin.

VIOLIN CONCERTO NO. 1

This intense, meditative concerto is really a lovely work. If your taste runs to romantic violin concertos, and you're a bit sated with the old standbys, you might try this soaring work.

* * WILKOMIRSKA, ROWICKI	*Warsaw Philharmonic*	HELIODOR (S) 25087 [Wieniawski, Violin Concerto No. 2]

Wanda Wilkomirska, a Polish violinist, plays with a singing tone and eloquent style. The sound is fine. [The coupling is with the extremely popular and romantic Wieniawski concerto.]

Tartini, Giuseppe (1692-1770)

One of the greatest music theorists of his day, Tartini was the founder of a famous school for the violin at Padua, and the composer of over 100 violin concertos. He is chiefly recalled today—rather unfairly—for the last movement of a sonata appropriately entitled *The Devil's Trill*.

Tartini is sophisticated, warm-hearted, and poetic; he is well worth investigation by lovers of 18th-century string music.

CONCERTOS FOR VIOLIN AND STRINGS IN D, Capri 79; IN F, C. 63; CONCERTO GROSSO IN A MINOR, C. 76

These concertos are but a fraction of the hoard of Tartini manuscripts preserved at Padau. The boom in Tartini's popularity has only recently begun, and the chances are good that our indefatigable record companies will exhume all the other concertos as well.

| * GULLI, ABBADO | *Angelicum Orchestra of Milan* | MUSIC GUILD | (M) | 33 |
| | | | (S) | 33 |

Three melodious works are played with dash and *galant* style. They are technically well reocrded.

CONCERTOS FOR VIOLIN AND STRINGS IN E; IN F; IN G; IN D

This is virtuoso music, full of dazzling cadenzas, but not particularly profound.

| * * GERTLER, De STOUTZ | *Zurich Chamber Orch.* | VANGUARD | (S) SRV 213 |

Four concertos are beautifully played by a remarkable violinist. Gertler has made many excellent records, and this is one of his best. The serene slow movements are particularly well done. The Swiss ensemble is impeccable. The disc is well recorded.

SONATA IN G FOR VIOLIN ("DEVIL'S TRILL")

This is a widely popular, extremely "violinistic" sonata that remains a favorite piece of most skillful fiddlers. The manuscript was lost for many years, and then appeared in print in a volume called "Cartier's Violin School."

SZERYNG

* * SZERYNG

VICTROLA VIC   (S) 1037
[Tchaikovsky, Violin Concerto]

Szeryng is one of our top jet-age violinists, and his performance of this fiddler's favorite is simply the best on records. The sound is fine.

CONCERTO FOR VIOLIN AND ORCHESTRA, IN D MINOR

It is estimated that Tartini composed about 140 concertos—not to mention 50 trios and 150 violin sonatas. This composition is graceful and lyrical, but hardly extraordinary.

* TOMASOW   *Chamber Orchestra of the Vienna State Opera*   VANGUARD (M) SRV   154
(S) SRV 154SD
[Sinfonia Pastorale, for Violin and Strings; Nardini, Concerto for Violin and Orchestra, in E Minor]

This recording features clean playing and clear sound. It includes works by both Tartini and his star pupil, Nardini. Tartini is the more interesting; but neither of the compositions is exceptional.

SONATA A QUATTRO, IN D

This is one of the composer's musical experimentations. Tartini, a violin master, constantly experimented with innovations for the violin, such as lighter bows, thicker strings, etc. He also experimented with "musical fashions," as was the vogue among Italian composers of his day.

*   *Stuyvesant String Quartet*   NONESUCH   (M) H 1114
(S) H 71114
[Purcell, Chacony for Strings, in G minor; Dittersdorf, Quartet for Strings, in D; Haydn, Quartet for Strings, in F minor, Opus 55, No. 2]

This album is called "Quartet Music of the 17th and 18th Centuries," and it's a hodge-podge. The Purcell can be called a quartet only by the wildest semantic license. What matters more is that the playing is only so-so.

TRIO SONATA IN F FOR TWO VIOLINS AND CONTINUO

Though not particularly gripping, this music is pleasant.

* * DAVID OISTRAKH,
IGOR OISTRAKH,
PISCHNER,
YAMPOLSKY

HELIODOR   (M)   25009
(S) HS 25009
[Trio Sonatas by Bach, Handel, and Benda]

This recording provides all that one might expect from the celebrated Oistrakh father-son duo. Here is utterly serious, yet gorgeous violin playing. Hans Pischner plays the harpsichord; Vladimir Yampolsky, the piano. [George Benda (1722-1795) was a Bohemian composer, and his music is suggestive of Corelli. The "Bach" sonata (S.1037)—no longer thought to be Bach—is nevertheless pleasing. The "enhanced stereo" is successful.]

Tchaikovsky, Peter Ilyich (1840-1893)

After a short period as a student of law and then as a clerk in the Russian Ministry of Justice, Tchaikovsky studied composition under Anton Rubinstein at the St. Petersburg Conservatory. In 1866, he became a teacher at Nicholas Rubinstein's new Moscow Conservatory.

Tchaikovsky's first three symphonies reveal his interest in Russian folksong. Yet he was never a fanatical nationalist as were the St. Petersburg group of "The Five," whom he regarded—with the exception of Rimsky-Korsakov—as mildly talented amateurs. They, in turn, shrugged him off with indifference.

Throughout his life a sensitive and neurotic man, Tchaikovsky, when he was thirty-seven, tried marriage only briefly. After a few months, he and his wife Antonia Milyukova agreed to regard their marital contract as null and void.

From 1877 to 1890, Tchaikovsky was provided with an income by his patroness, Nadezhda von Meck, with whom he corresponded but never met. This most inspired period of his career produced the last three of his six symphonies, his most appealing operas *Eugene Onegin* and *Pique Dame (The Queen of Spades)*, the *Concerto in D for Violin and Orchestra*, and the ballets *Sleeping Beauty* and *Casse-Noisette (Nutcracker)*.

He toured Europe in 1888, and he visited America as a conductor in 1891.

Nine days after the first performance of his *Sixth Symphony*, the "Pathetique," Tchaikovsky died of cholera.

PLACE AND ACHIEVEMENT   Tchaikovsky is so vastly popular and so taken for granted that one is tempted to be condescending toward his music. But the truth is, in the words of Shostakovich, "Tchaikovsky's music is not only one of the cornerstones of Russian musical culture and world music. . . . It is at the same time a creative and technical encyclopedia to which every Russian composer has reference in the course of his own work."

Tchaikovsky's warm, open-hearted melodies have suffered from overexposure. Yet in the entire history of music only Mozart, Schubert and Verdi have written melodies that move us so deeply and so immediately.

Tchaikovsky is one of the great masters of the symphonic form. But, above all, he is one of music's supreme romanticists. His *Concerto in D for Violin and Orchestra* and his *Concerto No. 1 in B-flat Minor for Piano and Orchestra* are among the most popular works in the repertory.

THE ESSENTIAL TCHAIKOVSKY

ORCHESTRAL MUSIC: *Symphony No. 4 in F Minor; Symphony No. 5 in E Minor; Symphony No. 6 in B Minor (Pathetique); Concerto in D Major for Violin and Orchestra; Romeo and Juliet Fantasy-Overture; Marche slav; 1812 Overture; Capriccio Italien; Nutcracker Suite.*

OTHER MAJOR WORKS

OPERAS: *Eugene Onegin; Pique Dame (The Queen of Spades).*
BALLETS: *Swan Lake; Sleeping Beauty.*
ORCHESTRAL MUSIC: *Manfred Symphony; Serenade for String Orchestra; Mozartiana Suite No. 4 for Orchestra; Hamlet Fantasy-Overture; Francesca da Rimini Symphonic Fantasy; Rococo Variations for Cello and Orchestra.*
CHAMBER MUSIC: *String Quartet No. 1 in D Major; Trio in A Minor.*
SONGS: *None But the Lonley Heart; One Small Word; He Loved Me Dearly. [There are many others, too numerous to mention.]*
CHAMBER MUSIC: *[There are many assorted short pieces.]*

CAPRICCIO ITALIEN (Opus 45)

This composition is a colorful, pleasing souvenir of Tchaikovsky's 1879 visit to Rome, where he lived next to an army barracks. He used bugle fanfares and Italian tunes as themes in the *Capriccio.*

* * STEINBERG	*Pittsburgh Symphony*	PICKWICK (S) 4027 [Mendelssohn, Symphony No. 4; Wolf, Italian]
* BEECHAM	*Columbia Symphony*	ODYSSEY (M) 32160117 [Bizet, Carmen Suite; Ponchielli]
SCHURICHT	*Paris Conservatory Orch.*	R'CHMOND (M) 19041 [Suite No. 3]

Steinberg's reading is the only modern recording here; it is a strong, vivid performance. [The disc includes Mendelssohn's sparkling *Fourth Symphony*, and is thus an especially worth-while buy.]

Beecham's interpretation is even more highly spirited, but faded sonics lessen its appeal.

Though the style is lively on the mono Schuricht recording, the sonics are poor.

In certain pieces of music, such as the *Capriccio Italien*, stereo is particularly effective. For this composition, stereo is a must.

CONCERTO NO. 1 IN B FLAT
FOR PIANO AND ORCHESTRA

Tchaikovsky wrote this vastly popular concerto in a month, in 1874. He gave a private performance for two colleagues at the Moscow Conservatory, one of them his friend and patron Nicholas Rubinstein. In a chilly classroom, the composer played through the work. When he had finished, Rubinstein plunged into a tirade of abuse, calling the work unpianistic, tawdry, and unoriginal.

Tchaikovsky describes the emotion-packed scene that followed: "I left the room without a word and went upstairs. I could not have spoken for anger and agitation. Presently Rubinstein came to me, and seeing how upset I was, called me into another room. There he repeated that my Concerto was impossible, pointed out many places where it had to be revised. . . . 'I shall not alter a single note,' I replied. 'I shall publish the work precisely as it stands.' "

ARRAU, GALLIERA	Philharmonia Orchestra	SERAPHIM	(S) 60020
BLUMENTHAL, GIELEN	Vienna Ensemble	VOX	(S) 511500
* * * GILELS, REINER	Chicago Symphony	VICTROLA	(S) 1039
RICHTER, ANCERL	Czech Philharmonic	PARLIAMENT	(S) 120
RICHTER, KONDRASHIN	Moscow Radio Orch.	PERIOD	(S) 2341

Arrau doesn't seem to have his heart in this performance; it is a curiously cool, correct reading, little more.

Blumenthal is hearable, and quite unremarkable.

Gilels delivers a sweeping, robustly romantic reading. The sound is crisp.

Richter-Ancerl is fuzzily recorded.

Richter-Kondrashin alos is marred by unacceptable sonics. If you're after Richter's tempestuous version, get his high-priced recording on the DGG label.

CONCERTO NO. 2 FOR PIANO AND ORCHESTRA
(Opus 44)

The sweeping Piano Concerto No. 2 has never really become popular—surprisingly, as it contains many fine pages. But it's not a stunning masterpiece such as No. 1.

MAGALOFF, DAVIS	London Symphony	WORLD SERIES	(M/S) 9007

Magaloff copes with the fiendishly difficult piano part; that is about all that can be said favorably about this rendition. The sound is muddy and booming.

CONCERTO IN D FOR VIOLIN AND ORCHESTRA
(Opus 35)

The Tchaikovsky *Concerto in D* is the most popular romantic violin concerto in today's repertory.

This work vividly demonstrates the changes in critical taste that occur from age to age: friends and foe alike were at first hostile to the concerto. Even Mme. von Meck, Tchaikovsky's unwavering "Beloved Friend," was appalled by it in 1881. Leopold Auer, the St. Petersburg virtuoso and legendary teacher, declared the work "impossible to play." Later, however, Auer changed his mind, and required his students to master the Tchaikovsky concerto.

* * OISTRAKH, KONWITSCHNY	*Saxon State Orch.*	HELIODOR (S) 25071 [Beethoven, Romances]	
* * KOGAN, SILVESTRI	*Paris Conservatoire Orch.*	SERAPHIM (S) 60075 [Meditation: Souvenir d'un lieu cher]	
* * SZERYNG, MUNCH	*Boston Symphony Orch.*	VICTROLA (S) 1037 [Tartini, Sonata in G ("Devil's Trill")]	
* RICCI, SARGENT	*New Symphony Orch.*	RICHMOND (M) 19011	
OISTRAKH, GAUK	*National Philharmonic*	PERIOD SHO (S) 307	
MORINI, RODZINSKY	*London Philharmonic*	WESTMINSTER (S) 1011	
CAMPOLI, ARGENTA	*London Symphony Orch.*	RICHMOND (S) 29085 (M) 19085	
SPIVAKOVSKY, GOEHR	*London Symphony Orch.*	EVEREST (S) 3049 (M) 6049	

Oistrakh's rendition of the Tchaikovsky concerto is unsurpassed. His reading with Konwitschny is pure and vibrant. Nevertheless, *Saturday Review's* Irving Kolodin grumbles: "My only complaint would be that Oistrakh is too often primarily playing the violin rather than Tchaikovsky." The sound is agreeable, although "electronically processed" for stereo. [The disc also includes Beethoven's ingratiating *Romances*.]

On Oistrakh's recording with Gauk, the sonics are poor.

A first-rate ultra-romantic approach, coupled with far better sonics, is heard from Leonid Kogan, ace violinist who among the Russians ranks just below "King David." The English publication *Records and Recordings* comments: "Kogan attacks the music with tremendous brio and

sinewy strength. The stereo is magnificently spacious and well focused."
[The Kogan disc also includes the elegiac *Meditation,* originally conceived
as the violin concerto's slow movement, and finally used by Tchaikovsky
as the first of three violin pieces collectively entitled *Souvenir d'un lieu
cher.*]

The Szeryng reading should not be slighted; he is a tremendous
fiddler. The imaginative work of the Boston symphony under Munch is
all that one could desire. The sound is exemplary.

In summary: the Oistrakh, Kogan, and Szering readings are all fine;
you won't go wrong buying any of them.

The other recordings are of much lesser interest.

EUGENE ONEGIN (Opus 24)
(Complete opera, sung in Russian)

Tchaikovsky adored opera; yet none of his operas are entirely successful.
Onegin contains some beautiful melodies and orchestration, but it lacks
dramatic tension. *Onegin* rambles, and the listener will find it heavy going
after half an hour.

MELIK-PASHAIEV	*Bolshoi Theatre Production* 3-PERIOD	(M) 1003

This hoary relic started its electronic career in the old days of 78 rpm
recordings, and it sounds it. Vocal expert Philip Miller's verdict, in *Guide
to Vocal Records:* "The big scenes . . . are messy and unclear, the solo
ensembles like so many catfights."

EUGENE ONEGIN (Opus 24)
(Excerpts, sung in Russian)

* VISHNEVSKAYA, ARDEYEVA, BELOV, KHAIKIN	*Bolshoi Theatre Production* MONTILLA	(S) 2072

Vishnevskaya is one of the best Russian singers today, and this record
shows her at her somber best. In other respects, the record is unexceptional.

FRANCESCA DA RIMINI (Opus 32)

Written in 1876, this comparatively uninspired work was originally
planned as an opera, but an impossible libretto made Tchaikovsky decide
to compose "an orchestral fantasy" instead. It is based on the celebrated
love story of Paolo and Francesca.

* * STOKOWSKI	New York Stadium Symphony	EVEREST	(S) 3011
			(M) 6011
		[Hamlet]	
* * MUNCH	Boston Symphony Orch.	VICTROLA	(S) 1197
		[Romeo and Juliet]	
JORDA	Paris Conservatory Orch. & Romeo and Juliet	RICHMOND	(M) 19027
		[Romeo and Juliet]	

Stokowski's lush, wide-screen treatment works well, though the conductor's own style is highly evident. One might even say the performance is more "Staikowsky" than "Tchaikovsky."

Munch gives a lean, vigoous reading. The sonics are excellent.

Against this competition, the mono reading with Jorda does not warrant purchasing.

HAMLET (Fantasy Overture) (Opus 67a)

This overture is a loose treatment of the Shakespeare play, similar to Tchaikovsky's *Romeo and Juliet* but far less appealing.

* * STOKOWSKI	New York Stadium Symphony	EVEREST	(S) 3011
			(M) 6011
		[Francesca da Rimini]	
* BOULT	London Philharmonic	RICHMOND	(M) 19014
		[1812 Overture]	

Stowkowski is preferred; his throbbing performance is highly successful. Boult is much more straight-forward.

MANFRED (Symphonic Poem) (Opus 58)

This tempestuous work is sporadic: the composer himself admitted that it was only "half-successful."

| GOOSSENS | London Symphony Orch. | EVEREST | (S) 3035 |
| | | | (M) 6035 |

The playing is barely acceptable, and the sound is foggy.

MARCHE SLAV (Opus 31)

The *Marche slav* was written for a war-benefit concert of the Russo-Turkish war in 1876. Stirring, loud, and feverish, it is one of the most popular patriotic pieces ever written.

* * REINER	Chicago Symphony Orch.	Victrola	(S) 1968
* * SARGENT	Royal Philharmonic	Seraphim	(S) 60023
* MITROPOULOS	New York Philharmonic	Odyssey	(S) 32160228
BARBIROLLI	Danish State Radio Symphony	Richmond	(M) 19053
TUXEN	Halle Orch.	Vanguard [Symphony No. 5]	(S) 139

Reiner and the Chicago orchestra deliver an exciting, full-bodied performance, resonantly recorded.

Sargent's players are much less glittering, but theirs is nevertheless a stirring performance.

Mitropoulos' reading is exuberant, and the sound is fair, but this disc is quite outclassed by Reiner's.

Barbirolli has first-rate sonics but indifferent playing.

Tuxen's performance is stirring, but the *Marche slav* really requires stereo for maximum effectiveness.

NUTCRACKER (Opus 71) (Complete ballet)

The *Nutcracker* was commissioned for the St. Petersburg Opera in 1891. Many listeners weary of the complete ballet, and prefer the orchestral suites—the selections usually played at concerts. The composer himself found the ballet "a little boring, despite the magnificence of the stage setting." Especially beloved by young people, the ballet music contains some delightful passages.

* * ABRAVANEL	Utah Symphony Orch., Chorus of University of Utah	2-Vanguard	(S) 168/9
* RODZINSKI	London Philharmonic	2-Westminster	(S) 203 (M) 1205
* ROZHDESTVENSKY	Bolshoi Theatre Production	2-Artia	(S) 180/1

Abravanel gives a meticulous performance, but often seems rhythmically too stiff. The sonics are good.

Rodzinski's interpretation seems stodgy. The sound is only fair.

Rozhdestvensky is very good, but the Russian sound is poor.

NUTCRACKER SUITE (Opus 71A)

Tchaikovsky made this ingratiating orchestral arrangement from his ballet music. It is one of themost popular works in the entire orchestral repertory, and a sure-fire children's favorite.

* * KURTZ	*Philharmonic Orch.*	3-SERAPHIM (S) 6011 (3-record album) [Swan Lake; Sleeping Beauty]	
* * DORATI	*Minneapolis Symphony Orch.*	MERCURY (S) 18011 (M) 14011	
* TOSCANINI	*NBC Symphony Orch.*	VICTROLA (M) 1263 [Bizet, Carmen Suite]	
* FISTOULARI	*Paris Conservatory Orch.*	RICHMOND (M) 19065 [Nutcracker Suite No. 2]	
* HOLLINGSWORTH	*London Symphony Orch.*	EVEREST (S) 3111 (M) 6111	
PERLA	*Bamberg Symphony Orch.*	VOX (M) (5)-11390 [R. Strauss, Rosen Kavalier Suite]	

Few conductors have surpassed Efrem Kurtz in ballet music. This warm, affectionate album, which contains Tchaikovsky's other two beloved ballets as well, is a solid buy for those who love this music. The respected English journal *The Gramaphone* characterized the album: "Pure gold . . . . irreproachably realized."

For those who wish only one record, Dorati is splendid. This recording was once considered the last word in sound, and even against today's competition, it is excellent.

In this particular work. Toscanini is too taut for my taste.

Fistoulari's interpretation moves with a pleasant, flowing rhythm appropriate to ballet music.

Hollingsworth's version is serviceable.

The Perlea recording is adequate, but unexceptional.

NUTCRACKER SUITE NO. 2

Completely overshadowed by the delightful *Nutcracker Suite No. 1,* this second suite is rarely heard in the concert hall. Nevertheless, Tchaikovsky lovers will enjoy it.

* DORATI	*Minneapolis Symphony Orch.*	MERCURY (S) 18011 (M) 14011 [Nutcracker Suite (Opus 71A)]	
* FISTOULARI	*Paris Conservatory Orch.*	RICHMOND (M) 19065 [Nutcracker Suite (Opus 71A)]	

Dorati gives a meticulous reading; the sound is early-era stereo, only mildly effective.

Fistoulari's interpretation is warm and romantic, with clean mono sound.

OVERTURE "1812" (Opus 49)

Another rousing patriotic piece, this overture is nearly as graphic as a film scenario in its portrayal of the stirring events of 1812. Tchaikovsky's music clearly depicts the French and Russians locked in mortal combat. The *Marseilles* rises, threateningly: the French are in Moscow. At last the enemy is hurled back as cathedral bells peal, massed drums roll, and a Russian hymn pours forth a paean of victory.

Many serious collectors disparage this music, yet millions enjoy it.

* * SARGENT	*Royal Philharmonic*	SERAPHIM (S) 60023 [Marche slav; Romeo and Juliet]
* * REINER		VICTROLA (S) 1025 [Debussy, Iberia; Liszt, Mephisto]
* ROSSI ,	*Vienna State Opera Orch.*	VANGUARD (M) 110 [Capriccio Italien; Rimsky-Korsakov, Capriccio Espagnol]
SCHERCHEN	*Vienna State Opera Orch. & mixed program*	WESTMINSTER (S) 1007
STUPKA	*Prague Symphony Orch. & mixed program*	PARLIAMENT (M) 145

Both the Sargent and Reiner discs are excellent. Your preferences among the other items on the records may help determine your choice.

Sargent is urbane and civilized, in an all-Tchaikovsky program.

Reiner is more sweeping and colorful, in a good mixed program.

Rossi is commendable, but outclassed.

The other performances have less appeal.

ROMEO AND JULIET

This "fantasy overture" includes some of the most glowing love music ever written. Balakirev, the founder of the "Russian Five," suggested to the young Tchaikovsky that he set the Shakespeare drama as an orchestral work. Balakirev even outlined the structure, which Tchaikovsky followed. Written in 1870, it was Tchaikovsky's first important piece.

* TOSCANINI	*NBC Symphony Orch.*	VICTROLA (M) VIC-1245 [Glinka, Kamarinskaya; Sibelius, Finlandia; Sinetana, Moldau]
* * MUNCH	*Boston Symhony Orch.*	VICTROLA (S) VIC-1197 [Francesca da Rimini]

* SARGENT	Royal Philharmonic	SERAPHIM (S) 60023 [Marche slav; 1812 Overture]
BOULT	London Philharmonic	SOMERSET ST. FI. 1600 [Hamlet]
VAN BEINUM	London Philharmonic	RICHMOND (M) 19027 [Francesca da Rimini]
SANDERLING	Saxon State Orch.	HELIODOR (S) 25061 [Bordoni, In the Steppes; Symphony No. 2]
SCHERCHEN	Vienna State Opera Orch.	3-WESTMINSTER (S) 1007 [& mixed program]

Toscanini was fond of *Romeo and Juliet* and played it often. This recording throbs with the Maestro's nervous energy, and I star it despite flaccid recording.

More modern sound (1957) is heard on the Munch reading, which *High Fidelity* reviewed as "whipped up with Munch's customary vigor and unabashed extroversion—and this is, of course, only just and right for such juicy music."

The Sargent disc is excellent.

The other entries are unremarkable.

SLEEPING BEAUTY (Opus 66) (Complete ballet)

This charming ballet is based on Perrault's famous fairy tale. Many listeners regard this music as superior to the more popular *Swan Lake*.

* FISTOULARI	Paris Conservatory Orch.	2-RICHMOND (M) 42001

Fistoulari leads a graceful, poised performance. The sound is a bit thin.

SLEEPING BEAUTY (Opus 66) (Excerpts)

* * KURTZ	Philharmonia Orch. & Nutcracker; Swan Lake	3-SERAPHIM	(S) 6011
* DORATI	Minneaolis Symphony Orch.	MERCURY	(S) 18012 (M) 14012
* VAN REMOORTEL	Vienna Symphony Orch. & Swan Lake	Vox (5)	(S) 11770
* LEVINE	Ballet Theatre Orch. & Romeo	PICKWICK	(S) 4002

| GOEHR | *Rome Opera Orch.*
& Swan Lake | HARMONY | (M) 7219 |
| DeCROSS | *Paris Promenade Orch.* | PERIOD | SHO 326 |

The Kurtz three-record album far outshines the others. (See detailed comments under *Nutcracker Suite.*)

Dorati, Van Remoortel and Levine are all suave, highly romantic, and fairly well recorded, though their sound is not the most recent.

The Goehr and DeCross performances are not outstanding.

SWAN LAKE (Opus 20) (Complete ballet)

The most popular of Tchaikovsky's three ballets, *Swan Lake* is a cornerstone of the classical dance.

| * * ABRAVANEL | *Utah Symphony Orch.* | 2-VANGUARD | (S) 223/4 |
| * FISTOULARI | *London Symphony Orch.* | 2-RICHMOND | (M) 42003 |

Abravanel is polished. His players are well-drilled and responsive; the stereo sound is spacious.

Fistoulari is light-fingered and keeps the music moving. The sound is agreeable.

SWAN LAKE (excerpts)

* * KURTZ	*Philharmonia Orch.*	3-SERAPHIM (S) 6011 [Nutcracker; Sleeping Beauty]
* * ALWYN	*London Philharmonic* *& Grieg: Peer Gynt*	RICHMOND (S) 29057 (M) 19057 [Grieg, Peer Gynt]
* * MOREL	*Royal Opera House Orch.* *Covent Garden*	VICTROLA VIC (S)-1002
* FISTOULARI	*London Symphony Orch.*	RICHMOND (M) 19084
VAN REMOORTEL	*Vienna Symphony Orch.*	Vox (5) 11770 [Sleeping Beauty]
DORATI	*Minneapolis Symphony Orch.*	MERCURY (S) 18025 (M) 14025
GOEHR	*Rome Opera Orch.*	HARMONY (M) 7219 [Sleeping Beauty]

The Kurtz three-record album leads in a superlative, glowing performance. (See comments under *Nutcracker Suite.*)

Alwyn, another sure hand with ballet scores, provides a graceful, satisfying reading.

Morel's version is delicate and polished, and contains more of the *Swan Lake* excerpts.

Fistoulari's interpretation is first-rate, but the mono sound has dimmed, and stereo is desirable for the *Swan Lake* music.

The readings by Van Remoortel, Dorati, and Goehr are pleasant but unexceptional.

SUITE NO. 3, Opus 55

This poignant suite met enormous success when the composer himself conducted it at his Carnegie Hall debut in 1891.

BOULT	*Paris Conservatory Orch.*	LONDON	STS-15034
SCHURICHT	*Paris Conservatory Orch.*	RICHMOND	(M) 19041
		Capriccio Italien]	
		[Theme and Variations only;	

Boult's reading is straightforward rather than hghly emotional. The sound is satisfactory.

Schuricht is workmanlike and efficient, but unspectacular. The sound is fair.

SYMPHONY NO. 4 in F minor (Opus 36)

Tchaikovsky's *Symphonies No. 4, 5,* and *6* are among the great romantic achievements of the 19th century.

In the winter of 1876-1877, when Tchaikovsky started working on his *Fourth Symphony,* he suddenly plunged into one of his "black moods," a state of mind so depressing that he wrote in despair to his friend, Klimentke, "Since we last met, I am very much changed—especially mentally. Not a kopek's worth of fun and gaiety is left in me. Life is terribly empty, tedious, and tawdry. . . . The only thing that has not changed is my love for composing. . . . I pray that I might write something really decent."

"Something decent" did come from his pen at this time: The great *Fourth Symphony*.

* * MRAVINSKY	*Leningrad Philharmonic*	MONTILLA	(M)	8001
* * MUNCH	*Boston Symphony Orch.*	VICTROLA (VIC)	(S)	1100
* * BEECHAM	*Royal Philharmonic*	PICKWICK	(S)	4033
* BARBIROLLI	*Halle Orch.*	VANGUARD	(S)	135

DENZLER	Orchestra Suisse Romande	RICHMOND	(S) 29082
			(M) 19082
HOLLREISER	Bamberg Symphony Orch.	VOX (5)	11190
IVANOV	USSR State Symphony Orch.	ARTIA	(M) 155

Mravinsky's reading most successfully conveys the gripping tension and excitement of the work. The English *Stereo Record Guide* comments: "a sympathetic and distinguished reading." However, the mono sound is only so-so.

Munch and Beecham both deliver confident, passionate conceptions, handsomely recorded.

Barbirolli is workmanlike, but on the dull side.

The other readings are outclassed.

SYMPHONY NO. 5 in E minor (Opus 64)

The first performances of the *Fifth Symphony*, which Tchaikovsky himself conducted in St. Petersburg in 1888, were a popular success. As usual, however, the composer considered his new work a failure. He declared that he found in it "something repellent, something superfluous, patchy and insincere, which the public instinctively recognizes." He did not accept the audience's applause as proof of enthusiasm; he was sure that they were only being polite. "Am I really played out, as they say?" he wrote to his benefactress Madame von Meck.

Today, Tchaikovsky's *Fifth Symphony* is one of the half-dozen most popular symphonies in the repertory. In many ways, the *Fifth Symphony* is the most beguiling of all Tchaikovsky's orchestral works. All of Tchaikovsky's best qualities are displayed: his Slavic eloquence, melancholy spirit, and, above all, his genius for melody.

* * STEINBERG	Pittsburgh Symphony Orch.	PICKWICK	(S) 4014
* KRIPS	Vienna Philharmonic	LONDON	STS-15017
* BOULT	London Philharmonic	SOMERSET ST. FI.	100000
HOLLREISER	Bamberg Symphony Orch.	VOX (5)	10380
SARGENT	London Symphony Orch.	EVEREST	(S) 3039
			(M) 6039
BARBIROLLI	Halle Orch. & Marche Slave [Marche slav]	VANGUARD	(S) 139

Steinberg and the Pittsburgh orchestra are most impressive. Theirs is a dynamic reading that sticks close to the score—an unusual accomplishment among interpreters of Tchaikovsky. The sound on the Steinberg recording is spacious.

Krips is impassioned, but not as impressive as Steinberg.

Boult delivers a workmanlike performance, without much eloquence.

Hollreiser is unexceptional.

Sargent is too matter-of-fact for this dark, brooding score.

Barbirolli is strangely dull here—in the words of *High Fidelity,* "down-right heavy-handed."

SYMPHONY NO. 6 in B minor (Opus 74) ("Pathetique")

This is perhaps the greatest of Tchaikovsky's symphonies, and certainly the most popular.

The composer had begun work on a sixth symphony upon his return from America in 1891. The work was already partially orchestrated, and then Tchaikovsky destroyed it in a fit of despair. He commented to his nephew, Vladimir Davidoff, that "it contained little that was fine — an empty patter of sounds without any inspiration."

Then, in 1892, on a train journey to Paris, he conceived a new symphony—the "Pathetique." "I composed all through my journey, in my mind," he wrote, "and frequently I shed tears."

* * * GIULINI	*Philharmonic Orch.*	SERAPHIM	(S) 60031
* * * TOSCANINI	*NBC Symphony Orch.*	VICTROLA	VIC-1268
* * STEINBERG	*Pittsburgh Symphony Orch.*	PICKWICK	(S) 4026
* TALICH	*Czech Philharmonic*	PARLIAMENT	(M) 113
* MUNCH	*Paris Conservatory Orch.*	RICHMOND	(M) 19002
* MONTEUX	*Boston Symphony Orch.*	VICTROLA	VIC (S) 1009
MARTINON	*Vienna Philharmonic*	LONDON	STS-15018
BARBIROLLI	*Halle Orch.*	VANGUARD	(S) 148
DIXON	*Rundfunk Symphony Orch.*	EVEREST	(S) 3115
			(M) 6115

These recordings provide a rich field.

The Giulini disc has been praised to the skies. *High Fidelity* called it "incandescent" and "among the very best available at any price." The English journal *The Gramophone* spoke of "masterly control of tension." Such a stunning Tchaikovsky disc is particularly remarkable coming from the baton of Maestro Giulini, who is noted almost exclusively for his opera conduction. The 1961 sound is clear.

Toscanini usually shrugged off Tchaikovsky, and the *Sixth Symphony* was one of the few Tchaikovsky works he would conduct, when pressed to do so. This 1947 recording is famous among collectors for its emotion-charged, whip-lashed eloquence. *High Fidelity* commented on this reissue: "This twenty year old performance of the Pathetique must still be one of the best in an overcrowded field."

Worthy performances of lesser impact are heard from Steinberg, Talich, Munch, and Monteux. Of these, Steinberg has by far the most successful sonics.

VARIATIONS ON A ROCOCO THEME FOR CELLO (Opus 33)

The composer wrote these delightful *Variations* for a colleague, the cellist Karl Friedrich Fitzenhagen. The theme is "Mozartian"; Tchaikovsky adored Mozart throughout his life. Since its premiere in 1877, cellists have loved playing this superb piece of music.

* ROSTROPOVICH	*Moscow State Orch.*	PERIOD	SHO (St-2)	337
CASSADO, PERLEA	*Vienna Pro Musica Symphony Orch.*	Vox		9360
		[Dvorak, Cello Concerto]		

The great Russian cellist Rostropovich is probably the finest player since Casals. However, this exciting reading is marred by rather harsh sound.

Cassado is competent, but far outclassed.

Telemann, George Philipp (1681-1767)

Telemann was born in Magdeburg, studied law at Leipsiz University, and taught himself music. He wrote church music for the Thomaskirche, and operas for the Leipzig Theatre. For a while he was organist of the Neukirche, and later in 1704, he became Kapellmeister to Prince Promitz at Sorau. In 1708, he became Konzertmeister at Eisenach where he made friends with J. S. Bach; he later became Kapellmeister there. He also held posts, at various times, in Frankfurt and Hamburg (where he was succeeded by C.P.E. Bach). He was one of the most prolific composers of all time, and probably wrote over a thousand works.

PLACE AND ACHIEVEMENT   Today, Telemann is very much an "in" composer. The French speak of *la Telemanie* (translatable as "Telemania"); and in the United States, there exists a whole Telemann record industry. Telemann has become for the sixties what Vivaldi was for the fifties: the baroque musician supreme. In his own day, Telemann was considered to be the outstanding composer of his time; his contemporary, Johann Sebastian Bach, was only a fairly obscure organist who worked in Leipsiz. Incidentally, Bach was given his post in Leipzig only after Telemann and another had turned it down; "none of the best men were available," as the city fathers grumpily noted for posterity's bemusement.

Telemann never reaches for the stars, as does Bach; we are not overcome by the sheer intellectual virtuosity of his work, as happens with Bach. What Telemann wrote was urbane, vivacious, and graceful music—music that pleases the ear, if offered in limited doses.

THE ESSENTIAL TELEMANN
The most industrious composer in an age of prodigious production, Telemann wrote 12 cycles of cantatas for the church year, 44 Passions, oratorios, much other church music, 40 operas, 600 French overtures (i.e. suites for orchestra), concertos, a great deal of chamber music in various forms, fantasies for harpsichord, and short fugues for organ.

From among this staggering output, one cannot point to any one or two towering masterpieces. As is the case with Vivaldi, Telemann's music is of enormous range, and yet one work is often indistinguishable from another. Every lover of baroque has his own favorite Telemann concerto or sonata. From among a vast storehouse, I note some delightful scores and performances; also, a few records to avoid.

CANTATA FOR SOPRANO AND ORCHESTRA ("INO")

Telemann wrote the *"Ino" Cantata* in 1765, two years before his death at eighty-six, inspired by the 1765 publication of a text by Karl Ramler. Several of Telemann's younger contemporaries had already set the same text to music. This is a masterful, mature and very dramatic work, quite unlike the rest of Telemann's output. Ever desirous of "keeping up with the times," the composer wrote the piece in answer to the new style of a younger generation. Contributing to it all the physical strength he had left, he produced an astonishingly "modern" piece of music—certainly one of his greatest.

* * CIANNELLA, RILLING *Bach Colleguim, Stuttgart*   TURNABOUT
(M/S) TV 34100

* STICH-RANDALL,   *Vienna State Opera Orch.*   NONESUCH   (S) 71182
BOETTCHER   [Bach, Cantata 151]

Rilling has the edge in this delightfully fresh music. Yvonne Ciannella sings with an attractive light touch. The sound is warm.

In the Nonesuch offering, Stich-Randall is in excellent voice, yet I prefer Ciannella's style. The sound is clean.

CANTATA: THE TIMES OF DAY (TAGESZEITEN)

Morning, noon, evening, and night are the subject of this rather solemn, pious work, a miniature hymn of praise of the world and its Creator. This work points up "the Telemann problem": to reach one jewel, you have to plow through hundreds of pages of empty *galanterie* that never would have been exhumed if Telemann were not so much in vogue. This piece is *not* a Telemann jewel.

* CZERNY, UNGER,   *Solistenvereinigung and*   HELIODOR   (M/S) H 25041
LEIB, KOCH   *Kammerorchester, Berlin*

The cantata is modestly but pleasantly realized. The sound is rather dark.

CONCERTOS

Telemann may have been the most prolific composer who ever lived; I, for one, have no intention of wading through all his concertos. I don't think there is too much point in doing so. I doubt that there are even a handful of scholars who can identify all of them. Here are some choice collections:

* * * AURIACOMBE	*Chamber Orch. of Toulouse*	NONESUCH	(S) H-71066	
* * * I. K. MATHIESEN, A. H. MATHIESEN	*Concentus Musicus of Denmark*	NONESUCH	(S) H-71065	
* * REDEL	*Pro Arte Orchestra, Munich*	WORLD SERIES	(M/S) PHC 9035	
* *	*Hamburg Camerata Instrumentale*	HELIODOR	(M/S) H 25006	
* * RISTENPART	*Chamber Orch. of the Saar*	NONESUCH H		1132
		H		71132
* * RAMPAL, DOUATTE	*Collegium Musicum of Paris*	NONESUCH H	(M)	1124
		H	(S)	1124

The Auriacombe disc is a real standout. The style and playing are impeccable. The sound is spacious.

The Mathiesens provide another remarkable winner—one of the best Telemann records to be had at any price. In certain places, this attractive music is pure champagne. The instrumentalists are flawless.

Redel and the Pro Arte Orchestra provide warm, intimate playing. The sound is good. (A point that might enrage purists: what is palmed off here as "Concerto for Flute and Oboe" is not a concerto at all; it is a *Trio Sonata* for recorder and violin, puffed up to orchestral size. That doesn't bother me, and it shouldn't bother you.

The Hamburg musicians give a highly spirited performance — especially trumpeter Adolf Scherbaum. His pianissimo effects are truly extraordinary. The sound is excellent.

The Ristenpart disc is worth having if only for the superb overture for three oboes. You might easily mistake this piece for vintage Mozart. The record features fine playing throughout.

Flutist Rampal does his usual civilized job in the Collegium Musicum disc. All the soloists excel, but the conducting is on the glum side.

FANTASIAS FOR KEYBOARD

Telemann wrote some three dozen *Fantasias,* intended for easy-to-play-*Hausmusik.*

* ELSNER	DOVER HCR [No. 13-24g]	5236
* HOKANSON	WORLD SERIES M/S	9061

Helma Elsner provides studious, Germanic harpsichord playing of the final dozen of the composer's keyboard sonatas. *Stereo Review:* "Performance: somewhat stolid; recording: good."

Leonard Hokanson offers six *Fantasias*—competently played.

MUSIC FOR FLUTE AND HARPSICHORD

The *Concerto for Flute and Harpsichord,* the highlight of this stylish album, sounds years ahead of its time.

* * RAMPAL,   Nonesuch   (S) H 71038
  VEYRON-LACROIX

Rampal is perhaps the greatest flute virtuoso of this century; teamed with Veyron-Lacroix, he has produced dozens of perfectly beguiling records. This is one of them—French culture at its sophisticated best.

OVERTURE FOR TRUMPET, OBOE, STRINGS AND CONTINUO, IN D

* ANDRE, PIERLOT,   *Collegium Musicum of Paris* Nonesuch   (M) 1091
  BARBOTEU,   (S) 71091
  COURSIER, DOUATTE   [Vivaldi, Concerto for Two
                                                 Horns, Strings, and Con-
                                                 tinuo]

Here is stylish and graceful playing, especially from trumpeter Andre. [The Vivaldi work is harmless.] The sound is clear stereo.

PIMPINONE (Opera)

Originally entitled *The Unequal Marriage,* this set of three comic interludes was first produced in 1725. It predated Pergolesi's *La Serva Padrona* by eight years, and is quite similar in plot and comic characterization.

* * CIANNELLA, WENK   *Bach Collegium, Stuttgart*   Turnabout   (S) TV 34123

* ROSCHER, SUESS,   *Berlin Chamber Orch.*   World Series
  KOCH   PHC (M/S) 9066

The Turnabout offering is the winner here, with a much more bubbly performance than its rival. Better sound, too. Yvonne Ciannella sketches Telemann's hussy down to the last scathing syllable. The hard-to-navigate appoggiaturas come off well.

The World Series recording is blighted by a stodgy, over-serious conception.

THREE ORCHESTRAL SUITES *(including*
DON QUICHOTTE)

Here is first-rate, satisfying Telemann.

* * BEAUCAMP	*Rouen Chamber Orch.*	WORLD SERIES PHI. WS (M/S) 9003

In their dynamic, vital playing, the Rouen players are quite astonishing. The group is made up of young instrumentalists in their twenties who won their posts in a nationwide competition in France.

FOUR SONATAS FOR FLUTE AND CONTINUO
(METHODICAL SONATAS)

These are baroque solo sonatas accompanied by a continuo, which in this performance is played by a harpsichord and cello. Telemann uses the continuo device as far more than just a harmonic support; the supporting instruments are constantly in imitation or in dialogue with the solo flute.

* * BARON, KOUGELL, CONANT	DOVER	SCR ST 7004 HCR 5241

This is one of Dover's best releases—with sensitive, even exquisite playing, by Sam Baron, one of the top flutists in America. The recording is clear.

SONATAS AND TRIOS: SONATA FOR FLUTE,
OBOE, AND CONTINUO IN D MINOR; TRIOS FOR
FLUTE, OBOE, AND CONTINUO IN E MINOR;
IN D; TRIO SONATA FOR OBOE, HARPSICHORD
AND CONTINUO, IN E-FLAT

* *	*Maxence Larrieu Quartet*	NONESUCH	(S) H 71061

This lovely record features glowing musicianship and flawless sound.

SUITE IN A MINOR FOR FLUTE AND STRINGS

The *A Minor Suite* is one of the most endearing of Telemann's works. In its style and facility, it reminds us of Bach's famous "B Minor Suite," which also features the flute.

* * MOEHRING, MUELLER-BRUEHL	*Cologne Soloists Ensemble*	NONESUCH H-71078 [Concerto in A Minor for Violin; Suite in F-Sharp Minor for Strings]

The music is elegantly played, and the sound is pleasant. Nevertheless, a definitive performance of this work has yet to appear on a low-priced label.

WATER MUSIC

Telemann's *Water Music,* unlike Handel's, is program music. *Neptune in Love, Naiads at Play*—all melodious, stylish, and quite charming.

* GENDRE, WALLEZ, LAROQUE, DOUATTE	*Collegium Musicum of Paris*	NONESUCH H (M/S) 1109 [Overture In C, "Hamburger Ebb und Fluht"; Musique de Table, 2nd production: Concerto for Three Violins, Strings and Continuo, in F]

From this pompous interpretation, you would never guess that Telemann was a man of wide culture who sought elegance in music.

Tinctoris, Johannes (c. 1445-1551)

Tinctoris, a Frenchman, was noted for his theoretical writings on music. He also published the first dictionary of musical terms. Particularly enjoyable is his smug remark (written in 1477): "No music written more than forty years before is worth hearing."

MISSA TRIUM VOCUM

This *Mass for Three Voices* is unrelentingly wearisome, and is primarily of historical interest to students of the period.

BLANCHARD	*Instrumental and Vocal Ensemble*	NONESUCH	(M) H 1048 (S) H 71048

The male voices are poor and often off-pitch. This recording is one of Nonesuch's lesser contributions.

Titelouze, Jean *(1563-1633)*

Titelouze, a virtuoso organist, lived in Rouen. He was organist at the Church of St. Jean and later at the Cathedral of Rouen. He visited Paris in 1604 to inaugurate the organ at the Abbey of St. Denis, and again in 1610, to inaugurate the organ at Notre Dame.

ORGAN WORKS

Historically, these organ hymns are interesting, but musically they are of little importance.

DARASSE	TURNABOUT (S) 34126
	[Attaignant, Dances]

The Turnabout disc features gorgeously recorded cathedral tones played by Xavier Darasse. The playing is acceptable, but this dullish music is hardly worth-while. [Another organist, Andre Isoir, plays the Attaignant dances on the reverse side.]

Torelli, Giuseppe (1659-1709)

This Italian was a violinist as well as composer, as were many musicians of his day. He was a violinist at the Church of San Petronio in Bologna from 1686 to 1695; he then became leader of the court orchestra of the Margrave of Brandenburg-Ansbach. He lived in Bologna from 1701 on. His music is light-weight and rather innocuous to modern ears—quite similar to the music of his contemporary Corelli. Together with Corelli, Torelli was largely responsible for the development of the concerto grosso form.

CONCERTO IN A FOR GUITAR, VIOLIN AND ORCHESTRA

This is most pleasant, unsubtle music, and entirely unimportant.

* * SCHIET, BOETTCHER	*Vienna Festival Chamber Orch.*	TURNABOUT (S) 34123 [Carulli; Paganini, Romanze for Guitar Solo]

This mild concerto is well played, with a sense of musical spontaneity that belongs here. This record of off-beat classical guitar music is highly refreshing and relaxing.

CONCERTO FOR TWO OBOES, TWO TRUMPETS AND TWO ORCHESTRAS

If you like the cute idea of two oboes pitted against two trumpets, this concerto is for you. Otherwise, steer clear.

Bologna Instrument Ensemble	MUSIC GUILD (S) 130

The playing is spirited, but unimpressive.

Vaughan Williams, Ralph (1872-1958)

Born in Down Ampney, England, Vaughan Williams was educated at Cambridge. He studied with Parry and Stanford and studied in Berlin with Max Bruch. He held rather few official appointments, but he conducted the Bach Choir between 1920 and 1926, and he became president of the English Folk Dance and Song Society in 1932.

PLACE AND ACHIEVEMENT Vaughan Williams was a staunch upholder of the classical tradition. Like Bartok, he was tremendously interested in folk song. His range of expression was remarkable: brutal violence, mystic serenity (as with Bartok, often in the same piece), and above all a sense of uncompromising honesty. Though Vaughan Williams is not much in vogue today, there is every chance he will be regarded as one of the distinguished composers of this century.

Vaughan Williams wrote difficult music, the appreciation of which increases with repeated hearing. Surprisingly archaic, yet paradoxically surprisingly modern, Vaughan Williams was unquestionably a master.

THE ESSENTIAL VAUGHAN WILLIAMS

ORCHESTRAL MUSIC: *Fantasia on a Theme by Thomas Tallis, for Double String Orchestra; A London Symphony; A Pastoral Symphony; Symphony No. 4 in F Minor; Symphony No. 6, in E Minor; Symphony No. 7, "Sinfonia Antartica"; Symphony No. 8; Symphony No. 9.*

OTHER WORKS

ORCHESTRAL MUSIC: *A Sea Symphony; Symphony No. 5, in D; Symphony No. 7; The Lark Ascending, for Violin and Orchestra; Concerto Accademico, for Violin and Orchestra; Concerto for Oboe and Strings; Serenade to Music.*

OPERAS: *Hugh the Drover; Sir John in Love; Riders to the Sea; The Pilgrim's Progress.*

MASQUE: *Job.*

CHURCH MUSIC: *Mass in G Minor.*

ORATORIO: *Sancta Givitas.*

SONGS: *On Wenlock Edge, Cycle for Tenor, String Quartet, and Piano.*

FANTASIA ON A THEME BY THOMAS TALLIS;
FIVE VARIANTS OF "DIVES AND LAZARUS";
FANTASIA ON "GREENSLEEVES";
FLOS CAMPI, FOR VIOLA, SMALL ORCHESTRA,
AND WORDLESS CHOIR

This is a choice collection of works by Vaughan Williams. The noble *Tallis Fantasia* and the evocative, affectionate *Greensleeves Fantasia* are both first-rate pieces. *Flos Campi*, an exotic, even sensual composition, is based on the Biblical *Song of Songs*.

* * * LENTZ, ABRAVANEL	*University of Utah* *Chamber Choir* *Utah Symphony Orch.*	VANGUARD CARDINAL (S) VCS 10025

Abravanel captures that elusive romantic, Vaughan Williams, in an unsentimental yet extremely moving rendition. The sound is very fine indeed, especially in the difficult-to-record *Tallis Variations* where a solo string quartet is used against the background of a large string orchestra. *Stereo Review* comments: "Performance: fine; recording: very good; stereo quality: first-rate."

FANTASIA ON "GREENSLEEVES" (1934)

The *Greensleeves Fantasia* has a cool beauty hard to resist. This charming little piece is a by-product of Vaughan Williams' opera *Sir John in Love* which is based loosely on Shakespeare's *Merry Wives of Windsor*.

* * BOULT	*Philharmonic Promenade* *Orch.*	VANGUARD (M) 1093 [English Folk Song Suite; Tallis Fantasy; Norfolk Rhapsody]

Here is bucolic English playing, appropriate for the work.

FANTASIA ON A THEME BY TALLIS

This truly first-rate music is the best introduction to Vaughan Williams. Thomas Tallis was probably born in 1505; he rose to be a Gentleman of the Chapel Royal under Henry VIII.

* * BOULT	*Vienna State* *Opera Orch.*	WESTMINSTER (M) 18928 (S) 14111 [English Folk Song Suite; Greensleeves Fantasia]

Here is dedicated playing by a noted interpreter of Vaughan Williams. The soloists of the second orchestra play beautifully; the central climax of the music, which is overwhelming, is handled well here.

SYMPHONY NO. 2, "LONDON"

One of the best of the symphonies, the *Second* is very ambitious program music. The composer tries to capture the "soul of a city." Vaughan Williams wrote: "The title might be called 'A symphony by a Londoner.' That is to say, various sights and sounds of London may have influenced the composer, but it would not be helpful to describe these. The work must succeed or fail as music, and in no other way. Therefore, if the hearers recognize a few suggestions of . . . Westminster chimes, or the lavender cry, these must be treated as accidents and not essentials of the music."

* * BARBIROLLI   *Halle Orch.*   VANGUARD   (S)   134

Barbirolli, very much at home in this music, offers a loving treatment. The sound is fair.

SYMPHONY NO. 8 IN D MINOR

The *Eighth Symphony* was written when the composer was in his eighties; yet it sounds utterly fresh and exciting.

* * * BARBIROLLI   *Halle Orch.*   VANGUARD EVERYMAN
                                                      SRV (M) 184
                                                      SRV (S) 184 SD
                                              [Elgar, "Enigma" Varia-
                                              tions]

This is a superb disc. Sir John Barbirolli has come up with two performances that will be studied by conductors for years to come. The sound is pleasant. [The Elgar is Victorian English writing at its best. Barbirolli is sweeping and grand.]

SYMPHONY NO. 9 IN E MINOR (1958)

The *Ninth* is one of the more tedious symphonies of this English composer; nevertheless, the *Ninth* is still impressive.

* BOULT   *London Philharmonic*   EVEREST   (M)   6006
                                                      (S)   3006

Boult provides competent playing. The sound is fair.

Vecchi, Orazio (1550-1605)

Vecchi's chief claim to fame is that, in the late Renaissance, he developed a new form called "Madrigal comedy." "Madrigal comedy" apparently included rustic scenes, imitative animal noises, and other quaint effects.

MADRIGALS: IL CONVITO MUSICALE

In *Festina*, his madrigal comedy, Vecchi told his listeners: "Observe this music of mine, enjoy it truly, sing cheerfully, and live happily!" God rest his soul for these sentiments, but the music is unfortunately hard to enjoy.

GIANI	*Nuovo Madrigaletto Italiano*	TURNABOUT	(M) 4067
			(S) 34067
		[Banchieri, Festina nella sera]	

Except for keen students of music history, this record is of little interest. The music is dull, and coyly sung.

Vejvanovsky, Pavel *(c. 1640-1693)*

Vejvanovsky was probably born in Hukvaldy, Bohemia; he entered the service of the Bishop of Kromeritz about 1664. Vejvanovsky was a successful musician, enjoying comfort and prosperity. He even married a burgomaster's daughter—quite an achievement for a lowly musician.

These days, every buff has his favorite "absolutely-unknown-composer." Vejvanovsky, the seventeenth-century Bohemian field trumpeter, is the pet of my friends Robert Braggalini and Lloyd Moss who hold forth at radio station WQXR in New York City. Some afternoons, it seems that Vejvanovsky has taken over the station.

WORKS FOR TRUMPETS, ORGAN AND ORCHESTRA

This music includes rousing outdoor ceremonial music, lovely fanfares for trumpet trios, and a variety of other works.

* * * PESEK	*Members of the Prague Wind Ensemble and The Prague Symphony Orch.*	CROSSROADS	(S) 22160034 (M) 22160033

The works are brilliantly and affectionately played. The stereo is first-rate.

Verdi, Giuseppe *(1813-1901)*

Verdi tried to enter the Milan Conservatory, but the directors rejected his application on the grounds that he had no talent. Rebuffed, Verdi studied with private teachers. In 1839, La Scala gave his first opera, *Oberto,* which was such a success that the Opera House asked him to write a second opera. The new work failed, but the one that followed it, *Nabucco,* performed in 1842, was such a triumph that Verdi was famous. In 1851, he wrote the first of his acknowledged masterpieces—*Rigoletto.* He followed *Rigoletto* with *La Traviata* and *Il Trovatore.* After *Aida,* he took a sixteen-year leave from opera composing. When he returned, it was to reveal a more profound nature in his operatic writing with *Otello* and *Falstaff.* He died following a paralytic stroke, and was given a state funeral.

PLACE AND ACHIEVEMENT   Forty years ago, the sophisticated music lover smiled at the suggestion that Verdi was a supremely great composer. His late and less popular masterpieces *Otello* and *Falstaff* were admired, but *Rigoletto, La Traviata, Il Trovatore,* and *Aida* were dismissed as "organgrinder hurdy-gurdy music." Today, due to the efforts of such champions as the writer Franz Werfel, Verdi's place in the sun has never stood higher.

He was a tough, straightforward peasant, and his music is blessed with a minimum of frills. Common sense breathes in his pages of genius. He developed his gifts stubbornly, grimly, moving from crude, noisy apprentice pieces to a row of blazing masterpieces that have no equal in the annuals of opera. Besides his divine gift of melody, there is a special, very Latin quality to Verdi, that Franz Werfel has astutely sketched: "The tingling agility of Rossini, the divinely gentle melancholy of Bellini, the sensually ecstatic melodiousness of Donizetti gradually faded into the shadows of the past. Quite beyond the purely musical values, suddenly something new struck a surprising chord: energy and angry passion. Roughness—"*Ruvidezza,*" the Italians call it. Hidden under this *ruvidezza,* a grindling, an underground rumbling which produced the amazing effect known to Italy under the apt name of *furore.*"

THE ESSENTIAL VERDI
OPERAS: *Rigoletto; Il Trovatore; La Traviata; Aida; Otello; Falstaff; Un Ballo in Maschera; La Forza del Destino; Don Carlos.*
CHORAL MUSIC: *Requiem Mass.*

OTHER WORKS

OPERAS: *Nabucco; I Lombardi; Ernani; Luisa Miller; I Vespri Siciliani; Simon Boccanegra.*

CHORAL MUSIC: *Quattro Pezzi Sacri.*

AIDA (Complete) (Sung in Italian)

First produced in 1871, Aida was commissioned by the Khedive of Egypt for the opening of the Italian Theatre, and not, as often stated on record liners, for the opening of the Suez Canal. This is one of Verdi's very greatest and most popular operas.

* * TEBALDI, STIGNANI, DEL MONACO, PROTTI, EREDE	*Radio Italiana Orch.*	3-RICHMOND	(M) 63002
* * NELLI, GUSTAVSON, TUCKER, VALDENGO, TOSCANINI	*NBC Symphony Orch.; Chorus*	3-VICTROLA VIC (S)	3611
CANIGLIA, STIGNANI,, GIGLI, BECHI, SERAFIN	*Rome Opera Orch.*	3-SERAPHIM	6016
CURTIS, VERNA, CORELLI, QUESTA	*Radio Italiana Orch.*	3-EVEREST/CETRA	(S) 401/3

Here the choice is simple: if you want marvelous singing—it's Tebaldi-Richmond all the way, with a strong cast and spirited conducting. When this set started its life on English Decca, Sackville-West called it "one of the best opera sets to come from Decca, and it is hard to see how a better cast could have been assembled." The mono sound is still highly listenable.

The Toscanini set offers surprisingly successful re-channeled stereo, nondescript singing (except for the arousing Radames of the young Richard Tucker)—and the fire, passion, drive, and insight of Maestro Toscanini.

Both Gigli and Caniglia sound very, very tired, and the conducting is hectic. (Basso Tancredi Pasero is terrific, though, if you collect bassos.)

AIDA (Excerpts)

* * TEBALDI, STIGNANI, DEL MONACO, PROTTI, EREDE	*Radio Italiana Orch.*	RICHMOND	23037
CORELLI, VERNA, PIRAZZINI, NERI, QUESTA	*Symphony Orch. and Chorus of Torino Della Radiotelevisione Italiana*	PICKWICK	(S) 4047

Richmond's is a single record containing excerpts of the notable Tebaldi set reviewed above.

The Pickwick abridgement is from the full-length set on Everest/Cetra. Maria Curtis Verna is a studied and stately Aida, but the real attraction here is the confident, ringing voice of Franco Corelli, the leading Italian tenor of our day. When you hear him knock off the aria *Celeste Aida,* you'll understand why Corelli can turn a hall of 3500 listeners to quivering jelly, and why he gets paid $8,000 a night. The synthetic "stereo" sound is rather metallic. This is a pleasant disc for Corelli buffs, but not for hi-fi enthusiasts.

UN BALLO IN MASCHERA (Complete)
(Sung in Italian)

Written in 1859, this is a masterpiece. In this period, Verdi's style is slowly changing: beautiful melody for its own sake gives way to musical characterization, and *bel canto* (smooth singing) is welded to emotional expression.

* * BARBIERI, CANIGLIA, RIBETTI, GIGLI, BECHI, SERAFIN	*Rome Opera House Orch.*	2-SERAPHIM	(M)	6026
LEIBOWITZ	*Paris Radio Orch., Chorus*	2-PERIOD	(M)	1082

The Gigli-Caniglia team is appealing, with the great tenor at the top of his explosive form. The rest of the cast is excellent, especially Bechi. The sound is what you would, or should, expect it to be, from a 1943 recording.

The Leibowitz set is serviceable, but French style and artists throw me off in Verdi. (It's sung in Italian, not French.)

LA BATTAGLIA DE LEGNANO (Sung in Italian)

Very early Verdi, written in 1849, *The Battle of Legnano,,* comes between *Macbeth* and *Luisa Miller,* and glorifies the struggle of the Milanese against the Emperor Barbarossa. At the premiere in Rome, there were demonstrations, emotional patriotic scenes, etc. It is weak Verdi, by his own standards; the opera is primarily of historical interest, but it also contains good blood-and-thunder arias and choruses.

* MANCINI, PANERAI, BERDINI, PREVITALI	*Radio Italiana Orch.*	EVEREST/CETRA	(S) 431/3

The erudite opera critic George Jellinek, in *Stereo Review,* comments on the "modernized" version of this set: "The performance is unsubtle, uninhibited, and sizzling—like the work itself."

DON CARLOS (Sung in Italian)

Set to a text by Schiller, *Don Carlos* was first performed at Paris in 1867, and in a revised version, in Milan in 1884. The opera is full of glorious music, and Verdi shows signs of reaching for the grandiose style of Meyerbeer, who had been a sensational success in Paris. The action and music are closely knit, naturally and profoundly.

* * * STELLA, NICOLAI,   *Rome Opera House Orch.*   3-SERAPHIM   (M) 6004
FILIPPESCHI, GOBBI,
CHRISTOFF, SANTINI

* * CANIGLIA,   *Radio Italiana Orch.*   4-EVEREST/CETRA
STIGNANI, PICCHI,   (S) 414/4
ROSSI-LEMINI

The Seraphim set is a plum: distinguished singers, and distinguished singing. The mono sound is highly hearable. Tito Gobbi and Boris Christoff together are something to hear. George Jellinek comments on this set, in *Stereo Review:* Tito Gobbi's sensitive art tops the vocal honor. . . . Antonietta Stella's Elizabeth is touchingly realized and sung with lovely tonal quality."

The Cetra set is not to be slighted. Caniglia sings with a vivid fire-eating style that has almost vanished from the boards. (She sometimes sings with shaky pitch, too.) Stignani is excellent. The indispensible Phililp Miller gives a survey of the male singers: "Rossi Lemeni is powerful, after the manner of Chaliapin. Neri's Grand Inquisitor is tremendous." The sound is acceptable.

ERNANI (Sung in Italian)

Ernani followed *I Lombardi*, in 1844. Here are more powerful unison choruses set to fiery words. This opera is lesser Verdi, but genius is genius.

* PENNO, TADDEI,   *Radio Italiana Orch.*   EVEREST/CETRA   (S) 448/3
MANCINI,
ROSSINI, PREVITALI

The old Cetra set is lusty and rough-and-ready. Mancini is a good soprano, with a voice reminiscent of the great Ponselle. Penno is a rousing tenor; Basso Taddei is admirable as always. The chorus is fine, but the sound is disappointing. *High Fidelity* comments: "Virtually every groove is riddled with distortion overload."

FALSTAFF (Sung in Italian)

Verdi's last opera (1893), is the happy smile with which the octogenarian composer bade farewell to the form. A stunning work, considered by many his very finest.

* * TADDEI, CARTERI,   *Radio Italiana Orch.*   EVEREST/CETRA (S) 416/3
    PAGLIUGHI, ROSSI

The reading of *Falstaff* by Toscanini (a 1950 radio broadcast preserved on high-priced Victor) must be regarded as near to definitive as we will ever get. But the performance led by Mario Rossi is first-rate, if not transcendental, and is blessed with much distinguished singing. Toscanini's buoyant lightness is hardly approached here, but the all-around, seasoned singing makes this one most worthwhile. The sound is dated but lively. Philip Miller commented on this one, way back when: "The Cetra recording still ranks among the best complete operas to come out of Italy, and in many ways it complements the Toscanini set."

Angel—are the ones to buy.

LA FORZA DEL DESTINO (THE FORCE OF DESTINY) (Sung in Italian)

First heard in St. Petersburg, in 1862, La Forza ranks just below the very best Verdi operas.

* CANIGLIA,   *Radio Italiana Orch.*   EVEREST/CETRA (S) 418/3
  TAGLIABUE,
  MASSINI, STIGNANI,
  PASERO, MARINUZZI

The women singers are honorable in this set, although Caniglia sometimes goes off-pitch in her free-wheeling style. The men are straightforward and not exactly exciting. As for sound, this set was by no means new when it came out ages ago on LP, and I don't mean the reconditioned "stereo LP."

Wait for the great Milanov set on Victor to drop down onto Victrola. With a new Price-Tucker set on the market, it's just a matter of time.

UN GIORNO DI REGNO (Sung in Italian)

Verdi's one early comedy, *King For A Day*, was composed in 1840, two years before *Nabucco* spread his fame throughout Italy. 1840 was also the year when Verdi's happy family life was smashed at one blow when he lost his young wife and both his little sons within a few months. This opera is smallish Verdi, but pleasant. He was not to try another comic opera until his great swan song, *Falstaff*.

* PAGLIUGHI, COZZI,	*Milan Radio-Tel.*	2-EVEREST/CETRA (S) 456
ONCINA, CAPECCHI,	*Italian Lyric Orch. and*	
CARLIN,	*Chorus*	
BRUSCANTINI,		
DALAMANGAS,		
SIMONETTO		

The Cetra cast here are all staunchly trained Italians, and you hear
it. The balance gets hectic sometimes. The 1951 sound is poor. *Stereo
Review:* "The performance is unpolished but spirited. . . . The poorish
sound will depress most opera lovers—except the specialist, who will want
to own a recording of Verdi's second opera, especially at an attractive
price."

I LOMBARDI ALLA PRIMA CROCIATA
(THE LOMBARDS IN THE FIRST CRUSADE)
(Sung in Italian)

This is an early Verdi work (1843), following his first success *Nabucco*,
when the patriotic crowd shouted "Viva Verdi" instead of the forbidden
"Viva l'Italia!" *I Lombardi* also had revolutionary overtones, and was
taken up by most Italian opera houses. This work is hardly top-drawer
Verdi, but there are some rousing arias and choruses.

BERTOCCI, PETRI,	EVEREST/CETRA (S) 454/3
PIRAZZINI, VITALE,	
WOLF-FERRARI	

On the Cetra set, Philip Miller commented (*Guide to Vocal LP Recordings,* Knopf, 1955): "The cast here brings together some excellent
voices, but the vocalism is uneven. . . . Vitale ranges from exquisite to
nasal. . . . The reproduction, marred by a hum, is fuller in the later sides
than in the first." Opera expert George Jellinek comments in *Stereo
Review,* on Everest's stereo surgery: "In sum, this is only an adequate
performance . . . fervent but unpolished. This reissue shows its age
badly, and the artificial stereo is no help."

LUISA MILLER (Sung in Italian)

This uneven, hot-blooded work followed *La Battaglia di Legnano* (1849).
Luisa Miller is based on a drama by Schiller (*Kabale und Liebe*).

| * VOLPI, KELSTON, | *Radio Italiana Orch.* | EVEREST/CETRA   (S) 433/3 |
| VAGHI, ROSSI | | |

This disc is primarily for vocal music lovers and appraisers. It features
a rich-voiced American soprano, Lucy Kelston—where is she?—as well as

the old pro Lauri-Volpi, who sang the leading tenor role in 1929, when
the Met gave this opera in New York with Rosa Ponselle. The rest of
the cast, and the sound, are only so-so.

NABUCCO *(Sung in Italian)*

Verdi's early smash, dating from 1842, is full of rousing music. The
famous chorus from this opera is heavenly, and this opera is well worth
owning.

* * MANCINI, GATTI, PREZIOSA, SILVERI, BINCI, CASSINELLI, GAGGI, FRANCARDI, PREVITALI	*Rome Radio-Tel. Italian Symphony Orch. and Chorus*	3-EVEREST/CETRA (S)	455

The old Cetra set is still vital, and will be enjoyed by anyone who
loves Verdi. The men singers are strong-voiced and assured. The women
have their ups and downs; Gabriella Gatti is excellent in a brief role, but
Mancini has many uncertain moments. All in all, the disc is recommendable, if only for the chance to hear this great early Verdi score.

A high-powered modern version is to be heard on expensive London,
with Suliotis and Gobbi.

OTELLO *(Complete) (Sung in Italian)*

Sixteen years passed between Verdi's *Aida* and his next opera, *Otello*,
although he composed the *Requiem* and some minor pieces in the mean-
time. *Otello* was produced in 1887, when Verdi was 74. This opera is
more than just an opera; it has been termed "the most complete realiza-
tion of character through the operatic medium." The libretto by Boito
is good poetry, and the libretto, as well as the music, veers more towards
the Wagnerian conception of music-drama. No oom-pah-pah Verdi, this.
That is, *Otello* is not made up of arias, duets, ensembles, etc. as is, for
example, *Traviata*. The long shadow of Wagner had fallen on the old
Italian master. The great *Otello* is the result, although still firmly in the
tradition, of Italian opera.

* * BROGGINI, CORSI, GUICHANDUT, MERCURIALI, TADDEI, SOLEY, STEFANONI, ALBERTINI, CONTE, CAPUANA	*Torino Radio-Tel. Italian Symphony Orch.*	3-EVEREST/CETRA (S)	460
* * TEBALDI, DEL MONACO, PROTTI, CORENA, EREDE	*St. Cecilia Accademia Orch. and Chorus*	3-RICHMOND	(M) 63004

There is much to admire on the Everest set conducted by Capuana. The conducting is hard-driving, despite some shaky moments in the "Kiss Motif" business in Act One; and Taddei is not exactly with the orchestra in the *Credo*. Carlo Guichandut's Otello is convincing (he has more or less built his career on this role); this is a dark, rough-edged voice, musical and intelligent, which rises well to Verdi's emotional storms. Cesy Broggini is a light-voiced Desdemona with a vibrato that sometimes disturbs me, but on the whole she is a sensitive singer.

The Richmond set here is maddening: a dream Desdemona in the lovely, gentle voice of Tebaldi, and a coarse, superficial Otello of Del Monaco. That wraps it up. The mono sound is good, but faded.

All Otellos are measured by the heady Toscanini set with Ramon Vinay; if it drops to Victrola, grab it.

OTELLO (Excerpts)

* * * MARTINELLI, TIBBETT, JEPSON, PELLETIER	*Metropolitan Opera Chorus and Orch.*	RCA VICTROLA VIC (M) 1365

This cast includes some of the best singers of the Metropolitan in the late 1930's. Martinelli sounds past his best days, but he is still a ringing Otello. The great Lawrence Tibbett's Iago was one of his famous roles, and this disc is worth having for his artistry alone, despite the fact that the sound is flat and frustrating.

RIGOLETTO (Complete) (Sung in Italian)

The text is based on a Victor Hugo play, *Le Roi s'Amuse,* first performed at Venice in 1851. Wild enthusiasm greeted the premiere, and this opera has been a sure-fire favorite ever since. This opera features sharp characterizations and radiant bel canto singing, which is often reduced, in scrappy performances, to barrel-organ Verdi.

* * GUEDEN, DEL MONACO, SIMIONATO, PROTTI, SIEPI, CORENA, EREDE	*St. Cecilias Accadimia* *Orch.*	3-RICHMOND	(M) 63005
* PAGLIUGHI, TADDEI, QUESTA		3-EVEREST/CETRA	(S) 407/3
	Patagonia Festival Orch. *and Chorus*	2-PERIOD-TE	(M) 1112

The Richmond set is good, honest singing, and a lot depends on whether you like the stand-up, let-'em-hear-it-in-the-balcony style of Del Monaco. For this singer, life begins at forte. The women are fresh and appealing. The sound is good mono.

The Cetra set, allegedly stereo, has the dependable Taddei, but little more.

The Period set cannot be taken seriously.

RIGOLETTO (Excerpts)

* TADDEI, TAGLIAVINI, *Torino Orch. and Chorus* PICKWICK PAGLIUGHI, NERI, QUESTA		(S) 4049

Here is an enjoyable, unremarkable abridgement from the complete version on the rugged Everest-Cetra set. The respected soloists were all famous a generation ago. The sound is metallic.

RIGOLETTO: ACT IV; UISA MILLER: OVERTURE, QUANDO LE SERE AL PLACIDO; I LOMBARDI: QUI, POSA IL FIANCO

* * * MILANOV, MERRIMAN, PEERCE, WARREN, MOSCONA, TOSCANINI	*NBC Symphony Orch.* *and Chorus*	VICTROLA VIC	(S) 1314

This disc is a splendid one-record souvenir of great days and great artists. Strongly recommended. *Stereo Review's* verdict: "Performance: exceptional; recording: mediocre; stereo quality: bad ersatz."

SIMON BOCCANEGRA

First performed in 1857, and revised in 1881, this opera, *Simon Boccanegra* has never enjoyed wide popularity, but it has much noble music.

* SILVERI, STELLA, PETRI, BERGONZI, PRADELLI	EVEREST/CETRA (S) 434/3

This set has all the virtues and vicissitudes of most of the historical lusty Cetra series. The Italians know how to sing, but their style is idiomatic; the singers are either raw-voiced and on the way up, or hoarsely on the way down. The sound is fair.

For a rousing, knocked-down performance, and great duet-singing, get the set on Angel with Gobbi-Christoff, and De los Angeles.

LA TRAVIATA

Just two months after the tremendous success of *Il Trovatore* in Rome, *La Traviata* had its 1853 premiere in Venice. This performance was a disaster—everything went wrong. It was revived the following year at the same theatre, this time with a brilliant cast, and ever since then, it has been one of the mainstays of opera companies throughout the world. The story here is based on the famous *Camille* drama of Alexandre Dumas the Younger.

* * CALLAS, ALBANESE, SANTINI	3-EVEREST/CETRA (S) 425/3

Cetra offers the early Maria Callas in the title role—the only *Traviata* she has recorded, by the way. She is good but uneven; the famous, much-admired Callas vocal line flashes out sometimes, but not always. Francesco Albanese is a strong tenor. The rest of the cast is competent, and the tempi are brisk. The sound is hard but passable.

NOTE: The much-heralded Toscanini set may soon be released from Victrola. If you want electric, tight-reined performance with singers who are much less relaxed and agreeable than in this Cetra set, watch for the Toscanini disc.

LA TRAVIATA (Excerpts)

* * CALLAS, ALBANESE, SANTINI	*Radio Italiana Orch.*	EVEREST (M) 6169 (S) 3169 [Ponchielli: Excerpts from Gioconda]
GUEDEN, WUNDERLICH, FISCHER-DIESKAU, BARTOLETTI	*Bavarian Radio Chorus and Symphony Orch.*	HELIODOR HS 25088

This single disc of excerpts is an important record for Callas fans. It is enjoyable throughout.

If you can get used to the idea of *Traviata* sung in German, the Heliodor is a striking disc. Hilde Gueden is warm and pensive, rather than flashingly dramatic, and she has a lovely cultured voice. Both Wunderlich and Fischer-Dieskau are virile-sounding, and seem entirely caught up in the opera. The conducting is very well-paced, with a continual sense of forward thrust. This disc is not the definitive *Traviata,* but a very satisfying job indeed. The sonics are first-class.

LA TRAVIATA (Selections)

* * * CALLAS, SANTINI	*Torino Symphony Orch.,* *Radio-Tel. Orch. and* *Chorus*	PICKWICK	(S) 4051

The Pickwick disc is a one-record selection from the old Cetra complete set that Everest has taken over. Callas is no less than superb—tigerish, intense, and always interesting. The sound, don't ask me how, is excellent (except for some massed choral moments) even though it has gone through several face-lifts. This record is one of a series of one-record opera highlights that Pickwick is merchandising, all based on the Cetra treasure-house. They can all be recommended for exciting, most Italianate performances.

IL TROVATORE (THE TROUBADOUR)

First heard in 1853, *The Troubadour* was for a long time the most popular Verdi opera. Today, people are somewhat condescending toward this work, dismissing it as barrel-organ Verdi, not to be compared with his later more exalted works such as *Otello* and *Falstaff.* But make no mistake, Verdi's unique genius shines powerfully in this story of passion and violence. Wonderful melodies tumble out one after the other, many with ringing high C's that have filled opera houses for generations.

VOLPI, MANCINI, TAGLIABUE, PIRAZZINI, PREVITALI	EVEREST/CETRA (S) 426/3

Slim pickings here: Mancini is nimble-voiced in the florid arias, and the work of veteran Lauri-Volpi is instructive and honorable. Not much else can be commended. The sound is acceptable.

OVERTURES AND PRELUDES

The Verdi overtures and orchestra preludes to his various operas are great favorites of the concert hall. Some of them, such as the preludes to *Traviata* and the overture *to La Forza del Destino,* are very fine in themselves.

* * * TOSCANINI	*NBC Symphony Orch.*	VICTROLA VIC	1248
		[Forza del Destino; Traviata, Acts 1, 3; Vespri Siciliani; Rossini, Overture]	
* * * TOSCANINI	*NBC Symphony Orch.*	VICTROLA VIC	(S) 1314
		[Luisa Miller; I Lombardi; Rigoletto]	
* * GAMBA	*London Symphony Orch.*	LONDON STS	(S) 15043
		[Traviata, Acts 1, 3; Vespri Siciliani]	
* * SOLTI		RICHMOND	(M) 19047
		[in collection]	
* * SOLTI		VICTROLA VIC	(S) 1119
		[in collection]	
* DORATI	*London Symphony Orch.*	PICKWICK	(S) 4043
* BARBIROLLI		VANGUARD	(S) 250
		[in collection]	
* GAVAZZENI		LONDON STS	15023
		[in collection]	
EREDE		RICHMOND	(M) 19048
		[in collection]	
PEDROTTI	*Czech Philharmonic Orch.*	PARLIAMENT	152
		[in collection]	

The Toscanini versions are classic, and take preference over all others. All the stereo entries are hearable.

Gamba and Solti are dramatic standouts.

Dorati and Barbirolli sound well, and the Gavazzeni record has much elan.

ARIAS

Great arias by Verdi are scattered on endless vocal recitals by celebrated artists.

* * MILANOV, PEERCE, WARREN, MOSCONA, CELLINI	*RCA Victor Orch., Shaw Chorus, Mitropoulos, Metropolitan Opera Orch.*	VICTROLA VIC	(S) 1336

```
* * FISCHER-DIESKAU,    Berlin Philharmonic Orch.    SERAPHIM        (S) 60014
    EREDE                                            [Arias from Falstaff, Il
                                                     Trovatore, Rigoletto, Don
                                                     Carlo, Un Ballo in Mas-
                                                     chera and I Vespri Siciliani]
```

The Victrola recording has first-rate singing and ensemble work from stars who just yesterday were the glories of the Metropolitan. The sound is not bad.

Impeccable singing and sharp characterization are heard from the distinguished German lieder singer Fischer-Dieskau—less convincing than the Verdi of native Italians but well worth having. The sound is good.

CHORUSES

Choruses from Verdi operas offer pleasant listening, good to dip into, if one's mood inclines. No low-price disc is available at the moment; best available is the Robert Shaw Chorale on high-priced Victor, or (with garlic) Serafin and the La Scala Chorus on Angel.

RELIGIOUS MUSIC

REQUIEM

This is a supreme Verdi work of 1874, and "his best opera," to quote more than one wag. The most full-blooded and glorious *Requiem* ever penned, it is a towering work of the nineteenth century.

```
* * VISHNEVSKAYA,      Moscow Philharmonic and   TURNABOUT TV    34210-11
    ISAKOVA,           State Academic Chorus
    IVANOVSKY,
    PETROV,
    MARKEVITCH

* * VISHNEVSKAYA,      Moscow Philharmonic and   PARLIAMENT     (S)   154
    ISAKOVA,           State Academic Chorus
    IVANOVSKY,
    PETROV,
    MARKEVITCH
```

Four dream soloists are needed for a recording; and all standards are set by the old, great Caniglia-Stignani-Gigli-Pinza quartet on Angel.

The present version is far from that exalted level, but it does offer good spirited singing. Some purists may quibble over a few nasal Slavic accents; but on the whole, it is highly hearable. Markevitch is very much the boss, with a tight, hard-driving performance in the Toscanini tradition. The sound is excellent on both sets of the same performance. For those bewildered by this duplication, the answer lies in the vagaries and opportunities presented by Russia having no copyright agreements with the West. *Stereo Review* went all out for this reading (the Parliament pressing), hearing more than I hear, "The turbulent and terrifying pages . . . come to life with a sweeping excitement no other recorded version can equal."

TE DEUM

Verdi's four *Sacred Pieces* (1898) form his very last work, or to be exact, group of works. He wrote these vital pages at the incredible age of 85. Here are pages that echo the great *Requiem* but are not quite in its class.

* TOSCANINI	*NBC Symphony Orch.,* *Shaw Chorus*	VICTROLA VIC (S) 1331 [Nabucco Excerpt; Hymn of the Nations]

Toscanini and the Shaw Chorale are all that one desires. [The *Nabucco* excerpts is lovely; the *Hymn of the Nations* is inconsequential.]

The sound is entirely hearable.

Victoria, Tomas Luis De *(ca. 1549-1611)*

Victoria was one of the most remarkable composers in the history of Spanish music. A friend of Palestrina who influenced him enormously, Victoria has sometimes been called "the Spanish Palestrina." A master of subtle and expressive polyphony, he confined himself to church music, and his choral writing sometimes reaches a highly polished beauty of style.

MOTETS & CHORAL WORKS

These sonorous works are a must for any lover of early seventeenth-century church music.

* * * STEVENS	*Ambrosian Consort and Singers*	DOVER	(M)	5271
			(S)	7271
		[Byrd; G. Gabriali; Morales]		
* LITTLE	*Montreal Bach Choir*	VOX	(50)	1090
		[Missa Alma]		
D'ALESSI	*Trevisco Catholic Chapel Choir*	PERIOD	(2)	765
DEISS	*St. Esprit Chevilly Schola*	MUSIC GUILD	(S)	143
		[Missa "Quarti"]		

Denis Stevens is not only an authority on seventeenth-century music, he also knows how to make singers and instrumentalists sound as if they are deeply interested in the music they are playing. This is an exceptionally fine performance. The sound is rich.

The Montreal Choir is well rehearsed, and they are accomplished singers. What is missing here is religious fervor. The *Stereo Record Guide* comments: "A fair disc, quite well but not stunningly recorded."

The chorus on the Period disc sounds too large and unwieldy. Or perhaps they were insufficiently rehearsed.

Music Guild provides dedicated singing, but somewhat filmy sound.

PSALMI

This is blissful music, for eight, nine, and twelve voices. If you enjoy Bach, you should give Victoria a try.

* *	*Blanchard Ensemble*	NONESUCH	(7)	1016

Unhurried serenity characterizes this performance and makes it appealing. The sound is warm.

Vieuxtemps, Henri *(1820-1881)*

A precocious violinist, Vieuxtemps was earning his living as a soloist at the age of 13. He traveled widely in Europe and in the United States, until a paralytic stroke in 1873 prevented him from playing and teaching. He wrote a good deal of violin music—dazzling display pieces which will probably survive as long as there are virtuosos to play it.

CONCERTO NO. 5 IN A FOR VIOLIN *(Opus 37)*

This is a lush and superficial piece, with expert writing fo rthe violin.

* KOGAN, *State Radio Orch.* MONTILLA (S) 2076
KONDRASHIN

Kogan gives a silky performance. The sound is acceptable.

Villa-Lobos, Heitor (1887-1959)

Villa-Lobos was born in Rio de Janeiro. Mainly self-taught, he lived in Paris from 1922 to 1926 on a fellowship from the Brazilian Government. In 1931, he became superintendent of Musical Education in schools in Rio de Janeiro. He was founder and director of the Orfeao de Professores, a teachers' training college. His compositions, which total over 2,000 pieces, show the influence of Brazilian folk song, and of Indian music which he studied in 1912.

PLACE AND ACHIEVEMENT   Villa-Lobos is a second-rate twentieth century composer, several steep rungs below Stravinsky and Bartok. It is too early to clearly assess all of his staggering output. The greatest composer South America has produced, Villa-Lobos had a vivid imagination, combined with a complete lack of self-consciousness; he composed with careless abandon. Villa-Lobos can be called the Thomas Wolfe of twentieth century music: he needed (but unlike Wolfe, never thought of employing) a firm editor. "I am Brazilian folk-lore," Villa-Lobos once remarked. Certainly no other composer ever made more extensive use of folk and popular songs.

His music has a direct appeal. Bravado and an exuberant verve are both his strengths and his weaknesses. This is an exotic composer whose music ranges enormously from simple harmony to a kind of do-it-yourself atonality.

ORCHESTRAL AND MISCELLANEOUS MUSIC: *Bachiana Brasileira No. 2; Bachiana Brasileira No. 5, for Soprano and Eight Cellos; Choros No. 6, Choros No. 10, for Orchestra and Mixed Chorus; Symphony No. 11.*

THE ESSENTIAL VILLA-LOBOS

ORCHESTRAL AND MISCELLANEOUS MUSIC: *Eleven Other Symphonies; Magdalena, Play with Music; Mandu Carara, Symphonic Poem or Ballet, for Two Pianos, Percussion, Large Chorus, and Children's Chorus; Choros No. 8, for Two Pianos and Orchestra; Choros No. 9 and 12, for Orchestra; Choros No. 11 and 13, for Piano and Orchestra; Choros No. 14 for Chorus, Band, and Orchestra; Amazonas; Concerto for Violin and Orchestra; Rudepoema, for Piano and Orchestra (also for Piano Solo); Concerto for Piano and Orchestra; Symphony No. 7, "Monthanhas do Brasil"; Madona, Symphonic Poem; Bachianas Brasileiras No. 1, 3, 4, 6, 7, 8, 9; Choros No. 1, 2, 3, 4, 7, for Various*

·

Chamber-Music Combinations; Nonetto; 15 String Quartets; Three Piano Trios; Cecilio Brasileiro; Alma Brasileira, (Choros No. 5); Prole do Bebe, for Piano; Songs; Two Cello Concertos, Harp Concerto.

CONCERTO FOR HARMONICA

John Sebastian and Larry Adler have raised the lowly harmonica to unheard-of heights. A number of modern composers have been so intrigued with their art they have written works especially for them; among these composers are Vaughan Williams, Darius Milhaud and Alan Hovhaness. This Villa-Lobos concerto is dedicated to John Sebastian.

* SEBASTIAN, SCHWIEGER	*Stuttgart Radio Symphony Orch.*	HELIODOR	(M) 25064 (S) 25064
		[Tcherepnin, Concerto for Harmonia]	

This is a slight work, and so is the Tcherepnin; but Sebastian plays with a refinement that is remarkable.

BACHIANAS BRASILEIRAS NO. 6; QUINTETTE EN FORME DE CHOROS

Villa-Lobos adored Bach. *Bachianas Brasileiras* can only be freely translated as "Bachian Brazilian Spirit." These compositions are not imitations of Bach, but rather the universal spirit of Bach transmuted into Brazilian idiom. *No. 6* is a duet for flute and bassoon which I find only mildly interesting.

The *Quintet* is far more exciting. Originally, the *choros* was a kind of Brazilian street dance. Villa-Lobos borrows its free, improvisatory feeling. The composer substitutes an English horn for the French horn used in the traditional woodwind ensemble; the result is a lush coloration that Villa-Lobos exploits to the hilt.

*	*New York Woodwind Quintet*	NONESUCH H	(S) 71030
		[Glazounov, Concerto for Saxophone; Ibert, Concertino da Camara]	

Baron and Garfield give very capable performances in the *Bachianas*. The wind playing in the *Quintet*, too, is excellent. The sound is good.

BACHIANAS BRASILIERAS NO. 1 FOR 8 CELLI; (1930) UIRAPURU

In the "Modinha" section of the *Bachianas No. 1,* eight cellos make a rich instrumental orchestra. This music is powerful.

Uirapuru, subtitled *A Symphonic Poem,* is one of the Brazilian composer's more important scores. This is early Villa-Lobos composed in 1917, but revised 31 years later. The work is a musical impression of a trip the composer took into the Brazilian interior, picturesque and bizarre. It is a gorgeous score.

| * * STOKOWSKI | *New York Stadium Orch.* | EVEREST | (M) 6016 |
| | | | (S) 3016 |

[Prokofiev, Cinderella Ballet Music]

Stokowski is in his element; the music is vividly played. The sound is effective. Arthur Cohn: "Stokowski is the ideal conductor for this score.

BACHIANAS BRASILIERAS NO. 3 (1938)

Here is more Brazil than Bach — rather picturesque solo piano with orchestral accompaniment.

| BLUMENTAL, TOFFOLO | *Trieste Philharmonic* | Vox | (M) 10070 |

The playing is hectic; so is the nasal recording.

BACHIANAS BRASILIERAS NO. 5, FOR SOPRANO AND EIGHT CELLI (1938-1945)

This is *the* celebrated *Bachianas,* with the haunting, exquisite melody.

| RENZI, SURINACH | *Chamber Ensemble* | HELIODOR | (S) 25037 |

This pedestrian reading will not do. Get the luscious version with De los Angeles on expensive Angel Records, or the old, unforgettably classic performance by Sayao on Columbia.

FANTASIA CONCERTANTE FOR ORCHESTRA OF CELLOS

Villa-Lobos's devotion to the cello dates back to his youth when he played that instrument in the cinemas of Rio. Here is a haunting slow movement, as well as bemusing sounds for 32 cellos; it is an impressive work.

* VILLA-LOBOS   *The Violincello Society*   EVEREST   (M) 6024
                                                        (S) 3024
[Bach Villa-Lobos; Preludes
and Fugues from The Well-
Tempered Clavier, tran-
scribed for orchestra of
cellos]

The playing is not at all impressive, considering that practically the foremost names of the Violincello Society are here, including the Juilliard Quartet's Claus Adam and Bernard Greenhouse. Sloppy intonations are heard, particularly in the high tessitura. [The Bach transcription is more or less what one would expect it to be — little more than an interesting curiosity.] The recording quality is all right.

Viotti, Giovanni Battista (1755-1824)

Viotti, who had a great reputation as a violinist, directed the Paris Opera from 1819 to 1822. He wrote 29 concertos whose first-movement forms were studied with interest by Mozart and Beethoven.

VIOLIN CONCERTO NO. 22 IN A MINOR

During the first half of the 19th century, the concertos of Spohr and Viotti were the staple fare of the concert violinist. However, *No. 22* is the only one of Viotti's works that is still played. For more than a century, *No. 22* has been used as a test piece at many conservatories, and many an aspiring violinist has had to sweat through it before being granted his *diplome*. This charming work has now vanished from the concert stage. One explanation for this, as given to me by a string player, is that every violinist hates to be reminded of his early, painful struggles with the piece.

* * LAUTENBACHER, GALLING, BUENTE	*Berlin Symphony Orchestra and Concerto for Piano, Violin, and Strings in A Major*	TURNABOUT (M/S) 34229

The cultured Susanne Lautenbacher provides solid, intelligent playing. In the double concerto, pianist Martin Galling is beautifully attuned to her conception. The sound is acceptable.

Vitali, Tommaso Antonio *(ca. 1665-?)*

Vitali, born in Bologna, was the son of the more famous Giovanni Vitali, who was also a violinist and composer. Tommaso Vitali entered the service of the Duke of Modena and became widely known in his time as a violinist and teacher.

CHACONNE FOR VIOLIN

This much-edited, much-truncated piece was attributed to Vitali by the great violinist Ferdinand David. It is a lovely set of variations, a monument of the baroque period. This is Vitali's most famous work.

* * TOMASOW	VANGUARD	(S)	197
* * SZERYNG	EVEREST	(M)	6154
		(S)	3154
* D. OISTRAKH, OBORIN	MONTILLA	(M)	2042

Tomasow is poised and most appealing on a first-rate disc of Baroque violin music.

Szeryng gives an assured, graceful interpretation. This is also a worthwhile disc.

The Oistrakh disc is marred by indifferent sound.

Vivaldi, Antonio (ca. 1675-1741)

Vivaldi was born in Venice. He became a pupil of his father Giovanni Battista Vivaldi and a pupil of Legrenzi. Composer and violinist, he was ordained a priest in 1703. From 1704, and for many years thereafter, he worked in the service of the Conservatorio dell'Ospedale della Pieta, a music school for girls in Venice; became a violin teacher in 1709, and maestro de'concerto in 1716. He was one of the most prolific composers of his time.

PLACE AND ACHIEVEMENT   Vivaldi's biography is in his music; we know little else about him, and nothing of his extensive travels. "The Red Priest," as he was called affectionately — an allusion to the color of his hair — was a humble man, extremely busy with his choir and his orchestra. A celebrated violinist, he was possessed by an uncontrollable passion to compose music. Nearly 500 of his concertos have been catalogued; there are many more. Vivaldi also wrote some 40 operas, and 100 religious works.

Until the end of World War II, the music of Vivaldi was hardly known. Unplayed for 200 years, his fame survived only because of Bach's admiration of the Venetian's music. It was Vivaldi who introduced the concerto form; and Bach at Wiemar, when twenty-five became acquainted with the form.

Much of Vivaldi sounds like Bach in a genial mood, and yet without the solid substance of Bach. This, perhaps, is why Vivaldi's music palls with repeated hearing. With the exception of some extremely moving choral pieces, his works are characterized by an evenness, a bland dexterity that leaves our intelligence unrewarded. Vivaldi's music, for the most part, is undemanding, and we tend to grow impatient with it. Yet today, despite this shortcoming, Vivaldi is one of the splendors of our baroque heritage. His works are back in the concert hall, and the number of his compositions in the record catalogues are legion. Those who discover him for the first time will be struck by his musical felicity, his bold harmonies, and his dramatic effects.

THE ESSENTIAL VIVALDI

CONCERTOS: *Opus 3, L'Estro Armonico; Opus 10, Flute Concertos; Opus 8, The Contest of Music and Fancy* (which includes the separately played "The Four Seasons"). [Beyond this, everyone has his favorite Vivaldi concerto, and it becomes a matter of personal taste.]

VOCAL WORKS: *Gloria; Psalm III (Beatus Virgine); Juditha Triumphans (Oratorio); Magnificat in E.*

OTHER WORKS

Vivaldi was hugely prolific in almost all forms popular in his time: concertos, chamber music, church music, opera, etc.

CONCERTOS: Vivaldi is largely remembered for his vivacious, rather unpretentious concertos, the best of them are delightful; the others can be wearisome.

L'ESTRO ARMONICO (Opus 3)

Vivaldi was an incredibly fast writer; it was said that he could compose music faster than the copyists could copy it out. This points up the problem of listening to three hours of concertos that admittedly are like peas in a pod. Vivaldi's music contains few of Mozart's surprises or inventions; Vivaldi is too often predictable.

Here is Vivaldi's first and most famous set of twelve concertos — "Musical Fancy," roughly translated.

* * TOMASOW, BOSKOWSKI, ROSSI	*Vienna State Opera Chamber Orch.*	3-VANGUARD	(S) 143/5
* BARCHET, REINHARDT	*Stuttgart Pro Musica String Orch.*	3-Vox	(M) VBX-20

The Vienna players are more assured and effective. The sound is acceptable.

Barchet is too stiff as a soloist. The sound is presentable.

CIMENTO DELL'ARMONIA D DELL'INVENZIONE (Opus 8)

Beauty mingles too freely with trivia in this "Contest of Music and Fancy," or "The Rivalry between Technique and Inspiration." It is said that Vivaldi never expected his hastily written music to be published along with his more thoughtful efforts, but the music was.

* BARCHET, ELSNER, REINHARDT	*Stuttgart Pro Musica String Orch.*	3-Vox VBX	(M) 32

Vox offers correct playing by Barchet and Reinhardt. The sound is decent.

CONCERTO IN D MINOR FOR VIOLA D'AMORE, GUITAR AND ORCHESTRA

This is an ingratiating piece, with melodious, soothing pages.

* LEMMEN, PROBST, RISTENPART	Chamber Orch. of the Saar	NONESUCH	H-71104 [Concertos: in E Minor for Bassoon; in G Minor for 2 Celli; In B Flat for Oboe and Violin; in A for Strings]

Here is solid, blameless playing, with lovely sounds from the viola d'amore. The disc is agreeably recorded.

SIX CONCERTI FOR FLUTE, STRINGS, AND CONTINUO (Opus 10)

Even though the baroque concerto was already in a highly advanced stage, these were the first flute concertos ever published (1730) — and some of the most satisfying flute music ever written.

* * EUSTACHE, BECKENSTEINER, DOUATTE	Collegium Musicum of Paris	NONESUCH	(S) 71042

Jean-Pierre Eustache is an elegant and spirited flute player, and the men of Paris perform with verve and style. The sound is all one could desire.

CONCERTOS FOR STRINGS

These are six pleasant Vivaldi concertos; one in D minor is nicknamed "Senza Cantin" because the soloist is called upon to play the entire piece without resource to the E string.

* * GOBERMAN	New York Sinfonietta	ODYSSEY	(S) 32160053

The playing is vivacious. The 1962 sound is acceptable and rather dry.

LUTE AND MANDOLIN CONCERTI

Here is pleasing music. Listeners will be struck by the similarity of the opening theme to that of Bach's Third Brandenburg Concerto. The specific works are the Concerto in C Major for Mandolin and String Orchestra, Concerto in G Major for Two Mandolins and String Orchestra, Concerto in D Major for Lute, Violins and Figured Bass, and Trio in G Minor for Violin, Lute and Figured Bass. The lute was a great favorite during the Renaissance, enormously popular as a home instrument, rather like the piano in later years. Today, French violin-makers are still called *luthiers*. Mandolin making was an Italian specialty and the mandolin was the instrument of Neopolitan street airs.

* FAERBER	*Wuerttemberg Chamber Orch.*	TURNABOUT TV	(S) 34153

The graceful sounds are gracefully played by the Wuerttembergers.

FOUR SEASONS (Opus 8, No. 1-4)

One of Vivaldi's masterpieces and easily his most popular composition *The Four Seasons* is a striking work, paraphrasing four descriptive sonnets in violin concerto form. The music, immediately attractive, epitomizes the felicity of baroque string music.

* * * BRONNE, MONOSOFF, KWALWASSER, KOUTZEN, GOBERMAN	*New York Sinfonietta*	ODYSSEY	(M) 3216 0131 (S) 3216 0132
* * WARCHAL	*Slovak Orch.*	CROSSROADS	(M) 22 16 0083 (S) 22 16 0084
* * BARCHET, MUENCHINGER	*Stuttgart Chamber Orch.*	RICHMOND	19056
* FERRARI, COURAUD	*Stuttgart Chamber Orch.*	MERCURY	(M) 14041 (S) 18041
* LAUTENBACHER, FAERBER	*Wuerttemberg Chamber Orch.*	TURNABOUT	(M) 4040 (S) 34040
* BARCHET, TILEGANT	*Southwest German Chamber Orch.*	NONESUCH	(M) 1070 (S) 71070
ALES, DOUATTE	*Collegium Musicum, Paris*	PERIOD SHO (St-2) 309 [Vivaldi, 2-Trumpet Concerto]	

We are presented with an embarrassment of riches in the low-priced field. Leading a formidable field is the late Max Goberman's superbly styled performance. Martin Bookspan, in *Stereo Review's* annual updating of "The Basic Repertory," calls this record the best of any available performance, bar none. Here is extraordinary ensemble playing delivered with an *elan* and inspiration that can hardly be bettered. The sound is excellent.

The Czech recording on Crossroads is first rate.

Muenchinger is authoritative — a memorable disc.

The Stuttgart players are splendid as well. These four are incredibly good choices!
The other versions, while quite pleasant, do not compare with the above.

OBOE CONCERTO IN C MAJOR; BASSOON CONCERTO IN A MINOR; CONCERTO FOR OBOE AND BASSOON IN G MAJOR; CONCERTO FOR TWO OBOES AND TWO CLARINETS IN C MAJOR

Vivaldi wrote 38 concertos for the bassoon; the *A Minor* is one of the best of this bewildering array. The other concertos are quite entertaining, which is exactly what they were meant to be.

* CAROLDI, BIANCHI, SANTI	*GLI Accademici Di Milano*	Vox PL	(M) 10740 (S) 510740

The disc is nicely played and fairly well recorded.

THREE CONCERTOS FOR VIOLIN D'AMORE; TWO CONCERTOS FOR MANDOLIN

* * GOBERMAN	*New York Sinfonietta*	ODYSSEY	(M) 3216 0131 (S) 3216 0138

Here is one of the remarkable contributions of Max Goberman, who set out to record Vivaldi *complet*. He had gotten through 17 works before his death in 1962. His readings have been widely respected by musicians as high-water marks of baroque recording. This is a most welcome disc, with good sound.

CONCERTOS FOR WOODWINDS AND STRING ORCHESTRA: FOR FLUTE, BASSOON, AND STRINGS, IN G MINOR ("LA NOTTE"); FOR BASSOON AND STRINGS, IN E-FLAT; FOR PICCOLO AND STRINGS, IN A MINOR; FOR TWO OBOES, TWO CLARINETS, AND STRINGS, IN C

* * GOBERMAN	*New York Sinfonietta*	ODYSSEY	(M) 3216 0011 (S) 3216 0012

Another of Goberman's fine recordings. See comments on the listing immediately above.

CONCERTOS FOR PICCOLO AND ORCHESTRA IN A MINOR: FOR PICCOLO AND ORCHESTRA, IN C; FOR VIOLIN AND ORCHESTRA IN A MINOR; FOR TWO VIOLINS AND ORCHESTRA, IN D MINOR; FOR THREE VIOLINS AND ORCHESTRA, IN F

These piccolo pieces are harmless pleasantries and little more.

RISTENPART   *Chamber Orch. of the Saar* NONESUCH   (M) H1022
   (S) H71022

These works are satisfactorily played but hardly worth-while. Skip this one.

CONCERTOS FOR FLUTE, OBOE, VIOLIN, AND CONTINUO, IN G MINOR: FOR FLUTE, OBOE, VIOLIN, AND CONTINUO, IN F; FOR FLUTE, OBOE AND CONTINUO, IN G MINOR; FOR FLUTE, VIOLIN, CELLO, AND CONTINUO, IN G MINOR; FOR FLUTE, OBOE, VIOLIN, BASSOON, AND CONTINUO, IN C

These are not concertos but rather small pieces for two to four instruments and continuo. They are smallish Vivaldi, but pleasant.

* MUNCLINGER   *Ars Rediviva Ensemble*   CROSSROADS (M) 22 16 0045
   (S) 22 16 0046

The works are very well played indeed, with a firm, sensible approach. The sound is good.

COLLECTIONS As with Telemann, too much of Vivaldi is too much hit and miss, up and down. The quip that Vivaldi wrote not 600 concertos but the same concerto 600 times is deadly accurate. An excellent idea for the collector, therefore, is to buy a Baroque sampler, or an anthology of various musical styles. Such a collection will provide contrast and avoid surfeit. The following albums, with attractive themes and outstanding Vivaldi choices, are warmly recommended.

THE ITALIAN BAROQUE: VIVALDI, CELLO CONCERTO IN G MAJOR; CORELLI, CONCERTO GROSSO (Opus 6, NO. 1); PERGOLESI, CONCERTINO II IN G MAJOR; CIMAROSA, CONCERTO FOR TWO FLUTES IN G MAJOR

These are superb selections.

* * MAINARDI, NOCOLET, DEMMLER, MARKEVITCH, BAUMGARTNER	*Lucerne Festival Strings*	HELIODOR	HS 25033

The soloists are unbeatable. The sound is harmonious, but on the dark side.

VIRTUOSO WIND CONCERTOS: ALBINONI, CONCERTO IN D FOR OBOE AND ORCHESTRA (Opus 9, No. 4); FASCH, CONCERTO IN D FOR TRUMPET AND ORCHESTRA; C. STAMITZ, CONCERTO IN B-FLAT FOR CLARINETTE AND ORCHESTRA; TELEMANN, CONCERTO IN D FOR HORN AND ORCHESTRA; VIVALDI, CONCERTO IN A MINOR FOR FLUTE AND ORCHESTRA

* * ANDRE. NICOLET, WINSCHERMANN, KLEIN, PENZEL, MUELLER-BRUEHL	*Cologne Soloists Ensemble*	NONESUCH	H (S) 71148

Here is more unimpeachable solo work; flutist Nicolet is particularly warm and ingratiating. The conducting is vigorous. The sound is good.

SONATAS: VIVALDI, SONATA IN G MINOR; ALBINONI, SONATA IN A (Opus 6, No. 11); T. A. VITALI, CHACONNE IN G MINOR; TARTINI, SONATAS (Opus 1: No. 4, IN G and No. 10, in G MINOR "DIDONE ABBANDONATA"); MARCELLO, SONATA IN D (Opus 1, No. 1)

The Vivaldi work is warmhearted; and the rest of the compositions are first-rate, elegant baroque pieces. All the composers played on this disc were sure-handed composers for the violin; many were themselves violin virtuosos.

* * * TOMASOW, HEILLER   VANGUARD   SRV 197SD

Violinist Jan Tomasow has a poised sense of baroque style; he is fresh and unhurried, and his rich tone is never syrupy. This disc made a recent "Best of the Year" list of *High Fidelity,* who commented: "Less sinuous and caressing in the slow movements than some, he sings and soars nevertheless, and in the fast movements is tremendously brilliant."

THE SPLENDOR OF BRASS: TELEMANN, OVERTURE IN D FOR TRUMPET, OBOE AND STRINGS; VIVALDI, CONCERTO IN F FOR TWO HORNS AND STRINGS

* DOUATTE   *Collegium Musicum of*   NONESUCH   H (S) 71091
                   Paris

The French horn playing is on the quavering side, with an annoying vibrato. The conducting is stylish and brisk. The sound is agreeable.

ITALIAN BAROQUE TRUMPET CONCERTI: MANFREDINI, CONCERTO IN D FOR TWO TRUMPETS; VIVALDI, CONCERTO IN C FOR TWO TRUMPETS; TORELLI, TRUMPET CONCERTO IN D; ALBINONI, TRUMPET CONCERTO IN C

The baroque revival in our time has brought about new interest and enjoyment in the splendors of trumpet playing. Popular taste altered so much in the last 200 years, it is difficult for us to realize that in the late seventeenth and early eighteenth centuries the solo trumpet was one of the glories of concert music. Today, the baroque trumpet has again become familiar. Highpitched *"clarini"* trumpets are taken out of museums and dusted off, and virtuoso trumpeters are courted by new *padronas* — the record companies.

* * FAERBER, KEHR   *Wuerttemberg Chamber*   TURNABOUT   TV 4057
                       Orch.   TV 34057S
                       Mainz Chamber Orch.   [Various Trumpeters]

The Turnabout collection offers good concertos played by various sturdy trumpeters — all with a sure grasp of the festive, outdoor nature of that instrument. The disc is well recorded.

VOCAL MUSIC By no means profound, Vivaldi's best efforts in this genre are nevertheless highly enjoyable, and stand as works of great musical dignity.

GLORIA IN D

The *Gloria* is one of the most appealing vocal pieces ever written. The work, for two soprano solos, chorus, and orchestra, was written for the girl's orphanage in Venice where Vivaldi was the music-master.

* * PIERRE, CHAMONIN, COLLARD, CAILLAT	*Paillard Orch. and Chorus*	MUSIC GUILD [Kyrie; Lauda]	(S) 128
* * SAILER, BENCE, COURAUD	*Stuttgart Pro Musica Orch.*	TURNABOUT [Mozart, Exsultate]	(3) 4029

Both sets are quite good, but the Paillard has an innocence that I prefer to the more polished version from Stuttgart. [The Paillard disc is backed by two vigorous examples of the old Venetian double orchestra-and-chorus mode, and the recording balances these forces with ringing, antiphonal sound.]

[The stylish Stuttgart version, however, has the extra attraction of being coupled with Mozart's famous "Miniature concerto for soprano" — the lovely *Exsultate,* commissioned by the famous castrato singer Venanzio Rauzzini.]

LA FIDA NINFA (Sung in Italian)

Vivaldi wrote 38 operas, but none have blossomed anew as has so much of his string music. Upon hearing this painstaking opera, the listener will readily understand why. It consists of long dreary sections of *secco* recitatives, and unmoving arias — of interest to musicologists only.

* SOLOISTS, MONTEROSSE	*Chamber Orch., Members of the Opera, Milan*	Vox	DL BX 210 STDL BX 5210

The Vox set is haphazardly sung. The choral tone is diffused in reproduction.

JUDITHA TRIUMPHANS (Complete)
(Sung in Latin)

This is an undeniably effective oratorio. Written in 1716, it is based on the Apochryphal story of *Judith.* There are moments of real beauty, but also two hours of less than gripping music.

| ** ZEDDA | Orch. of the Angelicum Mailand, Chorus of the Philharmonic Academy of Rome | VICTROLA VIC/VICS-6016 |
| EPHRIKIAN | Scuola Veneziana | 3-PERIOD   1043 |

The Victrola set features agreeable singing and sound. The florid passages come through with style, and the tempos are convincing.

The Period album is quite inferior, and hardly adequate. Philip Miller (1955): "The recording balance is not altogether satisfactory. . . . The performance is in many ways excellent, if uneven."

BEATUS VIRGINE (Psalm 111)

This is a work of great dignity and moving passages, it makes one wonder why Vivaldi's concertos have been so much preferred to his vocal music.

| SOLOISTS, GRISHKAT | Chamber Choir of Stuttgart, Pro Musica Orch. | LYRICHORD   (M) 95 |

Here is a very good performance by the dependable Grishkat, although the somewhat foggy choral reproduction betrays its age. This record, if I am not in error, was treasured by Vivaldi lovers when it was on the Vox label, some 15 years ago.

Wagner, Richard *(1813-1883)*

Richard Wagner, originally Wilhelm Richard, was born in Leipzig. Quite possibly, he was the natural son of a Jewish actor named Ludwig Geyer. At school in Leipzig, Wagner acquired a profound interest in drama and in Beethoven's symphonies.

His first appointment was as chorus master at Wuerzburg in 1833. In 1835, he was appointed conductor at Magdeburg, where his opera *Das Liebesverbot* was unsuccessfully performed in 1836.

In 1839, Wagner arrived in Paris where he supported himself through journalism and by making arrangements of other composers' works. In 1842, he moved to Dresden where he became second conductor. There, *Rienzi* was performed in 1842; *Der Fliegende Hollaender,* in 1843; and *Tannhaeuser,* in 1845. Because of his activity in the Revolution of 1894, he was forced to leave Dresden.

His friendship with Liszt led to the production of *Lohengrin* at Weimar in 1850. In 1860, after more than ten years of exile spent mainly in Switzerland, Wagner was allowed to re-enter Germany. In 1864, he settled in Munich under the protection of Ludwig II of Bavaria, where *Tristan und Isolde* was produced in 1865. Opposition at court compelled him to leave Munich for Switzerland, but *Die Meistersinger* was nevertheless performed at Munich in 1868.

In spite of financial hardships, Wagner planned the construction of a festival theater for his operas at Bayreuth. The foundation stone was laid in 1872; and the theater opened in 1876 with the first performance of *Der Ring des Nibelungen.*

Wagner was married to Minna Planer, an actress, in 1836; in 1870, he married Cosima, the illegitimate daughter of Liszt and the former wife of the conductor Hans von Buelow, who was Wagner's friend and disciple.

PLACE AND ACHIEVEMENT The eclipse of Wagner, predicted every few years for more than a century, has never quite arrived. Though his music has enraged millions, the Wagner cult thrives as never before. No other composer has garnered the contempt of so many other composers; Debussy, Stravinsky and many others have dismissed Wagner as a colossal fraud.

And yet his music lives today stronger than ever. Long-playing records enable us to enjoy Wagner's music without suffering for five hours in the opera house.

Why are people still fascinated with this Germanic madness, these unendurably long ravings of a demented genius? Because Wagner was, and remains, a sorcerer. We submit to his pretentious librettos — which he wrote himself — his helmeted supermen, his absurd Rhinemaidens, and the clouds of opaque gas that seem to enshroud his music-dramas, because the music itself is so compelling. He was a master-builder, one of the most daring of composers. Though most of his works may be summed up as glorious failures, we endure pages that are banal or worse, because we know that later on rare beauty awaits us.

Wagner took it for granted that he was a great man with a message for the world. And he expected a luxurious life in return. Mozart raged at the idea of being a prince's servant, but did not know how to break out of the system; Beethoven broke out of it once and for all. Liszt went further, and assumed the stance of the poet at the piano. Richard Wagner went still further; he struck the posture of a superman, believed it himself, and then convinced the world he was right.

In sum, Wagner's music is a unique jungle that not all music lovers care to enter. Love sacred and love profane are his great themes; and sublime sex permeates his great pages. The world of music has never been the same since *Tristan und Isolde*.

THE ESSENTIAL WAGNER

OPERAS: *Tannhaeuser; Lohengrin; Tristan und Isolde; Die Meistersinger; The Ring of the Nibelungs (The Rhinegold, The Valkyrie, Siegfried, and The Twilight of the Gods); Parsifal.*
ORCHESTRAL MUSIC: *Siegfried Idyll; Overture to the Flying Dutchman.*

OTHER MAJOR WORKS

OPERAS: *Rienzi; The Flying Dutchman.*
ORCHESTRAL MUSIC: *A Faust Overture.*
SONGS: *Five Wesendonck Songs, for Voice and Orchestra.*

EINE FAUST-OVERTURE (1840)

This is a product of the twenty-six-year-old Wagner's salad days in Paris when he was fighting off both hunger and creditors in an attic on the Rue de la Tonnelliere. It is unimportant music today, but it anticipated many features of the style of Franz Liszt.

* * TOSCANINI	*NBC Symphony Orch.*	VICTROLA VIC (M) 1247 [Lohengrin, Preludes; Meistersinger, Preludes; Siegfried Idyll]
* HORENSTEIN	*Southwest German Radio Symphony Orch.*	2-VOX (S) 2029 [Liszt, Faust Symphony]

Toscanini's performance is vital. The sound is indifferent. Horenstein's version is quite dramatic, quite unexceptional.

DER FLIEGENDE HOLLAENDER (Excerpts)
(Sung in German)

The legend of the Flying Dutchman, doomed to sail the seas forever, provided the first powerful stimulus to Wagner's imagination.

* * KUPPER, WAGNER, HAEFLIGER, GREINDL, WINDGASSEN, METTERNICH, FRICSAY	*Berlin RIAS Symphony Orchestra and Choir*	HELIODOR	(S) 25070

In this disc, conductor Ferenc Fricsay makes us keenly aware how great a blow to music was his untimely death. His reading is exciting from beginning to end. The singers are good, except for an unsteady soprano. Greindl is excellent as *Daland;* Windgassen makes a large-sized *Erik*. The sound is decent.

GOETTERDAEMMERUNG (Excerpts: SIEGFRIED'S RHINE JOURNEY; FUNERAL MARCH; BRUENNHILDE'S IMMOLATION SCENE)

Wagner's most colossal achievement was the famous tetralogy *The Ring of the Nibelung* which includes four ponderous operas: *Das Rheingold, Die Walkuere, Siegfried,* and *Goetterdaemmerung (Death of the Gods).* At times, this is absolutely great music, yet as a whole it is unbelievably wearisome. Only the fanatical Wagnerian can listen to five hours of *Goetterdaemmerung* without longing to escape. Yet once caught in Wagner's spell, "The Old Rattlesnake" (as Nietzsche called Wagner) has a cold fascination that grips the listener.

* * FLAGSTAD, FURTWAENGLER	*Vienna Philharmonic Orch.*	SERAPHIM	(M) 60003

Except for Toscanini, Furtwaengler stood head and shoulders above every conductor of his time. His Wagner is a full-blooded conception that is almost ideal. (His *Rhine Journey* includes the Toscanini interpolation of the Siegfried-Bruennhilde duet.) Flagstad is at the top of her form, and her *Immolation Scene* has poise and majesty. Here rapport with Furtwaengler can only be called glowing. This record was made from pre-1950 discs; though the sound is decent, it is hardly up to today's standards. However, if you want to hear great classic Wagner of a generation ago, the record is worthwhile.

DIE MEISTERSINGER VON NUERNBERG (Complete)

This is in many ways the most engaging of Wagner's music-dramas, as he called his solemn operas. *Die Meistersinger's* humor and mellowness make this opera less boring than Wagner's more sepulchral utterances.

* * FRANTZ, ALDENHOF, LEMNITZ, UNGER, KEMPE	*Saxon State Orch. and Dresden State Opera Chorus*	5-Vox OPBX	(M)	142
* * SCHWARTZKOPF, HOPF, UNGER, KUNZ, EDELMANN, VON KARAJAN	*Chorus and Orchestra of the Bayreuth Festival,* 1951	5-Seraphim IE	(M)	6030
* * GUEDEN, TREPTOW, DERMOTA, SCHOEFFLER, DOENCH, EDELMANN, KNAPPERTSBUSCH	*Vienna State Opera Chorus, Vienna Philharmonic Orch.*	Richmond RS	(M)	65002

Of all the conductors of this complex score, only Kempe has managed to elicit all the subtle glories. This is a lyric interpretation; there is a singing, flowing quality about this reading that is hard to equal. The legendary Tiana Lemnitz stands out as *Eva,* though rather past her best years when this recording was made; yet she possessed such a fine musical intelligence that her vocal flaws do not matter. Her lovely, delicate *Eva* should be pondered by all students of the vocal art. Ferdinand Franzt is perhaps the best *Hans Sachs* on records. The sound, just passable, rather goes to pieces toward the end.

The Karajan performance is a live taping from the first postwar Bayreuth Festival, and offers a wonderful flow of melody and lyrical playing by the orchestra. The singing is not remarkable; Edelmann's *Hans Sachs* is superficial; Elizabeth Schwartzkopf sounds young and fresh-voiced, but not much more. Still, the presence of Karajan and clear sonics lend a charismatic quality.

Knappertsbusch's version, more solid and straightforward, builds towards a thrilling third act in a very impressive performance. Hilde Gueden stands out with a light girlish charm. Dermota's *David* is impeccable; Paul Schoeffler's *Sachs* is more than memorable: a deeply moving, deeply thought out interpretation. The rest of the cast is strong and dedicated. The sound is better than on the Vox set — entirely acceptable, and surprisingly good for a live performance of 1951.

TANNHAEUSER (Complete)

Wagner, the showman, is at his best here: trumpeters, off-stage choruses, the orgiastic Venusberg scene, the lot. Compared to some of Wagner's works, this opera is easy to hear, but is not of the caliber of such later triumphs as *Tristan* and *Meistersinger*.

BAEUMER, SCHECH, SEIDER, HEGER	*Munich State Opera*	4-Vox OPBX	(M)	143

This set is a sorry job: with ragged playing, indifferent singing, and poor sound dating from 1951.

TANNHAEUSER (Excerpts)

BAEUMER, SCHECH, SEIDER, HEGER	*Munich State Opera*	Vox	(M) 15140

This is a one-record selection from the set reviewed above.

PARSIFAL (Complete)

Wagner's last opera is perhaps the longest opera ever composed, painfully intolerable in the opera house. With good cause, *Parsifal* has been called "a combination of megalomania and senility." The play, written by himself, of course, is pure claptrap, a mishmash of Christianity and Buddhism — a mystic, "consecrational stage play," he called it, ironically, Wagner, an unrepentant anti-Semite, picked the best man he could get to conduct the premiere: Hermann Levi, a Jew.

MOEDL, WINDGASSEN, LONDON, UHDE, WEBER, KNAPPERTSBUSCH	*Chorus and Orchestra of the Bayreuth Festival,* 1951	5-Richmond RS	(M) 65001

This set is a historical testament to the Knappertsbusch era of the 1960's at Bayreuth. Knappertsbusch was one of the many conductors whose studio recordings rarely matched their gifted work in live performances. Nevertheless, this is a firm, convincing reading. Windgassen stands out with a full-bodied, moving portrait. The sound is quite acceptable.

TRISTAN UND ISOLDE (Excerpts)

Tristan is one of the greatest operas ever written. For devotees, the five-record complete *Tristan,* available only on high-priced discs, is not a bar too long; its interminable length will cause other listeners to despair. This is love music, from beginning to end; the music glows and flames with passion. The famous *Liebesnacht* is nothing less than a prolonged orgasm in sound — remarkable music, indeed.

* * * TRAUBEL, MELCHIOR, JANSSEN, KURWENAL, RODZINSKI, LEINSDORF, KINSKY	*New York Philharmonic, Columbia Opera, and Colon Opera House Orchestras*	ODYSSEY	(M) 3216 0145

The sound on this very important record is bad — even for the 1940's. But you will hear the greatest *Tristan* ever, the one and only Lauritz Melchior. Here is a ringing, exultant voice; a *heldentenor* that was a dream. Helen Traubel was overshadowed by the awesome Kirsten Flagstad, but she was certainly the world's second best *Isolde*. Her large voice, beautifully colored, and comprehending, matches Melchior's tremendous sound. But the unbelievable Melchior is reason enough for buying this album.

DIE WALKUERE (Complete)

This absorbing work is the greatest opera in Wagner's *Ring* cycle. It contains pages of surpassingly beautiful music — and pages of maddening, windy music. That's Wagner.

* * MOEDL, RYSANEK, KLOSE, SUTHAUS, FRANTZ, FRICK, FURTWAENGLER	*Vienna Philharmonic Orch.*	5-SERAPHIM	(M) 6012

Furtwaengler probes Wagner's depths in a dramatic and intellectual way no one else has ever approached. The female voices are not outstanding. Frick is noble and unforgettable. Suthaus, though at times seemingly tired, was one of the best Wagnerian tenors since Melchior, but he has an annoying habit of now and then sliding into notes. The sound is passable.

For a very well-sung and sonically compelling *Walkuere* featuring Birgit Nilsson, buy the George Solti set on high-priced London.

DIE WALKUERE (Excerpts: ACT 1, SCENE 3; ACT III: RIDE OF THE VALKYRIES)

* * TRAUBEL, NBC Symphony Orch. Victrola VIC (S) 1316
MELCHIOR,   [Siegfried: Act II: Forest
TOSCANINI   Murmurs; Die Goetterdaem-
              merung: Act III: Siegfried's
              Death and Funeral Music]

The very Italian Toscanini would not seem to be the ideal interpreter of Wagner's Teutonic pronouncements. But after hearing this release, one realizes how disciplined was the genius of Toscanini. You'll find none of Furtwaengler's introspection and musical philosophizing in this reading, but rather a lean, whip-taut performance. Melchior is fine. Traubel here is rather stolid to my ears. Peter Davis disagrees somewhat with my estimate, and had this to say in *High Fidelity*: "For all the furious energy and fine revelation of detail in the Toscanini performance, it strikes me as nervous, edgy, and impatient." The sound is thin.

FIVE WESENDONCK SONGS

These lovely songs which include the poignant *Traeume* were written to lyrics Wagner composed to his mistress Mathilde Wesendonck, wife of Otto Wesendonck, his chief benefactor at the time.

* * FLAGSTAD, MOORE   Seraphim (M) 60046
              [Brahms, Two Songs with
              Viola, Opus 91; Grieg, Four
              Songs]

The great Norwegian singer, Kirsten Flagstad, one of the vocal miracles of the century, recorded these songs in 1948. This disc still casts her radiant spell. The sound is fair and quite bearable. [The Brahms songs on the reverse are haunting; the Grieg songs are not for me.]

WAGNER ORCHESTRAL CONCERTS In the low-priced field, there is a generous supply of what Sir Thomas Beecham used to call "bleeding chunks" of Wagner — that is, orchestral music, without singing, of various overtures, preludes, scenes, etc., from Wagner's music-dramas. Some of these recordings provide a good introduction to Wagner's music. You are probably better off beginning with one of these orchestral records to find out how much you like Wagner's music, rather than plunging into Wagnerian opera. The fact is that many music lovers enjoy these orchestral pieces, but can't stand the singing in the opera itself.

SIEGFRIED IDYLL

Originally played at the foot of the staircase in Wagner's home on the morning of Christmas Day, 1870, which also happened to be Cosima Wagner's thirty-third birthday, this music celebrates Wagner's joy at the birth of his son Siegfried. This is private music; Wagner consented to the publication of the piece some eight years after it was written only because he desperately needed cash.

* * * TOSCANINI	NBC Symphony Orch.	VICTROLA VIC (M) 1247 [Lohengrin, Preludes; Meistersinger: Preludes]
* * MONTEUX	San Francisco Symphony Orch.	VICTROLA VIC (S) 1102 [Beethoven, Symphony No. 4]
* * PARAY	Detroit Symphony Orch.	MERCURY (M) 14054 (S) 18054 [Goetterdaemmerung: Siegfried's Rhine Journey; Parsifal: Prelude; Tristan und Isolde: Prelude]
SCHURICHT	Bavarian Radio Symphony Orch.	VANGUARD (S) 220 [Lohengrin, Preludes; Meistersinger, Overture]

Toscanini is wonderfully authoritative. The sound is not bad.
Monteux is glowing here, rich in ambiance and sheer tonal wormth.
Paul Paray is impressive and the sonics are fine.
Schuricht's performance suffers from lack of tension.

DER FLIEGENDE HOLLAENDER: OVERTURE; LOHENGRIN: PRELUDE; DIE MEISTERSINGER: SUITE FROM ACT III; TRISTAN UND ISOLDE: PRELUDE AND LOVE-DEATH

* * BARBIROLLI	Halle Orch.	EVERYMAN SRV (M) 149 SRV (S) 149SD

The glowing Barbirolli disc would be near the top of the list at any price. The sound is good.

TRISTAN UND ISOLDE: PRELUDE AND LOVE-DEATH; PARSIFAL: PRELUDE, GOOD FRIDAY SPELL

* * TRAUBEL, MELCHIOR, TOSCANINI	NBC Symphony Orch.	VICTROLA VIC (M) 1278

Many critics still prefer "The Maestro's" personal and electric interpretation of Wagner above all competition. The sound is still fairly decent.

OVERTURES TO TANNHAEUSER, DER FLIEGENDE HOLLAENDER, AND DIE MEISTERSINGER; PRELUDE TO "LOHENGRIN"; RIDE OF THE VALKYRIES; SIEGFRIED IDYLL; PRELUDE AND LIEBESTOD FROM TRISTAN; PRELUDE AND GOOD FRIDAY MUSIC FROM PARSIFAL

* * FURTWAENGLER   *Berlin Philharmonic*   2-Seraphim IB   (M)   6024
                      Orch., Vienna
                      Philharmonic Orch.

Here are some of Furtwaengler's best performances. Most of the great Wagnerian orchestral excerpts are here; this set is a must for the faithful. These are glowing performances, rendered with the special rapt, dedicated quality of this greatest of Wagnerian conductors. This reissue was on the *Saturday Review's* list of "Best Recordings of 1968." Some of the recordings date as early as 1939, so don't expect anything in the way of high fidelity sound.

Walton, William (1902-   )

Walton has a curious reputation today: he is the most important British composer between Vaughan Williams and Benjamin Britten. Yet his music is seldom impressive; there is something unconvincing about his fastidious, neo-classicist efforts.

FACADE, SUITES NO. 1 AND 2

Ironically, this "Recitation With Chamber Orchestra," written when Walton was twenty, remains his most successful piece, not excepting his ambitious cantata *Belshazzar's Feast*.

Set to poems by Edith Sitwell, *Facade* was first given in 1923 as a semi-theatrical entertainment in Chelsea. The curtain was painted to represent a head; through the mouth of this head, with the assistance of a megaphone, the poems were declaimed to the commentary of Walton's music. The mood suggests the early works of Evelyn Waugh. A good performance of this satirical piece is a delight.

In 1926, Walton arranged the work into suites for a large orchestra, and it has since become a concert favorite in this form. It has also been made into a ballet.

* * FISTOULARI   *Royal Opera House Orch.*   VICTROLA VIC   (S)   1168
[Lecocq]

The music is well played and well recorded.

Weber, Carl Maria Friedrich Ernst Von
(1786-1826)

Weber studied with his father, and then with Michael Haydn under whom he became a chorister at Salzburg. After completing further study in Munich in 1798, Weber appeared as a solo pianist. His first opera, *Das Waldmaedchen,* was produced in Freiberg, in 1800. Weber conducted at the Breslau theatre, 1804 through 1806. After many more concert tours, in 1813 he was appointed conductor at Prague, and appointed conductor of the Dresden Opera in 1816. His most successful work, the opera *Der Freischuetz,* was presented at Berlin in 1821. In 1826, Weber visited London to produce *Oberon* which he had written for the Convent Garden Opera. He died there, about eight weeks after the first performance of his opera.

PLACE AND ACHIEVEMENT   Almost single-handedly, Weber created romantic German opera. Wagner called him, "this most German of German composers."

Of all of Weber's many works, the overtures to his three greatest operas, *Der Freischuetz, Euryanthe,* and *Oberon,* remain as durable pieces in the concert hall. The rest of his composition have sunk into what Philip Hale once called "that great graveyard of forgotten operas, symphonies, and Masses."

Weber's operas have pleasant moments, but with the exception of the great *Der Freischuetz,* most of them suffer from disastrous libretti and bad organization. His piano music reveals a fertile imagination and florid style, but usually the music no longer holds us. In his time, Weber was a distinguished pianist, conductor, and a lively critic. Today, like Franz Liszt, Weber is more spoken about than listened to. Yet his place as an innovator is undisputed, and he broke the ground for Wagner and music-drama, a debt that Wagner freely admitted.

THE ESSENTIAL WEBER
ORCHESTRAL MUSIC:*Overtures to Der Freischuetz, Euryanthe, Oberon; Invitation to the Dance (orchestrated by Hector Berlioz).*
OPERA: *Der Freischuetz.*

OTHER WORKS
OPERAS: *Euryanthe; Oberon.*
ORCHESTRAL MUSIC: *2 Symphonies; Konzertstueck, for Piano and Orchestra; 2 Concertos for Piano and Orchestra; 2 Concertos for Clarinet and Orchestra; Concerto for Bassoon and Orchestra; Concertino for Clarinet and Orchestra.*
CHURCH MUSIC: *Cantatas; Masses.*

PIANO MUSIC: *4 Sonatas for Piano; Valses; Fughetti; Variations; Ballades; Romances.*

SONGS: [*There are numerous short songs.*]

CONCERTO NO. 1 IN C MAJOR FOR PIANO (Opus 1); CONCERTO NO. 2 IN E-FLAT MAJOR FOR PIANO (Opus 32)

This agreeable, spontaneous music shows strong accents of Haydn and Mozart, and yet contains a personal romantic coloration that anticipates the great pages to come in *Freischuetz* and *Oberon*.

* WUEHRER, SWAROWSKY	*Pro Musica Symphony, Vienna*	TURNABOUT	(S) 34155

The works are handsomely played by Friedrich Wuehrer, a strong, assertive pianist who is highly respected on the Continent but little known in America. The remastered stereo sound is acceptable.

DER FREISCHUETZ (Sung in German)

This opera is a delight. Although it is rarely played in America, we now have no less than four inexpensive performances available on records— *mirabile dictu!*

* * * GRUEMMER, OTTO, SCHOCK, FRICK, KOHN, KEILBERTH	*Berlin Philharmonic and Municipal Opera Chorus*	2 SERAPHIM	(S)	6010
* CUNITZ, LOOSE, RUS, HOPF, EDELMANN, ACKERMANN	*Vienna Philharmonic*	2-RICHMOND		62016
TROETSCHEL, BOEHME, ALDENHOFF, THOMANN	*Saxon State Orchestra and Chorus*	3-VOX OPBX	(M)	149
BEIKE, TROETSCHEL, BOEHME, KEMPE	*Saxon State Orch.*	3-URANIA (5)	(M)	242/3

Keilberth easily leads all entries with an authoritative performance that sounds thoroughly rehearsed. The singers and orchestra sound as though they have been brought up on this music and have it in their bones. Elisabeth Gruemmer is splendid in her two arias. Frick's big, dark-toned voice never sounded better. Rudolf Schock, a great draw in Germany, is hardly known in this country. He is extraordinarily good here. The spoken dialogue is nearly completely cut—no loss. The musical score is complete.

The Ackermann set has a splendid chorus and excellent orchestra work, but some shaky singers. Rus and Reinhold are fine, but Maud Cunitz detracts from the set with dullish, even clumsy handling of Agathe's ravashing music. *High Fidelity's* verdict: "A rather ordinary evening at the Vienna State Opera, circa 1950."

The Vox set is heavy-handed and uneven in the quality of the performances.

In the Urania set, the singing is pedestrian and the sound is metallic.

DER FREISCHUETZ (Excerpts)

Here are selections from Weber's best-known opera.

* * SCHLEMM, STREICH, WINDGASSEN, UHDE, LEHMANN, LEITNER, ROTHER	*Various Orchestras*	HELIODOR	H (M) 25016 HS (S) 25016

The soloists, thoroughly German, are excellent. Windgassen and Rita Streich are in top form; Streich is a special delight. This disc seems to be a hodge-podge of selections from original masters; though hardly an ideal version, it is nevertheless quite pleasant. The sound is darkish in tone.

INVITATION TO THE DANCE (Opus 65)

This charming piece, once popular in the saloons of 1814, is now one of the supreme favorites of our Pops programs. Originally written for piano, it was orchestrated most brilliantly by Berlioz, and then again by the conductor Felix Weingartner.

* * * ANCERL	*Czech Philharmonic*	CROSSROADS	(M) 22 16 0105 (S) 22 16 0106 [Liszt, Les Preludes; Rimsky-Korsakov, Capriccio Italien]
* * * REINER	*Chicago Symphony Orch.*	VICTROLA LM/LSC	(M/S) 2112
* * TOSCANINI	*NBC Symphony*	VICTROLA	S-1024
* * KNAPPERTSBUSCH	*Vienna Philharmonic*	LONDON	STS 15045
* * BOSKOVSKY	*Vienna Philharmonic*	LONDON	STS 15070
* JORDA	*San Francisco Symphony Orch.*	VICTROLA VIC (S) 1024 [Mendelssohn, Piano Concerto; Rachmaninoff, Concerto No. 2]	

Ancerl delivers a polished, poetic, much praised reading. The sound is clean.

Reiner's version, all icy glitter, is also first-rate.

Toscanini's reading is incisive, but the rechanneled sound is murky.

Knappertsbusch is relaxed and expansive, and the sound is clean.

Boskovsky has superlative players for this music, and his touch is genial.

A neat, rather than poetic version, is to be had from Jorda.

KONZERTSTUECK IN F (Opus 79)

This *Concert-Piece* of 1821, according to Weber's diary, met with "unbelievable success, enormous applause." Tastes change, alas, and the romantic effects of this music hold but minor interest for us.

* * ARRAU, GALLIERA	*Philharmonic Orch.*	SERAPHIM	(S) 60020
		[Tchaikovsky, Piano Concerto No. 1]	

Arrau gives a vibrant, absorbing performance. *Stereo Record Guide* comments: "This is superb. Where in the Tchaikovsky *Concerto* Arrau sounds rather uninterested, here he gives one of the freshest performances imaginable of this unusual piece with its programme about knights and ladies." The sound is resonant.

OVERTURES

Weber's overtures to his operas are all that actively survive of his life's work.

* * TOSCANINI	*NBC Symphony*	VICTROLA	(S) 1341
* * ANSERMET	*Orchestra Suisse Romande*	LONDON	STS 15056
* CHALABALA	*Czech Philharmonic*	PARLIAMENT	(S) 622
LE CONTE	*Frankfurt Radio Symphony Orch.*	MONTILLA	(S) 2031
DOWNES	*London Symphony*	SOMERSET St/Fi	14700

Toscanini obtains discipline, excitement, and devotion to the text. The rechanneled sound is fair.

Ansermet is luminous in an early 1950's disc that, although far from today's stereo standard, holds up sonically. *Stereo Record Guide* comments: "Ansermet gives excellent performances, paying his usual scrupulous attention to the composer's markings."

Chalabala is presentable, but little more.

Le Conte is adequate, but his orchestra is ragged.
Downes, hearable, is quite unexceptional.

PIANO SONATAS (Opus 24; Opus 39)

Weber was the originator of the virtuoso piano piece; *Invitation to the Dance* was his most famous composition. Today, his piano music is neglected; why, I cannot tell you, for this music contains much romance, drama, and color.

* * WEBSTER	DOVER	(M) 5254
		(S) 7254

Beveridge Webster is a fine pianist of taste and sensibility. The sound is warm and realistic. A few more recordings like this, and a Weber boomlet may begin.

PIANO SONATA NO. 1 IN C (Opus 24); PIANO SONATA NO. 2 IN A-FLAT (Opus 39)

This is hardly earth-shaking music, yet much of it contains some interest.

* WEBSTER	DOVER HCR ST (S) 7006
	HCR ST (S) 7006

Beveridge Webster, with the intelligence we have learned to expect from him, negotiates his way in a poetic fashion.

QUINTET IN B-FLAT MAJOR FOR CLARINET AND STRINGS (Opus 34); CONCERTO NO. 1 IN F MINOR FOR CLARINET AND ORCHESTRA (Opus 73); CONCERTINO IN C MINOR FOR CLARINET AND ORCHESTRA (Opus 26)

Weber wrote much endearing music for his close friend, the clarinetist Heinrich Barmann. Weber's clarinet music ranks with his finest pieces; and is particularly suitable for the liquid, poetic sound of the instrument.

* * GLAZER, FAERBER	*Wuerttemberg Chamber Orch.,*	TURNABOUT TV (S) 34151

The Turnabout disc provides warm bravura playing by the noted clarinetist David Glazer. The sound is good. *Stereo Record Guide:* "Glazer is a capable and agile player, obviously a good musician."

Webern, Anton Von (1883-1945)

Webern, a pupil of Schoenberg, began as a theater conductor. Later, he served as choral and orchestral conductor at workers' concerts in Vienna. One of the "Infamous Three" — Schoenberg, Berg, and Webern — who set a bomb called twelve-tone music under standard musical structure, Webern is considered by some to be the prime exponent of that iconoclastic movement. He went further than Schoenberg in the search for new "systems" of sound.

His music takes getting used to; new ears are required — if you don't have them, your children will. Tenuous patterns, subdued dynamics, blendings of instruments so subtly that at times melodies can only be put together, as in a mosaic, from isloated notes in different parts — all this is the strange, significant music of Anton Webern.

Webern, a scholar who edited the music of Heinrich Isaac (circa 1450-1517), was an utterly serious musician, certainly not a faddist. His works include three cantatas, a symphony for small orchestra, a concerto for nine instruments, a string quartet, and a string trio.

CANTATA NO. 1 (Opus 29)

This substantial work features tone-row manipulation. This music seems at times like a staccato kind of shorthand — everything has been reduced or sifted, with significant silences. It is strange music; intriguing music.

* * WESTHOFF, GURZENICH, WAND	*Chorus and Symphony Orch. of Cologne, Members of the Lamoureux Concerts Orch.*	NONESUCH (S) 71192 [Schoenberg, 5 Pieces for Orchestra; Stravinsky, Dunbarton Oaks Concerto]

The solo soprano performs valiantly, and the forces under Wand are impressive. But, after hearing the stunning Heather Harper and the players on the expensive Angel set, this disc sinks into the shade.

STRING QUARTET (Opus 28)

"Static sound placements" would be the best definition of this quartet. Tone rows are spread and contrasted; structure is achieved, partially, by accentuation of the instrumental entrances and fading away. This music should be heard a few times; after a while, canonic patterns emerge — grey, blacks, and whites that seem an aural equivalent of pointillism by Monet or Seurat.

The Claremont Quartet   NONESUCH   (S) 71186
[Schoenberg, Ode to Napoleon Buonaparte; Stravinsky, Three Pieces for String Quartet; Concertino for String Quartet]

This performance has not much bite or conviction. The sound is clean.

Weill, Kurt (1900-1950)

Kurt Weill was a pupil of Humperdinck and Busoni. The *Three Penny Opera* was his most famous work. His other operas include *The One Who Says Yes, The Seven Cardinal Sins, Mahoggony,* etc. He wrote incidental music to Franz Werfel's *The Eternal Road,* presented in New York in 1936. Weill was married to the singing actress Lotte Lenya, who starred in many of his operas.

Refugees from Hitler, the Weills fled Germany in 1933, living in Paris until their emigration to America in 1935.

PLACE AND ACHIEVEMENT   Kurt Weill was Germany's leading theatre composer between World Wars I and II. Today, he is not taken seriously as an opera composer; we deem his works musical shows.

He gained a reputation for his skill in mixing modern idiom with jazz. The most striking example of this is his setting of Bertolt Brecht's updated German version of *The Beggar's Opera,* entitled *Die Dreigroschenoper (The Three Penny Opera),* produced in Berlin in 1928. Many of his works include haunting ballads, but Weill's one indisputable, undying success is *The Three Penny Opera.*

Ironically, Weill contributed more to American musical theatre than to serious music. Dozens of Broadway shows, including *Pal Joey* and *West Side Story,* owe a heavy debt to Weill's pioneering efforts to create a lyrical musical form of honesty and meaning.

His instrumental works include a symphony and a violin concerto.

DER JASAGER (sung in German)

Weill was thirty when he wrote this, his sixth opera, in 1930. The title is freely translatable as "The One Who Says Yes." Based on a Japanese Noh play, and written in collaboration with Bertolt Brecht, the opera has a Brechtian moral tacked on at the end.

Like much of Weill's work, this is an oddly touching score, yet hardly a masterpiece. It enjoyed tremendous vogue in pre-Hitler Germany, and then it faded away.

* PROTSCHKA, BERT, VOHLA, KOHLER, DUESSELDORF	*Children's Chorus and Chamber Orch.*	HELIDOR	H (M) 25025 HS (S) 25025

Lotte Lenya supervised this production, and the cast is excellent. The firm-voiced boy soprano, Josef Protschka, is outstanding. This work, called by the composer "a school opera," was intended as a stage piece for young students and talented amateurs. The rather dry sound in this recording seems appropriate.

JOHNNY JOHNSON (sung in English)

This 1936 opera marks a milestone in the American musical theatre. It was written when Kurt Weill and his wife, Lotte Lenya, fled Nazi Germany and fell into the arms of the Group Theatre, then America's most vital dramatic force.

Preceding *Oklahoma* by seven years, *Johnny Johnson* pointed the way to successful integration of story, song, and dance. The work contains some delicious, typically Weill tunes, but not enough outstanding melodies to hold up as a total musical unit. For Weill devotees, this recording will be a treat; for others, perhaps not.

* LENYA, MEREDITH, LEAR, STEWART, SHERMAN, MERRILL, MATLOWSKY	HELIODOR	H (M) 25024 HS (S) 25024

This disc features the famous opera star Evelyn Lear when she was just a young, rising singer. Lear, Burgess Meredith, Lotte Lenya, and Scott Merrill are most appealing. The dry sound of the recording fits well with the mordant dance-of-death humor.

Speaking of casts: theatre buffs may care to know that the original *Johnny Johnson* on Broadway included the following members of the Group Theatre: Lee J. Cobb, Elia Kazan, Luther Adler, Morris Carnovsky, and the late John Garfield.

THE THREE PENNY OPERA

Die Dreigroschenoper is irresistible. One of the true masterpieces of our time, this work ranks in significance with Stravinsky's *Le Sacre du Printemps (The Rite of Spring)* and Schoenberg's *Pierrot Lunaire*. *Die Dreigroschenoper* is more fun than either of the other two.

This is the old *Beggar's Opera* as revised by the trenchant Bertolt Brecht in 1928. It seems as if George Grosz's savage drawings of pre-Hitler Germany are set to unforgettable music: all is *kaput*. Today's hit musical *Cabaret* aims for a similar effect, but is light-years away from Kurt Weill's masterwork.

* * * LENYA	*Theatre de Lys Production* (sung in English)	MGM	31210C
* * LIANE, ANDAY, ROSWAENGE, JERGER, PREGER, ADLER	*Chorus and Orchestra of* *the Vienna State Opera* (sung in German)	VANGUARD EVERYMAN SRV (S) 273	

The famous Lenya production ran for years and years at the off-Broadway Theatre de Lys. Virgil Thomson called it "the finest thing of its kind in existence." Devout fans of Weill prefer the sacrosanct, Lenya-supervised, two-record set of this opera recorded in German in 1958—but the American production is every bit as good, in an irreverent, what-the-hell-does-it-all-matter mood. Marc Blitzstein did the excellent English adaptation and lyrics. The great Lotte is splendid—what a singing actress! Scott Merrill is superb as Mack the Knife. What a pity there are so few records available of this gifted artist. All other roles are excellently played. The sonics are not ideal—but so what? [NOTE: The fine-sounding mono edition of this MGM record has been officially discontinued by the company, and remaining stocks are sold in most record shops at under $2.00; the stereo version remains high-priced. Buy the low-priced mono version before they're all gone.]

Vanguard gives us a fine, acerbic reading largely casted by veterans of the Vienna State Opera of the 1930's. If you can get used to the idea of anyone else but Lenya doing the part, the Polly of the notable cabaret singer Liane is first-rate. The rechanneled stereo sound is not bad.

Wieniawski, Henryk *(1835-1880)*

This Polish violinist and composer studied at the Paris Conservatory. From 1850 he traveled extensively on concert tours throughout Europe. Appointed solo violinist to the Czar in 1859, he lived mainly in St. Petersburg for the next ten years. He is considered to have been one of the most brilliant violinists of the nineteenth century. Wieniawski composed for his instrument, and is especially remembered for his two concertos. His music contains much fiery temperament and shows off the virtuoso violinist in a romantic fashion.

CONCERTO NO. TWO FOR VIOLIN AND ORCHESTRA, IN D, OPUS 22

This is a most romantic and beautiful concerto, reminiscent of the style of Bruch and Lalo.

* * WILKOMIRSKA, ROWICKI	*Warsaw Philharmonic*	HELIODOR	(S) 25087

[Szymanowski, Concerto No. One]

The Polish violinist is superb, and we will certainly here much more of the name Wikomirska. The sound is warm and very good indeed. [The coupling is an impressive, neo-romantic work by a Polish composer who died in 1937.]

Willaert, Adrian (1490-1562)

Born in Flanders, Willaert studied law at the University of Paris. He moved to Italy, and in 1527 was appointed *maestro di capella* at St. Mark's in Venice, a post which he held until his death. (Among his successors were Andrea Gabrieli, Giovanni Gabrieli, and Monteverdi.)

Inspired by the presence of two great organs at St. Mark's, Willaert wrote some striking *cori spezzati,* or compositions for two antiphonal choirs. This was two separate groups of musicianse, seated in different parts of the church, and "musically opposed" to each other. This form became a Venetian specialty. He also wrote Masses, motets, madrigals, chansons, and other works.

MADRIGALS, MOTETS, RICERCARI

This music was boldly inventive in its day—Willaert experimented in form, and came up with daring, way-out works for his time. Willaert and his contemporaries also created some of the first madrigals—the most flourishing musical form of the late Renaissance. These early explorations are a must for the student of music history, but will not prove very rewarding for the casual listener.

STEVENS   *Ambrosian Singers*   ODYSSEY   (S) 32 16 0202

The singing is lachrymose and uninspired, although the sonics are rich and resonant. I cannot believe that I have been listening to the same disc as *High Fidelity's* reviewer, who summed up, "The performances are in all ways equal to the music."

Wolf, Hugo (1860-1903)

Hugo Wolf studied at the Vienna Conservatorium, 1875-77, but was compelled to leave because of a disagreement with the director. He began writing songs about 1876, and for the rest of his brief life this was his principal creative activity. He composed in fits and starts: a furiously productive period would be followed by despondency and torpor. For some years he earned a precarious living by teaching and by writing musical criticism for the *Wiener Salonblatt.*

In 1897, he lost his reason and had to enter an asylum, where he died. His long disease, financial wretchedness, hectic private life, and final mental collapse all contributed to the intense, desperate quality of his music.

PLACE AND ACHIEVEMENT   Wolf is one of that remarkable foursome—Schubert, Schumann, Brahms, and Wolf—whose lyric outburst in nineteenth-century Germany is one of the great triumphs of romanticism. Between them they wrote over a thousand songs of extraordinary range and diversity, the greatest songs ever written.

Wolf's lieder are far more intellectualized and more difficult to love than Schubert's; Wolf's music contains few of those pure Schubertian melodies that at once touch the heart. Wolf admired Wagner fanatically, and his songs, like much of Wagner's work, often seem to be independent instrumental works to which a vocal part has been appended.

But Wolf possessed a rare genius. Through repeated hearing, the lover of lieder will discover marvelous artistic subtleties and shadings. For example, the passion of his women in the Spanish songs is quite unlike the passion of those in his Goethe songs.

A tremendous artist has wedded words and music as no one else could. His reputation is growing from year to year, and the number of available recordings is certain to increase.

THE ESSENTIAL WOLF

VOCAL MUSIC: *Spanisches Liederbuch, Italienisches Liederbuch, Moerike Lieder, Eichendorff Lieder, Goethe-Lieder, other songs.*

OTHER MAJOR WORKS

OPERA: *Der Corregidor.*

ORCHESTRAL MUSIC: *Penthesilea, Tone Poem for Orchestra.*

CHAMBER MUSIC: *Italian Serenade, for Chamber Orchestra (also for String Quartet).*

DER CORREGIDOR (Opera)
(sung in German)

This work lacks design, continuity, and everything else that one expects in an opera, but it contains some extraordinary music. Wolf's forte was the art-song; and this opera consists of a charming, extended group of gemlike fragments. *Der Corregidor* is almost unknown in America, and rarely revived in Europe. Tasting this work on records—a bit here, and a bit there—seems to be the best way to enjoy this strange uneven work.

Wolf's opera *Der Corregidor* is based on the same story as de Falla's ballet *The Three Cornered Hat.* Both use Pedro de Alarcon's spicy tale of the magistrate and the miller's wife. The jealous miller repays the magistrate, who is surreptiously courting the miller's wife, by cuckolding the judge in return.

* FUCHS, TESCHEMACHER, ERB, HERMANN, BOEHME, FRICK, HANN, ELMENDORFF	*Saxon State Orch. and Chorus*	URANIA	(M) (5) 208/3

This album is ancient but honorable. Joseph Hermann stands out among the singers, and the sopranos are very impressive. Karl Erb oversings: he even seems to be trying to improve on Wolf's score. Students are warned that this recording contains many cuts, and may seem hectic in pace. The sound is indifferent in quality.

GOETHE-LIEDER

This is a cycle of 51 dark-hued songs, composed in 1888 and 1889, and based on poems by Goethe.

* * LOTTE LEHMANN, ULANOWSKY, piano	VICTROLA VIC (M) 1320 [Brahms Lieder]	

A generation ago, no singer had a greater reputation in lieder than did the great Lotte Lehmann, who was also famous for her Marschallin in Richard Strauss's *Rosenkavalier.*

This recording is a tribute to Lehmann's recent 80th birthday. Lovers of the vocal art, and those with nostalgic memories, will welcome this disc; others may wonder what all the fuss is about. To modern ears, Lehmann often sounds terribly mannered and over-dramatic. Hers was never a glorious voice, but rather a supreme musical and artistic intelligence. However, if lieder is your dish, there are spine-tingling moments here that are well worth-while.

ITALIENISCHES LIEDERBUCH (Opus 121)

This is not easy music, at first, but the "spiritual and worldly" *Italian Song-book* is one of the glories of the art-song repertory—fascinating music with rich poetic insight. The work is a cycle of songs: miniature, self-complete vocal jewels that hang like pearls on a necklace.

* * BERGER, PREY, WEISSENBORN, MAELZER		2-Vox	(M) LDL 532 (S) SLDL 5532 (2 records) [Brahms, Vier Ernste Ge-saenge]

This is one of the best performances of the *Italian Songbook* ever recorded, perhaps preferable to the Fischer-Dieskau—Seefried effort on DGG.

The mature Erna Berger is mellow; the young Prey is a dark, eager voice, that is extremely good. The sound is satisfactory. [The *Four Serious Songs* on the reverse side of the disc are vintage Brahms, dearly beloved by all lieder fans. Altogether, this is a poetic, remarkable record.]

ITALIAN SERENADE (1893-94)

An exhilarating work, the *Italian Serenade* is Wolf's only instrumental piece that has become widely popular. This serenade exists in two forms: for string quartet, and for small orchestra.

* * STEINBERG	*Pittsburgh Symphony Orch.*	PICKWICK	(S) 4027 [Mendelssohn, Symphony No. 4]

Steinberg and the Pittsburgh Orchestra are properly delicate and fanciful. The sonics are good.

Xenakis, Yannis (1922-   )

Xenakis, a Greek, is one of the bellwethers of "The New Music." Xenakis studied in Paris with Messiaen; and at Gravesano, with the conductor-theorist Hermann Scherchen. The Greek composer also collaborated for 12 years with Le Corbusier, designing the striking Phillips Pavilion at the Brussels Exposition of 1958.

In 1955, Xenakis introduced his theories of "mathematical music." The composer admits—even boasts—that this music is composed as the result of highly complex calculations.

Xenakis has a tremendous reputation in Europe today as an avant-garde composer. Many critics are convinced that the future in music lies along the lines spaded by this extraordinary mathematician-composer. Olivier Messiaen, the gifted composer, has written of Xenakis: "The surprising thing is that the preliminary calculations are completely forgotten at audition. There is no cerebral quality, no intellectual frenzy. The result in sound is a delicately poetic calm or violently brutal agitation, as the case may be." We shall certainly be hearing a good deal more from this innovator.

METASTASIS; PITHOPRAKTA; EONTA

Metastasis is derived from the Greek: meta = after; stasis = stationary state. Sixty-one players are used who pay 61 different parts. The composer set out to prove that "the human orchestra could outclass, in new sonorities and finesse, the new electronic means that had set out to eliminate it." The systematic employment of *glissandi* led the author, some years late, to the startling conception of the Phillips Pavilion at the Brussels Exposition.

Pithoprakta is more musical mathematics; in the composer's words, "a dense cloud of sound atoms." The perceptive critic Roland Gelatt called the effect of *Pithoprakta* "as exciting as anything in modern music."

Eonta is more mathematical symbolism in music—scored for piano, two trumpets, and three trombones, and calculated by the IBM 7090.

* * * LE ROUX, TAKAHASI, SIMONOVIC	*French National Radio Orch., Paris Instrumental Ensemble*	CARDINAL	(S) 10030

The players overcome the awesome technical difficulties with seeming ease. The sound is vivid. And on this chilling musical note of the programmed future, we close our volume and retreat. So be it.

Zandoni, Riccardo *(1883-1944)*

Zandoni, together with Respighi and Pizzetti, belongs to the Italian generation that came after Puccini. To escape Puccini's overpowering influence, these Italian composers attempted to utilize elements from the styles of Richard Strauss and other "foreign devils." Their operas for the most part have perished.

FRANCESCA DA RIMINI

Francesca, composed in 1914, is Zandoni's most noted work. This opera, which flourished for two seasons, 1917-1919, at the Metropolitan Opera in New York, is reminiscent of Montemezzi's *Love of Three Kings,* but is far less inspired. It contains no really remarkable music.

* CANIGLIA,   EVEREST/CETRA   (S) 405/3
TAGLIABUE,
PRANDELLI,
CARLIN,
GUARNIERI

Opera lovers will revel in the vocal expertise of the great Maria Caniglia, Gigli's co-star on many recordings in the 1930's and 40's. Although her best years were behind her when this set was recorded, and although she fails, now and then, in the high register, Caniglia was a finer singer—a consummate mistress in building an aria in a free-wheeling style. Prandelli is just fair. The rest of the cast sing spiritedly but erratically. The sound—don't ask me how—is still hearable.

Music before Bach

Music before Bach

This is usually vocal music, ranging from solo compositions to large choral ensembles. The most famous pieces by composers who flourished before Bach are religious in nature, but there was also much delightful secular composition, especially about love.

"AN EVENING OF ELIZABETHAN VERSE AND ITS MUSIC"

This is a good Elizabethan sampler, interspersed with lively poetry.

* *   *New York Pro Musica*   ODYSSEY   (M) 32 16 0171

The sound is dry, but the charm remains.

ANTHOLOGY OF RENAISSANCE MUSIC

This lively, first-rate collection provides an excellent introduction to the peculiar joys of Renaissance music. Here are 14 pieces by Dufay, Des Prez, Lassus, Morley, De Victoria, Palestrina, Van Berchem, and J. Mouton.

* * GREENBERG   *The Primavera Singers of*   DOVER   (M)   5248
                   the New York Pro Musica
                   Antiqua

Noah Greenberg's musicians provide impassioned ensemble singing.

BALLADES, RONDEAUX, AND VIRELAIS FROM THE 14th CENTURY

This is secular, winning music. The compositions are by Machaut, Landino, Baude Cordier, R. Gallo and De Insulis, De Haspre, Dufay, and Guglielmo Ebreo.

* MISKELL   *Ancient Instrument*   ODYSSEY   (S) 32 16 0178
              Ensemble of Zurich

The music is nicely sung, but it could have bee nmore spirited. The stereo sound is first-rate.

BRASS MUSIC OF THE RENAISSANCE

Here are good examples of a once immensely popular form: the brass choir. The works are by M. Franck, Scheidemann, Schuetz, Stoltzer, Attaignant, Adson, Paumann, G. Gabrieli, A. Gabrieli, Frescobaldi, and Banchieri.

| * MASSON | *Brass Ensemble* | NONESUCH H | (S) 71111 |

Gabriel Masson's musicians offer staunch brass playing. The sound is exemplary.

CANBY SINGERS: "O GREAT MYSTERY"

The title is taken from the first three entries—all settings of the text *O Magnum Mysterium*. Works by Victoria, Morales, Byrd, Guerrero, Lassus, Waelrant, Schuetz, Handel, Schein, M. Franck, and Monteverdi are included.

| * CANBY | *Canby Singers* | NONESUCH H | (S) 71026 |

Shaky intonation and pale recording mar this disc.

"COURT AND CEREMONIAL MUSIC OF THE EARLY 16th CENTURY"

Here are fine compositions by Deprez, A. Gabrieli, G. Gabrieli, Gesius, Fevin, Mouton, and others.

| * * * | *The Roger Blanchard Ensemble with the Pouleau Consort* | NONESUCH | (S) 71012 |

This is one of the best records ever made of early music. The singing is fervent. The sound is superb.

"DANCE MUSIC OF THE RENAISSANCE"

This is highly pleasant sixteenth-century instrumental music. Compositions are by Moderne, Susato, Gervaise, Phalese, Franck, Hassler, Attaignant, and Demantius.

| * CONRAD, BRIX-MEINERT, KOCH, LEMMEN | *Chamber Ensemble* | RCA VICTROLA (M/S) 1328 |

The playing is delightfully fresh, as well as expert. The sound is first-rate.

"DUETS FOR COUNTERTENORS"

Compositions are by Morley, Purcell, Schuetz, Jones, Monterverdi, Blow, and Deering.

* A. DELLER,	*Ensemble of Baroque*	VANGUARD CARDINAL VCS
M. DELLER	*Instruments*	(S) 10022

Alfred and Mark Deller, father and son, give a good demonstration of the high art of the countertenor. The great Alfred sounds rather tired here, but the total effect is fascinating for those who dote on this sort of thing. However, if two high-pitched male voices are not your dish, there are many who agree with you.

"DOUBLE CHORUS MOTETS OF THE OLD MASTERS"

Here are motets by Gallus, Dulichius, Schroter, Staden, Hassler, Pachelbel, and J. S. Bach. The seldom-heard selections are worthwhile.

* * THAMM	*Windbacher Boys Choir*	MACE	(M) 9054

A chorus of boys' voices has a purity unmatched by any other combination of sound, and these boys really sing. The sound is first-rate.

"ENGLISH MADRIGALS — FROM THE COURTS OF ELIZABETH I AND JAMES I"

These are chaste, romantic pieces with grave appeal.

* * BURGESS	*The Purcell Consort*	TURNABOUT	(S) 34202
	of Voices		

Here are appealing singing and pleasing sound—a superior album.

FLORENTINE CARNIVAL SONGS — AND OTHER MUSIC OF THE ITALIAN RENAISSANCE

Songs written especially for carnival goings-on in Florence are the highlight of this disc; they hold a certain charm.

The Antiqua Players   Classic   (M) 1042

The performance is good. The sound is thin.

"FRENCH CHANSONS AND DANCES OF THE 16th CENTURY"

This scintillating collection includes works by Non Papa, de Lassus Crecquillon, Gomberg, Sermisy, and others.

* * * CAPE   *Pro Musica Antiqua*   Dover   (M) 5221
                of Brussels

Don't miss this one. The music is done with verve and affection. The sound is dry.

"FRENCH TROUBADOUR SONGS"

These are poignant songs. The works are by Binchois, Dufay, Lantins, and Machaut.

* CUENOD, LEEB   Westminster W   9610

The music is impeccably sung. Hughes Cuenod is just the right singer for this sort of thing.

"GERMAN MUSIC OF THE RENAISSANCE"

Here is a sprightly collection of Renaissance tidbits. Also heard here is a solemn Mass by Isaac which alone is worth the price of the record. Composers represented are Isaac, Demantius, De Broda, Greiter, Senfl, Othmayr, Walter, Finck, Stolzer, and Lemlin.

* STEVENS   *The Ambrosian Consort,*   Dover HCR (M/S) 7270
          The In Nomine Players

The works are cheerfully sung and the singing is very enjoyable, except for a wobbly tenor. The stereo sound is just fair.

"IN A MEDIEVAL GARDEN"

This is a collection of instrumental and vocal music of the Middle Ages and the Renaissance.

Stanley Buetens   Nonesuch H   (S) 71120
Lute Ensemble

The musicians give a poetic rendition of these slight pieces; this lively record offers a glimpse of the age.

"ITALIAN AND SPANISH SONGS OF THE 16th AND 17th CENTURIES"

These are romantic yet virile songs, by Da Gagliano, Carissimi, de Mudarra, Fiorentino, Frescobaldi, Gagliano, Milan, Verdelot, Willaert, and others.

     * CUENOD, LEEB   WESTMINSTER   (M)   9611

The works are impressively sung by the tenor Hughes Cuenod, one of the best modern interpreters of early music.

"ITALIAN TROUBADOUR SONGS"

The songs are by Arcadelt, Caccini, Gogliano, and Peri; they are dolefully pleasing items.

     CUENOD, LEEB   WESTMINSTER   (M)   9609

The songs are tastefully done.

LAUDARIO 91 DI CORTONE: THE NATIVITY; THE PASSION

Medieval popular traditional religious songs have been edited and harmonized, somewhat in our own musical idiom, by the admirable harpsichordist and musicologist Sgrizzi.

     * * LOEHRER   *Soloists, Chorus and Orch.*   NONESUCH H   (S) 71086
                              of the Societa Cameristica
                              di Lugano

The songs are sung with moving dignity, and the sound is intimate and resonant.

"MASTERPIECES OF THE EARLY FRENCH AND ITALIAN RENAISSANCE"

The joys and sorrows of love, and obsession with death, are the themes of this most beautiful album.

* * *   Singers and   NONESUCH H   (H) 71010
                     Instrumentalists of
                     La Societe de Musique
                     d'Autrefois

The singing is admirable. The "enhanced stereo" sound is a success.

"MEDIEVAL SONGS OF PRAISE"

Here is little-known Italian devotional music of the thirteenth century.
These anonymous songs are something of an odd mixture of troubadour
song and Gregorian chant.

DEL FERRARO   Choir of the Papal   HELIODOR HS   (S) 25076
                    Chapel of St. Francis
                    of Assisi

The effect will intrigue enthusiasts of early music. The singing is fervent.

MISSA SALVE; MISSA DE SANCTA MARIA

Here are two fragmentary, anonymous thirteenth-century English and
Spanish masses. The English Mass was pieced together and edited by
Denis Stevens from scattered bits of music known as the "Worcester
Fragments." These works are nearly a century older than the earliest
known Mass written entirely by one composer (Guillaume de Machaut).

* * STEVENS   Ambrosian Singers   DOVER   HCR 5263

The music is sung with dignity and feeling by four male singers. For
those who love very old music, this record will be haunting; for others
it may be a bore. But it is certainly indispensable to students, or to music
lovers who wish to hear the first stirrings of Western music.

"MUSIC FROM THE CHAPEL OF CHARLES V"

This is pious choral music by Gombert, Crecquillon, and Schlick.

* * FROIDEBISE,   Roger Blanchard   NONESUCH H   (S) 71051
    BLANCHARD   Vocal Ensemble

The music is intensely sung. The Blanchard Ensemble are near-perfect
in these fairly interesting obscure items. The organ pieces, played by
Pierre Froidebise, are also rewarding.

"MUSIC FROM THE CHAPEL OF PHILIP II OF SPAIN"

Here are works by Cristobal de Morales, Tomas Luis de Victoria, Antonio Cabezon, and Alonso Mudarra.

* * FROIDEBISE, BLANCHARD	*The Roger Blanchard* *Ensemble*	NONESUCH H	(S) 71016

This disc offers a vocal paradigm of how to sing little-known religious music. The grave organ of the Laurenskerk, Alkmaar, played by Pierre Froidebise, is excellent. So is the sound.

"MUSIC FROM THE COURT OF BURGUNDY"

These are lovely examples of the rondeau and the ballade; Dufay's great *Lamentatio* is here as well. Included are compositions by Grenon, Fontaine, Binchois, Dufay, Mureau, Busnois, Morton, and Ghizeghem.

* * BLANCHARD	*Vocal and Instrumental* *Ensemble, Pierre Pouleau* *Recorder Trio*	NONESUCH H	(S) 71058

The singing is appealing; so is the recorder trio.

"MUSIC OF THE EARLY RENAISSANCE"

The works are by Dunstable, Dufay, Frye, and de Lantins.

* BURGESS	*Musica Reservata;* *Purcell Consort of Voices*	TURNABOUT TV	34058

Here is ancient music imbued with life and sung with devotion. The sound is clean.

"MUSIC OF THE RENAISSANCE"

These are noble pieces by Da Venosa, Marenzio, Lechner, di Lasso, Peurl, Othmayr, and Praetorius.

*	*The Vogelweide Chamber* *Choir of Innsbruck*	MACE	(M) 9062

The singing is good, but the sound is rather constricted.

"MUSIC OF SHAKESPEARE'S TIME"

The vocal and instrumental works of Elizabethan England are handsomely displayed. Included are pieces by Bartlet, Brade, Byrd, Campian, Corkine, Cornyshe, Dowland, Ferrabosco, Holborne, and others.

* * * LEPPARD	*Ensemble*	2-NONESUCH	(S) 73010

I know of no better sampler of Elizabethan Jacobean music or of the art of madrigal singing than this lovingly made album. The sound is warm.

"MUSIC FROM THE STUART MASQUE"

The courtly masque form combined elements of spectacle, dance, music, and drama in England's early seventeenth century. Here are works by Lawes, Coperario, Campian, Cutting, and others.

Concentus Musicus of Denmark	NONESUCH	(S) 71153

Recorders and ancient krummhorns provide the chief interest here; unless you dote on them, the effect is pallid.

"OLD ENGLISH VOCAL MUSIC"

Here are selections by Byrd, Tallis, Morley, Gibbons, Dowland, etc.

*	*Prague Chamber Ensemble*	CROSSROADS	(S) 22 16 0144

Full-throated, intense choral singing emanates from this large group.

"RECORDER MUSIC OF THE MEDIEVAL RENAISSANCE AND BAROQUE PERIODS"

Recorder works by Isaac, Gibbons, Fasch, Gervaise, and others are heard here. These are lively pieces—just the thing for recorder fanciers.

*	*The Manhattan Recorder Consort*	CLASSIC	(M) 1056

Tasteful playing marks this performance.

"RENAISSANCE CHORAL MUSIC FOR CHRISTMAS"

Here are fine compositions by Deprez A. Gabrieli, G. Gabrieli, Gesius, Handl (Gallus), Praetorius, Scheidt, Schuetz, Vulpius, and Walter.

* VOORBERG	*N.C.R.V. Vocal Ensemble,* Hilversum	NONESUCH H	(S) 71095

The works are chastely sung, but a whole side of unrelieved early choral excerpts can be wearisome.

RENAISSANCE VOCAL MUSIC — ENGLISH AND ITALIAN MADRIGALS, FRENCH CHANSONS, GERMAN LIEDER

The secular songs here—some of them 400 years old—are still fresh and winning. The composers represented are Morley, Dowland, Weelkes, Bennet, Pilington, Festa, Arcadelt, Rore, Beaulieu, Sandrin, Sermisky, Mornable, Layolle, Coste, Sweelinck, Jeep, and Peurl.

* * TRAEDER, KOPF-ENDRES, VOORBERG, HAHN	*Niedersaechsischer Singkreis, Hanover; Camerata Vocale, Bremen; N.C.R.V. Vocal Ensemble, Hilversum; Kaufbeurer Martinsfinken*	NONESUCH H	(S) 71097

The singing is intimate and good.

"SECULAR VOCAL MUSIC OF THE RENAISSANCE FROM SPAIN, ITALY AND FRANCE"

Four intriguing songs by the Spaniard Juan del Encina are extremely beautiful. Other fine works are by Vilches, Alonso, Aldomar, Badajoz, Wert, Rore, Luzzaschi, and Striggio.

* * * STEVENS	*The Ambrosian Singers and Players*	DOVER HCR	5262

The performance is a beauty; this is one of the best Renaissance records ever made. This record should not be missed by lovers of the period.

"SELECTIONS FROM THE FITZWILLIAM VIRGINAL BOOK"

The *Fitzwilliam Virginal Book* is a manuscript collection of English keyboard music of the late sixteenth and early seventeenth century.

* * WINOGRON   Dover HCR   (S) 7266

This disc is a real sleeper. The hushed dulcet tones of the virginal (an instrument much like a small harpsichord) have never been more intriguingly displayed.

"SHAKESPEAREAN SONGS AND CONSORT MUSIC"

The Elizabethan songs displayed here are plaintive. Composers are Morley, Wilson, Weelkes, Johnson, Cutting, and others.

* * A. DELLER, DUPRE   *Deller Consort,*   RCA Victrola (S/M) 1266
                       male voices

The lute and the countertenor form a haunting combination. The sound is warm and good.

"THE PLAY OF HEROD"

This "Twelfth-Century Christmas Drama" is a medieval ecclesiastical musical play reconstructed from ancient manuscripts and "realized" by Charles Ravier. It is a fascinating job. NOTE: This is not the edition made famous in the New York Pro Musica version; this is a much more unorthodox reconstruction which enraged some critics. I enjoy this version nevertheless.

* * RAVIER   *Ensemble Polyphonique*   Nonesuch   (S) 71181

The playing is fine.

"THE PLEASURES OF CERVANTES"

Here is a collection of vocal and instrumental music of Spain dating from the fifteenth, sixteenth, and seventeenth centuries. Works are by Aranes, Mena, Milan, Narvaez, Ribera, Romero, and Valderrabano, as well as an anonymous composer. This is fascinating record of secular Spanish *canarios jacaras,* and such.

* * * GAVALDA   *Polyphonic Ensemble*   Nonesuch H (S) 71116
                   of Barcelona

The singing is impassioned, and I for one am rooted by it. Most of it is for one or two voices and harpsichord, and there is a warm intimacy about the performance. What it all has to do with Cervantes is dubious, but if this sort of imaginative merchandising enables Nonesuch to produce such jewels, more power to them.

"THE TRIUMPH OF MAXIMILIAN I"

This is fifteenth- and sixteenth-century music from the court musicians of one of the great Renaissance patrons of the arts. Included are works by Festa, Hofhaimer, Isaac, and Senfl, as well as an anonymous composer.

* * McCARTHY, SCHMEISER	*The London Ambrosian Singers; The Vienna Renaissance Players*	NONESUCH HB (2-record set)	73016

This leisurely, well-planned album conjures up a vivid picture of the period. The singing and sound are fine.

Anthologies and Collections

Anthologies and Collections

Low-priced records today offer hundreds of collections of music for every conceivable combination of instruments and from every period. Many of these collections are discussed in detail in the body of this book and may be found under the name of the first composer listed on the record.

The discs noted in this section are mostly recommended performances of out-of-the-way music; they are also dealt with at length under the composer's listing. For example, the lover of organ music will find a review here of esoteric collections that he might not otherwise have noticed; he will, of course, find heaps of organ music discussed under J. S. Bach and other composers.

Outstanding discs of Elizabethan music are also listed here: much more is reviewed under Purcell, Blow, Morley, Gibbons, etc.

CLARINET

THE VIRTUOSO CLARINET

"Ah, if we only had some clarinets," Mozart wrote to his father in 1778. "You can't imagine what marvelous effects an orchestra produces with flutes, oboes, and clarinets!" Three minor but inventive composers, who were born roughly a half century before Mozart, can be heard here experimenting with the new-fangled instrument.

FRANZ POKORNY (1729-after 1770) was Bohemian and studied in Mannheim. There he met Stamitz and was converted to the "new music". He composed over 100 piano concertos.

JOHANN MOLTER (c. 1695-1765) worked at several courts in Germany. He wrote four concertos for clarinet that are among the first concertos we know for this instrument.

* JACQUES LANCELOT, CLARINET, ALBERT BEAUCAMP, ROUEN CHAMBER ORCHESTRA	PHILLIPS WS	S 9078

The playing is crisp and spirited.

FLUTE

SONATAS FOR FLUTE, VIOLA, AND VIOLA D'AMORE

KRAUS: Sonata for Viola and Flute; LORENZITI "La Caccia" for Viola D'Amore; C. P. E. BACH: Sonata in A Minor, for unaccompanied Flute; TELEMANN: Sonatas in Canon for Flute and Viola d'Amore.

* * CLAUDE MONTEAUX, FLUTE; WALTER TRAMPLER, VIOLA/VIOLA D'AMORE	MUSIC GUILD	S 147

Flute and viola d'amore is a new sound for us, and a pretty one. The playing is first-rate. The flutist is the son of the famous conductor Pierre Monteux, and the violinist is one of the best I have ever heard. The sonic balance could have been better on this recording.

FLUTE AND GUITAR — AN 18th CENTURY SERENADE

Here is an intriguing and felicitous combination of instruments which yield tranquilizing music.

MAURO GIULIAN (1781-1828) was a famous Italian guitarist virtuoso. He lived in Vienna, 1807-21, and his musicianship was much admired by Beethoven.

ROBERT DE VISSE (1650-1725) was a French guitarist as well as a singer and composer. He published two instruction books on the art of the guitar.

The playing is chaste and graceful.

* JEAN-PIERRE RAMPAL, FLUTE; REBE BARTOLI, GUITAR	ODYSSEY	S 32 16 0218

THE ROCOCO FLUTE

Works by: J. B. LOEILLET, BLAVET, PHILIBERT DE LAVIGNE, NAUDOT

* ANDREW LOLYA, FLUTE, SALLY ROSOFF, CELLO, ROY EATON, HARPSICHORD	MACE	S 9086

The playing is appealing and the selections are more satisfying than most rococo pieces.

EIGHTEENTH-CENTURY FRENCH FLUTE SONATAS

MICHEL DE LA BARRE: *Sonata in G Major* ("L'Inconnue"); MICHEL BLAVET; *Sonata No. 6 in A Minor* ("La Bouget"); ANNE DANICAN-PHILIDOR: *Sonata in D Minor;* FRANCOIS COUPERIN: ("le Grand"), *Concert Royal No. 7 in G Minor,* from "Les Gouts reunis."

* JEAN-PIERRE RAMPAL, AND ROBERT VEYRON-LACROIX, FLUTES	DOVER HCR	S 7238

Ornamental French music, played with Gallic grace by this celebrated team.

FRENCH HORN

THE ART OF DENNIS BRAIN, VOLUME 1

BEETHOVEN: *Horn Sonata in F Major, Opus 17;* MOZART: *Divertimento in E-Flat Major, K. 289;* DITTERSDORF (ed. Haas): *Partita in D Major;* SCHUMANN: *Adagio and Allegro, Opus 70;* HAYDN: *Symphony No. 31, in D major:* First Movement; MOZART: *Horn Concerto No. 2 in E-Flat major, K. 417,* DUKAS: *Villanette*

* * * DENNIS BRAIN, HORN, GERALD MORE AND DENIS MATTHEWS, PIANO; DENNIS BRAIN WIND ENSEMBLE	SERAPHIM	60040 M

The much-loved Dennis Brain was the great English horn player who died in an automobile accident in 1957. His supple style is incredible, and no one has approached it. This is one of the most popular entries in the Seraphim catalogue. The recordings date from 1944-53, and the sound is passable.

THE ART OF DENNIS BRAIN, VOLUME 2

MOZART: *Quintet in E-flat (K. 452);* BERKELEY: *Trio, Oput 44*

* DENNIS BRAIN, HORN, LEONARD BRAIN, OBOE, STEPHEN WATERS,	SERAPHIM	M 60073

CLARINET, CECIL
JAMES, BASSOON,
COLIN HORSLEY,
PIANO, MANOUG
PARIKIAN, VIOLIN

More of the Brain legacy. The Mozart Quintet is a masterpiece; the Berkeley Trio is not unappealing.

HARP

FOUR CENTURIES OF MUSIC FOR THE HARP

Works by: C. P. E. BACH, DUSSEK, NADERMANN, HANDEL, CABEZON, RIBAYAZ

SOPHIA DUSSEK (1775-1947) was a Scotch singer and pianist as well as harpist. She was the wife of Jan Dussek, one of the first piano virtuosi, whose chief claim to fame rests on the fact that he was the first pianist to place his instrument sideways upon the platform, thus enabling the audience to admire his profile.

FBANCOIS NADERMANN (c. 1773-1835) was a French harpist at the Paris Opera and was professor of harp at the Paris Conservatory.

* MARIE-CLAIRE   NONESUCH   H 71098 S
JAMET, HARP

The poignant-sounding, dulcet harp, once adored by young maidens as much as the piano is in our own day, is now, alas, sadly out of favor. But this disc provides a good anthology of the literature. The playing is sensitive; the sound, chaste.

HARPSICHORD

SPANISH KEYBOARD MUSIC

Works by: ALRENIZ, MATEC, ANGLES, CASANOVAS, GALLES, FREIXANET, RODRIGUEZ, CANTALLOS, SERRANO, FERNANDEZ

* * FERNANDO   WESTMINISTER COLLECTORS
VALENTI,   SERIES   W 9323
HARPSICHORD

A lovingly played assortment of almost entirely unknown musich.

Valenti's harpsichord style is free, unfussy, and full-bodied. This is a charming record with clear 1957 sound.

ORGAN

COMPENIUS ORGAN IN DENMARK

A sprightly, secular collection of works, played on a fantastic, extravagantly-made organ built in 1612.

SAMUEL SCHEIDT (1587-1654) was a pupil of Sweelinck, and organist at Halle, Germany. He left a historic collection of organ music, *Tabulatura Nova,* which influenced organ composers for the next two centuries.

ANTONIO CABEZON (1510-1566) came from a famous family of Spanish musicians. A blind organist, he served under Charles V and Philip II, and his music is remarkably advanced in technique for its period.

ANTONIO VALENTE (16th century) was a blind Italian composer and organist who worked in Naples.

* FRANCIS CHAPELET, ORGAN	ODYSSEY	32 16 0067 S

The playing is sprightly and ingratiating.

FRENCH ORGAN MASTERPIECES OF THE 17th AND 18th CENTURIES

Works by: PIROYE, MARCHAND, F. COUPERIN, DE GRIGNY AND CLERAMBOAULT

While the German composers for organ were largely concerned with architectonics in sound and with obstruse counterpoint, the French organ composers sought elegance and *panache.* Thus, the French organ music is often colored—or encrusted—with ornamentations: trills, turns, and other delicate devices that are supposed to make the music more palatable and subtle.

* * PIERRE FROIDEBISE ON THE GREAT ORGAN OF THE LAURENSKERK, ALKMAAR	NONESUCH	H 71020 S

The playing here and the noble organ are both admirable.

ITALIAN ORGAN MUSIC OF THE 17th AND 18th CENTURIES

Works of FRESCOBALDI, TRABAC|, MERULA, ROSSI, PASQUINI, D. SCARLQTTI, ZIPOLI.

GIROLAMO FRESCOBALDI (1583-1643) was the Italian "Prince of orgaists." It is said that when he was appointed organist of St. Peter's in Rome, 30,000 persons went to hear his first recital there.

GIOVANNI TRABACI (c. 1575-1647) was organist and Chapel master at the Court of Naples for more than thirty years.

MICHEL ROSSI (c. 1600-1674) was a pupil of Frescobaldi in Rome, and wrote operas as well as organ music.

BERNARDO PASQUINI (1637-1710) was a celebrated Italian composer in his day, profoundly influenced by Palestrina.

TARQUINO MERULA (c. 1590-1665) was organist at several celebrated Italian cathedrals. His works are early examples of the use of voices and instruments in combination.

| * * * LUIGI FERDINANDO TAGLIAVINI, AT THE SERASSI ORGAN, PISOGNE | MUSIC GUILD | S 129 |

A beauty—pensive, ruminative, obscure organ music that excites and pleases. Both the instrument and the organist are impressive.

MASTER WORKS FOR ORGAN, VOLUME 1

(The North German School): Works by: BUXTEHUDE, TUNDER, BRUHNS, KNELLER, HANFF, WECKMANN, BOEHM, RRUNCKHORST.

| * * JORGEN ERNST HANSEN, ORGAN | NONESUCH | (S) H 71100 |

MASTER WORKS FOR ORGAN, VOLUME 2

(The North German School): Works by: BOEHM, REINCKEN, SCHIEFER-DECKER, ERICH, LUEBECK, LEIDING, TELMANN, BRUHNS.

| * * JORGEN ERNST HANSEN, ORGAN | NONESUCH | (S) H 71105 |

MASTER WORKS FOR ORGAN, VOLUME 3

Works by: SWEELINCK, SCHILDT, J. PRAETORIUS, HASSE, STRUNGK, OTTER, SCHEIDEMANN, DECKER.

"The organ possesses and encompasses all other instruments of music—large and small, however named—in itself alone . . . when you hear this artful creation, you think nought but that you have all the other instruments one amongst another."

So wrote the master composer Praetorius in 1691. The appeal of organ music is not a ready one; one must yield to its cold discipline, its austerity. But once these are accepted, there is a nobility, and a philosophical mien to the instrument that exhilarates.

These three records, played on a marvelous old instrument, provide a more than good introduction into the sombre mysteries of the king of instruments. All the pieces are somber, pensive, speculative works of the greatest flourishing of organ music we have had: the German school of the seventeeth and eighteenth centuries, which culminated in J. S. Bach.

* * JORGEN ERNST HANSEN, ORGAN	NONESUCH	(S) H 71110

Organist Hansen is first-rate and never boring.

MUSIC FOR THE BAROQUE ORGAN

Works by: PACHELBEL, MURSCHAUSER, MUFFAT, FROBERGER, FUX, KERIL.

This is mostly eighteenth century music by German organ composers, some of whom were contemporaries of Bach. It is devoted, meditative music, played on four noble baroque organs of Germany.

* ERNST GUNTHERT, ORGAN	MACE	S 9042

The playing is good.

SPANISH ORGAN MUSIC

Works by: LLUSA, VIOLA, ELIAS, TOMAS DE SANTA MARIA, DE SOTO, CANANILES, CASANOVAS.

In the 16th century Spain's organists in the cities of the great cathedrals could rival the best of Europe. Most of these pieces written for them can be considered as specimens of Spanish Renaissance music at its best. There is also a worthwhile selection of eighteenth-century Spanish organ music. The instrument used is sonorous and serene; I can't tell you which organ it is, because Mace is maddeningly sloppy in their program notes.

* * PAUL BERNARD, ORGAN	MACE	M 9059

A worthwhile record for lovers of organ music.

BAROQUE MUSIC FOR RECORDERS

Works by: WIDMAN, DEMANTIUS, LOEILLET, HANDEL, FASCH

* CONCENTUS   NONESUCH   H 71064 S
  MUSICUS OF
  DENMARK UNDER
  THE DIRECTION
  OF I. K. AND A. H.
  MATHIESEN

You are not likely to hear more polished and spirited recorder playing than is produced here; whether you care to hear nearly an hour of it is another question.

EIGHTEENTH CENTURY RECORDER MUSIC

Works by: BACH, TELEMANN, etc.

* THE RECORDER   CLASSIC   M 1051
  CONSORT OF THE
  MUSICIAN'S
  WORKSHOP

Alto recorder is the "voice" here, with a chamber ensemble.

Nicely done, but nearly an hour of this can be soporific, unless you're a recorder fiend.

RECORDER MUSIC OF SIX CENTURIES
(see also: Collections: Music before Bach.)

Works by: PRAETORIUS, BYRD, MORLEY, GIBBONS, etc.

The recorder, a small, wooden straight-blown flute that is similar to a small clarinet, is booming after a lapse of nearly two centuries. It was one of the most widely used instruments from the Middle Ages to the late eighteenth century. The five "voices" of a recorder consort are here in rarely heard selections that are played with devotion.

Among the obscurities: TYLMAN SUSATO (?—before 1564) was a music printer and city musician at Antwerp in 1529. He lost his post upon the arrival of Phillip II in 1549.

* THE RECORDER   CLASSIC   M 1068
  CONSORT OF THE
  MUSICIAN'S
  WORKSHOP

The playing is earnest.

VIOLA D 'AMORE

"THE VIRTUOSO VIOLA D'AMORE"

Works by: HAYDN, STAMITZ, ARIOSTI, HINDEMITH, KAUFMAN, TOESCHI, LORENZITI.

This sweet instrument — literally "the love viola" — was a favorite in baroque and rococo music. Roughly resembling a viola, the viola d'amore is a bowed string instrument with six or seven principal strings, and a number of subsidiary strings made of wire that quiver in sympathy.

* KARL STUMPF, VIOLA D'AMORE, AND CHAMBER ENSEMBLE	MACE	S 9049

This record is well-played and will appeal to lovers of light, out-of-the-way chamber music.

VIOLIN

A FRENCH VIOLIN RECITAL

DEBUSSY: *Sonata in G-minor for Violin and Piano;* RAVEL: *Tzigane; Concert Rhapsody in D-major for Violin and Orchestra;* ENESCJ: *Sonata No. 3 in A-minor, Opus 25 for Violin and Piano.*

CHRISTIAN FERRAS, VIOLIN; PIERRE BARBIZET, PIANO	MACE	M 9045

Very French, very sec, and beautiful. Warm sound.

FOUR HUNDRED YEARS OF THE VIOLIN

* * * STEVEN STARYK, VIOLIN; ELOISE NIWA AND ADELE KOTOWSKA, PIANO; KENNETH GILBERT, HARPSICHORD	EVEREST [six discs]	S 3203/6

A remarkable achievement by the Canadian-born violinist, Steven Staryk. Six records of violin playing may not seem your dish, but the playing is first-rate, and the album is almost an encyclopedia, of the art of the violin. Staryk, a violinist with an arresting, intense tone and perfect control of his instrument, makes it all sound effortless. Staryk, by the way, was concert master for Sir Thomas Beecham, and later for Fritz Reiner— two formidable conductors who were one-man schools in themselves.

OISTRAKH VIOLIN RECITAL

CHAUSSON: *Poeme, Opus 25;* SAINT-SAENS: *Introduction and rondo capricioso, Opus 28;* LECLAIR: *Sonata for Violin and Piano, No. 3, in D;* LOCATELLI: *Sonata for Violin and Piano in F minor.*

* * DAVID OISTRAKH,   RCA VICTROLA VIC S 1058
VIOLIN; VLADIMIR
YAMPOLSKY, PIANO
(IN C AND D);
CHARLES MUNCH,
BOSTON SYMPHONY
ORCHESTRA

Collected from the great Russian's first two American-made recordings. Supreme violin playing, rather on the smooth side. The re-issue sounds better than the 1956 originals did.

SOUVENIERS OF FRITZ KREISLER

Schön Rosmarin, The Old Refrain, Liebesfreud, etc.

* *   VICTROLA   (M) 1372

Fritz Kreisler, who died in 1962, was one of the most beloved violinists who ever lived. Of present-day violinists, perhaps only Yehudi Menuhin evidences Kreisler's heart and humanity in his playing. These 14 short pieces, many of them composed by Kreisler himself, were universal favorites two generations ago. The sound is thin.

VIRTUOSO SHOWPIECES BY RUGGIERO RICCI

WIENIAWSKI: *Scherzo-Tarantelle;* SARASATE: *Jota Aragonesa;* SMETANA: *From the Homeland. No. 2, etc.*

* *   LONDON STS   15049 S

Ricci is an ex-child prodigy, an artist of intense temperament and lyrical vitality. He does this collection of 12 encore pieces with sweep and brilliance. The sound is excellent.

MISCELLANEOUS COLLECTIONS

BATTLE MUSIC

Works by: BIBER, DANDRIEU, MOZART, NEUBAUER
For those who collect battle music. This is good, camp fun, nothing more.

The playing is decent.

BAROQUE FANFARES AND SONATAS FOR BRASS

Works by: HAMMERSCHMIDT, LOWE VON EISENACH, MASSAINO, PEZEL, SPEER

Dazzling music, brilliantly played. One of the best brass rceordings ever. The sound is out of this world.

BAROQUE MASTERS OF VENICE, NAPLES, AND TUSCANY

Works by: BARSANTI, BOCCHERINI, BONPORTI, CIMAROSA, DALL'ABACO, DURANTE, PERGOLESI, PESCETTI, PORPORA, RUTINI, A. SCARLATTI, D. SCARLATTI, TARTINI, VERACINI, VIVALDI, VINCI, ZIPOLI

Some like science fiction, some like late-late movies, and some like jumbo-sized compilations of Italian baroque music. Personally, my tolerance point for this sort of musical macaroni runs low after a half hour; and this monster, if you play the whole thing, runs some two and a half hours. Of course, you might *want* to own a three-record album of the baroque masters of Venice, Naples, and Tuscany.

The playing is neat and stylish.

BRASS MUSIC

Works by: HOLBORNE, HARDING, FARNABY, BASSANO, BUSSANE, GUY, ANON, LOCKE, G. GABRIELI, TROMBONCINO, SCHEIN, LASSO

The anonymous *"Lauda"* played here apparently exists on no surviving manuscript; the music is from the detailed painting of a music manuscript in Cappaccio's "St. Jerome in his Study." *Note*: Music for brass only can be wearisome, unless you're an addict.

JAMES HARDING (?-1626) was a flutist at the English court from 1581 until his death. He wrote instrumental music chiefly.

ANTHONY HOLBORNE (?-1602) is known to have been "servant to her Most Excellent Majestie." He was Gentleman Usher to Queen Elizabeth, and wrote many short pieces and airs.

MATTHEW LOCKE (1630-1677) was composer-in-ordinary to Charles II, and later organist to Queen Catherine.

| * * THE LONDON GABRIELI BRASS ENSEMBLE | NONESUCH   7118 S/1118 M |

A resounding record. Modern trombones, trumpets, and tuba are used here, which may offend devotees of the sackbut. Splendidly spacious sound.

RECITALS BY FAMOUS SINGERS   One of the great pleasures offered by records is the chance to hear great singers of the past and present in recitals. The discs listed here include performances of opera arias, operetta, German lieder, and song recitals.

"A MOST UNUSUAL SONG RECITAL"

(Songs by Beethoven, Haydn, Rossini, Brahms, Reger, R. Strauss, Wolf.)

| * * LUDWIG, BERRY | *Gerald Moore, Piona* | SERAPHIM | (S) 60087 |

Christa Ludwig and Walter Berry are each famous opera singers in their own right, though thy happen to be husband and wife. A pleasant record.

CALLAS, MARIA

(Music by Verdi and Ponchielli)

| * CALLAS, SANTINI, VOTTO | *RAI Symphony Orch.* | EVEREST | (S) 3169 |

Very early Callas, and dramatically impressive. A few annoying pre-echos disturb, and the fake stereo is fair. This one is primarily for her fans.

DERMOTA, ANTON

(Arias and Lieder by Schumann, Wolf, R. Strauss, Mozart)

* * DERMOTA   *Various Ensembles*   EVEREST   (S) 3202

Dermota was a famous German tenor in the 1950's. This is a rich, virile voice, with much musical intelligence. Recommended for all vocal fans. As David Hall once said, "Dermota is one of those rare birds — a German lyric tenor who really sings instead of bleating." The sound is so-so.

EVANS, GERAINT

(Arias from oratorios by Handel, Mendelssohn, etc.)

* * EVANS   *BBC Welsh Orch.*   EVEREST   3238

The gifted Welsh singer Geraint Evans has one of the richest, darkly powerful male voices to be heard today. He is entirely at home in these hearty oratorio pieces. The sound is decent.

FABULOUS '40's AT THE METROPOLITAN

(Arias by Gluck, Rossini, Mozart, Gounod, Massenet, Bizet, Saint-Saens, Wagner)

* * VARIOUS ARTISTS   ODYSSEY   (S) 3216 0304

Here are Rise Stevens, Jenny Tourel, Helen Traubel, Lily Pons and other names already hallowed. The fake stereo is harmless.

GARDEN, MARY

* GARDEN   ODYSSEY   32 16 0079

If you can take the terrible scratching sound, you'll hear why Mary Garden was so highly regarded.

FOUR ROCOCO QUARTETS

Works by: ROSETTI, DITTERSDORF, RICHTER, ASPLMAYER
The Mannheim school and its followers are represented here, and a new language—called "classical music"—can be heard developing. These are

light, pleasing eighteenth century quartets, gracefully played.

FRANZ ASPLMAYR (1728-1786) lived and died in Vienna and was a follower of the Mannheim school of composition.

FRANZ ROSETTI (ROESSLER) (1746-1792) was Bohemian and is remembered chiefly for the *Requiem* he wrote to honor Mozart's memory.

FRANZ RICHTER (1709-1789) was a native of Moravia. He worked in Mannheim and was later Kapellmeister of the Cathedral of Strasbourg. He wrote more than 64 symphonies.

* OISTERSEK STRING QUARTET OF COLOGNE	PHILLIPS WS	S 9026

The playing is acceptable.

GERMAN DANCES OF MOZART, SCHUBERT AND BEETHOVEN

This is cheerful music, much of it intended for dancing. The advertisement for Beethoven's set of dances reads: "By the master hand of Hr. Ludwig van Beethoven, out of love for the artistic fraternity."

* NORTHERN SINFONIA ORCHESTRA, BORIS BROTT, CONDUCTOR	MACE	9070

Played here with gusto.

LIGHT MUSIC PROGRAM

TCHAIKOVSKY: *Nutcracker Suite, Opus 71a;* CATALANI: *Loreley, Dance of the Water Nymphs;* BIZET: *Carmen Suite, No. 1;* PONCHIELLI: *La Gioconda: Dance of the Hours.*
ALFREDO CATALANI (1854-1893) was an Italian opera composer. He is best known for *La Wally,* which is still heard in Italy. His *Loreley* was heard in New York in 1921-22.

* * NBC SYMPHONY ORCHESTRA, ARTURO TOSCANINI	RCA VICTROLA VIC	1263

Maestro Toscanini was supreme in orchestral trifles as well as in the more weighty repertory. This set is a good example of his crisp, exhilarating style even with bon-bons. The mono sound, dating from 1951-52, is fair.

"TWO HUNDRED YEARS OF BRASS MUSIC"

Works by: G. GABRIELI, PURCELL, SCHEIN, etc.

In the late Renaissance a wealthy nobleman would visit another court or city with his entourage of brass-wind musicians—and the size of his band often determined his rank. Later, when the bourgeoisie took over, every town boasted its *stadtpfeifers*—municipal pipers who performed daily from town hall towers.

* THE CHAMBER BRASS PLAYERS	CLASSIC	M 1039

The playing is polished here; the sound is rather dry.

VIENNESE WALTZES

Works by: LEHAR, LANNER, GUNGL

Among the veteran waltz masters represented, Joseph Gungl (1810-1889) was a Hungarian composer of dance music who visited America in 1849 with his own band.

* * PHILHARMONIA
  PROMENADE
  ORCHESTRA,
  HENRY KRIPS,
  COND.
	SERAPHIM M/S	60018

Out-of-the-way selections here, not the usual Strauss family bill-of-fare. The conducting glides smoothly and is charming. The Angel sound of 1959 is clean.

LEHMANN, LOTTE: OPERA ARIAS AND LIEDER

Arias and Lieder by Verdi, Puccini, Giordano, Massenet, Thomas, Offenbach, Godard, Wagner, R. Strauss).

* * * LEHMANN	*Various Ensembles*	SERAPHIM	(M) 60060

This is radiant, ecstatic-style singing from the great mistress of lieder and opera. The mono sound is from 1928-33, when Lehmann was the Vienna Staatsoper's adored reigning diva. These are originally Parlophone-Odeon masters and the sound is not bad, considering. The French and Italian items are sung in German, which may throw some people off.

[BENJAMIN GODARD was a French composer and violinist. He wrote several operas, two violin concertos, and over 100 songs, a handful of which still survive among sentimentalists.]

LEHMANN, LOTTE: SONGS OF VIENNA

(Works by J. Strauss, Leopoldi, Stolz, Benatzky, Arnold, Sieczynski, and Mendelssohn.)

* * LEHMANN,   ODYSSEY   (M) 32 16 0179
ULANOWSKY

Lotte and light music, recorded in 1941, somewhat after her best years. French and English songs are here as well, with excellent piano accompaniment, and they are served up with the same *gemuetlichkeit* as the Viennese favorites.

McCORMICK, JOHN

(Arias and Songs by Verdi, Donizetti, Puccini, Bizet, Wagner, Handel, Lotti, Kramer, Donaudy, Bantock, Hopper.)

* * McCORMACK   *Various Ensembles*   VICTROLA VIC   1393

The great Irish-American tenor John McCormack, who died in 1945, was widely beloved for his singing of simple sentimental songs. He was also an unusually natural artist in opera. The sound is adequate.

THE ART OF ZINKA MILANOV

(Arias by Verdi and Ponchielli.)

* * MILANOV   *Various Ensembles*   RCA VICTROLA VIC
(M/S) 1336

Here is 1951-55 Milanov, which were great years indeed for the fiery soprano. The high-register pianissimos are still unbelievable. Peerce, Warren, and Moscona are also admirable in their respective duties. The stereo is fake but hearable.

MILANOV, ZINKA—FAMOUS OPERATIC ARIAS

(Arias by Puccini, Verdi, Dvorak.)

* MILANOV, BASILE   *RCA Victor Orch.*   RCA VICTROLA VIC
(M/S) 1198

The great Yugoslavian soprano, recorded in 1958, when her voice was a bit past her prime. But luscious tones and sweeping style in the great tradition are still to be heard in this record.

GIGLI, BENJAMINO

(Arias by Verdi, Donizetti, Mozart, etc.)

* * GIGLI   *Various Ensembles*   SERAPHIM   60054

They don't make tenors like the great Gigli anymore, and if they did, we wouldn't let them get away with all those corny sobs. But it was a great voice, with a wonderful, caressing sound. These recordings range from 1927-1949 and sound all right, considering their age.

GIGLI, BENJAMINO: CANTI SACRI

(Sacred songs by Mozart, Schubert, Franck, Verdi, etc.)

* GIGLI   *Various Ensembles*   SERAPHIM   (M) 60036

Gigli's lachrymose style, for me, is far more acceptable in opera, but he was famous as well for this painted-madonna sort of thing. These numbers were recorded between 1932 and 1947.

GOBBI, TITO

(Operatic Arias, Italian and Neapolitan Songs)

* * GOBBI, EREDE,   *Philharmonia Orch.*   SERAPHIM SIB   6021
BIZELLI, JESSON,
MOORE

Gobbi is a full-throated actor-singer, one of the best in the business. Charisma here—that indefinable something that sets a voice apart.

HOTTER, HANS: GREAT GERMAN SONGS

Songs by Brahms, Wolf and Loewe)

* * * HOTTER, MOORE   SERAPHIM   (M) 60065

Here is Hotter at his best, which means voice colorations that few singers can manage, plus a deep sense of tragedy. There are many out-of-the-way songs here. The Hugo Wolf characterizations are beautifully done, with uncanny comprehension.

HOTTER, HANS: SONG RECITAL

(Songs by Schubert, Schumann, R. Strauss)

* * * HOTTER, MOORE   SERAPHLM   (S/M) 60025

Hans Hotter is one of the greatest lieder singers who ever lived, with a dark, compelling voice that roots the listener. The selections here are jewels of the lieder repertory. Altogether, an unforgettable album. Originally released in 1960.

KIPNIS, ALEXANDER

(Arias by Mozart, Rossini, Verdi, Wagner, and Songs by Schubert, Brahms, etc.)

* * * KIPNIS, basso   SERAPHIM   (M) 60076

Those who were lucky enough to have heard the Russian bass Alexander Kipnis will never forget him; for less fortunate mortals, this album is a stunning display of the gifts of one of the greatest voices of this century.

MOORE, GERALD

(Songs by Haydn, Mendelssohn, Bizet, Wolf, Granados, Lizst, Verdi, Brahm,s Schumann, Schubert, Mozart, Mahler.)

* * * MOORE, piano   (Accompanying various   SERAPHIM   (M) 60044
                        famous singers)

The Englishman Gerald Moore is the most famous piano accompanist of our century. This album is not only a tribute to his subtle art but a rare chance to hear the glittering singers with whom he has worked over the years. This is a superb anthology of the art of the song and its best interpreters. Included here, among other legendary names: Elisabeth Schumann, Kathleen Ferrier. Karl Erb, Hans Hotter, Kirsten Flagstad, Elisabeth Schwartzkopf, Christa Ludwig, etc. etc. Don't miss this one!

PEERCE, JAN: JOURNEY THROUGH OPERA

(Arias by Ponchielli, Mozart, Donizetti, Puccini, Verdi, etc.)

* PEERCE, RUDEL   *Orchestra of the Vienna*   VICTROLA VCS   10036
                     Festival

Toscanini's favorite tenor well after his great years, but the style is still authoritative. This is a popular program, and the sound is good.

PONS, LILY: GALA CONCERT

(Arias by Delibes, Bellini, Verdi, Rossini, Thomas, Meyerbeer, Faure, Ponce, Bachelet, etc.)

* PONS	ODYSSEY	32 16 0270

Lily Pons was a favorite coloratura soprano of the Metropolitan Opera a generation ago, and they used to line up to hear her sing *Lakme* the way they do today to hear Joan Sutherland do *Lucia*. Hers was an arresting voice, but not sweetly appealing.

ROBESON, PAUL: SONGS OF FREE MEN

(Spiritual and folksongs of many lands.)

* * * ROBESON	ODYSSEY	(S) 32 16 0268

The great Paul Robeson had one of the richest, most compelling voices of our century. This collection of first-rate revolutionary songs (in Russian, German, Spanish, etc.) and spirituals is easily his best record.

SIEPI, CESARE

(Arias by Verdi, Rossini, Mozart, etc.)

* * SIEPI, BASILE	*Turino Symphony Orch.*	EVEREST	3228

Cesare Siepi is considered Ezio Pinza's successor at the Metropolitan. He has much the same warmly glowing voice, and a marvelous *cantabile* flowing, melodious sty e. This record was made when Siepi was on the way up, and the sound is just fair. But this is a worthwhile disc.

TAUBER, RICHARD: VIENNA, CITY OF MY DREAMS

(Works by Lehar, J. Strauss, and others.)

* * TAUBER	*Various Orchestras*	SERAPHIM	(M) 60015

Richard Tauber stands almost alone as a sympathetic interpreter of German and Central European operettas, even though he now and then stoops to crowd-pleasing *kitsch*. The sound is dated and thin.

TEBALDI, RENATA

(Works by Verdi, Mozart, Puccini, Catalani, etc.)

* TEBALDI Various orchestras EVEREST (S) 3205

The great, dulcet voice of La Tebaldi, caught when she was young and up-and-coming. The orchestral sound is just fair, and the faked stereo is a mess. But Tebaldi is Tebaldi.

TIBBETT, LAWRENCE

(Works by Bizet, Gounod, Rossini, Verdi, Puccini, etc.)

* * TIBBETT Various ensembles VICTROLA VICS
(S/M) 1340

With the possible exception of Leonard Warren and Paul Robeson, Lawrence Tibbett had the best dramatic style of any American male singer. It's an exaggerated style, but it's still great. The synthetic stereo is a mess. *Stereo Review* featured this reissue with the headline "Lawrence Tibbett: a baritone for all time."

UNFORGETTABLE VOICES IN UNFORGOTTEN PERFORMANCES, I

(Arias by Italian Composers: BELLINI, VERDI, DONIZETTI, MEYERBEER, PUCCINI)

* * VARIOUS ARTISTS VICTROLA VIC 1395

This is a first-rate collection of ten arias, featuring such legendary singers as Rosa Ponselle, Milanov, Caruso, etc. The sound, on the whole, is acceptable.

UNFORGETTABLE VOICES IN UNFORGOTTEN PERFORMANCES, II

(Arias by French composers: RAMEAU, DAVID, THOMAS, MASSE, HALEVY, MEYERBEER, OFFENBACH, BIZET, SAINT-SAENS, CHARPENTIER, MASSENET)

* * VARIOUS ARTISTS VICTROLA VIC 1394

Twelve arias here, sung by stars of earlier eras. Ruffo, Swarthout, Kirsten, Peerce are some of the luminaries.

WUNDERLICH, FRITZ IN MOZART OPERA

* * * WUNDERLICH,   *Bavarian State Opera Orch.*   HELIODOR HS   25075
JOCHUM

The German lyric tenor Fritz Wunderlich died in 1966 after an accident. He was 35. He showed every sign of becoming *the* lyric tenor of our age; no one else around today has that arresting virile quality that was Wunderlich. He never sang in America, although his debut at the Met was scheduled for October, 1966, and he is known chiefly to record devotees. How devoted they remain—the number of Wunderlich admirers grows from year to year—can be seen from the spate of records available to us.

This disc is one of Wunderlich's best, and you can hear the fast-rising Evelyn Lear and James King as well.

WUNDERLICH IN VIENNA: TRADITIONAL VIENNESE SONGS AND FOLK SONGS

* * WUNDERLICH,   *Vienna State Opera Chorus*   HELIODOR HS   25051
STOLZ

Done to the hilt, and conducted by one of the illustrious veterans of this field.

WUNDERLICH—OPERA, OPERETTA, AND SONG RECITAL

(Music by Kallmann, Lehar, Puccini, etc.)

* * WUNDERLICH   *Various Orchestras*   SERAPHIM   (S) 60043

This record contains operatic arias, operetta and songs. The glorious voice of Wunderlich shines here in 1960-65 recordings.

WUNDERLICH—OPERATIC RECITAL

(Works by Mozart, Puccini, Verdi, etc.)

* * * WUNDERLICH   *Various orchestras*   VICTROLA VICS
(M/S)   1235

A beauty, and my personal favorite of the several worthy Wunderlich discs.

WUNDERLICH RECITAL

(Opera arias by Handel, Mozart, Boieldieu, Donizetti, Verdi, Thomas, Massenet, Tchaikovsky, Lortzing.)

* * WUNDERLICH   *Various ensembles*   SERAPHIM   (S) 60078

Here are more warm, moving performances from the unforgettable Wunderlich. The operas are sung in German.

CHORAL MUSIC   These collections feature various composers on the same disc and, usually, sacred or romantic pieces.

A CHORAL RECITAL BY THE VIENNA ACADEMY KAMMERCHOIR

(Works by Mozart, Schubert, Brahms, and others.)

* * * MEYER   *Vienna Academy*   MACE   9061
Kammerchoir

This disc is one of the best choral recordings to appear in the last few years. The sound is good.

CHAMBER MUSIC FOR VOICES

Here are some fascinating capella choral pieces, including the *Crucifix* of Antonio Lotti, and some way-out harmonic experiments by Orazio Vecchi (1550-1603).

Other works are by Gallus, Des Pres, Bruckner, Hasselboeck, David, Heiller, Widmann, Wilbye, Jannequin, Burkhardt, Hindemith and Distler.

* * MITTERGRAD   *Klagenfurt Madrigal Chorus* MACE MCS   (M/S) 9078

The music is handsomely sung.

GERMAN LITURGICAL MUSIC

(Works by J. S. Bach, Mortiz von Hessen, Johann Staden, Heinrich Isaac, and Tilman Susato.)

* * ALTMEYER,   *The RIAS Chamber Choir,*   MACE   (M) 9022
BRENNECKE,   *Consortium Musicum*
ZARTNER, ARNDT

Sensitive choral singing is offered here. The German Elektrola sound is resonant—not at all boxed or shrill as is so often the case with choral recordings.

GREGORIAN CHANT

This term applies to one of the monodic and rhythmically free ritual melodies in the liturgical chants of the Roman Catholic Church.

The term "Gregorian Chant" was first used about the thirteenth century. Pope Gregory I became concerned with the codification of the various responsories of the Office, and all Latin unaccompanied and monodic church songs were named after him.

Some music lovers find Gregorian chant unspeakably boring; others like myself, are hooked for life on this serene, tranquilizing music. Formerly confined to divine services, the beauties of Gregorian chant have recently enjoyed a tremendous new popularity with the advent of the long playing record. Little other Western music can sustain and humble the spirit as effectively as Gregorian chant at three o'clock in the morning. Gregorian chant is also, perhaps, the closest approach of Western music to the infinite-reaching religious music of the East.

* * ST. THOMAS ABBEY MONKS	Vox	(S)	6420
* * BENEDICTINE MONKS	Phillips WS	(S)	9004
* * VIENNA HOFBURGKAPELLE CHOIR	Turnabout WS	(S)	3070
* * ENCALCAT ABBEY CHOIR	Music Guild	(S)	137
* * BENEDICTINE MONKS	Everest [4 records]	(S)	3159

All the above are good examples of this esoteric music, sung with dedication and purity. The sound is good on all of them.

LITURGICAL MUSIC FROM THE RUSSIAN CATHEDRAL

(Works by: GRETCHANINOFF, KALINIKOFF, KASTALSKY, KOMPANEJSKY, TCHESNOKOFF, etc.)

Russian church music has a stern, virile dignity all its own.

* GILLES, GIESEN, TRUBETZKOI, LINKE	*Johannes-Damascenus Choir, Essen*	Nonesuch H	(S) 71073

If you love deep-throated male voices, try this one.

SACRED MUSIC OF THE MASTERS

(Works by: MOZART, HANDEL, PALESTRINA, LASSUS, NEKES,
VAN NUFFEL, DE MONTE, MANGON, VON BINGEN, HASSLER, etc.)

* * GRAFF, VOSS, Organ   *Aachen Domchor*   MACE   (M) 9030
REHMANN

A thoroughly drilled chorus performs on this disc, with Aschen Cathedral sounds thrown in.

THE CHRISTMAS CAROLS OF EUROPE

Carols that are entirely unknown to me predominate here and they
are most beautiful.

* * * VENHODA   *The Prague Madrigal*   CROSSROADS   (S) 2215 0054
Singers

If you love music—any kind of music—don't overlook this superb disc.
The singing and sound are both lovely.

THE DOVE DESCENDING

(Works by: BRAHMS, CARTER, GESUZLDO, HASSLER, HINDEMITH,
MONTEVERDI, SERMISY, STARVINSKY AND WARLOCK.)
This collection offers a good chance to hear short choral pieces of all
periods—a form that has virtually vanished from our concert halls. This
sort of thing can pall after a few minutes, unless it's your thing.

* CANBY   *The Canby Singers*   NONESUCH H   7

The performance is decent; the sound is just fair.

VESPERS AND MATINS OF THE EASTERN ORTHODOX CHURCH

This sombre liturgical music grow on you, in a tranquilizing way.

* RUSSIAN CHOIR   MUSIC GUILD   138
(Potorjinsky)

The music is movingly sung.

The "New Music" and Electronic Music

There is nothing in modern music more bewildering, more difficult to comprehend, and yet more important than what we call the "New Music." I would like to begin with a few postulates for the reader to mull over.

Pioneering composers have always been denounced as radicals and anarchists, and have been accused of taking music to hell in a barrel. Yet posterity sees them as logical developers of the art. Against the perspective of time we have seen the revolutionaries of our own century—Stravinsky, Schoenberg, et al.—as predictable, almost inevitable continuations of the composers who came before them.

But the men of the New Music are not continuations of anybody else. They have deliberately kissed goodbye almost 400 years of music; we are witnessing today the most decisive break, the most agonizing wrench in the development of Western music since 1600, when revolutionists in music began writing something new called monody melodies for solo voice with instrumental accompaniment.

Until a hundred years ago composers wrote music to be enjoyed. They wanted to please their patron or their audience. Mozart longed for a *schlager,* a hit opera. But since Schoenberg and the New Schoo of Vienna began work in our century, composers have loftily decreed that it wasn't important whether or not the audience liked their music. Ten years ago a "new" composer, Milton Babbitt, even wrote an essay, "Who Cares if You Listen." Consequently, audiences have begun staying away in droves when a new, living piece of music is scheduled by any symphony orchestra. People do not want to endure a painful evening, even though it might be "good for them."

But with the New Music (of which Electronic Music is but one aspect), a curious thing has happened—people like it.

What people? The disbelieving reader asks. Young people, college-age people——they dig it.

The New Music is generally not to be heard in our staid concert halls. It is rarely listed on programs of symphony orchestras. It is heard from college orchestras, from the sound laboratories of our big universities — although *not,* usually, at the traditional music conservatories. It is heard on tape at discotheques and at such hip places as New York's Electric Circus.

And more significantly: the kids—college students and the under-thirties, in general—are buying records of the New Music, and buying them by the armload. Record companies, which are not subsidized and are not in business for their health, are producing more and more way-out records of the New Music, and the companies *are making money on them.*

This is incredible. It is astounding. A new, eager young audience has sprung up that is willing, even enthusiastic, about the new music of their time. I don't know whether the kids smoke pot when they listen, or use this music as a backdrop to conversation or meditation or LSD sessions. But it seems to be *their music*—along with pop-rock, of course.

That is what's happening; where it's at; and that's where we are at.

So—what's all the noise about? Why don't the new noise-making composers just go away and let us continue to pay homage to Beethoven and company?

Because musicians everywhere are searching for new tools, new ways of expression to expand musical horizons. It's taking place on the pop scene as well, by the way, and with a vengeance. Pop music is so way-out it is becoming a serious art form, and is drawing closer to what the serious musicians are writing today. The walls are tumbling down between concert and pop music.

"Why should I like all this noise?" a listener may ask. "I love Beethoven and Tchaikovsky and a lot of Stravinsky. I'm happy."

For now, don't worry about liking the New Music. Rather, I urge you to consider with an open mind what the new composers are trying to do. We must try to *understand* this new music, and that isn't easy. The first step to understanding a new art form is to try to comprehend *why* the artist wants it this way. You say you love Beethhoven and the traditional way of writing music. So does the composer of electronic music. He cou dn't agree with you more. But, he asks, what is the young composer of today supposed to do? Copy Beethoven? He wouldn't want to try—and if he did, you wouldn't want to hear it. The new composer is saying that the old forms are exhausted, that Beethoven and company said all that there was to be said in their kind of music.

The composer of today is forced to seek new roads to explore new avenues. When you hear Stravinsky, you are really tuned in with a say, three or four different "classical" composers, you automatically as- different set of ears than when you listen to Mozart. If styles did not become exhausted, there would be only one style and one form in each art, from its beginning to today, and that would be very boring.

*   *   *

But how did this electronic music start?

Some seventy years ago a Russian inventor named Leon Theremin came up with a new machine. It was electrically controlled and it looked like a radio receiver with an antenna. It produced music by high-frequency circuits and emitted sounds similar to the human voice. It could also be made to sound like various musical instruments. All the player had to do was jiggle the dials. Theremin's machine, along with a contraption by an American named Cahill, was just about the first famous electronic instrument. Today there are vast, complicated, musical monsters (magnetrons) at places such as the Columbia-Princeton Electronic Music Center. These machines can suggest just about any sound known on earth —or in outer space, for that matter. There are also "second generation" magnetrons that are portable and easy to use.

The electronic composer starts with these sound-giving machines — or anything else that makes sound—and creates as he pleases. There is no performer, usually. It's straight from the composer to the consumer—you. The tape-recorder sets down the musical "happening" and you listen to it. Think of the way a painter works directly on canvas. The new composer is doing the same thing, only on a tape-recorder.

A few composers wrote music for the theremin, (the inventor named the machine after himself) but these were just curiosity pieces; it was too early. Then, with the advent of electrical recording techniques, and the miraculous tape-recorder, the time was right. A whole new world opened up for the living composer. He didn't have to scribble black notes on white paper and then beg a conductor to play it with an orchestra. He could start out with musical sounds fed into the tape; then he could manipulate it, alter it, blend it as he pleased. In a way, it's a technique we take for granted in photography—enlargements, montages, distortions —they're all possible ways of creating new beauty. The modern composer asked himself: *Why not in music?*

The first big breakthrough happened in France in 1948. A group of young composers started writing something they called *musique concrete*. They started with "natural" sounds—a drop of rain, a railroad, ping-pong balls, famous voices, anything. With a new machine called the Phonogene, they mixed these sounds, spliced them, and ran them backwards, or altered them completely. The theory was that they would start with "noise" (also called "junk music") and try to refine the sound enough to make it usable for a piece of music. This school never got very far, but they are still at it.

Much more interesting, and much more respected today, is a new German school that starts with "pure sound" from a machine, and then tries to p ot music as precisely as though it were being programmed on an IBM machine. The most successful, thus far, is the composer Stockhausen. It's interesting to note that he also is a keen student of mathematics. Unlike the "Concrete" school, these new composers are not interested in natural sounds distorted by machines. Rather, they are interested in creating geometric patterns in sound, in exploring all that they can, in creating new ways to hear beauty in tone. In a way, it's very similar to abstract painting.

For example, you know that there are modern painters who say you can look at their pictures upside down; the angle doesn't matter. Similarly, Stockhausen says, "In my electronic music, there is no beginning and no end; the listener may begin on whatever page he pleases, but he must then play a complete cycle in a given succession."

There are also American composers who work the same way and who are exploring all these new devices. The most noted is John Cage, who was born in Los Angeles in 1912. He uses both the "concrete" and the true electronic method. He writes pieces that can be played singly, or together at the same time on two loudspeakers. He doesn't care if you hear one or both together, it's up to you.

"Well," the reader says dubiously, "it's all sort of interesting, and I appreciate what you said about listening with new ears, but all this so-called 'music' sounds terrible. It's just noise!"

"Just noise" has been the most common complaint in the history of music. Not only Berlioz and Wagner, but also Haydn and even Mozart were attacked by critics who stuffed their ears and yelled, "Noise!" There's something called the time lag that has to work before our ears get accustomed to new ways of writing. We're not smarter than the old critics who scoffed at Mozart—we're just *used* to his music.

Something is goingon. We are witnessing the birth of a new school — and what we must endure now are the cries and squawks of the new infant. It may be fifty years before it reaches a stage of aesthetic beauty. I am not saying that the mainstream of music can flow *only* through "junk-tapes" and the magnetron and the electronic music synthesizer. But electronic music is here, and it's in its second generation now. It is without question the true music of our time. More than in any other form of art today, the medium is the message. It can also be a shattering experience.

One last word, before you put this down and say, "I don't care. I don't like the idea of a music-making machine. It can't be good—it's not natural!"

The best answer I know to that common remark was made by the perceptive Jacques Barzun: "The moment man ceased to make music with his voice alone the art became machine-ridden. Orpheus's lyre was a machine, a symphony orchestra is a regular factory for making artificial sounds, and a piano is the most appalling contrivance of levers and wires this side of the steam engine."

CONSULT LISTINGS UNDER BOULEZ, CAGE, GABURO, MESSIAEN, PENDERECKI, STOCKHAUSEN, SOBOTNICK, XENAKIS.

COMPUTER MUSIC FROM THE UNIVERSITY OF ILLINOIS

This disc has the honor of containing the first large-scale work ever written by a computer, the *Illiac Suite for string quartet,* generated by a machine called *Illiac.* Live performance here—by a computer, that is—and this inspired computer can scare the hell out of you. Total serialism is used in parts; scales of nine to fifteen tones in the octave.

McKENZIE   *Contemporary Chamber Players*   HELIODOR   HS 25053

The computer used here has since been sold for scrap. Which caused one critic to comment: "This was doubtless the first time in history that a composer has brought a price on the open market as sheer junk."

ELECTRONIC MUSIC FROM THE UNIVERSITY OF ILLINOIS:

More musicotechnology. Lejaren Hiller (1924 –), Kenneth Gaburo (1926 –), Charles Hamm (1925 –), and Herbert Brun (1918 –) are all highly trained musicians connected with the Studio for Experimental Music at the University of Illinois.

GILBERT   *Chamber Players of the University of Illinois*   HELIODOR   S 25074

Not my cup of tea.

"NEW MUSIC FROM JAPAN"

Akira Miyoshi (1923-); Toru Takemitsu (1930-); Toshiro Mayuzumi (1929-) are leaders of avant-garde music in Japan. From the evidence of this record, they are all highly skilled craftsmen.

* * * IWAKI   *The NHK Symphony Orch.*   ODYSSEY   (M/S) 3216 0151

An adventurous record, to put it mildly, and more impressive than most of the pieces from contemporary American composers. There is little here of the sterile quality of so much of the neo-music of the past ten years. This is sonorous, imaginative composition that contains vitality and exuberance. This disc reminds me of the experiments of Xenakis. If you want only one or two "new" records, try this one. The sound is superb.

Writing in *Stereo Review,* composer Eric Salzman commented: "Japanese music is right up there with it these days and, in the field of new music, the Japanese orchestras put our own to shame. These are excellent, idiomatic performance of difficult new music."

"NEW MUSIC IN QUARTER-TONES"

This record contains pieces by Charles Ives, Ted Macero, Calvin Hampton, and Donald Lybbert.

* MACERO   *Chamber Ensemble from*   ODYSSEY   (M/S) 32160161
                   the University of Syracuse

Pandemonium to my ears, but fun, once you accept the quartertone pitch relationship. *Triple Play* has a rhythmic quotation from a novelty song called *I'm in Love with Tootsie Oodles.* Ted Macero, Calvin Hampton, and Donald Lybbert are loyal Americans all.

"NEW SOUNDS IN ELECTRONIC MUSIC"

Steve Reich (1936-   ) is a New Yorker and studied with Berio and Milhaud; Pauline Oliveros (1932-   ) is from Texas and is a lecturer in Electronic Sound at the University of California; Richard Maxfield (1927-   ) was born in Seattle and studied with Babbitt, Sessions, and Dallapiccola, and has taught experimental music at the New School in New York.

Come Out is a repeated loop with a single phrase spoken for 13 minutes. It will drive you mad. According to the composer, it was "inspired" by the arrest for murder of six boys during the Harlem riots of 1964. The repeated voice imparts a nightmarish quality.

* * STEVE REICH: ODYSSEY   (S) 32 16 0160
     Come Out;
   RICHARD MAXFIELD:
     Night Music;
   PAULINE OLIVEROS:
     I of IV

This is a strong record, one of the best of the new crop in avant-garde music technology.

The only credit listing on this set is "'Engineering, George Engfer." In other words, we have McLuhan-age composers getting their message straight onto tape and straight to the listener—short-cutting soloists, orchestras, conductors, and other old-fashioned means. From what I make of it, much of this is sound-distortion, aptly dubbed in the trade as "junk sound environs", sounds twisted and blended precisely like way-out sculpture is handled today.

NONESUCH GUIDE TO ELECTRONIC MUSIC

This is a helpful compendium to the vocabulary of the New Noise (no sneer intended), edited by cognoscenti Paul Beaver and Bernard L. Krause. It is extremely enlightening for anyone who cares to be initiated into the mysteries of our curious age, in which the muse is the Moog Series III synthesizer, and the Dolby A 301 noise-reduction system is the handmaiden of art.

* *	*2 records*	NONESUCH	(S) 73018

This album was conceived "because responsible critics often refer to the new taped sounds as 'drips, bird whistles, squiggles, burps, coughs, and other sorts of effects'." Also included is a carefully prepared booklet that is in itself an introduction to electronic-music theory. This 2-record album lists for $7.50, and does not belong, strictly speaking, in our low-priced discography. But as it is unique, still modestly priced, and a most helpful guide, I feel it should be noted here and Nonesuch saluted for their enterprise. The sound is magnificent. A minority report from *Stereo Review:* "The album begins and ends with a painful piece of electronic *Kitsch* which I actually thought for a while was a put-on. But no, it's for real—an honest-to-Gawd attempt to produce electronic Muzak. . . . ."

THE NEW MUSIC—Volume 1

The following compositions are included in this album: STOCKHAUESN *Kontra-Punket for Ten Instruments;* PENDERECKI *Threnody for the Victims of Hiroshima;* BROWN *Available Forms;* POUSSER *Rimes.*

* * * MADERNA	*Rome Symphony Orch.*	VICTROLA	(S) 1239

THE NEW MUSIC—Volumes 2 and 3

Volume II contains the following compositions: BOULEZ *Sonaine for flute for piano;* HAUBENSTOCH-RAMATI *Interpolation;* MODERNA *Concerto for oboe and chamber orchestra.*
Volume III contains the following: NONOY *su Sangre ya Viene Cantando;* FUKISHIMA *Hi-kyo;* BERIO *Serenade No. 1;* LEHMANN *Quanti.*

These three albums comprise an excellent survey of what is going on with composers "since Hiroshima," the dividing line for young composers today.

Luigi Nono (1924-   ) is a leading figure of serialism and musical revolution; he is married to Arnold Schoenberg's daughter. His piece here, a section from a large, 12-tone piece, is in the Schoenberg tradition, if that is the correct term.

Luciano Berio (1925-   ) represented by a fascinating "Serenade I for Flute and 14 Instruments", is another serial composer. There is a light-heartedness in his music that is refreshing after the solemn sounds of all the serial composers today.

Karlheinz Stockhausen (1928-   ) stands out above most post-war composers; he is the *enfant terrible* of electronic music, endlessly involved with theories and experimentation. (See also under alphabetical listing of Stockhausen.) Each opus is *newer* new music. The dessicated music of Webern is the big influence here, although Stockhausen seems indifferent to any formal musical writing. He is an absolutely serious, marvelously inventive composer. One cannot help but be impressed with his brilliant mind.

* * * GAZZELLONI,	*Soloists of the Rome*	RCA Victrola VIC
RZEWSKI, FABER,	*Symphony Orch.*	(M/S) 1312/13
MADERNA		

The playing is exciting throughout—often dazzling. Special mention must be made of the dauntless, and quite beautiful "bent-tone" playing of Severine Gazzelloni, featured on six of the seven compositions in *Volumes Two* and *Three*. The sound is good on all three records.

TUDOR: A SECOND WIND FOR ORGAN
KAGEL: IMPROVISATION AJOUTEE
WOLFF: FOR 1, 2, OR 3 PEOPLE
MUMMA: MESA, FOR 4 CYBERSONIC BANDONEON

Christian Wolff (1933-   ), a Frenchman, came to the United States in 1941 and presently teaches at Harvard. His piece is intriguing. He says of it: "It's as though you take a walk with a friend or friends, going by whatever way you like . . . .". According to the composer, any instrument may be used for this work.

here, a section from a large, 12-tone piece, is in the Schoenberg tradi-
listing of Stockhausen.) Each opus is *newer* new music. The dessicated

Luigi Nono (1924-   ) is a leading figure of serialism.

Maurice Kagel (1931-   ) was born in Buenos Aires and was a composer and pianist there. Since 1957 he has lived in West Germany.

Gordon Mumma (1935-   ) is from Massachusetts and is one of the founders of the Cooperative Studio for Electronic Music and Merce Cunningham Dance Company. His *Mesa* is a duo for bandoneon (an accordion-like instrument of the organ family).

David Tudor is a leading pianist of the New Music. He has experimented with piano works that require playing directly on the strings, framework and case, and that introduce new tone colors by "preparing" the strings with objects of various materials. Since 1948 he has devoted himself to the performance of contemporary music, both instrumental and electronic.

In this record Tudor is working with an organ. But is it music? Alfred Frankenstein has dismissed it as "on the silly, solemn side of music." I don't know, and neither does anyone else. But it has something, and it seems that this school of music is here, whether we like it or not.

* TUDOR   *Organ and Bandoneon*   ODYSSEY   (S) 32 16 0158

The technical work is impressive. The sound is fine.

VARIOUS "ALTERED" PIECES FOR CHORUS AND ORCHESTRA

These are new pieces for chorus and orchestra that have been altered electronically by sound synthesizer and Vocorder.

All these works extend the human voice physically. Several types of lip, throat, and cup microphones are fed into a complex configuration of electronic equipment, and then processed during the performance. Pre-recorded tapes are also used as accompanying material. This is highly experimental music, breaking through our known sound barriers. The Vocorder encodes speech sounds and was designed by Sylvania Electronic Systems.

* LUCIER   *Brandeis University*   ODYSSEY   S 32 16 0156
                     Chamber Choir

The sound is stunning, as it is on most records of "new music" reported here. One might consider the dictum of the knoweledgeable Arthur Cohn who said "A recording is no place for musical vaudeville."

The Basic Repertory

THE 100 CLASSICAL COMPOSITIONS PLAYED MOST FREQUENTLY BY MODERN ORCHESTRAS

J. S. Bach
Brandenburg Concertos X
Chaconne, in D Minor, from Violin Partita No. 2
Magnificat, in D
Cantata No. 4
Cantata No. 80
Cantata No. 140

Bartok
Concerto for Orchestra X

Beethoven
Piano Concerto No. 3, in C Minor X
Piano Concerto No. 4, in G X
Piano Concerto No. 5, in E-flat, "Emperor" X
Violin Concerto in D X
Piano Sonata No. 14, "Moonlight" X
Symphony No. 1, in C X
Symphony No. 2, in D X
Symphony No. 3, in E-flat, "Eroica" X
Symphony No. 4, in B-flat X
Symphony No. 5, in C Minor X
Symphony No. 6, in F, "Pastoral" X
Symphony No. 7, in A X
Symphony No. 8, in F X
Symphony No. 9, in D Minor X
Trio No. 6, in B-flat, "Archduke" X

Berlioz
Symphonie fantastique X
Harold in Italy, for Viola and Orchestra

Bizet
Symphony No. 1, in C

Brahms
Piano Concerto No. 1, in D Minor ✗
Piano Concerto No. 2, in B-flat ✗
Violin Concerto, in D ✗
Concerto, in A Minor, for Violin and Cello
Symphony No. 1, in C Minor ✗
Symphony No. 2, in D ✗
Symphony No. 3, in F ✗
Symphony No. 4, in E Minor ✗

Bruckner
Symphony No. 7, in E ✗
Symphony No. 9, in D Minor

Chopin
Piano Concerto No. 1, In E
Piano Concerto No. 2, in F
Nocturnes, for Solo Piano ✗
Waltzes, for Solo Piano ✗

Copland
Ballet Suites—Billy the Kid and Rodeo

Debussy
La Mer ✗

Dvorak
Cello Concerto, in B Minor ✗
Symphony No. 8, in G ✗
Symphony No. 9, in E Minor, "From the New World" ✗

Franck
Violin and Piano Sonata, in A ✗
Symphony, in D Minor ✗

Gershwin
An American in Paris
Piano Concerto, in F
Rhapsody in Blue

Grieg
Piano Concerto, in A Minor ✗

Handel
Messiah
Water Music X

Haydn
Symphony No. 94, in G, "Surprise"
Symphony No. 101, in D, "Clock" X
Symphony No. 104, in D, "London" X

Liszt
Piano Concerto No. 1, in E-flat X

Mahler
Das Lied von der Erde
Symphony No. 1, in D X
Symphony No. 4, in G X
Symphony No. 9, in D X

Mendelssohn
Violin Concerto, in E Minor X
Symphony No. 3, in A Minor, "Sctoch"
Symphony No. 4, in A, "Italian" X

Moussorgsky-Ravel
Pictures at an Exhibition X

Mozart
Piano Concerto No. 20, in D Minor X
Clarinet Quintet, in A \
Sinfonia Concertante in E-flat, for Violin and Viola
Symphony No. 35, in D, "Haffner" X
Symphony No. 39, in E-flat X
Symphony No. 40, in G Minor X
Symphony No. 41, in C, "Jupiter" X
Requiem X
String Quintet in G, K. 516

Prokofiev
Peter and the Wolf
Symphony No. 5

Rachmaninoff
Piano Concerto No. 2, in C Minor
Piano Concerto No. 3, in D Minor

Ravel
Bolero
Daphnis and Chloe

Rimsky-Korsakov
Scheherazade

Rossini
Overtures

Saint-Saens
Carnival of the Animals
Symphony No. 3, in C Minor

Schubert
String Quintet, in C
Piano Quintet, in A, "Trout"
Symphony No. 8, in B Minor, "Unfinished"
Symphony No. 9, in C, "The Great"
String Quintet in C, Opus 163
String Quartet in D, "Death and the Maiden"

Schumann
Cello Concerto, in A Minor
Piano Concerto, in A Minor
Symphony No. 1, in B-flat, "Spring"

Shostakovich
Symphony No. 5

Sibelius
Symphony No. 1, in E Minor
Symphony No. 2, in D
Symphony No. 5, in E-flat

Smetana
The Moldau, from my Fatherland

Strauss ✗
Don Juan ✗
Till Eulenspiegel's Merry Pranks ✗

Stravinsky
Petrouchka (complete) ✗
Le Sacre du printemps

Tchaikovsky
Piano Concerto No. 1, in B-flat Minor ✗
Violin Concerto, in D ✗
The Nutcracker
Symphony No. 4, in F Minor ✗
Symphony No. 5, in E Minor ✗
Symphony No. 6, in B Minor "Pathétique" ✗

Vivaldi
The Four Seasons, From Cimento dell' Armonia e dell' Invenzione ✗

Wagner
Overtures, and orchestral excerpts from his operas. ✗

The Great Works of Western Music

Medieval and Renaissance

The men who composed between the twelfth century and the sixteenth century were the founding fathers of Western music. This music, which is mostly choral, is strikingly similar in its emotive beauty to the work of medieval and renaissance painters. The sacred works are severe and formal; the secular music (madrigals, ayres, etc.) is gay, rhythmic and dance-like.

THE MOST IMPORTANT WORKS OF THIS EARLY PERIOD ARE:

Byrd, William
Mass in 4 parts; Keyboard music.

Des Prez, Josquin
Masses; Motets.

Dowland, John
Ayres; Lute Music.

Dufay, Guillaume
Hymns, Choruses, Songs, Motets, "L'Homme Armé" Mass.

Gabrieli, Giovanni
Canzoni for Brass, Sonata pian'e forte, Motets.

Gesualdo, Don Carlo
Madrigals.

Gibbons, Orlando
Anthems, Church Music.

Gregorian Chant
(before the 13th century) Various collections.

Isaac, Heinrich
Choral Music; Missa Carminum.

Lassus, Orlandus
Madrigals; Masses; etc.

Machut, Guillaume De
Mass: Notre-Dame.

Medieval & Renaissance
Various Collections.

Monteverdi, Claudio
Ballo delle Ingrate; Combattimento di Tancredi e Clorinda; Il Lagrime d'Amante; Madrigals; Orfeo; Incoronazione de Poppea.

Morley, Thomas
Madrigals; First Book of Ayres.

Obrecht, Jacob
Missa Fortuna desperata.

Ockeghem, Johannes
Chansons; Motets.

Palestrina, Giovanni
Choral Music; Masses; Missa Papae Marcelli.

Praetorius, Michael
Canticum Trium Puerorum; Terpsichore.

Tallis, Thomas
Lamentations of Jeremiah; Church Music.

Victoria, Tomás Luis De
Choral Music.

The Baroque Period

The Baroque period runs roughly from 1600 to the death of Johann Sebastian Bach in 1750. This era is characterized by its marked departure from the grave, vocal polyphony of medieval and Renaissance music. Highly developed melody, brilliant counterpoint, and large-scaled instrumental works are the characteristic glories of this period.

THE MOST IMPORTANT BAROQUE WORKS ARE:

Albinoni, Tomaso
Concerti a cinque; Concerti for Oboe.

Bach, Carl Philipp Emanuel

Concerto in A for Cello; Concerto in E flat for Harpsichord and Piano; Magnificat.

Bach, Johann Christian

Flute Sonatas.

Bach, Johann Sebastian

Brandenburg Concerti; Cello Suites (unaccompanied); Cantatas No. 4, 51, 140, 202, 80, 56, 8, 76, 106; Chromatic Fantasy and Fugue for Harpsichord; Concerti for Harpsichord (1, 4, 5); Concerti for Violin (1, 2); Concerto in D for 2 Violins; Fantasia and Fugue in G for Organ; Flute Sonatas; Goldberg Variations for Harpsichord; Italian Concerto for Harpsichord; Jesu, Joy of Man's Desiring; Magnificat; Mass in B; Musical Offering; Partitas for Harpsichord; Passacaglia and Fugue in C for Organ; St. John Passion; St. Matthew Passion; Sonatas and Partitas for Violin unaccompanied; Suites for Orchestra; Toccata and Fugue in D for Organ; Well-Tempered Clavier (for Harpsichord).

Boyce, William

Symphonies (1-8).

Buxtehude, Dietrich

Organ Music; Cantatas.

Corelli, Arcangelo

Concerti grossi, Opus 6.

Couperin, Francois

Concerts royaux; Harpsichord Music.

Frescobaldi, Girolamo

Harpsichord/Organ Music.

Gay & Pepusch

Beggar's Opera.

Handel, George Frederick

Alcina; Arias; Concerti grossi, Opus 6; Concerti for Organ; Flute Sonatas; Israel in Egypt; Messiah; Royal Fireworks Music.

Schutz, Heinrich
Eastern Oratorio; Motets; Symphoniae Sacre.

Sweelinck, Jan Pieterszoon
Choral and Organ Music.

Tartini, Giuseppe
Sonata in G for Violin; "Devil's Trill."

Telemann, Georg Philipp
Concerti (various); Musique de Table (Suites); Sonatas for Flute, Oboe and Continuo; Suite in A for Flute and Strings.

Torelli, Giuseppe
Concerti grossi, Opus 8.

Vivaldi, Antonio
Concerti for Violin ("L'Estro armonico," "Four Seasons," "La Cetra"); Concerti (for various instruments); Gloria.

The Classic Era

This period runs from the exploratory music of Bach's son, Karl Philipp Emanuel Bach, through the early period of Beethoven. The composers of this period were absorbed with developing great musical forms—the symphony, the string quartet, the concerto. The music of Haydn and Mozart and the early work of Beethoven epitomize the aims and achievements of this era.

THE MOST IMPORTANT WORKS OF THIS PERIOD ARE:

Beethoven, Ludwig van
An die ferne Geliebte; Concerti for Piano (1, 2, 3, 4, 5); Concerto for Violin; Fidelio; Missa Solemnis; Octet in E flat for Winds; Overtures; Quartets (7-16); Quintet in E flat for Piano and Winds; Sextet in E flat for Winds; Sonatas for Piano (8, 12, 14, 21, 23, 28, 29, 30, 31, 32); Sonatas for Violin and Piano (5, 9); Symphonies (1, 2, 3, 4, 5, 6, 7, 8, 9); Trio in B flat "Archduke."

Boccherini, Luigi
Concerto in B flat for Cello; Cello Sonatas.

Cimarosa, Domenico
Concerto for Oboe.

Gluck, Christoph Willibald
Orfeo ed Euridice.

Haydn, Franz Joseph
Concerto in D for Cello; Concerto in D for Harpsichord; Concerto in E flat for Trumpet; Creation; Mass No. 7 (In Time of War, "Paukenmesse"), Mass No. 9 (Nelson); Quartets Opus 76, 77 (Opus 76, No. 3, "Emperor"); Sonatas (miscellaneous) for Piano; The Seasons; Symphonies (45, 88, 92, 94, 96, 100, 101, 103, 104).

Mozart, Wolfgang Amadeus
Arias; Concerto for Bassoon; Concerto for Clarinet; Concerti for Flute; Concerti for Horn (1-4); Concerti for Piano (16, 17, 19, 20, 21, 22, 23, 24, 25, 26, 27); Concerto No. 10 in E flat for 2 Pianos; Concerti for Violin (3, 4, 5, 7); Così fan tutte; Divertimenti in D for Strings; Don Giovanni; Exsultate Jubelate; Magic Flute; Marriage of Figaro; Mass in C, "The Great"; Overtures; Quartet for Oboe; Quartets (14, 16, 17, 18, 23); Quintet for Clarinet; Quintet in E flat for Piano and Winds; Quintet in G; Requiem; Serenade "Eine kleine Nachtmusik"; Serenades No. 6 "Serenata Notturna," No. 7 "Haffner," No. 9 "Posthorn"; Serenade No. 10 for 13 Wind Instruments; Sinfonia Concertante for Violin & Viola; Sonatas for Piano (8, 11, 13, 15, 16); Sonatas for Violin; Symphonies (35, 36, 38, 39, 40, 41).

Rossini, Gioacchino
Barber of Seville; Overtures.

Stamitz, Karl
Quartet in E flat for Woodwinds; Trios for Orchestra.

Weber, Carl Maria von
Der Freischuetz; Invitation to the Dance; Overtures.

Romanticism

This era extends roughly from the mature Beethoven through the French impressionist school of Debussy and Ravel—from 1800 until the end of World War I. Composers of this school revolted against the restrictions imposed by the formal patterns of the classical school. This epoch is marked by poetic, sweeping imagination.

THE MOST IMPORTANT WORKS OF THIS PERIOD ARE:

Adam, Adolphe-Charles
Giselle.

Albéniz, Isaac
Iberia.

Bellini, Vincenzo
Norma; I Puritani; La Sonnambula.

Berlioz, Hector
Damnation of Faust; Harold in Italy; Overtures; Requiem; Nuits D'Eté, song cycle; Romeo et Juliette; Symphonie fantastique.

Bizet, Georges
L'Arlésienne: Suites 1 and 2; Carmen; Symphony No. 1 in C.

Borodin, Alexander
In the steppes of Central Asia; Polovtsian Dances from "Prince Igor".

Brahms, Johannes
Academic Festival Overture; Alto Rhapsody; Concerti for Piano (1, 2); Concerto for Violin; Concerto for Violin and Cello; German Requiem; Hungarian Dances; Piano Music; Piano Trio No. 1; Quintet for Clarinet and Strings; Quintet in F for Piano and Strings; Sextet No. 1 for Strings; Sonata No. 3 for Violin and Piano; Symphonies (1, 2, 3, 4); Tragic Overture; Trio in E flat for Horn, Violin and Piano; Variations on a Theme by Haydn.

Bruch, Max
Concerto No. 1 for Violin; Kol Nidrei for Cello and Orchestra; Scottish Fantasy for Violin and Orchestra.

Bruckner, Anton
Symphonies (4, 7, 9).

Chabrier, Emmanuel
Espana.

Chausson, Ernest
Poème for Violin and Orchestra.

Chopin, Frédéric
Andante Spianato and Grande Polonaise; Concerti for Piano (1, 2);
Ballades, Etudes, Impromptus, Mazurkas, Nocturnes; Polonaises, Pre-
ludes, Scherzos, Waltzes; Fantasie in F; Sonatas for Piano (2, 3); Les
Sylphides.

Debussy, Claude
Clair de lune; Images for Orchestra; La Mer; Nocturnes for Orches-
tra; Prélude à L'aprés-midi d'un faune; Preludes for piano; Quartet;
Sonata No. 3 for Violin and Piano.

Delibes, Léo
Coppélia (ballet suite); Sylvia (ballet suite).

Delius, Frederick
Briggs Fair; On Hearing the First Cuckoo in Spring.

Donizetti, Gaetano
Don Pasquale; Lucia de Lammermoor; L'eliser d'amore.

Dukas, Paul
Sorcerer's Apprentice.

Dvorák, Antonin
Carnival Overture; "American" Quartet; Concerto for Cello; Slavonic
dances; Symphonies (7, 8, 9).

Elgar, Edward
Enigma Variations; Pomp and Circumstance Marches.

Enesco, Georges
Roumanian Rhapsody No. 1.

Falla, Manuel de
El Amor brujo; Nights in the Gardens of Spain; Three-Cornered Hat.

Fauré, Gabriel
Pelléas et Mélisande; Requiem.

Franck, César
Chorales for Organ; Quintet for Piano and Strings; Sonata for Violin and Piano; Symphonic Variations; Symphony in D.

Glazounov, Alexander
Concerto for Violin.

Glinka, Mikhail
Russlan & Ludmilla: Overture.

Gounod, Charles
Faust.

Grieg, Edvard
Concerto for Piano; Peer Gynt Suites 1, 2.

Humperdinck, Englebert
Hansel and Gretel.

D'Indy, Vincent
Symphony on a French Mountain Air.

Ippolitov-Ivanov, Mikhail
Caucasian sketches.

Lalo, Édouard
Symphonie espagnole.

Leoncavallo, Ruggero
Pagliacci.

Liszt, Franz
Concerti for Piano (1, 2); Hungarian Rhapsodies; Mephisto Waltz; Les Préludes; Sonata in B for piano.

Mascagni, Pietro
Cavalleria Rusticana.

Massenet, Jules
Le Cid (ballet suite); Manon.

Mendelssohn, Felix
Concerto for Violin; Elijah; Midsummer Night's Dream, Incidental music; Octet in E flat for Strings; Overtures; Symphonies (3, 4, 5).

Mussorgsky, Modest
Boris Godounov; Night on Bald Mountain; Pictures at an Exhibition; Songs and Dances of Death.

Offenbach, Jacques
Gaîté Parisienne; Orpheus in Hades; Tales of Hoffman.

Paganini, Niccolo
Concerto No. 1 for Violin; Caprices.

Puccini, Giacomo
La Bohème; Madame Butterfly; Tosca; Turandot.

Rachmaninoff, Sergei
Concertos for Piano (2, 3); Preludes for Piano; Rhapsody on a Theme of Paganini; Symphony No. 2.

Ravel, Maurice
Alborada del gracioso; Bolero; Concerto for the Left Hand; Concerto in G for Piano; Daphnis et Chloé; Introduction and Allegro; Ma Mère l'Oye (suite); Pavane pour une infante défunte; Quartet; Rapsodie espagnole; Tombeau de Couperin; Tzigane for Violin and Orchestra; La Valse; Valses nobles et sentimentales.

Resphighi, Ottorino
Boutique fantasque (Ballet, after Rossini); Fountains of Rome; Pines of Rome.

Rimsky-Korsakov, Nikolai
Capriccio espagnol; Coq d'Or (ballet suite); Russian Easter Overture; Scheherazade.

Saint-Saens, Camille
Carnival of the Animals; Concerto No. 2 for piano; Danse macabre; Havanaise for Violin and Orchestra; Introduction and Rondo Capriccioso; Symphony No. 3, "Organ".

Sarasate, Pablo de
Zigeunerweisen.

Schubert, Franz
Impromptus; Marche militaire No. 1; Mass No. 6 in E flat; Octet in F; Quartet No. 14 "Death and the Maiden"; Quintet in A, "Trout"; Quintet in C; Rosamunde; Incidental Music; Sonatas for Piano (D. 960, 959, 664); Songs; Symphonies (5, 8, 9); Trio No. 1 (Piano); Trio No. 2 (Piano); Wanderer Fantasie.

Schumann, Robert
Carnaval; Concerto for Cello; Concerto for Piano; Dichterliebe; Kinderscenen; Manfred Overture; Quintet in E flat for Piano and Strings; Songs; Symphonic Etudes; Symphonies (1, 2, 3, 4).

Smetana, Bedrich
The Bartered Bride; The Moldau.

Strauss, Johann
Die Fledermaus; Waltzes.

Tchaikovsky, Peter Ilyich
Capriccio Italien; Concerto No. 1 for Piano; Concerto for Violin; Marche slav; Nutcracker (ballet suite); Overture 1812; Romeo and Juliet; Serenade for Strings; Sleeping Beauty; Swan Lake; Symphonies (4, 5, 6).

Thomas, Ambroise
Mignon.

Verdi, Giuseppe
Aida; Otello; Requiem; Trovatore; Falstaff; Rigoletto; Traviata.

Wagner, Richard
Der fliegende Hollaender; Tanhaueser; Die Meistersinger; Siegfried Idyll;Die Walküre; Siegfried; Goetterdaemmerung; Tristan und Isolde; Parsifal.

Wieniawski, Henri
    Concerto No. 2 for Violin.

Wolf, Hugo
    Italian Serenade; Songs.

Twentieth Century Music (1900-1960)

The great men of this period—Stravinsky, Bartok, Schoenberg — made great strides in broadening the scope of music. A dozen schools sprang up, often overlapping each other: expressionism, serial music, atonal music, neo-classicism, are some of the leading developments of this era.

THE MOST IMPORTANT WORKS OF THIS PERIOD ARE:

Barber, Samuel
    Adagio for Strings; Concerto for Violin.

Bartók, Béla
    Concerto for Orchestra; Concerto for Violin (1938); Miraculous Mandarin (ballet suite); Music for Strings; Percussion and Celesta; Sonata for 2 Pianos and Percussion; 6 Quartets.

Berg, Alban
    Concerto for Violin; Lyric Suite for String Quartet; Wozzeck.

Bernstein, Leonard
    Fancy Free; West Side Story (ballet music).

Bloch, Ernest
    Sacred Service; Schelomo.

Britten, Benjamin
    Ceremony of Carols; Serenade for Tenor, Horn and Strings; Symphony for Cello and Orchestra; Young Persons Guide to the Orchestra; Peter Grimes.

Copland, Aaron
Appalachian Spring; Billy the Kid; Rodeo; Piano Sonata; Piano Fantasy; El Salón México.

Gershwin, George
American in Paris; Concerto in F for Piano; Porgy and Bess; Rhapsody in Blue.

Gould, Morton
Spirituals for Orchestra.

Grofé, Ferde
Grand Canyon Suite.

Hanson, Howard
Symphony No. 2 "Romantic".

Harris, Roy
Symphony No. 3.

Hindemith, Paul
Kleine Kammermusik; Mathis der Maler, Symphony; Symphonic Metamorphosis of Themes by Weber.

Holst, Gustav
The Planets.

Honegger, Arthur
Pacific 231; Roi David; Joan of Arc.

Hovhaness, Alan
Mysterious Mountain.

Ibert, Jacques
Divertissement; Escales (Ports of Call).

Ives, Charles
Central Park in the Dark; Three Places in New England; Holidays.

Janácek, Leos
Slavonic Mass.

Khachaturian, Aram
Gayne, Ballet: Suite.

Kodály, Zoltán
Háry János: Suite; Peacock Variations.

Mahler, Gustav
Kindertotenlieder; Das Lied von der Erde; Songs of a Wayfarer; Symphonies (1, 2, 4, 9).

Menotti, Gian Carlo
Amahl and the Night Visitors; The Medium; The Consul.

Milhaud, Darius
La Création du monde; Suite provencale.

Nielsen, Carl
Symphony No. 5.

Orff, Carl
Carmina Burana; Carmina Catullus.

Poulenc, Francis
Concerto in G for Organ, Strings and Timpani; Concerto for 2 pianos; Gloria in G; Sextuor for Piano and Winds.

Prokofiev, Serge
Alexander Nevsky; Classical Symphony; Concerto No. 3 for Piano; Concertos for Violin (1, 2); Lieutenant Kije Suite; Love for 3 Oranges: Suite; Peter and the Wolf; Romeo and Juliet; Symphony No. 5.

Schoenberg, Arnold
Chamber Symphony in E flat; Five Pieces for Orchestra; Verklaerte Nacht.

Shostakovich, Dmitri
Age of Gold; Concerto No. 1 for Piano, Trumpet and Orchestra; Symphony No. 5; Symphony No. 9.

Sibelius, Jean
Concerto for Violin; Finlandia; Pohjola's Daughter; Swan of Tuonela; Symphonies (1, 2, 5); Tapiola; Valse Triste.

Strauss, Richard
Also sprach Zarathustra; Death and Transfiguration; Don Juan; Ein Heldenleben; Der Rosenkavalier; Salome; Songs; Till Eulenspiegel.

Stravinsky, Igor
Concerto for Violin; Firebird: Suite; l'Histoire du soldat: Suite; Les Noces; Petrouchka; Pulcinella: Suite; Oedipus Rex; Sacre du printemps; Symphony of Psalms; Symphony in Three Movements.

Varese, Edgard
Ionisation.

Vaughan Williams, Ralph
Fantasia on Greensleeves; Fantasia on a Theme by Tallis; Symphonies (2,8).

Webern, Anton
Five movements for string quartet; five orchestral pieces.

Weill, Kurt
The Three Penny Opera.

Electronic Music (1950-   )

Around 1950, a tremendous revolution in music occurred. Musical tradition was cast to the winds, and many composers felt free to "begin from a new beginning," with an entirely new conception of what sounds constitute music.

In fact, new sounds have been employed; new rhythms have been tested. What has been produced is light years away from the old classical patterns.

SOME OF THE MOST IMPORTANT PRODUCTIONS OF THE ELECTRONIC AGE ARE:

Boulez, Pierre
Le Marteau sans Maitre; Structures for two pianos.

Cage, John
Solos for Voice 2.

Penderecki, Krzysztof
The Passion according to Saint Luke; Threnody for the Victims of Hiroshima.

Schuller, Gunther
Seven Studies on themes of Paul Klee.

Stockhausen, Karlheinz
Kontra-Punkte for 10 Instruments; Momente.

Xenakis, Yannis
Metastasis, for Orchestra; Eonta for piano and strings.

The Leading Low-Priced Record Labels

CROSSROADS A product of CBS under the aegis of Paul Myers, Crossroads are high-quality records that are made in Czechoslovakia and pressed in the United States. Many of them first appeared on the imported Supraphon label. The Crossroads catalogue has grown by leaps and bounds and seems to contain something for everyone. There is a special emphasis on Czech composers. The orchestral recordings range from good to excellent; the best buys are those records in which Karl Ancerl conducts. Some of the chamber music on Crossroads is little less than extraordinary. Stereo sonics are generally first-rate.

DOVER is a quiet little company and a favorite of knowledgeable chamber music fans. This label is hard to find in many record shops, but the company will send you its catalogue for $2.00, if you write to them directly at 180 Varick Street, New York, N. Y. 10014. The bulk of the records listed is European, and these are usually very good indeed. Highlights are collections of Renaissance music by such notables as Denis Stevens. Dover also has an outstanding series of piano recordings by Beveredge Webster. Records may be ordered by mail.

EVEREST is basically a conglomeration of many small companies that could not survive the fierce economics of the record industry. Under Bernard Solomon's sharp direction, Everest is very much on the track today. In the orchestral field the company offers new, worthwhile stereo releases originating chiefly from Pye Records, England. Also some good Russian material as well. But the backbone of the Everest catalogue is its opera releases. For the low-priced market, Everest has recirculated the famous Cetra series of recordings which consist of some 90 operas, some of them off-beat works, unavailable in any other recording. Most of these records were made in nonstop sessions for Radio Italiana during the early 1950's. They feature such now-famous stars as Callas, Tebaldi, etc. and there is a hectic, do-or-die enthusiam about the series that is usually irresistible. The sound varies widely in Everest-Cetra, ranging from excellent to atrocious.

In addition to its massive relaunching of the Cetra opera catalogue, Everest is also presenting the opera recordings of the Italian firm, Ricordi. These true-stereo items were also recorded in the late 1950's; the famous Maria Callas "Medea" is included. Opera lovers owe a deep debt to Everest records for having had the vision and the courage to introduce such a staggering number of operas on a low-priced label.

HELIODOR is the low-priced label of Deutsche Gramophon Gesellschaft (DGGG) records, one of the most prestigious labels in the world Heliodor boasts items from the impressive DGG catalogue. Authoritative artists are to be found here: conductors Fricsay, Furtwaengler, and Lorin Maazel, violinist David Oistrakh, and lieder-singer Fischer-Dieskau. Heliodor has also taken over some outstanding MGM recordings, such as Douglas Moore's opera "The Ballad of Baby Doe," and some of conductor Arthur Winograd's notable releases. The sound is usually first-rate DGG quality.

LONDON STEREO TREASURY. This is just what it says. London's early-era plums of the 1950's are to be had here, with such stalwart conductors as Ansermet and von Beinum, Solti, Krips, etc. In the orchestral repertory LST entries are almost invariably near the head of anybody's list of best low-cost buys. The sound is usually excellent, in keeping with London's formidable reputation for sonics.

MACE is a little offshoot of Sceptre Records, which is better known for its million-seller discs of Dionne Warwick. Under the guidance of Joseph Zerga, Mace has built a nice collection that is chiefly drawn from the catalogues of Electrola, Germany, and Qualiton, Hungary. (Electrola is the German arm of the famous English EMI recording complex.) The covers are *kitsch,* but the recordings and sound are generally solid Mittel-Europa quality. A series of great recordings by the famous blind organist and keyboard artist Helmut Walcha leads the attractions.

MERCURY WING is the low-priced line of Mercury Records. Mercury made a name for itself with sonically superior discs; Mercury-Wing are these famous discs of five to ten years ago. Orchestral music is the forte here, under such outstanding conductors as Paul Paray, Antal Dorati, and Raphael Kubelik.

MONITOR specializes in behind-the-Iron-Curtain tape. This energetic firm is easily the leader of the many small labels in this area. The company offers a wealth of outstanding material: Russian artists, of course, but also some excellent chamber music discs by American artists. If you've shied away from Russian recordings because of poor quality, listen to some of the Monitor titles recommended in this book. The sound is surprisingly good.

MUSICAL HERITAGE SOCIETY records are available by mail order only. Address: 1991 Broadway, New York, N. Y. 10023. Free catalogue on request. American pressings of European masters are the goods here, and they range from good to excellent. French and German artists are featured and the catalogue is made up of 18th century music (Bach, Haydn, Mozart) for the most part, and little-heard works from other periods.

NONESUCH the classical division of Elektra, is regarded by many as the best low-priced label on the market today. Imagination, taste, and a spirit of high adventure are to be found here, as well as recordings that are usually outstanding and true stereo sound. Nonesuch really launched the low-priced record revolution (although Paul Myers of Crossroads has the low-priced record revolution. Although Paul Myers of Crossroads also has a good claim to this honor, we all owe a debt to the dynamic Jac about everything is to be found in this impressive catalogue, which is made up largely of recent-vintage European performances in true stereo. Nonesuch has recently gone all out for original production of electronic music, with some spectacular results.

ODYSSEY is a low-priced label of CBS Records, and it offers famous CBS records of from five to twenty years ago (when CBS was called "Columbia"), at less than half the price. Under the astute direction of Paul Myers, Odyssey specializes in "Legendary Performances"—discs by Bruno Walter, Casals, Sir Thomas Beecham, Max Goberman, etc. Equally important in the Odyssey catalogue are way-out discs that venture into the realms of "new music" and electronic music; as a series these are as good or better than any recordings of new music I have heard. Sonically, this electronic series is dazzling.

PHILIPS WORLD SERIES is a subsidiary label of Phillips Records. This is a small catalogue thus far, but an excellent one. Specialties: chamber music and music of the baroque era. A remarkable series of chamber music recordings by the Beaux Arts Trio is to be found here; many critics rate these performances tops at any price. Also outstanding: a host of recordings by one of the best chamber music orchestras in the world, "I Musici." Leading European artists are to be heard on the World Series line.

PICKWICK is a fast-growing firm that does not produce its own records; it utilizes masters from Capitol, Mercury, and Everest. Pickwick Records are often to be found in startling places such as drugstores. The company offers solid recordings of popular orchestral works, and features such conductors as Steinberg and Dorati. The sound is usually more than good.

RICHMOND is the budget line of the famous London Records label. And London is the same as the world-famous British Decca label. Opera recordings by famous stars are the attraction here—Tebaldi, Del Monaco, etc. La Tebaldi did all her famous roles *first* on what are now Richmond records; she did them all over again years later in stereo. This is what you get on expensive London Records. There are many critics who prefer Tebaldi's fresh-voiced performances on Richmond.

SERAPHIM—"Angels of the highest order"—is the budget line of the respected Angel Records catalogue. Known in the trade as "fallen Angels," Seraphim, record for record, offers the best $2.50 worth of musical performance to be had in the American marketplace. The parent company of both Seraphim and Angel Records is E.M.I., the great English recording complex. Thus Seraphim has access to a treasurehouse of recordings by such legendary greats as Gigli, Flagstad, Lotte Lehman, etc. Having a new extensive low-priced market to tap has enabled Brown Meggs of Seraphim to bring out brand-new stereo recordings of European artists that otherwise would never have seen the light of day over here. For example, the Seraphim *"Marriage of Figaro"* is a superb performance, one of the best Figaros to be had regardless of price. But as its stars are comparatively unknown in America, it would have had no chance whatsoever here in the high-priced, glitteringly packaged, glamorous-name market. So you get this recording on Seraphim at $2.50 *list*. Seraphim has also come out with a series of new recorded-in-U.S.S.R. material, on the Seraphim-Melodiya label, and the first releases are good.

VANGUARD — EVERYMAN — CARDINAL is another pioneer firm dating back to the pre-dawn of the long playing record. Vanguard has a reputation for admirable taste in its selection of artists, Countertenor Alfred Deller, conductor Mogens Woldike, etc. Chamber music and baroque lovers have known for years that Vanguard means just about the best performances you can get in this field. Technically, the Vanguard-Everyman releases are almost always admirable; on the Cardinal line they are sonically as good as anything to be had on records.

VICTROLA, of course, needs little introduction. For late starters, Victrola was the venerable trade name of the Victor Talking Machine Company before its absorption by RCA. The knowledgeable Roger Hall of RCA is backing low-price Victrola issues to the hilt; he believes that the day is not far off in the record trade when an outstanding release on a high-priced label will be released as a matter of course a year later in "paperback"—precisely as is done in the book business. Victrola has a formidable catalogue, boasting such conductors as Charles Munch, Fritz Reiner, Pierre Monteux, and one of America's top orchestras, The Boston Symphony. The historic Toscanini recordings are to be found here as well. Roger Hall has injected new stereo recordings from Europe into the Victrola list. The outstanding item thus far in this department is a remarkable set of way-out music called, simply, "The New Music."

VOX - TURNABOUT. Vox is a pioneer firm in recording low-priced records (despite their ostensibly high list price), and at least one generation of record lovers has grown up on inexpensive Vox releases. The catalogue is huge, surprisingly varied, and the majority of the releases emanate from Europe. Vox has never been afraid of the off-beat, the little-known work—in fact, it has made a specialty of adventuresome recordings that the more staid labels would have avoided. In recent years Vox has refurbished its image with a new label, Turnabout, that ranks with Nonesuch in quality and range of production. Vox has recently brought out a new $3.98 line, "Candide", to do battle with Vanguard's "Cardinal" label. Both of these "medium lines" present stereo only, and feature the highly praised Dolby System of virtually noise-free recording technique.

WESTMINSTER is another venerable firm, as recording companies go. This label was *the* label for chamber music buffs in the 1950's, and the youthful exuberance of those famous recordings is now preserved on Westminster's "Collector's Series" line (mono only). Westminster also has a small, choice stereo budget line, "Music Guild", specializing in baroque, renaissance music.

LIST PRICE OF LOW-PRICED CLASSICAL RECORDS

THESE PRICES ARE CORRECT AS OF MAY 1, 1969. CHANGES
IN LIST PRICES MAY OCCUR FROM TIME TO TIME.

LABEL	MONO	STEREO
Audio Fidelity	$2.50	$2.50
Crossroads	2.98	2.98
Dover	2.00	2.00
Everest-Cetra	2.98	2.98
Heliodor	2.98	2.98
London Stereo Treasury Series	—	2.49
Lyrichords LLS	1.98	—
Mace	2.50	2.50
Melodiya Seraphim	2.49	2.49
Mercury Wing	1.89	2.89
Monitor 2000	2.50	2.50
Music Guild	2.39	2.39
Musical Heritage Society	2.50	2.50
Nonesuch	2.98	2.98
Odyssey	2.98	2.98
Parliament	1.98	2.98
Philips World Series	—	2.98
Pickwick	—	1.79
RCA Victrola	2.98	2.98
Richmond	2.49	2.49
Seraphim	2.49	2.49
Somerset	1.89	—
Turnabout	2.98	2.98
Vanguard	2.50	2.50
Westminster	1.98	1.98

List prices are not adhered to for the most part. Most record stores sell these discs at some discount; just how much of a discount depends on the store. Records bought in the New York area and through discount mail order houses can be purchased at times as low as $1.49.

The record industry has decided to abandon mono recordings for the most part. As a result, many record shops are offering mono discs for around $1.00. There are some great bargains to be picked up at this price.

RECORDS WHICH ARE LIST-PRICED OVER $2.50 BUT ARE NA-
TIONALLY AVAILABLE, FOR THE MOST PART, AT $2.50 OR LESS

Artia	Esoteric
Baroque	Everest
Collector's Series	Period
Concertdisc	Vox
Counterpoint	Westminister

The firms listed above issue records which bear a list price of as much as $5.95. But, in fact, records with these labels can be bought in most discount stores at around $2.00 or even less. Why all this hanky-panky?

There are several reasons. A record store in Kansas may order, let us say, two records of a particular title. The order will be billed at full list price less a 40% dealer's discount. A huge New York chain will order 500 records of the very same title; because of the large order, that store's discount will be considerably greater. Thus the dealer in Kansas is not overcharging his customer; he just has to pay more for the record himself.

Still another reason why some record companies maintain a high list price is that they do considerable business with schools, libraries, etc., who will buy just one record of a title; and the manufacturer, in order to retrieve the cost of handling, packing, shipping, etc., for that single record, must maintain a high list price while offering a small discount.

Each and every one of the records issued by the above companies may not be available at a low price. Nevertheless, you will find hundreds of goodies at bargain basement prices. For example, Westminster sells only their Collector's Series at low prices. But as far as I am concerned, there are as many top records in their Collector's Series as there are to be found among the higher-priced Westminster issues.

A NOTE ON "REPROCESSED" STEREO

"Reprocessed" stereo sound came into being seven or eight years ago and is becoming more and more popular in an all-stereo industry. Reprocessing—or "electronic enhancement"—involves filtering the highs from one channel and the lows from the other channel to create the illusion of separation — in other words, taking one good monophonic high-fidelity recording and separating it into two bad low-fidelity channels. Many comparisons of the original monophonic and the reprocessed stereo have shown that the original recording is far superior to the "re-mix".

Thus, electronically reprocessed stereo is usually inferior in fidelity and reproduction to the original monaural versions. There seems to be no satisfactory way to make processed stereo sound as good as true stereo. However, the industry wants to phase out mono. The past year has seen wholesale dumpings on the market of mono records of all artists and whole catalogues. The companies are selling off the records cheaply and rapidly. This is why so many stores are now offering huge mono inventories at prices like $1-$2 per disc.

The advantage of a company having no mono lies in terms of cost and trouble. When you carry both stereo and mono, you must have two masters and press two different versions of each release. You also need separate record jackets and cover, one labeled "mono" and one labeled "stereo". This is only part of the headache: two lines for one product means double work in stock control, bookkeeping, price structures, catalogues, shipping, and all the other complexities of the record industry.

In sum, if you are a high fidelity fan, avoid reprocessed stereo where possible, and stick to true mono and true stereo. "Mono only" is nothing to be feared, or to be sheepish about. Of course, music such as symphonic works is more pleasant to the ear with stereo, but solo works, chamber music, and most vocal music sound perfectly good on mono.